Steven Holzner

SAMS
Teach Yourself
Microsoft®
Visual Basic®
.NET 2003

in 21 Days

SAMS

800 E. 96th St., Indianapolis, Indiana, 46240 USA

Sams Teach Yourself Microsoft® Visual Basic® .NET 2003 in 21 Days

Copyright © 2003 by Sams Publishing

International Standard Book Number: 0-672-32531-4

Library of Congress Catalog Card Number: 2003102956

Printed in the United States of America

First Printing: May 2003

07 06 05   10 9 8 7

Trademarks

All terms mentioned in this book that are known to be trademarks or service marks have been appropriately capitalized. Sams Publishing cannot attest to the accuracy of this information. Use of a term in this book should not be regarded as affecting the validity of any trademark or service mark.

Warning and Disclaimer

Every effort has been made to make this book as complete and as accurate as possible, but no warranty or fitness is implied. The information provided is on an "as is" basis. The author and the publisher shall have neither liability nor responsibility to any person or entity with respect to any loss or damages arising from the information contained in this book.

Bulk Sales

Sams Publishing offers excellent discounts on this book when ordered in quantity for bulk purchases or special sales. For more information, please contact:

U.S. Corporate and Government Sales
1-800-382-3419
corpsales@pearsontechgroup.com

For sales outside of the U.S., please contact:

International Sales
international@pearsoned.com

ASSOCIATE PUBLISHER
Michael Stephens

EXECUTIVE EDITOR
Candace Hall

DEVELOPMENT EDITOR
Songlin Qiu

MANAGING EDITOR
Charlotte Clapp

PROJECT EDITOR
Elizabeth Finney

COPY EDITORS
Chuck Hutchinson
Rhonda Tinch-Mize
Mike Henry

INDEXER
Ginny Bess

PROOFREADER
Linda Seifert

TECHNICAL EDITOR
Karl Hilsmann

TEAM COORDINATOR
Cindy Teeters

INTERIOR DESIGNER
Gary Adair

COVER DESIGNER
Aren Howell

PAGE LAYOUT
Bronkella Publishing

Contents at a Glance

Contents

About the Author

STEVEN HOLZNER is the award-winning author of 78 books on programming, and has been writing bestsellers on Visual Basic topics ever since Visual Basic has been around. His books have sold nearly 2 million copies and have been translated into 16 languages around the world. He has a Ph.D. from Cornell University, has been on the faculty of both Cornell and MIT, and is a former contributing editor to *PC Magazine*. He was writing about Visual Basic before version 1.0 even came out, and it's his favorite all-time development package. He uses it almost daily for commercial development and Web hosting.

Dedication

To Nancy, as always and forever (for all the reasons she already knows!).

Acknowledgments

A book like the one you're reading is the product of many people's hard work. I'd especially like to thank Candy Hall, the acquisitions editor; Songlin Qiu, the development editor; Elizabeth Finney, the project editor; Chuck Hutchinson and Rhonda Tinch-Mize, the copy editors; Linda Seifert, the proofreader; and Karl Hilsmann, the tech editor.

We Want to Hear from You!

As the reader of this book, *you* are our most important critic and commentator. We value your opinion and want to know what we're doing right, what we could do better, what areas you'd like to see us publish in, and any other words of wisdom you're willing to pass our way.

As an associate publisher for Sams Publishing, I welcome your comments. You can e-mail or write me directly to let me know what you did or didn't like about this book— as well as what we can do to make our books better.

Please note that I cannot help you with technical problems related to the *topic* of this book. We do have a User Services group, however, where I will forward specific technical questions related to the book.

When you write, please be sure to include this book's title and author as well as your name, e-mail address, and phone number. I will carefully review your comments and share them with the author and editors who worked on the book.

E-mail: `feedback@samspublishing.com`

Mail: Michael Stephens
Associate Publisher
Sams Publishing
800 E. 96th St.
Indianapolis, IN 46240 USA

For more information about this book or another Sams Publishing title, visit our Web site at `www.samspublishing.com`. Type the ISBN (excluding hyphens) or the title of a book in the Search field to find the page you're looking for.

Introduction

Welcome to our grand tour of Visual Basic .NET 2003. This book has been designed to open up Visual Basic and make it more accessible than any other book can. There's as much Visual Basic crammed into this book as will fit.

We're going to center what we do around seeing Visual Basic *in action*, because that's the best way to master the topic—hands-on, not with dry theoretical lectures. Here, you're going to see everything at work, from the basics all the way to deploying finished applications, from simple text boxes to installing ad rotators in Web applications, from the easiest Windows application to advanced Web services and distributed data applications. You'll find a working example for every programming topic in the book.

All of which is to say that this is the book for people who want to get the most out of Visual Basic .NET 2003. That's our goal, and we're going to push the envelope to get there.

What's in This Book

From cover to cover, this book is pure Visual Basic .NET. It covers the full Visual Basic language and hundreds of skills from using visual tools when dropping data adapters into windows to connecting Windows applications to Web applications at runtime. Here are a few of the topics we're going to see:

- Using the Visual Basic .NET Integrated Development Environment (IDE)
- Reviewing the complete Visual Basic .NET syntax
- Creating Windows applications
- Creating Web applications
- Showing and hiding controls such as text boxes and buttons
- Handling multiple windows at once
- Implementing exception handling and filtering
- Creating owned and always-on-top forms
- Anchoring and docking controls
- Creating controls at runtime
- Using smart device applications
- Sending keystrokes to other applications
- Handling every Windows and Web control available, from text boxes to Web validation controls

- Creating menus, submenus, context menus, and owner-drawn menus
- Printing
- Creating toolbars
- Object-oriented programming (OOP)
- Employing class inheritance and overloading
- Creating OOP interfaces and polymorphism
- Drawing and coloring graphics
- Handling images
- Creating nonrectangular windows
- Opening and creating files
- Detecting browser type and capabilities in Web applications
- Preserving data over server roundtrips
- Creating database-handling applications
- Using SQL and parameterized SQL with databases
- Creating data connections, datasets, and data adapters
- Handling relational databases and data views
- Implementing simple and complex data binding
- Creating multitier distributed database applications
- Establishing master/detail data relationships
- Writing and reading database data in XML
- Creating custom controls for use in Windows and on the Web
- Handling multithreaded applications
- Synchronizing and joining threads in code
- Creating Windows services and installers
- Creating Web services and connecting to them
- Deploying your applications

You can also download the code for this book from http://www.samspublishing.com/. All the code in this book has been tested on at least two separate computers and verified to work as it should. (Note that in the past, Microsoft has made unannounced changes to Visual Basic without changing the version number, which has made previously working code stop working. If you have problems with the code or receive errors when you try to run it, check whether Visual Basic itself has changed. And check the Web site for updates.)

To download the code on the Sams Web site at `http://www.samspublishing.com/`, enter this book's ISBN (without the hyphens) in the Search box and click Search. When the book's title is displayed, click the title to go to a page where you can download the code.

The Conventions Used in This Book

There are some conventions that you should know about, and the Introduction is a good place to get acquainted with them. For instance:

- When we've added a new piece of code and are discussing it, it will appear shaded, and when there's more code to come, you'll see three dots. Here's what that looks like:

```
Private Sub Button1_Click(ByVal sender As System.Object, _
    ByVal e As System.EventArgs) Handles Button1.Click

    TextBox1.Text = "No problem."
        .
        .
        .

End Sub
```

- Occasionally, we'll discuss Visual Basic .NET syntax in the compact form you'll see in the Microsoft documentation, and you should know how to decipher that. For example, in this description of the `Dim` statement (which you use to declare variables and arrays), items in brackets ([and]) are optional, upright bars(|) mean *or*, curly braces ({ and }) indicate that you select only one of the enclosed items, and the items in italic are not keywords built into Visual Basic—they're just placeholders, meant to be replaced with your own terms:

```
[ <attrlist> ] [{ Public | Protected | Friend | Protected Friend
| Private | Static }] [ Shared ] [ Shadows ] [ ReadOnly ] Dim [ WithEvents ]
```

- Code lines, commands, statements, variables, and any text you type or see onscreen appears in a monospace typeface.

- Italic text and a new term icon highlight technical terms when they're being defined.

- The ➡ icon is used before a line of code that is really a continuation of the preceding line. Sometimes a line of code is too long to fit as a single line on the page. If you see ➡ before a line of code, remember that it's part of the line immediately preceding it. Most of the time, however, we'll use the Visual Basic underscore character (_) at the end of a line of code to indicate that the line is continued on the following line. This is discussed in Day 1.

- We'll also refer to the items in menus the same way you'll see in many computer books; for example, the File, New Project menu item refers to the New Project item in the File menu.

- You'll see tips throughout the book, which are meant to give you something more, a little more insight or a pointer to some new technique. Here's what a tip looks like:

> You can create a simple animation by moving forms or controls around with a loop in code and the SetBounds method.

- You'll also see notes, which are there to give you additional information. Here's what a note looks like:

> Although you can use threads to run the code, for user interface controls such as buttons and text boxes, using threads is not a good idea. Sooner or later, your code will freeze up. The user interface code should be run by an application's main thread.

What You'll Need

To use this book, you'll need Visual Basic .NET; the version we'll be using in this book is Visual Basic .NET 2003. Besides Visual Basic itself, there are some additional software packages you might want.

To create Web applications and Web services, you'll need access to a Web server that runs the Microsoft Internet Information Server (IIS), as discussed in Day 11. If you choose, you can run IIS on the same machine Visual Basic .NET is on, and IIS comes with many Windows versions (although you may have to install it from the CDs that come with Windows).

> If you're running IIS on the same machine as Visual Basic .NET, you should install IIS before installing Visual Studio .NET so that Visual Basic can register the presence of IIS properly.

We'll also work with databases in this book. To work with a database, you need a data provider such as SQL Server. You can use other data providers, but Visual Basic .NET is most often connected to SQL Server, so we'll use that data provider here. A knowledge of Structured Query Language (SQL) will also help, but it's not necessary; we'll see a complete SQL primer in Day 16.

And that's about it. Just about everything else that you need comes with Visual Basic .NET itself. We'll be writing and testing our code in the Visual Basic Integrated Development Environment (IDE), which we'll see in Day 1, and the IDE will give us all the other tools we need. There will be detours into occasional side topics, such as JavaScript and regular expressions for checking text strings, but if you have Visual Basic .NET, IIS, and a data provider like SQL Server, you're fully prepared for all we'll be doing.

Visual Basic .NET Resources Online

Plenty of Visual Basic .NET resources are available online, and you can turn to them for additional information and to stay in touch with the Visual Basic community. You can find many groups on Usenet that discuss Visual Basic topics (be careful what you read on those groups; there's no guarantee of accuracy), such as these groups hosted by Microsoft:

- `microsoft.public.dotnet.languages.vb`
- `microsoft.public.vb.addins`
- `microsoft.public.vb.bugs`
- `microsoft.public.vb.controls`
- `microsoft.public.vb.database`
- `microsoft.public.vb.installation`
- `microsoft.public.vb.syntax`
- `microsoft.public.vsnet.general`
- `microsoft.public.vsnet.ide`

Some non-Microsoft Usenet groups are out there as well, like these:

- `comp.lang.basic.visual`
- `comp.lang.basic.visual.3rdparty`
- `comp.lang.basic.visual.announce`
- `comp.lang.basic.visual.database`
- `comp.lang.basic.visual.misc`

As you would expect, you can find many Web pages out there on Visual Basic .NET. Here's a starter list of pages hosted by Microsoft:

- `http://msdn.microsoft.com/vbasic/`—The main Visual Basic page
- `http://msdn.microsoft.com/vbasic/techinfo/default.asp`—The tech page for Visual Basic .NET
- `http://msdn.microsoft.com/vbasic/support/default.asp`—The support page for Visual Basic .NET
- `http://msdn.microsoft.com/vbasic/community/default.asp`—A listing of Visual Basic .NET online communities
-
  `http://msdn.microsoft.com/vbasic/productinfo/vbasic03/faq/default.asp` —The Visual Basic .NET 2003 Frequently Asked Questions (FAQ) page
- `http://msdn.microsoft.com/vbasic/downloads/default.asp`—Free downloads for Visual Basic .NET
- `http://msdn.microsoft.com/howto/visualbasic.asp`—A page of how-to projects covering common Visual Basic .NET tasks

And that's all the introduction we need. Now we have all we need to start our in-depth tour of Visual Basic .NET. If you have comments, suggestions, or problems, please e-mail them to me, Steve Holzner, at `feedback@samspublishing.com`. I want to make sure this book stays at the top of the field, and I'll implement your suggestions in upcoming editions.

PART I

At a Glance

Visual Basic .NET Essentials

In this part, we begin with Visual Basic .NET programming, getting the essentials under our belts before pressing on. We see our first programs here and get a taste of what Visual Basic .NET can do.

Besides Windows and Web applications, you get an introduction to console applications, which are easy to create and provide us with a basic platform for our examples. We'll use console applications until Part II to bring us up to speed on the Visual Basic .NET essentials, such as seeing how to handle data, work with operators, write conditional statements, loops, and more.

We'll also add procedures and exception handling to deal with runtime errors to our programming arsenal in this part, giving us the effective and powerful foundation we'll need throughout the rest of the book.

1

2

3

DAY 1

Getting Started with Visual Basic .NET!

Welcome to Visual Basic .NET 2003. Over the next 21 days, you'll get an in-depth guided tour of the ins and outs of Visual Basic .NET. From the most basic to the most advanced, we're going to become masters of Visual Basic in this book. You've come to the right place.

If you want to create Windows applications, or if you want to create Web programming on the server, there's just nothing like Visual Basic .NET. Visual Basic is easy to get started with, and yet it has almost incredible programming power behind it, so there's just no limit to how far you can go.

We'll dig into Visual Basic .NET immediately. This is our first day on the job, and we're not only going to get an overview of Visual Basic, but we'll also create working applications and get a thorough understanding of the parts of our main programming tool—the Visual Basic Integrated Development Environment (IDE). The IDE is what you see when you start Visual Basic, and it presents you with the dozens of toolbars, windows, menus, and tabs that we'll unravel today. The IDE is the essential tool we'll use on nearly every page of this book, and learning how to use it will give us the essential foundation and mastery we'll need for the coming days. Here are today's topics:

- The history of Visual Basic
- Putting Visual Basic .NET to work in examples
- Creating a Windows application
- Creating a Web application
- Creating a Console application
- Understanding the .NET Framework and the common language runtime
- Developing Visual Basic solutions and projects
- Using the Visual Basic .NET Integrated Development Environment (IDE)
- Dissecting the Visual Basic .NET IDE in depth

There's practically no limit to what you can do with Visual Basic .NET 2003. To see how we got here, and to get started, we'll take a look at the history of Visual Basic first.

The History of Visual Basic

Visual Basic 1.0 appeared in 1991 (I got a pre-release version of version 1.0, which is when I first started writing books about Visual Basic—and that's when I first decided that Visual Basic was the way of the future). Up to that point, the only way to do Windows programming was to use C code, and lots of it—you had to write five pages of C code to produce even a blank window. And you could only create visual elements, like buttons in code, with a lot of work.

The genius of Visual Basic changed all that. Now if you want a button, you just draw it in place. Want a text box? Just draw one. That was a total revolution, and one that programmers by the thousands embraced. It changed Windows programming forever.

Until Visual Basic, the user interface (UI) of a program was very difficult to create and manage. Now, it was not only simple, it was *fun*. Programmers loved it.

NEW TERM The original Visual Basic lived up to its name in the sense that it was fairly basic. But that changed with new versions, and with third-party vendors that introduced Visual Basic eXtension (VBX) controls. In Windows programming, user interface elements such as buttons, text boxes, and check boxes are called *controls*, and third-party vendors started producing new controls that Visual Basic then included.

Visual Basic 3.0 changed the picture again, adding support for database access with Data Access Objects (DAO). That turned out to be a major turning point for Visual Basic: Up to that point, many programmers had thought of it as a toy, but when it started to work with databases, people took it more seriously.

Visual Basic 4.0 and 5.0 were targeted at Windows 95, and started making the way you write code in Visual Basic more modular, introducing some object-oriented programming (OOP).

Version 6.0 introduced many new features, including ActiveX Data Objects (ADO), which let you work with databases in a variety of sources, including on the Internet.

The Web development in Visual Basic 6.0 paved the way for the future—and for a whole new type of Visual Basic. Microsoft decided that the Web was the way to go, and several years after Visual Basic 6.0 came out, it introduced Visual Basic .NET 2002.

Visual Basic .NET made Visual Basic's connection to the Web integral to the whole package. The language itself grew up as many old syntax features were removed and replaced. The process of creating applications changed radically. In fact, the change meant that for the first time, you couldn't automatically upgrade older code so that it would run in the new version. (Visual Basic .NET does have a migration tool that opens automatically when you try to open a Visual Basic 6.0 application, but the programming differences between Visual Basic version 6.0 and Visual Basic .NET 2002 were so profound that this tool is practically useless for all but the most simple applications.)

The biggest change in Visual Basic .NET 2002 was that Web programming became as important as Windows programming. Creating a Windows application in Visual Basic had always been easy: You just drew the user interface you wanted, added some code, and ran it. Now creating Web applications is just as easy: You just draw the user interface you want, add some code, and run it. Visual Basic .NET handles uploading and maintaining the Web application automatically, making Web development as easy as Windows development. We'll take a look at that topic today in more depth.

The current version, Visual Basic .NET 2003, introduces still more innovations. Here's a list of what's new. If you're new to Visual Basic programming, some of these items will be new to you. In that case, just treat this list as a reference to come back to as these various new topics are covered throughout the book. Don't be concerned that you have to understand these items at this point. Visual Basic .NET 2003 now supports the following features:

- Nonrectangular windows
- Mobile Web applications (for PDAs)
- Data providers for ODBC and Oracle
- New code in the .NET Framework

- A folder dialog for your applications to handle Windows folders
- Better support for migrating VB6 code to Visual Basic .NET
- The capability to track who has access to an application's code in the Visual Basic .NET Solution Explorer
- Improved security in the debugger (as well as better error messages)
- The capability to allow side-by-side installations of different versions of Visual Studio
- Arithmetic left and right shift operations on integral data types
- The capability to declare a loop variable as part of a For or For Each loop
- Support for Smart Devices (like Pocket PCs)
- Improved security, including automatically scanning user input in Web applications for embedded (and possibly malicious) HTML
- Improved access to Web services
- The capability to deploy applications with installers that target a specific version of the .NET Framework

We're at the cutting edge of Visual Basic now, pushing the envelope. In this book, we're going to put Visual Basic .NET 2003 through its paces. In fact, the simplest way to introduce Visual Basic .NET 2003 is to let it introduce itself. And we can do that by putting it to work right now.

Putting Visual Basic to Work

Take a look at Figure 1.1; that's Visual Basic .NET 2003. More correctly, it's the Visual Basic .NET 2003 Integrated Development Environment, the IDE. The version of Visual Basic .NET 2003 you see in Figure 1.1 is part of Visual Studio .NET 2003 (you may have another edition of Visual Basic .NET, such as the Standard Edition, which doesn't include the full toolset that comes with Visual Studio .NET 2003), and appears when you start Visual Studio .NET 2003. Visual Studio includes more than just Visual Basic; it also supports other languages such as Visual C++, Visual C#, and now, in Visual Studio .NET 2003, Visual J#.

When you start Visual Studio for the first time, you see the Start Page that appears in Figure 1.1, showing the contents of the My Profile tab (one of the three tabs at the top of the Start Page—Projects, Online Resources, and My Profile). Your profile allows you to set various options for Visual Basic, including how to display help information.

FIGURE 1.1

The Visual Basic IDE.

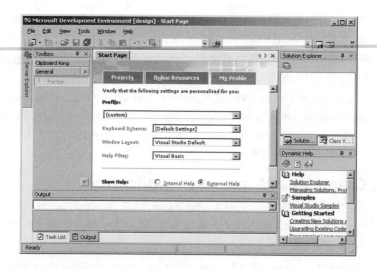

In fact, customizing how you view help information here is worthwhile. The Visual Studio help system will look up answers for you, searching through all its help files, and may return help that is really only relevant to, say, Java programming in Visual J#. To avoid that problem, you would be wise to restrict help information to Visual Basic help, which you can do by selecting Visual Basic in the Help Filter drop-down box you see in the center of Figure 1.1.

Requesting external help windows is also a good idea, as opposed to displaying help information in the IDE itself. By default, when you look something up in the Visual Studio help system, the results are displayed in a cramped window at the upper right in the IDE, about 2-by-2 inches or so, nearly impossible to be useful—especially because this tiny space is often broken up into subwindows by the help system. As Microsoft itself often recommends, it's best to display help information in its own window, switching back and forth between the IDE and the help window as needed. To make sure the help system gets its own window, click the External Help radio button that you see in the Start Page in Figure 1.1.

Tip

You can also switch to an external help window at any time if you don't want to do it now. You can either click the External Help radio button in the Start Page's My Profile tab, or select the Tools, Options menu item to open the Options dialog box. Then select the Help item in the Environment folder that appears at right, and click the External Help radio button, followed by the OK button.

That's what the IDE looks like. Before we discuss things abstractly, it's a good idea to actually put the IDE to work, getting a feel for Visual Basic, and we can do that by creating a few introductory examples. Seeing things actually work is the best introduction to a programming topic, so let's see what Visual Basic can do for us.

The standard types of Visual Basic .NET applications are Windows applications, Web applications, and Console applications. To get a feel for Visual Basic .NET, we'll take a minute to create a quick example of each of these applications here, starting with Windows applications.

Creating a Windows Application

We'll put together our first Visual Basic .NET Windows application now to get us on the right track. There's a great deal to learn about such applications, but creating a simple one is just that—simple.

NEW TERM To create a Windows application, select the File, New, Project menu item in the IDE, opening the New Project dialog you see in Figure 1.2. To create a new Visual Basic Windows application, click the Visual Basic Projects folder you see at left in the Project Types box in Figure 1.2, and select the Windows Application icon you see at right in the Templates box. Visual Basic will suggest the name WindowsApplication1 for this first application, which is fine. A Windows application like this is considered a new *project* in Visual Basic, and you might want to specify a directory where you can store the new project's files, using the Location box you see at the bottom of the New Project dialog. (If you don't specify a location for the new project, Visual Basic will store it in C:\Documents and Settings*username*\My Documents\Visual Studio Projects.)

And that's it! Now click OK to create the new WindowsApplication1 project.

FIGURE 1.2

The New Project dialog.

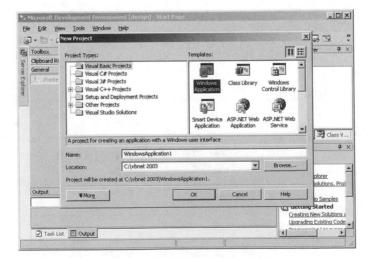

NEW TERM   When you click the OK button in the New Project dialog, the new Windows
application is created and displayed as you see in Figure 1.3. You can see the
window for the new application in the center of the IDE in that figure. A window under
design like this is called a *form* in Visual Basic, and you can see a grid of dots on this
form, allowing you to align the controls such as buttons and text boxes you add to the
form. Forms like this one are displayed in a Visual Basic Windows form *designer*, also
called a Windows form *design window*. You can see the tab named Form1.vb[Design]
displayed at the top of the designer, as well as a tab for the Start Page. If you have other
designers open, you can use these tabs to navigate to the designer you want.

FIGURE 1.3

*A new Windows
application.*

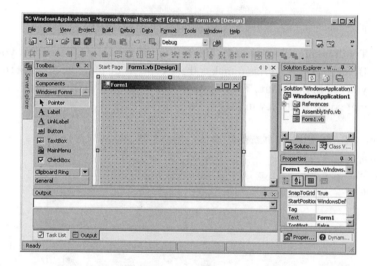

We can actually run this application now; the application is already so complete that it will
display the blank form as a window. To run the application, select Visual Basic's Debug,
Start menu item, or press F5. That's it. When the application runs, you won't see any controls in the window, but, as you see in Figure 1.4, the window has a title bar displaying the
minimize, maximize, and close buttons that you see in standard Windows applications.
You have a functioning, but not very interesting, Windows application already. To close
this application, click the close button (marked with an X) in the application's title bar.
Doing so will close the window and return you to the Visual Basic .NET IDE.

The next step is to add a few controls—a button and a text box—to the form in the
Visual Basic .NET IDE. You do that using the Visual Basic toolbox, which appears
directly to the left of the application's form in Figure 1.3 (it has the caption `Toolbox`).
You can add new controls to a form by finding the control you want in the toolbox and
either double-clicking it or dragging it to the form (more on how this feature works in
Day 4, "Creating Windows Forms").

FIGURE **1.4**

A blank window.

Try dragging a button and a text box to the application's form, as you see in Figure 1.5. By default, Visual Basic makes these controls display the text Button1 and TextBox1, as you see in the figure. That's fine for this example; we'll see how to customize the text that controls display in Day 4.

FIGURE **1.5**

Adding controls to a new Windows application.

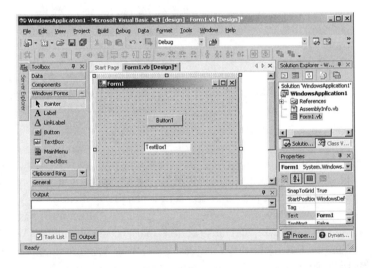

To make these controls do something, you can use Visual Basic code; for example, you can use code to display a message in the text box when the user clicks the button. To add some code that will be executed when the button is clicked, double-click the button now, opening a code designer as you see in Figure 1.6.

FIGURE 1.6

A code designer.

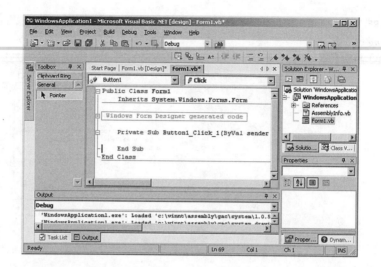

The code designer in Figure 1.6 displays the code for the button. Take a look at this part of the code that you see in the Figure 1.6(note the use of an underscore, _, here in the text, which is used to break up the first line of code so that it will fit on the page; you use an underscore at the end of a line of code to tell Visual Basic that the code is continued on the next line):

```
Private Sub Button1_Click(ByVal sender As System.Object, _
    ByVal e As System.EventArgs) Handles Button1.Click

End Sub
```

This is the place to put the code to run when the button is clicked. For example, to place the text "Hello there!" into the text box, you use the line of Visual Basic code TextBox1.Text = "Hello there!", typing it like this directly into the code designer:

```
Private Sub Button1_Click(ByVal sender As System.Object, _
    ByVal e As System.EventArgs) Handles Button1.Click
    TextBox1.Text = "Hello there!"
End Sub
```

You can see the results in Figure 1.7, where this new code appears in the code designer.

FIGURE 1.7

Adding code to a Windows application.

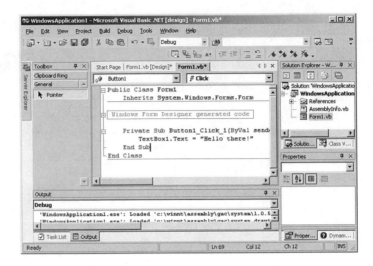

Now try running the application by selecting Visual Basic's Debug, Start menu item, or by pressing F5. When the application appears, click the button to which you've just added code. When you do, the message Hello there! is displayed in the text box, as you see in Figure 1.8.

FIGURE 1.8

Running a new Windows application.

Congratulations! you've created your first Visual Basic .NET 2003 Windows application. And you've added controls to it so that the application actually does something. To end the application, click the close button (marked with an X) in the application's title bar. When you do, the application will end and the Visual Basic .NET IDE will reappear automatically.

Creating a Web Application

Creating a Web application is as easy as creating a Windows application with Visual Basic .NET. As we'll see in Day 11, "Creating Web Forms with ASP.NET," you need a Web server with Microsoft Internet Information Server (IIS), as well as the .NET Framework, installed on it to create Web applications. Working with such a server to create Web applications is not hard. You select Visual Basic's File, New, Project menu item to open the New Project dialog as before, but instead of selecting the Windows Application icon, you select the ASP.NET Web Application icon, as you see in Figure 1.9.

FIGURE **1.9**

Creating a Web application.

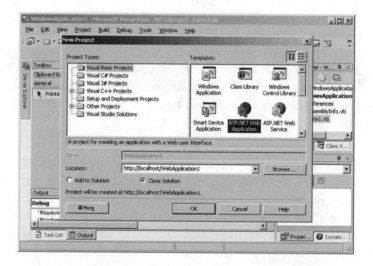

By default, Visual Basic gives this first Web application the name WebApplication1. Just as we did with our Windows application, you can add buttons and text boxes to Web applications from the toolbox and add code to these controls in just the same way as well.

When you run the new Web application, it'll appear in a Web browser such as the Microsoft Internet Explorer, as you see in Figure 1.10. When you click the button, the message Hello there! appears in this Web application just as it did in the Windows application, as you can also see in Figure 1.10. To end the application, close the browser window, which makes the Visual Basic .NET IDE reappear.

These capabilities are very impressive. In this way, Visual Basic .NET enables us to create a Web application with the same steps as a Windows application. You just drag the controls you want onto a form (a Web form this time, not a Windows form), double-click the button to open a code designer, add the same code as we used for the Windows form (TextBox1.Text = "Hello there!"), and then run the application in the same way, selecting Visual Basic's Debug, Start menu item, or by pressing F5.

FIGURE 1.10

*Running a Web
application.*

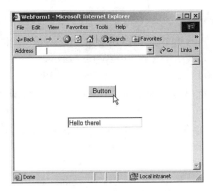

Instead of a Windows application appearing, though, the result appears in your Web browser. The application's files are stored on the Web server, and Visual Basic handles the task of maintaining it, uploading, and downloading data as needed automatically. And if the server is publicly available, anyone who enters its URL into a browser will see your application run.

In this way, as you'll see in Day 11, Visual Basic .NET enables you to create Web applications in the same way as you create Windows applications. There are some differences, though. Web applications support only some of the controls that Windows applications do, for example, and you'll need a round-trip back to the server if you want to handle button clicks and so on in your application. But on the whole, Visual Basic .NET Web applications are an amazing achievement. The details on Web applications are coming up in Days 11 to 15.

Creating a Console Application

NEW TERM — Another common type of Visual Basic .NET application is the *console applica-tion*, and we'll be using such applications during the next two days as we study the Visual Basic language. To create a console application, you select the File, New, Project menu item, and click the Console Application icon in the New Project dialog, as you see in Figure 1.11. The default name suggested by Visual Basic for this new console application is ConsoleApplication1, as you can also see in Figure 1.11, and that name is fine. Click OK to create this new application.

There's no user interface in a console application; the output of such an application simply appears directly in a DOS window as text. That means that instead of a user interface appearing in some form designer in the IDE, we go straight to a code designer when you open a console application. You can see the code designer for this new console application in Figure 1.12.

FIGURE 1.11

Creating a console application.

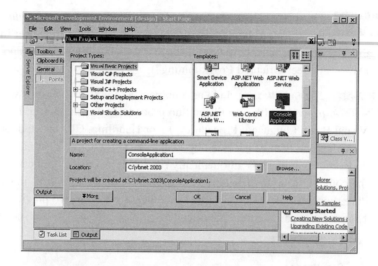

FIGURE 1.12

A new console application.

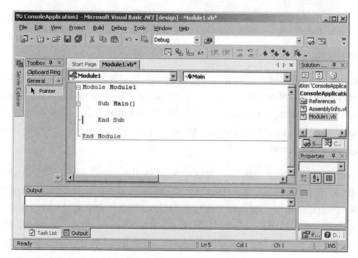

Here's the code in the new console application:

```
Module Module1

    Sub Main()

    End Sub

End Module
```

NEW TERM   This code is wrapped up in a Visual Basic module. A *module* is what Visual Basic uses to hold code not directly associated with a user interface, and it's exactly what we need here (you'll see all the details on modules and where they fit in Day 9, "Object-Oriented Programming").

NEW TERM   The `Sub Main()` and `End Sub` part here is Visual Basic's way of creating a *Sub procedure* (the details on Sub procedures are coming up in Day 3, "Mastering the Visual Basic Language: Procedures, Error Handling, Classes, and Objects"), which holds code that can then be accessed by Visual Basic by name. That name is `Main` here, and code with that name is automatically run when a console application starts. We can put the code we want to execute when the console application runs in the `Main` Sub procedure. For example, to display the same message as our two previous examples—`Hello there!`—we can use this line of code:

```
Module Module1

    Sub Main()
        Console.WriteLine("Hello there!")
    End Sub

End Module
```

Because console applications don't have text boxes or other user-interface elements, you can't display text in such elements. Instead, you can use `Console.WriteLine` to write lines of text to the console (DOS) window; this new line of code, `Console.WriteLine("Hello there!")`, writes the text `"Hello there!"` to the console window.

You can now run this new application in the usual way—selecting the Debug, Start menu item, or by pressing F5. But if you do, you'll get a disappointing result: A DOS window will appear with the text `"Hello there!"` in it, but it'll close just as fast as it opened, and all you'll really see is a flicker on the screen. You can solve this problem by intentionally keeping the console window open until you're ready to dismiss it—for example, until you press the Enter key. And you can do that by making the console application wait until you press that key, using `Console.ReadLine()`. As you'll see tomorrow, console applications can use `Console.ReadLine()` to read a line of text you type in the console window; such lines of text are read when you press the Enter key, ending your input. To make this work, we can display a prompt saying `"Press Enter to continue..."` and then use `Console.ReadLine()` to wait until the Enter key is pressed:

```
Module Module1

    Sub Main()
        Console.WriteLine("Hello there!")
```

```
        Console.WriteLine("Press Enter to continue...")
        Console.ReadLine()
    End Sub

End Module
```

And that's all we need! You can see this new code in your console application in Figure 1.13.

FIGURE 1.13

Adding code to a new console application.

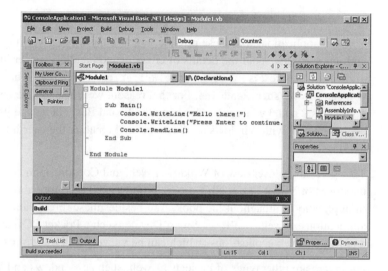

When you run this new application using Debug, Start, you see the results in Figure 1.14—a new DOS window displaying the text we want and waiting for you to press the Enter key. (You can also close this application by clicking the close button at upper right in the title bar.)

FIGURE 1.14

Running a new console application.

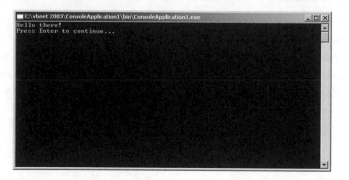

Tip

In fact, you can avoid using the `Console.ReadLine()` statement altogether if you start the application with the Debug, Start Without Debugging menu item. If you do, the console application will not close the DOS window until you press a key. While you're developing applications, however, it's best to leave the debugger active (which we do when we use the Debug, Start menu item) because that enables you to recover more easily if a serious problem occurs.

Console applications like these provide you an easy way of working with Visual Basic without worrying about the details of creating and handling a user interface. All you have to do to display text is to use `Console.WriteLine`, and to read what the user has typed, you can use `Console.ReadLine`. For that reason, we'll use simple console applications in both Days 2 and 3 while we're learning the Visual Basic language itself. In Day 4, we'll begin working with Windows applications, and creating the user interface will be the main issue.

That gives us an overview of Windows, Web, and Console applications, three of the cornerstones of Visual Basic .NET programming; we'll see more about each of these types of applications throughout the book. And besides these three, there are two other types of applications as well. You'll see Smart Device (such a Pocket PCs) applications in Day 4 and Mobile Web applications (which can be viewed in PDAs, for example) in Day 11.

And there are other types of projects as well, such as Windows and Web services (which we'll see in Day 21, "Creating Windows Services, Web Services, and Deploying Applications"). A Windows service runs in the background in Windows (although it can display an icon in the Windows taskbar), providing some service such as scanning files for viruses, and a Web service provides the same functionality on the Web, giving your Web applications shared access to the code and data in that Web service.

That gives us a good taste of Visual Basic .NET at work, and we've created some sample applications, so we have a feel for our topic. It's time to step back to see some of the bigger picture, getting more of the foundation we'll need in the coming days. For example, what's the .NET part of Visual Basic .NET about? We'll take a look at that and other issues next, as we get the bigger picture about the innovations in Visual Basic .NET from a programmer's perspective. These are concepts we'll need in the coming days.

Visual Basic .NET from a Programmer's Perspective

We should become familiar with a number of concepts before digging into Visual Basic .NET programming in depth so that we have the programming framework we need. The first thing to take a look at is the .NET Framework itself.

In the early days of Visual Basic programming, a great deal of the functionality built in to Visual Basic was stored in Windows dynamic link libraries (DLL files). That was fine when you were developing your programs. When you installed Visual Basic, all the DLL files you needed were also installed, even though they could run too many megabytes.

But this way of doing things became a problem when you were finished creating your applications and wanted to distribute them to others. You may have the needed DLL files on your computer, but the people who wanted to use your new application may not. That meant that you would have to package the needed DLLs in your installation package to be installed on the target machine as well as your application. But what DLLs would your application need? How would you know? Visual Basic started to include all kinds of tools to discover what DLLs your application would need and to include them in your application's deployment package.

But that wasn't good enough. Because you had to include those huge DLLs in your installation package, that package could easily run to 40MB or more. Imagine that situation— just the simplest of applications, like the ones we've developed already today would need dozens of megabytes of space, far more than you could fit onto a disk. And what if the DLLs you were installing on the target machine conflicted with other versions of the same DLLs that were already there? Would the user's current software continue to work?

The .NET Framework solved this problem by including all the support your application needs and packaging it as part of Windows. That meant the code in those DLLs that you originally needed to distribute to target systems along with your application was already installed in those target systems. Now all you have to do is to distribute your application's code—making your installation package much smaller.

The .NET Framework provides what your application needs in two parts: the .NET Framework class library and the common language runtime.

The .NET Framework Class Library

The first major part of the .NET Framework is the .NET Framework class library. The class library holds an immense amount of prewritten code that all the applications you create with Visual Basic, Visual C++, Visual C#, Visual J#, and other Visual Studio languages build on.

For example, say that your application displays a Windows form such as the sample application you've created today. To actually create and draw that Windows form takes thousands of lines of code—something you probably wouldn't want to be responsible for writing each time you wanted to display a window. And because of the .NET Framework's class library, you don't have to. All the code you need is already available in the class library for your application to use.

All your application needs to do is to search the class library for the particular type of form that it needs and use it. In this way, you don't have to create the form from scratch. This means your code can be very small; all the power you need is already available to you in the .NET Framework's class library. The class library comes built in with all the code your application needs to draw, handle memory, create Windows forms, perform input/output (I/O) operations, manage security, and more.

The Common Language Runtime

Although the .NET Framework class library is a great resource, packed full of an immense amount of prewritten code for you, you need some way of getting that code to run, and that's what the .NET Framework's common language runtime is all about. The common language runtime is what actually runs your Visual Basic .NET application.

NEW TERM When you build a Visual Basic .NET application, your code is translated—that is, *compiled*—into the language that the common language runtime actually understands, the Microsoft Intermediate Language, or more commonly MSIL or just IL. When you run the application, the common language runtime reads the MSIL for your application and quickly translates it into the actual binary codes that your computer works with. In this way, Microsoft can one day create a common language runtime for operating systems other than Windows, and your Visual Basic .NET applications, compiled into IL, will run on them.

This has a very powerful side effect: The common language runtime can run programs created not only in Visual Basic, but also in Visual C++, Visual C#, and other Visual Studio languages. Applications written in those other languages are also translated into IL. This means they all look alike to the common language runtime, which is what's actually responsible for running them.

And there's another powerful side effect as well: Because your application is stored in IL, you can also easily mix various Visual Studio languages in the same application. When you build an application, everything is translated into the same language anyway, and that's IL.

New Term In fact, because everything is stored in IL, the applications you build are not like the applications you build using other packages besides Visual Studio. Those applications are stored in the binary format that a computer runs directly. Visual Studio applications, however, are built using IL, and they're built to interact with the common language runtime. For that reason, they're called *assemblies*.

Assemblies are the fundamental unit of deployment for applications in Visual Studio, and although we won't use the term often, knowing it is good because you'll see it used frequently in the Visual Basic documentation.

Assemblies

An assembly holds the IL modules for your application. When you create an application in Visual Basic .NET and run it, Visual Basic .NET creates one or more assemblies, which are run by the common language runtime. That is, assemblies are the way your applications interact with the .NET Framework instead of the EXE or DLL files of VB6.

New Term What's in a .NET assembly? Each assembly has a *manifest*, which is like a table of contents, giving the name and version of the assembly. The manifest also lists what other assemblies are needed to support this one, if any, and how to handle security issues.

New Term The core of the assembly is made up of *modules*, which are internal files of IL code, ready to run. That's how Visual Basic .NET stores the IL it creates—in modules inside assemblies.

That, then, is what an assembly is—the package that holds the IL for your application, the information that the common language runtime needs to handle your application. We won't deal with assemblies directly a great deal, but you can configure them to a substantial degree. For example, each project contains a file named AssemblyInfo.vb, which holds, among other things, the version number for your application.

New Term The common language runtime looks at applications in terms of assemblies, which are how applications are stored after they've been built. But what about while you're developing and creating them? As you've seen, when you create a new application in Visual Basic .NET, you actually create a new project, selecting the File, New, Project menu item. In fact, there's more to the story than that because each project is also part of a Visual Basic *solution*, which can hold several projects.

Solutions and Projects

New Term When you created applications in Visual Basic 6.0, you simply created projects. Each project held the code and data for an application. If you wanted to combine projects, you created a *project group*. In Visual Basic .NET, however, project groups have become far more integral to the development process, and now they're called *solutions*.

When you create a new project in Visual Basic .NET, Visual Basic will actually create a new solution first and make the new project a part of that solution. You can see how this works in the Solution Explorer, which is the window that appears in the IDE at upper right, as you see in Figure 1.15.

FIGURE 1.15

The Solution Explorer in the IDE.

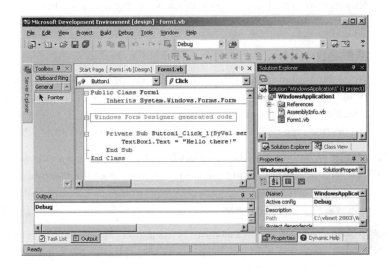

In this case, the Solution Explorer is displaying the Windows application we created earlier today. You can see in the Solution Explorer that the solution has been given the same name, WindowsApplication1, as the contained project. The top line in the Solution Explorer holds the name of the current solution, and below it is the line containing the name of the contained project, which in this case is also WindowsApplication1. (You can change either the solution name or a project's name simply by editing them in the Solution Explorer.)

Under the project's name, the Solution Explorer displays the files in the current project. For example, Form1.vb stores the form in the application, and AssemblyInfo.vb holds data about the current assembly, as discussed in the previous section. You can use the Solution Explorer to get an overview of the files in an application, switching between them just by double-clicking them in the Solution Explorer (making them open in form or code designers as appropriate).

> **Tip**
>
> You can look at and edit the information in AssemblyInfo.vb using the Solution Explorer. Just double-click the AssemblyInfo.vb file in the Solution Explorer to open it, and you'll see where Visual Basic .NET stores the version number for your application.

Why would you want to add more than one project to a solution? As you'll see in Day 20, "Creating User Controls, Web User Controls, and Multithreading," you can create your own Windows and Web controls for use in applications. Each new control becomes a new project in an application, and if you have multiple custom controls, you'll have multiple projects in one solution. And you can also add another simple Windows or Web form project to the solution to test the custom controls.

> **Tip**
>
> How do you add a new project to a solution? When you have a solution open, you just select the File, New, Project menu item to create a new project, and click the Add to Solution radio button in the New Project dialog to add the new project to the current solution. When you have multiple projects in the same solution, you can specify which project you want to have run when you start the application. As you'll see in Day 20, you do that by right-clicking the project you want in the Solution Explorer and selecting the Set As Startup Project item in the menu that appears.

Solution and Project Files

As you can see in the Solution Explorer, each Visual Basic .NET project has a number of files connected with it. It's a good idea to get an overview of this file structure for future reference because you'll be dealing with it a lot in your own programming. Each project is stored in its own folder, which is given the name of the project; for example, the project WindowsApplication1 is stored in a folder of the same name. (Multiple projects in the same solution aren't stored in the same folder by default, although you can store them that way if you prefer.)

The file structure for the WindowsApplication1 project looks like this, including what each file does:

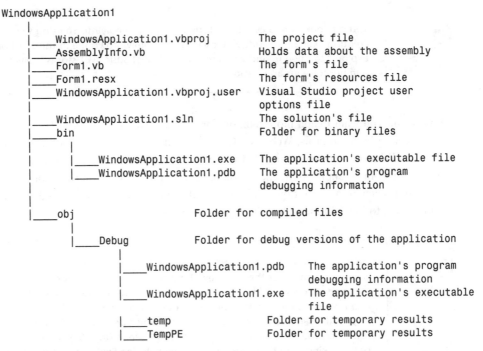

```
WindowsApplication1
      |
      |____WindowsApplication1.vbproj          The project file
      |____AssemblyInfo.vb                      Holds data about the assembly
      |____Form1.vb                             The form's file
      |____Form1.resx                           The form's resources file
      |____WindowsApplication1.vbproj.user      Visual Studio project user
      |                                         options file
      |____WindowsApplication1.sln              The solution's file
      |____bin                                  Folder for binary files
      |    |
      |    |____WindowsApplication1.exe         The application's executable file
      |    |____WindowsApplication1.pdb         The application's program
      |                                         debugging information
      |
      |____obj                    Folder for compiled files
           |
           |____Debug             Folder for debug versions of the application
                |
                |____WindowsApplication1.pdb    The application's program
                |                               debugging information
                |____WindowsApplication1.exe    The application's executable
                |                               file
                |____temp         Folder for temporary results
                |____TempPE       Folder for temporary results
```

Note in particular the WindowsApplication1.vbproj file, which is the project file that contains the names of all files in this project, and other project information, as well as the WindowsApplication1.sln file, which is the solution file that holds the names and locations of the various projects in the current solution.

As you can see, many different file types are involved in a typical Visual Basic .NET project. It's a good idea to familiarize yourself with the types of files you'll see in a Visual Basic project. Here's a list, arranged by file extension. This list is intended as a reference you can use as needed when you develop your Visual Basic projects; don't feel you have to know all this information at this point.

- **.asax**—A global application class, used to handle global ASP.NET application-level events.
- **.asmx**—A Web service class.
- **.asp**—An Active Server Page.
- **.aspx**—A Web form.
- **.bmp**—A bitmap file.
- **.css**—A cascading style sheet file.
- **.exe**—An executable file holding the application's assembly.

- **.htm**—An HTML document.
- **.js**—A JScript file (Microsoft's version of JavaScript).
- **.pdb**—A file that holds program debug data.
- **.resx**—A resource file used to store resource information.
- **.rpt**—A Crystal Report.
- **.sln**—A solution file.
- **.suo**—A file that holds options for a solution.
- **.txt**—A text file.
- **.vb**—A Visual Basic source code file. It can be a basic Windows form, a code file, a module file, a user control, a data form, a custom control, an inherited form, a Web custom control, an inherited user control, a Windows service, a custom setup file, an image file for creating a custom icon, or an AssemblyInfo file (used to store assembly information such as versioning and assembly name).
- **.vbproj**—A Visual Basic project file.
- **.vbs**—A VBScript file.
- **.vsdisco**—A dynamic discovery project, which provides a means to describe all Web services in a Web project.
- **.web**—A Web configuration file, which configures Web settings for a Web project.
- **.wsf**—A Windows scripting file.
- **.xml**—An XML document file.
- **.xsd**—An XML schema provided to create typed datasets.
- **.xslt**—An XSLT style sheet file, used to transform XML documents and XML schemas.

In addition, you might have noticed that the application's executable file is built in a directory called Debug. By default, you can build Visual Basic .NET applications in two ways: in debug or release versions. And now that we're discussing applications in general, it's important that we take a look at these versions.

Debug and Release Versions

So far, we've started our programs from the Debug menu's Start item, which causes Visual Basic to launch the program while staying in the background. If a problem occurs, the Visual Basic IDE will reappear to let you debug the program's code. And when you end the program, the Visual Basic IDE will automatically reappear to let you continue your development work.

That capability is useful for development, of course, but when your program is ready to go and to be used for others, you hardly want them to have to launch your program from Visual Basic. In addition, applications set up for easy debugging have a great deal of data stored in them that users won't need in general. For example, all the names you use in your code will be stored in the application so the Visual Basic .NET debugger can display them as needed. But the end user doesn't need to know all those internal names, so that information is useless in the version of your application that you release to the public.

NEW TERM That's where the difference between *debug* and *release* versions of your program comes in. In a debug version of your program, Visual Basic stores a great deal of data needed to interface with the debugger in your program when it runs. Storing all this data not only makes the corresponding assembly larger, but also slower. In the release version of your program, the program doesn't have all that added data and can run as a standalone program, without needing to be launched from Visual Basic (although it still needs the .NET Framework, of course).

When you create a new solution, Visual Basic creates it in Debug mode by default, which means that you launch it from the Debug menu as you've been doing. However, you can switch to Release mode in several ways (like many things in Visual Basic .NET, there's more than one way to do this). Here are some of them:

- You can select the Configuration Manager item in the Build menu, select Release in the Active Solution Configuration list box, and then click OK.
- You can select the solution by clicking it in the Solution Explorer and then selecting the Properties item in the Project menu. Select the Configuration Properties folder on the left in the dialog that opens, followed by the Configuration item in that folder. Then select Release from the drop-down list box in the configuration column of the table that appears and click OK.
- Here's the easiest way—just use the drop-down list box that appears in the Visual Basic .NET standard toolbar, at the top of the IDE. By default, this list box displays the word Debug, and all you need to do to switch to Release mode is to select Release instead.

When you've set the mode for a solution to Release, you can build it using the Build menu's Build Solution item (the Build Solution menu item causes Visual Basic to compile only items it thinks have been newly changed; to force it to compile *all* items in the solution, choose the Rebuild Solution item instead of Build Solution). This builds the solution in a way that others can use it, and you can deploy your program this way (usually with the help of a deployment project that you build in Visual Basic, as we'll do in Day 21).

When you build an application in Release mode, a new folder named Release is added to the obj folder for the project, and the new application executable file goes there:

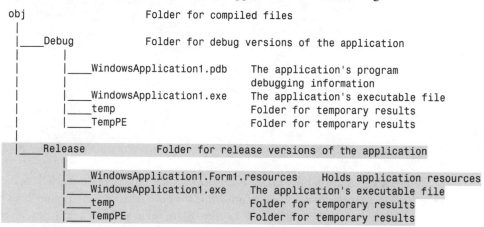

```
obj                          Folder for compiled files
 |
 |____Debug                  Folder for debug versions of the application
 |      |
 |      |____WindowsApplication1.pdb    The application's program
 |      |                               debugging information
 |      |____WindowsApplication1.exe    The application's executable file
 |      |____temp                       Folder for temporary results
 |      |____TempPE                     Folder for temporary results
 |
 |____Release                 Folder for release versions of the application
        |
        |____WindowsApplication1.Form1.resources    Holds application resources
        |____WindowsApplication1.exe      The application's executable file
        |____temp                         Folder for temporary results
        |____TempPE                       Folder for temporary results
```

We now have the background we need on Visual Basic .NET solutions and projects as we head into the following days, where we'll assume this knowledge and put it to work. We'll also take for granted that you know your way around the central programming tool itself—the Visual Basic .NET IDE. We're going to be using the IDE on nearly every page to come in this book, so we're going to need to know all about it in detail; after all, it's our primary programming tool. Because using the IDE is going to become second nature to us, we'll take the rest of today to understand it.

The Visual Basic .NET Integrated Development Environment

The skill we're going to work on for the rest of today is using the IDE, which you can see in Figure 1.16. The original Visual Basic IDE was very simple, containing not much more than a Windows form designer and the toolbox. That's changed today, as Visual Basic has changed—and as other languages have been added to Visual Studio, which uses the same IDE for them.

FIGURE 1.16

*The Visual Basic .NET
Integrated
Development
Environment.*

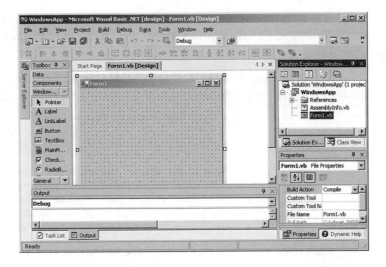

We've already used parts of the IDE today, but now it's time to build the IDE foundation we'll need in the coming days. We're going to cover all the IDE windows here, so it's important to know that you don't have to know all of them at this stage. Just scan the various topics and decide which ones you want to read; then come back to the others later. For completeness, you'll see everything here, but at this point, you should just read the parts that seem useful to you now instead of trying to memorize everything at once.

Here's something else to know: There are so many independent windows in the IDE that you can easily misplace or rearrange them inadvertently (you can move and arrange each IDE window easily, and that can happen by mistake if Visual Studio thinks you wanted to drag an IDE window when you actually didn't). The IDE windows are docking windows, which means you can use the mouse to move windows around as you like. When the windows are near an edge, they'll "dock"—adhere—to that edge, so you can reconfigure the IDE windows as you like. If you move IDE windows inadvertently, don't panic, just use the mouse to drag them back.

Tip

Here's something else that's good to know: You can restore the default window layout by selecting the Tools, Options menu item, then selecting the General item in the Environment folder, and clicking the Reset Window Layout button. This tip turns out to be really useful to know, because sooner or later, Visual Basic .NET will dock some window you didn't even want to move in a place where other windows are docked already, rearranging all your other windows. And trying to fix that problem manually can take a long time! If all the IDE windows appear to jump and shuffle themselves suddenly, leaving you with something you hardly recognize, you know it has happened to you.

Here's another feature that's useful: As you can see in Figure 1.16, the various IDE windows often have an X at the upper right so you can close them. Sooner or later, most people close a window in the IDE by mistake (and all other windows often slide around to fill the gap). That makes it easy to panic—the toolbox is gone! You might think, "Oh no, I'll have to reinstall everything!" In fact, that's not true; you just have to reopen the closed window again.

You can open that closed window using the View menu. Just open that menu, find the window that you closed, and select it (such as View, Toolbox) to make it reappear. Some windows are listed in the View, Other Windows menu item, which opens a submenu of additional windows. The IDE simply has too many windows to fit them all into one menu without using a submenu. So, if you close a window by mistake, just look at the View menu to open it again.

Also note that there's so much in the IDE that Visual Studio now makes many windows share the same space (you might get the impression sometimes that the best option for Visual Studio is to use a wall-sized screen). To let a number of windows share the same space, Visual Studio adds tabs at the edge of that space, as you can see in Figure 1.16. For example, notice the Properties and Dynamic Help tabs at the lower right, or the Start Page and Form1.vb[Design] tabs above the form under construction in the middle of the IDE. You can switch among the various windows sharing the same space by clicking these tabs.

And you should be aware of yet another space-saving device that the IDE uses. In addition to the close buttons (marked with X) at the top right of many IDE windows, you'll also see a small thumbtack button. For example, you can see this thumbtack above the toolbox and the Solution Explorer. This is the auto hide feature, which allows you to reduce a window to a tab connected to the edge on which it's docked.

For example, in Figure 1.16, the Server Explorer (which lets you explore data sources on other servers) is hidden and has become a tab at the upper left in the IDE. If you move the mouse over that tab, the full Server Explorer window will open, covering most of the toolbox. You can auto-hide most windows like this; for example, if you were to click the thumbtack button in the toolbox, it would close and become a tab under the Server Explorer tab in the IDE. To restore a window to fully open status, just click the thumbtack again.

You can customize the IDE as well. For example, to customize menus and toolbars, such as specifying which toolbars to display (there are 25 toolbars to choose from), or what buttons go on what toolbars, select the Tools, Customize menu item. To customize IDE options such as the fonts and colors used to display code, you select the Tools, Options menu item and use the various items in the Environment folder.

That's it for our overview of the IDE. Now it's time to get to the IDE details themselves, starting, appropriately enough, with the Start Page.

The Start Page

When you start Visual Basic .NET, you'll see the Start Page, as you see outlined in Figure 1.17. As you can see, the Start Page has three tabs: Projects, Online Resources, and My Profile.

The Projects Tab

The Projects tab of the Start Page lists your most recent projects, as you can see in Figure 1.17, and just clicking a project name will open that project.

FIGURE 1.17

The Start Page, Projects tab.

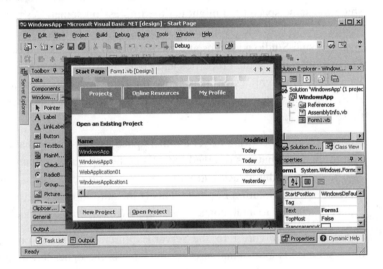

You can also create a new project here by clicking the New Project button. This is the tab you'll see when you start Visual Basic .NET after you've created at least one project. Until that time, and the first time you open Visual Basic .NET, you'll see the My Profile tab.

The Online Resources Tab

The next tab in the Start Page is the Online Resources tab, which gives you access to Visual Basic .NET online resources as long as your computer is connected to the Internet. You can see this tab at work in Figure 1.18.

FIGURE 1.18

The Start Page, Online Resources tab.

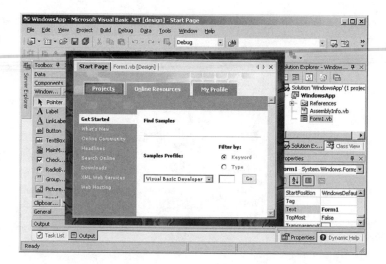

This tab is useful because it keeps you in touch with the Visual Basic .NET community. You can check for online Visual Basic samples by clicking the Get Started subtab, selecting Visual Basic Developer in the drop-down list box, and clicking Go. The Online Community subtab gives you access to various discussion groups online. For more detailed information on Visual Basic .NET online resources, see the section "Online Resources" coming up later today.

The My Profile Tab

We've already put the My Profile tab, which you can see in Figure 1.1, to work. Using this tab, you can filter help topics, select internal or external help windows, and specify other aspects of your Visual Studio environment.

The Menus and Toolbars

The IDE's menu and toolbar system is fairly extensive, and you can see both the main menu and default toolbars outlined in Figure 1.19.

In fact, the items in the menu system can change depending on what you're doing. For example, the Project menu will display 16 items if you first select a project in the Solution Explorer, but only 4 if you have selected a solution, not a project.

You can even make whole menus disappear and appear just by what you're working on. If you have a Windows form designer open, for example, you'll see a Data menu (for connecting to databases) and a Format menu (for arranging the controls in the window), as you see in Figure 1.3. But if you have a code designer open instead, those menus will disappear, as you see in Figure 1.6.

FIGURE 1.19

*The IDE menus and
default toolbars.*

There are hundreds of menu items here, and many useful ones that will quickly become
favorites, such as the most recently used (MRU) list of files and projects that you can
access from the Recent Files or Recent Projects items near the bottom of the File menu.

> **Tip**
>
> In Visual Studio, you can set the number of items that appear in MRU lists by
> selecting the Tools, Options menu item, clicking the Environment folder,
> selecting the General item, and entering a value in the Most Recently Used
> Lists text box.

The menu system also allows you to set many IDE options with the Tools, Options menu
item, and set which toolbars to view with the Tools, Customize menu item, both of which
we've already mentioned. You'll see more and more menu items throughout the book as
appropriate.

The toolbars you see under the main menu in Figure 1.19 are the default toolbars that
Visual Basic .NET displays. Twenty-five toolbars are available, however, and you can
choose which ones you want displayed by using the Tools, Customize menu item or the
View, Toolbars menu item, and even which buttons appear in which toolbar. You can also
customize which toolbars appear by right-clicking a toolbar and selecting the toolbars
you want from the menu that appears. Sometimes Visual Basic .NET displays new toolbars automatically; for example, the Debug toolbar automatically appears after you start
debugging an application (as when you select the Debug, Start menu item).

Tip

How can you tell what all those buttons in the various toolbars do? The IDE will display a tool tip—those small yellow windows with explanatory text—when you let the mouse hover over each button.

Each button in a toolbar corresponds to an item in a menu, by the way. Toolbars simply present you with a quick alternative to selecting various menu items.

Designers

NEW TERM   What makes Visual Basic visual is that you can see what you're creating as you create it, and it does that with *designers*. For example, a Windows form designer allows you to see what a window will look like when you run an application. You can see a Windows form designer in Figure 1.20.

FIGURE 1.20

A Windows form designer.

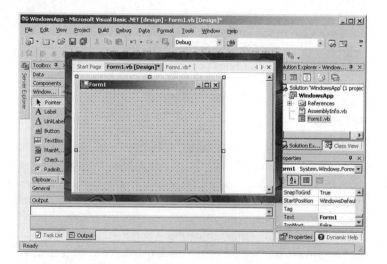

Tip

Note the asterisk (*) in the tab for the Windows form designer in Figure 1.20. The asterisk means that you've made changes in the designer that have not yet been saved to disk. To save those changes to disk, select the File, Save *xxxx* menu items, where *xxxx* is the item you want to save, or click the toolbar button with a disk to save the current file, or the toolbar button with a stack of disks, which saves all files in the project.

Visual Basic has several types of designers. Windows form designers are one type; Web form designers are another type. Other designer types are available as well, such as user control designers (which enable you to create custom controls), XML designers (which enable you to work with Extensible Markup Language, XML), code designers, and others. When you're working with several designers at once, you can select one by clicking its tab. And you can close a designer by selecting it and clicking the close button (marked with an X) you see to the right of the designer tabs in Figure 1.20.

We've already seen code designers at work and entered our own code, as in Figure 1.7. Using a code designer, you can add code for a particular element, like a button, as in Figure 1.7. To open a code designer, you only have to double-click an element in a visual designer like a form designer. After a code designer is open, you can reach it by clicking its tab, labeled Form1.vb in Figure 1.7. Here's the code we worked on in that code designer:

```
Public Class Form1
    Inherits System.Windows.Forms.Form

'Windows Form Designer generated code

    Private Sub Button1_Click_1(ByVal sender As System.Object, _
        ByVal e As System.EventArgs) Handles Button1.Click
        TextBox1.Text = "Hello there!"
    End Sub
End Class
```

Note the section labeled "Windows Form Designer generated code" in Figure 1.7; the plus sign (+) in front of it means that it holds a collapsed section of code. The Windows form designer actually writes a fair amount of code for you when you create a Windows form, and the code designer shows that code collapsed by default—another space-saving feature of the crowded IDE. To see what's in this collapsed code section, click the +, opening that section (and turning the + into a –). Here's the code that was hidden and that performs setup for the form (more on what this code does in Day 4):

```
Public Class Form1
    Inherits System.Windows.Forms.Form

#Region " Windows Form Designer generated code "

    Public Sub New()
        MyBase.New()

        'This call is required by the Windows Form Designer.
        InitializeComponent()

        'Add any initialization after the InitializeComponent() call

    End Sub
```

```vb
'Form overrides dispose to clean up the component list.
Protected Overloads Overrides Sub Dispose(ByVal disposing As Boolean)
    If disposing Then
        If Not (components Is Nothing) Then
            components.Dispose()
        End If
    End If
    MyBase.Dispose(disposing)
End Sub

'Required by the Windows Form Designer
Private components As System.ComponentModel.IContainer

'NOTE: The following procedure is required by the Windows Form Designer
'It can be modified using the Windows Form Designer.
'Do not modify it using the code editor.
Friend WithEvents Button1 As System.Windows.Forms.Button
Friend WithEvents TextBox1 As System.Windows.Forms.TextBox
<System.Diagnostics.DebuggerStepThrough()> Private Sub InitializeComponent()
    Me.Button1 = New System.Windows.Forms.Button
    Me.TextBox1 = New System.Windows.Forms.TextBox
    Me.SuspendLayout()
    '
    'Button1
    '
    Me.Button1.Location = New System.Drawing.Point(112, 56)
    Me.Button1.Name = "Button1"
    Me.Button1.TabIndex = 0
    Me.Button1.Text = "Button1"
    '
    'TextBox1
    '
    Me.TextBox1.Location = New System.Drawing.Point(104, 120)
    Me.TextBox1.Name = "TextBox1"
    Me.TextBox1.TabIndex = 1
    Me.TextBox1.Text = "TextBox1"
    '
    'Form1
    '
    Me.AutoScaleBaseSize = New System.Drawing.Size(5, 13)
    Me.ClientSize = New System.Drawing.Size(292, 273)
    Me.Controls.Add(Me.TextBox1)
    Me.Controls.Add(Me.Button1)
    Me.Name = "Form1"
    Me.Text = "Form1"
    Me.ResumeLayout(False)

End Sub

#End Region
```

```
    Private Sub Button1_Click_1(ByVal sender As System.Object, _
        ByVal e As System.EventArgs) Handles Button1.Click
        TextBox1.Text = "Hello there!"
    End Sub
End Class
```

> **Tip**
>
> Note the #Region and #End Region keywords here; they enclose a code sec-
> tion that the code designer knows can be collapsed or expanded by clicking +
> and –. You can use the #Region and #End Region keywords in your own code
> as well, to enable the code designer to hide sections of already-tested code.

IntelliSense

NEW TERM   One powerful feature of code designers is Microsoft's *IntelliSense*. IntelliSense is
responsible for displaying helpful boxes that open as you write your code, listing
all the possible options and even completing your typing for you.

For example, the code we entered into the code designer in our Windows form example
was TextBox1.Text = "Hello there!"; this code will assign text to the Text property
of the text box (more on properties when we discuss the Properties window in a few
pages). When you type **TextBox1.** (it's important to include the dot [.] here) in the code
designer, IntelliSense will open a box for you showing you all the possibilities such as
TextBox1.ReadOnly, TextBox1.TextAlign, TextBox1.Text, and so on, as you see in
Figure 1.21. You can either just keep typing or select an option from the IntelliSense box,
as you see in Figure 1.21.

FIGURE 1.21

Using IntelliSense.

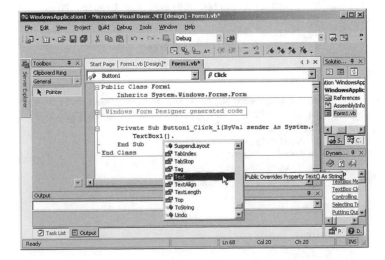

Because IntelliSense is a useful feature, you can easily start relying on it. If you forget the name of some property, say the Text property, you can just type **TextBox1.** and IntelliSense will give you a list of all available options. All you need to do is to scroll up and down the list until you find the one you want.

IntelliSense performs all kinds of tasks for you, such as listing the members of objects (such as the properties of our text box), displaying information about items when you let the mouse hover over those items (try letting the mouse hover over the word TextBox1, for example), completing words you're typing, automatically adding additional parentheses to make sure there's a closing parenthesis for each opening parenthesis, and more. Don't be surprised when IntelliSense offers syntax tips that display the correct Visual Basic syntax when you're typing something.

Visual Studio's IntelliSense is something you quickly get used to and usually find useful or, at least, ignorable. But if you want, you can turn off the various parts of IntelliSense. To do that, first select the Tools, Options menu item; then select the Text Editor folder, then the Basic subfolder, and finally the General item in the Basic subfolder. You'll see a number of IntelliSense options you can turn on and off with check boxes.

Note

When you're typing Visual Basic .NET code, you might enter what Visual Basic considers an error (**TextBox1.Txt**, for example). Visual Basic will add a wavy line under the error, and if you let the mouse rest over the error, Visual Basic will tell you what it thinks is wrong. This capability is also useful, but it's not technically part of IntelliSense.

The Toolbox

NEW TERM A lot of Visual Basic action centers around the *toolbox*, which holds various items such as the controls that you can add to forms. We've already used the toolbox to add a button and text box to a Windows form, in fact. You can see the toolbox outlined in Figure 1.22.

More and more tools appear in the toolbox with each new version of Visual Basic. To fit everything in, the toolbox is now divided up using tabs, and you can see these tabs, marked Data, Components, Windows Forms, and General, in Figure 1.22. The Data tab holds items you can use to make connections to data sources, and the Windows Forms tab holds buttons, list boxes, radio buttons, and the other user-interface controls you use in Windows forms. To add an item from the toolbox to a form, you simply double-click the item in the toolbox or drag it to the form. In this way, the toolbox gives you a palette of items you can use to design your user interface.

FIGURE 1.22

The toolbox.

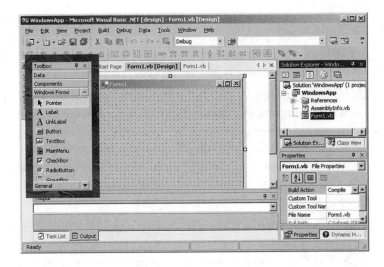

Which tabs are available depends on what type of designer you're working with. For example, when you're working on a Web form, you'll see Data, Web Forms, Components, HTML, Clipboard Ring (which displays the recent items you've put into the clipboard), and General tabs, but when you open a Windows form in a code designer, you'll see only the General and Clipboard Ring tabs. The General tab is empty by default, and is a place to store general components, controls, and fragments of code (you can even add more tabs to the toolbox by right-clicking the toolbox and selecting the Add Tab item).

Despite the fact that the toolbox is now divided into tabs, it's still likely that the tab you want to use, such as the Windows Forms tab, will hold more items than it can display at once, so you'll end up scrolling up and down in that tab. That's just another artifact of a very crowded IDE.

The Solution Explorer

We've seen the Solution Explorer at work already. This tool gives you an overview, file by file, of what files are in a project and what projects are in a solution. You can see the Solution Explorer outlined in Figure 1.23.

As you see in Figure 1.23, the Solution Explorer presents the file organization of a solution hierarchically, starting with the solution itself, followed by the project(s) in the solution, followed by the project files. To open a file in a designer, you just locate it in the

Solution Explorer and double-click it. And it works the other way too—when you select
a designer to work with, the matching file in the Solution Explorer is highlighted. (This
capability is new in Visual Basic .NET 2003; you can turn this option on and off by
selecting the Tools, Options menu item, which opens the Options dialog; selecting the
Projects and Solutions folder; and selecting the Track Active Item in Solution Explorer
check box.)

1

FIGURE 1.23

The Solution Explorer.

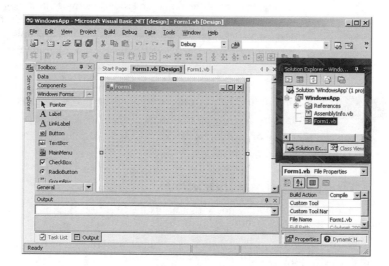

Here's something else that's useful to know about the Solution Explorer: If you've
selected something in the Solution Explorer that has both a visual designer and a code
designer, say a Windows form, you can switch between those designers using the buttons
in the Solution Explorer toolbar, which you see in Figure 1.23. The leftmost button in the
toolbar opens the code designer for the form, and the button second from the left opens
the form's visual designer.

You can also manage your projects and solutions in the Solution Explorer. For example,
you can right-click a solution and add a new project to it by selecting the Add, New,
Project menu item in the pop-up menu that appears. And you can specify which of multiple projects runs first—that is, the startup project or projects—by right-clicking the project and selecting the Set As Startup Object item, or by right-clicking the solution and
selecting the Set Startup Projects item.

Tip

> The Solution Explorer has a big effect on the item in the Visual Basic Project menu. When you select a project in the Solution Explorer, it becomes the current project as far as Visual Basic is concerned, so that's the project the items in the Project menu will work with. For example, you can set the Windows icon for a single-project application by selecting that project in the Solution Explorer, selecting Properties from the Project menu, then selecting the Build item of the Common Properties folder in the dialog that appears, and browsing to the new icon file you want to use. (Icon files have the extension .ico, and a good selection of them is available in the common\graphics\icons folder that comes with Visual Basic.)

NEW TERM The Solution Explorer arranges things in terms of files, as you can see in Figure 1.23, and that's one way to look at Visual Basic solutions and projects. However, there's another way of looking at object-oriented programs—in terms of *classes*—and the Class View window does that.

The Class View Window

If you look at the IDE window that holds the Solution Explorer, you'll see two tabs at the bottom—Solution Explorer and Class View—as shown in Figure 1.23. Clicking the Class View tab opens the Class View window, as you see in Figure 1.24, and gives you a new way to look at projects.

FIGURE 1.24

The Class View window.

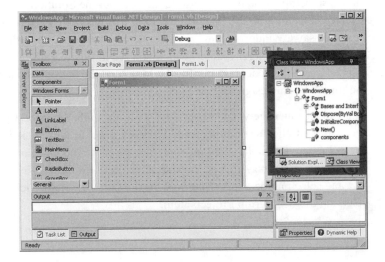

The Solution Explorer enables you to see an overview of your application in terms of the files in the application. From a programmer's point of view, however, what's often more important is to see how an application is arranged in programming terms, and that's what the Class View window is all about.

As you're going to see in the coming days, items like Windows forms are built using classes in Visual Basic .NET. You'll see the details later, but each class contains members that you work with in your program. For example, the `TextBox` class contains the `Text` member that you've already seen. The Class View window looks at your program in these terms, displaying what classes you have in your program and what members each class has.

This way of looking at a program will become more useful as we get into the programming aspects of Visual Basic .NET—especially in Day 9, where we're going to see a great deal on classes. What's important to know at this point is that the Class View window displays your program in programming terms, not just in terms of what files your program uses as the Solution Explorer does.

The Properties Window

The Properties window is a programmer's favorite, and you'll find yourself using this window a great deal in Visual Basic programming. You can see the Properties window outlined in Figure 1.25.

FIGURE 1.25

The Properties window.

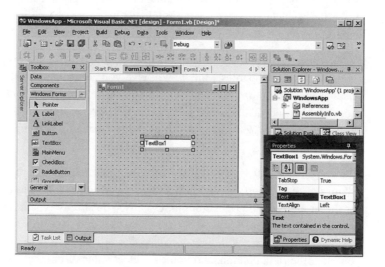

As we already know, items like text boxes have properties such as the Text property, which holds the text displayed in a text box. Such properties enable you to configure the items in your programs; for example, you can use properties to set the size and color of forms, the text and text alignment in text boxes, the caption in a button, and so forth.

NEW TERM When you're working on a form in the IDE and setting properties of various items in your program, that's called *design time*. When your program is running, that's called *runtime*. Some properties are available only at runtime (such as the current selection made by the user in a list box), some are available only at design time (such as the name a control is known by in your code), but most properties (such as the Text property of a text box) are available at both design time and runtime. To set the value of a property at runtime, you can use code like TextBox1.Text = "Hello there!". To set the value of a property at design time, you use the Properties window. The settings you make in the Properties window at design time set the values of the properties that elements in your program will have when the program starts to run.

When you select an item such as a form or a text box in a visual designer, the current values of its properties are displayed in the Properties window (give it a try). If you look at the Properties window in Figure 1.25, you'll see it's divided into two columns. The column on the left lists the properties available at design time, and the column on the right lists those properties' current values. Note also that the name of the item whose properties are displayed appears in the drop-down list box at the top of the Properties window. This list box contains the name of all items in the current designer that has properties, which means you can use this list box to select the item whose properties you want to set.

When you select a property, such as the Text property of a text box that you see in Figure 1.25, the Properties window will give you an explanation of the property in the panel at the bottom of the Properties window. Note also that you can display the list of properties alphabetically by clicking the second button from the left at the top of the Properties window. You can also display them in categories by clicking the leftmost button.

You can change a property's value easily. You just select that property's name in the left column of the Properties window, as you see in Figure 1.25, and then enter the new value for the property in the right column. Usually, you simply type in the value of the new property. Sometimes, however, certain properties can have only a few allowed values; in this case Visual Basic will display a drop-down list box next to the property's name when you click the right column, and you can select values from that list. Sometimes, Visual Basic requires more information, as when you create data connections, and a button with an ellipsis (…) appears. When you click that button, Visual Basic will usually walk you through the steps it needs to get that information.

As you can see, the Properties window is a useful tool, and you use it to configure the items in your application at design time, setting the values that those items' properties will have when the program first starts running.

The Dynamic Help Window

Another useful window—the window that shares the Properties window's space, in fact—is the Dynamic Help window. The Visual Basic .NET IDE often bends over backward to be helpful, and the Dynamic Help window is an example of that. You can reach this window, shown in Figure 1.26, by clicking the Dynamic Help tab next to the Properties tab.

FIGURE 1.26

The Dynamic Help window.

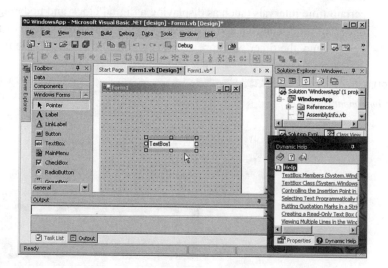

There are many ways of getting help in Visual Basic .NET, which contains an extensive help system. Visual Basic .NET has a Help menu with such items as Contents, Index, and Search to help you track down help on what you're looking for. But it also has the Dynamic Help window, which looks up information for you automatically.

If the Dynamic Help window is open and you select a control in a visual designer, as you see in Figure 1.26 where a text box has been selected, or if a code designer is open and you've selected a term like TextBox1, the Dynamic Help window will *automatically* look up help information for you.

If you click a help link in the Dynamic Help window, the corresponding help topic is opened in the help system in an internal window in the IDE by default, or in an external help window if you've set the IDE to use external help instead. This makes looking up information a great deal easier; you just select an item, and various help topics are automatically displayed in the Dynamic Help window, enabling you to select among the options.

Component Trays

NEW TERM   Another term you should know is *component trays*. When you add a visual item like a text box or a button to a form, you can see it in the form and select that element as needed to work on it and set its properties. However, some items that you can add to a form do not appear at runtime; for example, you can add a *timer* control from the toolbox to a form, as you see in Figure 1.27. You can use timers to make things happen at certain time intervals (such as displaying a digital clock and updating the time every second), but timer controls do not appear at runtime. To give you something to work with at design time, the timer will appear in a component tray, as you see in Figure 1.27.

FIGURE 1.27

A component tray.

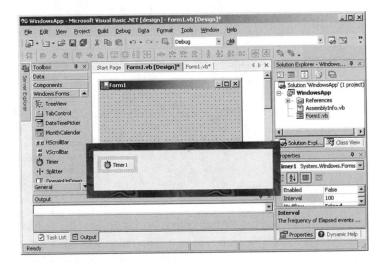

Component trays are added to visual designers to display items that aren't visible at runtime, but that you want to work with at design time. For us, that will include not only clocks, but also connections to databases, as well as datasets used to hold data from databases.

The Server Explorer

While we're speaking of data connections, we should take a look at the Server Explorer. As you can guess from its name, you use the Server Explorer to explore servers. It's a good tool because it makes what are really distant servers feel very close. You can see the Server Explorer in Figure 1.28.

FIGURE 1.28

The Server Explorer.

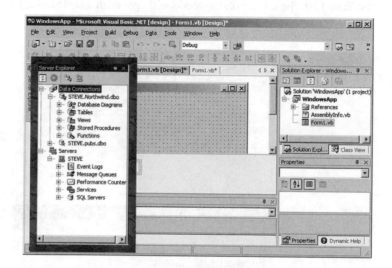

If you don't see the Server Explorer, select the View, Server Explorer menu item. The Server Explorer is usually stored as a tab on the left of the IDE, using the auto hide thumbtack button. When you let the mouse cursor hover over that tab, the Server Explorer will open, gliding out automatically.

In Figure 1.28, the Server Explorer has found a server named STEVE, which is my SQL Server, and it has examined the databases on that server. It has detected two data connections I've made to databases, named STEVE.Northwind.dbo and STEVE.pubs.dbo, and lets you examine the corresponding databases. You'll learn about data connections and how to work with the Server Explorer in Days 16 through 19.

> **Tip**
>
> You can do more than just look using the Server Explorer. You can drag and drop items onto Windows forms or Web forms from the Server Explorer. For example, if you drag a database table onto a form, Visual Basic .NET will create the code you need to access that table automatically, as you'll see in Day 16, "Handling Databases with ADO.NET."

The Task List and Output Window

The Task List displays things that Visual Basic .NET thinks you have to do, such as correcting errors in your code. For example, say you make a typo and try to run a program before fixing it. In that case, the Task List will appear as you see in Figure 1.29, listing the errors Visual Basic found when trying to run your program. If you click an error in the Task List, the corresponding code will appear in a code designer, as you see in Figure 1.29.

FIGURE 1.29

The Task List.

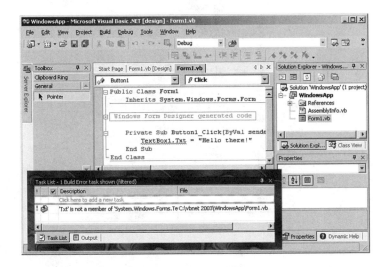

The Task List has other uses as well. For example, if you open a VB6 project in Visual Basic .NET, the migration tool will appear automatically and let you update the VB6 project as much as possible. Because so much is different from VB6, however (for example, all graphics and drawing work are just about completely different), the migration tool will leave many "TO DO" items in your code. They will all appear in the Task List, and you can click them one by one to work on them in your code.

The Task List shares space with the Output window, which you can see in Figure 1.30. The Output window displays Visual Basic's progress as it's trying to do something you've asked it to do. In Figure 1.30, you can see the output generated by starting and running a program. Here, Visual Basic is telling us that the program was started and has ended successfully.

FIGURE 1.30

The Output window.

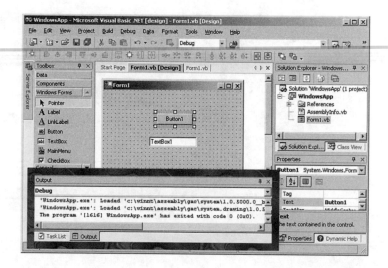

 Tip

You can send messages to the Output window directly using `System.Diagnostics.Debug.Write` like this: `System.Diagnostics.Debug.Write("Hello there from the Output window!")`.

We've finished our overview of the Visual Basic .NET 2003 IDE. As you can see, there's a great deal here. Knowing how to use the IDE is a skill that becomes second nature to Visual Basic programmers, and that's going to happen as we use it throughout the book.

Online Resources

We'll end our first day of Visual Basic .NET work by taking a look at some of the resources available online. These resources are available for free, they're there to augment your Visual Basic .NET arsenal, and they're worth knowing about. For example, the Visual Basic home page itself is at http://msdn.microsoft.com/vbasic/, and you'll find fairly recent material and discussions there.

Microsoft has done a good job of putting together many other Visual Basic resources online—and has given you access to those resources in the IDE. For example, if you select the Online Resources tab in the Start Page and then select the Online Community subtab, you'll see a number of selections, as shown in Figure 1.31.

...e Start Page, Online Resources tab.

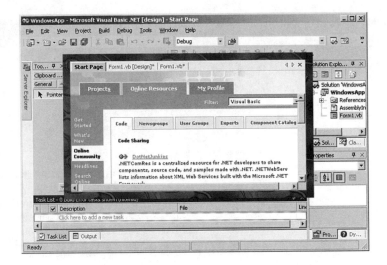

Here are the new tabs that appear in Figure 1.31 and what they do:

- **Code**—Lists code-sharing groups
- **Newsgroups**—Lists Usenet groups that discuss Visual Basic
- **User Groups**—Allows you to search for local Visual Basic .NET user groups
- **Experts**—Lists some recent technical articles available online
- **Component Catalog**—Lists Visual Basic components (such as new controls) available from component vendors

The Code Sharing section has a lot of code available for free download. Here are some sample sites you'll find in this section:

- `http://www.dotnetjunkies.com/comreswhatis.aspx`—The Dotnetjunkies site, a centralized repository for code to share with others
- `http://www.gotdotnet.com/userarea/default.aspx`—The Gotodotnet site's user examples
- `http://www.123aspx.com/directory.aspx?dir=1`—An overview of code-sharing resources on the Internet

The Newsgroups section lists a few Usenet groups that discuss Visual Basic .NET, including

- `microsoft.public.dotnet.languages.vb`
- `microsoft.public.dotnet.languages.vb.upgrade`

- `microsoft.public.vsnet.general`
- `microsoft.public.vsnet.ide`

Usenet groups like these can be a good place to post questions and to discuss various programming issues. You're more likely to get answers to general questions here, though, instead of help with in-depth problems.

Another important part of the online resources available in the IDE is a list of Internet service providers (ISPs) that support .NET and allow you to host your Web applications and services. You can develop Web applications and services on the same computer that has Visual Basic installed, but to make them accessible to others on the Internet, you can host them with an ISP. When you click the Web Hosting subtab in the Online Resources tab, you'll see a list of .NET-enabled ISPs, including

- `https://logon.vs.k2unisys.net/signup1.asp`—The Unisys .NET ISP
- `http://www.innerhost.com/default.asp?main=vsdotnetfree.asp`—The INNERHOST .NET ISP
- `http://www.brinkster.com/Join.asp?vsuser`—The Brinkster .NET ISP
- `http://www.eraserver.net/vsb2form.asp`—The EraServer.NET ISP
- `http://www.hostbasket.com/dotnet_hosting.shtml`—The Hostbasket .NET ISP
- `http://www.hostworks.com.au/signup.asp`—The Hostwork .NET ISP (currently including a three-month free trial)
- `http://www.ico.com.au/dotnetapplication.aspx`—The ICO .NET ISP in Australia (which advertises free .NET hosting)
- `http://www.maximumasp.com/signup.aspx?p=DotNet`—The MaximumASP .NET ISP
- `http://1ch.protier.com/`—The ProTier .NET ISP
- `https://admin-au.server-secure.com/dotnet/signup.cfm`—The WebCentral .NET ISP

As you can see, many online resources are available on Visual Basic to keep you connected with the Visual Basic community. Take a look!

Summary

In this, our first day working with Visual Basic .NET, we've come far. We've gotten an idea of what Visual Basic .NET is good for and how it's used. We've also taken a look at where Visual Basic came from and its history.

We started by putting Visual Basic .NET to work immediately, seeing how easy it was to create a simple Windows application, Web application, and Console application. We were able to use the toolbox to drag new controls onto a Windows form and to add code to a button in a Windows form so that clicking the button would display a message in a text box.

After putting Visual Basic .NET to work, we stepped back to get the big picture from a programmer's point of view, getting an overview of the .NET Framework and the common language runtime and how they fit into the picture for us. We also discussed Visual Basic solutions and projects, and how they're related.

Much of today's work involved cultivating an essential skill for Visual Basic .NET programmers—using the Visual Basic Integrated Development Environment, the IDE. This is the tool that we'll be using throughout the book, and we got a good foundation for that work today.

After getting an overview of the IDE, we dug into the individual parts of the IDE, including the Start Page, the menu and toolbar systems, designers, including visual and code designers, the toolbox, the Solution Explorer, the Class View window, the Properties window, the Dynamic Help window, the Server Explorer, and more.

We've started our in-depth guided tour of Visual Basic .NET and built the foundation we'll need in the coming days. Tomorrow, you'll see more details, seeing how to work with data and operators in Visual Basic .NET as we start to write some real code.

Q&A

Q When I put controls onto a form at design time, they align themselves to the grid of dots on the form—but I need finer control. Isn't there some way to let me position controls exactly as I want them, independent of that grid?

A Yes. Just set the form's SnapToGrid property in the Properties window to False, which enables you to set the position of a control to anything you want. Incidentally, when you're adding controls to forms using the toolbox, you can use the items in the Format menu and the Layout toolbar to align, make the same size, and set the spacing for controls. You can also select multiple controls and move and resize them all at once.

Q How can I find out whether my current Internet service provider supports Visual Basic .NET?

A The best way is simply to ask your ISP's tech support staff. If they don't support Visual Basic .NET, suggest to them that they consider it. Tell them that Visual

Basic .NET is growing all the time and that other users will soon be asking. Keep in mind that you can get an account at one of the ISPs listed earlier in this chapter that do support .NET. You don't have to dial directly; just connect to your local ISP and let Visual Basic .NET connect to the remote ISP.

Workshop

This workshop tests whether you understand the concepts you saw today. It's a good idea to make sure you can answer these questions before pressing on to tomorrow's work.

Quiz

1. How do you create a new project in Visual Basic .NET?

2. After you've added a control to a form in a visual designer, how do you open a code designer to add or edit the control's code?

3. Name four different types of applications that Visual Basic .NET can create.

4. Name the two major elements of the .NET Framework that are essential for Visual Basic .NET.

5. What's the name of the IDE window that allows you to see the hierarchical arrangement of the files in your project?

Quiz Answers

1. The most common way to create a new project is to select the File, New, Project menu item and to use the New Project dialog that opens. You can also, however, click the New Project button in the Start Page, or right-click a solution in the Solution Explorer and select Add, New Project.

2. You can double-click the control to open a code designer. You can also select the control and click the View Code button in the Solution Explorer's toolbar (the left-most button), or select the View, Code menu item. Another alternative is to right-click the control and select the View Code menu item in the pop-up menu that appears.

3. Visual Basic .NET 2003 can create five types of applications: Windows applications, Web applications, Console applications, Smart Device applications (such as Pocket PCs), and Mobile Web applications (for PDAs).

4. The two essential components of the .NET Framework for Visual Basic .NET are the .NET Framework class library that supports items such as Windows forms, and the common language runtime, which is what actually runs your program.

5. The Solution Explorer.

Exercises

1. Look at the Windows application we developed today. Using the Properties window at design time, change the caption of the button to `Click Me` and delete the text in the text box (which is `TextBox1` when you first create the text box). You can do this by altering the `Text` property of both the button and the text box. Now run the application to make sure that the button has the caption `Click Me` and the text box is empty when the application starts. (More details on how to do this are coming up in Day 4.)

2. In the Windows application we developed today, the text box displays new text when you click the button. But the button itself can also display new text if you change the button's `Text` property at runtime. Add the code `Button1.Text = "Clicked!"` to the Windows application now so that the button's caption changes to `Clicked!` after it has been clicked.

DAY 2

Mastering the Visual Basic Language: Data, Operators, Conditionals, and Loops

Today and tomorrow, we'll be working on what really makes a Visual Basic .NET program tick—the Visual Basic language itself. Before we can deal with all kinds of user interfaces such as Windows and Web applications, we need to understand how to deal with data and how to write Visual Basic code. Today, we'll be

- Looking at Visual Basic keywords and statements
- Commenting code
- Declaring Visual Basic .NET constants, enumerations, and variables
- Examining the Visual Basic data types
- Converting between data types

- Declaring arrays and dynamic arrays
- Handling text strings
- Using Visual Basic operators
- Examining Visual Basic operator precedence
- Making decisions with `If`, `Select`, `Switch`, and `Choose`
- Using the `Do`, `For`, `For Each`, and `While` loops
- Using the `With` statement
- Ending a program in code

Today is all about storing data in Visual Basic and starting to work with that data in code. Everything we see today is essential for our upcoming work. Because we're focusing on the actual Visual Basic language here, the emphasis is on the code, not the user interface, and we're going to keep things simple by using console applications of the type we saw yesterday:

```
Module Module1

    Sub Main()
        Console.WriteLine("Hello there!")
        Console.WriteLine("Press Enter to continue...")
        Console.ReadLine()
    End Sub

End Module
```

This code just displays the follow message:

```
Hello there!
Press Enter to continue...
```

And it waits for you to press Enter, at which point it'll close its DOS window. By using console applications today and tomorrow, we won't have to worry about the user-interface details, such as how to display multiple-line text in a Windows form. We'll spend all of Day 4, "Creating Windows Forms," figuring out how Windows forms work.

Visual Basic .NET Keywords

NEW TERM   Let's get started now. The Visual Basic .NET language itself is made up of *keywords*, which are reserved words that you can use in your code and that have special meaning in Visual Basic. These are the words we'll use to write our programs. You can find a list of these keywords in Table 2.1, and you'll see plenty of them at work today and tomorrow.

TABLE 2.1 The Reserved Visual Basic Keywords

AddHandler	AddressOf	AndAlso	Alias
And	Ansi	As	Assembly
Auto	Boolean	ByRef	Byte
ByVal	Call	Case	Catch
CBool	CByte	CChar	CDate
CDec	CDbl	Char	CInt
Class	CLng	CObj	Const
CShort	CSng	CStr	CType
Date	Decimal	Declare	Default
Delegate	Dim	DirectCast	Do
Double	Each	Else	ElseIf
End	Enum	Erase	Error
Event	Exit	False	Finally
For	Friend	Function	Get
GetType	GoSub	GoTo	Handles
If	Implements	Imports	In
Inherits	Integer	Interface	Is
Let	Lib	Like	Long
Loop	Me	Mod	Module
MustInherit	MustOverride	MyBase	MyClass
Namespace	New	Next	Not
Nothing	NotInheritable	NotOverridable	Object
On	Option	Optional	Or
OrElse	Overloads	Overridable	Overrides
ParamArray	Preserve	Private	Property
Protected	Public	RaiseEvent	ReadOnly
ReDim	REM	RemoveHandler	Resume
Return	Select	Set	Shadows
Shared	Short	Single	Static
Step	Stop	String	Structure
Sub	SyncLock	Then	Throw

2

TABLE 2.1   continued

To	True	Try	TypeOf
Unicode	Until	Variant	When
While	With	WithEvents	WriteOnly
Xor			

NEW TERM   How do you use these keywords to write programs? You put them together into lines of code, called *statements*.

Visual Basic .NET Statements

A Visual Basic .NET statement is a complete Visual Basic instruction, and you usually give each statement its own line in your code. Statements can contain

- **Keywords**—Words reserved for Visual Basic's use.
- **Operators**—Symbols used to perform operations. For example, + performs addition operations, and – performs subtraction operations, and so on. We're going to see these operators in use today.
- **Variables**—Symbolic names given to values stored in memory and declared using the Dim keyword. We'll also see these variables in use today.
- **Literal values**—Simple numeric or text values, such as 24 or "Hello there!".
- **Constants**—The same as variables, except that you can't change the value stored in a constant (hence the name).
- **Expressions**—Combinations of any of the items in this list that Visual Basic can evaluate to yield a value. For example, the expression 5 + 2 yields the value 7.

Each statement is one of the following types:

- A *declaration statement*, which can name and create a variable, constant, array, or procedure.
- An *executable statement*, which can perform an action.

The following example shows both types of statements that will introduce the use of variables. Say, for example, that you want to store the current temperature, 60 degrees, in a program and also display that temperature. You can store the value 60 in a variable, which functions as a name you give to a data item stored in memory. To declare the variable, you use the Visual Basic Dim statement. In this case, you can indicate that the variable named Temperature will store integer values; this is a declaration type of statement:

```
Dim Temperature As Integer
    .
    .
    .
```

Now you can assign a value of 60 to this variable in an execution statement. This
statement uses the = *assignment operator* to assign 60 to Temperature:

```
Dim Temperature As Integer
Temperature = 60
    .
    .
    .
```

2

Now you can use the Temperature variable in your code, and Visual Basic will automatically substitute the value stored in it, 60, for the variable itself. You can see how to display that value in the sample project named Declaration in the code for this book, as you
see in Listing 2.1.

LISTING 2.1   Declaring and Using a Variable (Declaration project, Module1.vb)

```
Module Module1

    Sub Main()
        Dim Temperature As Integer
        Temperature = 60
        Console.WriteLine(Temperature)
        Console.WriteLine("Press Enter to continue...")
        Console.ReadLine()
    End Sub

End Module
```

You can see the results of this program in Figure 2.1, where, indeed, the value 60 is
displayed.

FIGURE 2.1

*Declaring and using a
variable.*

There's more to know about statements. For example, statements can become too long to fit onto a single line, and you can divide them using an underscore (_) at the end of each line like this, where the code is using the + addition operator to assign the value 1 + 2 + 3 + 4 + 5 + 6 + 7 + 8 + 9 + 10 (= 55) to the variable Temperature:

```
Dim Temperature As Integer
Temperature = 1 + 2 + 3 _
+ 4 + 5 + 6 _
+ 7 + 8 + 9 + 10
```

> **Tip**
>
> You can actually put multiple statements on the same line in Visual Basic .NET if you separate them with a colon (:), like this:
>
> `Dim Temperature As Integer : Temperature = 60.`

Commenting Your Code

NEW TERM　　You can also add *comments* to your code to make it easier to understand. Comments are descriptive text meant to be read by programmers only—Visual Basic ignores them. Comments in Visual Basic start with an apostrophe ('). Here's an example with comments added to our previous code to make it easier to read; note that comments can appear at the end of a line of code or on their own line:

```
Sub Main()
    'Declare the Temperature variable
    Dim Temperature As Integer
    Temperature = 60      'Assign a value of 60 to Temperature
    'Display the value in the Temperature variable
    Console.WriteLine(Temperature)
    Console.WriteLine("Press Enter to continue...")
    Console.ReadLine()
End Sub
```

> **Tip**
>
> Here's a little known Visual Basic fact: Instead of an apostrophe, you can use the keyword REM in your code to create a comment. This convention is left over from Visual Basic's early days.

That gives us our start. Now it's time to start taking a systematic look at one of the main topics in this chapter—working with variables.

Declaring Variables

You declare variables in Visual Basic with the Dim statement, and like many of the built-in Visual Basic statements, this statement has many components. Here's the Visual Basic syntax for this statement:

```
[ <attrlist> ] [{ Public | Protected | Friend | Protected Friend |
Private | Static }] [ Shared ] [ Shadows ] [ ReadOnly ] Dim [ WithEvents ]
name[ (boundlist) ] [ As [ New ] type ] [ = initexpr ]
```

Note the [and], { and }, and | in this statement, which we'll see as we describe the syntax of many Visual Basic statements. All the items in square brackets ([and]) are optional, and you choose only one of the items in curly braces ({ and }). The upright bar (|) separates options, and you're expected to use your own values for the items in italics. (The use of [and], { and }, and | is also discussed in the Introduction.)

Most of the options here, like Public and Protected, aren't going to make any sense at this point, and they won't until you've mastered object-oriented programming later in this book. For example, the keywords Public, Private, Protected, and Friend all have to do with how data in classes and objects may be accessed inside and outside those classes and objects (we'll get the full details in Day 9, "Object-Oriented Programming"). For the sake of reference, here's what the various parts of the Dim statement mean; refer to this list as needed throughout the book:

- *attrlist*—Specifies a list of attributes that apply to the variables you're declaring in this statement. Attributes are an advanced topic; they let you add more in-depth information, such as version numbering.

- Public—Gives variables public access, which means there are no restrictions on their accessibility. You can use Public only at module, namespace, or file level (not inside a procedure). If you specify Public, you can omit the Dim keyword.

- Protected—Gives variables protected access, which means they are accessible only from within their own class or from a class derived from that class. You can use Protected only at class level (not inside a procedure). If you specify Protected, you can omit the Dim keyword.

- Friend—Gives variables friend access, which means they are accessible from within the program that contains their declaration, as well as anywhere else in the same assembly. You can use Friend only at module, namespace, or file level (not inside a procedure). If you specify Friend, you can omit the Dim keyword.

- Protected Friend—Gives variables both protected and friend access.

- Private—Gives variables private access, which means they are accessible only from within their own class. You can use Private only at module, namespace, or file level (not inside a procedure). If you specify `Private`, you can omit the `Dim` keyword.

- `Static`—Makes variables static, which means they'll retain their values even after the procedure in which they're declared finishes. You can declare static variables inside a procedure or a block within a procedure, but not at class or module level. If you specify `Static`, you can omit the `Dim` keyword.

- `Shared`—Declares a shared variable, which means it is not associated with a specific object but can be shared across many objects. You can use `Shared` only at module, namespace, or file level (not at the procedure level). If you specify `Shared`, you can omit the `Dim` keyword.

- `Shadows`—Makes this variable a shadow of an identically named programming element in a base class. You can use `Shadows` only at module, namespace, or file level (not inside a procedure). If you specify `Shadows`, you can omit the `Dim` keyword.

- `ReadOnly`—Means this variable can only be read and not written. This can be useful for creating constants. You can use `ReadOnly` only at module, namespace, or file level (not inside procedures). If you specify `ReadOnly`, you can omit the `Dim` keyword.

- `WithEvents`—Means that this variable is used to respond to events. You cannot specify both `WithEvents` and `New` in the same variable declaration.

- *name*—Specifies the name of the variable. Note that you separate multiple variables with commas. If you specify multiple variables, each variable will be of the data type given in the `As` clause that follows the *name* part.

- `boundlist`—Used to declare arrays; gives the upper bounds of the dimensions of an array variable (an array can have up to 60 dimensions). Multiple upper bounds are separated by commas.

- `New`—Means you want to create a new object. If you use `New`, a new object is created. Note that you cannot use both `WithEvents` and `New` in the same declaration.

- *type*—Specifies the data type of the variable. Can be `Boolean`, `Byte`, `Char`, `Date`, `Decimal`, `Double`, `Integer`, `Long`, `Object`, `Short`, `Single`, or `String`; or the name of an enumeration, structure, class, or interface. You use a separate `As` clause for each variable, or you can declare a number of variables of the same type by using common `As` clauses. If you do not specify *type*, the variable takes the data type of *initexpr*. If you don't specify either *type* or *initexpr*, the data type is set to `Object`.

- *initexpr*—Indicates an initialization expression that is assigned to the variable when it is created. If you declare more than one variable with the same `As` clause, you cannot supply *initexpr* for those variables.

Let's make sense of all this with a few examples, like these:

```
Dim ID As Integer
Dim Name As String
Dim Address As String
```

This code creates a variable named ID that holds integer values and variables named Name and Address that hold text strings. You can also initialize variables when they're created by assigning a value to them this way:

```
Dim ID As Integer = 1234
Dim Name As String = "Cary Grant"
Dim Address As String = "1313 Mockingbird Lane"
```

And you can declare multiple variables of the same data type like this:

```
Dim Name, Address As String
```

You can also omit the As part, which will make Visual Basic guess what data type you want to use, as here, which has the same effect as our previous declarations:

```
Dim ID = 1234
Dim Name = "Cary Grant"
Dim Address = "1313 Mockingbird Lane"
```

You can even combine these declarations like this:

```
Dim ID = 1234, Name = "Cary Grant", Address = "1313 Mockingbird Lane"
```

If you want to be more explicit, you can list the type of each variable like this:

```
Dim ID As Integer = 1234, Name As String = "Cary Grant", _
    Address As String = "1313 Mockingbird Lane"
```

By convention, you usually use capitalized names for variables in Visual Basic, like Temperature, and if you want to make up a variable name from several words, capitalize the first letter of each this way:

```
Dim TheNumberOfVotes As Integer
```

At this point, we've seen that variables can hold integers and strings. So what other data types are available?

What Data Types Are Supported?

NEW TERM   Visual Basic .NET supports a wide variety of data types for variables (and the same data types are supported in all Visual Studio .NET languages). You can see the available data types in Table 2.2. The Single and Double types handle floating-point values, which the Integer types (such as Short, Integer, and Long) do not. The names

Single and Double mean *single precision floating point* and *double precision floating point*, respectively. Also note the Boolean data type, which only takes values like True or False.

TABLE 2.2 Visual Basic Data Types

Type	Storage Size	Value Range
Boolean	2 bytes	True or False
Byte	1 byte	0 to 255 (unsigned)
Char	2 bytes	0 to 65,535 (unsigned)
Date	8 bytes	January 1, 0001 to December 31, 9999
Decimal	16 bytes	+/–79,228,162,514,264,337,593,543,950,335 with no decimal point; +/–7.9228162514264337593543950335 with 28 places to the right of the decimal; smallest nonzero number is +/–0.0000000000000000000000000001
Double	8 bytes	–1.79769313486231E+308 to –4.94065645841247E–324 for negative values; 4.94065645841247E–324 to 1.79769313486231E+308 for positive values
Integer	4 bytes	–2,147,483,648 to 2,147,483,647
Long	8 bytes	–9,223,372,036,854,775,808 to 9,223,372,036,854,775,807
Object	4 bytes	Any type can be stored in a variable of type Object
Short	2 bytes	–32,768 to 32,767
Single	4 bytes	–3.402823E+38 to –1.401298E–45 for negative values; 1.401298E–45 to 3.402823E+38 for positive values
String	Varies	0 to approximately 2 billion Unicode characters
User-defined type (structure)	Varies	Each member of the structure has a range determined by its data type

If you do not specify an initialization value for a variable, Visual Basic gives variables a default value depending on the variable's data type:

- 0 for all numeric types and Byte.
- Binary 0 for Char.
- Nothing for Object, String, and arrays. (Nothing means there is no object associated with the variable.)
- False for Boolean.
- 12:00 AM January 1 of the year 1 for Date.

Some programmers like to use prefixes for variable names to indicate the data type of the variable. If you come across a variable in the middle of someone else's code, a prefix makes it easy to know what data type the variable can hold. Table 2.3 lists some of the variable prefixes that have become conventional (but optional) for the Visual Basic data types.

TABLE 2.3   Variable Prefixes

Data Type	Prefix
Boolean	bln
Byte	byt
Collection object	col
Date (Time)	dtm
Double	dbl
Error	err
Integer	int
Long	lng
Object	obj
Single	sng
String	str
User-defined type	udt

Here are some prefixed variable names as examples:

```
blnYesNo                'Boolean data type variable
intNumberOfVotes        'Integer data type variable
dblSolarRadiationValue  'Double data type variable
```

One of the most important types of data is the String type, which handles text strings. This data type has a lot of support in Visual Basic .NET, and it deserves a closer look.

Working with Strings

You declare a string just as you would other variables:

```
Dim Directions As String
```

As with other types of variables, you can also initialize a string when you declare it, like this:

```
Dim Directions = "Follow the Yellow Brick road."
```

2

In Visual Basic, strings are stored using Unicode (which you can learn more about at http://www.unicode.org/) and can contain about two billion characters. Visual Basic comes with many functions built in to work with strings. For example, you can use the Len function to determine a string's length:

```
Dim Directions As String = "Follow the Yellow Brick road."
Dim Length As Integer = Len(Directions)
```

Another function, UCase, changes a string to uppercase; after you run this code, the variable Directions will hold the text "FOLLOW THE YELLOW BRICK ROAD.":

```
Dim Directions = "Follow the Yellow Brick road."
Directions = UCase(Directions)
```

For reference, you can find the popular Visual Basic string-handling functions organized by task in Table 2.4; we'll see more about these functions throughout the book.

TABLE 2.4 String-Handling Functions and Methods

To Do This	Use This
Compare two strings	StrComp, String.Compare, String.Equals, String.CompareTo
Convert strings	StrConv, CStr, String.ToString
Convert to lowercase or uppercase	Format, Lcase, Ucase, String.Format, String.ToUpper, String.ToLower
Convert to and from numbers	Str, Val, Format, String.Format
Copy strings	=, String.Copy
Create an array of strings from one string	String.Split
Create a string of a repeating character	Space, String, String.String
Find the length of a string	Len, String.Length
Format a string	Format, String.Format
Get a substring	Mid, String.SubString
Insert a substring	String.Insert
Join two strings	&, +, String.Concat, String.Join
Justify a string with padding	LSet, RSet, String.PadLeft, PadRight
Manipulate strings	InStr, Left, LTrim, Mid, Right, RTrim, Trim, String.Trim, String.TrimEnd, String.TrimStart
Remove text	Mid, String.Remove
Replace text	Mid, String.Replace

TABLE 2.4 continued

To Do This	Use This
Search strings	InStr, String.Chars, String.IndexOf, String.IndexOfAny, String.LastIndexOf, String.LastIndexOf Any
Set string comparison rules	Option Compare
Trim leading or trailing spaces	LTrim, RTrim, Trim, String.Trim, String.TrimEnd, String.TrimStart
Work with character codes	Asc, AscW, Chr

Here's something else to know: To concatenate (join) strings, you can use the & or + operators (Visual Basic can use either, but Microsoft recommends the & operator). For example, here's how to assign a long string, broken up over several lines, to a variable:

```
Dim Message As String
Message = "Well, I'm not sure what the problem is " _
& "but there's definitely something wrong with " _
& "your data. Better check it twice."
```

> **Tip**
>
> Note the use of single quotation marks in the preceding text string. Using them is fine, but if you use a double quotation mark in your text, Visual Basic will think you're ending the text string. Instead, use two double quotation marks ("") to stand for a double quotation mark, like this, "I said ""Hello"" to him.".

The & operator is a good one to know about because you can use it to break up a text string over different lines. Visual Basic will object if you try to do something like this without concatenating the sections of this text into one text string (in fact, it'll try to add a double quotation mark to the end of the first line and will not understand the other lines at all):

```
Dim Message As String
Message = "Well, I'm not sure what the problem is
but there's definitely something wrong with
your data. Better check it twice."
```

Performing Data Conversions

Take a look at Listing 2.2, which you'll find in the Conversions project in the code for this book.

LISTING 2.2 Converting Between Data Types (Conversions project, Module1.vb)

```
Module Module1

    Sub Main()
        Dim dblValue As Double
        Dim intValue As Integer
        dblValue = 1.2345678
        intValue = dblValue
        Console.WriteLine(intValue)
        Console.WriteLine("Press Enter to continue...")
        Console.ReadLine()
    End Sub

End Module
```

Here, the code assigns a double value of 1.2345678 to an integer variable, which can't store numbers with decimal parts. So what happens? The decimal part is truncated, and when the code displays the result, all you see is 1:

```
1
Press Enter to continue...
```

So you've lost the .2345678 part of your data, and Visual Basic didn't even tell you that was going to happen. In fact, Visual Basic converted the double value into an integer automatically. To stop these kinds of automatic conversions from happening, you can use the statement `Option Strict On` in your code like this:

```
Option Strict On
Module Module1

    Sub Main()
        Dim dblValue As Double
        Dim intValue As Integer
        dblValue = 1.2345678
        intValue = dblValue
        Console.WriteLine(intValue)
        Console.WriteLine("Press Enter to continue...")
        Console.ReadLine()
    End Sub

End Module
```

With `Option Strict On`, Visual Basic won't automatically convert between data types if there's a possibility of data loss, such as when you convert a `Long` (which has twice the storage of an `Integer`) to an `Integer` (although converting an `Integer` to a `Long` is okay). Now there's no chance that automatic data conversions will change your data without you knowing it. If you want a data conversion where data loss could occur to happen now, you have to explicitly make it happen, as in this case, which converts the double value to an integer:

```
Option Strict On
Module Module1

    Sub Main()
        Dim dblValue As Double
        Dim intValue As Integer
        dblValue = 1.2345678
        intValue = CInt(dblValue)
        Console.WriteLine(intValue)
        Console.WriteLine("Press Enter to continue...")
        Console.ReadLine()
    End Sub

End Module
```

NEW TERM Here, the code uses the `CInt` Visual Basic *function* to convert a number to `Integer` format. You pass data to a function by enclosing the data in parentheses like this: `CInt(dblValue)`. The function then returns a value, which in this case is the integer value of `dblValue`.

Visual Basic provides the following conversion functions:

- `CBool`—Converts to `Bool` data type
- `CByte`—Converts to `Byte` data type
- `CChar`—Converts to `Char` data type
- `CDate`—Converts to `Date` data type
- `CDbl`—Converts to `Double` data type
- `CDec`—Converts to `Decimal` data type
- `CInt`—Converts to `Int` data type
- `CLng`—Converts to `Long` data type
- `CObj`—Converts to `Object` type
- `CShort`—Converts to `Short` data type
- `CSng`—Converts to `Single` data type
- `CStr`—Converts to `String` type

You can also use the `CType` function, which allows you to specify a type to convert to:

```
Option Strict On
Module Module1
    Sub Main()
        Dim dblValue As Double
        Dim intValue As Integer
        dblValue = 1.2345678
        intValue = CType(dblValue, Integer)
        Console.WriteLine("intValue = " & Str(intValue))
        Console.WriteLine("Press Enter to continue...")
        Console.ReadLine()
    End Sub
End Module
```

In fact, Visual Basic supports a number of functions for converting between various data types, and they come in handy. You'll find them in Table 2.5 for reference.

TABLE 2.5   Visual Basic Data Conversion Functions

To Convert	Use This
Character code to character	Chr
Character to character code	Asc
Date to a number	DateSerial, DateValue
Decimal number to other bases	Hex, Oct
Number to string	Format, Str
One data type to another	CBool, CByte, CDate, CDbl, CDec, CInt, CLng, CObj, CSng, CShort, CStr, Fix, Int
String to lowercase or uppercase	Format, LCase, UCase, String.ToUpper, String.ToLower, String.Format
String to number	Val
Time to serial number	TimeSerial, TimeValue

Converting Strings to Numbers

One very important conversion to know about is converting strings to numbers and numbers to strings. When you read a number the user has typed into a text box, for example, that data is a string. You have to convert it to a number (such as an integer) before you can treat it as a number (adding another number to it, for example). To convert a string to a number, you can use the `Val` function; to convert a number to a string, you can use the `Str` function. Here's how you might read the text in one text box, convert it to a number, convert it back to a string, and display it in another text box:

```
Dim intValue as Integer
intValue = Val(TextBox1.Text)
TextBox2.Text = Str(intValue1)
```

Declaring Constants

NEW TERM   Besides variables, you can also declare *constants* in Visual Basic .NET. As you can gather from their names, you can change the values in variables, but you can't change the value in a constant after it's been created. Constants are good to use when you have a value that you never want to let code change inadvertently.

You declare constants in Visual Basic with the `Const` statement, which looks like this in general:

```
[ <attrlist> ] [{ Public | Protected | Friend | Protected Friend |
Private }] [ Shadows ] Const name [ As type ] = initexpr
```

The various parts of this statement are the same as the `Dim` statement; see coverage of `Dim` earlier today in the "Declaring Variables" section for the details. The example in Listing 2.3, the Constants project in the code for this book, creates a constant named `Pi` and assigns it the value 3.1415926535.

LISTING 2.3   Declaring a Constant (Constants project, Module1.vb)

```
Module Module1

    Sub Main()
        Const Pi = 3.1415926535
        Console.WriteLine(Pi)
        Console.WriteLine("Press Enter to continue...")
        Console.ReadLine()
    End Sub

End Module
```

Here's what you see when you run this project:

```
3.1415926535
Press Enter to continue...
```

NEW TERM   So far, we've seen how to create both constants and variables, both of which are single data items. The next step is to start creating *groups* of data items, which we'll do today with Visual Basic enumerations and arrays.

Creating Enumerations

NEW TERM   Say that you have a number of constants that you want to group together. For example, you want to assign the value 0 to a constant named Sunday, the value 1 to the constant Monday, and so on. You could declare separate constants, but using an *enumeration*, you can create all seven constants at once.

You create such an enumeration like this—with the Enum statement:

```
[ <attrlist> ] [{ Public | Protected | Friend | Protected Friend | Private }]
[ Shadows ] Enum name [ As type ]
   [<attrlist1>] membname1 [ = initexpr1 ]
   [<attrlist2>] membname2 [ = initexpr2 ]
       .
       .
       .
   [<attrlistn>] membnamen [ = initexprn ]
End Enum
```

The parts of this statement are the same as for constants (see the preceding section), but this time, the situation is a little more involved because you're declaring multiple items. In addition, the type for the constants in the enumeration must be one of the integer types (Byte, Short, Long, or Integer—Integer is the default). For example, Listing 2.4 shows how you can set up and use an enumeration that assigns a constant to every day of the week; this is from the Enumerations example in the code you can download for this book.

LISTING 2.4   Creating an Enumeration (Enumerations project, Module1.vb)

```
Module Module1

    Enum Days
        Sunday = 0
        Monday = 1
        Tuesday = 2
        Wednesday = 3
        Thursday = 4
        Friday = 5
        Saturday = 6
    End Enum

    Sub Main()
        Console.WriteLine("Saturday is day " & Days.Saturday & ".")
        Console.WriteLine("Press Enter to continue...")
        Console.ReadLine()
    End Sub

End Module
```

That's how you create the enumeration named Days here. When you want to refer to a constant in the Days enumeration, you do so like this: Days.Sunday, Days.Tuesday, and so on. Here's what you see when you run this program:

```
Saturday is day 6.
Press Enter to continue...
```

The next step up from enumerations is arrays, and we'll see them next.

Declaring Arrays and Dynamic Arrays

Arrays enable you to group your data into a single programming construct, letting you access individual data items with a numeric index. Here, we'll see how to create arrays with the statements named Dim (which originally stood for "dimension" because it was used to specify the dimensions of an array—you didn't need to declare simple variables in earlier versions of Visual Basic) and ReDim (to redimension an array at runtime). The best starting place is with the Dim statement, so let's turn to it now.

Creating an Array

You can use the Dim statement to create an array, just as you can a simple variable. For example, say you want to keep track of the student test scores in a class you're teaching. You might start with an array named Scores like this:

```
Dim Scores(20) As Integer
```

This statement creates an array named Scores of 21 integers. You can now access each element of the array with a numeric index that ranges from 0 to 20 (0 is always the lower bound for arrays in Visual Basic). You can access these elements as Scores(0) to Scores(20). For example, you can store some data in this array and then retrieve the data stored in Scores(1) like this:

```
Dim Scores(20) As Integer
Scores(0) = 25
Scores(1) = 75
Scores(2) = 95
Console.WriteLine("Student 1 scored " & Scores(1))
Console.WriteLine("Press Enter to continue...")
Console.ReadLine()
```

In this way, you can treat an array as a set of variables indexed with an integer that is 0 or positive. This capability is very useful because that numeric index is under your code's control, which means you can easily access all the data in an array just by adding 1 to the numeric index to access each successive element. (This is very powerful in loops, which we'll see later today.)

You can find the upper bound of an array (that's 20 here) with the Visual Basic UBound function. For example, the expression UBound(Scores) would return a value of 20 in this example.

NEW TERM   What if the students took a second test? You can add another *dimension* to the Scores array like this: Dim Scores(1, 20) As Integer. Now the first index, which can be either 0 or 1, indicates which test score you want, and the second index can be the number of the student whose score you want. Listing 2.5 shows how that might look in code where you want to display the score of student 1 on the first test; this is taken from the Arrays example in the code you can download for this book.

LISTING 2.5   Creating an Array (Arrays project, Module1.vb)

```
Module Module1

    Sub Main()
        Dim Scores(1, 20) As Integer
        Scores(0, 0) = 25
        Scores(0, 1) = 75
        Scores(0, 2) = 95
        Scores(1, 0) = 35
        Scores(1, 1) = 65
        Scores(1, 2) = 85
        Console.WriteLine("On the first test, student 1 scored " & Scores(0, 1))
        Console.WriteLine("Press Enter to continue...")
        Console.ReadLine()
    End Sub

End Module
```

You can see the results in Figure 2.2.

You can also initialize the data in an array if you don't give an array an explicit size; here's the syntax to use, where this code is initializing an array with the values 1, 3, 5, 7, and 9:

```
Dim Data() As Integer = {1, 3, 5, 7 , 9}
```

Now Data(0) will hold 1, Data(2) will hold 3, and so on.

You can initialize a two-dimensional array as follows:

```
Dim Data2( , ) As Integer = {{1, 2, 3}, {4 , 5, 6}}
```

This statement creates a two-dimensional array of two rows and three columns:

```
1 2 3
4 5 6
```

Now `Data(0, 0)` holds 1, `Data(1, 1)` holds 5, `Data(0, 2)` holds 3, and so on.

FIGURE 2.2

Declaring and using an array.

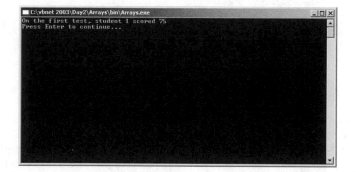

Creating a Dynamic Array

NEW TERM You can also create *dynamic* arrays that you can redimension at runtime. This capability is useful if you don't know how much data you want to store in an array before your program runs. To create a dynamic array, you use the `Dim` statement, declaring the array with empty parentheses like this:

```
Module Module1

    Sub Main()
        Dim Scores() As Integer
            .
            .
            .
    End Sub

End Module
```

Before you can use this new array, you have to dimension it, which you can do with `ReDim`. Here's how you use `ReDim`:

```
ReDim [Preserve] ArrayName(subscripts)
```

You use the `Preserve` keyword to preserve the data in an existing array when you change the size of the last dimension. The *ArrayName* parameter holds the name of the array to redimension. The *subscripts* parameter specifies the new upper bounds of the various dimensions of the array. For example, here's how you would give this array two elements and store values in those elements:

```
Module Module1

    Sub Main()
        Dim Scores() As Integer
        ReDim Scores(1)
        Scores(0) = 25
        Scores(1) = 75
            .
            .
            .
    End Sub

End Module
```

Now say that you want to add more data to this array. You can redimension the array again, using the `Preserve` keyword to preserve the data already in the array, as in Listing 2.6. (If you don't use `Preserve`, the data already in the array won't be preserved.) You can see how this task works in the DynamicArrays project in the code for this book, which you see in Listing 2.6.

LISTING 2.6   Creating a Dynamic Array (DynamicArrays project, Module1.vb)

```
Module Module1

    Sub Main()
        Dim Scores() As Integer
        ReDim Scores(2)
        Scores(0) = 25
        Scores(1) = 75
        ReDim Preserve Scores(5)
        Scores(2) = 95
        Scores(3) = 35
        Scores(4) = 65
        Scores(5) = 85
        Console.WriteLine("Scores(3) = " & Scores(3))
        Console.WriteLine("Press Enter to continue...")
        Console.ReadLine()

    End Sub

End Module
```

The result of this code is

```
Scores(3) = 35
Press Enter to continue...
```

Now we have an essential understanding about how to work with data using variables, constants, and arrays. How about doing something with that data next?

Using Visual Basic Operators

2

NEW TERM To allow you to work on your data, Visual Basic comes with plenty of built-in *operators*. In Visual Basic, operators perform *operations* on *operands*. For example, say that you want to add two numbers and display the results. You can do that with the addition operator, +, like this:

```
Dim intItem1 As Integer = 1111
Dim intItem2 As Integer = 2222
Dim intItem3 As Integer
intItem3 = intItem1 + intItem2
Console.WriteLine(intItem3)
Console.WriteLine("Press Enter to continue...")
Console.ReadLine()
```

This code displays the sum of 1111 + 2222, which is 3333. In this case, 1111 is the first operand, + is the operator, 2222 is the second operand, and the operation is addition.

Various types of operators are used in Visual Basic, and we'll see them all here. The arithmetic operators are as follows:

- ^—Exponentiation (2 ^ 3 = 8)
- *—Multiplication (2 * 3 = 6)
- /—Division (6.2 / 2 = 3.1)
- \—Integer division (8.9493 \ 2 = 4)
- Mod—Modulus, the remainder after integer division (16 Mod 5 = 1)
- +—Addition (2 + 3 = 5)
- – —Subtraction (6 – 4 = 2)
- >>—Performs an arithmetic right shift on a bit pattern. For example, 8 >> 1 moves the bits in 8 one place to the right, which results in 4. This is not a "circular" shift—bits shifted off are not introduced at the beginning of operand1. This operator is new in Visual Basic .NET 2003.

- <<—Performs an arithmetic left shift on a bit pattern. For example, 8 << 1 moves the bits in 8 one place to the left, which results in 16. This is not a "circular" shift—bits shifted off are not introduced at the end of operand1. This operator is new in Visual Basic .NET 2003.

The assignment operators are as follows (for example, Temperature = 60 stores the value 60 in the variable Temperature; Temperature += 5 adds 5 to the value in Temperature and stores the result in Temperature, and so on):

- =—Assignment
- ^=—Exponentiation followed by assignment
- *=—Multiplication followed by assignment
- /=—Division followed by assignment
- \=—Integer division followed by assignment
- +=—Addition followed by assignment
- –=—Subtraction followed by assignment
- &=—String concatenation followed by assignment

Here are the comparison operators, which we'll see later today. These operators yield true or false values (for example, 6 > 3 yields a value of True) that are used in the branching statements we're going to see soon:

- <—Less than. True if operand1 is less than operand2.
- <=—Less than or equal to. True if operand1 is less than or equal to operand2.
- >—Greater than. True if operand1 is greater than operand2.
- >=—Greater than or equal to. True if operand1 is greater than or equal to operand2.
- =—Equal to. True if operand1 equals operand2.
- <>—Not equal to True if operand1 is not equal to operand2.
- Is—True if two object references refer to the same object.
- Like—Performs string pattern matching.

The string concatenation operators are as follows (for example, the expression "Hi " & "there" results in the string "Hi there".):

- &—String concatenation
- +—String concatenation (using & is preferred)

Next come the logical/bitwise operators, where *bitwise* means working bit by bit with numerical values. We'll see how to use these operators, like the comparison operators, when we work with branching statements today. These types of operators can work on logical (True/False) values (for example, if blnItem1 is set to True and blnItem2 is set to False, then blnItem1 Or blnItem2 returns a value of True). They also can work on numbers for bitwise operations, which work on their operands bit by bit (for example, if intItem1 is set to 2 and intItem2 is set to 1, then intItem1 Or intItem2 yields 3).

- And—Performs an "And" operation. (For logical operations, the result is true if both operands are true, false otherwise; the same applies for bit-by-bit operations where you treat 0 as false and 1 as true.)

- Not—Reverses the logical value of its operand, from true to false and false to true; for bitwise operations, turns 0 into 1 and 1 into 0.

- Or—Performs an "Or" operation. (For logical operations, the result is true if either operand is true, false otherwise; the same applies for bit-by-bit operations where you treat 0 as false and 1 as true.)

- Xor—Performs an "Exclusive-Or" operation. (For logical operations, the result is true if either operand, but not both, is true, and false otherwise; the same applies for bit-by-bit operations where you treat 0 as false and 1 as true.)

- AndAlso—A "short-circuited" And operator; if the first operand is false, the second operand is not tested. Otherwise, it is the same as And.

- OrElse—A "short-circuited" Or operator; if the first operand is true, the second is not tested. Otherwise, it is the same as Or.

And here are the remaining two operators:

- AddressOf—Gets the address of a procedure
- GetType—Gets information about a type

We'll gain experience with these various operators throughout the book.

Operator Precedence

Say your three students have scored 50, 60, and 70 points on the exam, and, naturally, you want to use Visual Basic .NET to figure out the average score. You might use this code:

```
Dim intScore1, intScore2, intScore3, intNumberStudents As Integer
intScore1 = 50
intScore2 = 60
intScore3 = 70
```

2

```
intNumberStudents = 3
Console.WriteLine("Average grade = " &
    intScore1 + intScore2 + intScore3 / intNumberStudents)
Console.WriteLine("Press Enter to continue...")
Console.ReadLine()
```

However, this is the result you see, which makes your students, but not you, happy:

```
Average grade = 133.333333333333
Press Enter to continue...
```

What happened? The problem lies in this line:

```
Console.WriteLine("Average grade = " &
    intScore1 + intScore2 + intScore3 / intNumberStudents)
```

Visual Basic evaluates division operations before addition operations, so 50 + 60 + 70 / 3
becomes 50 + 60 + 23.333333333333 or 133.333333333333. To fix this problem, you
can put parentheses around the scores to make Visual Basic add them before performing
the division like this: (50 + 60 + 70) / 3. Here's what the expression looks like in code:

```
Dim intScore1, intScore2, intScore3, intNumberStudents As Integer
intScore1 = 50
intScore2 = 60
intScore3 = 70
intNumberStudents = 3
Console.WriteLine("Average grade = " &
    (intScore1 + intScore2 + intScore3) / intNumberStudents)
Console.WriteLine("Press Enter to continue...")
Console.ReadLine()
```

And here's the result, as expected:

```
Average grade = 60
Press Enter to continue...
```

NEW TERM   When several operations occur in an expression at once, each part is evaluated
and resolved in a predetermined order called *operator precedence*. When the
operators come from different categories, they may be evaluated in a different order; for
example, * is evaluated before +. (Operators with the same precedence are evaluated
from left to right in an expression.)

The arithmetic and concatenation operators are evaluated before the comparison and logical operators, for example. And comparison operators are evaluated before the logical
operators. Here are the precedence rules—the arithmetic and concatenation operators have
the highest precedence, and are arranged this way, from highest precedence to lowest:

- Exponentiation (^)
- Negation (–) (for example, -intItem reverses the sign of the value in intItem)
- Multiplication and division (*, /)
- Integer division (\)
- Modulus arithmetic (Mod)
- Addition and subtraction (+, –)
- String concatenation (+)
- String concatenation (&)
- Arithmetic bit shift (<<, >>)

After that come the comparison operators, which all have the same precedence:

- Equality (=)
- Inequality (<>)
- Less than, greater than (<, >)
- Greater than or equal to (>=)
- Less than or equal to (<=)
- Like
- Is

Finally come the logical/bitwise operators, which have this precedence order, from highest to lowest:

- Negation (Not)
- Conjunction (And, AndAlso)
- Disjunction (Or, OrElse, Xor)

NEW TERM The next step up after using operators is to start using *branching statements*, which allow you to make decisions and take different paths in your code, depending on the results of those decisions. And now that we've taken a look at what Visual Basic has to offer us with operators, it's time to take a look at branching statements.

Making Decisions with If Statements

NEW TERM We'll look at the powerful branching statements, also called *conditional statements*, next. These statements allow you to use comparison and logical operators

2

to examine your data and make decisions based on the results; for example, you might want to turn on the air conditioning if `Temperature` holds a value higher than 76 but turn on the heat instead if `Temperature` holds a value of 60 or lower. We'll start with the `If` statement, which is the bread and butter of branching statements. Here's how the `If` statement works:

```
If condition Then
    [statements]
[ElseIf condition-1 Then
    [elseifstatements-1]]
        .
        .
        .
[ElseIf condition-n Then
    [elseifstatements-n]]
[Else
    [elsestatements]]
End If
```

You can use comparison and logical operators in *condition* here to generate a logical result that's true or false; for example, if *condition* is `intItem > 5`, then *condition* will be true if the value in `intItem` is greater than 5. If *condition* is true, the statements immediately following the `Then` keyword in the body of the `If` statement will be executed, and the `If` statement will terminate before the code in any `ElseIf` or `Else` statement is executed. If *condition* is false, the following `ElseIf` statements are evaluated, if there are any; this statement allows you to test additional conditions, and if any are true, the corresponding code (*elseifstatements* above) is executed and the `If` statement terminates. If there are no `ElseIf` statements, or if none of their conditions are true, the code in the `Else` statement (*elsestatements* above), if there is one, is executed automatically.

Let's see an example to make this clear. In this case, we can ask the user to enter a temperature and respond with messages like `"Too hot!"`, `"Too cold!"`, or `"Just right!"` To read input from the user, we use `Console.ReadLine()`, which returns whatever the user typed as a string. We can convert that string to a number with the `Val` function; if that number is greater than 75 degrees, we can display the message `"Too hot!"`:

```
Sub Main()
    Dim intInput As Integer
    Console.WriteLine("Enter a temperature...")
    intInput = Val(Console.ReadLine())
    If intInput > 75 Then
        Console.WriteLine("Too hot!")
        .
        .
        .
```

Otherwise, if the temperature entered was less than 55, which we can check with an
ElseIf clause (using ElseIf is optional in an If statement), we can display "Too
cold!":

```
Sub Main()
    Dim intInput As Integer
    Console.WriteLine("Enter a temperature...")
    intInput = Val(Console.ReadLine())
    If intInput > 75 Then
        Console.WriteLine("Too hot!")
    ElseIf intInput < 55  Then
        Console.WriteLine("Too cold!")
    .
    .
    .
```

If the temperature was neither too hot nor too cold, we can display the message "Just
right!" in an Else clause (which is also optional in an If statement) in the If project in
the code for this book. That code appears in Listing 2.7.

LISTING 2.7   Using an If Statement (If project, Module1.vb)

```
Module Module1

    Sub Main()
        Dim intInput As Integer
        Console.WriteLine("Enter a temperature...")
        intInput = Val(Console.ReadLine())
        If intInput > 75 Then
            Console.WriteLine("Too hot!")
        ElseIf intInput < 55  Then
            Console.WriteLine("Too cold!")
        Else
            Console.WriteLine("Just right!")
        End If
        Console.WriteLine("Press Enter to continue...")
        Console.ReadLine()
    End Sub

End Module
```

You might see these results (press Enter after entering your temperature):

```
Enter a temperature...
32
Too cold!
Press Enter to continue...
```

Besides the comparison operators like > and >=, you can also use logical operators like And and Or to link logical conditions. For example, if the temperature is greater than 75 degrees *or* less than 55, you can display the message "No good!"—and the message "Just right!" otherwise—like this:

```
If intInput > 75 Or intInput < 55 Then
    Console.WriteLine("No good!")
Else
    Console.WriteLine("Just right!")
End If
```

You can do the same thing by displaying the message "Just right!" if the temperature is less than or equal to 75 *and* the temperature is greater than or equal to 55—and the message "No good!" otherwise:

```
If intInput <= 75 And intInput >= 55 Then
    Console.WriteLine("Just right!")
Else
    Console.WriteLine("No good!")
End If
```

Besides If statements, you can also use the Select branching statement, coming up next.

Making Decisions with Select

If you have a number of conditions to check, you can do so with a number of If statements, or an If statement with many ElseIf statements. But there's an easier way—you can use a Select statement. Here's what Select looks like in general:

```
Select Case testexpression
[Case expression-1
    [statements-1]]
        .
        .
        .
[Case expression-n
    [statements-n]]
[Case Else
    [elsestatements]]
End Select
```

You use multiple Case statements in a Select statement, each specifying a different expression to test against *testexpression*. If the value of *testexpression* matches the value of a Case statement's expression, the code in the Case statement is executed. If no Case statement matches the text expression, the code in Case Else (if there is such a

Case statement) is executed. In this statement, *testexpression* and *expression-1* to *expression-n* must be one of the simple data types (Boolean, Byte, Char, Date, Double, Decimal, Integer, Long, Object, Short, Single, or String).

Here's an example using Select. This example checks an integer the user enters. If the value entered is 1, the program will display the message "Thank you for the 1.":

```
Dim intInput As Integer
Console.WriteLine("Enter an integer...")
intInput = Val(Console.ReadLine())
Select Case intInput
    Case 1
        Console.WriteLine("Thank you for the 1.")
    .
    .
    .
```

If the value entered is in the range 2–5, which you can check with the case 2 To 5, the program says "Your value was 2, 3, 4, or 5":

```
Select Case intInput
    Case 1
        Console.WriteLine("Thank you for the 1.")
    Case 2 To 5
        Console.WriteLine("Your value was 2, 3, 4, or 5")
    .
    .
    .
```

You can also use logical expressions, such as Case Is > 5, this way to check if the entered value was greater than 5:

```
Select Case intInput
    Case 1
        Console.WriteLine("Thank you for the 1.")
    Case 2 To 5
        Console.WriteLine("Your value was 2, 3, 4, or 5")
    Case Is > 5
        Console.WriteLine("That was greater than 5.")
    .
    .
    .
```

If none of these cases match, you can use an optional Case Else to perform some action anyway, which in this example—the Select project in the code for the book—displays the message "Sorry, I can't deal with that." You can see how this works in Listing 2.8.

2

LISTING 2.8   Using a Select Statement (Select project, Module1.vb)

```
Module Module1

    Sub Main()
        Dim intInput As Integer
        Console.WriteLine("Enter an integer...")
        intInput = Val(Console.ReadLine())
        Select Case intInput
            Case 1
                Console.WriteLine("Thank you for the 1.")
            Case 2 To 5
                Console.WriteLine("Your value was 2, 3, 4, or 5")
            Case Is > 5
                Console.WriteLine("That was greater than 5.")
            Case Else
                Console.WriteLine("Sorry, I can't deal with that.")
        End Select
        Console.WriteLine("Press Enter to continue...")
        Console.ReadLine()
    End Sub

End Module
```

Here's the kind of output you might see when you run this code:

```
Enter an integer...
2
Your value was 2, 3, 4, or 5
Press Enter to continue...
```

Making Decisions with Switch and Choose

Although not in common use (that is, you can skip this topic if you want), two other Visual Basic functions can help you make decisions in code: Microsoft.VisualBasic.Switch and Choose.

The Microsoft.VisualBasic.Switch function evaluates a list of expression/value pairs and returns the value associated with the first expression in the list that is true. Here's the syntax:

```
Microsoft.VisualBasic.Switch(expr-1, value-1[, expr-2, value-2 ...
[, expr-n, value-n]])
```

Here, *expr-1* is the first expression to evaluate; if true, Microsoft.VisualBasic.Switch returns *value-1*. If *expr-1* is not true but *expr-2* is, this function returns *value-2* and so on. The next example, shown in Listing 2.9, the Switch project in the code for this book, uses `Microsoft.VisualBasic.Switch` to calculate the absolute value of the variable `intValue` (having temporarily forgotten how to use the built-in Visual Basic absolute value function, `Abs`).

LISTING 2.9   Using a `Switch` Statement (Switch project, Module1.vb)

```
Module Module1

    Sub Main()
        Dim intValue As Integer
        Console.WriteLine("Enter an integer...")
        intValue = Val(Console.ReadLine())
        Console.WriteLine("Absolute value: " & _
            Microsoft.VisualBasic.Switch(intValue < 0, -1 * intValue, intValue
>= 0, intValue))
        Console.WriteLine("Press Enter to continue...")
        Console.ReadLine()
    End Sub

End Module
```

Tip

Using the negation operator, –, you can write `-1 * intValue` as `-intValue`.

Here's what you might see when you run this code:

```
Enter an integer...
-3
Absolute value: 3
Press Enter to continue...
```

You can also use the `Choose` function to return one of a number of choices based on an index, which is a whole number. Here's the syntax:

```
Choose(index, choice-1[, choice-2, ... [, choice-n]])
```

If _index_ is 1, the first choice is returned; if index is 2, the second choice is returned; and so on. Here's an example using `Choose`. In this case, we have three horses—Sea Biscuit, Valiant, and Flier—that finished the race in places 1, 2, and 3. This code enables you to get the name of the horse that finished in a particular place, based on the value in the variable `intFinish`:

```
strHorse = Choose(intFinish, "Sea Biscuit", "Valiant", "Flier")
```

NEW TERM   That finishes the branching statements in Visual Basic .NET; next we'll look at
            loops. You use loops to execute a series of statements repeatedly. That doesn't
mean you perform one identical task repeatedly, of course, because you might be operating on different data items each time through the loop.

Computers are great at handling loops—providing you with a way of executing repetitive
code quickly.

Using the For Loop

The first loop we'll see is the For loop, the most popular of all Visual Basic loops. Here's
the syntax for the For loop:

```
For index [As dataType] = start To end [Step step]
    [statements]
    [Exit For]
    [statements]
Next [index]
```

NEW TERM   The *index* variable is originally set to *start* automatically when the loop begins.
            Each time through the loop, *index* is incremented by *step* (*step* is set to a
default of 1 if you don't specify a value), and when *index* equals *end*, the loop ends. You
can use the Exit For statement to terminate the For loop at any time. Note also that you
can declare the *index* variable in a For loop using the optional As *dataType* clause, as
long as the *index* variable isn't already declared elsewhere (this is new in Visual Basic
.NET 2003).

The next example, which you see in Listing 2.10, will put this loop to work. Because For
loops use a loop index that can be incremented each time through the loop, they're particularly good to use with arrays, which use an index to access their data. For example,
say that you want to display all the elements of an array named Scores. You could do
that with a For loop that loops from 0 to UBound(Scores) (which is the upper bound of
the array) like this in the For project in the code for this book.

LISTING 2.10   Using a For Statement (For project, Module1.vb)

```
Module Module1

    Sub Main()
        Dim Scores(2) As Integer
        Scores(0) = 45
        Scores(1) = 55
```

LISTING 2.10 continued

```
            Scores(2) = 65
        For intLoopIndex As Integer = 0 To UBound(Scores)
            Console.WriteLine("Score(" & intLoopIndex & ") = _
                " & Scores(intLoopIndex))
        Next intLoopIndex
        Console.WriteLine("Press Enter to continue...")
        Console.ReadLine()
    End Sub

End Module
```

Here's what you see when you run this code (note that each time through the loop, the loop index was incremented, which means we see the next element in the array):

```
Score(0) = 45
Score(1) = 55
Score(2) = 65
Press Enter to continue...
```

This example declared its loop index, `intLoopIndex`, in the loop itself, but you can also use a variable that's already been declared as the loop variable like this:

```
Dim intLoopIndex As Integer
For intLoopIndex = 0 To UBound(Scores)
    Console.WriteLine("Score(" & intLoopIndex & ") = " & Scores(intLoopIndex))
Next intLoopIndex
```

There's another, closely allied type of loop—the `For Each` loop.

Using the For Each Loop

You use the `For Each` loop to loop over elements in an array or other type of collection of elements. This loop is great because it automatically loops over all the elements in the array; you don't have to worry about getting the loop indices just right to make sure you get all elements as you do with a `For` loop. Here's the syntax for this loop:

```
For Each element [As dataType] In group
    [statements]
    [Exit For]
    [statements]
Next [element]
```

Here, `element` will be filled with the next successive element from `group` each time through the loop. You can terminate this loop, like the `For` loop, at any time by executing the Exit For statement. And you can declare the *element* variable in this loop, like the For loop, by specifying a data type, as long as the *element* variable has not already been declared elsewhere (this is new in Visual Basic .NET 2003).

Listing 2.11 shows this loop in action in the ForEach project in the code for this book, where the code displays all the elements of the Scores array.

LISTING 2.11   Using a For Each Statement (ForEach project, Module1.vb)

```
Module Module1

    Sub Main()
        Dim Scores(2) As Integer
        Scores(0) = 45
        Scores(1) = 55
        Scores(2) = 65
        For Each Score As Integer In Scores
            Console.WriteLine("Score = " & Score)
        Next Score
        Console.WriteLine("Press Enter to continue...")
        Console.ReadLine()
    End Sub

End Module
```

And here are the results of this code (note that because For Each statements don't have a numeric loop index, this example doesn't display the index number of each item as in the For example):

```
Score = 45
Score = 55
Score = 65
Press Enter to continue...
```

The next loop to look at is the popular While loop.

Using the While Loop

Like the For Each loop, the While loop doesn't need a loop index (of course, you can add one yourself by simply incrementing the value in a variable each time through the loop if you want to). You give a While loop a condition to test, and it will keep looping while that condition remains true. Here's the syntax of the While loop:

```
While condition
    [statements]
End While
```

Listing 2.12 shows an example putting the While loop to work in the While project in the code for this book, which keeps looping until the user enters a **q** to quit.

LISTING 2.12   Using a While Loop (While project, Module1.vb)

```
Module Module1

    Sub Main()
        Console.WriteLine("Please enter 'q' to quit...")
        Dim strInput As String = Console.ReadLine()

        While (strInput <> "q")
            Console.WriteLine("You typed " & strInput)
            Console.WriteLine("Please enter 'q' to quit...")
            strInput = Console.ReadLine()
        End While
        Console.WriteLine("Quitting now.")
        Console.WriteLine("Press Enter to continue...")
        Console.ReadLine()
    End Sub

End Module
```

You can see the results in Figure 2.3, where the While loop keeps looping until the user enters a **q** to quit.

FIGURE 2.3

Using a While loop.

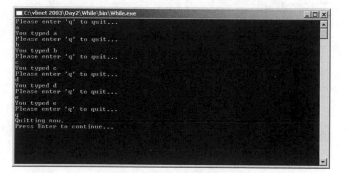

Tip

> Many built-in Visual Basic functions, such as EOF (which returns a value of True when you've read all the data in a file and have reached the end of the file—which is what EOF stands for), are made so they'll return values of True or False, allowing you to use them as the conditions in While loops and the upcoming loop, the Do loop. In a While loop, that might look like this: While(Not EOF(...)) [Read more data] End While. You'll learn more about EOF in Day 10, "Graphics and File Handling."

You might have noticed that, in this example, we needed to read a character from the user before even entering the While loop because you need to test the While loop's condition first thing in that loop. In the While loop, we need to read another character from the user to keep seeing whether we should keep looping. But there's an easier way to do this—we can use a Do loop and test the loop's condition at the end of the loop, not the beginning.

Using the Do Loop

You can use the Do loop to keep executing Visual Basic statements while or until (depending on which keyword you use, While or Until) its *condition* is true. With a Do loop, unlike a simple While loop, you can end the loop at any time with an Exit Do statement. The Do loop has two versions. First, you can evaluate *condition* at the beginning (remember that, as discussed earlier today, you use only one of the items in curly braces):

```
Do [{While | Until} condition]
    [statements]
    [Exit Do]
    [statements]
Loop
```

Or you can evaluate it at the end, like this (note that this form of Do loop ensures that the code in its body is run at least once, unlike While loops):

```
Do
    [statements]
    [Exit Do]
    [statements]
Loop [{While | Until} condition]
```

Listing 2.13 shows how to adapt the While loop example we just saw in the preceding section to use a Do loop, where we have to use code to read a character from the user in only one place.

LISTING 2.13 Using a Do Loop (Do project, Module1.vb)

```
Module Module1
    Sub Main()
        Dim strInput As String

        Do
            Console.WriteLine("Please enter 'q' to quit...")
            strInput = Console.ReadLine()
            Console.WriteLine("You typed " & strInput)
        Loop While (strInput <> "q")

        Console.WriteLine("Quitting now.")
        Console.WriteLine("Press Enter to continue...")
        Console.ReadLine()
    End Sub
End Module
```

That covers the four loops in Visual Basic .NET—For, For Each, While, and Do. While we're talking about loops, it's important to cover another statement—the With statement. Although this statement is not, properly speaking, a loop, it can be as useful as a loop.

Using the With Statement

NEW TERM You use a With statement to make a Visual Basic object the *default* object for a set of enclosed Visual Basic statements. For example, a text box is considered an object in Visual Basic, and when you make a text box the default object, you can access its properties more easily—for example, just using the term .Text instead of TextBox1.Text. Here's the syntax for this statement:

```
With object
    [statements]
End With
```

The following example shows how to put With to work. This example uses a text box, TextBox1, and a With statement to set the text box's Height, Width, and Text properties in the With statement:

```
With TextBox1
    .Height = 30
    .Width = 300
    .Text = "Hello there!"
End With
```

2

Ending a Program in Code

We have one last statement to look at today. Say that you want to end a program from code—that is, close its window. How can you do that? You can use the End statement. In console applications, as with other applications, End will stop the application and close the application's window(s).

Listing 2.14 shows an example, the End project in the code for this book. This example has a loop that will run forever if left to itself: While (True)...End While. (This is called an endless loop, and it's not a good idea to create an endless loop unless you've added some foolproof way to stop it.) This loop will run until the user types **End** to end the program. (Note that this example uses the UCase Visual Basic function to convert the user input to uppercase, so the user can type **END**, **end**, **EnD**, and the code will still work.)

LISTING 2.14   Using an End Statement (End project, Module1.vb)

```
Module Module1

    Sub Main()

        Dim strInput As String

        While (True)
            Console.WriteLine("Type End to quit.")
            strInput = Console.ReadLine()
            If (UCase(strInput) = "END") Then
                End
            End If
        End While

    End Sub

End Module
```

When the user runs this application and types **End**, the application will end and the console window will close immediately.

In fact, there's another statement similar to End: the Stop statement. If you've started a Visual Basic .NET application from the Debug menu, however, Stop will do more than just end the application—it will bring up the Visual Basic .NET debugger to the location of the Stop statement, allowing you to debug your code.

Summary

Today, we started programming in Visual Basic .NET. We got an overview of Visual Basic statements and keywords. And we saw that we can add comments to Visual Basic code that Visual Basic won't read; such comments are entirely for the convenience of programmers.

Then we started working with data by seeing how to name and declare variables with the Dim statement. Variables are the fundamental unit of data storage in Visual Basic programming. We saw that there are various different data types, such as strings, integers, doubles, and Booleans (which hold only the values True or False). We also saw that we can initialize the value of a variable while declaring it.

Declaring variables gave us an introduction to working with different data types, and that brought up the issue of converting between data types. We saw that Visual Basic converts between data types automatically as needed but that we can turn off that feature with Option Strict On, in which case we're responsible for data conversions ourselves in those cases where there's a possibility of data loss.

Besides declaring variables, we also saw how to declare constants and enumerations. Constants are just like variables except that we declare them with the Const statement, and after they're created, we cannot change their value. Enumerations, declared with the Enum statement, function as sets of constants.

The next step up for us in data handling was working with arrays and dynamic arrays. We saw how to create arrays, including multidimensional arrays, using the Dim statement, and how to initialize them. We also saw how to store and access data in arrays.

We also saw how to redimension an array at runtime with the ReDim statement. Redimensioning an array makes sense for those times when we don't know until a program is running how many data items we have to work with.

After spending time trying to understand the basics of data storage, we worked with Visual Basic operators. Using operators, we can handle data in various ways, as when we use the arithmetic operators to add, subtract, multiply, divide, and so on. We also saw that there is such a thing as operator precedence, which means Visual Basic will execute some operators before others.

We then turned to making decisions in code with the branching statements—If, Select, Switch, and Choose. We saw how to use conditional and logical operators to create conditions these statements test and then execute code accordingly.

2

We also saw how to use the four Visual Basic .NET loops today, including the Do, For, For Each, and While loops. We saw examples of each, as well as looked at the differences between these loops. For example, we saw that the code in a While loop doesn't have to be executed even once, whereas the code in a Do loop where the condition is checked at the end of the loop always is. And we saw how to use the With statement today to make an object the default object.

Finally, we saw how to end a program in code at any time with the End statement. And we saw that the Stop statement ends a program as well—and brings up the debugger if we launched the program from the Debug menu.

Tomorrow, we're going to continue our work with the Visual Basic language when we take an in-depth look at creating procedures and handling errors, and get an introduction to classes and objects.

Q&A

Q What's the difference between comparison operators and logical operators?

A Comparison operators such as <= and >= enable you to create logical clauses, like intInput <= 75 and intInput >= 55. You can connect logical clauses using logical operators such as And this way: intInput <= 75 And intInput >= 55.

Q Can I change the data type used in an array or the number of dimensions in an array with ReDim?

A No. Although you can change the number of elements in an array with ReDim, you can't change the number of dimensions or the data types used.

Workshop

This workshop tests whether you understand the concepts you saw today. It's a good idea to make sure you can answer these questions before pressing on to tomorrow's work.

Quiz

1. What character do you use at the end of a line to indicate to Visual Basic that the current statement is continued on the next line?

2. What value does the statement Dim a As Double = 1 + 2 + 3 + 4 / 4 * 5 leave in the variable a?

3. How can you declare and initialize an array of integers named a so that it holds the values 1, 2, 3, and 4 in one statement?

4. How can you write an If statement to check whether the integer variable intDayOfTheMonth holds a day of the month in the second week of the month?

5. How many times does For intLoopIndex As Integer = 0 To 5 Console.WriteLine("Hello") Next intLoopIndex display "Hello"?

Quiz Answers

1. You use the underscore character (_). Note that you shouldn't break text strings over lines unless you end with a double quotation mark, begin the next section of the string with a double quotation mark, and use & to connect them, as discussed in the text.

2. 11. The 4 / 4 * 5 part is evaluated left to right to give 5, which is added to 1 + 2 + 3 to give 11.

3. You can use this statement: Dim a() As Integer = {1, 2, 3, 4}.

4. Here's one way: If(intDayOfTheMonth > 7 and intDayOfTheMonth < 15) Then ... End If.

5. Six times.

Exercises

1. Using If statements, write a game in which the users have to guess a positive integer from 0 to 100 while your code displays the messages "Higher" or "Lower" until they enter the correct value. (If you want to have your code select the number to guess randomly, you can use the Visual Basic Randomize() statement followed by the statement Dim intGuessMe As Integer = 101 * Rnd() to place a random positive integer from 0 to 100 in the variable intGuessMe.)

2. Using one For loop inside another (*nesting* two For loops), display all the elements of a 3 × 3 two-dimensional array (that is, an array of three rows and three columns).

DAY 3

Mastering the Visual Basic Language: Procedures, Error Handling, Classes, and Objects

Today, we're going to look at some crucial aspects of the Visual Basic language: procedures such as Sub procedures and functions, procedure scope, and exception (runtime error) handling. We'll also get an introduction to a topic that's become central to Visual Basic: classes and objects.

NEW TERM Now that our code is growing larger, it's good to know about procedures, which allow us to break up our code into manageable chunks. In fact, in Visual Basic, all executable code must be in procedures. There are two types of procedures: *Sub procedures* and *functions*. In Visual Basic, Sub procedures do not return values when they terminate, but functions do.

NEW TERM If you declare variables in your new procedures, those variables might not be accessible from outside the procedure, and that fact is new also. The area of your program in which a data item is visible and can be accessed in code is called *scope*, and we'll try to understand scope—a crucial aspect of object-oriented programming—in this chapter.

NEW TERM We'll also look at handling runtime errors today. In Visual Basic, a runtime error is the same as an exception (that's not true in all languages), so we're going to look at *exception handling*. We'll see that there are two ways of heading off errors that happen at runtime before they become problems.

Finally, we'll get an introduction to classes and objects in this chapter. Visual Basic .NET programming is object-oriented programming (OOP), a fact you need to understand in depth to be a Visual Basic programmer. Today, we'll start by discussing classes and objects in preparation for our later work (such as Day 9, "Object-Oriented Programming," which is all about OOP). Here's an overview of today's topics:

- Creating Sub procedures and functions
- Passing arguments to procedures
- Returning data from functions
- Preserving data values between procedure calls
- Understanding scope
- Using unstructured exception handling
- Using structured exception handling with `Try`/`Catch`
- Using exception filtering in `Catch` blocks
- Using multiple `Catch` statements
- Throwing an exception
- Throwing a custom exception
- Understanding classes and objects
- Supporting properties and methods in objects

All these topics are powerful ones, and they're all related. And today, the best place to start is with Sub procedures.

Sub Procedures

Procedures give you a way to break up your Visual Basic code, which is invaluable as that code grows longer and longer. Ideally, each procedure should handle one discrete task. That way, you break up your code by task; having one task per procedure makes it easier to keep in mind what each procedure does.

You can place a set of Visual Basic statements in a procedure, and when that procedure is *called*, those statements will be run. You can *pass* data to procedures for that code to work on and read that data in your code. The two types of procedures in Visual Basic are *Sub procedures* and *functions*, and both can read the data you pass them (the name *Sub procedure* comes from the programming term *subroutine*). However, only one type, functions, can also *return* data.

In fact, we've been creating Sub procedures in our code already (not surprisingly, because all Visual Basic code has to be in a procedure). All the code we developed yesterday went into the Sub procedure named Main, created with the keyword Sub:

```
Module Module1

    Sub Main()
        Console.WriteLine("Hello there!")
        Console.WriteLine("Press Enter to continue...")
        Console.ReadLine()
    End Sub

End Module
```

This Main Sub procedure is special because when a console application starts, Visual Basic calls Main automatically to start the program. When Main is called, the code is run as we wanted.

You can also create your own Sub procedures, giving them your own names. Those names should give an indication of the procedure's task. For example, to show the "Hi there!" message, you might create a new Sub procedure named ShowMessage by simply typing this text into the code designer:

```
Module Module1

    Sub Main()

    End Sub

    Sub ShowMessage()

    End Sub

End Module
```

In the ShowMessage Sub procedure, you place the code you want to execute, like this code to display the message:

```
Module Module1

    Sub Main()

    End Sub

    Sub ShowMessage()
        Console.WriteLine("Hi there!")
    End Sub

End Module
```

How do you make the code in the ShowMessage Sub procedure run? You can do that by calling it; to do so, just insert its name, followed by parentheses, into your code:

```
Module Module1

    Sub Main()
        ShowMessage()
        Console.WriteLine("Press Enter to continue...")
        Console.ReadLine()
    End Sub

    Sub ShowMessage()
        Console.WriteLine("Hi there!")
    End Sub

End Module
```

And that's it! Now when you run this code, Visual Basic will call the Main Sub procedure, which in turn will call the ShowMessage Sub procedure, giving you the same result as before:

```
Hi there!
Press Enter to continue...
```

Tip

If you want to, you can use a Visual Basic Call statement to call a Sub procedure like this: Call ShowMessage(). This usage is still supported, although it goes back to the earliest days of Visual Basic, and there's no real reason to use it here.

Note the parentheses at the end of the call to ShowMessage like this: ShowMessage(). You use those parentheses to pass data to a procedure, and we'll take a look at that task next.

Passing Data to Procedures

Say you want to pass the message text you want to display to the ShowMessage Sub procedure, allowing you to display whatever message you want. You can do that by passing a text string to ShowMessage, like this:

```
Module Module1

    Sub Main()
        ShowMessage("Hi there!")
        Console.WriteLine("Press Enter to continue...")
        Console.ReadLine()
    End Sub

    Sub ShowMessage()

    End Sub

End Module
```

NEW TERM A data item you pass to a procedure in parentheses this way is called an *argument*. Now in ShowMessage, you must declare the type of the argument passed to this procedure in the procedure's *argument list*:

```
Module Module1

    Sub Main()
        ShowMessage("Hi there!")
        Console.WriteLine("Press Enter to continue...")
        Console.ReadLine()
    End Sub

    Sub ShowMessage(ByVal Text As String)

    End Sub

End Module
```

NEW TERM This creates a new string variable, Text, which you'll be able to access in the procedure's code. The ByVal keyword here indicates that the data is being passed *by value*, which is the default in Visual Basic (you don't even have to type ByVal, just Text As String here, and Visual Basic will add ByVal automatically).

NEW TERM Passing data by value means a copy of the data will be passed to the procedure. The other way of passing data is *by reference*, where you use the ByRef keyword. Passing by reference (which was the default in VB6) meant that the *location* of the data in memory will be passed to the procedure. Here's an important point to know: Because objects can become very large in Visual Basic, making a copy of an object and passing that copy can be very wasteful of memory, so objects are automatically passed by reference. We'll discuss passing by value and passing by reference in more detail in a page or two.

Visual Basic automatically fills the Text variable you declared in the argument list in this example with the string data passed to the procedure. This means you can access that data as you would the data in any other variable, as you see in the SubProcedures project in the code for this book, as shown in Listing 3.1.

LISTING 3.1   Passing Data to a Sub Procedure (SubProcedures project, Module1.vb)

```
Module Module1

    Sub Main()
        ShowMessage("Hi there!")
        Console.WriteLine("Press Enter to continue...")
        Console.ReadLine()
    End Sub

    Sub ShowMessage(ByVal Text As String)
        Console.WriteLine(Text)
    End Sub

End Module
```

And that's all you need! Now you're passing data to Sub procedures and retrieving that data in the procedure's code. You can pass more than one argument to procedures as long as you declare each argument in the procedure's argument list. For example, say you want to pass the string to show and the number of times to show it to ShowMessage; that code might look like this:

```
Module Module1

    Sub Main()
        ShowMessage("Hi there!", 3)
        Console.WriteLine("Press Enter to continue...")
        Console.ReadLine()
    End Sub

    Sub ShowMessage(ByVal Text As String, ByVal Times As Integer)
        For intLoopIndex As Integer = 1 To Times
```

```
        Console.WriteLine(Text)
    Next intLoopIndex
End Sub
```

```
End Module
```

Here's the result of this code:

```
Hi there!
Hi there!
Hi there!
Press Enter to continue...
```

If you pass arguments by reference, using the ByRef keyword, Visual Basic passes the memory location of the passed data to the procedure (which gives the code in that procedure access to that data). You can read that data just as you do when you pass arguments by value:

```
Sub ShowMessage(ByRef Text As String, ByRef Times As Integer)
    For intLoopIndex As Integer = 1 To Times
        Console.WriteLine(Text)
    Next intLoopIndex
End Sub
```

The code in the procedure has access to the data's location in memory, however, and that's something to keep in mind. So far, we've passed two literals ("Hello there!" and 3) to ShowMessage, and literals don't correspond to memory locations. But see what happens if you pass a variable by reference, like this:

```
Dim NumberOfTimes As Integer = 3
ShowMessage("Hi there!", NumberOfTimes)
        .
        .
        .
Sub ShowMessage(ByRef Text As String, ByRef Times As Integer)
    For intLoopIndex As Integer = 1 To Times
        Console.WriteLine(Text)
    Next intLoopIndex
End Sub
```

The code in the procedure has access to that variable, and if you change the value of the passed argument, you'll also change the value in the original variable:

```
Dim NumberOfTimes As Integer = 3
ShowMessage("Hi there!", NumberOfTimes)
        .
        .
        .
```

```
Sub ShowMessage(ByRef Text As String, ByRef Times As Integer)
    For intLoopIndex As Integer = 1 To Times
        Console.WriteLine(Text)
    Next intLoopIndex
    Times = 24
End Sub
```

After this code is finished executing, for example, the variable `NumberOfTimes` will be left holding 24. This side effect is not unintentional; it's intentional. Being able to change the value of arguments is a primary reason to pass arguments by reference.

Changing the value of arguments passed by reference is one way to pass data from a procedure back to the calling code, but it can be troublesome. You can easily change an argument's value unintentionally, for example. A more structured way of passing data back from procedures is to use functions, which is the next topic.

You should also know that an `Exit Sub` statement, if you use one, causes an immediate exit from a Sub procedure in case you want to leave before executing all code. For example, say you have a Sub procedure that displays reciprocals of numbers you pass to it, but you want to avoid trying to find the reciprocal of 0. You could display an error message and exit the procedure like this if 0 is passed to the procedure:

```
Sub Reciprocal(ByVal dblNumber As Double)
    If dblNumber = 0 Then
        Console.WriteLine("Cannot find the reciprocal of 0.")
        Console.WriteLine("Press Enter to continue...")
        Console.ReadLine()
        Exit Sub
    End If
    Console.WriteLine("The reciprocal is " & 1 / dblNumber)
    Console.WriteLine("Press Enter to continue...")
    Console.ReadLine()
End Sub
```

Sub Procedure Syntax

Like other Visual Basic statements, Sub procedures require a formal declaration. You declare Sub procedures with the `Sub` statement:

```
[ <attrlist> ] [{ Overloads | Overrides | Overridable |
NotOverridable | MustOverride | Shadows | Shared }]
[{ Public | Protected | Friend | Protected Friend | Private }]
Sub name [(arglist)]
[ Implements interface.definedname ]
    [ statements ]
```

```
    [ Exit Sub ]
    [ statements ]
End Sub
```

And like other Visual Basic statements, many of the keywords here won't make sense at this point, so you can treat this information as reference material to come back to later. (Many of the keywords here deal with OOP, but we can't cover OOP in the detail needed here before knowing how to work with procedures, so it's impossible to avoid slightly circular definitions.) The parts of this statement are as follows:

- *attrlist*—This is an advanced (and optional) topic; this is a list of attributes for use with this procedure. Attributes can add more information about the procedure, such as copyright data and so on. You separate multiple attributes with commas.

- Overloads—Specifies that this Sub procedure overloads one (or more) procedures defined with the same name in a base class. An overloaded procedure has multiple versions, each with a different argument list, as we'll see in Day 9. The argument list must be different from the argument list of every procedure that is to be overloaded. You cannot specify both Overloads and Shadows in the same procedure declaration.

- Overrides—Specifies that this Sub procedure overrides (replaces) a procedure with the same name in a base class. The number and data types of the arguments must match those of the procedure in the base class.

- Overridable—Specifies that this Sub procedure can be overridden by a procedure with the same name in a derived class.

- NotOverridable—Specifies that this Sub procedure may not be overridden in a derived class.

- MustOverride—Specifies that this Sub procedure is not implemented. This procedure must be implemented in a derived class.

- Shadows—Makes this Sub procedure a shadow of an identically named programming element in a base class. You can use Shadows only at module, namespace, or file level (but not inside a procedure). You cannot specify both Overloads and Shadows in the same procedure declaration.

- Shared—Specifies that this Sub procedure is a shared procedure. As a shared procedure, it is not associated with a specific object, and you can call it using the class or structure name.

- Public—Procedures declared Public have public access. There are no restrictions on the accessibility of public procedures.

3

- Protected—Procedures declared Protected have protected access. They are accessible only from within their own class or from a derived class. You can specify Protected access only for members of classes.

- Friend—Procedures declared Friend have friend access. They are accessible from within the program that contains their declaration and from anywhere else in the same assembly.

- Protected Friend—Procedures declared Protected Friend have both protected and friend accessibility. They can be used by code in the same assembly, as well as by code in derived classes.

- Private—Procedures declared Private have private access. They are accessible only within the element in which they're declared.

- *name*—Specifies the name of the Sub procedure.

- *arglist*—Lists expressions representing arguments that are passed to the Sub procedure when it is called. You separate multiple arguments with commas.

- Implements *interface.definedname*—Indicates that this Sub procedure implements an interface. We'll see interfaces, which allow you to derive one class from several others, in Day 9.

- *statements*—Specifies the block of statements to be executed within the Sub procedure.

In addition, each argument in the argument list, *arglist*, has this syntax:

```
[ <attrlist> ] [ Optional ] [{ ByVal | ByRef }]
[ ParamArray ] argname[( )] [ As argtype ] [ = defaultvalue ]
```

Here are the parts of *arglist*:

- *attrlist*—Lists (optional) attributes that apply to this argument. Multiple attributes are separated by commas.

- Optional—Specifies that this argument is not required when the procedure is called. If you use this keyword, all following arguments in *arglist* must also be optional and be declared using the Optional keyword. Every optional argument declaration must supply a *defaultvalue*. Optional cannot be used for any argument if you also use ParamArray.

- ByVal—Specifies passing by value. ByVal is the default in Visual Basic.

- ByRef—Specifies passing by reference, which means the procedure code can modify the value of the original variable in the calling code.

- ParamArray—Acts as the last argument in *arglist* to indicate that the final argument is an optional array of elements of the specified type. The ParamArray keyword allows you to pass an arbitrary number of arguments to the procedure. ParamArray arguments are always passed by value.

- *argname*—Specifies the name of the variable representing the argument.

- *argtype*—Specifies the data type of the argument passed to the procedure; this part is optional unless Option Strict is set to On. It can be Boolean, Byte, Char, Date, Decimal, Double, Integer, Long, Object, Short, Single, or String, or the name of an enumeration, structure, class, or interface.

- *defaultvalue*—Specifies the default value for an optional argument, required for all optional arguments. It can be any constant or constant expression that evaluates to the data type of the argument. Note that if the type is Object, or a class, interface, array, or structure, the default value must be Nothing.

That gives us what we need to know about Sub procedures, we'll move on to functions next.

Creating Functions

You can also create functions in Visual Basic .NET. They are just like Sub procedures except that they can return a value. You declare a function in much the same way as a Sub procedure, except that you use the Function keyword instead of Sub.

Let's look at an example. In this case, we'll create a function named Summer that calculates the sum of two integers and returns that sum; this project is named Functions in the code for the book. To create this new function, you use the Function keyword:

```
Module Module1

    Sub Main()

    End Sub

    Function Summer(ByVal int1 As Integer, ByVal int2 As Integer) As Long

    End Function

End Module
```

This example looks just like creating a Sub procedure, except for the Function keyword and the As Long at the end. The As Long part is there to indicate that this function returns a Long value. (Long is a better return value choice than Integer here because two integers could be passed to Summer such that their sum exceeds the capacity of the Integer data type.)

 Tip   It's worth realizing that function names can use the same type prefixes that variable names use to indicate return type, such as intSummer.

You return a value from a function with the Return statement, as here, where the code is returning the sum of the two arguments passed to the function:

```
Module Module1

    Sub Main()

    End Sub

    Function Summer(ByVal int1 As Integer, ByVal int2 As Integer) As Long
        Return int1 + int2
    End Function

End Module
```

Now when you call Summer with two integers, like Summer(2, 3), Visual Basic will treat that function call as an expression and replace it with the value returned by the function, which is 5 here. Listing 3.2 shows how this might look in code.

LISTING 3.2   Returning Data from a Function (Functions project, Module1.vb)

```
Module Module1

    Sub Main()
        Dim intItem1 As Integer = 2
        Dim intItem2 As Integer = 3
        Console.WriteLine(intItem1 & " + " & _
            intItem2 & " = " & Summer(intItem1, intItem2))
        Console.WriteLine("Press Enter to continue...")
        Console.ReadLine()
    End Sub

    Function Summer(ByVal int1 As Integer, ByVal int2 As Integer) As Long
        Return int1 + int2
    End Function

End Module
```

When you run this code, you see this result:

```
2 + 3 = 5
Press Enter to continue...
```

Function Syntax

Here's the formal syntax for functions; you use the Function statement:

```
[ <attrlist> ] [{ Overloads | Overrides | Overridable |
NotOverridable | MustOverride | Shadows | Shared }]
[{ Public | Protected | Friend | Protected Friend |
Private }] Function name[(arglist)] [ As type ]
[ Implements interface.definedname ]
    [ statements ]
    [ Exit Function ]
    [ statements ]
End Function
```

The various parts of this statement are the same as for Sub procedures (see the previous topic) except for the As *type* clause, which specifies the type of the return value from the function. This clause indicates the data type of the value returned by the function. That type can be Boolean, Byte, Char, Date, Decimal, Double, Integer, Long, Object, Short, Single, or String, or the name of an enumeration, structure, class, or interface.

The Return statement, if there is one, sets the return value and exits the function; any number of Return statements can appear anywhere in the function, but as soon as one of them is executed, you return from the function to the calling code. You can also use the Exit Function statement to exit the function at any time. If you use Exit Function, how can you return a value from a function? You just assign that value to the function name itself, like this:

```
Function Summer(ByVal int1 As Integer, ByVal int2 As Integer) As Long
    Summer = int1 + int2
    Exit Function

        .
        .
        .

End Function
```

If you use Exit Function without setting a return value, the function returns the default value appropriate to *argtype*. That's 0 for Byte, Char, Decimal, Double, Integer, Long, Short, and Single; Nothing for Object, String, and all arrays; False for Boolean; and 1/1/0001 12:00 AM for Date.

Using Optional Arguments

You can make some arguments in a procedure call *optional*, which means that if the calling code doesn't specify a value for them, a default value will be used. To make an argument optional, you use the Optional keyword and supply a default value like this, where the strText argument of the ShowMessage function is optional and the default value is "Hello there!":

```
Module Module1

    Sub Main()

    End Sub

    Sub ShowMessage(Optional ByVal strText As String = "Hello there!")
        Console.WriteLine(strText)
    End Sub

End Module
```

Now if you call ShowMessage with no arguments, as shown in Listing 3.3 and the Optional project in the code for this book, the message "Hello there!" will be displayed.

LISTING 3.3   Using Optional Arguments (Optional project, Module1.vb)

```
Module Module1

    Sub Main()
        ShowMessage()
        Console.WriteLine("Press Enter to continue...")
        Console.ReadLine()
    End Sub

    Sub ShowMessage(Optional ByVal strText As String = "Hello there!")
        Console.WriteLine(strText)
    End Sub

End Module
```

Note that if you declare one argument optional in a procedure's argument list, all following arguments must be optional too (otherwise, Visual Basic wouldn't know which argument had been omitted).

Passing a Variable Number of Arguments

Here's another valuable technique: You can create procedures that can accept a varying number of arguments. You do that with the `ParamArray` keyword in the argument list, which makes all the arguments passed at that point in the list and after it part of an array. If you use a `ParamArray` argument, it must be the *last* argument in the argument list. Here's an example; in this case, the `ShowMessage` Sub procedure is able to handle a variable number of arguments:

```
Module Module1

    Sub Main()

    End Sub

    Sub ShowMessage(ByVal ParamArray Text() As String)
        .
        .
        .
    End Sub

End Module
```

This means that the `Text` argument here is really an array of arguments. In this example, we can loop over all the arguments in this array, displaying them like this:

```
Module Module1

    Sub Main()

    End Sub

    Sub ShowMessage(ByVal ParamArray Text() As String)
        Dim intLoopIndex As Integer
        For intLoopIndex = 0 To UBound(Text)
            Console.Write(Text(intLoopIndex))
        Next intLoopIndex
        Console.WriteLine("")            'Skip to the next line
    End Sub

End Module
```

Now you can call `ShowMessage` with different numbers of arguments, as you see in Listing 3.4.

LISTING **3.4**   Using Variable Numbers of Arguments (VariableArgs project, Module1.vb)

```
Module Module1

    Sub Main()
        ShowMessage("Hello there!")
        ShowMessage("Hello", " there!")
        Console.WriteLine("Press Enter to continue...")
        Console.ReadLine()
    End Sub

    Sub ShowMessage(ByVal ParamArray Text() As String)
        Dim intLoopIndex As Integer
        For intLoopIndex = 0 To UBound(Text)
            Console.Write(Text(intLoopIndex))
        Next intLoopIndex
        Console.WriteLine("")
    End Sub

End Module
```

Here's what you see when this code runs:

```
Hello there!
Hello there!
Press Enter to continue...
```

Preserving Data Between Procedure Calls

Suppose that you want to keep track of the number of times you've called a procedure.
You might write a function like Tracker in this code, which has a variable named
intCount that it increments each time you call the function:

```
Module Module1

    Sub Main()
        For intLoopIndex As Integer = 0 To 5
            Console.WriteLine(Tracker())
        Next intLoopIndex
        Console.WriteLine("Press Enter to continue...")
        Console.ReadLine()
    End Sub

    Function Tracker() As Integer
        Dim intCount As Integer
        intCount += 1
```

```
        Return intCount
    End Function
```

```
End Module
```

Because the code calls Tracker six times and displays its return value each time, you might expect to see this program display 1, 2, 3, 4, 5, and 6. But you actually get this result:

```
1
1
1
1
1
1
Press Enter to continue...
```

The problem here is that the intCount variable in Tracker is re-initialized to 0 each time the procedure is called, so the return value, after intCount is incremented, is always 1. The solution is to declare intCount as *static*, as shown in Listing 3.5 and the Static project in the code for this book.

LISTING 3.5   Using Static Variables (Static project, Module1.vb)

```
Module Module1

    Sub Main()
        For intLoopIndex As Integer = 0 To 5
            Console.WriteLine(Tracker())
        Next intLoopIndex
        Console.WriteLine("Press Enter to continue...")
        Console.ReadLine()
    End Sub

    Function Tracker() As Integer
        Static intCount As Integer
        intCount += 1
        Return intCount
    End Function

End Module
```

Now the value in intCount is preserved between calls to the Tracker function, and you do indeed see the result 1, 2, 3, 4, 5, and 6.

Besides using the Static keyword, you can also make intCount a module-level variable to do the same thing, by taking it out of any procedure:

```
Dim intCount As Integer

Function Tracker() As Integer
    intCount += 1
    Return intCount
End Function
```

The result here is the same as using Static to declare the variable; because the variable is outside any procedure, its value isn't reset when you call a procedure.

Tip

> To declare module-level variables, you place the declaration outside any procedure in the module. You can also select the module in the left drop-down list box at the top of the code designer and the (Declarations) item in the right drop-down box, which will place the cursor at the beginning of the module, outside any procedure.

Making a variable into a module-level variable outside any procedure like this introduces the idea of *scope*. Here, the scope of this new variable is module-level scope. The scope of an item in your program is the area in which it's accessible in your code, and there are all different types of scope—module-level, procedure-level, block-level, and more. And we'll look at this issue next.

Understanding Scope

Now that we're dividing our code into procedures, it's a good idea to look at the issue of scope because putting code in procedures restricts that code's scope. Now that Visual Basic .NET is emphasizing OOP more than ever before, scope has become even more important because much of the power of classes and objects is all about restricting scope and hiding implementation details to make things simpler.

The *scope* of a programming element in your code is all the code that can access it. In other words, an element's scope is its *accessibility* in your code. In Visual Basic .NET, where you declare an element determines its scope, and an element can have one of the following levels of scope:

- **Block scope**—The item is available only within the code block in which it is declared.

- **Procedure scope**—The item is available only within the procedure in which it is declared.

- **Module scope**—The item is available to all code within the module, class, or structure in which it is declared.

- **Namespace scope**—The item is available to all code in the namespace.

Let's look at these various levels of scope.

Block Level

A code block is the body of a compound statement. A compound statement is one that can hold other statements, such as an `If` statement. Here's an `If` statement in which a variable, `strText`, is declared. Note that `strText` is *inaccessible* outside the `If` statement, so code that tries to display its value won't work:

```
Module Module1

    Sub Main()

        Console.WriteLine
        Console.WriteLine("Enter a letter...")
        Dim strInput = Console.ReadLine()
        If strInput = "q" Then
            End
        Else
            Dim strText As String = "Please type q to quit."
            Console.WriteLine(strText)
        End If

        Console.WriteLine(strText)          'Will not work!
        Console.WriteLine("Press Enter to continue...")
        Console.ReadLine()
    End Sub

End Module
```

Procedure Level

NEW TERM   An element declared in a procedure is not available outside that procedure, which means that only the code in the procedure that contains the declaration can access it. Elements at this level are called *local* elements, and you declare them with the `Dim` or `Static` statements. In the following example, the variable `strText` declared in the `ShowMessage` Sub procedure cannot be accessed in the `Main` Sub procedure:

```
Module Module1

    Sub Main()
        ShowMessage()
        Console.WriteLine(strText)              'Will not work!
        Console.WriteLine("Press Enter to continue...")
        Console.ReadLine()
    End Sub

    Sub ShowMessage()
        Dim strText = "Hi there!"
        Console.WriteLine(strText)
    End Sub

End Module
```

Module Level

NEW TERM   Visual Basic .NET uses the term *module level* to apply to three programming ele-
            ments: modules, classes, and structures. (We'll see classes later today and struc-
tures in Day 9.) You declare elements at this level by placing the declaration outside any
procedure or block in the module, class, or structure.

Unlike in blocks or procedures (where you can use only `Dim` or `Static`), at the module
level you can also use these keywords to restrict or enlarge scope. (Don't feel you have
to memorize these definitions at this stage; we'll see more on these terms throughout the
book.)

- `Public`—The `Public` statement declares elements to be accessible anywhere. This
  includes inside the same project, from other projects that reference the current project, assemblies built from the project, and so on.

- `Protected`—The `Protected` statement declares elements to be accessible only
  from within the same class or from a class derived from this class. You can use
  `Protected` only at class level and only when declaring a member of a class.

- `Friend`—The `Friend` statement declares elements to be accessible from within the
  same project, but not from outside the project.

- `Protected Friend`—The `Protected` statement with the `Friend` keyword declares
  elements to be accessible either from derived classes or from within the same project, or both. You can use `Protected Friend` only at class level.

- `Private`—The `Private` statement declares elements to be accessible only from
  within the same module, class, or structure.

Let's look at module-level scope with some examples. For example, you can create a new code module, Module2, like this:

```
Module Module1

    Sub Main()

    End Sub

End Module

Module Module2

End Module
```

Tip Although this example declares two modules in the same file (Module1.vb), you can also add a module in a new file to a Visual Basic project by selecting the Project, Add Module menu item (which will create Module2.vb, Module3.vb, and so on).

3

And if you declare a new Sub procedure, ShowMessage, in the new module, you can access it from the first module:

```
Module Module1
    Sub Main()
        ShowMessage()
        Console.WriteLine("Press Enter to continue...")
        Console.ReadLine()
    End Sub
End Module

Module Module2
    Sub ShowMessage()
        Console.WriteLine("Hello there!")
    End Sub
End Module
```

However, if you declare the Sub procedure Private to the new module, you cannot access it in the first module:

```
Module Module1
    Sub Main()
        ShowMessage()                'Will not work!
```

```
        Console.WriteLine("Press Enter to continue...")
        Console.ReadLine()
    End Sub
End Module

Module Module2
    Private Sub ShowMessage()
        Console.WriteLine("Hello there!")
    End Sub
End Module
```

In module scope, you can also make variables—not just procedures—public or private; this example declares strText in the second module using a Dim statement:

```
Module Module1
    Sub Main()
        Console.WriteLine(strText)         'Will not work!
        Console.WriteLine("Press Enter to continue...")
        Console.ReadLine()
    End Sub
End Module

Module Module2
    Dim strText = "Hello there!"
End Module
```

By default, module-level variables are declared Private when you use Dim, so strText cannot be accessed outside its module. However, if you declare this new variable Public, it can be accessed in the first module with no problem:

```
Module Module1
    Sub Main()
        Console.WriteLine(strText)
        Console.WriteLine("Press Enter to continue...")
        Console.ReadLine()
    End Sub
End Module

Module Module2
    Public strText = "Hello there!"
End Module
```

Namespace Scope

NEW TERM   You can also declare elements at namespace level in Visual Basic. A *namespace* is an OOP feature used to keep elements with the same name from conflicting with each other in larger programs. (If you don't use a Namespace statement in your code, all your code is in the same namespace.) Declaring a module-level element Friend or Public makes it available to all procedures throughout the namespace.

We now have the background we'll need on procedures and scope, two very important programming concepts. Next, let's tackle handling the runtime errors that may crop up because the Visual Basic language puts special emphasis on this topic.

Handling Runtime Errors

NEW TERM You may have taken all the bugs out of your code, but there's another kind of problem that is often impossible to head off—runtime errors, called *exceptions* in Visual Basic .NET. A runtime error occurs when your program is asked to do something it can't do—divide a number by zero, for example, or open a file that doesn't exist. Tomorrow we'll start working with Windows forms programming and creating programs ready for public release, so it's a good idea to know how to handle runtime errors; otherwise, they'll crash your program.

Visual Basic .NET has good support for handling runtime errors. In fact, there are two ways of handling exceptions in Visual Basic .NET: unstructured (the VB6 way) and structured (the Visual Basic .NET way). We'll see them both today.

Unstructured exception handling centers on the `On Error GoTo` statement, whereas structured exception handling centers on the `Try/Catch` statement. "Unstructured" exception handling is called that because you can handle it anywhere in your code with the `On Error GoTo` statement, whereas "structured" exception handling with the `Try/Catch` statement restricts exception handling to specific code blocks (as an `If` statement does). We'll see unstructured exception handling first.

Unstructured Exception Handling

In Visual Basic, unstructured exception handling revolves around the `On Error GoTo` statement. Here's how the `On Error GoTo` statement works:

```
On Error { GoTo [ line | 0 | -1 ] | Resume Next }
```

The parts of this statement are as follows:

- `GoTo line`—Calls the error-handling code that starts at the line specified at *line*. Here, *line* is a line label or a line number. If a runtime error occurs, program execution goes to the given location. The specified line must be in the same procedure as the `On Error` statement.

- `GoTo 0`—Disables the enabled error handler in the current procedure.

- `GoTo -1`—Same as `GoTo 0`.

3

- `Resume Next`—Specifies that when an exception occurs, execution skips over the statement that caused the problem and goes to the statement immediately following. Execution continues from that point.

The following example shows how to use the `On Error GoTo` statement that uses division by zero to create an overflow error. In this case, the code redirects execution to the label `Handler`. You can create this label by placing it on a line of its own followed by a colon:

```
Module Module1

    Sub Main()
        On Error GoTo Handler
        .
        .
        .
        Exit Sub
Handler:

    End Sub

End Module
```

Note that we've used an `Exit Sub` statement here so that in normal execution, the procedure stops before reaching the error-handling code that follows the `Handler` label. Now we can add the code that causes the overflow error:

```
Module Module1
    Sub Main()
        On Error GoTo Handler
        Dim intItem1 As Integer = 0
        Dim intItem2 As Integer = 128
        Dim intResult As Integer
        intResult = intItem2 / intItem1
        Console.WriteLine("Press Enter to continue...")
        Console.ReadLine()
        Exit Sub
Handler:

    End Sub
End Module
```

When the overflow error occurs, control is transferred to the `Handler` label, and we can add code there to display an error message to the user, as shown in Listing 3.6 and the OnError project in the code for this book.

LISTING 3.6   Using Unstructured Exception Handling (OnError project, Module1.vb)

```
Module Module1
    Sub Main()
        On Error GoTo Handler
        Dim intItem1 As Integer = 0
        Dim intItem2 As Integer = 128
        Dim intResult As Integer
        intResult = intItem2 / intItem1
        Console.WriteLine("Press Enter to continue...")
        Console.ReadLine()
        Exit Sub
Handler:
        Console.WriteLine("An overflow error occurred.")
        Console.WriteLine("Press Enter to continue...")
        Console.ReadLine()
    End Sub
End Module
```

3

Now when you run this code, you'll see this result:

```
An overflow error occurred.
Press Enter to continue...
```

In this way, you were able to handle the exception without having Visual Basic display all kinds of error message boxes.

Here's something else to know: If you call procedure B from procedure A, and B doesn't have any On Error exception-handling code but A does, then if an exception occurs in B, control will transfer back to A, where the exception will be handled.

Getting an Exception's Number and Description

A built-in error object named Err has a Number property that enables you to determine an error's number. While testing your program, you can use Err.Number to determine the numbers of the errors you might run into and can then use those numbers to handle those errors in different ways. For example, this code handles only overflow errors, which are error number 6:

```
Module Module1
    Sub Main()
        On Error GoTo Handler
        Dim intItem1 As Integer = 0
        Dim intItem2 As Integer = 128
        Dim intResult As Integer
```

```
            intResult = intItem2 / intItem1
            Console.WriteLine("Press Enter to continue...")
            Console.ReadLine()
            Exit Sub
Handler:
            If (Err.Number = 6) Then
                Console.WriteLine("An overflow error occurred.")
            End If
            Console.WriteLine("Press Enter to continue...")
            Console.ReadLine()
    End Sub
End Module
```

 Tip

As of this writing, the Visual Basic documentation no longer includes a list of errors by error number. To find a runtime error's number, you can always create that error yourself and have your code display the value of `Err.Number`.

You can also use the `Err` object's `Description` property to get a short description of the error, as in this code:

```
Module Module1
    Sub Main()
        On Error GoTo Handler
        Dim intItem1 As Integer = 0
        Dim intItem2 As Integer = 128
        Dim intResult As Integer
        intResult = intItem2 / intItem1
        Console.WriteLine("Press Enter to continue...")
        Console.ReadLine()
        Exit Sub
Handler:
            Console.WriteLine(Err.Description)
        Console.WriteLine("Press Enter to continue...")
        Console.ReadLine()
    End Sub
End Module
```

This code displays this message:

```
Arithmetic operation resulted in an overflow.
Press Enter to continue...
```

> **Tip**
>
> You can determine more details about the source of an error by using the Err object's Source property. This property holds the name of the object or application that caused the error. For example, if you connect your program to Microsoft Excel and it generates an error, Err.Source will hold "Excel.Application".

Using Exception Objects

You can also use Err.GetException to get an exception object that enables you to determine what kind of runtime error occurred. Visual Basic .NET has many exception objects, and you can see a sampling in Table 3.1.

TABLE 3.1 Some Visual Basic Exceptions

AppDomainUnloadedException	ArgumentException
ArgumentException	ArgumentNullException
ArgumentOutOfRangeException	ArithmeticException
ArrayTypeMismatchException	BadImageFormatException
CannotUnloadAppDomainException	ComponentException
DivideByZeroException	DllNotFoundException
DuplicateWaitObjectException	EntryPointNotFoundException
ExecutionEngineException	ExternalException
FieldAccessException	FormatException
IndexOutofRangeException	InvalidCastException
InvalidOperationException	InvalidProgramException
MissingFieldException	MissingMemberException
MissingMethodException	MulticastNotSupportedException
NotFiniteNumberException	NotImplementedException
NotSupportedException	NullReferenceException
ObjectDisposedException	OperationException
OutOfMemoryException	OverflowException
PlatformNotSupportedException	RankException
SafeArrayTypeMismatchException	StackOverflowException

TABLE 3.1   continued

TypeInitializationException	TypeLoadException
TypeUnloadedException	UnauthorizedAccessException
UriFormatException	

For example, to test for an overflow error, you can check if the type of the exception is OverflowException. To do that, you use the TypeOf and Is keywords, which are specifically designed for just this purpose to be used in If statements to work with objects:

```
Module Module1
    Sub Main()
        On Error GoTo Handler
        Dim intItem1 As Integer = 0
        Dim intItem2 As Integer = 128
        Dim intResult As Integer
        intResult = intItem2 / intItem1
        Console.WriteLine("Press Enter to continue...")
        Console.ReadLine()
        Exit Sub
Handler:
        If (TypeOf Err.GetException() Is OverflowException) Then
            Console.WriteLine("An overflow error occurred.")
        End If
        Console.WriteLine("Press Enter to continue...")
        Console.ReadLine()
    End Sub
End Module
```

If the type of exception that occurred is OverflowException, the message "An overflow error occurred." will be displayed here.

Even though structured exception handling is newer than unstructured exception handling, you can still do things with unstructured exception handling that you can't with structured exception handling. The main thing is that you can resume execution of the part of your code that caused the error (after skipping the problematic line) using the Resume statement.

Using the Resume Statement

After an exception occurs, you can use the Resume statement to resume program execution in unstructured exception handling. Here are the possibilities:

- Resume resumes execution with the statement that caused the error.
- Resume Next resumes execution with the statement after the one that caused the error.
- Resume line resumes execution at line, a line number or label that specifies where to resume execution.

Listing 3.7 is an example using Resume Next; this is the Resume project in the code for this book. It enables you to skip over the line that caused the problem and keep going with the following line.

LISTING 3.7   Using the Resume Statement (Resume project, Module1.vb)

```
Module Module1
    Sub Main()
        On Error GoTo Handler
        Dim intItem1 As Integer = 0
        Dim intItem2 As Integer = 128
        Dim intResult As Integer
        intResult = intItem2 / intItem1
        Console.WriteLine("Press Enter to continue...")
        Console.ReadLine()
        Exit Sub
Handler:
        Console.WriteLine("An overflow error occurred.")
        Resume Next
    End Sub
End Module
```

Here's what you see when you run this application:

```
An overflow error occurred.
Press Enter to continue...
```

And here's an example using Resume line to do exactly the same thing. Here, we're using a line label, LineAfter, which is just a (nonreserved) word followed by a colon that can be used to label a line of code:

```
Module Module1
    Sub Main()
        On Error GoTo Handler
        Dim intItem1 As Integer = 0
        Dim intItem2 As Integer = 128
        Dim intResult As Integer
        intResult = intItem2 / intItem1
```

3

```
LineAfter:
        Console.WriteLine("Press Enter to continue...")
        Console.ReadLine()
        Exit Sub
Handler:
        Console.WriteLine("An overflow error occurred.")
        Resume LineAfter
    End Sub
End Module
```

> **Tip**
>
> You can use the statement `On Error Resume Next` or `On Error Resume` at the beginning of your code when you don't want to add explicit exception-handling code. These statements will make Visual Basic .NET continue execution after an exception has occurred.

Turning Off Exception Handling

To turn off unstructured error handling, you can use the `On Error GoTo 0` or `On Error GoTo -1` statements (they do the same thing). Here's an example:

```
Module Module1
    Sub Main()
        On Error GoTo Handler
        Dim intItem1 As Integer = 0
        Dim intItem2 As Integer = 128
        Dim intResult As Integer
        intResult = intItem2 / intItem1
        On Error GoTo 0
        Console.WriteLine("Press Enter to continue...")
        Console.ReadLine()
        Exit Sub
Handler:
        Console.WriteLine("An overflow error occurred.")
        Resume Next
    End Sub
End Module
```

Now that we have a good understanding of unstructured exception handling, we'll look at structured exception handling next.

Structured Exception Handling

In addition to unstructured exception handling, Visual Basic .NET also supports structured exception handling. It's important to know about structured exception handling because not only does it allow you to handle exceptions, but in some circumstances, Visual Basic will insist that you handle possible exceptions using structured exception handling before running your code.

NEW TERM In Visual Basic .NET, structured exception handling centers on the `Try/Catch` statement. In this statement, you put sensitive, exception-prone code in a `Try` block, and if an exception occurs, the code in the `Try` block will *throw* the exception (actually an exception object), which will then be *caught* by a following `Catch` block. The code in the `Catch` block handles the exception. Unlike unstructured exception handling, where exception handling can be spread throughout your code, structured exception handling all takes place inside a `Try/Catch` statement. Here's the syntax of that statement:

```
Try
    [ tryStatements ]
    [Catch [ exception1 [ As type1 ] ] [ When expression1 ]
        catchStatements1
        [Exit Try]
    [Catch [ exception2 [ As type2 ] ] [When expression2 ]
        catchStatements2
        [ Exit Try ]
        .
        .
        .
    [Catch [ exceptionn [ As typen ] ] [ When expressionn ]
        catchStatementsn ]
        [ Exit Try ]
    [ Finally
        [ finallyStatements ] ]
End Try
```

The parts of this statement are as follows:

- `Try`—Starts the `Try` block.
- `tryStatements`—Specifies the sensitive statements where you anticipate possible exceptions.
- `Catch`—Starts the block that catches and handles the exception(s).
- `exception`—Specifies a variable that you give to the exception.
- `type`—Indicates the type of the exception you want to catch in a `Catch` block.
- `When expression`—Specifies a `Catch` block clause that means the `Catch` block will catch exceptions only when `expression` is `True`. The `expression` is an expression

3

used to select exceptions to handle; it must be convertible to a `Boolean` value. It is often used to select errors by number.

- *catchStatements*—Specifies statements that handle exceptions occurring in the `Try` block.
- `Exit Try`—Exits a `Try`/`Catch` statement immediately. Execution moves to the code immediately following the `End Try` statement.
- `Finally`—Starts a `Finally` block that is always executed when execution leaves the `Try`/`Catch` statement. If a `Try` statement does not contain any `Catch` blocks, it must contain a `Finally` block. `Exit Try` is not allowed in `Finally` blocks.
- *finallyStatements*—Specifies statements that are executed after all other exception processing has occurred.

Here's an example, the Exception project in the code for this book, to get us started. In this case, the exception-prone code in the `Try` block executes a division by zero, which generates an overflow exception:

```
Module Module1
    Sub Main()
        Dim intItem1 As Integer = 0
        Dim intItem2 As Integer = 128
        Dim intResult As Integer
        Try
            intResult = intItem2 / intItem1
            Console.WriteLine("The answer is " & intResult)
            Console.WriteLine("Press Enter to continue...")
            Console.ReadLine()
            .
            .
            .
    End Sub
End Module
```

When an exception occurs, control leaves the `Try` block and enters the `Catch` block, where you can handle the exception something like you see in Listing 3.8.

LISTING 3.8   Using Structured Exception Handling (Exception project, Module1.vb)

```
Module Module1
    Sub Main()
        Dim intItem1 As Integer = 0
        Dim intItem2 As Integer = 128
        Dim intResult As Integer
```

LISTING 3.8   continued

```
        Try
            intResult = intItem2 / intItem1
            Console.WriteLine("The answer is " & intResult)
            Console.WriteLine("Press Enter to continue...")
            Console.ReadLine()
        Catch
            Console.WriteLine("An overflow exception occurred.")
            Console.WriteLine("Press Enter to continue...")
            Console.ReadLine()
        End Try
    End Sub
End Module
```

When you run this application, you'll see this result:

```
An overflow exception occurred.
Press Enter to continue...
```

You can also get Visual Basic's error message for an exception. To do that, you can create a variable, called e here, which will hold the exception:

```
Try
    intResult = intItem2 / intItem1
        .
        .
        .
Catch e As Exception
    Console.WriteLine("An overflow exception occurred.")
    Console.WriteLine("Press Enter to continue...")
    Console.ReadLine()
End Try
```

Now that you have the actual Visual Basic exception object corresponding to the exception that occurred in the variable named e, you can use e.ToString to display the exception as text like this:

```
Try
    intResult = intItem2 / intItem1
        .
        .
        .
Catch e As Exception
    Console.WriteLine(e.ToString())
    Console.WriteLine("Press Enter to continue...")
    Console.ReadLine()
End Try
```

Here's what you might see when a division by zero takes place:

```
System.OverflowException: Arithmetic operation resulted in an overflow.
   at Filters.Module1.Main() in C:\vbnet 2003\Day3\Filters\Module1.vb:line 7
Press Enter to continue...
```

Although this result is good for programmers because it indicates the location of the problem, this exception description isn't very helpful to users. Instead, you can use the exception object's Message property to display a better error message:

```
Try
    intResult = intItem2 / intItem1
        .
        .
        .
Catch e As Exception
    Console.WriteLine(e.Message)
    Console.WriteLine("Press Enter to continue...")
    Console.ReadLine()
End Try
```

Here's what you'll see in this case:

```
Arithmetic operation resulted in an overflow.
Press Enter to continue...
```

NEW TERM The generic Catch e As Exception block in this example catches all types of exceptions, but, as with unstructured exception handling, you can narrow down an exception handler to catching only a single type of exception, a process called *filtering*.

Exception Filtering in the Catch Block

A Catch e As Exception block catches all types of exceptions and stores the exception object in a variable named e. However, you can specify that a Catch block catch only certain types of exceptions with the As *type* clause. (Table 3.1 contains a list of some of the Visual Basic .NET exception types.) For example, to catch only exceptions of the type OverflowException, you can add a Catch block as in Listing 3.9.

LISTING 3.9   Filtered Exception Handling (Filters project, Module1.vb)

```
Module Module1
    Sub Main()
        Dim intItem1 As Integer = 0
        Dim intItem2 As Integer = 128
        Dim intResult As Integer
```

LISTING 3.9 continued

```
        Try
            intResult = intItem2 / intItem1
            Console.WriteLine("The answer is " & intResult)
            Console.WriteLine("Press Enter to continue...")
            Console.ReadLine()
        Catch e As OverflowException
            Console.WriteLine("An overflow exception occurred.")
            Console.WriteLine("Press Enter to continue...")
            Console.ReadLine()
        End Try
    End Sub
End Module
```

Tip

If you want to get the name of an exception and you're able to cause that exception while testing your program, call e.getType() to get the type of the exception as a string. When you know the name of the exception, you can provide a Catch block for it.

3

You can also use a When clause in a Catch block to further filter exception handling. For example, your code may have multiple sections that may cause overflows, and you want to handle the overflows only when intItem1 is 0 in a particular Catch block. You can do that in a When clause that uses the logical expression intItem1 = 0:

```
Try
    intResult = intItem2 / intItem1
        .
        .
        .
Catch e As OverflowException When intItem1 = 0
    Console.WriteLine("An overflow exception occurred.")
    Console.WriteLine("Press Enter to continue...")
    Console.ReadLine()
End Try
```

You can also filter on error numbers like this:

```
Try
    intResult = intItem2 / intItem1
        .
        .
        .
```

```
Catch e As OverflowException When Err.Number = 6
    Console.WriteLine("An overflow exception occurred.")
    Console.WriteLine("Press Enter to continue...")
    Console.ReadLine()
End Try
```

But what about handling the other overflow exceptions caused by your code. Can you have multiple Catch blocks in the same Try/Catch statement? You certainly can.

Using Multiple Catch Statements

If you want to handle a number of different exceptions, you can use multiple Catch blocks. In the following example, different Catch blocks handle overflow exceptions, out-of-memory exceptions, and array index out-of-range exceptions (which occur when an array index has been set to a negative value or to a value greater than the upper bound of the array):

```
Module Module1
    Sub Main()
        Dim intItem1 As Integer = 0
        Dim intItem2 As Integer = 128
        Dim intResult As Integer
        Try
            intResult = intItem2 / intItem1
            Console.WriteLine("The answer is " & intResult)
            Console.WriteLine("Press Enter to continue...")
            Console.ReadLine()
        Catch e As OverflowException
            Console.WriteLine("An overflow exception occurred.")
            Console.WriteLine("Press Enter to continue...")
            Console.ReadLine()
        Catch e As OutOfMemoryException
            Console.WriteLine("Out of memory.")
            Console.WriteLine("Press Enter to continue...")
            Console.ReadLine()
        Catch e As IndexOutOfRangeException
            Console.WriteLine("Array index out of range.")
            Console.WriteLine("Press Enter to continue...")
            Console.ReadLine()
        End Try
    End Sub
End Module
```

Using multiple Catch blocks like this gives you a good handle on handling exceptions of various types. Each Catch block serves as a different exception handler, and you can place exception-specific code in each such block.

Using `Finally`

Another part of the Try/Catch statement that you should know about is the `Finally` block. The code in the `Finally` block, if there is one, is always executed in a `Try/Catch` statement, even if there was no exception, and even if you execute an `Exit Try` statement. This allows you to make sure that even if there was an exception you'll be sure of running this code (as long as the whole program is still running). Listing 3.10 shows an example with a `Finally` block, the Finally example in the code for the book.

LISTING 3.10 Using the `Finally` Statement (Finally project, Module1.vb)

```
Module Module1
    Sub Main()
        Dim intItem1 As Integer = 0
        Dim intItem2 As Integer = 128
        Dim intResult As Integer
        Try
            intResult = intItem2 / intItem1
            Console.WriteLine("The answer is " & intResult)
        Catch e As OverflowException
            Console.WriteLine("An overflow exception occurred.")
        Catch e As OutOfMemoryException
            Console.WriteLine("Out of memory.")
        Catch e As IndexOutOfRangeException
            Console.WriteLine("Array index out of range.")
        Finally
            Console.WriteLine("Press Enter to continue...")
            Console.ReadLine()
        End Try
    End Sub
End Module
```

In this case, you'll always see the `"Press Enter to continue..."` prompt, and the code will wait for you to press Enter whether or not an exception was thrown. Here's what you might see:

```
An overflow exception occurred.
Press Enter to continue...
```

Throwing an Exception Yourself

You can throw an exception yourself in your code by using the `Throw` statement. In this example the code explicitly throws an overflow exception:

```
Module Module1
    Sub Main()
```

```
        Try
            Throw New OverflowException()
            Console.WriteLine("Press Enter to continue...")
            Console.ReadLine()
        Catch e As Exception
            Console.WriteLine(e.Message)
            Console.WriteLine("Press Enter to continue...")
            Console.ReadLine()
        End Try
    End Sub
End Module
```

Throwing your own exceptions like this gives you a great deal of control over the exception-handling process. And you're not limited to just the exceptions that Visual Basic has already defined either, as we'll see next.

Creating and Throwing Custom Exceptions

You can, in fact, customize and create your own exceptions. To do that, you throw an exception using the ApplicationException object. Listing 3.11 shows an example, the CustomException example in the code for this book, where we're creating a custom exception and giving it the text "This is a new exception".

LISTING 3.11   Creating Custom Exceptions (CustomException project, Module1.vb)

```
Module Module1
    Sub Main()
        Try
            Throw New ApplicationException("You threw this custom exception.")
        Catch e As Exception
            Console.WriteLine(e.Message)
        Finally
            Console.WriteLine("Press Enter to continue...")
            Console.ReadLine()
        End Try
    End Sub
End Module
```

Here's what you see when you run this application:

```
You threw this custom exception.
Press Enter to continue...
```

Note the New keyword in the statement Throw New ApplicationException("You threw this custom exception."). You use this keyword when you create new objects.

As we head into tomorrow's work with Windows forms, which will take us through five days, we'll need to know something about classes and objects. For that reason, we'll get a good introduction to them here.

Introducing Classes and Objects

Object-oriented programming (OOP) is a topic that is central to Visual Basic, and we're going to take it step by step, getting an introduction to classes and objects today and continuing our OOP work throughout the book.

Yesterday, we worked with simple variables, like this integer variable:

```
Dim intItem1 As Integer
```

NEW TERM Here, `intItem1` is the variable and `Integer` is the variable's *type*. In the same way, you can declare *objects*, using a *class* as the object's type:

```
Dim TheObject As TheClass
```

NEW TERM Here, `TheObject` is an object of `TheClass` class. In this way, you can think of a class as an object's *type*. What's different about a class from a simple type like an `Integer`? The difference is that classes and objects can contain *members*. As we've already seen, one type of member is a *property*, which holds data, and you access an object's properties with a dot followed by the property name like this:

```
TheObject.TheProperty = "Hello!"
```

NEW TERM Classes and objects can also contain built-in procedures, called *methods*. A method can either be a Sub procedure or a function, and you call it as you would any other procedure, except that you need to preface the method name with the class or object name and a dot like this, where `TheMethod` returns a message as a text string:

```
Dim Message As String = TheObject.TheMethod()
```

NEW TERM In practice, you usually use the properties and methods of objects only. Classes can support properties and methods directly, without needing to create an object, but you have to make special provisions in the class, as we'll see in Day 9. Those members of a class that you can use with the class directly without needing to create an object first are called *class members*; for example, if `TheMethod` was a class method, you could use it with the class name, no object needed:

```
Dim Message As String = TheClass.TheMethod()
```

3

Encapsulation

NEW TERM So now you know the relation of an object to a class; it's much like the relation of a cookie to a cookie cutter or a variable to the variable's type. What's good about this is that you can pack a great deal into an object, and the programmer no longer has to deal with a great many separate properties and procedures; they're all wrapped up in an easily-thought-of object. All the internal details are out of sight, out of mind. In fact, OOP was first created to help you deal with code as programs grew longer and longer by wrapping up that code into objects to simplify things, a process called *encapsulation.*

For example, think of a car. Under the hood, dozens of things are going on: The fuel pump is pumping, the pistons are firing, the distributor and timing belt are timing the power sent to the pistons, oil is circulating, voltage is being regulated, and so on. If you had to attend to all those operations yourself, there's no way you could drive at the same time. But the car takes care of those operations for you, and you don't have to think about them (unless they go wrong and have to be "debugged," of course…). Everything is wrapped up into an easily handled concept—a car. You get in, you drive.

You don't have to say that you're going to drive off and regulate oil pressure, pump water, feed gas to the engine, and time the spark plugs. You just drive off. The car presents you with a well-defined "interface" where the implementation details are hidden; you just have to use the pedals, steering wheel, and gear shift, if there is one, to drive.

That's similar to the objects you'll see in Visual Basic. For example, the user-interface elements we'll see tomorrow—text boxes, buttons, even Windows forms—are all objects. They all have properties and methods that you can use. Behind the scenes, there's a lot going on, even in a text box object, which has to draw itself when required, store data, format that data, respond to keystrokes, and so on. But you don't have to worry about any of that; you just add a text box to your program and it takes care of itself. You can interact with it by using a well-defined programming interface made up of properties like the `Text` property (as in `TextBox1.Text = "Hello!"`), which holds the text in a text box, and methods like the `Clear` method, which erases all text in the text box (and which you call like this: `TextBox1.Clear()`).

An Example in Code

The Windows forms that we'll be creating in the next five days are all classes, created with the `Class` statement, as we'll see tomorrow. For that reason, let's look at an example that creates a class and an object in code. This example will be much simpler than the

Visual Basic TextBox class, but it's similar in many ways: Both the TextBox class and our new class are created with a Class statement, and both will support properties and methods. This example will start giving us the edge we need when dealing with OOP.

Creating a Class

How do you actually create a class? You use the Class statement:

```
[ <attrlist> ] [ Public | Private | Protected | Friend | Protected Friend ]
[ Shadows ] [ MustInherit | NotInheritable ] Class name
 [ Implements interfacename ]
   [ statements ]
End Class
```

We saw most of these terms described with the Sub statement earlier today. Here are what the new items mean:

- MustInherit—Indicates that the class contains methods that must be implemented by a deriving class, as we'll see in Day 9.

- NotInheritable—Indicates that the class is one from which no further inheritance is allowed, as we'll see in Day 9.

- name—Specifies the name of the class.

- statements—Specifies the statements that make up the code for the class.

Here's how we might create a new class named TheClass in a project named Classes (which is in the code for this book):

```
Module Module1

    Sub Main()

    End Sub

End Module

Class TheClass
        .
        .
        .
End Class
```

Creating a Data Member

We can now add members to this class, making them Public, Private, or Protected. Public makes them accessible from code outside the class, Private restricts their scope to the current class, and Protected (which we'll see in Day 9) restricts their scope to the present class and any classes derived from the present class. For example, we can add a public data member to our new class just by declaring a variable `Public` like this:

```
Module Module1

    Sub Main()

    End Sub

End Module

Class TheClass
    Public ThePublicData = "Hello there!"
        .
        .
        .
End Class
```

This is not a property of the new class. You need special code to create a property, as we'll see. However, this new data member is accessible from objects of this class like this: `TheObject.ThePublicDataMember`. By default, data members are private to a class, but you can make them public—accessible outside the object—with the `Public` keyword as done here.

Creating an Object

NEW TERM Let's see how to access our new data member by creating an object, `TheObject`, from `TheClass`. Creating an object is also called *instantiating* an object, and an object is also called an *instance* of a class. Unlike the declaration of a simple variable like an `Integer`, this line of code doesn't create a new object; it only declares the object:

```
Dim TheObject As TheClass
```

To create a new object in Visual Basic, you need to use the `New` keyword:

```
Dim TheObject As New TheClass
```

This line creates the new object `TheObject` from `TheClass`. You can also create the new object this way:

```
Dim TheObject As TheClass
TheObject = New TheClass
```

NEW TERM Some classes are written so that you can pass data to them when you create objects from them. What you're actually doing is passing data to a special method of the class called a *constructor*. For example, as we'll see tomorrow, you can create a `Size` object to indicate a Windows form's size, and to make that form 200 by 200 pixels, you can pass those values to the `Size` class's constructor this way:

```
Size = New Size(200, 200)
```

We'll often use constructors when creating objects, but our current example doesn't use one. Here's how we can create a new object—`TheObject`—using the class `TheClass`, and display the text in the public data member `TheObject.ThePublicDataMember`:

```
Module Module1

    Sub Main()
        Dim TheObject As New TheClass
        Console.WriteLine("ThePublicData holds """ & _
            TheObject.ThePublicData & """")
        .
        .
        .
    End Sub

End Module

Class TheClass
    Public ThePublicData = "Hello there!"
        .
        .
        .
End Class
```

You can use public data members like this instead of properties if you like, but properties were invented to give you some control over what values can be stored. You can assign any value to a public data member like this, but you can use internal code to restrict possible values that may be assigned to a property (for example, you might want to restrict a property named `Color` to the values `"Red"`, `"Green"`, and `"Blue"`). Properties are actually implemented using code in *methods*, not just as data members. And we'll look at methods next.

Creating a Method

Let's add a method to our class now. This method, `TheMethod`, will simply be a function that returns the text `"Hello there!"`, and we can call that method as `TheObject.TheMethod()` to display that text:

```
Module Module1

    Sub Main()
        Dim TheObject As New TheClass
```

```
        Console.WriteLine("ThePublicData holds """ & _
            TheObject.ThePublicData & """")
        Console.WriteLine("TheMethod returns """ & _
            TheObject.TheMethod() & """")
            .
            .
            .
    End Sub

End Module

Class TheClass
    Public ThePublicData = "Hello there!"

    Function TheMethod() As String
        Return "Hello there!"
    End Function
            .
            .
            .
End Class
```

That's all it takes! Just adding a Sub procedure or function to a class like this adds a new method to the class. Although such methods are public by default, you can make methods private (declaring them like this: `Private Function TheMethod() As String`), which restricts their scope to the present class. You do that for methods that are used only internally in a class. (To continue the car analogy, such internal methods might be the ones entirely internal to the car, such as the ones that regulate oil pressure or battery voltage.)

Creating a Property

Let's see how to create a property now. You declare properties using `Get` and `Set` methods in a `Property` statement:

```
[ <attrlist> ] [ Default ] [ Public | Private | Protected | Friend |
Protected Friend ] [ ReadOnly | WriteOnly ] [Overloads | Overrides ]
[Overridable | NotOverridable] | MustOverride | Shadows | Shared]
Property varname([ parameter list ]) [ As typename ]
[ Implements interfacemember ]
    [ <attrlist> ] Get
        [ block ]
    End Get
    [ <attrlist> ] Set(ByVal Value As typename )
        [ block ]
    End Set
End Property
```

Here are the parts of this statement that are different from the keywords we've already seen in the Sub statement:

- Default—Makes this a default property. Default properties can be set and retrieved without specifying the property name.

- ReadOnly—Specifies that a property's value can be retrieved, but it cannot be modified. ReadOnly properties contain Get blocks but no Set blocks.

- WriteOnly—Specifies that a property can be set, but its value cannot be retrieved. WriteOnly properties contain Set blocks but no Get blocks.

- *varname*—Specifies a name that identifies the property.

- *parameter list*—Specifies the parameters you use with the property.

- *typename*—Specifies the type of the property. If you don't specify a data type, the default type is Object.

- *interfacemember*—When a property is part of a class that implements an interface (covered in Day 9), this is the name of the property being implemented.

- Get—Starts a Get property procedure used to return the value of a property. Get blocks are optional unless the property is ReadOnly.

- End Get—Ends a Get property procedure.

- Set—Starts a Set property procedure used to set the value of a property. Set blocks are optional unless the property is WriteOnly. Note that the new value of the property is passed to the Set property procedure in a parameter named Value when the value of the property changes.

- End Set—Ends a Set property procedure.

The Set block enables you to set the value of a property, and the Get block enables you to return the value of the property. When you assign a value to a property (as in TheObject.TheProperty = "Hello there!"), the Set block is called, and when you read a property's value (as in Dim strText As String = TheObject.TheProperty), the Get block is called.

You can add code to both blocks to restrict the data stored in a property. Visual Basic passes a parameter named Value to the Set block during property assignments, and the Value parameter contains the value that was assigned to the property when the Set block was called. You usually store the actual value of the property in a private data member in the class.

Here's how this looks in the example. First, you create the new property procedure to handle the property TheProperty, which will hold string data:

```
Module Module1

    Sub Main()
        Dim TheObject As New TheClass
        Console.WriteLine("ThePublicData holds """ & _
            TheObject.ThePublicData & """")
        Console.WriteLine("TheMethod returns """ & _
            TheObject.TheMethod() & """")
        Console.WriteLine("TheProperty holds """ & _
            TheObject.TheProperty & """")
        Console.WriteLine("Press Enter to continue...")
        Console.ReadLine()
    End Sub

End Module

Class TheClass
    Public ThePublicData = "Hello there!"

    Function TheMethod() As String
        Return "Hello there!"
    End Function

    Public Property TheProperty() As String
        Get

        End Get
        Set(ByVal Value As String)

        End Set
    End Property

End Class
```

Tip

When you type the first line of a property procedure—that's Public Property TheProperty() As String here—Visual Basic .NET will add a skeleton for the Get and Set procedures automatically.

The next step is to add the code for this property. In this case, we can store the property's value in a private data member named TheInternalData. All we have to do is add code to the Set block to store values in this data member and the Get block to return this data member's value when needed, as shown in Listing 3.12.

LISTING 3.12   Classes and Objects (Classes project, Module1.vb)

```
Module Module1

    Sub Main()
        Dim TheObject As New TheClass
        Console.WriteLine("ThePublicData holds """ & _
            TheObject.ThePublicData & """")
        Console.WriteLine("TheMethod returns """ & _
            TheObject.TheMethod() & """")
        Console.WriteLine("TheProperty holds """ & _
            TheObject.TheProperty & """")
        Console.WriteLine("Press Enter to continue...")
        Console.ReadLine()
    End Sub

End Module

Class TheClass
    Public ThePublicData = "Hello there!"
    Private TheInternalData As String = "Hello there!"

    Function TheMethod() As String
        Return "Hello there!"
    End Function

    Public Property TheProperty() As String
        Get
            Return TheInternalData
        End Get
        Set(ByVal Value As String)
            TheInternalData = Value
        End Set
    End Property

End Class
```

And that's all we need! Now we've created a new class, given that class a public data member, method, and property, and displayed the data from each of these elements. Here's what you see when you run this example:

```
ThePublicData holds "Hello there!"
TheMethod returns "Hello there!"
TheProperty holds "Hello there!"
Press Enter to continue...
```

And that gives us the foundation we'll need when we start working with classes and objects tomorrow.

3

Summary

Today, we saw a great deal about the Visual Basic language. We started by looking at how to create procedures in Visual Basic .NET.

There are two types of procedures: Sub procedures and functions. They can both contain sets of Visual Basic statements that may be called, but only functions can return values. We saw that we can pass arguments to procedures, including optional arguments. We also saw how to support variable-length argument lists. And we also saw how to preserve data values between calls to procedures—both with static variables and module-level variables.

That introduced us to the idea of scope. An element's scope is the area in a program where that element is accessible. We saw that there are four levels of scope: block level, procedure level, module level, and namespace level.

We also looked at runtime error handling today. Runtime errors are called exceptions, and the two types of exception handling in Visual Basic are structured and unstructured exception handling. Structured exception handling centers around the Try/Catch statement, and unstructured exception handling uses the On Error statement. We saw how to catch exceptions, throw our own exceptions, filter exceptions, and more.

We also got an introduction to classes and objects in OOP today. We saw how to create a class, create an object of that class, and create public data members, properties, and methods in a class. That information will come in handy throughout the book.

And that's it! We now have the foundation in the Visual Basic language we'll need for the coming days. Tomorrow, we're going to begin putting to work what we've seen so far as we start working with Windows applications.

Q&A

Q How can I pass an array to a procedure?

A Say you create an array like this: Dim Array(4) As Integer. Then you assign a value to one element like this: Array(1) = 1. Now you can pass the array to a function named TheFunction as follows: TheFunction(Array). The function is declared like this: Function TheFunction(ByVal PassedArray() As Integer) As Integer. And finally you can refer to the passed array using the name PassedArray as follows: Return PassedArray(1).

Q Can I mix structured and unstructured exception handling?

A Only up to a point. You can't mix the On Error and Try/Catch statements, but you can, for example, access the Err.Number property in Catch blocks.

Workshop

This workshop tests whether you understand the concepts you saw today. It's a good idea to make sure you can answer these questions before pressing on to tomorrow's work.

Quiz

1. What's the difference between a function and a Sub procedure?

2. How can a Sub procedure pass data back to the calling code?

3. List three statements that will cause an immediate exit from a procedure.

4. What level of scope does a variable defined in a For loop have?

5. By default, what type of access do data members and methods have in classes?

Quiz Answers

1. A function can have a formal return value, whereas a Sub procedure cannot.

2. You can pass data back to the calling code if you pass a variable by reference. In that case, the code in the Sub procedure can assign a new value to that variable.

3. Return, Exit Sub/Function, and End Sub/Function.

4. Block-level scope.

5. Data members are private by default (that is, if declared with the Dim statement), and methods are public by default.

Exercises

1. Modify the Summer function discussed today to use the ParamArray keyword so that it will add as many integers as you pass to this function and return the total sum (not just the sum of two integers, as the version we've already seen today does).

2. As discussed in the text, add a new property, Color, to TheClass in the Classes example that will accept only the values "Red", "Green", and "Blue". If any other value is assigned to the Color property, store the word "Undefined" in that property.

PART I

In Review

Visual Basic .NET Essentials

In Part 1, we've worked through the Visual Basic .NET essentials that we'll need for the rest of the book. We got an overview of the .NET framework and Visual Basic .NET's place in it. And we also took a look at Visual Basic .NET's primary tool—the IDE—in depth.

Most importantly, these first three chapters gave us the coding skills we'll use over and over in the coming chapters. Using console applications to make the coding easier, we've seen how to store and work with data in our programs, declaring variables and understanding the range of various Visual Basic .NET data types.

After working with simple variables, we continued on to assemble data items into arrays, seeing how to declare and use them and creating dynamic arrays that can be resized at runtime. And we also worked with strings and text handling.

After getting down the essentials of data handling, we took a look at the Visual Basic .NET operators to start doing something with that data, including working with and understanding all the available operators and operator precedence.

The next step was to begin making decisions in our code with the If, Select, Switch, and Choose statements. And from there, we added more power with loops, such as the Do, For, For Each, and While loops.

From loops, we continued on to writing our own procedures—in particular, Sub procedures and functions—and saw how to compartmentalize our code into easily handled pieces. You saw not only how to pass data to procedures, but also how to return data from functions.

Another skill we mastered was exception handling—both structured and unstructured. We focused on structured exception handling with the Try/Catch statement, putting sensitive code in a Try block and handling exceptions in a Catch block. We also saw how to support exception filtering with multiple Catch blocks and even how to throw in our own exceptions.

Here's an example that ties together many of the concepts we've seen in Part I. Let's assume that someone has heard of your Visual Basic .NET skills and has hired you to create a program to drive his car—entering the command left makes the car turn left, the command right makes the car turn right, and quit ends the program.

You can handle multiple commands like this with a Select statement, reading the commands the user gives and implementing them by displaying messages such as "Turning left..." and "Turning right...". If the user enters an invalid command, we can throw an exception that will be caught in a Catch block.

We'll wrap our Select statement in a Do loop to make it keep executing until the user types quit; here's what that looks like:

```
Dim blnRun As Boolean = True
Dim DoThis As String

Do
    System.Console.Write("Type left, right, or quit: ")
    DoThis = System.Console.ReadLine()
    Try
        Select Case DoThis
            Case "left"
                System.Console.WriteLine("Turning left...")
            Case "right"
                System.Console.WriteLine("Turning right...")
            Case "quit"
                System.Console.WriteLine("Quitting...")
                blnRun = False
        End Select
    End Try
Loop While (blnRun)
```

And we can add the Try/Catch part to handle invalid responses this way:

```
Dim blnRun As Boolean = True
Dim DoThis As String
```

```
Do
    System.Console.Write("Type left, right, or quit: ")
    DoThis = System.Console.ReadLine()
    Try
        Select Case DoThis
            Case "left"
                System.Console.WriteLine("Turning left...")
            Case "right"
                System.Console.WriteLine("Turning right...")
            Case "quit"
                System.Console.WriteLine("Quitting...")
                blnRun = False
            Case Else
                Throw New ApplicationException(_
                    "Sorry, that's not a valid choice.")
        End Select
    Catch e As ApplicationException
        System.Console.WriteLine(e.Message)
    End Try
Loop While (blnRun)
```

That's all we need. Now when the driver types `left`, he'll see `"Turning left..."`; when he types `right`, he'll see `"Turning right..."`, and when he types `quit`, the program will quit:

```
Type left, right, or quit: left
Turning left...
Type left, right, or quit: right
Turning right...
Type left, right, or quit: quit
Quitting...
```

On the other hand, if he enters an invalid response, our custom exception will be thrown and he'll see an error message:

```
Type left, right, or quit: left
Turning left...
Type left, right, or quit: right
Turning right...
Type left, right, or quit: up
Sorry, that's not a valid choice.
Type left, right, or quit:
```

And that's it—if you're up to speed on code like this, you're ready to turn to the next part of this book, where we start constructing Windows applications.

PART II

At a Glance

Creating Windows Applications in Visual Basic .NET

In Part II, we start getting *visual*. We're going to see what Visual Basic .NET is really good at as we create our own Windows applications. Creating your own Windows applications will only take a few keystrokes and mouse clicks, as we're going to see.

After working with the ins and outs of creating windows, multi-window applications, owned windows, always-on-top windows, and more, we'll take a look at the kinds of *controls* you use in windows. Controls include buttons, text boxes, and all the other elements the user types into, clicks, and scrolls.

In Part II, we're going to get our start with not only buttons and text boxes, but also check boxes, radio buttons, list boxes, combo boxes, picture boxes, scrollbars, splitters, tool tips, menus, printing, status bars, toolbars, progress bars—and lots more. We'll be adding all those controls to our Windows applications and connecting them to our code.

4

5

6

7

8

PART II

DAY 4

Creating Windows Forms

Today, we go visual. We're going to begin our work on Windows forms today and continue that work over the next four days. Today we're going to learn about Windows forms, and in the coming days, we'll focus on the great variety of controls we can support in Windows forms and how to use them.

As you might expect, there's a great deal to Windows forms. We'll see not only how to create forms and work with them in code, but also how to add controls to forms, support multiple forms, develop forms for smart devices (such as Pocket PCs—this capability is new in Visual Basic .NET 2003), create nonrectangular windows (also new in Visual Basic .NET 2003), create multiple-document interface (MDI) applications, display dialogs, and more. Here's an overview of today's topics:

- Creating and working with Windows forms
- Working with multiple forms
- Building multiple-document interface (MDI) applications
- Creating nonrectangular windows
- Creating smart device applications
- Setting tab order for a form's controls

- Setting the Startup form and initial positions for forms
- Moving and sizing forms and controls in code
- Using built-in dialogs: MsgBox, MessageBox.Show, and InputBox
- Communicating between windows
- Creating dialogs and owned forms
- Anchoring and docking controls
- Creating always-on-top forms
- Handling mouse and keyboard events
- Sending keystrokes to other programs

Windows forms are our first real experience in programming user interfaces, and there's a lot going on today. We'll start by taking a look at the big picture: Windows forms in overview.

Windows Forms in Overview

NEW TERM   You can see a Windows form at work in Figure 4.1. Let's get the terminology down first. At the top of the form is the *title bar*, also called the *caption bar*, which displays the form's title (Form1 in this case, the default name Visual Basic gives to the first form in your Windows application). The title bar also includes the *control box*, which holds the (reading left to right) minimize, maximize, and close buttons.

FIGURE 4.1

A Windows form.

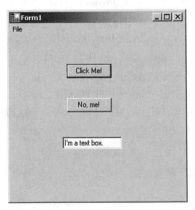

NEW TERM   You can also see that this form has a *menu bar*, which in this case has only one menu, the File menu (we'll see menus in Day 7, "Windows Forms: Working with Menus, Built-in Dialogs, and Printing"). Under the menu bar, forms can also have *toolbars*, with buttons that correspond to menu items, as we've seen already in the Visual Basic IDE itself.

NEW TERM You can also see three *controls* in Figure 4.1—two buttons and a text box. These controls are placed in the form's *client area*—the area under the title bar and under any menu bars and toolbars if there are any, and excluding the form's *border* (you can just see the border, a few pixels thick at the top of the title bar in Figure 4.1). The client area, in other words, is your program's workspace. While the border, title bar, menu bar, and toolbars are maintained by Windows, you get to work in the client area.

The form in Figure 4.1 has the standard, default Windows form border, which the user can resize with the mouse, but you can select from various borders with the FormBorderStyle property in the Properties window, including the fixed, nonresizable borders you use in dialogs, and 3D borders.

Those are the parts of a form as far as Visual Basic is concerned. Let's see a form in action now, as we create a new Windows application.

Creating a Windows Application

4

We created Windows applications as far back as Day 1, "Getting Started with Visual Basic .NET!"; in fact, that was the first example in the book. Creating a Windows application is easy: You just open the New Project dialog by clicking the New Project button in the Start page or selecting the File, New, Project menu item. Next, you select the Visual Basic Projects folder in the Project Types box at right in the dialog, click the Windows Application icon in the Templates box, give the new application a name (this example will be called FirstWin in the code for the book), and click OK. This creates a Windows project and solution, as you see in Figure 4.2. The name of the first form that Visual Basic creates for you by default, and that you can see in Figure 4.2, is Form1 (you can change that name in the Properties window). To refer to the form in code, you'll use that name—Form1.

Creating this new FirstWin Windows application creates a directory named FirstWin automatically, with these files in it:

```
FirstWin
    |
    |____WindowsApp.vbproj      A Visual Basic project
    |____AssemblyInfo.vb        Information about an assembly, including
    |                           version information
    |____Form1.vb               The form's code file
```

```
|____Form1.resx            An XML-based resource template
|____WindowsApp.vbproj.user  Project user options
|____WindowsApp.sln        Solution file—the solution's configuration
|____bin                   Directory for binary executables
|____obj                   Directory for debugging binaries
```

FIGURE 4.2

Creating a Windows application.

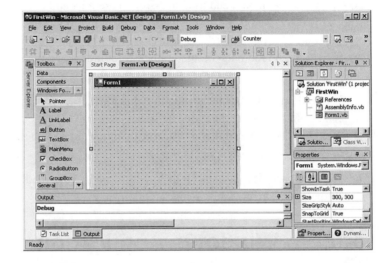

These are the essential files Visual Basic uses to support a Windows application. At this point, all we have is a blank window, however. As we saw in Day 1, we can run this application and see that window—but we can only resize or close it. In Day 1, we added a few controls to our Windows form—a button and a text box—and we can do the same thing today. Today, however, we're also going to take the resulting code apart piece by piece to see what makes it tick.

Adding Controls

Using the toolbox, add a button and a text box to Form1 in the FirstWin application now, as we did in Day 1 (that is, double-click the control you want in the toolbox and drag the new control to the place where you want it in the form, or just drag the control from the toolbox), as you see in Figure 4.3. The button will be named Button1 by default (a second button would be named Button2, and so on) and the text box TextBox1, and you use these names to refer to these objects in code (you can change these names in the Properties window if you want).

Select the button and change its caption to "Click Me" using the Text property in the Properties window; then select the text box and delete the text in it (TextBox1) with the same property in the Properties window, giving you the customized controls you see in Figure 4.3. As you can see in the Properties window, Visual Basic gives the new button object the name Button1 and the new text box object the name TextBox1.

FIGURE 4.3

Adding controls to a Windows application at design time.

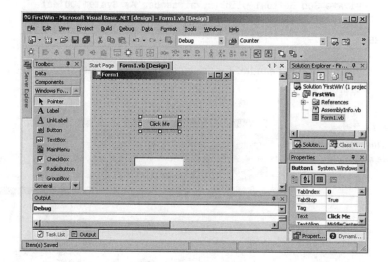

NEW TERM Note the dotted border around the button with the small white boxes in Figure 4.3. These boxes are called *sizing handles*. Using the mouse, you can resize controls you've added to a form by using these sizing handles. And, of course, you can drag controls around to new positions using the mouse as well.

NEW TERM In Day 1, we made the text box display a message when the user clicked the button, and we can do the same thing here—but today, we're going to dissect the resulting code. To make this application do something when the button is clicked, we need to add code to the button's Click *event*.

Working with Events

The Windows user interface relies on events to know when the user has done something. For example, when the user clicks a button, a Click event occurs. When the user double-clicks the mouse, a DoubleClick event occurs. When the user presses a key, a KeyPress event occurs. By responding to user-interface events like these, your application allows the user to take the lead—and that's the way Windows applications work. In addition to properties and methods, events are also members of classes like the Form class we'll see today; we'll see that forms themselves support a number of events, including the Click event.

To handle the button click in our application, we need to work with the button's `Click` event. To access that event, just double-click the button, opening a code designer to the `Button1_Click` Sub procedure:

```
Private Sub Button1_Click(ByVal sender As System.Object, _
    ByVal e As System.EventArgs) Handles Button1.Click

End Sub
```

This is the event handler for the button's `Click` event. You can see this code designer in Figure 4.4.

FIGURE 4.4

A Windows application code designer.

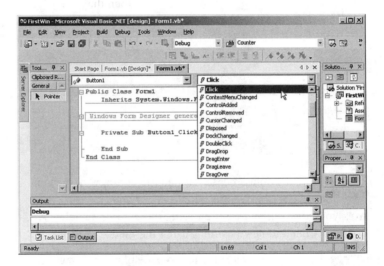

When you double-click a control or form in a visual designer, a code designer with an event handler for the control or form's *default event* appears. The default event for buttons is the `Click` event, so that event's handler appears when you double-click a button in a visual designer. Besides the `Click` event, buttons have many other events, such as `MouseUp` and `MouseDown`. To add code to such events, you first select the object causing the event (such as `Button1` or `TextBox1`) in the left drop-down list box at the top of the code designer, and the event you want to add code to in the right drop-down list box in the code designer, as you see in Figure 4.4. Selecting an event this way makes the code designer add an event handler for the event to the code automatically.

The event handler `Button1_Click` is called when the button is clicked at runtime. This Sub procedure is passed the object that caused the event (the button object itself) and an

EventArgs object that has more information about the event. Note also the Handles Button1.Click clause at the end, which is the way you indicate this Sub procedure in an event handler, handling the Click event of Button1. As we saw in Day 1, to display a message in TextBox1 when the button is clicked, we just need to add this code, which assigns the message "No problem." to the text box's Text property:

```
Private Sub Button1_Click(ByVal sender As System.Object, _
    ByVal e As System.EventArgs) Handles Button1.Click
    TextBox1.Text = "No problem."
End Sub
```

That's all it takes! Now this code will run when the button is clicked. You can see the results in Figure 4.5 when you run the application (either by pressing F5 or by selecting the Debug, Start menu item) and click the button. To end the application, click the X (close) button in the title bar.

FIGURE 4.5

A running Windows application.

The actual executable file for this application is named FirstWin.exe (which you can find in the application's bin directory). If you simply double-click FirstWin.exe in Windows Explorer, it'll start. You can even copy this file to other, suitably prepared computers that have the .NET Framework installed, and it'll run there (but you should first create a release, not debug, version of the application, as discussed in Day 1). Note that we'll also see how to create deployment packages for our applications in Day 21, "Creating Windows Services, Web Services, and Deploying Applications."

Now that we've created a Windows application, it's time to take it apart, line by line. That's coming up next.

4

Windows Forms in Code

Windows forms are based on the `Form` class—technically speaking, the `System.Windows.Forms.Form` class. This class is based on the `System.Windows.Forms.ContainerControl` class, which in turn is based on the `System.Windows.Forms.ScrollableControl` class, and so on back like this:

```
System.Object
    System.MarshalByRefObject
        System.ComponentModel.Component
            System.Windows.Forms.Control
                System.Windows.Forms.ScrollableControl
                    System.Windows.Forms.ContainerControl
                        System.Windows.Forms.Form
```

NEW TERM   Each class in this hierarchy *inherits* the functionality of its predecessors (we'll see all about object-oriented inheritance in Day 9, "Object-Oriented Programming"). And if you look at this class hierarchy, you'll see something interesting: Forms are actually just modified controls; they're based on the `Control` class (`System.Windows.Forms.Control`) like any other control (such as buttons or text boxes). This means that you can do just about anything with a form that you can do with a control (for example, like other controls, forms have a `Text` property; in forms, this property sets the text in the title bar).

Form Properties, Methods, and Events

As you would expect, the `Form` class is a big one, with many properties (such as `BackColor`, which holds the background color), methods (such as `Hide` and `Show`, which hide and show the window), and events (such as `Click`, which occurs when the form is clicked). You can see the highlights of the `Form` class's public properties in Table 4.1, the highlights of the public methods in Table 4.2, and the highlights of the public events in Table 4.3. Taking a moment to look through these tables to see what's available is worthwhile (you can find the full set of properties, methods, and events in the Visual Basic documentation).

TABLE 4.1   The Significant Public Properties of the `Form` Class

Property	Description
AcceptButton	Returns or sets the button automatically clicked when the Enter key is pressed.
ActiveControl	Returns or sets the active control in the form.
ActiveForm	Returns the currently active form in the application.
ActiveMdiChild	Returns the active multiple-document interface (MDI) child window.
AllowDrop	Returns or sets whether the form will accept data that the user drags onto it.

TABLE 4.1 continued

Property	Description
AutoScale	Returns or sets whether the form adjusts to fit the font used and scales its controls.
AutoScroll	Returns or sets whether the form enables autoscrolling.
BackColor	Sets the background color.
BackgroundImage	Returns or sets the background image in the form.
Bottom	Returns the location of the bottom of the form (measured in pixels).
Bounds	Returns or sets the size and location of the form.
CancelButton	Returns or sets the button control automatically clicked when the Esc key is pressed.
CanFocus	Returns whether the form can accept the input focus.
ClientRectangle	Returns the rectangle holding the form's client area.
ClientSize	Returns or sets the client area size of the form.
ContainsFocus	Returns whether the form has the input focus.
ControlBox	Returns or sets whether a control box is displayed.
Controls	Returns the collection of controls in the form.
Cursor	Returns or sets the mouse cursor when the mouse is over the form.
DialogResult	Returns or sets the dialog result for the form.
DisplayRectangle	Returns the rectangle that represents the display area of the control.
Font	Returns or sets the text font in the form.
ForeColor	Returns or sets the foreground color of the form.
FormBorderStyle	Returns or sets the form's border style.
HasChildren	Returns whether the form contains child controls.
Height	Returns or sets the form's height (measured in pixels).
Icon	Returns or sets the form's icon.
IsMdiChild	Returns whether the form is a multiple-document interface (MDI) child.
IsMdiContainer	Returns or sets whether the form is a container for multiple-document interface (MDI) child forms.
Left	Returns or sets the x coordinate of a control's left edge (measured in pixels).
Location	Returns or sets the coordinates of the upper-left corner of the form with respect to the upper-left corner of the screen.
MaximizeBox	Returns or sets whether the maximize button is displayed.

4

TABLE 4.1 continued

Property	Description
MaximumSize	Returns the maximum size the form can be resized to.
MdiChildren	Returns an array of forms holding the multiple-document interface (MDI) child forms for this form.
MdiParent	Returns or sets the multiple-document interface (MDI) parent form for this form.
Menu	Returns or sets the menu that is in the form.
MinimizeBox	Returns or sets whether the minimize button is displayed.
MinimumSize	Returns or sets the minimum size the form can be resized to.
Modal	Returns whether this form is displayed modally.
Name	Returns or sets the name of the form.
Opacity	Returns or sets the opacity for the form.
OwnedForms	Returns an array of forms that are owned by this form.
Owner	Returns or sets the form that owns this form.
Right	Returns the position of the right edge of the form.
ShowInTaskbar	Returns or sets whether the form is displayed in the Windows taskbar. Set this to False for dialogs.
Size	Returns or sets the size of the form.
StartPosition	Returns or sets the starting position of the form at runtime.
Text	Returns or sets the text in the title bar.
Top	Returns or sets the y coordinate of the control's top edge (measured in pixels).
TopMost	Returns or sets whether the form should be displayed as the topmost form in the application.
TransparencyKey	Returns or sets the color that represents transparent areas of the form.
Visible	Returns or sets whether the form is visible.
Width	Returns or sets the width of the form (measured in pixels).
WindowState	Returns orsets the form's window state—normal, minimized, or maximized.

TABLE 4.2 The Significant Public Methods of the Form Class

Method	Description
Activate	Activates the form, giving it the input focus.
AddOwnedForm	Adds a new owned form to the form.

TABLE 4.2   continued

Method	Description
BringToFront	Brings a form to the front of others.
Close	Closes the form.
CreateGraphics	Creates the Graphics object for the form, which you can use to draw in the form.
DoDragDrop	Starts a drag-and-drop operation.
Focus	Sets input focus to the form.
Hide	Hides the form.
LayoutMdi	Arranges the multiple-document interface (MDI) child forms inside an MDI parent form.
Refresh	Forces the form to redraw itself.
RemoveOwnedForm	Removes an owned form.
SendToBack	Sends the form to the back.
SetBounds	Sets the bounds of the control.
SetDesktopBounds	Sets the bounds of the form in desktop coordinates.
SetDesktopLocation	Sets the location of the form in desktop coordinates.
Show	Shows the form, making it visible.
ShowDialog	Shows the form as a dialog.
Update	Causes the control to redraw the invalidated parts of its client area.

4

TABLE 4.3   The Significant Public Events of the Form Class

Event	Description
Activated	Occurs when the form is activated and gets the input focus.
Click	Occurs when the form is clicked.
Closed	Occurs when the form is closed.
Closing	Occurs when the form is closing.
ControlAdded	Occurs when a new control is added.
ControlRemoved	Occurs when a control is removed.
CursorChanged	Occurs when the cursor has changed.
Deactivate	Occurs when the form loses the focus.
DoubleClick	Occurs when the form is double-clicked.

TABLE 4.3   continued

Event	Description
DragDrop	Occurs when a drag-and-drop operation finishes.
DragEnter	Occurs when an object is dragged onto the form.
DragLeave	Occurs when an object has been dragged out of the form.
DragOver	Occurs when an object has been dragged over the form.
Enter	Occurs when the form is entered by the mouse.
ForeColorChanged	Occurs when the ForeColor property value has changed.
GotFocus	Occurs when the form receives focus.
KeyDown	Occurs when a key is pressed down while the form has focus.
KeyPress	Occurs when a key is pressed while the form has focus.
KeyUp	Occurs when a key is released while the form has focus.
Load	Occurs before a form is displayed for the first time.
LostFocus	Occurs when the form loses the focus.
MouseDown	Occurs when a mouse button is pressed and the mouse is over the form.
MouseEnter	Occurs when the mouse pointer enters the form.
MouseHover	Occurs when the mouse pointer hovers over the form.
MouseLeave	Occurs when the mouse pointer leaves the form.
MouseMove	Occurs when the mouse pointer is moved over the form.
MouseUp	Occurs when a mouse button is released and the mouse pointer is over the form.
MouseWheel	Occurs when the mouse wheel moves while the form has focus.
Move	Occurs when the form is moved.
Paint	Occurs when the form is redrawn.
Resize	Occurs when the form is resized.
SizeChanged	Occurs when the Size property value has changed.
TextChanged	Occurs when the Text property value has changed.

That gives us an overview of working with forms; now we'll look at forms from the programmer's point of view. The code for each form is what Visual Basic uses to create and display the form, and each form has its own .vb file. For example, the code support for the form in our application is in Form1.vb, which appears in the form's code designer (refer to Figure 4.4). To see what makes a form work in code, we'll take that file apart now.

Dissecting a Form's Code

If you look at the top of the code for Form1 in Form1.vb, the first thing you see is that Form1 is a class, and it is based on the standard Visual Basic Windows Form class:

```
Public Class Form1
    Inherits System.Windows.Forms.Form
        .
        .
        .
```

NEW TERM As we'll see in Day 9, the Inherits keyword allows you to "inherit" all the functionality of another class in your current class, including that class's nonprivate members. Not surprisingly, this process is called *inheritance*. This code makes Form1 a new class that inherits all nonprivate members of the System.Windows.Forms.Form class.

Next comes the code that Visual Basic writes for you (usually hidden, but as discussed in Day 1, you can toggle this code open or closed with the +/– button that appears in the code designer). This code initializes the window and positions the controls in it as you've placed them. Here's the first part of the code, including the New Sub procedure, which is called to create the new window:

```
Public Class Form1
    Inherits System.Windows.Forms.Form

#Region " Windows Form Designer generated code "

    Public Sub New()
        MyBase.New()

        'This call is required by the Windows Form Designer.
        InitializeComponent()

        'Add any initialization after the InitializeComponent() call

    End Sub

    'Form overrides dispose to clean up the component list.
    Protected Overloads Overrides Sub Dispose(ByVal disposing As Boolean)
        If disposing Then
            If Not (components Is Nothing) Then
                components.Dispose()
            End If
        End If
        MyBase.Dispose(disposing)
    End Sub
```

4

```
'Required by the Windows Form Designer
Private components As System.ComponentModel.IContainer

'NOTE: The following procedure is required by the Windows Form Designer
'It can be modified using the Windows Form Designer.
'Do not modify it using the code editor.
Friend WithEvents Button1 As System.Windows.Forms.Button
Friend WithEvents TextBox1 As System.Windows.Forms.TextBox
    .
    .
    .
```

Note in particular the two lines at the end that declare the button and text box objects in this application, Button1 and TextBox1, based on the System.Windows.Forms.Button and System.Windows.Forms.TextBox classes. As we'll see in Day 9, declaring these objects Friend gives them access to the code and data of the form, and using the WithEvents keyword means that they support events.

The next part of the code is all about setting up the controls in the form. You can see here how those controls are initialized and sized and then added to the form:

```
Public Class Form1
    Inherits System.Windows.Forms.Form

#Region " Windows Form Designer generated code "
    .
    .
    .
    <System.Diagnostics.DebuggerStepThrough()> _
    Private Sub InitializeComponent()
        Me.Button1 = New System.Windows.Forms.Button
        Me.TextBox1 = New System.Windows.Forms.TextBox
        Me.SuspendLayout()
        '
        'Button1
        '
        Me.Button1.Location = New System.Drawing.Point(104, 80)
        Me.Button1.Name = "Button1"
        Me.Button1.TabIndex = 0
        Me.Button1.Text = "Click Me"
        '
        'TextBox1
        '
        Me.TextBox1.Location = New System.Drawing.Point(88, 160)
        Me.TextBox1.Name = "TextBox1"
        Me.TextBox1.Size = New System.Drawing.Size(104, 20)
        Me.TextBox1.TabIndex = 1
        Me.TextBox1.Text = ""
        '
```

```
          'Form1
          '
          Me.AutoScaleBaseSize = New System.Drawing.Size(5, 13)
          Me.ClientSize = New System.Drawing.Size(292, 273)
          Me.Controls.Add(Me.TextBox1)
          Me.Controls.Add(Me.Button1)
          Me.Name = "Form1"
          Me.Text = "Form1"
          Me.ResumeLayout(False)

       End Sub

#End Region

       Private Sub Button1_Click(ByVal sender As System.Object, _
          ByVal e As System.EventArgs) Handles Button1.Click
          TextBox1.Text = "No problem."
       End Sub
End Class
```

The Me keyword in the code here is a Visual Basic keyword that stands for the current object whose code you're executing; in this case, Me stands for the form itself. That means that a line of code like Me.Text = "Form1" sets the caption of the form in the title bar (and if you change the Text property in the Properties window, this line of code will be altered to match). Because the current object is the default object in code, you could simply write lines like this as Text = "Form1".

At the end of the preceding code, you can see the Button1_Click event handler that's been added. That's where all the event handlers you create will go—at the end of the code in Form1.vb. The rest of the code is managed by Visual Basic itself, and although Microsoft says you shouldn't alter that code directly, if you know what you're doing, you certainly can.

That gives us an overview of the code Visual Basic uses to create and initialize a Windows form. But that's just the beginning. The next step is to work with Windows forms in our own code.

Handling Windows Forms in Code

You can make Windows forms do great deal, using your own code. For example, you can start a form at a certain location, you can make forms appear and disappear, you can add new controls at runtime, and more. Let's look at some of what you can do, first by setting a form's starting position.

4

Setting a Form's Starting Positions

You can use a form's StartPosition property at design time or runtime to specify its initial position on the screen. You assign this property values from the FormStartPosition enumeration. Here are the possible values:

- FormStartPosition.CenterParent—The form is centered within the bounds of its parent form.

- FormStartPosition.CenterScreen—The form is centered on the current display and has the dimensions specified in the form's size.

- FormStartPosition.Manual—The Location and Size properties of the form will determine its starting position.

- FormStartPosition.WindowsDefaultBounds—The form is positioned at the Windows default location (which Windows will decide) and has the bounds determined by Windows default.

- FormStartPosition.WindowsDefaultLocation—The form is positioned at the Windows default location (which Windows will decide) with the dimensions specified in the form's Size property.

Here's how you can set a form's StartPosition property from code, making a form appear in the center of the screen:

```
Form1.StartPosition = FormStartPosition.CenterScreen
```

Setting and Getting Forms' and Controls' Sizes and Locations

In Visual Basic, you can use the Size and Location properties to set the size and location of forms and controls, or the SetBounds method to do the same thing.

You can assign a new Size object to the Size property of forms or controls. If you want to set the location, you assign a new Point object to the Location property. To create a new Size object, you use the Size class's constructor like this: Size(x_size, y_size). To create a new Point object, you use the Point class's constructor like this: Point(x_location, y_location).

As with all measurements on the screen in Visual Basic .NET, these positions are measured in pixels. The Location property places the upper-left point of the control or form to the new location specified by the Point object you use. The Point object's location is measured with respect to the form's or control's container. A form's container is the screen itself, and the point (0, 0) is at upper left of the screen. Positive X is to the right, and positive Y is downward. A control's container is the form it's in, and (0, 0) is at upper left of the client area.

For example, the Mover project in the code for this book moves and resizes both a form and a control when you click a button. Listing 4.1 shows how it does that.

LISTING 4.1   Moving and Sizing a Form and a Control (Mover project, Form1.vb)

```
Private Sub Button1_Click(ByVal sender As System.Object, _
    ByVal e As System.EventArgs) Handles Button1.Click
    Size = New Size(200, 200)
    Location = New Point(0, 0)
    Button1.Size = New Size(100, 100)
    Button1.Location = New Point(0, 0)
End Sub
```

Tip

To determine the width and height of the screen in pixels, use System. Windows.Forms.Screen.GetBounds(Me).Width and System.Windows.Forms. Screen.GetBounds(Me).Height.

4

Note that this code refers simply to the `Size` and `Location` properties without qualifying them as `Form1.Size` and `Form1.Location`. That's fine because the form is the default object here, so Visual Basic knows that you are referring to properties of the form. If you want to qualify these properties explicitly, you could use this code instead:

```
Form1.Size = New Size(200, 200)
Form1.Location = New Point(0, 0)
Button1.Size = New Size(100, 100)
Button1.Location = New Point(0, 0)
```

In this example, the form will be resized and moved to the upper left of the screen, and the button will be resized and moved to the upper left of the client area when you click the button.

You can also read the current values in the `Size` and `Location` properties. A `Size` object supports `Width` and `Height` properties, so to determine a form's or control's width and height in pixels, you can check *xxxx*`.Size.Width` and *xxxx*`.Size.Height`, where *xxxx* is the name of the form or control (such as `Form1.Size.Width`). A `Point` object has `X` and `Y` properties, so you can get the location of the upper left of a form or control in its container (the container is the screen for a form and a form for a control) as *xxxx*.Location.X and *xxxx*.Location.Y.

If you prefer, you can use the SetBounds method to do the same thing. Here's what the SetBounds method looks like:

```
Sub SetBounds(ByVal x As Integer, ByVal y As Integer, _
    ByVal width As Integer, ByVal height As Integer)
```

Here are the arguments you pass to SetBounds:

- *x*—The new X location of the upper left of the form or control.
- *y*—The new Y location of the upper left of the form or control.
- *width*—The new width of the form or control.
- *height*—The new height of the form or control.

Using SetBounds, you can resize and move the form and button the same way we did in the Mover example:

```
Private Sub Button1_Click(ByVal sender As System.Object, _
    ByVal e As System.EventArgs) Handles Button1.Click
    SetBounds(0, 0, 200, 200)
    Button1.SetBounds(0, 0, 100, 100)
End Sub
```

Tip	You can create simple animation by moving forms or controls around with a loop in code and the SetBounds method.

Displaying and Hiding Forms and Controls

You can also use the Visible property to display forms and controls, which you set to True or False. For example, say that you want to make a form disappear when the user clicks a button in that form (probably really surprising the user); you could do that like this:

```
Private Sub Button1_Click(ByVal sender As System.Object, _
    ByVal e As System.EventArgs) Handles Button1.Click
    Form1.Visible = False
End Sub
```

The same works for controls. To make the button disappear when the user clicks it, you can use this code:

```
Private Sub Button1_Click(ByVal sender As System.Object, _
    ByVal e As System.EventArgs) Handles Button1.Click
    Button1.Visible = False
End Sub
```

You can also use the Show and Hide methods of forms and controls to show and hide them. For example, when the user clicks Button1, we can hide Form1 this way:

```
Private Sub Button1_Click(ByVal sender As System.Object, _
    ByVal e As System.EventArgs) Handles Button1.Click
    Form1.Hide()
End Sub
```

To show this form again, you could call Form1.Show().

Customizing a Form's Border and Title Bar

As we already know, you can set the text in a form's title bar using the Text property like this:

```
Form1.Text = "A new form"
```

NEW TERM   You can further customize the title bar in a form with the ControlBox property. The control box refers to the maximize and minimize buttons that appear at right in the title bar, and you can remove them by setting the form's ControlBox property to False (the default is True). For example, when you create dialogs, as we'll do later today, you should remove the control box, as well as add OK and Cancel buttons. You should also make the dialog's border *fixed*, not resizable, which is the default.

You can set a form's border style with its FormBorderStyle property; here are the possible values from the FormBorderStyle enumeration that you can assign to that property (either in code at runtime or in the Properties window at design time):

- FormBorderStyle.Fixed3D—A fixed, three-dimensional border.
- FormBorderStyle.FixedDialog—A thick, fixed dialog-style border.
- FormBorderStyle.FixedSingle—A fixed, single line border.
- FormBorderStyle.FixedToolWindow—A tool window border that is not resizable.
- FormBorderStyle.None—No border.
- FormBorderStyle.Sizable—A resizable border; this is the default for Windows forms.
- FormBorderStyle.SizableToolWindow—A resizable tool window border.

4

Tabbing Between Controls

If you have multiple controls in a form, the user can move between them using the mouse or the Tab key. When the user presses the Tab key, a new control receives the input focus and is highlighted (in the case of controls like buttons) or displays a blinking cursor (in the case of controls like text boxes). When a control has the input focus, it means that this control is the target of keyboard keystrokes (only one control can have the focus at a time).

 The order in which the focus moves from control to control when the user presses the Tab key is called the *tab order*. To set the tab order yourself, you first select a control and make sure its TabStop property is True. If this property is False, the control is not accessible by pressing the Tab key. Next, you set the control's position in the tab order by entering a number in the TabIndex property. The tab index starts at 0, and the control with the TabIndex set at 0 is the control that has the focus when the form first appears.

> **Tip**
>
> By default, the first control you add to a form has TabIndex 0.

And that's all you need! Now you've given your program a keyboard interface.

Setting a Form's State—Minimized, Maximized, Enabled, or Disabled

You can also maximize and minimize a form in code with the WindowState property, which can take these values from the FormWindowState enumeration:

- FormWindowState.Maximized—The window becomes maximized.
- FormWindowState.Minimized—The window becomes minimized.
- FormWindowState.Normal—The window is set to its normal state.

For example, here's how you might maximize a form when the user clicks a button:

```
Private Sub Button1_Click(ByVal sender As System.Object, _
    ByVal e As System.EventArgs) Handles Button1.Click
    WindowState = FormWindowState.Maximized
End Sub
```

In addition, you can also set the Enabled property to enable or disable a window. When a form is disabled, it will beep only if the user tries to give it the focus. You can set the Enabled property to True to enable a window and to False to disable it.

Adding Controls at Runtime

NEW TERM You can also add and remove controls on a form at runtime. For example, you might be writing a calendar application and want to display a new button for every day of the month—and the number of buttons will vary by month. Using the `Add` and `Remove` methods of the `Controls` *collection* of a form, you can add and remove controls at runtime.

Visual Basic collections, such as the `Controls` collection, enable you to manage multiple objects, like the controls in a form (VB also has a `Forms` collection that holds all the forms in your application). You can use a collection's `Add` and `Remove` methods to add and remove items from a collection, and refer to items by index number (as you would in an array). For example, if you have only one control, `Button1`, in `Form1`, you can refer to that button as `Form1.Controls(0)`.

We'll put this into practice by seeing how to add a new button to a form at runtime. To do that, we'll create a new button object in code (not by using the toolbox at design time).

This new project will be called AddControls in the code for this book; when the user clicks a button in this project, a new button will appear. Start this project by adding a new button, `Button1`, with the caption `"Click Me"` to a form; then double-click the button to open the form's code designer and create the `Button1_Click` event handler. When the user clicks this button, we can create a new button, `Button2`. `Button2` will be a new object of the Visual Basic `Button` class (just as a new text box would be an object of the `TextBox` class), and we can make it a module-level object (so it can be accessed from multiple Sub procedures) like this:

```
Public Class Form1
    Inherits System.Windows.Forms.Form

' Windows Form Designer generated code

    Dim WithEvents Button2 As Button

    Private Sub Button1_Click(ByVal sender As System.Object, _
        ByVal e As System.EventArgs) Handles Button1.Click
        .
        .
        .
    End Sub

End Class
```

4

Note the WithEvents keyword here; you need to use this special keyword when an object you're declaring will support events, like the Click event of this new Button object. When the user clicks the first button, Button1, we can create the new Button2 object and give it a size, location, and caption:

```
Public Class Form1
    Inherits System.Windows.Forms.Form

' Windows Form Designer generated code

    Dim WithEvents Button2 As Button

    Private Sub Button1_Click(ByVal sender As System.Object, _
        ByVal e As System.EventArgs) Handles Button1.Click
        Button2 = New Button
        Button2.Location = New Point(104, 104)
        Button2.Size = New Size(75, 23)
        Button2.Text = "And Me!"
        .
        .
        .
    End Sub

End Class
```

NEW TERM   This code creates the new button, but when you click this new button, nothing happens. How can we add an event handler to it in code? You can do that by creating a new Sub procedure yourself, Button2_Click, and giving it the same argument list as the first button's Click event handler. Then you use the AddHandler statement to connect this new event handler to Button2 by specifying the event you want to add an event handler to, which is Button2.Click, and the *address* in memory of the event handler Button2_Click, which you can find with the AddressOf operator. In this case, the code in the new event handler might just display some text in a text box, so add a new text box, TextBox1, to the form now, as well as this code:

```
Public Class Form1
    Inherits System.Windows.Forms.Form

' Windows Form Designer generated code

    Dim WithEvents Button2 As Button

    Private Sub Button1_Click(ByVal sender As System.Object, _
        ByVal e As System.EventArgs) Handles Button1.Click
        Button2 = New Button
        Button2.Location = New Point(104, 104)
        Button2.Size = New Size(75, 23)
```

```
        Button2.Text = "And Me!"

        AddHandler Button2.Click, AddressOf Button2_Clicked
        .
        .
        .
    End Sub

    Private Sub Button2_Clicked(ByVal sender As Object, ByVal e As
System.EventArgs)
        TextBox1.Text = "No problem!"
    End Sub

End Class
```

All that's left is to add the new `Button2` object to the `Controls` collection for the form, which will display the new button, as you see in Listing 4.2.

LISTING 4.2   Adding a New Button to a Form at Runtime (AddControls project, Form1.vb)

```
Public Class Form1
    Inherits System.Windows.Forms.Form

' Windows Form Designer generated code

    Dim WithEvents Button2 As Button

    Private Sub Button1_Click(ByVal sender As System.Object, _
        ByVal e As System.EventArgs) Handles Button1.Click
        Button2 = New Button
        Button2.Location = New Point(104, 104)
        Button2.Size = New Size(75, 23)
        Button2.Text = "And Me!"

        AddHandler Button2.Click, AddressOf Button2_Clicked
        Controls.Add(Button2)
    End Sub

    Private Sub Button2_Clicked(ByVal sender As Object, _
        ByVal e As System.EventArgs)
        TextBox1.Text = "No problem!"
    End Sub

End Class
```

4

You can see the results in Figure 4.6. When the user clicks a button, a new button appears in the form, and when the user clicks the new button, the message "No problem!" appears in the text box.

FIGURE 4.6

Adding controls to a Windows application at runtime.

There's another way to add an event handler without using AddHandler if you know exactly which control an event handler will handle. You can add a Handles clause to the event handler, like this, where the code indicates this event handler handles the Click event of Button2:

```
Private Sub Button1_Click(ByVal sender As System.Object, _
    ByVal e As System.EventArgs) Handles Button1.Click
    Button2 = New Button
    Button2.Location = New Point(104, 104)
    Button2.Size = New Size(75, 23)
    Button2.Text = "And Me!"

    Controls.Add(Button2)
End Sub

Private Sub Button2_Clicked(ByVal sender As Object, _
    ByVal e As System.EventArgs) Handles Button2.Click
    TextBox1.Text = "No problem!"
End Sub
```

Now the Click event of Button2 is connected to Button2_Clicked. When you add an event handler to a control using a code designer, you'll see that Visual Basic uses a Handles clause by default.

Using the Built-in Message and Input Dialogs

It's time to take the next step up beyond simple forms now, working toward multiple-form applications. In our progress toward multiple-form applications, we'll first see how to use the built-in dialogs that Visual Basic supports and you can access with the MsgBox, MessageBox.Show, and InputBox functions; then we'll see true multiple-form applications, followed by multiple-document interface (MDI) applications, owned forms, and more.

> **Tip**
>
> Besides the MsgBox, MessageBox.Show, and InputBox functions, Visual Basic includes a number of built-in dialogs to open files, save files, set colors, and so on. We'll see them in Day 7.

Working with the MsgBox Function

The handy MsgBox function displays a message box as needed. Here's how you use this function (note that the default values for various parameters appear after the equals signs):

```
Function MsgBox(Prompt As Object [, Buttons As MsgBoxStyle = MsgBoxStyle.OKOnly
[, Title As Object = Nothing]]) As MsgBoxResultArguments
```

Here are the arguments you pass to this function:

- *Prompt*—A string that holds the message in the message box.
- *Buttons*—The sum of values specifying the number and type of buttons to display, the icon style to use, and more. See Table 4.4 for the possible values.
- *Title*—The title of the dialog, displayed in the title bar of the dialog. If you omit *Title*, the application name is placed in the title bar.

 NEW TERM Using the *Buttons* argument, you can customize the buttons and appearance of the message box, and you can find the possible values to use from the MsgBoxStyle enumeration in Table 4.4. Note that you can set the *modality* of the message box to MsgBoxStyle.ApplicationModal or MsgBoxStyle.SystemModal. The first constant means that the user must dismiss the message box before continuing with the application, and the second means the user can't do anything else with the whole system until dismissing the message box.

4

TABLE 4.4   The `MsgBoxStyle` Enumeration

Constant	Description
MsgBoxStyle.OKOnly	Displays an OK button only.
MsgBoxStyle.OKCancel	Displays both OK and Cancel buttons.
MsgBoxStyle.AbortRetryIgnore	Displays Abort, Retry, and Ignore buttons.
MsgBoxStyle.YesNoCancel	Displays Yes, No, and Cancel buttons.
MsgBoxStyle.YesNo	Displays Yes and No buttons.
MsgBoxStyle.RetryCancel	Displays Retry and Cancel buttons.
MsgBoxStyle.Critical	Displays the Critical Message icon.
MsgBoxStyle.Question	Displays the Warning Query icon.
MsgBoxStyle.Exclamation	Displays the Warning Message icon.
MsgBoxStyle.Information	Displays the Information Message icon.
MsgBoxStyle.DefaultButton1	First button will be the default (chosen if the user presses Enter).
MsgBoxStyle.DefaultButton2	Second button will be the default (chosen if the user presses Enter).
MsgBoxStyle.DefaultButton3	Third button will be the default (chosen if the user presses Enter).
MsgBoxStyle.ApplicationModal	Application modal, which means the user must respond to the message box before continuing work in the current application.
MsgBoxStyle.SystemModal	System modal, which means all applications are unavailable until the user dismisses the message box.
MsgBoxStyle.MsgBoxSetForeground	Makes the message box the foreground window.
MsgBoxStyle.MsgBoxRight	Right-aligns the text.
MsgBoxStyle.MsgBoxRtlReading	Specifies text should appear right-to-left (such as Hebrew and Arabic).

The `MsgBox` function also returns a value from the `MsgBoxResult` enumeration. You can see the values in this enumeration in Table 4.5. Using these values, you can determine which button the user clicked.

TABLE 4.5   The `MsgBoxResult` Enumeration

Constant	Description
MsgBoxResult.OK	The OK button was clicked.
MsgBoxResult.Cancel	The Cancel button was clicked.

TABLE 4.5 continued

Constant	Description
MsgBoxResult.Abort	The Abort button was clicked.
MsgBoxResult.Retry	The Retry button was clicked.
MsgBoxResult.Ignore	The Ignore button was clicked.
MsgBoxResult.Yes	The Yes button was clicked.
MsgBoxResult.No	The No button was clicked.

You can see an example in the Messages project in the code for the book. Here's how it displays a message box with the message "This is a message box!" and displays a message in a text box if the user clicked the OK button in the message box:

```
Private Sub Button1_Click(ByVal sender As System.Object, _
    ByVal e As System.EventArgs) Handles Button1.Click
        Dim intReturnValue As Integer
        intReturnValue = MsgBox("This is a message box!", _
        MsgBoxStyle.OKCancel + MsgBoxStyle.Information + _
        MsgBoxStyle.SystemModal, "Message Box")
        If (intReturnValue = MsgBoxResult.OK) Then
            TextBox1.Text = "You clicked the OK button."
        End If
End Sub
```

You can see this message box at work in Figure 4.7.

FIGURE 4.7

Using the MsgBox *function.*

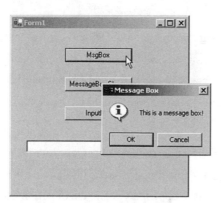

Working with the **MessageBox.Show** Method

You can also use the .NET Framework's MessageBox class's Show method to display message boxes in Visual Basic. Here's how to use this method:

```
Function Show( ByVal text As String, _
    ByVal caption As String, ByVal buttons As MessageBoxButtons, _
    ByVal icon As MessageBoxIcon, ByVal defaultButton As _
    MessageBoxDefaultButton, ByVal options As MessageBoxOptions) _
As DialogResult
```

The arguments you pass to this method are as follows:

- *text*—The message to display in the message box.
- *caption*—The text to display in the title bar of the message box.
- *buttons*—One of the MessageBoxButtons enumeration values that specifies which buttons to display in the message box. See the following lists.
- *icon*—One of the MessageBoxIcon enumeration values that specifies which icon to display in the message box. See the following lists.
- *defaultButton*—One of the MessageBoxDefaultButton enumeration values that specifies which is the default button for the message box. See the following lists.
- *options*—One of the MessageBoxOptions enumeration values that specifies which display and association options will be used for the message box. See the following lists.

Here are the MessageBoxButtons enumeration values:

- AbortRetryIgnore—The message box will show Abort, Retry, and Ignore buttons.
- OK—The message box will show an OK button.
- OKCancel—The message box will show OK and Cancel buttons.
- RetryCancel—The message box will show Retry and Cancel buttons.
- YesNo—The message box will show Yes and No buttons.
- YesNoCancel—The message box will show Yes, No, and Cancel buttons.

Here are the MessageBoxIcon enumeration values:

- Asterisk—Shows an icon displaying a lowercase letter *i* in a circle.
- Error—Shows an icon displaying a white *X* in a circle with a red background.
- Exclamation—Shows an icon displaying an exclamation point in a triangle with a yellow background.
- Hand—Shows an icon displaying a white *X* in a circle with a red background.
- Information—Shows an icon displaying a lowercase letter *i* in a circle.

- None—Shows no icons.
- Question—Shows an icon displaying a question mark in a circle.
- Stop—Shows an icon displaying a white *X* in a circle with a red background.
- Warning—Shows an icon displaying an exclamation point in a triangle with a yellow background.

Here are the MessageBoxDefaultButton enumeration values:

- Button1—Makes the first button on the message box the default button.
- Button2—Makes the second button on the message box the default button.
- Button3—Makes the third button on the message box the default button.

Here are the MessageBoxOptions enumeration values:

- DefaultDesktopOnly—Displays the message box on the active desktop.
- RightAlign—Right-aligns the message box text.
- RtlReading—Specifies that the message box text should be displayed with right-to-left text.

The result of the Show method is a value from the DialogResult enumeration, showing what button the user clicked:

- Abort—The Abort button was clicked.
- Cancel—The Cancel button was clicked.
- Ignore—The Ignore button was clicked.
- No—The No button was clicked.
- None—Nothing is returned from the dialog. (This means that a modal dialog continues running.)
- OK—The OK button was clicked.
- Retry—The Retry button was clicked.
- Yes—The Yes button was clicked.

The following example, from the Messages example in the code for this book, puts this method to work. This code checks the returned result to see if the user clicked the OK button and, if so, displays a message:

```
Private Sub Button2_Click(ByVal sender As System.Object, _
    ByVal e As System.EventArgs) Handles Button2.Click
    Dim intReturnValue As Integer
    intReturnValue = MessageBox.Show("This is also a message box!", _
```

4

```
            "Message Box", MessageBoxButtons.OKCancel, _
            MessageBoxIcon.Information, MessageBoxDefaultButton.Button1, _
            MessageBoxOptions.DefaultDesktopOnly)
        If (intReturnValue = DialogResult.OK) Then
            TextBox1.Text = "You clicked the OK button."
        End If
End Sub
```

You can see the results in Figure 4.8. As you can see, this message box looks just like the one created with the MsgBox function in the preceding section.

FIGURE 4.8

Using the
MessageBox.Show
function.

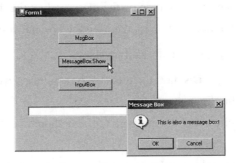

Working with the InputBox Function

You can use the InputBox function to display a dialog. This dialog enables the user to enter a string of text. Here's the syntax for this function:

```
Public Function InputBox(Prompt As String [, Title As _
String = "" [, DefaultResponse As String = "" [, _
XPos As Integer = -1 [, YPos As Integer = -1]]]]) As String
```

The arguments for the InputBox function are as follows:

- *Prompt*—A string holding the prompt for the dialog.
- *Title*—A string for the title bar of the dialog. Note that if you omit *Title*, the application name is placed in the title bar.
- *DefaultResponse*—A string displayed in the text box as the default response. If you omit *DefaultResponse*, the displayed text box is empty.
- *XPos*—The distance (in pixels) of the left edge of the dialog from the left edge of the screen. If you omit *XPos*, the dialog is centered horizontally.
- *YPos*—The distance (in pixels) of the upper edge of the dialog from the top of the screen. If you omit *YPos*, the dialog is positioned vertically about one third of the way down the screen.

Input boxes allow you to display a prompt and read a line of text typed by the user, and the InputBox function returns the string result. The following example is pulled from the Messages example in the code for the book:

```
Private Sub Button3_Click(ByVal sender As System.Object, _
    ByVal e As System.EventArgs) Handles Button3.Click
    TextBox1.Text = "You typed: " & InputBox("Please type something...")
End Sub
```

You can see the results of this code in Figure 4.9 (although the input box works, it looks pretty ugly).

FIGURE 4.9

Using the InputBox *function.*

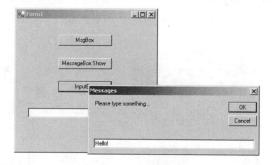

When the user enters text and clicks OK, the InputBox function returns that text, and the code displays it in the text box in the Messages example, as you see in Figure 4.10.

FIGURE 4.10

Getting text from the InputBox *function.*

This example introduces us to our first use of multiple windows, but all we're really doing so far is using various functions and letting Visual Basic do the rest. How about some true multiple-form applications?

Creating Applications with Multiple Forms

To see how to work with multiple-form applications, create a new Windows application named TwoForms. As you can gather from the name, the TwoForms example (also in the code for the book) will use two forms, and you'll be able to display and hide the second form by clicking buttons in the first.

By default, TwoForms has a single Windows form, Form1. To add the second form, select the Project, Add Windows Form item to open the Add New Item dialog you see in Figure 4.11. Then select the Windows Form icon in the Templates box and click Open, adding a new form, Form2, to the project, as you see in the IDE in Figure 4.12. Also add a text box with the text "Welcome to Form2" in it to the second form, as you see in Figure 4.12.

FIGURE 4.11

The Add New Item dialog.

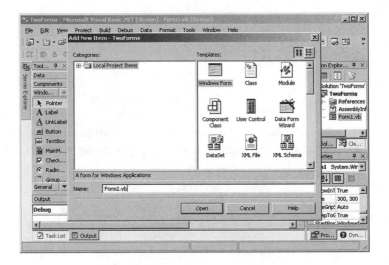

Let's make our new application do something. In Form1, the first form, add a button marked Show that will make the second form visible (it's invisible by default) and a button marked Hide that will make the second form disappear. We can add a button marked Get Text to read the text from the second form, showing us how to communicate between forms. Finally, add a text box, TextBox1, to the first form to display the text we read from the second form.

FIGURE 4.12

A second form in a Windows application.

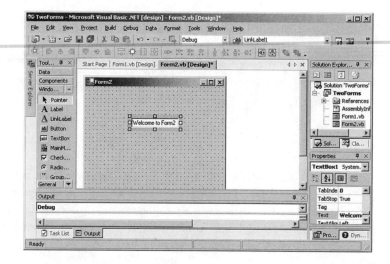

NEW TERM Although Visual Basic creates an object by default from the *startup form* (the form that appears when the application starts), which is Form1 here, and displays that form, Form2 remains just a class—there's no Form2 object when the program starts. To display and hide the second form, we'll need an object of the Form2 class in our code, so we can create that object now, calling it frmTwo in the code for the first form:

```
Public Class Form1
    Inherits System.Windows.Forms.Form

' Windows Form Designer generated code

    Dim frmTwo As New Form2
        .
        .
        .
End Class
```

Now we can add code for the Show and Hide buttons to show and hide the second form:

```
Public Class Form1
    Inherits System.Windows.Forms.Form

' Windows Form Designer generated code

    Dim frmTwo As New Form2
    Private Sub Button1_Click(ByVal sender As System.Object, _
        ByVal e As System.EventArgs) Handles Button1.Click
```

4

```
        frmTwo.Show()
    End Sub

    Private Sub Button2_Click(ByVal sender As System.Object, _
        ByVal e As System.EventArgs) Handles Button2.Click
        frmTwo.Hide()
    End Sub
        .
        .
        .
End Class
```

All that's left is to read the text from the second form when the user clicks the Get Text button in the first form. How do we do that? The name of the text box in the second form is TextBox1. TextBox1 is a subobject of the frmTwo object, so we can reach that text box as frmTwo.TextBox1 and the text in the text box as frmTwo.TextBox1.Text. Listing 4.3 shows how we copy the text in the text box in the second form into the text box in the first form.

LISTING 4.3 Working with Multiple Forms (TwoForms project, Form1.vb)

```
Public Class Form1
    Inherits System.Windows.Forms.Form

' Windows Form Designer generated code

    Dim frmTwo As New Form2
    Private Sub Button1_Click(ByVal sender As System.Object, _
        ByVal e As System.EventArgs) Handles Button1.Click
        frmTwo.Show()
    End Sub

    Private Sub Button2_Click(ByVal sender As System.Object, _
        ByVal e As System.EventArgs) Handles Button2.Click
        frmTwo.Hide()
    End Sub

    Private Sub Button3_Click(ByVal sender As System.Object, _
        ByVal e As System.EventArgs) Handles Button3.Click
        TextBox1.Text = frmTwo.TextBox1.Text
    End Sub
End Class
```

That's all you need! Now when you run this application, the first form will appear. Clicking the Show button displays the second form, as you see in Figure 4.13.

FIGURE 4.13

Displaying a second form in a Windows application.

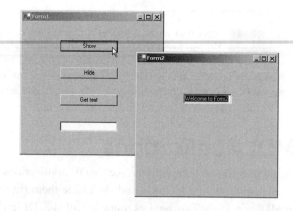

In addition, when you click the Get Text button in the first form, the text from the text box in the second form will be read and displayed in the first form, as you see in Figure 4.14. Congratulations! You're working with multiple forms in a Windows application.

FIGURE 4.14

Getting text from a second form in a Windows application.

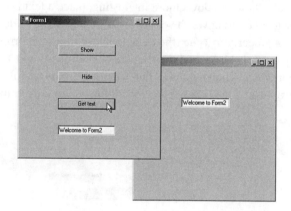

Note that Form1 was the startup form here. But what if you wanted another form, such as Form2, to be the startup form? You can set the startup form by right-clicking the project in the Solutions Explorer, selecting Properties, and then selecting the Common Properties folder and the General item in the box at left. Next, select the form you want to be the startup form from the Startup Object drop-down list on the right, click OK, and that's all you need.

Tip

New Term Now that we're working with multiple forms, here's another tip you need to know: You can make sure a form stays on top of all others at runtime by setting its `TopMost` property to `True`. You can also change the order in which your forms appear on top of each other (called the *stacking order*) with the `BringToFront` and `SendToBack` methods.

Creating MDI Applications

You can also create multiple-document interface (MDI) applications in Visual Basic. MDI windows can display multiple child windows inside them (in fact, the Visual Basic IDE itself is an MDI window). This next example is called MDI in the code for this book. First, create this new Windows application, calling it MDI. Next, set the `IsMdiContainer` property of `Form1` to `True` (the default is `False`) to make it the MDI window that will contain the MDI child windows.

Next, add a second form, `Form2`, to the project; `Form2` will be the class of our MDI child windows. To make these windows more interesting, place a text box on `Form2` now. We can stretch this text box to cover the entire form's client area. To do that, just set the text box's `MultiLine` property to `True` (the default, as we'll see tomorrow, is `False`, making text boxes only one line high), and then set the `Dock` property to `Fill` for the text box, as you see in Figure 4.15. Knowing about the `Dock` property is useful because it allows you to dock a control to an edge of a window or fill the window, as in this case.

Figure 4.15

Docking a text box.

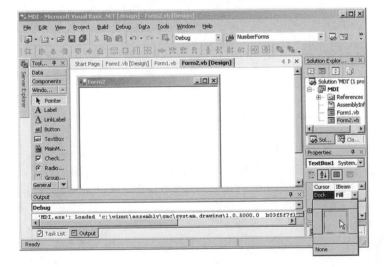

When the MDI form is first displayed, we can create a few MDI child windows and display them as well. To do that in a loop, you can declare an array of forms, each of the Form2 class, in Form1's Load event handler. The Load event occurs when a form is about to be displayed and you want to initialize that form. To bring up the Load event's event handler in a code designer, Form1_Load, just double-click Form1 itself (the Load event is the default event for a form, just as the Click event is the default event for buttons). Now add an array of Form2 objects named Forms:

```
Public Class Form1
    Inherits System.Windows.Forms.Form

' Windows Form Designer generated code

    Private Sub Form1_Load(ByVal sender As System.Object, _
        ByVal e As System.EventArgs) Handles MyBase.Load
        Dim Forms(4) As Form2
        .
        .
        .
    End Sub
End Class
```

Next, you can create, customize, and display five new MDI child forms. To make each new form a child of the main MDI form, this code sets the MdiParent property of each child to the current form, Form1:

```
Public Class Form1
    Inherits System.Windows.Forms.Form

' Windows Form Designer generated code

    Private Sub Form1_Load(ByVal sender As System.Object, _
        ByVal e As System.EventArgs) Handles MyBase.Load
        Dim Forms(4) As Form2
        For intLoopIndex As Integer = 0 To 4
            Forms(intLoopIndex) = New Form2
            Forms(intLoopIndex).Text = "Document" & Str(intLoopIndex)
            Forms(intLoopIndex).MdiParent = Me
            Forms(intLoopIndex).Show()
        Next intLoopIndex
        .
        .
        .
    End Sub
End Class
```

4

You can also arrange the MDI child windows, using the `MdiLayout` method:

```
Sub LayoutMdi(ByVal value As MdiLayout)
```

This Sub procedure takes one argument, *value*, which is one of the `MdiLayout` enumeration values that defines the layout of MDI child forms:

- `MdiLayout.ArrangeIcons`—All MDI child icons (which are displayed when you minimize an MDI child window) will be arranged.
- `MdiLayout.Cascade`—All MDI child windows will be cascaded.
- `MdiLayout.TileHorizontal`—All MDI child windows will be tiled horizontally.
- `MdiLayout.TileVertical`—All MDI child windows will be tiled vertically.

In Listing 4.4, we'll cascade the child forms, which is typical for MDI applications.

LISTING 4.4   Supporting MDI (MDI project, Form1.vb)

```
Public Class Form1
    Inherits System.Windows.Forms.Form

' Windows Form Designer generated code

    Private Sub Form1_Load(ByVal sender As System.Object, _
        ByVal e As System.EventArgs) Handles MyBase.Load
        Dim Forms(4) As Form2
        For intLoopIndex As Integer = 0 To 4
            Forms(intLoopIndex) = New Form2
            Forms(intLoopIndex).Text = "Document" & Str(intLoopIndex)
            Forms(intLoopIndex).MdiParent = Me
            Forms(intLoopIndex).Show()
        Next intLoopIndex
        Me.LayoutMdi(MdiLayout.Cascade)
    End Sub
End Class
```

As you can see in Figure 4.16, five MDI children are displayed inside the MDI parent, and each child's client area is covered by a multiline text box.

Tip

> Any kind of form—including different types in the same application—can be an MDI child in the same MDI window. To manage the MDI children, you can use the `Show` and `Hide` methods as you like. More on handling MDI applications is coming up in Day 7.

FIGURE 4.16

An MDI application.

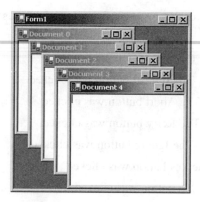

Creating Dialogs

As we've seen, Visual Basic supports message boxes and input boxes, but they're very basic. In real applications, you'll need to create your own custom dialogs. To see how that works, create a new Windows application now named Dialogs. Add a button marked Show Dialog to Form1 and add a text box. When the user clicks the Show Dialog button, the new dialog will appear. The user can enter text into a text box in the dialog, click OK, and that text will appear in the text box in Form1.

To create the new dialog, add a new form, Form2, to the project now. Set the new form's ControlBox property to False (to remove the control box minimize and maximize buttons), its FormBorderStyle property to FixedDialog (so the dialog can't be resized), and, optionally, its ShowInTaskbar property to False (so an icon for the dialog doesn't appear in the Windows taskbar, which is customary behavior for dialogs). Also, change the caption of Form2 to "Dialog"; add a text box, TextBox1; a button marked OK; and a button marked Cancel, as you see in Figure 4.17.

To turn the OK button in this dialog into a real OK button, set the AcceptButton property of Form2 to Button1 (the OK button) in the Properties window; that means when the user presses Enter, the OK button will be clicked. And set the CancelButton property of Form2 to Button2 (the Cancel button). If the user presses Esc, this button will be clicked.

In addition, set the DialogResult property of the OK button to OK and the same property of the Cancel button to Cancel. This property returns a value from the DialogResult enumeration when the dialog is closed, so you can determine which button the user has clicked. The possible settings for this property from the `DialogResult` enumeration are as follows:

- `DialogResult.OK`—The OK button was clicked.
- `DialogResult.Cancel`—The Cancel button was clicked.
- `DialogResult.Abort`—The Abort button was clicked.
- `DialogResult.Retry`—The Retry button was clicked.
- `DialogResult.Ignore`—The Ignore button was clicked.
- `DialogResult.Yes`—The Yes button was clicked.
- `DialogResult.No`—The No button was clicked.
- `DialogResult.None`—The None button was clicked.

FIGURE 4.17

Creating a dialog.

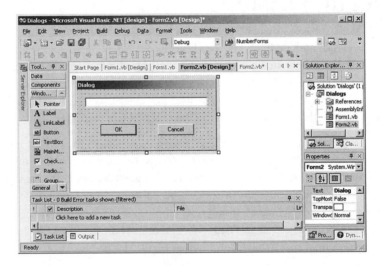

Finally, to make sure that the dialog is closed when the user clicks the OK or Cancel button, add this code to both buttons; it just uses the Form's `Close` method to close the dialog:

```
Public Class Form2
    Inherits System.Windows.Forms.Form

' Windows Form Designer generated code

    Private Sub Button1_Click(ByVal sender As System.Object, _
        ByVal e As System.EventArgs) Handles Button1.Click
        Me.Close()
    End Sub
```

```
        Private Sub Button2_Click(ByVal sender As System.Object, _
            ByVal e As System.EventArgs) Handles Button2.Click
                Me.Close()
        End Sub
End Class
```

Our dialog, Form2, is set. All that we need to do now is to display it when the user clicks
the Show Dialog button in Form1. To create a new dialog, you can create an object,
frmDialog, of the Form2 class:

```
Public Class Form1
    Inherits System.Windows.Forms.Form

' Windows Form Designer generated code
    Dim frmDialog As New Form2
        .
        .
        .

End Class
```

Now you can use the Form class's ShowDialog method, which will return the button the
user clicked as a DialogResult enumeration value. If the user clicked the OK (not
Cancel) button, we'll read the text he or she entered and display it, as you see in
Listing 4.5.

LISTING 4.5   Creating Dialogs (Dialogs project, Form1.vb)

```
Public Class Form1
    Inherits System.Windows.Forms.Form

' Windows Form Designer generated code
    Dim frmDialog As New Form2

    Private Sub Button1_Click(ByVal sender As System.Object, _
        ByVal e As System.EventArgs) Handles Button1.Click
            If frmDialog.ShowDialog() = DialogResult.OK Then
                TextBox1.Text = "You typed: " & frmDialog.TextBox1.Text
            End If
    End Sub
End Class
```

And that completes the code! Now run the application, as shown in Figure 4.18. The dialog appears when you click the Show Dialog button in Form1, and you can enter text in
it. When you click the OK button, the dialog disappears and the text you entered appears
in the text box in Form1, as you see in Figure 4.19. That's it. Now you're creating and
using dialogs.

4

FIGURE 4.18

Displaying a dialog.

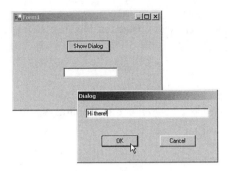

FIGURE 4.19

Getting data from a dialog.

 Note

When you're creating dialogs, the Windows convention is to always add a Cancel button. This way, if the user has opened the dialog by mistake, he or she can close it without problems.

Creating Owned Forms

NEW TERM Visual Basic also enables you to create *owned forms*. An owned form is tied to the form that owns it. For example, if the user minimizes the owner form, the owned form will also be minimized. If the user closes the owner form, the owned form will be closed, and so on. Owned forms are good if, for example, you want to display help at the same time the user is using your application.

You can add an owned form with the AddOwnedForm method and remove an owned form with the RemoveOwnedForm method. Listing 4.6 shows an example, OwnedForms in the code for this book; in this case, Form1 owns frmTwo, which is an object of the Form2 class.

LISTING 4.6   Creating Owned Forms (OwnedForms project, Form1.vb)

```
Public Class Form1
    Inherits System.Windows.Forms.Form

' Windows Form Designer generated code

    Dim frmTwo As New Form2
    Private Sub Form1_Load(ByVal sender As System.Object, _
        ByVal e As System.EventArgs) Handles MyBase.Load
        Me.AddOwnedForm(frmTwo)
        frmTwo.Show()
    End Sub
End Class
```

When you run this example, you'll see two forms with the captions Form1 and Form2. Minimizing Form1 will minimize Form2 as well; closing Form1 will close Form2 as well.

Using Nonrectangular Forms

You're not limited to rectangular windows in Visual Basic; you can use windows of any shape, which is new in Visual Basic .NET 2003. For example, the Ellipse project in the code for this book displays an elliptical window.

So how do you create a nonrectangular form? You first set the form's FormBorderStyle property to None. Next, you set the BackgroundImage property of the form to the image you want to use for the shape of the form. In this case, that's an ellipse, which you'll find in the background.jpg file in the Ellipse project. Finally, you set the TransparencyKey property to the background color of the image. In background.jpg, the background is white, so the TransparencyKey property for Form1 is set to white (a palette of colors to select from appears when you choose this property in the Properties window).

You can see the elliptical window in Figure 4.20, complete with a Close button added to close the window.

FIGURE 4.20

A nonrectangular form.

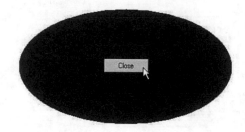

Note that because this window doesn't have a title bar, you'll have to provide some other way for the user to move it if you want to support that functionality. Later today, we'll look at working with the mouse, and that provides a good solution because you can add code to the window to allow the user to drag it with the mouse. (Also, look at the `PointToScreen` method coming up tomorrow in Table 5.1; this method can be helpful because it enables you to convert mouse coordinates in a form to a point in screen coordinates, which you can use to move the form using the `SetBounds` method.)

Note   Visual Basic nonrectangular windows can have display problems in screens set to use more than 24-bit color. (According to Microsoft, the solution is to reset the screen to use color values that are 24 bits or less.)

Creating Smart Device Applications

In Visual Basic .NET 2003, you can also create applications for smart devices such as Pocket PCs or computers running Windows CE, as long as those machines have the .NET Compact Framework installed.

To create a new smart device application, like the SmartDevices example in the code for this book, open the New Project dialog as usual. Next, select the Smart Device Application icon in the Templates box. The Smart Device Application Wizard appears, as you see in Figure 4.21, enabling you to configure the project. In this case, just leave the default values selected and click OK to create a Pocket PC Windows application.

FIGURE 4.21

Starting a smart device application.

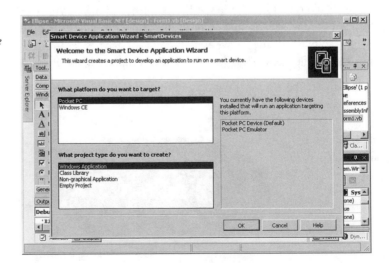

Now you can add buttons and text boxes to this new application, as you see in Figure 4.22. You can use the same coding that we've seen in other Visual Basic programs.

FIGURE 4.22

*Creating a smart
device application.*

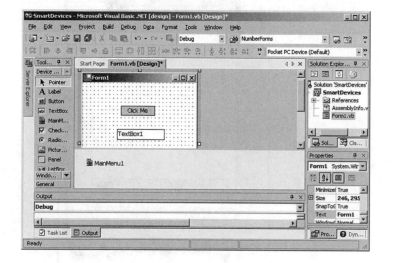

When you run the application, the Deploy SmartDevices dialog appears, allowing you to deploy your application. In this case, just choose the Pocket PC Emulator item and click Deploy (if you have a smart device available on your network, you can choose it instead). That starts the application in the emulator, as you can see in Figure 4.23.

And that's all it takes! Now you're programming for smart devices.

You can add controls to forms to interact with the user, but you can also use the events built into a form to interact with the user directly. Forms support a number of user interface events that you can use with the mouse and keyboard, and that discussion is coming up next. And because the Form class is based on the Control class, these events will also work with the controls we'll start working with tomorrow.

4

FIGURE 4.23

A smart device application.

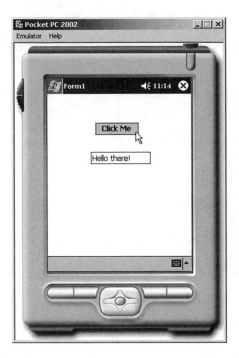

Handling Mouse Events

Besides the `Click` and `DoubleClick` events, you can handle several mouse events in forms and controls; here they are:

- `MouseDown`—Occurs when the mouse is over the form's client area or control and a button is pressed.
- `MouseEnter`—Occurs when the mouse enters the control or the form's client area.
- `MouseHover`—Occurs when the mouse hovers over the form's client area or control.
- `MouseLeave`—Occurs when the mouse leaves the form's client area or the control.
- `MouseMove`—Occurs when the mouse is moved over the form's client area or control.
- `MouseUp`—Occurs when the mouse is over the form's client area or control and a mouse button is released.
- `MouseWheel`—Occurs when the mouse wheel moves while the form or control has focus.

These mouse events occur in forms when the mouse is over the form's client area. In fact, if you put a control on a form and the mouse enters that control, you'll get a MouseLeave event in the form. Future mouse events will be targeted to the control until the mouse leaves the control again.

You use the MouseEventArgs object passed to mouse event handlers to find out more about a mouse event; here are the properties of this object (not all properties will be filled for all mouse events):

- Button—Specifies which mouse button was pressed (see the following list).
- Clicks—Indicates the number of times the mouse button was clicked.
- Delta—Specifies a signed number of *detents* the mouse wheel was rotated. A detent is the rotation of the mouse wheel one notch.
- X—Indicates the x coordinate of a mouse event.
- Y—Indicates the y coordinate of a mouse event.

You can determine which mouse button was involved with the Buttons property, which holds one of these values from the MouseButtons enumeration:

- MouseButtons.Left—The left mouse button
- MouseButtons.Middle—The middle mouse button
- MouseButtons.None—No mouse button
- MouseButtons.Right—The right mouse button
- MouseButtons.XButton1—The first XButton (Microsoft IntelliMouse Explorer only)
- MouseButtons.XButton2—The second XButton (Microsoft IntelliMouse Explorer only)

As we discussed earlier today, to add an event handler for any event—including mouse events—to a form, select the form, say Form1, and click the View Code button in the Solution Explorer. Select (Form1 Events) in the left drop-down list box of the code designer, and select the mouse event for which you want to add an event handler in the right drop-down list box. Visual Basic will add an event handler for that event automatically.

Listing 4.7 shows an example, the Mouser project in the code for this book, that looks at all mouse events in a form. (For those events that involve button presses, it checks only the left mouse button.) This application displays mouse events in a text box.

LISTING 4.7   Handling Mouse Events (Mouser project, Form1.vb)

```
Public Class Form1
    Inherits System.Windows.Forms.Form

' Windows Form Designer generated code

    Private Sub Form1_MouseEnter(ByVal sender As Object, _
        ByVal e As System.EventArgs) Handles MyBase.MouseEnter
        TextBox1.Text = "The mouse entered the client area."
    End Sub

    Private Sub Form1_MouseDown(ByVal sender As Object, _
    ByVal e As System.Windows.Forms.MouseEventArgs) _
    Handles MyBase.MouseDown
        If e.Button = MouseButtons.Left Then
            TextBox1.Text = "The left mouse button is down at (" & _
                CStr(e.X) & ", " & CStr(e.Y) & ")"
        End If
    End Sub

    Private Sub Form1_MouseHover(ByVal sender As Object, _
        ByVal e As System.EventArgs) Handles MyBase.MouseHover
        TextBox1.Text = "The mouse is hovering."
    End Sub

    Private Sub Form1_MouseMove(ByVal sender As Object, _
        ByVal e As System.Windows.Forms.MouseEventArgs) _
        Handles MyBase.MouseMove
        TextBox1.Text = "The mouse moved to: (" & CStr(e.X) & _
            ", " & CStr(e.Y) & ")"
    End Sub

    Private Sub Form1_MouseUp(ByVal sender As Object, _
        ByVal e As System.Windows.Forms.MouseEventArgs) _
        Handles MyBase.MouseUp
        If e.Button = MouseButtons.Left Then
            TextBox1.Text = "The left mouse button went up at (" & _
                CStr(e.X) & ", " & CStr(e.Y) & ")"
        End If
    End Sub

    Private Sub Form1_MouseWheel(ByVal sender As Object, _
        ByVal e As System.Windows.Forms.MouseEventArgs) _
        Handles MyBase.MouseWheel
        TextBox1.Text = "The mouse wheel rotated " & CStr(e.Delta) & " detents"
    End Sub

    Private Sub Form1_MouseLeave(ByVal sender As Object, _
    ByVal e As System.EventArgs) Handles MyBase.MouseLeave
        TextBox1.Text = "The mouse left the client area."
    End Sub
End Class
```

You can see the Mouser example at work in Figure 4.24, where it's reporting a
MouseDown event.

FIGURE 4.24

The Mouser
application.

Handling Keyboard Events

Besides working with the mouse, you can handle keyboard events in forms and controls
with these three events:

- KeyDown—Occurs when a key goes down.
- KeyPress—Occurs when a key is pressed.
- KeyUp—Occurs when a key is released.

In the KeyDown and KeyUp event handlers, you're passed an argument of type
KeyEventArgs containing data related to this event, with these properties:

- Alt—True if the Alt key was down.
- Control—True if the Ctrl key was down.
- Handled—Gets or sets whether the event was handled.
- KeyCode—Contains the keyboard code for a KeyDown or KeyUp event.
- KeyData—Contains the key data for a KeyDown or KeyUp event.
- KeyValue—Contains the keyboard value for a KeyDown or KeyUp event.
- Modifiers—Holds the modifier flags for a KeyDown or KeyUp event. This indicates
  which modifier keys (Ctrl, Shift, and/or Alt) were pressed. These values can be
  ORed together (using the Ctrl, Shift, and Alt properties is usually easier).
- Shift—True if the Shift key was down.

In KeyPress event handlers, you're passed an argument of type KeyPressEventArgs,
which supports the following properties:

4

- `Handled`—Gets or sets whether the `KeyPress` event was handled. If you set this value to `True`, Visual Basic will not handle this key; for example, to delete it, set `Handled` to `True` and do no further processing.
- `KeyChar`—Contains the character for the pressed key.

The `KeyDown` and `KeyUp` events are harder to work with than the `KeyPress` events. In `KeyDown` and `KeyUp`, the `keyCode` property holds character codes, which you can change to standard characters with the `Chr` function. You're responsible for checking the modifier keys here yourself, though, determining which modifier key—Ctrl, Shift, or Alt—was down when the key was pressed or released (the `keyCode` property corresponds to an uppercase character if you typed a letter). Here's an example showing how hard it is to work with these events. This code, from the Keyer example in the book's code, handles letters by first checking the key code to make sure a letter was typed (by checking `keyCode` against the enumeration values `Keys.A` to `Keys.Z`) and then by converting the letter to lowercase with the `Char.ToLower` method if the Shift key was not pressed:

```
Private Sub Form1_KeyDown(ByVal sender As Object, _
    ByVal e As System.Windows.Forms.KeyEventArgs) Handles MyBase.KeyDown
    If e.KeyCode >= Keys.A And e.KeyCode <= Keys.Z Then
        If e.Shift Then
            Label1.Text &= Chr(e.KeyCode)
        Else
            Label1.Text &= Char.ToLower(Chr(e.KeyCode))
        End If
    End If
End Sub
```

NEW TERM   You might also notice that this example displays the letters you type in a *label* control, which we'll work with tomorrow. The code uses a label because you can't give the focus to a label, which means the form has the focus instead, and so is the target of keystrokes. Like text boxes, labels have a `Text` property, but unlike text boxes, they don't have a border or white background by default. You'll learn more about labels tomorrow.

It's much easier to use the `KeyPress` event, which takes the data passed to the `KeyUp` and `KeyDown` events and processes that data so that you can work with characters where, for example, the Shift key has already been taken into account. That means to get the typed character—including both lowercase and uppercase letters—you just need to look at the `keyChar` property, as you see in Listing 4.8.

LISTING 4.8   Handling Mouse Events (Mouser project, Form1.vb)

```
Private Sub Form1_KeyPress(ByVal sender As Object, _
    ByVal e As System.Windows.Forms.KeyPressEventArgs) _
    Handles MyBase.KeyPress
    Label1.Text &= e.KeyChar
End Sub
```

You can see the Keyer example at work in Figure 4.25, where it's displaying text typed while the form has the focus, using form keystroke events.

FIGURE 4.25

The Keyer application.

Typing Keys in Other Programs

Here's something extraordinarily useful to know while we're discussing the keyboard: You can use Visual Basic to send keys to another program. When you send keys to other programs, you can use your Visual Basic application to control and automate those programs. For example, you might want to load several hundred spreadsheet files into a spreadsheet program and have that program print them out one by one—a prohibitive waste of time if done by hand.

You can use the System.Windows.Forms.SendKeys.Send method to send keystrokes to the program that currently has the focus (and note that using Alt+*key*, you can reach the menu items in that program). You can send a string of text and embed other keys, such as the Backspace key or Caps Lock key, in that text. For keys that do not correspond to simple text, you use the codes shown in Table 4.6.

TABLE 4.6   SendKeys Codes

Key	Code
Alt	%
Backspace	{BACKSPACE}, {BS}, or {BKSP}
Break	{BREAK}
Caps Lock	{CAPSLOCK}
Ctrl	^
Del or Delete	{DEL} or {DELETE}
Down Arrow	{DOWN}
End	{END}
Enter/Return	{ENTER} or ~
Esc	{ESC}
F1	{F1}
F10	{F10}
F11	{F11}
F12	{F12}
F13	{F13}
F14	{F14}
F15	{F15}
F16	{F16}
F2	{F2}
F3	{F3}
F4	{F4}
F5	{F5}
F6	{F6}
F7	{F7}
F8	{F8}
F9	{F9}
Help	{HELP}
Home	{HOME}
Ins or Insert	{INSERT} or {INS}
Left Arrow	{LEFT}
Num Lock	{NUMLOCK}
Page Down	{PGDN}

TABLE 4.6 continued

Key	Code
Page Up	{PGUP}
Print Screen	{PRTSC}
Right Arrow	{RIGHT}
Scroll Lock	{SCROLLLOCK}
Shift	+
Tab	{TAB}
Up Arrow	{UP}

Let's put SendKeys to work. This example, the SendKeys project in the book's code, will type the text "Visual Basic says Hello!" to Windows WordPad. To run this example, start the SendKeys application, start WordPad, and then click the Send Keys button in the SendKeys application. In Listing 4.9, the code uses the Visual Basic AppActivate function to give WordPad the focus (it does this by giving the focus to the application with the title bar text "Document - WordPad") and then types its text directly into WordPad.

LISTING 4.9 Sending Keys to WordPad (SendKeys project, Form1.vb)

```
Public Class Form1
    Inherits System.Windows.Forms.Form

'Windows Form Designer generated code

    Private Sub Button1_Click(ByVal sender As System.Object, _
        ByVal e As System.EventArgs) Handles Button1.Click
        AppActivate("Document - WordPad")
        System.Windows.Forms.SendKeys.Send("Visual Basic says Hello!")
    End Sub
End Class
```

Tip   Is there a way to start WordPad from your code if it's not already running? Yes, just call System.Diagnostics.Process.Start("WordPad").

You can see the result in Figure 4.26. Now you're able to send keystrokes to another program, controlling that program with a Visual Basic application.

4

FIGURE 4.26

*Typing in another
program.*

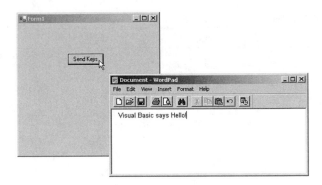

 Tip

Another handy function is the Beep function. Calling Beep() in your code
makes the computer beep. You can find many uses for Beep, from indicating
an error to the user to helping debug an application where the user interface isn't being displayed (if you place Beep() in your code at a specific
point and you hear a beep, you know that code is being run).

Summary

We've come far today, working with Windows forms and applications. We got our start
working with Windows applications in depth, seeing how to create them and dissecting
their code. And we got an introduction to the Form class and its members.

We also looked at how to work with the MsgBox, MessageBox.Show, and InputBox methods as easy techniques to display dialogs. The MsgBox and MessageBox.Show methods
display message boxes, and the InputBox method displays a functional, if ugly, box that
can take typed input from the user.

From that point, we started working with multiple-form applications, seeing how to communicate between forms, show and hide forms, and move and resize them as well. We
also looked at multiple-document interface (MDI) applications, seeing how to create MDI
windows and child windows, as well as how to arrange the child windows in a cascade.

We saw how to create true dialogs, customizing them with nonresizable borders, adding
OK and Cancel buttons, and launching them with the ShowDialog method. And we were
introduced to various other types of forms, including owned forms, as well as always-on-
top forms. We also looked at two topics new in Visual Basic .NET 2003—nonrectangular
windows and smart device applications. In particular, we created an application with an
elliptical window and a smart device application that ran in a Pocket PC emulator.

We ended today's work by looking at handling mouse and keyboard events, seeing how to handle both in forms. And we also saw how to send keystrokes to other programs, automating those programs under the control of a Visual Basic application.

Tomorrow, we're going to continue our work with Windows applications as we start adding controls to those applications—text boxes, buttons, labels, check boxes, and radio buttons—and working with those controls in depth.

Q&A

Q How can I pass a form to a procedure?

A You can treat a form like any other object in this case. You can pass this Sub procedure to a form and it will turn the form green:

```
Sub ColorFormGreen(ByVal frmForm As Form)
    frmForm.BackColor = System.Drawing.Color.Green
End Sub
```

Q What happened to the control arrays that were supported in earlier versions of Visual Basic?

A Control arrays, which enabled you to put selected controls into an array and access them by index number, are no longer supported. But you can use the Controls collection, which holds all the controls in a form, selecting the type of control you want like this:

```
If TypeOf Controls(intLoopIndex) Is Button Then...
```

Workshop

This workshop tests whether you understand the concepts you saw today. It's a good idea to make sure you can answer these questions before pressing on to tomorrow's work.

Quiz

1. What does the Me keyword stand for?

2. If you want to display a form in the center of the screen when it first appears, what value would you assign the form's StartPosition property?

3. Give two ways to move a form at runtime.

4. How do you make a form appear always on top of others?

5. List the three steps you need to make a form nonrectangular.

4

Quiz Answers

1. The `Me` keyword stands for the present object whose code is being executed—that is, the default object.

2. You should assign it the value `FormStartPosition.CenterScreen`.

3. You can use the `SetBounds` method or assign a new `Point` object to the form's `Location` property.

4. You can set the form's `TopMost` property to `True`.

5. 1) Set the form's `FormBorderStyle` property to `None`. 2) Set the form's `BackgroundImage` property to the image you want to use for the new form shape. 3) Set the `TransparencyKey` property to the background color of the image.

Exercises

1. Create a new multiple-form application that displays two forms when it starts, each with a text box. Add code to each text box's `TextChanged` event (this is the default event for text boxes, which occurs when the text in the text box changes; just double-click a text box to bring this event handler up in a code designer) so that when you change the text in one text box, the new text also appears automatically in the text box in the other form, keeping the two text boxes in the two different forms synchronized.

2. Write a new MDI application that displays *two* kinds of MDI child windows—one in which a multiline text box covers the client area and one in which a button that beeps when you click it covers the client area.

DAY 5

Windows Forms: Working with Text Boxes, Buttons, Labels, Check Boxes, and Radio Buttons

Today, we're going to start working in depth with the controls that can appear in Windows forms. Visual Basic supports a rich variety of such controls, and we've already been using two of them—buttons and text boxes. Today, we'll get the full story on those controls, as well as handle other varieties of text-displaying and button controls, such as rich text boxes, labels, check boxes, and so on. Here are today's topics:

- Text boxes
- Rich text boxes
- Labels
- Link labels
- Buttons

- Check boxes
- Radio buttons
- Panels
- Group boxes

All the Windows form controls we see in this and the next few days are based on the `Control` class (as are forms, which we saw yesterday). Much of the functionality of controls and forms comes from this class, which makes it the logical place to start our work with Windows controls.

Overview of the `Control` Class

The `Control` class—technically, the `System.Windows.Forms.Control` class—is the base class for all Windows forms controls. Here is the class hierarchy for this class, which is based on the `System.ComponentModel.Component` class, which is based on `System.MarshalByRefObject`, and so on:

```
System.Object
    System.MarshalByRefObject
        System.ComponentModel.Component
            System.Windows.Forms.Control
```

Windows controls are based on the `Control` class, and they inherit many properties, methods, and events from that class. You can find the significant public properties of the `Control` class in Table 5.1, the significant methods in Table 5.2, and the significant events in Table 5.3. The controls we'll be seeing in the coming days are based on the `Control` class, so when we review the significant properties, methods, and events of those controls, we'll omit those that come from the `Control` class because you can see them here.

TABLE 5.1   Significant Public Properties of `Control` Objects

Property	Means
AllowDrop	Returns or sets whether the control will accept data dropped onto it.
Anchor	Returns or sets which edge(s) of the control is(are) anchored.
BackColor	Returns or sets the control's background color.
BackgroundImage	Returns or sets the control's background image.
Bottom	Gets the distance between the bottom of the control and the bottom of its container (in pixels).
Bounds	Returns or sets the control's bounding rectangle.
CanFocus	Returns whether the control can receive the focus.

TABLE 5.1   continued

Property	Means
CanSelect	Returns whether the control can be selected.
Capture	Returns or sets whether the control has captured the mouse for mouse events outside its area.
ContainsFocus	Returns whether the control has the focus.
ContextMenu	Returns or sets the control's shortcut menu.
Controls	Returns or sets the collection of controls in this control.
Cursor	Returns or sets the cursor used when the user moves the mouse over this control.
DataBindings	Gets the control's data bindings.
Dock	Returns or sets the edge of the control's parent that a control is docked to.
Enabled	Returns or sets whether the control is enabled.
Focused	Returns whether the control has the focus.
Font	Returns or sets the font in the control.
ForeColor	Returns or sets the foreground color of the control.
HasChildren	Returns whether the control has child controls.
Height	Returns or sets the control's height.
Left	Returns or sets the x coordinate of the control's left edge (in pixels).
Location	Returns or sets the coordinates of the upper-left corner of the control with respect to the upper-left corner of its container (using a Point object).
Name	Returns or sets the control's name.
Parent	Returns or sets the control's parent container.
Right	Returns the distance between the right edge of the control and the left edge of its container (in pixels).
Size	Returns or sets the height and width of the control (in pixels).
TabIndex	Returns or sets the tab order of this control.
TabStop	Returns or sets whether the user can tab to this control by pressing the Tab key.
Tag	Returns or sets data about the control.
Text	Returns or sets the text in this control.
Top	Returns or sets the top coordinate of the control (in pixels).
Visible	Returns or sets whether the control is visible.
Width	Returns or sets the width of the control (in pixels).

5

TABLE 5.2   Significant Public Methods of `Control` Objects

Method	Means
BringToFront	Brings the control to the front of other controls that may be stacked on top of it.
Contains	Gets whether a particular control is a child of this control.
CreateGraphics	Creates a `Graphics` object for this control, used to draw in the control.
DoDragDrop	Starts a drag-and-drop operation.
FindForm	Returns the control's form.
Focus	Gives the focus to the control.
GetChildAtPoint	Gets the child control, if one exists, at the specified coordinates.
GetNextControl	Returns the next control in the tab order.
GetType	Gets the type of this control.
Hide	Hides the control.
Invalidate	Invalidates the control and sends a message to the control to make it redraw itself.
PointToClient	Translates the given screen point to client coordinates.
PointToScreen	Translates the given point in client coordinates to screen coordinates.
RectangleToClient	Translates the given screen rectangle to client coordinates.
RectangleToScreen	Translates the given client rectangle to screen coordinates.
Refresh	Forces the control to invalidate itself (actually its client area) and redraw itself.
Select	Activates this control, giving it the focus.
SendToBack	Sends the control to the back of the stacking order in case other controls are stacked on top of it.
SetBounds	Sets the bounds (location and size) of the control.
Show	Displays the control and sets its `Visible` property to `True`.
ToString	Returns a string that represents the current control (usually includes the data in the control).
Update	Forces the control to redraw any invalid areas.

TABLE 5.3   Significant Public Events of `Control` Objects

Event	Means
BackColorChanged	Occurs when the `BackColor` property changes.
BackgroundImageChanged	Occurs when the `BackgroundImage` property changes.
Click	Occurs when the control is clicked.
ControlAdded	Occurs when a new control is added.

TABLE 5.3   continued

Event	Means
ControlRemoved	Occurs when a control is removed.
CursorChanged	Occurs when the Cursor property value changes.
DoubleClick	Occurs when the control is double-clicked.
DragDrop	Occurs when a drag-and-drop operation finishes.
DragEnter	Occurs when an object is dragged into the control.
DragLeave	Occurs when an object is dragged out of the control.
DragOver	Occurs when an object is dragged over the control.
EnabledChanged	Occurs when the Enabled property value changes.
Enter	Occurs when the control is entered.
FontChanged	Occurs when the Font property changes.
ForeColorChanged	Occurs when the ForeColor property changes.
GotFocus	Occurs when the control receives focus.
Invalidated	Occurs when a control's display is updated.
KeyDown	Occurs when a key is pressed down while the control has focus.
KeyPress	Occurs when a key is pressed while the control has focus.
KeyUp	Occurs when a key is released while the control has focus.
Leave	Occurs when the control is left.
LocationChanged	Occurs when the Location property changes.
LostFocus	Occurs when the control loses the focus.
MouseDown	Occurs when the mouse is over the control and a mouse button is pressed.
MouseEnter	Occurs when the mouse enters the control.
MouseHover	Occurs when the mouse hovers over the control.
MouseLeave	Occurs when the mouse leaves the control.
MouseMove	Occurs when the mouse is moved over the control.
MouseUp	Occurs when the mouse is over the control and a mouse button is released.
MouseWheel	Occurs when the mouse wheel moves while the control has focus.
Move	Occurs when the control is moved.
Paint	Occurs when the control is redrawn.
ParentChanged	Occurs when the Parent property changes.
Resize	Occurs when the control is resized.
TextChanged	Occurs when the text in the control is changed.
VisibleChanged	Occurs when the Visible property changes.

5

It's worth taking a look through Tables 5.1, 5.2, and 5.3 to get an overview of what important properties, methods, and events are in the `Control` class. For example, you can use the `Font` property to set the font in a control (which we'll do later today), the `CreateGraphics` method enables you to create a `Graphics` object that you can use to draw your own figures in any control (the `Graphics` object is coming up in Day 10, "Graphics and File Handling"), and when a control is hidden or shown, a `VisibleChanged` event occurs, allowing you to keep track of what's going on.

We've already worked with controls in general—seeing how to use the toolbox to add controls to a form at design time and even seeing how to add controls to a form at run-time (see "Adding Controls at Runtime" in Day 4, "Creating Windows Forms"). Now it's time to get more specific, covering in depth the most powerful controls Visual Basic offers us. And we'll start with one we've already been using in an informal way: text boxes.

Using Text Boxes

Just about every Windows user knows about text boxes—those boxes into which you can type. Programs use them to read and display text data. From a programmer's point of view, you can assign text to a text box or read the text already in a text box with the `Text` property:

```
strText = TextBox1.Text
TextBox1.Text = srtText
```

Text boxes are powerful in Visual Basic. Besides the traditional one-line text boxes, you can create multiline text boxes, text boxes with scrollbars, read-only text boxes, password text boxes, and more. The `System.Windows.Forms.TextBox` class, which you can refer to in your code simply as the `TextBox` class, is based on the `TextBoxBase` class, which is based on the `Control` class:

```
System.Object
    System.MarshalByRefObject
        System.ComponentModel.Component
            System.Windows.Forms.Control
                System.Windows.Forms.TextBoxBase
                    System.Windows.Forms.TextBox
```

By default, you can enter up to 2,048 characters in a text box. If you set the `MultiLine` property to `True` to make the text box hold multiple lines of text, a text box can store up to 32KB of text. And you can limit the text in a `TextBox` control by setting the `MaxLength` property to a specific number of characters.

You can see the significant properties, methods, and events of the TextBox class in Tables 5.4, 5.5, and 5.6. (These tables do not include the significant properties, methods, and events this class inherits from the Control class. You'll find them in Tables 5.1, 5.2, and 5.3. In particular, note that the main event for text boxes, TextChanged, which occurs when the text in a text box changes, appears in Table 5.3.)

TABLE 5.4   Significant Public Properties of TextBox Objects

Property	Means
AutoSize	Returns or sets whether the height of the text box automatically changes to match the font.
BackColor	Returns or sets the background color of the text box.
BorderStyle	Returns or sets the border style of the text box.
CanUndo	Returns whether the user can undo a previous operation.
ForeColor	Returns or sets the foreground (text) color.
HideSelection	Returns or sets whether selected text remains highlighted when the text box loses the focus.
Lines	Returns or sets an array of strings that contains the text in a text box.
MaxLength	Returns or sets the maximum number of characters the user can enter.
Multiline	Returns or sets whether the text box can hold multiple lines of text (the default is False). It must be set to True if you want to display vertical scrollbars.
PasswordChar	Returns or sets the character used to mask characters of a password (single-line text boxes only).
ReadOnly	Returns or sets whether the text is read-only.
ScrollBars	Returns or sets which scrollbars should appear (multiline text boxes only).
SelectedText	Returns or sets the currently selected text in the control.
SelectionLength	Returns or sets the number of characters in the currently selected text.
SelectionStart	Returns or sets the starting point of text selected in the text box.
Text	Returns or sets the text in the text box.
TextAlign	Returns or sets text alignment in a text box.
TextLength	Gets the length of text in the text box.
WordWrap	Indicates whether a multiline text box control automatically wraps words from line to line. It must be set to False if you want to display horizontal scrollbars.

5

TABLE 5.5   Significant Public Methods of `TextBox` Objects

Methods	Means
AppendText	Appends text to the text currently in the text box.
Clear	Clears the text from the text box (setting it to an empty string, " ").
ClearUndo	Clears all data about the most recent text box operation.
Copy	Copies the selected text to the clipboard.
Cut	Deletes the selected text in the text box and places it in the clipboard.
Paste	Replaces the selected text in the text box with the text in the clipboard.
Select	Selects text in the text box.
SelectAll	Selects all the text in the text box.
Undo	Undoes the last operation in the text box.

TABLE 5.6   Significant Public Events of `TextBox` Objects

Event	Means
AutoSizeChanged	Occurs when the `AutoSize` property is changed.
ReadOnlyChanged	Occurs when the `ReadOnly` property is changed.

Taking a look through Tables 5.4, 5.5, and 5.6 is worthwhile. For example, note the Cut, Copy, and `Paste` methods, which allow you to send text to the clipboard and read text back from the clipboard, or the Undo method, which allows you to undo the most recent editing operation.

We'll look at a few specific tasks with text boxes next.

Aligning Text

Aligning text in a text box is easy enough with the `TextAlign` property, which you can set to these members of the `HorizontalAlignment` enumeration: `HorizontalAlignment.` `Left`, `HorizontalAlignment.Center`, and `HorizontalAlignment.Right`. You can see these possible options at work in Figure 5.1.

FIGURE 5.1

Aligning text in a text box.

Creating Read-Only Text Boxes

Say that you're using a text box to display the result of some long calculation. In that case, you might not want the user to change the text that you're displaying. To make sure that doesn't happen, you can create a read-only text box. You can do this in a few different ways:

- Set the text box's ReadOnly property to True (the default is False). This locks the text box so that the user can't enter any text, but you can still change the text in code.

- Disable a text box by setting the Enabled property to False (the default is True). This grays out the text box and does not allow the user to enter any text. This option is best saved for those cases in which you want to make the control appear inaccessible.

- Use a label (coming up later today) instead of a text box because labels are read-only by default. Just use the Text property of the label as you would in a text box.

 Tip

> To make a label look like a text box, set its BorderStyle property to Fixed3D and its BackColor property to System.Drawing.Color.White. At design time, you can set the BackColor property to white using the Web tab of the pop-up dialog that appears when you select the BackColor property in the Properties window, or the Window color using the System tab.

Creating Multiline Text Boxes

5

By default, text boxes display only a single line of text, but you can change that with the MultiLine property. Setting this property to True enables the text box to accept multiple lines of text. Just size the text box as you want it, vertically as well as horizontally, to allow multiple lines of text. In fact, multiline text boxes even wrap words from one line to the next automatically like a word processor (you can turn off word wrap by setting the WordWrap property to False). Now the user can enter multiple lines of text in your text box.

You can have a multiline (but not a single-line) text box display scrollbars by using the ScrollBars property. You can add scrollbars to a text box in four ways, using members of the ScrollBars enumeration; here are the possible values:

- ScrollBars.None—No scrollbars (the default)
- ScrollBars.Horizontal—Horizontal scrollbars

- `ScrollBars.Vertical`—Vertical scrollbars
- `ScrollBars.Both`—Both horizontal and vertical scrollbars

You can see a multiline text box in Figure 5.2, complete with a vertical scrollbar. This is the TextBoxes example in the code for this book. For a multiline text box to show a horizontal scrollbar, the `WordWrap` property must be set to `False` (the default is `True`).

FIGURE 5.2

A multiline text box.

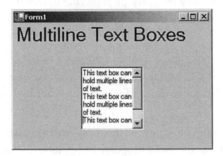

 Note   For scrollbars to appear at all, the text box's `MultiLine` property must be True.

Creating Password Controls

You can make a normal single-line text box into a password control that masks the password the user types by using the `PasswordChar` property. You assign a character to this property, usually an asterisk (*), that the control will use to display each character the user types instead of the character itself. You can see an example, the Passwords project from the book's code, in Figure 5.3.

FIGURE 5.3

Using a password control.

This example, shown in Listing 5.1, copies the masked text in the password control and displays it in a normal text box in the way you would expect when you click the Read Text button.

LISTING 5.1   Reading Text from a Password Control (Passwords project, Form1.vb)

```
Private Sub Button1_Click(ByVal sender As System.Object, _
    ByVal e As System.EventArgs) Handles Button1.Click
    TextBox2.Text = TextBox1.Text
End Sub
```

 Tip   You may wonder whether someone can copy the text in a password control and paste it somewhere else to read that text directly. The answer is no. Copying to the clipboard is disabled if you are using a password control.

Selecting Text

You can even make text boxes into mini–word processors (even more so if you use rich text boxes, coming up next), letting the user select and copy text. You can copy, cut, and paste text using the clipboard with the Copy, Cut, and Paste methods. The SelectingText example in the code for the book, which you can see in Listing 5.2 and in use in Figure 5.4, allows you to copy text and paste it between text boxes with the click of a button.

LISTING 5.2   Copying Text from a Text Box (SelectingText project, Form1.vb)

```
Private Sub Button1_Click(ByVal sender As System.Object, _
    ByVal e As System.EventArgs) Handles Button1.Click
    TextBox1.Copy()
    TextBox2.Paste()
End Sub
```

You can also select text and work with it in code, using these three properties:

- SelectionLength—Returns or sets the number of characters that are selected.
- SelectionStart—Returns or sets the starting point of the selected text. Also gives you the position of the insertion point if no text is selected.
- SelectedText—Returns or sets the string containing the currently selected text. If no characters are selected, it holds an empty string (" ").

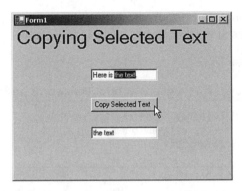

Here's how you might select all the text in a text box and replace it with `"Hello there!"` (note the use of the `Len` function to get the length of the text in the text box):

```
Private Sub Button1_Click(ByVal sender As System.Object, _
    ByVal e As System.EventArgs) Handles Button1.Click
    TextBox1.SelectionStart = 0
    TextBox1.SelectionLength = Len(TextBox1.Text)
    TextBox1.SelectedText = "Hello there!"
End Sub
```

Using Rich Text Boxes

Want a complete word processor built into your application? Use a rich text box control. Rich text boxes can use various fonts and formatted text (including italic, bold, and more), and you can save that text in rich text format (RTF) files and read in RTF files. Commercial word processors such as Microsoft Word can read RTF files, allowing you to interface to those word processors.

In Visual Basic, you use rich text boxes to support rich text; they're just like text boxes but with added power. Here's the class hierarchy for the `RichTextBox` class:

```
System.Object
    System.MarshalByRefObject
        System.ComponentModel.Component
            System.Windows.Forms.Control
                System.Windows.Forms.TextBoxBase
                    System.Windows.Forms.RichTextBox
```

Many Visual Basic programmers know about the rich text control, but few programmers actually know how to work with the rich text in it. Although you access text in a standard text box with the `Text` property, two such properties are used in rich text boxes: `Text` and `Rtf`. The `Text` property will return unformatted text, just as if you were working with a standard text box, and the Rtf property will return the text as formatted rich text, including the RTF codes that hold the RTF formatting. We'll also see how to format individual words in a rich text control today.

For reference, Tables 5.7, 5.8, and 5.9 show the significant properties, methods, and events of the RichTextBox class. (These tables do not include the significant properties, methods, and events this class inherits from the Control class; you can find them in Tables 5.1, 5.2, and 5.3.)

TABLE 5.7   Significant Public Properties of RichTextBox Objects

Property	Means
AutoSize	Returns or sets whether the rich text box automatically adjusts its size when the font changes.
BorderStyle	Returns or sets the border style of the rich text box.
BulletIndent	Returns or sets the indentation used in the rich text box when you display bullets in the text.
CanRedo	True if the previously undone action in a rich text box can be re-applied.
CanUndo	True if the previous action in a rich text box can be undone.
DetectUrls	Returns or sets whether the rich text box underlines and supports URLs.
HideSelection	Returns or sets whether the selected text should stay highlighted when the control loses the focus.
Lines	Returns or sets an array of the lines of text in a rich text box.
MaxLength	Returns or sets the maximum number of characters the rich text box can hold.
Multiline	Returns or sets whether this is a multiline rich text box, capable of holding multiple lines of text.
ReadOnly	Returns or sets whether text in the text box is read-only.
RightMargin	Returns or sets the right margin in a rich text box.
Rtf	Returns or sets the text of the RichTextBox control, including all Rich Text Format (RTF) codes.
ScrollBars	Returns or sets the scrollbars to display in the rich text box.
SelectedRtf	Returns or sets the currently selected Rich Text Format (RTF) formatted text in the control.
SelectedText	Returns or sets the selected text in the rich text box.
SelectionAlignment	Returns or sets the alignment for the current selection.
SelectionBullet	Returns or sets the bullet style applied to the current selection.

5

TABLE 5.7   continued

Property	Means
SelectionCharOffset	Returns or sets if text in the rich text box is a superscript or a subscript.
SelectionColor	Returns or sets the text color of the current text selection.
SelectionFont	Returns or sets the font of the current text selection.
SelectionHangingIndent	Returns or sets the distance (in pixels) between the left edge of the first line of text in the selected paragraph and the left edge of the following lines in the paragraph.
SelectionIndent	Returns or sets the indentation (in pixels) of the current text selection.
SelectionLength	Returns or sets the number of characters selected.
SelectionRightIndent	Returns the distance (in pixels) between the right edge of the rich text box and the right edge of the selected text.
SelectionStart	Returns or sets the starting point of text selected in the rich text box, measured in characters (0-based).
Text	Returns or sets the current text in the text box; treats text as unformatted text.
TextLength	Gets the length of text in the rich text box.
WordWrap	Indicates whether a multiline rich text box automatically wraps words.
ZoomFactor	Returns or sets the current zoom level of the rich text box.

TABLE 5.8   Significant Public Methods of RichTextBox Objects

Method	Means
AppendText	Appends the specified text to the current text in a rich text box.
CanPaste	True if you can paste text from the clipboard.
Clear	Deletes all text from the text box control.
ClearUndo	Indicates that the most recent operation cannot be undone.
Copy	Copies the current selection in the rich text box to the clipboard.
Cut	Deletes and places the current selection in the text box in the clipboard.
Find	Searches for text in a rich text box.
LoadFile	Loads the contents of a file into the rich text box.
Paste	Pastes the text contents of the clipboard into the control.
Redo	Reapplies the last operation that was undone.
SaveFile	Saves the contents of a rich text box to a file.
Select	Selects text in the rich text box.
SelectAll	Selects all text in the rich text box.
Undo	Undoes the last edit operation in the rich text box.

TABLE 5.9   Significant Public Events of `RichTextBox` Objects

Event	Means
LinkClicked	Occurs when the user clicks a link in a rich text box.
ReadOnlyChanged	Occurs when the ReadOnly property is changed.
SelectionChanged	Occurs when the text selection is changed.
VScroll	Occurs when the user clicks the vertical scrollbar.

If you look through Tables 5.7, 5.8, and 5.9, you'll see an amazing amount of programming power packed into this single control. For example, note the `LoadFile` and `SaveFile` methods, which enable you to load and save files, or the `ZoomFactor` property, which allows you to zoom in and out, or the `Find` method, which enables you to find text in the control. Truly, you have a whole word processor in a single control here.

Tip

Rich text boxes can support hyperlinks if you set the `DetectUrls` property to `True` and write code to handle the `LinkClicked` event.

Formatting Rich Text

You can customize the font displayed in a rich text box at design time by clicking the `Font` property in the Properties window, opening the Font dialog you see in Figure 5.5.

FIGURE 5.5

The Font dialog.

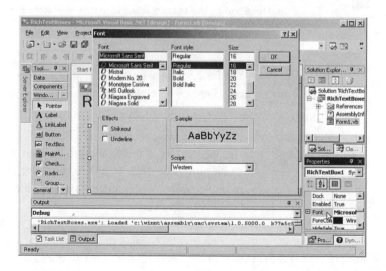

5

For example, using the Font dialog, you can make the text in a rich text control larger, as you see in Figure 5.6, which is the RichTextBoxes project in the code for this book.

FIGURE 5.6

A rich text box.

The Font dialog is fine if you want to format all the text in a rich text box at once at design time, but what if you want to format individual text or words? You must first select the text you want to format, which you can let the user do, or you can do it in code. For example, say you want to add bold to the word *bold* in Figure 5.6, underline to the word *underlined*, and so on, using code. You can search for those words with the Find method, which will select them (you can determine what's been selected by using the SelectionStart, SelectionLength, SelectedRtf, and SelectedText properties). If Find doesn't find a match, it will return a value of –1.

Tip

You can also use the Select method to select text, passing it the start and end location of the text to select (the first character is at location 0, the next at location 1, and so on).

After you select the text to format, you can change that text's font by assigning a new Visual Basic Font object to the rich text box's SelectionFont property.

Let's see how this works, adding code to the Format Text button you see in Figure 5.6. The rich text box you see in the figure is named RichTextBox1, and its font is held in the RichTextBox1.Font property. To add underlining to the font, you can create a new Font object, passing the current font and a new style to the Font class's constructor. The possible styles to use are in the FontStyle enumeration, and here are the possible values: FontStyle.Bold, FontStyle.Italic, FontStyle.Regular, FontStyle.Strikeout, and FontStyle.Underline. This means that to create a new Font object using the same font currently in the rich text box—only underlined—you can assign Font(RichTextBox1.Font, FontStyle.Underline) to the RichTextBox1.Font property. Listing 5.3 shows what all this looks like in code, in the RichTextBoxes example in the book's code.

LISTING 5.3   Formatting Text in a Rich Text Box (RichTextBoxes project, Form1.vb)

```
Private Sub Button1_Click(ByVal sender As System.Object, _
    ByVal e As System.EventArgs) Handles Button1.Click

    RichTextBox1.Find("bold")
    Dim fntBold As New Font(RichTextBox1.Font, FontStyle.Bold)
    RichTextBox1.SelectionFont = fntBold

    RichTextBox1.Find("italic")
    Dim fntItalic As New Font(RichTextBox1.Font, FontStyle.Italic)
    RichTextBox1.SelectionFont = fntItalic

    RichTextBox1.Find("strikeout")
    Dim fntStrikeout As New Font(RichTextBox1.Font, FontStyle.Strikeout)
    RichTextBox1.SelectionFont = fntStrikeout

    RichTextBox1.Find("underlined")
    Dim fntUnderline As New Font(RichTextBox1.Font, FontStyle.Underline)
    RichTextBox1.SelectionFont = fntUnderline
End Sub
```

You can see the result in Figure 5.7, where the individual words are formatted as we want them.

FIGURE 5.7

Formatting text in a rich text box.

Note that Find(*String*) returns only the first match. How can you find others? You can call Find with a different argument list to start searching at any point in the text, like

5

this: Find(*String*, *Start*, *Options*). Here, *String* is the string to search for, *Start* is the 0-based starting character location in the rich text box's text, and the *Options* argument is a value from the RichTextBoxFinds enumeration:

- RichTextBoxFinds.MatchCase—Makes the search case sensitive.
- RichTextBoxFinds.NoHighlight—Makes sure the match is not highlighted.
- RichTextBoxFinds.None—Searches for matches anywhere, not just whole-word matches.
- RichTextBoxFinds.Reverse—Starts at the end of the text and searches toward the beginning of the document.
- RichTextBoxFinds.WholeWord—Finds only matches that are whole words.

Saving and Loading RTF Files

You use the SaveFile method to save the text in a rich text box to disk and the LoadFile method to read it back. For example, we might add a new button, Save Text, to the RichTextBoxes example; clicking that button will save the text in the file text.rtf. (Unless you specify a path for this file, such as C:\text\text.rtf, the file will be saved in the same directory as the file RichTextBoxes.exe—that's the project's bin directory here.)

```
Private Sub Button2_Click(ByVal sender As System.Object, _
    ByVal e As System.EventArgs) Handles Button2.Click
    RichTextBox1.SaveFile("text.rtf")
End Sub
```

Now you can click the Save Text button to save the text in a rich text box control, as you see in Figure 5.8.

FIGURE 5.8

Saving an RTF file.

RTF-aware programs, such as Windows WordPad, can read the new text.rtf file, complete with formatting, as you see in Figure 5.9.

FIGURE 5.9

A new RTF file in WordPad.

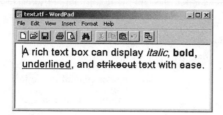

To load the file back into the rich text box, you use code like this:

```
RichTextBox1.LoadFile("text.rtf").
```

Using Labels

Like text boxes, labels can display text. Unlike text boxes, labels don't allow the user to edit that text directly. And by default, labels just present text in your applications without a border and using the default background color of forms. Here's the class hierarchy for the System.Windows.Forms.Label class:

```
System.Object
    System.MarshalByRefObject
        System.ComponentModel.Component
            System.Windows.Forms.Control
                System.Windows.Forms.Label
```

A label's text is stored in the Text property, and you can align text in a label with the TextAlign property. Labels can display images with the Image property and align that image with the ImageAlign property.

Because you can change the text in a label in code, but the user can't touch that text directly, labels are often used to display read-only text. For example, if you've written a calculator application, you might want to use a label to display numeric results. As we've seen, you can also make a label look just like a read-only text box, setting its BorderStyle property to Fixed3D and its background to white.

You can see the significant public properties of labels in Table 5.10. (This table does not include the significant properties, methods, and events this class inherits from the Control class; you can find them in Tables 5.1, 5.2, and 5.3.)

5

TABLE 5.10   Significant Public Properties of Label Objects

Property	Means
AutoSize	Returns or sets whether the label will automatically resize itself so as to display all its contents.
BorderStyle	Returns or sets the label's border style.
FlatStyle	Returns or sets whether the label looks flat.
Image	Returns or sets whether the image is displayed in the label.
ImageAlign	Returns or sets the alignment of an image in the label.
TextAlign	Returns or sets the alignment of the label's text.
UseMnemonic	Returns or sets whether the label makes the character following the ampersand character (&) in the Text property into an access character.

Aligning Text

You can align text in labels using the label's TextAlign property at both design time and runtime. This property takes values from the ContentAlignment enumeration; the members of that enumeration are as follows:

- ContentAlignment.BottomCenter — Vertically aligned at the bottom, horizontally aligned to the center.
- ContentAlignment.BottomLeft — Vertically aligned at the bottom, horizontally aligned to the left.
- ContentAlignment.BottomRight — Vertically aligned at the bottom, horizontally aligned to the right.
- ContentAlignment.MiddleCenter — Vertically aligned in the middle, horizontally aligned to the center.
- ContentAlignment.MiddleLeft — Vertically aligned in the middle, horizontally aligned to the left.
- ContentAlignment.MiddleRight — Vertically aligned in the middle, horizontally aligned to the right.
- ContentAlignment.TopCenter — Vertically aligned at the top, horizontally aligned to the center.
- ContentAlignment.TopLeft — Vertically aligned at the top, horizontally aligned to the left.
- ContentAlignment.TopRight — Vertically aligned at the top, horizontally aligned to the right.

You can see the various options in the Labels sample project in the code for this book, which you see at work in Figure 5.10. (To make the text alignment visible, these labels have had their `BorderStyle` property set to `BorderStyle.FixedSingle`.)

FIGURE 5.10

Label text alignment.

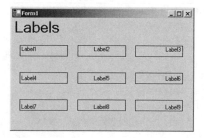

Using Labels to Support Access Keys

Labels do not have a `TabStop` property and cannot accept the focus. But they do have a `TabIndex` property, which adds them to the tab order. The reason is that you can use labels to support mnemonic characters, which are single characters accessed by pressing Alt and that character, such as Alt+X. (You make a character a mnemonic character by prefacing it with the & character in the `Text` property like this: `E&xit`.) When the user presses Alt and the mnemonic character, the focus goes not to the label, but to the control in the tab order after the label—that is, the control that the label labels. That's useful if that control doesn't have a caption (most don't), but you want to give it an access character.

To set up an access character for a control, make sure the label is just before the control you want to add the access character to in the tab order, set the label's `UseMnemonic` property to `True`, and place an ampersand (&) character right before the access character in the label's `Text` property like `E&xit`, which makes the access character for the next control Alt+X.

> **Tip**
>
> When using labels to label other controls, you might not want the label to be aligned along the default dotted grid in a form; you might want to place the label along the control's top edge, for example. To let you place a label (or any control) wherever you want, turn off the default alignment to the grid by setting the form's `SnapToGrid` property to `False`.

Using Link Labels

Link labels are much like labels in appearance, but they also enable you to support hyperlinks, both to other forms and to the Web. In fact, because the hyperlinks are supported in code, you can add any code you want to them. Here's the class hierarchy for link labels:

```
System.Object
    System.MarshalByRefObject
        System.ComponentModel.Component
            System.Windows.Forms.Control
                System.Windows.Forms.Label
                    System.Windows.Forms.LinkLabel
```

Link labels can function as labels, displaying simple text just like any other label. To support hyperlinks, several properties have been added to this control. To set the color of a link, you use the LinkColor property; to set the color of a link after it has been clicked, use VisitedLinkColor; and to set the color of a link while it's clicked, use the ActiveColorLink property. The LinkArea property sets the text in the link that makes up the actual link the user can click. When the link is clicked, a LinkClicked event occurs. You can set the behavior of a link with the LinkBehavior property, which takes these properties from the LinkBehavior enumeration:

- LinkBehavior.AlwaysUnderline—The link is always displayed as underlined text.
- LinkBehavior.HoverUnderline—The link displays underlined text only when the mouse hovers over the link.
- LinkBehavior.NeverUnderline—The link is never underlined. (You can still distinguish the link from other text using the LinkColor property.)
- LinkBehavior.SystemDefault—Makes the behavior of this setting dependent on the options the user sets in the Internet Options dialog of the Control Panel or Internet Explorer.

You can see the significant properties and events of link labels in Tables 5.11 and 5.12. (These tables do not include all the significant properties, methods, and events this class inherits from the Control class; you can find them in Tables 5.1, 5.2, and 5.3. For the significant properties it inherits from the Label class, see Table 5.10.)

TABLE 5.11 Significant Public Properties of LinkLabel Objects

Property	Means
ActiveLinkColor	Returns or sets the color for an active link.
DisabledLinkColor	Returns or sets the color for a disabled link.
LinkArea	Returns or sets the range in the text to treat as a link.

TABLE 5.11   continued

Property	Means
LinkBehavior	Returns or sets a value that represents the behavior of a link.
LinkColor	Returns or sets the color for a normal link.
Links	Gets the collection of links in the LinkLabel control.
LinkVisited	Returns or sets whether a link should be displayed as though it had been visited.
VisitedLinkColor	Returns or sets the color used for links that that have been visited.

TABLE 5.12   Significant Public Event of LinkLabel Objects

Event	Means
LinkClicked	Occurs when a link is clicked inside the link label.

In a link label, each hyperlink is an object of the LinkLabel.Link class and is stored in a collection called Links. To create hyperlinks in a link label, you can use the Add method of the Links collection. Let's take a look at that now.

Making a Link Label Work

To add hyperlinks to a link label at design time, you select the LinkArea property in the Properties window and click the ellipsis (...) button that appears to open the LinkArea editor you see in Figure 5.11. Then you can select the section of the link label's text you want to make into a hyperlink and click OK.

FIGURE 5.11

The LinkArea editor.

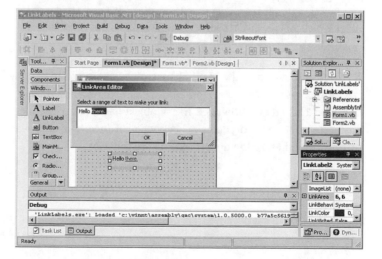

By default, the section of the text in the link label that you've designated as a hyperlink
will appear underlined when the link label appears. When it's clicked, a `LinkClicked`
event occurs. Here's an event handler that sets the link's color to the `LinkVisited` color
by setting the `LinkLabel1.LinkVisited` property to `True` and that navigates to
`www.microsoft.com` when the user clicks the hyperlink. To navigate to that URL, the
code uses the `System.Diagnostics.Process.Start` method to launch the user's
browser:

```
Private Sub LinkLabel1_LinkClicked(ByVal sender As System.Object, _
    ByVal e As System.Windows.Forms.LinkLabelLinkClickedEventArgs) _
    Handles LinkLabel1.LinkClicked
    LinkLabel1.LinkVisited = True
    System.Diagnostics.Process.Start("www.microsoft.com")
End Sub
```

Supporting Multiple Links

You can also support multiple links in one link label and navigate to other forms as well
as URLs. We'll see how that works in the LinkLabels sample project in the code for this
book. In that example, the link label will display the text "Get more information locally
or on the web." where the underlined text is linked; *locally* is linked to a new form, and
web is linked to www.microsoft.com.

You can support multiple links in one link label in code, using the `Add` method of the
`Links` collection. You pass this method the 0-based location in the link label's text
where a link starts, the number of characters in the link, and the link text. To make
the links in this example active, you can use code like this in the `Form1_Load` event
handler:

```
Private Sub Form1_Load(ByVal sender As System.Object, _
    ByVal e As System.EventArgs) Handles MyBase.Load
    LinkLabel1.Links.Add(21, 7, "locally")
    LinkLabel1.Links.Add(39, 3, "web")
End Sub
```

To determine which of the two links were clicked, you can use the `Link.LinkData` property of the `System.Windows.Forms.LinkLabelLinkClickedEventArgs` object passed to
the `LinkClicked` event handler. Every object has a `ToString` method that converts the
object's data to text, so you can check whether *locally* or *web* was clicked, as shown in
Listing 5.4, and take the appropriate action this way.

LISTING 5.4   Supporting Multiple Links in a Link Label (LinkLabels project, Form1.vb)

```
Public Class Form1
    Inherits System.Windows.Forms.Form

' Windows Form Designer generated code

    Private Sub Form1_Load(ByVal sender As System.Object, _
        ByVal e As System.EventArgs) Handles MyBase.Load
        LinkLabel1.Links.Add(21, 7, "locally")
        LinkLabel1.Links.Add(39, 3, "web")

    End Sub

    Private Sub LinkLabel1_LinkClicked(ByVal sender As System.Object, _
        ByVal e As System.Windows.Forms.LinkLabelLinkClickedEventArgs) _
        Handles LinkLabel1.LinkClicked

        LinkLabel1.Links(LinkLabel1.Links.IndexOf(e.Link)).Visited = True

        If (e.Link.LinkData.ToString() = "locally") Then
            Dim InfoWindow As New Form2
            InfoWindow.Show()
        Else
            System.Diagnostics.Process.Start("www.microsoft.com")
        End If
    End Sub
End Class
```

You can see the results of this code in Figure 5.12, where the *locally* link was clicked to bring up a second form.

FIGURE 5.12

Using link labels.

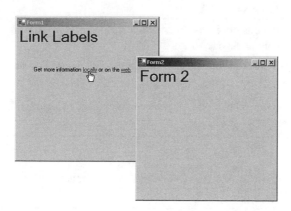

Clicking link labels makes something happen and so represents a bridge between the standard text-displaying controls such as text boxes and rich text boxes and the controls that we're about to dig into: buttons.

Using Buttons

Together with text boxes, buttons are the most popular controls in Visual Basic .NET. They're the easiest user interface element to use when you want to communicate with the user with events. We've seen the button Click event throughout this book, starting in Day 1, "Getting Started with Visual Basic .NET!"

As all other Windows controls are, the Button class is based on the Control class. Here's the class hierarchy for the Button class:

```
System.Object
    System.MarshalByRefObject
        System.ComponentModel.Component
            System.Windows.Forms.Control
                System.Windows.Forms.ButtonBase
                    System.Windows.Forms.Button
```

You can find the more significant public properties of the Button class in Table 5.13 and the more significant methods in Table 5.14. (Note that these tables do not include the significant properties, methods, and events Button inherits from the Control class, such as the Click event; you can see those properties, methods, and events in Tables 5.1, 5.2, and 5.3.)

TABLE 5.13   Significant Public Properties of Button Objects

Property	Means
DialogResult	Returns or sets the value sent to the parent form when the button is clicked. Used only in dialogs.
FlatStyle	Returns or sets whether the button has a flat appearance.
Image	Returns or sets an image displayed in a button.
ImageAlign	Returns or sets the alignment of the image in a button.
TextAlign	Returns or sets the alignment of the text in the button.

TABLE 5.14   Significant Public Method of Button Objects

Method	Means
PerformClick	Clicks the button, causing a button Click event.

We've already put buttons to work; we know the Click event well, as handled with a Button_Click event handler. And we know that you can use the Text property to hold the button's caption, which you can change at runtime. This is shown in the following example, which changes a button's caption when you click it:

```
Private Sub Button1_Click(ByVal sender As System.Object, _
    ByVal e As System.EventArgs) Handles Button1.Click
    Button1.Text = "You clicked me."
End Sub
```

As you can imagine, it's useful to be able to change the caption of buttons at runtime this way. For example, if a button's caption reads "Connect", then, when connected to the Internet, you could change the button's caption to "Disconnect".

You can also use the Font property to set the font used in the button, both at design time and at runtime. The ForeColor property sets the color of text in the button, and the BackColor property sets the color of the background (for example, in a red PANIC button). And as with other controls, you can show and hide buttons with the Visible property and the Show and Hide methods. You can also enable and disable buttons (a disabled button is grayed out and will not respond to the mouse) with the Enabled property.

Buttons are also very popular in dialogs. As you saw yesterday, you can set the AcceptButton or CancelButton property of a form to let users click a button by pressing the Enter or Esc keys even if the button does not have focus. And when you display a form using the ShowDialog method, it's treated as a dialog. You can use the DialogResult property of a button to specify the return value of ShowDialog.

You can change a button's look, giving it an image or aligning text and images in it. You can even make it look flat for a "Web" look, setting the FlatStyle property to FlatStyle.Flat. Or you can set the FlatStyle property to FlatStyle.Popup, which means the button appears flat until the mouse pointer passes over it, in which case the button pops up to give it the usual button appearance.

And as with other controls that display captions, you can use access characters in buttons. Just preface the character you want to make into an access character in the caption with an ampersand (&) like this "&Quit", and when the user presses Alt+Q, that button will be clicked automatically. In fact, you can click a button yourself, in code.

Clicking a Button in Code

To click a button in code, you can use the PerformClick method. For example, look at the Buttons example in the code for the book. You'll see two buttons there; the first has the caption "Click Me to Click the Other Button", and the second button has the

5

caption "The Other Button". When you click the first button, the code executes
Button2.PerformClick() to click the other button. The other button's event handler is
called, and the code in that event handler changes the caption of the second button to
"I've been clicked!" as you can see in Listing 5.5.

LISTING 5.5   Clicking a Button in Code (Buttons project, Form1.vb)

```
Public Class Form1
    Inherits System.Windows.Forms.Form

' Windows Form Designer generated code

    Private Sub Button1_Click(ByVal sender As System.Object, _
        ByVal e As System.EventArgs) Handles Button1.Click
        Button2.PerformClick()
    End Sub

    Private Sub Button2_Click(ByVal sender As System.Object, _
        ByVal e As System.EventArgs) Handles Button2.Click
        Button2.Text = "I've been clicked!"
    End Sub
End Class
```

You can see the results in Figure 5.13.

FIGURE 5.13

*Clicking a button in
code.*

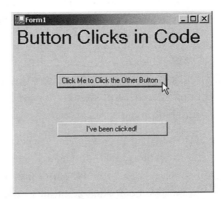

Adjusting the Focus After Button Clicks

Say that you have a rich text box and you want to let users search the text. You might add
a button marked Search to do that. When the user clicks the Search button, your program
can read the text to search for from a text box and use the rich text box's Find method to

find and select that text. The user will then probably want to keep working in the rich text box, perhaps editing the selected text. But the clicked Search button still has the focus, so the user will have to switch the focus back to the rich text box manually.

To give the rich text box (or any other control) the focus automatically after clicking the Search button, you can use the Focus method, which is a method supported by most controls that can accept the focus:

```
Private Sub Button1_Click(ByVal sender As System.Object, _
    ByVal e As System.EventArgs) Handles Button1.Click
    RichTextBox1.Find(TextBox1.Text)
    RichTextBox1.Focus()
End Sub
```

> **Tip**
>
> Like other controls, buttons have two events—GotFocus and LostFocus—that tell you when a button has gotten or lost the focus.

Displaying a Picture in a Button

Like a number of other controls in Visual Basic .NET, such as labels, buttons can display images. At design time, you only need to set the Image property in the Properties window to an image file. You can see an example in the ImageButtons project in the code for the book, which you see at work in Figure 5.14.

FIGURE 5.14

Using an image in a button.

You can load an image into a button at runtime if you use the Image class's FromFile method and assign the resulting Image object to the button's Image property. That might look something like this in code (you can use the same members of the ContentAlignment enumeration we saw for labels to align images):

```
Button1.Image = Image.FromFile("C:\vbnet\images\button.jpg")
Button1.ImageAlign = ContentAlignment.TopLeft
Button1.Text = ""
TextBox1.Text = "You clicked the button"
```

You'll learn more on the Image class and how to use it in Day 10.

That finishes our work on standard buttons for the moment. Next, we'll look at another kind of button: check boxes.

Using Check Boxes

Like buttons, check boxes are familiar controls in Windows. You can click a check box to select it and click it again to deselect it. When selected, a check box displays a check mark. Using check boxes, you can allow the user to select various options, such as what to put in a sandwich, or what options you want to support in a program, such as automatic spellchecking or left-alignment of text. In Visual Basic .NET, check boxes can also display a caption, which you store in the Text property, or an image, which you store in the Image property. The class hierarchy of the CheckBox class is as follows:

```
System.Object
    System.MarshalByRefObject
        System.ComponentModel.Component
            System.Windows.Forms.Control
                System.Windows.Forms.ButtonBase
                    System.Windows.Forms.CheckBox
```

You can find the more significant public properties of the CheckBox class in Table 5.15 and the more significant events in Table 5.16. (Note that these tables do not include the significant properties, methods, and events CheckBox inherits from the Control class, such as the Click event; you can see them in Tables 5.1, 5.2, and 5.3.)

TABLE 5.15   Significant Public Properties of CheckBox Objects

Property	Means
Appearance	Returns or sets the appearance of a check box.
CheckAlign	Returns or sets the alignment, horizontal and vertical, of the check box in this control.
Checked	Gets or sets whether the check box is checked.
CheckState	Returns or sets the state of a three-state check box.
FlatStyle	Returns or sets the flat-style appearance of the check box.
Image	Returns or sets the image that is displayed in a check box.
ImageAlign	Returns or sets the alignment of the image in a check box.
ThreeState	Specifies if the check box supports three check states instead of two.

TABLE 5.16 Significant Public Events of `CheckBox` Objects

Event	Means
AppearanceChanged	Occurs when the `Appearance` property changes.
CheckedChanged	Occurs when the `Checked` property changes.
CheckStateChanged	Occurs when the `CheckState` property changes.

You can make check boxes look like buttons that stay down when you click them and pop up when you click them again if you set the `Appearance` property to `Button`; see the section "Creating Toggle Buttons" later today. Also, the `ThreeState` property determines whether the control supports two or three states, as we'll see.

The main event here is the `CheckChanged` event, which occurs when the check box is clicked:

```
Private Sub CheckBox1_CheckedChanged(ByVal sender As System.Object,
ByVal e As System.EventArgs) Handles CheckBox1.CheckedChanged
    TextBox1.Text = "You clicked check box 1."
End Sub
```

This event occurs when the state of the check box changes, but what if you want to know whether a particular check box is checked at some particular time?

Getting and Setting a Check Box's State

You can use a check box's `Checked` property, which holds either `True` or `False`, to see whether a check box is checked. You can see an example in the CheckBoxes example in the code for the book; that example displays a number of check boxes, and when you click one, a message appears in a text box indicating whether that check box is currently checked. Listing 5.6 shows what the code for the `CheckChanged` event looks like for first check box, `CheckBox1`, using the `Checked` property.

5

LISTING 5.6 Clicking Check Boxes (CheckBoxes project, Form1.vb)

```
Private Sub CheckBox1_CheckedChanged(ByVal sender As System.Object,
ByVal e As System.EventArgs) Handles CheckBox1.CheckedChanged
    If CheckBox1.Checked Then
        TextBox1.Text = "Check box 1 is checked."
    Else
        TextBox1.Text = "Check box 1 is not checked."
    End If
End Sub
```

You can see this example at work in Figure 5.15.

FIGURE 5.15

*The CheckBoxes
example.*

You can also set a check box's state by setting its `Checked` property to `True` or `False`, as in this code:

```
Private Sub Button1_Click(ByVal sender As System.Object, _
    ByVal e As System.EventArgs) Handles Button1.Click
    CheckBox1.Checked = True
End Sub
```

And you can specify whether a check box should appear checked when it first appears by setting the `Checked` property to `True` at design time.

Using Three-State Check Boxes

Besides checked and unchecked, you can set check boxes to an "indeterminate" state. The indeterminate state is a sort of a middle state between checked and unchecked. In this state, a check box is checked with a gray background, to show that neither the checked nor the unchecked state applies. You need to set the check box's `ThreeState` property to `True` to indicate that you want it to support three states. You can see all three possible states for check boxes in the ThreeStates project in the code for the book, which you see at work in Figure 5.16.

FIGURE 5.16

*The three states of
check boxes.*

In standard check boxes you use the Checked property to get or set the value of a two-state check box. However, you use the CheckState property to get or set the value of the three-state check box. The three states are represented by the members of the CheckState enumeration (if the ThreeState property is set to True, the Checked property will return True for either a checked or indeterminate state):

- CheckState.Checked—A check appears in the check box.
- CheckState.Unchecked—No check appears in the check box.
- CheckState.Indeterminate—A check appears in the check box on a gray background.

If you've set the check box's ThreeState property to True, you can set its CheckState property to a value such as CheckState.Indeterminate at design time or runtime to set the check box to the indeterminate state:

```
Private Sub CheckBox1_CheckedChanged(ByVal sender As System.Object, _
    ByVal e As System.EventArgs) Handles CheckBox1.CheckedChanged
    CheckBox1.CheckState = CheckState.Indeterminate
End Sub
```

To handle changes in the CheckState property, use the CheckStateChanged event.

And that completes our coverage of check boxes for the moment. Next up is an allied control: radio buttons.

Using Radio Buttons

Radio buttons—also called option buttons—are another familiar Windows control. The user can click them to select them, which displays a dot inside them, and click them again to deselect them. The difference between radio buttons and check boxes is that radio buttons are designed to be used in a group, whereas check boxes need not be.

While check boxes display a set of nonexclusive options (like toppings on a pizza), radio buttons allow the user to select one option among mutually exclusive options (such as the day of the week). Because the options that radio buttons present are mutually exclusive, when the user selects one of a set of radio buttons, the others are cleared automatically. By default, all the radio buttons in a form act together in this way. To create multiple radio button groups on one form, you place each group in its own container, such as a group box or panel control. We'll see how to do that later today.

5

Here is the class hierarchy of the `RadioButton` class:

```
System.Object
   System.MarshalByRefObject
      System.ComponentModel.Component
         System.Windows.Forms.Control
            System.Windows.Forms.ButtonBase
               System.Windows.Forms.RadioButton
```

You can find the more significant public properties of the `RadioButton` class in Table 5.17, the significant methods in Table 5.18, and the significant events in Table 5.19. (Note that as with other controls, these tables don't list the significant properties, methods, and events `RadioButton` inherits from the `Control` class; you can see them in Tables 5.1, 5.2, and 5.3.)

TABLE 5.17   Significant Public Properties of `RadioButton` Objects

Property	Means
Appearance	Gets or sets the appearance of the radio button.
Checked	Returns or sets whether the radio button is checked.
FlatStyle	Returns or sets the flat-style appearance of the radio button.
Image	Returns or sets the image displayed in a radio button.
ImageAlign	Returns or sets the alignment of an image in a radio button.
TextAlign	Returns or sets the alignment of the text in a radio button.

TABLE 5.18   Significant Public Method of `RadioButton` Objects

Method	Means
PerformClick	Generates a `Click` event for the radio button.

TABLE 5.19   Significant Public Events of `RadioButton` Objects

Event	Means
AppearanceChanged	Occurs when the `Appearance` property changes.
CheckedChanged	Occurs when the value of the `Checked` property changes.

Like check boxes, radio buttons support a `Checked` property that indicates whether the radio button is selected. The chief event here is the `CheckedChanged` event, which occurs when the `Checked` property changes.

And like check boxes, radio buttons can display text, an image, or both. A radio button's appearance may be altered to appear as a toggle-style button or as a standard radio button by setting the Appearance property, and we'll see how to create toggle buttons here.

Getting and Setting a Radio Button's State

As mentioned, you can determine a radio button's state with the Checked property. You can see an example of this in the RadioButtons example in the code for this book. That example displays six radio buttons and supports them all with CheckChanged event handlers. The event handlers display a message indicating what the state of a radio button is when you click it:

```
Private Sub RadioButton1_CheckedChanged(ByVal sender As System.Object,
ByVal e As System.EventArgs) Handles RadioButton1.CheckedChanged
    If RadioButton1.Checked Then
        TextBox1.Text = "Radio button 1 is selected."
    Else
        TextBox2.Text = "Radio button 1 is no longer selected."
    End If
End Sub
```

You can see the results in Figure 5.17.

FIGURE 5.17

The RadioButtons example.

You can also set the radio button's checked state using the Checked property. The Checked property can take two values: True or False. Here's an example, setting a radio button, RadioButton1, to its selected state by setting its Checked property to True:

```
Private Sub Button1_Click(ByVal sender As System.Object, _
    ByVal e As System.EventArgs) Handles Button1.Click
    RadioButton1.Checked = True
End Sub
```

5

You make a radio button appear checked when your program first starts by setting its Checked property to True at design time.

Creating Toggle Buttons

Toggle buttons look like standard buttons but act like the check boxes or radio buttons they really are. When you click a check box toggle button, for example, it stays clicked until you click it again. You can turn both check boxes or radio buttons into toggle buttons if you set their Appearance property to Button (the default is Normal).

As an example, you can see three radio buttons that have been made into toggle buttons in Figure 5.18. When you click one, any other button that was down pops back up. These buttons are just like radio buttons, except that they look like standard buttons.

FIGURE 5.18

The ToggleButtons example.

You can change the appearance of radio buttons at runtime. Here's some code that does that:

```
Private Sub Button1_Click(ByVal sender As System.Object, _
    ByVal e As System.EventArgs) Handles Button1.Click
    RadioButton1.Appearance = Appearance.Button
    RadioButton2.Appearance = Appearance.Button
    RadioButton3.Appearance = Appearance.Button
End Sub
```

And that finishes our work with radio buttons for the moment. From a programmer's point of view, they're much like check boxes, except that they are used to present mutually exclusive options. The last two controls today—panels and group boxes—are all about taking controls like the ones we've seen and grouping them together, organizing the way those controls are presented to the user.

Using Panels

NEW TERM You can use panels to group controls in a form, organizing them by function. For example, a restaurant application might list sandwiches in one panel and pasta options in another. Panels, like group boxes, are used as *control containers*.

One thing panels, and group boxes, are good for is creating radio button groups. You can see two panels at work in Figure 5.19 in the Panels example in the book's code. Each panel contains three radio buttons, and each set of radio buttons acts independently. As you see in the figure, one radio button is selected in each group.

FIGURE 5.19

The Panels example.

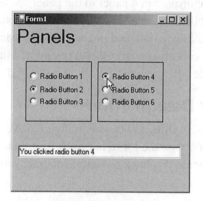

By default, panels don't display the borders you see in Figure 5.19; they function simply as control containers, invisible at runtime. However, you can set their BorderStyle property to FixedSingle or Fixed3D (the default is None). What's the difference between panels and group boxes? They're actually very similar. Both function as control containers, but only panels can display scrollbars, and only group boxes can display captions.

Here is the class hierarchy of the Panel class:

```
System.Object
   System.MarshalByRefObject
      System.ComponentModel.Component
         System.Windows.Forms.Control
            System.Windows.Forms.ScrollableControl
               System.Windows.Forms.Panel
```

You can find the more significant public properties of the Panel class in Table 5.20. (Note that as with other controls, this table does not list the significant properties, methods, and events Panel inherits from the Control class; you can find them in Tables 5.1, 5.2, and 5.3.)

5

TABLE 5.20   Significant Public Properties of `Panel` Objects

Property	Means
AutoScroll	Specifies whether the panel will display scrollbars if needed.
AutoScrollMargin	Returns or sets the size of the autoscroll margin (in pixels).
AutoScrollMinSize	Returns or sets the minimum size of the autoscroll.
AutoScrollPosition	Returns or sets the location of the autoscroll position.
DockPadding	Gets the dock padding settings for all edges of the panel.

You can dock the controls you display in a panel to the panel's sides using the controls' `Dock` property. To display scrollbars as needed in a panel, set the `AutoScroll` property to `True`. You can use panels to display colors and images with the `BackImage` and `BackColor` properties. And panels also support the `Click` event and the other standard control events you see in Table 5.3.

Creating Panels at Design Time

When you create panels at design time, as you see in Figure 5.20, they'll have a dotted border so you can see their extent on the form, but by default their `BorderStyle` property is set to `None`. If you want them to display a border at runtime, you'll need to change that property's value.

FIGURE 5.20

Creating a panel at design time.

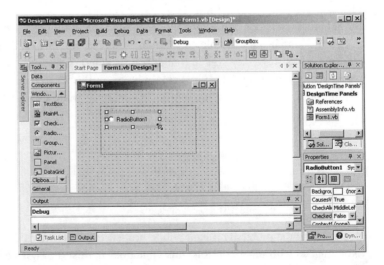

To add controls to a panel at runtime, you just drag those controls and drop them onto the panel, which automatically makes them child controls of the panel. For example, at runtime, the radio buttons you've dropped onto a panel will be coordinated into a radio

button group. When you drag the panel around at design time, all its child controls come with it.

Creating Panels at Runtime

You can also create panels at runtime and add controls to them. In fact, that's how the Panels example you saw in Figure 5.19 works. This example creates two new panels using the Panel class and, using the Add method of the panels' Controls collections, adds radio buttons to each panel. The code also adds a CheckChanged event handler to each radio button and adds each panel to the form's Controls collection to display the panel and its child radio buttons. Listing 5.7 shows the code that makes it all work (note that the location of each radio button is measured with respect to the upper-left corner of its container—that is, the panel control it's in).

LISTING 5.7   Creating Panels at Runtime (Panels project, Form1.vb)

```vb
Public Class Form1
    Inherits System.Windows.Forms.Form

    Dim Panel1 As New Panel
    Dim Panel2 As New Panel
    Dim WithEvents RadioButton1 As New RadioButton
    Dim WithEvents RadioButton2 As New RadioButton
    Dim WithEvents RadioButton3 As New RadioButton
    Dim WithEvents RadioButton4 As New RadioButton
    Dim WithEvents RadioButton5 As New RadioButton
    Dim WithEvents RadioButton6 As New RadioButton

    Private Sub Form1_Load(ByVal sender As System.Object, _
        ByVal e As System.EventArgs) Handles MyBase.Load

        Panel1.Location = New Point(20, 60)
        Panel1.Size = New Size(110, 100)
        Panel1.BorderStyle = BorderStyle.FixedSingle

        Panel2.Location = New Point(140, 60)
        Panel2.Size = New Size(110, 100)
        Panel2.BorderStyle = BorderStyle.FixedSingle

        RadioButton1.Location = New Point(6, 16)
        RadioButton1.Text = "Radio Button 1"
        RadioButton1.Size = New Size(120, 16)

        RadioButton2.Location = New Point(6, 36)
        RadioButton2.Text = "Radio Button 2"
        RadioButton2.Size = New Size(120, 20)

        RadioButton3.Location = New Point(6, 56)
        RadioButton3.Text = "Radio Button 3"
```

5

LISTING 5.7   continued

```
            RadioButton3.Size = New Size(120, 20)

            RadioButton4.Location = New Point(6, 16)
            RadioButton4.Text = "Radio Button 4"
            RadioButton4.Size = New Size(120, 16)

            RadioButton5.Location = New Point(6, 36)
            RadioButton5.Text = "Radio Button 5"
            RadioButton5.Size = New Size(120, 20)

            RadioButton6.Location = New Point(6, 56)
            RadioButton6.Text = "Radio Button 6"
            RadioButton6.Size = New Size(120, 20)

            Panel1.Controls.Add(RadioButton1)
            Panel1.Controls.Add(RadioButton2)
            Panel1.Controls.Add(RadioButton3)

            Panel2.Controls.Add(RadioButton4)
            Panel2.Controls.Add(RadioButton5)
            Panel2.Controls.Add(RadioButton6)

            Controls.Add(Panel1)
            Controls.Add(Panel2)

            AddHandler RadioButton1.CheckedChanged, AddressOf _
                RadioButton1_CheckedChanged
            AddHandler RadioButton2.CheckedChanged, AddressOf _
                RadioButton2_CheckedChanged
            AddHandler RadioButton3.CheckedChanged, AddressOf _
                RadioButton3_CheckedChanged
            AddHandler RadioButton4.CheckedChanged, AddressOf _
                RadioButton4_CheckedChanged
            AddHandler RadioButton5.CheckedChanged, AddressOf _
                RadioButton5_CheckedChanged
            AddHandler RadioButton6.CheckedChanged, AddressOf _
                RadioButton6_CheckedChanged
        End Sub

        Private Sub RadioButton1_CheckedChanged(ByVal sender As _
            System.Object, ByVal e As System.EventArgs)
            TextBox1.Text = "You clicked radio button 1"
        End Sub

        Private Sub RadioButton2_CheckedChanged(ByVal sender As _
            System.Object, ByVal e As System.EventArgs)
            TextBox1.Text = "You clicked radio button 2"
        End Sub

        Private Sub RadioButton3_CheckedChanged(ByVal sender As _
            System.Object, ByVal e As System.EventArgs)
```

LISTING 5.7   continued

```
            TextBox1.Text = "You clicked radio button 3"
        End Sub

        Private Sub RadioButton4_CheckedChanged(ByVal sender As _
            System.Object, ByVal e As System.EventArgs)
            TextBox1.Text = "You clicked radio button 4"
        End Sub

        Private Sub RadioButton5_CheckedChanged(ByVal sender As _
            System.Object, ByVal e As System.EventArgs)
            TextBox1.Text = "You clicked radio button 5"
        End Sub

        Private Sub RadioButton6_CheckedChanged(ByVal sender As _
            System.Object, ByVal e As System.EventArgs)
            TextBox1.Text = "You clicked radio button 6"
        End Sub
    End Class
```

You can see this example at work in Figure 5.19. When the program starts, the example's code, which is in the Form1_Load event handler, runs and creates the panels you see in the figure.

Using Group Boxes

Like panels, group boxes function primarily as control containers. However, you can give a group box a caption, which you set with the Text property. (On the other hand, group boxes can't display scrollbars as panels can.) Group boxes always have a border, as you can see in the GroupBoxes example in the book's code, shown at work in Figure 5.21; they don't even have a BorderStyle property that you could use to remove that border.

5

FIGURE 5.21

Using group boxes.

Here is the class hierarchy of the `GroupBox` class:

```
System.Object
    System.MarshalByRefObject
        System.ComponentModel.Component
            System.Windows.Forms.Control
                System.Windows.Forms.GroupBox
```

Group boxes don't have any special properties, methods, or events beyond the basic set you see in Tables 5.1, 5.2, and 5.3. The `Text` property you use for a group box's caption, for example, appears in Table 5.1.

You can create group boxes and add controls to them at design time or runtime. The GroupBoxes example you see at work in Figure 5.21 was created at runtime, but you can simply modify the Panels example we just saw in the preceding section to create group boxes at runtime. To do that, use the `GroupBox` class instead of the `Panel` class, don't set the `BorderStyle` property, and use the group box's `Text` property to set the caption of the group boxes. That's all you need.

Summary

Today, we've seen many of the primary Windows controls, including their properties, methods, and events. We began with an overview of the `Control` class on which such controls are based on and then started our in-depth work with text boxes. We saw how to align text in text boxes, create multiline text boxes, select text and copy it to the clipboard, handle text box events, display scrollbars, and even create password controls.

We saw that rich text boxes function just like text boxes, except that we can also support Rich Text Format (RTF) text. We saw how to use the `Rtf` property to handle RTF text, search for text, select text, format text using different font attributes such as italic and underline, as well save and load RTF text using files. All in all, the rich text control is very impressive. If you want a word processor in a control, here it is.

We saw that labels allow us to display text that the user can't alter, although we can alter that text in our code. We saw how to align text and support access keys using labels and how they can function much as read-only text boxes.

Link labels let us support all the functionality of labels as well as hyperlinks. We saw that the `LinkClicked` event allows us to handle hyperlink clicks with code that can open a new form, browse the Internet, or perform any other action that can be implemented with Visual Basic code. And we saw how to support multiple links in the same link label control.

From that point, we turned to buttons, the most common control to use when we need to support user-interface events. We saw how to use the `Click` event for buttons, as well as change a button's caption at runtime, create flat buttons and image buttons, click a button in code, and reset the focus after a button was clicked.

Check boxes let the user select one of a number of nonexclusive options, like fillings in a sandwich. We saw how to get and set a check box's state using the `Checked` property. We also saw how to work with three-state check boxes.

Radio buttons let the user select one of a set of mutually exclusive options, such as the day of the week. When one radio button in a radio button group is selected, the others in the same group are automatically deselected.

Finally, we looked at two controls meant to function as control containers: panels and group boxes. We saw that we can place child controls inside these controls to organize those child controls in our forms. As we've seen, the difference between these controls is that panels can support scrollbars and don't display a border by default; group boxes can display captions and always have a border.

That's it for the many powerful controls we've seen today. Tomorrow, we're going to add more Visual Basic power when we get all the details on list boxes, combo boxes, picture boxes, scrollbars, splitters, tool tips, and timers.

Q&A

Q Is there some way to discard typed keys before they're displayed in a text box or rich text box?

A Yes, use the argument named e by default (a `System.Windows.Forms.KeyPressEventArgs` object) passed to the `KeyPress` event handler. Just set `e.Handled` to `True` in your code, and Visual Basic will think you've handled the key press yourself.

Q When I add controls to a form and want to handle their events, do I have to supply a separate event handler for each one?

A No. You can use the same event handler for multiple controls if you want. In the event handler, make sure you don't use a `Handles` clause (for example, `Handles RadioButton3.CheckedChanged`) so the event handler is not tied to one control. Then use `AddHandler` to connect the event handler to as many controls as you want. To determine which control actually caused the event, you can check the caption of the control. The control itself is passed as an argument named `sender` to the event handler, so you can use code like this: `If sender.Text = "Radio Button 1" Then....` You can also store text in a control's `Tag` property (which is designed for this use) to distinguish between controls.

Workshop

This workshop tests whether you understand the concepts you saw today. It's a good idea to make sure you can answer these questions before pressing on to tomorrow's work.

5

Quiz

1. You set a text box's `ScrollBars` property to `ScrollBars.Vertical`, but no scroll-bar appears. What other property must you set to a nondefault value before the scrollbar will appear?

2. How do you convert a text box into a password control?

3. How would you search text backward in a rich text box for the text *Visual Basic*?

4. How do you convert a check box into a three-state check box? How do you determine whether it has been checked?

5. How do you convert a radio button or a check box into a toggle button?

Quiz Answers

1. You must also set the `Multiline` property to `True`. For a horizontal scrollbar to appear if you've set the text box's `ScrollBars` property to `ScrollBars.Horizontal` or `ScrollBars.Both`, you must set the `WordWrap` property to `False`.

2. You assign a character to the text box's `PasswordChar` property.

3. You can use `Find` to search backward, starting at the end of the text in the text box like this: `Find("Visual Basic", Len(RichTextBox1.Text), RichTextBoxFinds.Reverse)`.

4. You assign a check box's `ThreeState` property a value of `True` to convert it into a three-state check box. At runtime, you can examine the value in the check box's `CheckState` property, which will be `CheckState.Checked`, `CheckState.Unchecked`, or `CheckState.Indeterminate`.

5. You can set its `Appearance` property to `Button` (the default is `Normal`).

Exercises

1. Implement multiple links in a single link label to both the Visual Basic main page, `http://msdn.microsoft.com/vbasic/`, and the Gotodotnet site examples page, `http://www.gotdotnet.com/userarea/default.aspx`. Before displaying these sites, display a message box asking the users whether it's okay to start their browsers.

2. Add some text like "A noisy noise annoys an oyster, does it not?" to a rich text box; then use a `While` loop to convert all instances of *no* in that text to italic. Remember that the `Find` method will return –1 when no more matches are found.

DAY 6

Windows Forms: Working with List Boxes, Combo Boxes, Picture Boxes, Scrollbars, Splitters, Tool Tips, and Timers

Today, we're going to master some important Windows controls: list boxes, scrollbars, picture boxes, and more. Here are today's topics:

- List boxes
- Checked list boxes
- Combo boxes
- Picture boxes
- Scrollbars
- Track bars

- Splitters
- Notify icons
- Tool tips
- Timers

We'll jump right in, starting immediately with list boxes in Windows forms.

Using List Boxes

List boxes are those controls that display a list of items, allowing the user to select one or more. You can see a list box in Figure 6.1 in the ListBoxes project in the code for this book. If there are too many items to be seen at once, a scrollbar will appear, as you see in the figure.

FIGURE 6.1

A list box.

A lot of power is built into list boxes, and we'll see it all today. Here's the class hierarchy for the ListBox class:

```
System.Object
   System.MarshalByRefObject
      System.ComponentModel.Component
         System.Windows.Forms.Control
            System.Windows.Forms.ListControl
               System.Windows.Forms.ListBox
```

You can find the significant public properties of the ListBox class in Table 6.1, the significant methods in Table 6.2, and the significant events in Table 6.3, including those members inherited from the ListControl class. (Note that these tables do not include the significant properties, methods, and events ListBox inherits from the Control class; you can see them in Tables 5.1, 5.2, and 5.3.)

TABLE 6.1   Significant Public Properties of `ListBox` Objects

Property	Means
ColumnWidth	Returns or sets the width of columns (only for multicolumn list boxes).
HorizontalExtent	Returns or sets the width the horizontal scrollbar of a list box can scroll.
HorizontalScrollbar	Returns or sets whether a horizontal scrollbar should be displayed.
IntegralHeight	Returns or sets whether the list box should resize to avoid showing partial items.
ItemHeight	Returns or sets the height of list box items.
Items	Returns a collection of the list box items.
MultiColumn	Returns or sets whether the list box supports multiple columns.
ScrollAlwaysVisible	Returns or sets whether the vertical scrollbar is always visible.
SelectedIndex	Returns or sets the zero-based index of the currently selected item.
SelectedIndices	Returns a collection containing the (zero-based) indices of all currently selected items.
SelectedItem	Returns or sets the currently selected item in the list box.
SelectedItems	Returns a collection containing the currently selected items in the list box.
SelectionMode	Returns or sets the method in which items are selected in the list box.
Sorted	Returns or sets whether the items in the list box are sorted alphabetically.
Text	Returns or searches for the text of the currently selected item in the list box.
TopIndex	Returns or sets the index of the first visible item in the list box.

TABLE 6.2   Significant Public Methods of `ListBox` Objects

Methods	Means
BeginUpdate	Prevents the list box from redrawing itself until the `EndUpdate` method is called.
ClearSelected	Deselects all items in the list box.
EndUpdate	Resumes visual updating of the list box control after updating is halted by the `BeginUpdate` method.
FindString	Finds the first item in the list box that starts with the indicated string.
GetItemHeight	Returns the height of an item in the list box.
GetSelected	Returns whether the indicated item is selected.
SetSelected	Selects or clears the selection for the indicated item in a list box.

6

TABLE 6.3   Significant Public Event of ListBox Objects

Event	Means
SelectedIndexChanged	Occurs when the SelectedIndex property has changed.

Creating a List Box

You can create a list box the same way as you would create any other control in a Windows form: Just drag a list box from the toolbox onto a Windows form. The next step is to add items to the list box for the user to select from, and you can do that at either design time or runtime.

The items in a list box are stored in the list box's Items collection, and at design time, you can click the ellipsis (...) button in the Items property entry in the Properties window to open the String Collection Editor you see in Figure 6.2.

FIGURE 6.2

Adding items to a list box at design time.

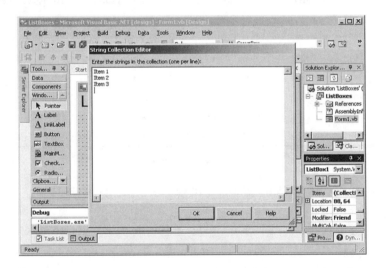

Just enter the items you want in the list box in this editor, as you see in Figure 6.2. Those items will appear when the list box first appears at runtime.

Let's look at how to add items to a list box at runtime. The items in list boxes are stored in the Items collection; the Items.Count property holds the number of items in the list. To add or delete items in a ListBox control, you can use the Items.Add, Items.Insert, Items.Clear, or Items.Remove methods. You can also add a number of objects to a list box at one time by using the AddRange method. For example, Listing 6.1 shows how we can add 10 items to the list box you see in Figure 6.1, the ListBoxes example, in the Form1_Load event handler.

LISTING 6.1   Adding Items to a List Box (ListBoxes project, Form1.vb)

```
Private Sub Form1_Load(ByVal sender As System.Object, _
    ByVal e As System.EventArgs) Handles MyBase.Load
    For intLoopIndex As Integer = 0 To 9
        ListBox1.Items.Add("Item " & intLoopIndex.ToString())
    Next intLoopIndex
End Sub
```

This code adds 10 items to the list box, items 0 to 9. Besides the Add method, you can use the Insert method, which enables you to specify the index location at which to insert an item like this: ComboBox1.Items.Insert (3, "A New Item"). And you can also use the AddRange method to add a collection of objects to a list box all at once; here's an example that adds an array of strings to a list box all at once:

```
Private Sub Form1_Load(ByVal sender As System.Object, _
    ByVal e As System.EventArgs) Handles MyBase.Load
    Dim strArray(9) As String

    For intLoopIndex As Integer = 0 To 9
        strArray(intLoopIndex) = New String("Item " & intLoopIndex)
    Next intLoopIndex

    ListBox1.Items.AddRange(strArray)
End Sub
```

Tip

When you add many items to a list box in code, the display in the list box can flicker on some systems. If that's a problem, you can use the BeginUpdate method to stop visual updating of the list box and the EndUpdate method to redraw the control when you're ready.

When you add items to a list box, each item is given an index, and you can refer to the item in the list box with this index by using the Items property like this: ListBox1. Items(7). The first item added to a list box gets the index 0; the next, index 1; and so on.

6

Tip

How do you remove items from a list box? You can use the RemoveAt method, passing the index of the item to remove this way: ListBox1.Items. Remove(6). You can also use the Items.Clear method to remove all items from the list box.

Handling List Box Events

The default event for list boxes is the SelectedIndexChanged event, which handles the case where a new item is selected. When a new selection is made, you can get the index of the newly selected item with the list box's SelectedIndex property. For example, the ListBoxes example indicates which item was clicked using the SelectedIndexChanged event like this:

```
Private Sub ListBox1_SelectedIndexChanged(ByVal sender As _
    System.Object, ByVal e As System.EventArgs) Handles _
    ListBox1.SelectedIndexChanged
    TextBox1.Text = "You selected item " & ListBox1.SelectedIndex
End Sub
```

You can see the results in Figure 6.1. When the user clicks an item in the list box, the selected item is displayed in the text box.

List boxes also support Click and DoubleClick events. Although you can use the Click event, you usually use the SelectedIndexChanged changed event, which occurs when the user clicks the list box in a new place anyway. However, the DoubleClick event does have a use, because double-clicking an item indicates that the user wants you to initiate some action; for example, if you list programs in a list box, double-clicking one might start that program.

Tip

> A DoubleClick event also causes a Click event to occur in the list box. To double-click an item, you must first click it.

Working with a List Box's Items

You can keep track of the number of items in a list box with the Items collection's Count property. For example, here's how you can copy the name of each item into a text box in a loop when the user clicks a button:

```
Private Sub Button1_Click(ByVal sender As System.Object, _
    ByVal e As System.EventArgs) Handles Button1.Click
    For intLoopIndex As Integer = 0 To ListBox1.Items.Count - 1
        TextBox1.Text &= ListBox1.Items(intLoopIndex) & " "
    Next
End Sub
```

Note that this code uses the Items collection to access the items in the list box; all you need to do to refer to an item with its index is to use that index with the Items collection like this: Items(7).

We've already seen that you can get the index of the currently selected item in a list box with the `SelectedIndex` property:

```
Private Sub ListBox1_SelectedIndexChanged(ByVal sender As _
    System.Object, ByVal e As System.EventArgs) Handles _
    ListBox1.SelectedIndexChanged
    TextBox1.Text = "You selected item " & ListBox1.SelectedIndex
End Sub
```

You can also set the selected item by assigning its index to the `SelectedIndex` property, and you can also use the `SetSelected` method. For example, `ListBox1.SetSelected(4, True)` selects the item with index 4, and `ListBox1.SetSelected(5, False)` deselects the item with index 5.

To get the text of the selected item in a list box, you can use the expression `ListBox1.Items(SelectedIndex)`. Another way to get the text of the selected item's text from a list box is to use the list box's `Text` property like this:

```
Private Sub ListBox1_SelectedIndexChanged(ByVal sender As _
    System.Object, ByVal e As System.EventArgs) Handles _
    ListBox1.SelectedIndexChanged
    TextBox1.Text = "You selected " & ListBox1.Text
End Sub
```

There's also another way to work with the selected item in a list box: as an object. When you add an item to a list box using the `Items` collection's `Add` method (or the `AddRange` method), you're really adding an object (or an array of objects) to the list box. Although our examples so far have added `String` objects to list boxes, you can add virtually any type of object, as long as it has a `ToString` method. (All Visual Basic .NET objects are supposed to support the `ToString` method; Visual Basic .NET will use this method to display the item's caption in the list box.) Besides getting just the index of the selected item, you can get the actual object that index corresponds to by using the `SelectedItem` property. Here's how you might use the object's `ToString` method to display the caption of a selected object:

```
Private Sub ListBox1_SelectedIndexChanged(ByVal sender As _
    System.Object, ByVal e As System.EventArgs) Handles _
    ListBox1.SelectedIndexChanged
    TextBox1.Text = "You selected " & ListBox1.SelectedItem.ToString()
End Sub
```

6

Being able to store objects in a list box is useful; for example, you might display client names in the list box, but have each entry actually be an object complete with contact information, past orders, and credit history for each client.

Sorting and Searching List Boxes

You can also sort the items in a list box alphabetically for easy user access by setting the list box's Sorted property to True (this property is False by default). Here's how that might look when the user clicks a button:

```
Private Sub Button1_Click(ByVal sender As System.Object, _
    ByVal e As System.EventArgs) Handles Button1.Click
    ListBox1.Sorted = True
End Sub
```

You can set the Sorted property at both runtime and design time.

| Tip | Sorting a list box can change the indices of the items in that list box (unless they were already in alphabetical order). After the sorting operation finishes, the new first item is given index 0; the next, index 1; and so on. |

You can also use the FindString method to search for an item in the list that contains a specific search string; this method returns the index of the matching item, or −1 if there was no match. You can call FindString as shown here to search for text—in this case, for the text "Item 4"—after which the code selects the matching item in the list box:

```
Private Sub Button1_Click(ByVal sender As System.Object, _
    ByVal e As System.EventArgs) Handles Button1.Click
    ListBox1.SelectedIndex = ListBox1.FindString("Item 4")
End Sub
```

You can also specify the index at which to start searching, like this, which begins the search at index number 2: ListBox1.FindString("Item 4", 2).

Creating Multiple-Selection List Boxes

List boxes can support multiple selections; the SelectionMode property determines how many list items can be selected at a time. You can set this property to these values from the SelectionMode enumeration:

- SelectionMode.MultiExtended—Multiple items can be selected, and the user can use the Shift, Ctrl, and arrow keys to make multiple selections.
- SelectionMode.MultiSimple—Multiple items can be selected.
- SelectionMode.None—No items may be selected.
- SelectionMode.One—Only one item may be selected at a time.

In single-selection list boxes, you use the Items collection's SelectedIndex and SelectedItem properties to determine which item has been selected. On the other hand, when you support multiple selections, you use the Items collection's SelectedIndices property to get the selected indices (stored as an array) and the SelectedItems property to access the selected items themselves (stored as a collection of objects).

For example, here's how you might use a For Each loop to loop over and display the selected items in a multiple-selection list box:

```
For Each intIndex In ListBox1.SelectedIndices
    TextBox1.Text &= ListBox1.Items(intIndex).ToString() & " "
Next
```

And here's how you might do the same thing using the SelectedItems collection:

```
For Each objItem In ListBox1.SelectedItems
    TextBox1.Text &= objItem.ToString() & " "
Next
```

You can see an example in the MultiSelectListBoxes project in the code for this book. This example, shown in Listing 6.2, creates a new list box in code and makes it a multiple-selection list box by setting the SelectionMode property to SelectionMode. MultiExtended. It also lets the list box support multiple columns by setting the list box's MultiColumn property to True, adds a number of items to the list box, and selects some of those items.

LISTING 6.2   Creating a Multiple-Selection List Box (MultiSelectListBoxes project, Form1.vb)

```
Dim ListBox1 As ListBox

Private Sub Form1_Load(ByVal sender As System.Object, _
    ByVal e As System.EventArgs) Handles MyBase.Load

    ListBox1 = New ListBox
    ListBox1.Size = New Size(270, 100)
    ListBox1.Location = New Point(10, 60)
    AddHandler ListBox1.SelectedIndexChanged, AddressOf _
        ListBox1_SelectedIndexChanged
    Me.Controls.Add(ListBox1)
    ListBox1.MultiColumn = True
    ListBox1.SelectionMode = SelectionMode.MultiExtended

    For intLoopIndex As Integer = 0 To 19
        ListBox1.Items.Add("Item " & intLoopIndex.ToString())
    Next intLoopIndex
```

6

LISTING 6.2   continued

```
    ListBox1.SetSelected(2, True)
    ListBox1.SetSelected(4, True)
    ListBox1.SetSelected(8, True)
    ListBox1.SetSelected(10, True)
End Sub
```

The `SelectedIndexChanged` event handler also contains code to display the selected items in two text boxes—one for the items themselves and one for their indices:

```
Private Sub ListBox1_SelectedIndexChanged(ByVal _
sender As System.Object, ByVal e As System.EventArgs)
    Dim Item As String
    Dim Index As Integer

    TextBox1.Text = "Here are the selected items: "
    For Each Item In ListBox1.SelectedItems
        TextBox1.Text &= Item.ToString() & " "
    Next

    TextBox2.Text = "Here are the selected indices: "
    For Each Index In ListBox1.SelectedIndices
        TextBox2.Text &= Index.ToString() & " "
    Next
End Sub
```

And that's it! You can see the results in Figure 6.3. As you see in that figure, the next list box supports multiple columns and selections.

FIGURE 6.3

Supporting multiple selections in a list box.

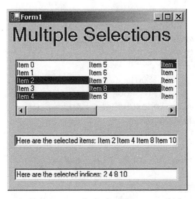

Using Checked List Boxes

Besides list boxes, Visual Basic .NET also supports *checked* list boxes, as you can see in Figure 6.4; that's the CheckedListBoxes example in the code for this book.

FIGURE 6.4

A checked list box.

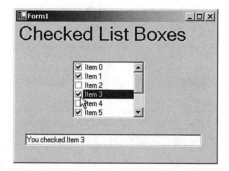

Checked list boxes are useful because they allow the user to check or uncheck items in a list (for example, you might want to let the user specify what directories to search, and so on), which is great if you're working with many items. Here's the hierarchy of the CheckedListBox class:

```
System.Object
   System.MarshalByRefObject
      System.ComponentModel.Component
         System.Windows.Forms.Control
            System.Windows.Forms.ListControl
               System.Windows.Forms.ListBox
                  System.Windows.Forms.CheckedListBox
```

As with list boxes, you can access the items in a checked list box by using the Items property. To check an item, the user must first select an item and then check or uncheck the item's check box. This is true unless you set the CheckOnClick property to True (as in the CheckedListBoxes example), in which case it takes only one click (you don't have to select an item before accessing the check box).

You can access the checked items using the CheckedItems property (which holds a collection of objects) and the CheckedIndices property (which holds an array). The GetItemChecked method determines whether an item is checked, and the SetItemChecked method can check or uncheck items. The ItemCheck event handles check box events.

Like check boxes themselves, checked list boxes can also support the three states of the CheckState enumeration: CheckState.Checked, CheckState.Indeterminate, and

6

CheckState.Unchecked. To use three-state check boxes, you use the GetItemCheckState and SetItemCheckState methods instead of the GetItemChecked and SetItemChecked methods.

You can find the significant public properties of the ListBox class in Table 6.4, the significant methods in Table 6.5, and the significant events in Table 6.6. (Note that these tables do not include the significant properties, methods, and events ListBox inherits from the Control class; you can find them in Tables 5.1, 5.2, and 5.3.)

TABLE 6.4   Significant Public Properties of CheckedListBox Objects

Property	Means
CheckedIndices	Returns an array of checked indices in this checked list box.
CheckedItems	Returns a collection of checked items (objects) in this checked list box.
CheckOnClick	Returns or sets whether the check box should be toggled when an item is selected.
ColumnWidth	Returns or sets the width of columns in a multicolumn checked list box.
HorizontalScrollbar	Returns or sets whether a horizontal scrollbar should be displayed.
IntegralHeight	Returns or sets whether the checked list box should resize to avoid showing partial items.
ItemHeight	Returns the height of the item area.
Items	Returns the collection of items in this checked list box.
MultiColumn	Returns or sets whether the checked list box supports multiple columns.
ScrollAlwaysVisible	Returns or sets whether the vertical scrollbar is always visible.
SelectedIndex	Returns or sets the (zero-based) index of the currently selected item in a checked list box.
SelectedIndices	Returns an array of the (zero-based) indices of all currently selected items in the checked list box.
SelectedItem	Returns or sets the currently selected item in the checked list box.
SelectedItems	Returns a collection containing the currently selected items in the checked list box.
SelectionMode	Returns or sets the selection mode.
Sorted	Returns or sets whether the items in the checked list box should be sorted alphabetically.
Text	Returns the text of the currently selected item in the checked list box.
ThreeDCheckBoxes	Returns or sets whether the check boxes should be displayed as flat or normal.
TopIndex	Returns or sets the index of the first visible item in the checked list box.

TABLE 6.5   Significant Public Methods of `CheckedListBox` Objects

Method	Means
BeginUpdate	Prevents the checked list box from redrawing itself until the `EndUpdate` method is called.
ClearSelected	Unselects all items in the checked list box.
EndUpdate	Resumes visual updating of the checked list box after updating is suspended by the `BeginUpdate` method.
FindString	Finds the first item in the checked list box that starts with the indicated string.
GetItemChecked	Returns whether the indicated item is checked.
GetItemCheckState	Returns a value specifying the check state of the current item.
GetItemHeight	Returns the height of an item in the checked list box.
GetItemText	Returns an item's text.
GetSelected	Returns whether the indicated item is selected.
SetItemChecked	Sets the item at the indicated index to `CheckState.Checked`.
SetItemCheckState	Sets the check state of the item at the indicated index.
SetSelected	Selects or clears the selection for the indicated item in a checked list box.

TABLE 6.6   Significant Public Events of `CheckedListBox` Objects

Event	Means
ItemCheck	Occurs when the checked state of an item changes.
SelectedIndexChanged	Occurs when the `SelectedIndex` property has changed.

Creating a Checked List Box

You can add items to a checked list box at design time with the String Collection Editor, just as you can with normal list boxes. You can also use the `Add` method of the `Items` collection, as with normal list boxes. In fact, the `Add` method has a form that you can use to set check marks when you add new items. Passing a value of `True` makes the item checked (the default is `False`), as in this code from the CheckedListBoxes example that checks all the new items:

```
Private Sub Form1_Load(ByVal sender As System.Object, _
ByVal e As System.EventArgs) Handles MyBase.Load
```

6

```
    For intLoopIndex As Integer = 0 To 9
        CheckedListBox1.Items.Add("Item " & intLoopIndex.ToString(), True)
    Next intLoopIndex
End Sub
```

So how do you work with check marks in code? That topic is coming up in the next two sections.

Setting an Item's Check State

You can use the SetItemChecked method to check or uncheck items by passing a value of True or False, respectively. You pass this method the index of the item to check or uncheck, and True or False. In the following example, the code checks the current selection in a checked list box when the user clicks a button:

```
Private Sub Button1_Click(ByVal sender As System.Object, _
    ByVal e As System.EventArgs) Handles Button3.Click
    CheckedListBox1.SetItemChecked(CheckedListBox1.SelectedIndex, True)
End Sub
```

To work with three-state check boxes, you use the SetItemCheckState method. You pass this method the index of the item to change and a value from the CheckState enumeration:

- CheckState.Checked—The check box is checked.
- CheckState.Indeterminate—The check box is in the indeterminate state, with a shaded appearance.
- CheckState.Unchecked—The check box is unchecked.

For example, CheckedListBox1.SetItemCheckState(0, CheckState.Checked) checks the item with index 0.

Getting an Item's Check State

The GetItemChecked method allows you to determine whether a check box is checked, returning True if it is. Here's an example that loops over all items in a checked list box and displays those that are checked:

```
Private Sub Form1_Load(ByVal sender As System.Object, _
ByVal e As System.EventArgs) Handles MyBase.Load
    For intLoopIndex As Integer = 0 To (CheckedListBox1.Items.Count - 1)
        If CheckedListBox1.GetItemChecked(intLoopIndex) = True Then
            TextBox1.Text &= CheckedListBox1.Items(intLoopIndex).ToString & " "
        End If
    Next
End Sub
```

The `CheckedItems` collection also gives you a handy way to access all checked items. Here's some code that does the same thing as the preceding code but uses the `CheckedItems` collection to make life a little easier:

```
Private Sub Form1_Load(ByVal sender As System.Object, _
ByVal e As System.EventArgs) Handles MyBase.Load
    For Each strObject In CheckedListBox1.CheckedItems
        TextBox1.Text &= strObject.ToString() & " "
    Next
End Sub
```

In addition to `CheckedItems`, you can also use a `CheckedIndices` property, which holds a collection containing the indices of the checked items in the checked list box:

```
Private Sub Form1_Load(ByVal sender As System.Object, _
ByVal e As System.EventArgs) Handles MyBase.Load
    For Each intIndex In CheckedListBox1.CheckedIndices
        TextBox1.Text &= "Index " & intIndex & " "
    Next
End Sub
```

If you're using three-state check boxes, you can use the `GetItemCheckState` method to determine how an item is checked. This method returns a value from the `CheckState` enumeration, as in this example:

```
Dim chkState As CheckState
chkState = CheckedListBox1.GetItemCheckState(CheckedListBox1.SelectedIndex)
```

Handling Check Events

You can track what's going on with the check boxes in a checked list box by using the `ItemCheck` event. This event occurs when the check state of any check box changes. How can you determine which check box of the many in the list caused the event? You can use the `SelectedIndex` property because the user can't change a check box in an item unless that item is also selected.

Alternatively, note that an `ItemCheckEventArgs` object is passed to the `ItemCheck` event handler, and that object has an `Index` property that gives you the index of the item whose check mark is about to change. The `NewValue` property of this object holds the check state about to be assigned to the item, which is a value from the `CheckState` enumeration: `CheckState.Checked`, `CheckState.Indeterminate`, or `CheckState.Unchecked`. Note that the check box does not actually have this new value; that value will be assigned to it when the `ItemCheck` event handler terminates.

6

Listing 6.3 shows how the code in the CheckedListBoxes example in the code for this book determines what item was checked and what its new check state is.

LISTING 6.3   Handling List Boxes (CheckedListBoxes project, Form1.vb)

```
Private Sub CheckedListBox1_ItemCheck(ByVal sender As Object, _
    ByVal e As System.Windows.Forms.ItemCheckEventArgs) _
        Handles CheckedListBox1.ItemCheck
    Select Case e.NewValue
        Case CheckState.Checked
            TextBox1.Text = "You checked Item " & e.Index
        Case CheckState.Unchecked
            TextBox1.Text = "You unchecked Item " & e.Index
    End Select
End Sub
```

You can see the results in Figure 6.4. When you check a check box, you'll see the new setting in the text box at the bottom of the window.

And that's it for list boxes! Next, we're going to look at a control that combines a list box and a text box: the combo box.

Using Combo Boxes

Combo boxes are also familiar controls; they combine a text box and a drop-down list, as you can see in Figure 6.5, the ComboBoxes example from the code for this book. The user can enter text into a combo box or can select an item from the drop-down part.

FIGURE 6.5

Using a combo box.

After the user selects an item in a combo box, the selected item's index and text are displayed, as you can see in Figure 6.6.

FIGURE 6.6

Displaying a combo box's selection.

The ComboBox class is actually derived from the ListBox class, as you can see in the class hierarchy:

```
System.Object
   System.MarshalByRefObject
      System.ComponentModel.Component
         System.Windows.Forms.Control
            System.Windows.Forms.ListControl
               System.Windows.Forms.ComboBox
```

True to their name, combo boxes combine aspects of both text boxes and list boxes. For example, you can access the text in a combo box by using the Text property like a text box. And as with list boxes, you can use the SelectedIndex and SelectedItem properties to access the selected item in a combo box (unlike with list boxes, however, you can select at most one item in a combo box; you use the mouse to open a combo box's drop-down list, and when you click the list once, the list immediately closes). The Items.Count property contains the number of items in the drop-down list.

To manage the drop-down list, you can use the Items.Add, Items.Insert, Items.Clear, Items.AddRange, and Items.Remove methods. You can also add items to and remove them from the list by using the Items property at design time. And as in list boxes, you can use the FindString method to search for an item in the list that contains a particular search string. You can also sort a combo box's list if you set the Sorted property to True (the default is False).

You can find the significant public properties of the ComboBox class in Table 6.7, the significant methods in Table 6.8, and the significant events in Table 6.9. (Note that these

6

tables don't include the significant properties, methods, and events ComboBox inherits from the Control class; you can see them in Tables 5.1, 5.2, and 5.3.)

TABLE 6.7　Significant Public Properties of ComboBox Objects

Property	Means
DropDownStyle	Returns or sets the style of the combo box.
DropDownWidth	Returns or sets the width of the drop-down part of a combo box.
DroppedDown	Returns or sets whether the combo box is displaying its drop-down part.
IntegralHeight	Returns or sets whether the combo box should resize to avoid showing partial items.
ItemHeight	Returns the height of an item in the combo box.
Items	Returns the collection of the items contained in this combo box.
MaxDropDownItems	Returns or sets the maximum number of items to be shown in the drop-down part of the combo box.
MaxLength	Returns or sets the maximum number of characters in the text box of a combo box.
PreferredHeight	Returns the preferred height of the combo box.
SelectedIndex	Returns or sets the (zero-based) index specifying the currently selected item.
SelectedItem	Returns or sets the currently selected item in the combo box.
SelectedText	Returns or sets the text that is selected in the text box part of a combo box.
SelectionLength	Returns or sets the number of characters selected in the text box of the combo box.
SelectionStart	Returns or sets the starting index of text selected in the combo box.
Sorted	Returns or sets whether the items in the combo box are sorted.

TABLE 6.8　Significant Public Methods of ComboBox Objects

Method	Means
BeginUpdate	Suspends drawing of the combo box when items are added to the combo box one at a time.
EndUpdate	Resumes drawing the combo box control after drawing was suspended by the BeginUpdate method.
FindString	Finds the first item in the combo box that starts with the indicated string.

TABLE 6.8   continued

Method	Means
GetItemText	Returns an item's text.
Select	Selects a range of text.
SelectAll	Selects all the text in the text box of the combo box.

TABLE 6.9   Significant Public Events of ComboBox Objects

Event	Means
DropDown	Occurs when the drop-down part of a combo box is shown.
DropDownStyleChanged	Occurs when the DropDownStyle property has changed.
SelectedIndexChanged	Occurs when the SelectedIndex property has changed.

Creating a Combo Box

At design time you can simply drag a combo box onto a form, and at runtime you can create a combo box using the ComboBox class. You can set the text in a combo box by using the Text property at runtime or design time. To add the items in a combo box's list, you can click the Items property at design time, opening the String Collection Editor discussed for list boxes.

At runtime, you can use the Items.Insert, Items.Add, and Items.AddRange methods to add items to the list part of a combo box. The following code from the ComboBoxes example in the book's code adds items to a combo box as well as the text prompt "Choose one..." to the text box in the combo box:

```
Private Sub Form1_Load(ByVal sender As System.Object, _
    ByVal e As System.EventArgs) Handles MyBase.Load
    For intLoopIndex As Integer = 0 To 10
        ComboBox1.Items.Add("Item " + intLoopIndex.ToString())
    Next
    ComboBox1.Text = "Choose one..."
End Sub
```

Handling Combo Box Events

Now that you have a new combo box, how do you handle events? Because combo boxes are combinations of text boxes and list boxes, the primary events are TextChanged events when the user types into the text box, and SelectedIndexChanged when the user uses the list box part of the combo box.

6

When the user changes the text in a combo box, a `TextChange` event occurs, exactly as it does when the user types in a text box. You can read the new text in the text box by using the `Text` property; for example, here's how you might display the new text in the combo box every time the user changes that text by typing:

```
Private Sub ComboBox1_TextChanged(ByVal sender As Object, _
ByVal e As System.EventArgs) Handles ComboBox1.TextChanged
    TextBox1.Text = ComboBox1.Text
End Sub
```

When the selection changes in a combo box, a `SelectionChanged` event occurs, and you can use the `SelectedIndex` and `SelectedItem` properties to get the index of the newly selected item and the item itself. Listing 6.4 shows the code from the ComboBoxes example that reports the new selection when the user makes a new selection in the combo box, as you can see in Figure 6.6.

LISTING 6.4   Handling Combo Boxes (ComboBoxes project, Form1.vb)

```
Private Sub ComboBox1_SelectedIndexChanged(ByVal sender _
As System.Object, ByVal e As System.EventArgs) Handles _
ComboBox1.SelectedIndexChanged
    Dim intSelectedIndex As Integer
    intSelectedIndex = ComboBox1.SelectedIndex
    Dim objSelectedItem As Object
    objSelectedItem = ComboBox1.SelectedItem

    TextBox1.Text = "Item's index: " & intSelectedIndex & _
    ". Item's text: " & objSelectedItem.ToString()
End Sub
```

 Tip

Here's an easy way to get text of the current selection in a combo box: When you make a selection, that new selection appears in the combo box's text box. That means you can easily get the text of the current selection: Just use the combo box's `Text` property.

Combo boxes also support `Click` events, which occur when the user makes a selection in the list box using the mouse. You can determine which item the user clicked by using the combo's `SelectedIndex` property, which holds the index of the clicked item. Or you can get that item directly by using the `SelectedItem` property, because when you click an item, it is made the new selected item in the text box.

You might think it's impossible to have `DoubleClick` events in combo boxes, because when you click the items in the list once, the list closes. That's true except for one type of combo box—simple combo boxes, where the list stays open all the time, and which can support `DoubleClick` events. How do you make a combo box into a simple combo box? You use the `DropDownStyle` property, coming up next.

Configuring Combo Boxes

You can configure the drop-down list in a combo box to act in one of three different ways, using the `DropDownStyle` property. Here are the possible settings for this property:

- `ComboBoxStyle.DropDown`—The Dropdown Combo style (the default) includes a drop-down list and a text box. With this style, the user can select from the list or type into the text box.

- `ComboBoxStyle.Simple`—The Simple Combo style includes a text box and a list that doesn't drop down. The user can select from the list or type into the text box.

- `ComboBoxStyle.DropDownList`—The Dropdown List style allows selection only from the drop-down list.

> By default, a simple combo box is sized so that none of the list is displayed. Increase the `Height` property to display the list.

And that completes our work with combo boxes today. Next up is the essential control for displaying images: picture boxes.

Using Picture Boxes

In Visual Basic .NET, you can use picture boxes to display graphics in bitmap, icon, JPEG, GIF, or other image formats. You can see a picture box, from the PictureBoxes example in the code for this book, at work in Figure 6.7.

FIGURE 6.7

Displaying an image in a picture box.

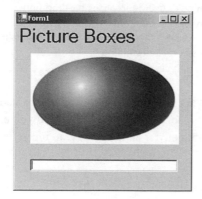

6

The `PictureBox` class is derived directly from the `Control` class:

```
System.Object
  System.MarshalByRefObject
    System.ComponentModel.Component
      System.Windows.Forms.Control
        System.Windows.Forms.PictureBox
```

You can find the significant public properties of the `PictureBox` class in Table 6.10 and the significant events in Table 6.11. (Note that these tables don't list the significant properties, methods, and events `PictureBox` inherits from the `Control` class; you can find them in Tables 5.1, 5.2, and 5.3.)

TABLE 6.10 Significant Public Properties of `PictureBox` Objects

Property	Means
BorderStyle	Sets the border style for the picture box.
Image	Sets the image that the picture box displays.

TABLE 6.11 Significant Public Events of `PictureBox` Objects

Event	Means
Resize	Occurs when the picture box is resized.
SizeModeChanged	Occurs when `SizeMode` changes.

 Note

In earlier versions of Visual Basic, picture boxes were power-intensive controls, enabling you to draw whole images as well as display them. Picture boxes no longer support all kinds of drawing methods directly; instead, all those methods have been removed and are now built into the `Graphics` class. Although picture boxes no longer have drawing methods built in, you can use a picture box's `CreateGraphics` method (inherited from the `Control` class) to get a `Graphics` object for the picture box, which allows you to draw in the image as picture boxes used to do. We'll discuss more on this topic in Day 10, "Graphics and File Handling."

By default, a picture box does not have any borders, but you can add a standard or three-dimensional border by using the `BorderStyle` property. And you can even handle events such as `Click` and `MouseDown` to convert an image into an imagemap, as we'll see.

Creating a Picture Box

After adding a picture box to a form, you can use the `Image` property to specify the image you want to display. At design time, you can do that by selecting the `Image` property in the Properties window. Then you click the button with an ellipsis (…) in it to open a dialog that enables you to select an image file to load into a picture box. That's how the image you see in Figure 6.7, ellipse.jpg, was loaded into the picture box there.

At runtime, you can load an image into the `Image` property, assigning an `Image` object to that property. We'll see how to work with `Image` objects in Day 10. To create an `Image` object from an image file, you can use the `Image` class's `FromFile` method (this method is a class method, not an object method, so you can use it with the name of the class, `Image`) like this:

```
Private Sub Button1_Click(ByVal sender As System.Object, _
    ByVal e As System.EventArgs) Handles Button1.Click
    PictureBox1.Image = _
        Image.FromFile("c:\vbnet 2003\Day6\PictureBoxes\ellipse.jpg")
End Sub
```

The powerful `FromFile` method can load images from bitmap (.bmp), icon (.ico), JPEG (.jpg), and GIF (.gif) files, as well as metafiles (.wmf) and other types of image files.

Sizing Picture Boxes to Contents

After you load an image into a picture box, you might want to size the picture box to match the image. Picture boxes don't do that by default, but you can make them resize themselves automatically to fit the image they're displaying by using the `SizeMode` property. This property may be assigned values from the `PictureBoxSizeMode` enumeration:

- `PictureBoxSizeMode.AutoSize`—Sizes the picture box to the image.

- `PictureBoxSizeMode.CenterImage`—Centers the image in the picture box.

- `PictureBoxSizeMode.Normal`—Places the upper-left corner of the image at upper left in the picture box.

- `PictureBoxSizeMode.StretchImage`—Allows you to stretch the image in code.

The `SizeMode` property of the picture box in Figure 6.7 is set to `PictureBoxSizeMode.AutoSize`, but you could also stretch the image if you set the `SizeMode` property to `PictureBoxSizeMode.StretchImage` and resize the picture box in code like this:

```
Private Sub Form1_Load(ByVal sender As System.Object, _
    ByVal e As System.EventArgs) Handles MyBase.Load
```

6

```
    PictureBox1.SizeMode = PictureBoxSizeMode.StretchImage
    PictureBox1.ClientSize = New Size(200, 200)
End Sub
```

You can see the new, stretched image in Figure 6.8, where the elliptical shape in Figure 6.7 has become nearly spherical.

FIGURE 6.8

Stretching an image in a picture box.

 Tip

At runtime (only), you can also change the size of the image using the `ClientSize` property.

Handling Picture Box Events

Like other controls, picture boxes support events, such as mouse events. In fact, you can use mouse events to create imagemaps using picture boxes. Imagemaps allow the user to click various "hot spots" in an image, launching new applications or Web pages, depending on what was clicked. To create an imagemap, you shouldn't use the `Click` event because that event's handler isn't passed the actual location of the click; instead, you should use the `MouseDown` event that we first saw in Day 4, "Creating Windows Forms." Listing 6.5 shows how the PictureBoxes example in the book's code uses the `MouseDown` event to display the location at which the user clicked an image.

LISTING 6.5   Handling Picture Box Clicks (PictureBoxes project, Form1.vb)

```
Private Sub PictureBox1_MouseDown(ByVal sender As Object, _
ByVal e As System.Windows.Forms.MouseEventArgs) _
Handles PictureBox1.MouseDown
    TextBox1.Text = "You clicked the image at (" & e.X & ", " & e.Y & ")."
End Sub
```

You can see the results of this code in Figure 6.9, after the user has clicked the image in the picture box.

FIGURE 6.9

Handling MouseDown *events in a picture box.*

And that's it for our work with picture boxes until Day 10, when we'll work with graphics in an in-depth way. The next control we'll see today is the scrollbar control.

Using Scrollbars

Scrollbars are another familiar control in Windows; they're those vertical or horizontal bars with a scroll box, also called a thumb, that you can drag. We saw how to add scrollbars to text boxes yesterday.

Besides attaching them to other controls, you can also use free-standing scrollbars in Visual Basic .NET. You can see two scrollbars—a vertical one and a horizontal one—from the ScrollBars example in this book's code in Figure 6.10. When the user moves a scrollbar, the new position of that scrollbar is displayed in the text boxes you see in the figure.

FIGURE 6.10

Handling scrollbar events.

6

In Visual Basic .NET, there are two types of scrollbars: horizontal and vertical. Horizontal scrollbars are supported with the `HScrollBar` class, and the hierarchy for that class is as follows:

```
System.Object
   System.MarshalByRefObject
      System.ComponentModel.Component
         System.Windows.Forms.Control
            System.Windows.Forms.ScrollBar
               System.Windows.Forms.HScrollBar
```

Vertical scrollbars are supported with the `VScrollBar` class, and the hierarchy for that class is as follows:

```
System.Object
   System.MarshalByRefObject
      System.ComponentModel.Component
         System.Windows.Forms.Control
            System.Windows.Forms.ScrollBar
               System.Windows.Forms.VScrollBar
```

You can find the significant public properties of the `HScrollBar` and `VScrollBar` classes in Table 6.12 and the significant events in Table 6.13. (Note that these tables do not list the significant properties, methods, and events `HScrollBar` and `VScrollBar` inherit from the `Control` class; you can find them in Tables 5.1, 5.2, and 5.3.)

TABLE 6.12   Significant Public Properties of `HScrollBar` and `VScrollBar` Objects

Property	Means
LargeChange	Returns or sets the amount the `Value` property changes when you click the scrollbar itself (outside the scroll box and arrow buttons).
Maximum	Returns or sets the upper limit of possible values of the scrollable range.
Minimum	Returns or sets the lower limit of possible values of the scrollable range.
SmallChange	Returns or sets the amount the `Value` property changes when an arrow button is clicked.
Value	Returns or sets the value indicating the current position of the scroll box.

TABLE 6.13   Significant Public Events of `HScrollBar` and `VScrollBar` Objects

Event	Means
Scroll	Occurs when the scroll box has been moved.
ValueChanged	Occurs when the `Value` property has changed, either in a `Scroll` event or programmatically.

Most of the controls that use scrollbars come with them built in, such as multiline text boxes, combo boxes, or list controls. However, scrollbars still pop up by themselves in some applications, such as when you want to let the user select red, green, and blue color values for a drawing color (although you can use a Color dialog for that; see Day 7, "Windows Forms: Working with Menus, Built-in Dialogs, and Printing"). We'll also see how to use scrollbars to scroll the contents of a picture box in Day 10.

Scrollbars are also perfect controls to dock to the edge of forms because that's where users expect to see them. To dock a scrollbar, use the Dock property.

You can set or get the current value of a scrollbar by using the Value property, which is the property you use to determine the new value the user has scrolled the scrollbar to. You can also set the Value property yourself in code, which moves the scroll box to match.

The two main events for scrollbars are the Scroll event, which happens continuously as the scrollbar is scrolled, and the ValueChanged event, which occurs every time the scrollbar's value changes by even one unit (which means it'll occur many times during a normal scroll operation).

Creating a Scrollbar

You can create horizontal and vertical scrollbars by dragging them onto a form from the toolbox at design time or by creating objects of the HScrollBar or VScrollBar classes at runtime. After you've created a scrollbar, you use the Minimum and Maximum properties to set the range of values the user can select using the scrollbar. The Minimum property is set to 0 by default, and the Maximum property is set to 100. You can set the Minimum and Maximum properties for scrollbars at design time or at runtime; here's how the ScrollBars example sets these properties at runtime:

```
Private Sub Form1_Load(ByVal sender As System.Object, _
    ByVal e As System.EventArgs) Handles MyBase.Load
    HScrollBar1.Minimum = 0
    HScrollBar1.Maximum = 100
        .
        .
        .
End Sub
```

6

Tip

Here's something to know when setting the Maximum property for a scrollbar: A scrollbar can scroll only up to its maximum value minus the width of the scroll box. For example, if you set the Minimum property to 0 and the Maximum property to 100, the actual maximum value the user can scroll to is 91.

When the user clicks the scrollbar itself, not the scroll box and not an arrow button, the
scroll box should move in that direction by the amount set by the scrollbar's
LargeChange property. You can set the LargeChange property at design time or at runtime; here's how the code in the ScrollBars example sets this property when the form
first loads:

```
Private Sub Form1_Load(ByVal sender As System.Object, _
ByVal e As System.EventArgs) Handles MyBase.Load
    HScrollBar1.Minimum = 0
    HScrollBar1.Maximum = 100
    HScrollBar1.LargeChange = 20
        .
        .
        .

End Sub
```

The user can also click the arrow buttons at either end of the scrollbar (see Figure 6.10),
and doing so makes the scrollbar's value change by the value in the SmallChange property. For example, here's how the code in the ScrollBars example sets this property for
the horizontal scrollbar when the form first loads:

```
Private Sub Form1_Load(ByVal sender As System.Object, _
    ByVal e As System.EventArgs) Handles MyBase.Load
    HScrollBar1.Minimum = 0
    HScrollBar1.Maximum = 100
    HScrollBar1.LargeChange = 20
    HScrollBar1.SmallChange = 5
        .
        .
        .

    End Sub
```

Now when the user clicks the arrow buttons, the setting of the horizontal scrollbar will
change by 5.

 Tip

> You might want to change the LargeChange and SmallChange properties
> while a program is running. For example, if you're using scrollbars to scroll
> through documents and the user alternates between 200- and 20,000-line
> documents, you might want to change these properties appropriately.

Now you've configured the settings needed for a scrollbar—the minimum and maximum
values, as well as the amount the scrollbar changes when the user clicks the scrollbar or
the arrow buttons. All that's left is to make the scrollbar active, and you can do that by
handling scrollbar events.

Handling Scrollbar Events

As already discussed, the two events you use most with scrollbars are the Scroll and ValueChanged events. The ValueChanged event occurs each time the Value property of the scrollbar changes, and in the course of normal scrolling, that event can happen hundreds of times. It's usually better to use the Scroll event (which is the default event for scrollbars), which also happens as the user scrolls the scrollbar, but not every time the Value property changes by 1.

When a Scroll event occurs, a ScrollEventArgs object is passed to the event's handler. You can use the NewValue property of this object to determine the new value the scrollbar is about to be scrolled to. You can also use the Type property, which tells you the type of the scroll operation, using a value from the ScrollEventType enumeration:

- ScrollEventType.EndScroll—The scroll box has stopped moving.
- ScrollEventType.First—The scroll box was moved to the Minimum position.
- ScrollEventType.LargeDecrement—The user clicked the scrollbar to the left (horizontal scrollbars) or above (vertical scrollbars) the scroll box, or pressed the Page Up key.
- ScrollEventType.LargeIncrement—The user clicked the scrollbar to the right (horizontal scrollbars) or below (vertical scrollbars) the scroll box, or pressed the Page Down key.
- ScrollEventType.Last—The scroll box was moved to the Maximum position.
- ScrollEventType.SmallDecrement—The user clicked the left (horizontal scrollbars) or top (vertical scrollbars) scroll arrow or pressed the up-arrow key.
- ScrollEventType.SmallIncrement—The user clicked the right (horizontal scrollbars) or bottom (vertical scrollbars) scroll arrow or pressed the down-arrow key.
- ScrollEventType.ThumbPosition—The scroll box was moved.
- ScrollEventType.ThumbTrack—The scroll box is currently being moved.

The ScrollBars example that you can see in Figure 6.10 uses the Scroll event to display the new values of the horizontal and vertical scrollbars in the application after they've been scrolled. For example, when the horizontal scrollbar has been scrolled, you can get the new value the scrollbar is about to be set to by using the NewValue property of the ScrollEventArgs object. You can also get the current location of the vertical scrollbar, which hasn't been changed, by using that scrollbar's Value property. Listing 6.6 shows what it looks like in code.

6

LISTING 6.6   Handling Scrollbars (ScrollBars project, Form1.vb)

```
Private Sub VScrollBar1_Scroll(ByVal sender As System.Object, _
ByVal e As System.Windows.Forms.ScrollEventArgs) Handles VScrollBar1.Scroll
    TextBox1.Text = "Horizontal scroll value: " & HScrollBar1.Value
    TextBox2.Text = "Vertical scroll value: " & e.NewValue
End Sub

Private Sub HScrollBar1_Scroll(ByVal sender As System.Object, _
ByVal e As System.Windows.Forms.ScrollEventArgs) Handles HScrollBar1.Scroll
    TextBox1.Text = "Horizontal scroll value: " & e.NewValue
    TextBox2.Text = "Vertical scroll value: " & VScrollBar1.Value
End Sub
```

You can see the results in Figure 6.10, where the application reports the locations of the scrollbars as you scroll them.

Note in particular the use of the NewValue property to get the new scroll setting. We used NewValue to get the value the scrollbar was *about* to be scrolled to in the Scroll event handler (the Value property, on the other hand, holds the scrollbar's *current* value).

Tip

> Actually, it wouldn't have been too bad if we had used the Value property instead of NewValue in this case, because when the user releases the mouse button (after having already completed the scroll operation), a final Scroll event occurs, and in that event, Value will indeed hold the scrollbar's final value.

That finishes our work with scrollbars for the moment. Next, we'll look at an allied control: track bars.

Using Track Bars

NEW TERM   Track bars, also called sliders, are very much like scrollbars in code, but they look different. Track bars look more like the controls you would see on a stereo, for example, as you can see in Figure 6.11, which is the TrackBars example from the code for this book. The scroll box here is called a *slider* (which is confusing because that's what some people call the entire control).

FIGURE 6.11

Handling track bar events.

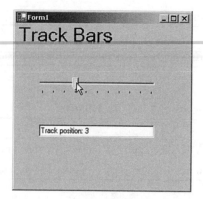

You use track bars when you want to let the user select a number from a continuous range of values (such as setting color values or sound level). Here is the class hierarchy for the TrackBar class:

```
System.Object
    System.MarshalByRefObject
        System.ComponentModel.Component
            System.Windows.Forms.Control
                System.Windows.Forms.TrackBar
```

You can find the significant public properties of the TrackBar class in Table 6.14, the significant methods in Table 6.15, and the significant events in Table 6.16. (Note that these tables do not list the significant properties, methods, and events TrackBar inherits from the Control class; you can find them in Tables 5.1, 5.2, and 5.3.)

TABLE 6.14 Significant Public Properties of TrackBar Objects

Property	Means
LargeChange	Returns or sets the amount the Value property changes when the track bar (not the slider) is clicked.
Maximum	Returns or sets the upper limit of the range of this track bar.
Minimum	Returns or sets the lower limit of the range of this track bar.
Orientation	Returns or sets the horizontal or vertical orientation of the track bar.
SmallChange	Returns or sets the value the amount the Value property changes when the user presses arrow keys.
TickFrequency	Returns or sets the distance between ticks drawn on the control.
TickStyle	Returns or sets how to display the tick marks on the track bar.
Value	Returns or sets the current position of the slider on the track bar control.

6

TABLE 6.15   Significant Public Method of `TrackBar` Objects

Method	Means
SetRange	Sets the `Minimum` and `Maximum` values for the track bar.

TABLE 6.16   Significant Public Events of `TrackBar` Objects

Event	Means
Scroll	Occurs when the slider has been moved by either a mouse or keyboard action.
ValueChanged	Occurs when the `Value` property of a track bar changes.

Creating Track Bars

You can create track bars at design time by dragging them onto a form or at runtime by creating an object of the `TrackBar` class. Although track bars are not based on scrollbars, they are very similar in code.

As in scrollbars, the `Value` property holds the track bar's current setting, which you can set or get with the `Value` property. And you can use the `Scroll` and `ValueChanged` events to handle track bar events. You can set a track bar's range of values with the `Minimum` (default = 0) and `Maximum` (default = 10) properties. You can specify how much the `Value` property should change when the user clicks the sides of the slider by using the `LargeChange` (default = 5) property and how much that property should change when the user presses arrow keys by using the `SmallChange` property (default = 1).

NEW TERM   Unlike scrollbars, however, a track bar can be displayed horizontally or vertically; you set its orientation by using the `Orientation` property. Track bars also can display *ticks*, giving the user an idea of the scale used to set the control's value. The `TickStyle` property allows you to determine how ticks are displayed; this property can take values from the `TickStyle` enumeration:

- `TickStyle.Both`—Tick marks on both sides of the track bar.
- `TickStyle.BottomRight`—Tick marks on the bottom of a horizontal track bar or on the right side of a vertical track bar.
- `TickStyle.None`—No tick marks.
- `TickStyle.TopLeft`—Tick marks on the top of a horizontal track bar or on the left of a vertical track bar.

In addition, you can set the tick *frequency*, actually the distance between ticks, with the `TickFrequency` property (the default is 1). For example, if the `Minimum` is 0, the `Maximum` is 10, and `TickFrequency` is set to 1, you'll see 11 ticks in the track bar, as in Figure 6.11.

Handling Track Bar Events

As with scrollbars, track bars support the Scroll and ValueChanged events. But unless you want to know every time the track bar value changes by one unit, you're usually better off using the Scroll event (like scrollbars, Scroll is the default event for track bars).

As we've seen, the Scroll event handler for scrollbars is passed a ScrollEventArgs object that has a NewValue property containing the new value about to be assigned to the scrollbar. However, the EventArgs (not ScrollEventArgs) object passed to the Scroll event handler does not have a NewValue property. The reason for this is that in track bar events, unlike scrollbars, the Value property is updated *before* the Scroll event occurs. That means we can display the current setting of the track bar like this:

```
Private Sub TrackBar1_Scroll(ByVal sender As System.Object, _
    ByVal e As System.EventArgs) Handles TrackBar1.Scroll
    TextBox1.Text = "Track position: " & TrackBar1.Value
End Sub
```

You can see the results of this code in Figure 6.11.

Using Splitters

Splitters enable you to resize controls at runtime. You can see a splitter at work in Figure 6.12, in the Splitters example in the code for this book, where it's letting the user use a mouse to resize a text box.

FIGURE 6.12

Using a splitter.

6

Space is usually tight in Windows applications, and because splitter controls allow you to resize other controls, extending them as needed and contracting them when their job is over, knowing about them is useful. Here is the class hierarchy for the Splitter class:

```
System.Object
   System.MarshalByRefObject
      System.ComponentModel.Component
         System.Windows.Forms.Control
            System.Windows.Forms.Splitter
```

You can find the significant public properties of the `Splitter` class in Table 6.17 and the significant events in Table 6.18. (Note that these tables do not list the significant properties, methods, and events `Splitter` inherits from the `Control` class; you can find them in Tables 5.1, 5.2, and 5.3.)

TABLE 6.17   Significant Public Properties of `Splitter` Objects

Property	Means
BorderStyle	Returns or sets the type of border.
MinSize	Returns or sets the minimum size of the target of the splitter.
SplitPosition	Returns or sets the position of the splitter.

TABLE 6.18   Significant Public Events of `Splitter` Objects

Event	Means
SplitterMoved	Occurs when the splitter has moved.
SplitterMoving	Occurs while the splitter is moving.

Creating Splitters

To create a splitter at design time, you add the control you want to resize to a container and then dock it in that container. The container could be a form, panel, group box, or other such control. In the Splitters example, a text box is docked to the left side of a panel. The panel is sized to be the same height as the text box, but about twice as wide, as you see in Figure 6.13 (the panel appears in dotted outline in that figure). Next, you dock a splitter in the container as well, docking it the same way (in other words, to the panel's left edge in the Splitters example), as you see in Figure 6.13; the splitter is the small, vertical dotted box in the middle.

Now, when you run the program, the splitter is invisible until the mouse passes over it. At that point, the splitter changes the mouse cursor, indicating that the control can be resized, as you see in Figure 6.12. The user can then expand or contract the control simply by dragging the splitter.

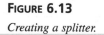

FIGURE 6.13

Creating a splitter.

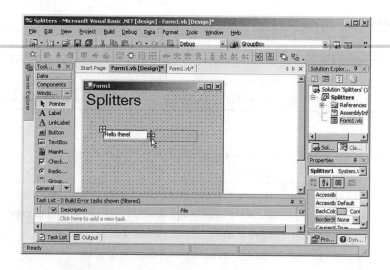

Using Notify Icons

Notify icons add an impressive touch to Windows applications; they enable you to display an icon in the Windows taskbar, in the area called the Windows system tray. Figure 6.14 is from the NotifyIcons example in the book's code, and that example is responsible for the red dot (black and white in the figure, of course) at right in the system tray.

FIGURE 6.14

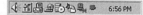

A notify icon.

Notify icons are great for applications that run in the background or don't have a formal user interface, like the Windows services we'll see in Day 21, "Creating Windows Services, Web Services, and Deploying Applications." Not only can such services flash an icon if there's an urgent message, but you can also open a dialog when you click them; for example, if you double-click the notify icon from the NotifyIcons example, it'll open a message box.

Here's the class hierarchy of the `NotifyIcon` class:

```
System.Object
   System.MarshalByRefObject
      System.ComponentModel.Component
         System.Windows.Forms.NotifyIcon
```

You can find the significant public properties of the `NotifyIcon` class in Table 6.19 and the significant events in Table 6.20.

6

TABLE 6.19 Significant Public Properties of `NotifyIcon` Objects

Property	Means
Icon	Returns or sets the current icon.
Text	Returns or sets the tool tip text displayed when the mouse hovers over the icon.
Visible	Returns or sets whether the icon is visible in the Windows system tray.

TABLE 6.20 Significant Public Events of `NotifyIcon` Objects

Event	Means
Click	Occurs when the user clicks the icon in the system tray.
DoubleClick	Occurs when the user double-clicks the icon in the system tray.
MouseDown	Occurs when the user presses a mouse button.
MouseMove	Occurs when the user moves the mouse.
MouseUp	Occurs when the user releases the mouse button.

Creating Notify Icons

To create a notify icon at design time, just drag one from the toolbox to a form. Because the new notify icon does not appear on the form at runtime, it will be added to a component tray under the form, as you see in Figure 6.15.

FIGURE 6.15

Creating a notify icon.

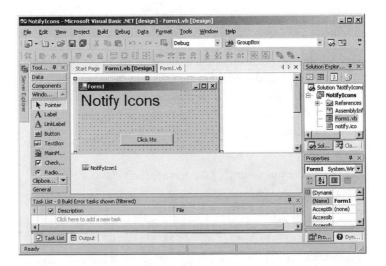

NEW TERM To create a notify icon, you need an icon file to assign to this control's `Icon` property, and you can create new icons with an *icon designer*. To open an icon designer, just select the Project, Add New Item menu item to open the Add New Item dialog; then select Icon File in the Templates box and click Open. This will create a new icon and open it for design in an icon designer, as you see in Figure 6.16.

FIGURE 6.16

Using an icon designer.

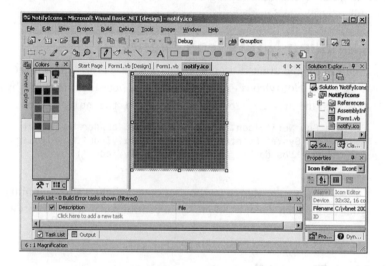

To design your icon, you can use the icon designer you see in Figure 6.16, saved as notify.ico (this is the icon the NotifyIcons example will use).

Tip Many icons are ready for you to use, and they come with Visual Basic .NET. Look at the Common7\graphics\icons directory.

To assign this new icon to the notify icon control, just set the `Icon` property of the notify icon to the name of the icon file to use, such as notify.ico (a dialog will appear when you select this property in the Properties window, allowing you to select whatever .ico file you want). Any text you store in the notify icon's `Text` property becomes the tool tip text for the icon when the mouse hovers over it in the system tray. Also, by default, the notify icon's `Visible` property is set to `True`; in the NotifyIcons example, however, it's set to `False` so the notify icon doesn't appear when the program starts. You can let the user display the icon with the Click Me button you see in Figure 6.15 by using this code:

6

```
Private Sub Button1_Click(ByVal sender As System.Object, _
    ByVal e As System.EventArgs) Handles Button1.Click
    NotifyIcon1.Visible = True
End Sub
```

When the user clicks this button, the notify icon appears in the system tray, as you see in Figure 6.14. Besides showing and hiding a notify icon, you can also handle events for this control—and that's coming up next.

Handling Notify Icon Events

You can handle events for notify icons such as `Click` and `DoubleClick`. For example, the code in the NotifyIcons example handles the `DoubleClick` event by displaying a message box with the message `"You double clicked the notify icon."` this way:

```
Private Sub NotifyIcon1_DoubleClick(ByVal sender As Object, _
ByVal e As System.EventArgs) Handles NotifyIcon1.DoubleClick
    MsgBox("You double clicked the notify icon.")
End Sub
```

In this way, you're able to let the user open a dialog, allowing him or her to interact with your code. Such dialogs can present a control panel, a set of options the user can select from, on-off buttons for your application, and more.

Using Tool Tips

Another control that is very useful—and very popular—is the tool tip. You've undoubtedly seen tool tips before; they're those small rectangular windows with a yellow background that display helpful text when the mouse hovers over some visual element in a program. For example, you can see a tool tip at work in Figure 6.17, in the ToolTips project in the code for this book.

FIGURE 6.17

A tool tip.

In earlier versions of Visual Basic, many controls had a `ToolTipText` property that allowed you to set tool tip text. These days, however, tool tips are supported by their own control—the ToolTip control. Here is the class hierarchy of the `ToolTip` class:

```
System.Object
   System.MarshalByRefObject
      System.ComponentModel.Component
         System.Windows.Forms.ToolTip
```

You can find the significant public properties of the `ToolTip` class in Table 6.21 and the significant methods in Table 6.22.

TABLE 6.21   Significant Public Properties of `ToolTip` Objects

Property	Means
Active	Returns or sets whether the tool tip control is active.
AutomaticDelay	Returns or sets the time (in milliseconds) before the tool tip appears.
InitialDelay	Returns or sets the initial delay for the tool tip.
ReshowDelay	Returns or sets the length of time (in milliseconds) that it takes other tool tips to appear as the mouse moves from one tool tip area to others.
ShowAlways	Returns or sets whether the tool tip appears even if its parent control is not active.

TABLE 6.22   Significant Public Methods of `ToolTip` Objects

Event	Means
GetToolTip	Returns the tool tip text connected to the indicated control.
SetToolTip	Associates tool tip text with the indicated control.

Creating Tool Tips

Because tool tips appear only when you make them appear, they aren't treated as standard controls at design time; they appear in the component tray, not on the form, as you see in Figure 6.18.

You can connect a tool tip with a control and assign text to a tool tip by using the `SetToolTip` method like this: `ToolTip1.SetToolTip(Button1, "This is a text box.")`. You can also use the `GetToolTip` method to get information about a tool tip object. Here's how that looks in the ToolTips example in the book's code:

```
Private Sub Form1_Load(ByVal sender As System.Object, _
    ByVal e As System.EventArgs) Handles MyBase.Load
    ToolTip1.SetToolTip(TextBox1, "This is a text box.")
End Sub
```

6

FIGURE 6.18

Creating a tool tip.

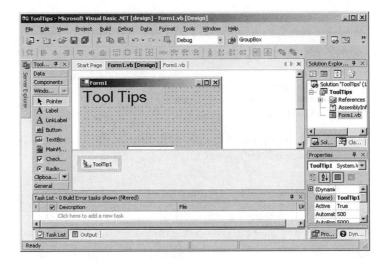

You can see the result in Figure 6.17, where the tool tip for the text box, `"This is a text box."`, is displayed. That's all it takes! As you can see, it's fairly easy to add tool tips to the visual elements in your applications.

Using Timers

Timers are powerful controls because they enable you to create and handle periodic events. For example, you might want to have a program check the status of an Internet connection every few seconds, schedule various tasks in order, or even display an alarm clock, as you see in Figure 6.19.

FIGURE 6.19

Creating an alarm clock.

The application you see at work in Figure 6.19 is the Timers example project in the code for this book. You can enter a time in the text box, click the Alarm On radio button, and when the displayed time exceeds the alarm time, the program will beep once per second. Behind the scenes, a Timer control is running the show, and it causes a Tick event once per second that makes this clock tick. Here is the class hierarchy of the Timer class:

```
System.Object
    System.MarshalByRefObject
        System.ComponentModel.Component
            System.Windows.Forms.Timer
```

You can find the significant public properties of the Timer class in Table 6.23, the significant methods in Table 6.24, and the significant events in Table 6.25.

TABLE 6.23   Significant Public Properties of Timer Objects

Property	Means
Enabled	Returns or sets whether the timer is running.
Interval	Returns or sets the time (in milliseconds) between timer ticks.

TABLE 6.24   Significant Public Methods of Timer Objects

Method	Means
Start	Starts the timer.
Stop	Stops the timer.

TABLE 6.25   Significant Public Event of Timer Objects

Event	Means
Tick	Occurs when the timer interval has elapsed (and the timer is enabled).

Creating a Timer

When you add a timer to a form, that timer goes into the component tray. You set how often you want the timer to generate Tick events by setting the Interval property (in milliseconds, one thousandths of a second—the default is 100, one tenth of a second). Each time a Tick event occurs, you can execute code in a handler for this event, just as you would any other event.

6

> **Tip**
>
> Timers use the computer's built-in clock, which ticks only about 18 times per second. That means timer ticks won't happen faster than that, no matter what the Interval property is set to.

You use a timer's Enabled property to turn the timer on (meaning Tick events will occur) or off (meaning they won't). In fact, you can also use the Start and Stop methods to do the same thing.

Let's see how this works in the Timers application you see in Figure 6.19. The user can turn the alarm on and off with radio buttons, which sets a Boolean variable named blnAlarmOn to True or False:

```
Dim blnAlarmOn As Boolean = False

Private Sub RadioButton1_CheckedChanged(ByVal sender As System.Object, _
    ByVal e As System.EventArgs) Handles RadioButton1.CheckedChanged
    If RadioButton1.Checked Then
        blnAlarmOn = True
    End If
End Sub

Private Sub RadioButton2_CheckedChanged(ByVal sender As System.Object, _
    ByVal e As System.EventArgs) Handles RadioButton2.CheckedChanged
    If RadioButton2.Checked Then
        blnAlarmOn = False
    End If
End Sub
```

The Interval property of the Timer control in this application is set to 1000 milliseconds, or 1 second. When the form first loads, the timer's Enabled property is set to True to start the clock:

```
Private Sub Form1_Load(ByVal sender As System.Object, _
    ByVal e As System.EventArgs) Handles MyBase.Load
    Timer1.Enabled = True
End Sub
```

A special property available to your code in Visual Basic .NET — TimeOfDay — enables you to get the current time so you can display it in a label (set to use 48-point size font) like this in the timer's Tick event handler:

```
Private Sub Timer1_Tick(ByVal sender As System.Object, _
    ByVal e As System.EventArgs) Handles Timer1.Tick
    Label1.Text = TimeOfDay
    .
    .
    .
End Sub
```

The user can enter a time, like **11:00:00**, in the text box you see in Figure 6.19 to set the time when the timer will start beeping. We can create a Visual Basic .NET DateTime object corresponding to the time the alarm should go off by first extracting the hour, minute, and seconds from the time in the text box. You can do that with the Split function, which "splits" a string into an array based on a delimiter character. The delimiter character is a colon (:) here, so here's how you can create the DateTime object containing the alarm time (the DateTime constructor needs the year, month, and day, which we can get from the Today object also available to your code):

```
Private Sub Timer1_Tick(ByVal sender As System.Object, _
    ByVal e As System.EventArgs) Handles Timer1.Tick
    Label1.Text = TimeOfDay
    If blnAlarmOn Then
        Dim strTimes() As String = Split(TextBox1.Text, ":")
        Dim dteAlarmTime = New DateTime(Today.Year, Today.Month, Today.Day, _
        Val(strTimes(0)), Val(strTimes(1)), Val(strTimes(2)))
        .
        .
        .

    End If
End Sub
```

Now you can do a direct comparison between the time the alarm is supposed to go off and the current time, which you can find by using the special built-in Now property. If the current time exceeds the time at which the alarm should go off, you can make the program beep once per second (because Timer1_Tick is called once per second) as shown in Listing 6.7.

LISTING 6.7   Creating an Alarm Clock (Timers project, Form1.vb)

```
Private Sub Timer1_Tick(ByVal sender As System.Object, _
    ByVal e As System.EventArgs) Handles Timer1.Tick
    Label1.Text = TimeOfDay
    If blnAlarmOn Then
        Dim strTimes() As String = Split(TextBox1.Text, ":")
        Dim dteAlarmTime = New DateTime(Today.Year, Today.Month, Today.Day, _
        Val(strTimes(0)), Val(strTimes(1)), Val(strTimes(2)))
        If Now > dteAlarmTime Then
            Beep()
        End If
    End If
End Sub
```

6

And that's all it takes! You can see the results in Figure 6.19. Now we're using timers to create a working alarm clock.

Summary

Today, we saw more of the controls we can use in Windows forms. We started with list boxes, which have a great deal of power packed into them. We saw how to create list boxes at design time and runtime; add items to a list box's Items collection; handle list box events; get the current selection in a list box; create multicolumn list boxes, multiple-selection list boxes, search and sort list boxes; and more.

We also saw that checked list boxes act much like standard list boxes, except that each item in the list is displayed with a check box in front of it. This control is good if you want to let the user select items from a list, such as the directories you want to search for data files, and so on. We saw how to handle these check boxes in code, checking them, unchecking them, and handling check box events.

Combo boxes combine list boxes with text boxes and so give you and the user more capability. In a combo box, the user can select items from the list or enter text into the text box, and we saw how to handle both such actions. We saw how to add items to combo boxes and configure combo boxes as drop-down combo boxes, simple combo boxes, and drop-down list combo boxes.

Picture boxes allow you to display and load images. We saw how to size a picture box to the image it's displaying, handle picture box mouse events (letting us create imagemaps), and stretch images in picture boxes.

Scrollbars are ubiquitous Windows controls and usually come attached to the controls that use them. However, we also saw how to create them ourselves today, both horizontal and vertical scrollbars, and how to configure them with properties such as Minimum and Maximum. We also saw that docking scrollbars to other controls or to the edge of a form is a good idea and saw how to handle scroll events.

Track bars work much like scrollbars, except that their appearance is different; they look much like the controls you see in stereo equipment rather than traditional scrollbars. We saw that in code, track bars work in just about the same way as scrollbars, and we saw how to configure track bars and handle their events.

Splitters allow the user to expand or contract other controls at runtime. You associate a splitter with a control by adding the splitter to the control's container and docking it the same way as the control. Splitters are handy, but there's not usually very much going on in code with these controls.

Notify icons enable you to display a small icon in the taskbar, which is good if your program doesn't have a user interface that is meant to stay open. We saw how to draw an icon, use it in the taskbar, and respond to events such as double-clicks.

Tool tips enable you to display helpful text when the mouse hovers over a control. We saw how to create tool tips, associate them with controls, and set their text.

Finally, we looked at timers, which allow you to create periodic Timer events. Today, we saw how to use timers to create an alarm clock application that not only displayed the current time, but also let the user specify the time for an alarm to go off.

And that's it for the controls we've seen today. Tomorrow, we're going to add more Visual Basic .NET power to our arsenal when we start working with menus, built-in dialogs, and printing.

Q&A

Q Is there any reason *not* to use timers?

A Yes, theoretically, Windows programs are meant to be user-driven, responding to events. When one works with timers, there's the risk that one might use them to wrest control away from the user and do whatever processing the code wants to do. Keep in mind that timers are for specific, timed sequences, not just to take control away from the user.

Q What happens if I don't confine a splitter to a container like a panel control, but just dock it to a form?

A You can still use the splitter to expand or contract controls in the form, but if you dock it to the entire form, the vertical dotted line that appears when the user resizes the control will extend from the top of the form to the bottom, much bigger than the control the user is resizing. The best technique is to add the control and a splitter to a container and then resize the container's height to match the control's height.

Workshop

This workshop tests whether you understand the concepts you saw today. It's a good idea to make sure you can answer these questions before pressing on to tomorrow's work.

Quiz

1. What collection do you work with when you add items to a list box?

2. How can you access an individual item in a list box? And how can you find out how many items are in the list?

3. What are the two primary events most used with combo boxes?

6

4. How do you make a picture box size itself to its contents?

5. What property holds the amount a scrollbar will change when the user clicks an arrow button?

Quiz Answers

1. You use the `Items` collection (and usually a method of this collection, such as `Add`).

2. You can refer to the item in the list box by using an index and the `Items` property like this: `ListBox1.Items(3)`. The number of items in the list is `Items.Count`.

3. The `TextChanged` and `SelectedIndexChanged` events.

4. You assign the value `PictureBoxSizeMode.AutoSize` to the `SizeMode` property of the picture box.

5. The `SmallChange` property.

Exercises

1. Using the `Location` property of a picture box, write a program that uses two scrollbars, docked to the right and bottom edges of a form, to move an image around the form. You might set the `BackColor` property of the form to match the background color of the image for added effect.

2. Create a multiple-selection list box that copies its selections into another (previously empty) list box when the user clicks a button.

DAY 7

Windows Forms: Working with Menus, Built-in Dialogs, and Printing

Today, we're going to look at a powerful set of Windows controls: menus, built-in dialogs, and the printing controls. For example, you wouldn't get far in Windows without using menus. Instead of filling your applications with dozens of buttons or check boxes, you normally use menus that open as needed to present the user with various options. Because space in Windows applications is always at a premium, menus offer a great way of packing those options into a program in a space-conserving way. We'll also see the built-in dialogs today, such as the Open File and Save File dialogs (which will prepare us for the file-handling work we'll do in Day 10, "Graphics and File Handling"). And we'll look at how to handle printing in Visual Basic .NET as well. Here's an overview of today's topics:

- Creating menus and submenus
- Adding check marks to menu items

- Creating menu access keys and shortcuts
- Handling multiple-document interface (MDI) menus
- Creating context menus
- Creating Open File dialogs
- Creating Save File dialogs
- Creating Font dialogs
- Creating Color dialogs
- Creating Folder Browser dialogs
- Printing
- Creating Print Preview dialogs
- Creating Page Setup dialogs

Our first topic is all about working with menus in Visual Basic .NET.

Using Menus

As you know, menu systems can become pretty complex. Take a look at the Visual Basic .NET IDE's File menu that appears in Figure 7.1. You can see all kinds of menu items here, including submenus (those menu items with a small black arrow let you open submenus), access keys (the underlined characters in various menu items), shortcuts (the codes like Ctrl+Shift+A you see in the menu), as well as menu separators (the horizontal lines that serve to divide menu items into functional groups). We'll see how to create all these elements and more today.

FIGURE 7.1

The Visual Basic .NET IDE File menu.

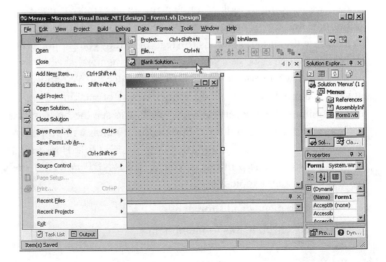

Creating Menus

So how do you create menus for your own applications? You can use two classes here: the `MainMenu` class, which supports the menu system itself, and the `MenuItem` class, which supports the actual items in each menu. As we'll see, you just have to drag a `MainMenu` control from the toolbox to a form at design time; filling in the names of the various menu items will be easy. Here's the class hierarchy for the `MainMenu` class:

```
System.Object
    System.MarshalByRefObject
        System.ComponentModel.Component
            System.Windows.Forms.Menu
                System.Windows.Forms.MainMenu
```

You can find the significant public properties of `MainMenu` objects in Table 7.1 and the significant public methods of this class in Table 7.2.

TABLE 7.1 Significant Public Properties of `MainMenu` Objects

Property	Means
IsParent	Returns whether this menu contains any menu items.
MdiListItem	Returns the `MenuItem` that is used to display a list of MDI child windows.
MenuItems	Returns the collection of `MenuItem` objects for use with the menu.

TABLE 7.2 Significant Public Methods of `MainMenu` Objects

Method	Means
GetForm	Returns the `Form` that contains this menu.
GetMainMenu	Returns the `MainMenu` that contains this menu.
MergeMenu	Merges the `MenuItem` objects of a menu with the current menu.

The `MainMenu` class enables you to add a menu system to a form. The actual menus in that system, such as File, Edit, Help, and so on, are supported by the `MenuItem` class. The menu items in those menus, such as Open, Close, Exit, and so on, are also supported by the `MenuItem` class.

Nearly all our menu work will have to do with the `MenuItem` class. For example, to work with `Click` events in menus, you'll be using the `MenuItem` class's `Click` event. And the `Select` event occurs when a menu item is selected (that is, highlighted; this enables you to perform tasks such as displaying help for menu items when the user places the mouse cursor over those items). Here's the hierarchy of the `MenuItem` class:

7

```
System.Object
    System.MarshalByRefObject
        System.ComponentModel.Component
            System.Windows.Forms.Menu
                System.Windows.Forms.MenuItem
```

You can see the significant public properties of objects of the MenuItem class in Table 7.3, the significant methods in Table 7.4, and the significant events in Table 7.5.

TABLE 7.3   Significant Public Properties of MenuItem Objects

Property	Means
Break	Returns or sets whether the item is displayed on a new line (for a menu item in a MainMenu object) or in a new column (for a menu item in a context menu).
Checked	Returns or sets whether a check mark appears in front of the text of a menu item.
Enabled	Returns or sets whether the menu item is enabled.
Index	Returns or sets the position of the menu item in its parent menu.
IsParent	Returns whether the menu item contains child menu items.
MdiList	Returns or sets whether the menu item will display a list of the MDI child windows.
MdiListItem	Returns the menu item that displays a list of MDI child forms, if there is one.
MenuItems	Returns the collection of menu item objects associated with the menu.
MergeOrder	Returns or sets the relative position of the menu item when it is merged with another.
MergeType	Returns or sets the behavior of this menu item when its menu is merged with another.
OwnerDraw	Returns or sets whether the menu item is drawn in code.
Parent	Returns the menu that contains this menu item.
RadioCheck	Returns or sets whether the menu item, if checked, should display a radio button instead of a check mark.
Shortcut	Returns or sets the shortcut key associated with the menu item.
ShowShortcut	Returns or sets whether the shortcut key that is associated with the menu item is displayed next to the menu item caption.
Text	Returns or sets the caption of the menu item.
Visible	Returns or sets whether the menu item is visible.

TABLE 7.4   Significant Public Methods of `MenuItem` Objects

Method	Means
MergeMenu	Merges this menu item with another menu item.
PerformClick	Creates a `Click` event for the menu item.
PerformSelect	Creates a `Select` event for this menu item.

TABLE 7.5   Significant Public Events of `MenuItem` Objects

Event	Means
Click	Occurs when the menu item is clicked (or selected using a shortcut key or access key defined).
DrawItem	Occurs when the `OwnerDraw` property of a menu item is `True` and a request is made to draw the menu item.
MeasureItem	Occurs when the menu needs to know the size of a menu item before drawing it (occurs before the `DrawItem` event).
Popup	Occurs before a menu item's list of contained menu items is displayed.
Select	Occurs when the user places the cursor over a menu item.

To add a menu system to a form, just drag a `MainMenu` control to the form at design time. Doing so adds a `MainMenu` control to the component tray under the form and opens the menu system in the form as you see in Figure 7.2.

FIGURE 7.2

Creating a menu.

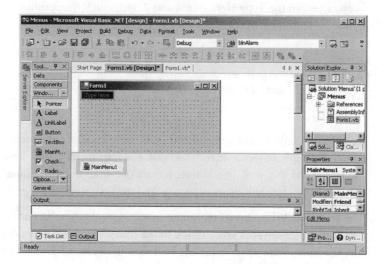

7

Note the text Type Here in Figure 7.2. To create a new menu, you just click that text to
open a text box; in that text box, you can enter captions for menus and menu items. For
example, you can see how this process works in Figure 7.3, where the menu has been
named File.

FIGURE 7.3

*Creating a menu
caption.*

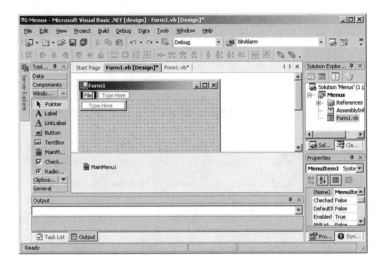

When you're creating a new menu, Type Here boxes of the kind you see in Figure 7.3
appear in all the places you can enter text—both for menu items in the current menu and
additional menus, as you see in the figure. Using this control is easy; all you have to do
is enter text in the Type Here boxes and double-click the resulting menus and menu items
to add code to their Click events in the corresponding code designer.

Tip

> To move menus and menu items around at design time, just drag the menus
> and menu items around.

You can see how to add a new menu item, Item 1, to the File menu in Figure 7.4. The
Menus example in the code for this book has four menu items, Item 1 to Item 4, added to
the File menu this way. In addition, there's one final item you should add to the File
menu—Exit—because users expect to find the Exit item at the end of the File menu.

The Exit item brings up an important point: Now that you're naming menu items, don't
forget that users expect you to stick to the many Windows menu conventions. For example, if a menu item opens a dialog, you should add an ellipsis (...) after its name (such as
Print Preview...). The File menu should be the first menu on the left, and an Exit item

should be at the bottom of that menu. Also, many shortcuts are already standard, such as Ctrl+S for Save, Ctrl+X for Cut, Ctrl+V for Paste/View, Ctrl+C for Copy, and so on.

FIGURE 7.4

Creating a menu item's caption.

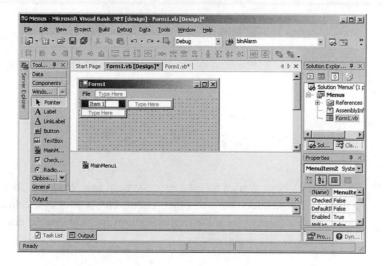

 Tip
You can change a menu item's caption at runtime. To do that, you just have to set its Text property like this: MenuItem3.Text = "You clicked the menu item.".

Handling Menu Item Events

You make menu items active by adding code to their Click events. To open a menu item's Click event, just double-click that item at design time. For example, you can add this code to the Exit item in the Menu example's File menu:

```
Private Sub MenuItem6_Click(ByVal sender As System.Object, _
    ByVal e As System.EventArgs) Handles MenuItem6.Click
    End
End Sub
```

Adding this code means that when the user clicks the Exit menu item, the program will end. Note that the File, Exit menu item is MenuItem6 in the Menus program. The File menu itself (which you can add Click event handlers to) is MenuItem1. The four items in the File menu, Item 1 to Item 4, are MenuItem2 to MenuItem5, which means that the final item in the File menu, the Exit item, is MenuItem6. You can see this new menu system at work in Figure 7.5.

7

FIGURE 7.5

A new menu system.

And that's it! Now you've added a menu system to a Windows form, added menu items to the menu, and added code to a menu item. That's all it takes. Just drag a `MainMenu` control onto a form, type in the captions you want, and double-click menu items to open the associated code designers.

Creating Submenus

NEW TERM So far, we've created a simple menu system, but far more is possible. For example, you can also create *submenus*. When a menu item has a small black arrow at right, as you see in Figure 7.1, selecting that item opens a submenu, as you can also see in that figure.

Creating submenus is easy. You just create the menu item you want to add a submenu to and then select that item in a form designer. Doing so opens a Type Here box to the right of that menu item, and you can enter the captions for the submenu items, as you see in Figure 7.6. Selecting the first item in the submenu opens a Type Here box for the next item under it, as well as another Type Here box for a new submenu to the right of it. All you have to do is enter the caption of the submenu items you want and then double-click them to open their `Click` event in the matching code designer.

For example, we can add code to display a message box when a menu item is selected, like this:

```
Private Sub MenuItem9_Click(ByVal sender As System.Object, _
    ByVal e As System.EventArgs) Handles MenuItem9.Click
    MsgBox("You clicked Item 7.")
End Sub
```

To see our submenus in action, take a look at Figure 7.7.

FIGURE 7.6

Creating submenus.

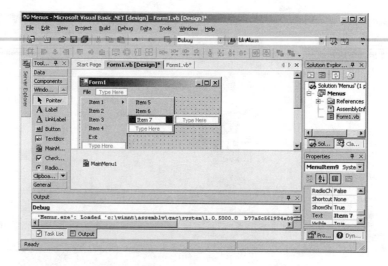

FIGURE 7.7

Using submenus.

Creating Check Mark Items

Menu items in Visual Basic .NET can also support check marks. Check marks are useful for menu items that can be toggled on and off, like Automatic Spell Checking, or indicating which MDI window in a list is currently open. You can add a check mark to a menu item at design time simply by clicking in front of the menu item, as you see in Figure 7.8. Doing so means the item will appear initially checked at runtime.

7

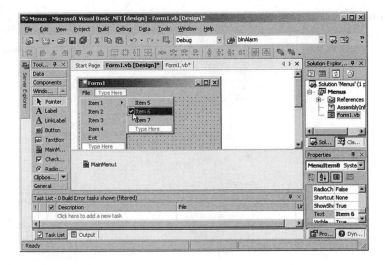

You can also work with check marks in code, using the MenuItem class's Checked property. For example, you can toggle a check mark in front of a menu item when you click that item like this (recall that the Not operator flips the logical value of its operand):

```
Private Sub MenuItem8_Click(ByVal sender As System.Object, _
    ByVal e As System.EventArgs) Handles MenuItem8.Click
    MenuItem8.Checked = Not MenuItem8.Checked
End Sub
```

You can see the new check mark in front of Item 6 in the Menus example in Figure 7.9.

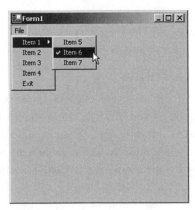

Tip

Want to use radio buttons instead of check boxes? Set your menu items' `RadioCheck` property to `True`.

Creating Menu Shortcuts and Access Keys

A menu shortcut is a key combination, which, when pressed, will cause the corresponding menu item to be selected. The menu containing the item need not even be open for the user to use a shortcut.

You can set a shortcut with the `Shortcut` property, and to display the shortcut next to the menu item's caption at runtime, you set the `ShowShortcut` property to `True`. When you select a menu item's `Shortcut` property in the Properties window, a list of possible shortcuts opens, as you see in Figure 7.10. In that figure, the shortcut Ctrl+X is being given to the Exit item in the Menus example in the code for this book.

FIGURE 7.10

Creating a menu shortcut.

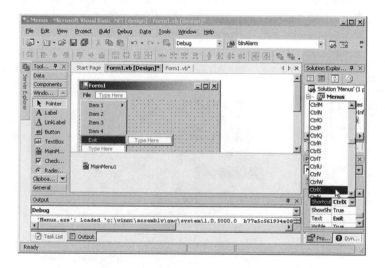

You can see this new shortcut at work in Figure 7.11. When the user presses Ctrl+X, the Exit item is activated.

You can assign a shortcut key combination to a menu item at runtime. To do that, you use members of the `Shortcut` enumeration, like this, which also assigns Ctrl+X to the Exit item:

```
menuItem6.Shortcut = Shortcut.CtrlX
```

7

FIGURE **7.11**

A menu shortcut.

You can use access keys to select menu items from the keyboard using the Alt key. For example, if you make the *x* in the Exit menu item an access key, as well as the *F* in the File menu, the user can select the Exit item by pressing Alt+F to open the File menu and then Alt+X to select the Exit item. To give an item an access key, you simply precede the access key in the menu item's caption with an ampersand (&). In this example, that means using the captions &File and E&xit. Access keys are underlined in menu captions when the user presses the Alt key, as you see in Figure 7.12, as visual cues to the user.

FIGURE **7.12**

A menu access key.

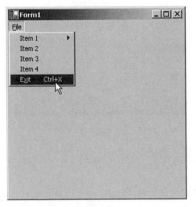

To use an access key, you still have to open the containing menu. If you want to assign a key to a menu item that can be used without first opening that item's menu, use a shortcut instead.

Creating Menu Separators

In Figure 7.13, you can see that we've changed Item 4 in the File menu into a menu separator, which appears as a horizontal line separating menu items into groups. In this case, the menu separator divides the Exit item from the other items in the File menu.

FIGURE 7.13

A menu separator.

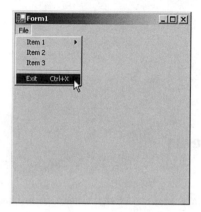

How do you convert a menu item into a menu separator? You simply make its caption into a single hyphen (-). That's all it takes. At runtime, you can do the same thing just by assigning - to a menu item's Text property.

Making Menu Items Visible or Invisible

Menu items don't have Show and Hide methods, but they do have a Visible property. You can use that property to make menu items appear and disappear at runtime. For example, to make the File, Item 3 menu item (that's actually MenuItem4 in code because the File menu itself is MenuItem1) disappear when you select it, you just need to set its Visible property to False:

```
Private Sub MenuItem4_Click(ByVal sender As System.Object, _
    ByVal e As System.EventArgs) Handles MenuItem4.Click
    MenuItem4.Visible = False
End Sub
```

You can see the results in Figure 7.14. After the user selects Item 3, it disappears, as shown in the figure.

7

Figure 7.14

Making a menu item disappear.

Disabling Menu Items

You can disable menu items by setting their `Enabled` property to `False` (the default is `True`). When a menu item is disabled, its caption appears gray. Here's an example: When the user selects Item 2 from the File menu of the Menus example, that menu item will be disabled:

```
Private Sub MenuItem3_Click(ByVal sender As System.Object, _
    ByVal e As System.EventArgs) Handles MenuItem3.Click
    MenuItem3.Enabled = False
End Sub
```

You can see the results in Figure 7.15, where Item 2 appears grayed out.

Figure 7.15

Disabling a menu item.

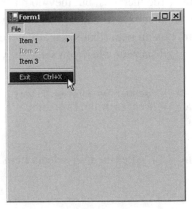

It's your choice whether you want to make menu items disabled or simply make them disappear, as in the preceding section. Although a few disabled menu items are okay, presenting the user with menus filled with grayed-out items is very frustrating. It's better to simply make those items disappear in that case.

Drawing Menu Items in Code

You can draw the appearance of a menu item in code, if you want. That's great if you want to draw icons or images in your menu items, for example.

Let's see how this works. To draw a menu item, you first set that item's OwnerDraw property to True. Then you must add code to the MeasureItem event, which occurs when Visual Basic .NET wants to know how much space to allow for your menu item. To pass this information back to Visual Basic .NET, you are passed an object of the MeasureItemEventArgs class, and you set this object's ItemHeight and ItemWidth properties to new values (measured in pixels) something like this in the Menus example:

```
Private Sub MenuItem7_MeasureItem(ByVal sender As Object, _
    ByVal e As System.Windows.Forms.MeasureItemEventArgs) _
    Handles MenuItem7.MeasureItem
    e.ItemHeight = 15
    e.ItemWidth = 60
End Sub
```

Your next task is to actually draw the item when requested, and you do that by handling the item's DrawItem event. This event's handler is passed a Bounds object, which gives you the bounds for the menu item. You can use the Height and Width properties of this object to get the actual extent of the drawing area you have to work with. And you are passed a Graphics object to do the actual drawing (we'll see Graphics objects in Day 10). For example, here's how we can draw a red ellipse for our menu item:

```
Private Sub MenuItem7_DrawItem(ByVal sender As Object, _
    ByVal e As System.Windows.Forms.DrawItemEventArgs) _
    Handles MenuItem7.DrawItem
    Dim penRed As New Pen(Color.Red)
    e.Graphics.DrawEllipse(penRed, e.Bounds)
End Sub
```

You can handle other standard events for this menu item, such as the Click event, like this:

```
Private Sub MenuItem7_Click(ByVal sender As System.Object, _
    ByVal e As System.EventArgs) _
    Handles MenuItem2.Click
    MsgBox("You clicked the red ellipse item.")
End Sub
```

You can see the results in Figure 7.16, where our new ellipse menu item appears. Now you're drawing your own menu items!

7

FIGURE 7.16

Drawing a menu item.

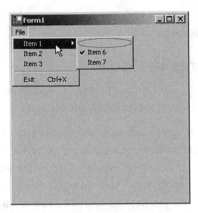

Creating Menus and Menu Items in Code

You can also create an entire menu system in code. To do that, all you have to do is create a MainMenu object, add the MenuItem objects you want to it, and assign the MainMenu object to a form's Menu property.

You can see an example in the CodeMenus project in the code for this book. All you really have to do is create MenuItem objects, configure them as you like them, and use the MenuItems collection's Add method to add them to menus or other menu items, as shown in Listing 7.1.

LISTING 7.1   Creating Menus in Code (CodeMenus project, Form1.vb)

```
Dim mainMenu1 As New MainMenu

Dim WithEvents menuItem1 As New MenuItem
Dim WithEvents menuItem2 As New MenuItem
Dim WithEvents menuItem3 As New MenuItem
Dim WithEvents menuItem4 As New MenuItem

Private Sub Form1_Load(ByVal sender As System.Object, _
    ByVal e As System.EventArgs) Handles MyBase.Load
    menuItem1.Text = "File"
    menuItem2.Text = "Item 1"
    menuItem3.Text = "Item 2"
    menuItem3.Checked = True
    menuItem4.Text = "Exit"
    menuItem4.Shortcut = Shortcut.CtrlX
    menuItem2.MenuItems.Add(menuItem3)
    menuItem1.MenuItems.Add(menuItem2)
    menuItem1.MenuItems.Add(menuItem4)
    AddHandler menuItem4.Click, AddressOf MenuItem4_Click
```

LISTING 7.1   continued

```
      mainMenu1.MenuItems.Add(menuItem1)
      Menu = mainMenu1
   End Sub

   Private Sub MenuItem4_Click(ByVal sender As System.Object, _
      ByVal e As System.EventArgs)
      End
   End Sub
```

You can see the menu system the CodeMenus project creates in Figure 7.17.

FIGURE 7.17

Creating a menu system in code.

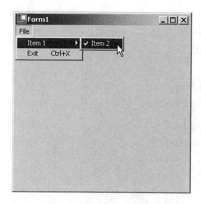

Working with Menus and MDI

Say that you have an MDI application and that each MDI child window contains a text box. You might want to add an Edit menu with one item, Auto Format, which formats the text in an MDI child window automatically. But you wouldn't want the Edit menu to appear unless any MDI child windows were actually open.

The way to make this work is to add an Edit menu to the MDI child window, with the Auto Format item in it. When an MDI child window appears, its menu is *merged* with the MDI parent window (so no menu system appears in the child).

You can specify how menu items should be added to the MDI parent window by using the `MenuItem` class's `MergeType` and `MergeOrder` properties. The `MergeType` property specifies how a menu item will be merged with its parent's menu system and can take these values from the `MenuMerge` enumeration:

- `MenuMerge.Add`—This is the default. The menu item should be added to other menu items in a merged menu.

7

- `MenuMerge.MergeItems`—All submenu items of this menu item should be merged with those of other menu items at the same position in a merged menu.
- `MenuMerge.Remove`—The menu item should not be included in a merged menu.
- `MenuMerge.Replace`—The menu item should replace an existing menu item at the same position.

The `MergeOrder` property sets the order of the merged items, in case you want to specify that order. To see how this works, look at the MdiMenus example in the book's code. In this example, the MDI child windows have an Edit menu whose `MergeType` property is set to `MenuMerge.Add`. When you start the application, you just see the MDI parent window with a File menu, as in Figure 7.18.

FIGURE 7.18

An MDI parent window.

When you use the File, New item to create an MDI child window, you'll see that the child window's Edit menu has been added to the MDI parent's menu system, as in Figure 7.19. In this way, you can update MDI parent menus as needed.

FIGURE 7.19

A merged MDI menu.

If you have two menus of the same name, such as Edit, in both the MDI parent and child windows, you can set the `MergeType` property of various items in the child menu to Add and the `MergeType` property of the MDI parent's menu to `MenuMerge.MergeItems`. Then, when a child window appears, the items you've specified will be added to the MDI parent's Edit menu (and the child window will not have an Edit menu).

Here's something else to know about MDI applications: You can support a Window menu in an MDI parent that automatically lets the user select between MDI child windows, giving the selected window the focus. All you have to do is add a new menu to the MDI parent with the caption `Window` and set the corresponding `MenuItem` object's `MdiList` property to `True` (the default is `False`). When you do, the Window menu will display a list of the open MDI child windows automatically, as you see in Figure 7.20.

FIGURE 7.20

Creating a Window MDI menu.

Using Context Menus

NEW TERM You can also create *context menus* in Visual Basic .NET. These menus are the ones that pop up when you right-click a control or form. You use them to give users access to frequently used menu commands. They're supported by the `ContextMenu` class, which has this class hierarchy:

```
System.Object
    System.MarshalByRefObject
        System.ComponentModel.Component
            System.Windows.Forms.Menu
                System.Windows.Forms.ContextMenu
```

You can find the significant public properties of `ContextMenu` objects in Table 7.6, their significant methods in Table 7.7, and their significant events in Table 7.8.

7

TABLE 7.6   Significant Public Properties of ContextMenu Objects

Property	Means
IsParent	Returns whether this menu contains any menu items.
MdiListItem	Returns the MenuItem that is used to display a list of MDI child forms.
MenuItems	Returns the collection of MenuItem objects associated with the menu.

TABLE 7.7   Significant Public Method of ContextMenu Objects

Method	Means
Show	Displays the context menu at the specified position.

TABLE 7.8   Significant Public Event of ContextMenu Objects

Event	Means
Popup	Occurs before the context menu is displayed.

Creating Context Menus

You create a context menu in much the same way as you create a standard menu, but you use a context menu control instead of a main menu control. Just drag a context menu control onto a form and add the items you want to this new menu, as you see in Figure 7.21.

FIGURE 7.21

Creating a context menu.

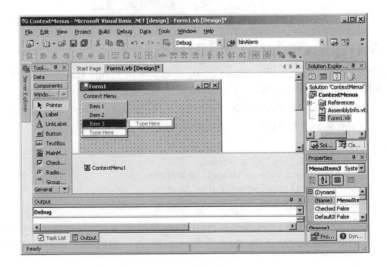

Next, assign the context menu control (that's ContextMenu1 in the ContextMenus example) to the ContextMenu property of the control or form (Form1 in the ContextMenus example) you want to connect it to.

In addition, you can connect code to the context menu items as you can with any other menu item. For example, here's how the ContextMenus example sets up the menu items' Click events:

```
Private Sub MenuItem1_Click(ByVal sender As System.Object, _
ByVal e As System.EventArgs) Handles MenuItem1.Click
    MsgBox("You clicked Item 1.")
End Sub

Private Sub MenuItem2_Click(ByVal sender As System.Object, _
ByVal e As System.EventArgs) Handles MenuItem2.Click
    MsgBox("You clicked Item 2.")
End Sub

Private Sub MenuItem3_Click(ByVal sender As System.Object, _
ByVal e As System.EventArgs) Handles MenuItem3.Click
    MsgBox("You clicked Item 3.")
End Sub
```

And that's all it takes! Now when you run the ContextMenus example and right-click the form, you'll see the context menu appear, as in Figure 7.22. (You can also make a context menu appear by using code; just set its Visible property to True.)

FIGURE 7.22

A context menu.

Using the Built-in Dialogs

Several Windows controls support Windows dialogs, such as a Font Selection dialog, an Open File dialog, and so on. These dialogs are very useful because they're the same dialogs used by other Windows applications, so they give the users what they're used to.

7

And they save you a lot of programming too (it's surprising how much programming is necessary to make a good Open File dialog). Here are the dialogs available to you through Windows controls in Visual Basic .NET:

- Open File dialogs
- Save File dialogs
- Folder Browser dialogs
- Font dialogs
- Color dialogs
- Print Preview dialogs
- Page Setup dialogs
- Print dialogs

At runtime, you can use the `ShowDialog` method to display a dialog. The return value from this method indicates what buttons were clicked; here are the possibilities, from the `DialogResult` enumeration:

- `DialogResult.Abort`—The dialog return value is Abort.
- `DialogResult.Cancel`—The dialog return value is Cancel.
- `DialogResult.Ignore`—The dialog return value is Ignore.
- `DialogResult.No`—The dialog return value is No.
- `DialogResult.None`—Nothing is returned from the dialog. This means that the modal dialog continues running.
- `DialogResult.OK`—The dialog return value is OK.
- `DialogResult.Retry`—The dialog return value is Retry.
- `DialogResult.Yes`—The dialog return value is Yes.

We'll see each of the available dialogs here, starting with the File Open and Save File dialogs, which allow the user to specify what files to open and where to save files. We'll need these dialogs in Day 10, when we work with file handling in code.

Using Open File Dialogs

Like the other Windows controls we've seen to this point, the Open File dialog is a familiar one. You can see one displayed by the OpenFileDialogs example in the code for this book in Figure 7.23.

FIGURE 7.23

An Open File dialog.

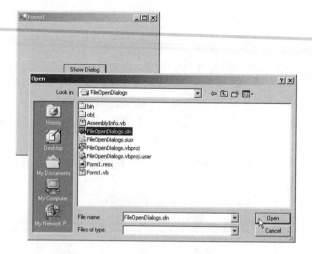

Open File dialogs are based on the `OpenFileDialog` class, which has this class hierarchy:

```
System.Object
   System.MarshalByRefObject
      System.ComponentModel.Component
         System.Windows.Forms.CommonDialog
            System.Windows.Forms.FileDialog
               System.Windows.Forms.OpenFileDialog
```

You can find the significant public properties of `OpenFileDialog` objects in Table 7.9, the significant public methods in Table 7.10, and the significant public events in Table 7.11.

TABLE 7.9   Significant Public Properties of `OpenFileDialog` Objects

Property	Means
AddExtension	Returns or sets whether the dialog adds an extension to filenames if the user doesn't give an extension.
CheckFileExists	Returns or sets whether the dialog shows a warning if the user indicates a file that does not exist.
CheckPathExists	Returns or sets whether the dialog displays a warning if the user indicates a path that does not exist.
DefaultExt	Returns or sets the default file extension.
FileName	Returns or sets the filename selected in the file dialog.
FileNames	Returns the filenames of all selected files in the dialog.
Filter	Returns or sets the filename filter string. This string sets the choices that appear in the Save as File Type or Files of Type box.

7

TABLE 7.9   continued

Property	Means
InitialDirectory	Returns or sets the starting directory.
Multiselect	Returns or sets whether the dialog allows multiple files to be selected.
ReadOnlyChecked	Returns or sets whether the read-only check box is checked.
RestoreDirectory	Returns or sets whether the dialog should restore the current directory when the dialog is closed.
ShowHelp	Returns or sets whether a Help button should be displayed.
ShowReadOnly	Returns or sets whether the dialog contains a read-only check box.
Title	Returns or sets the file dialog title.
ValidateNames	Returns or sets whether the dialog allows only valid Windows filenames.

TABLE 7.10   Significant Public Methods of OpenFileDialog Objects

Method	Means
OpenFile	Opens the selected file with read-only permission.
Reset	Resets all properties to their default values.
ShowDialog	Shows the dialog.

TABLE 7.11   Significant Public Events of OpenFileDialog Objects

Event	Means
FileOk	Occurs when the user clicks the Open or Save button.
HelpRequest	Occurs when the user clicks the Help button.

Some of the properties listed in Table 7.9 are very useful. For example, the name and path the user selected are stored in the FileName property. You can use the ShowReadOnly property to determine whether a read-only check box appears in the dialog. You can let users select multiple files by using the Multiselect property. The ReadOnlyChecked property specifies that files may be opened only as read-only. And you can use the dialog's OpenFile method to open files. Now let's look at putting one of these dialogs to work.

Creating Open File Dialogs

To support an Open File dialog, the OpenFileDialogs example has a button that calls the ShowDialog method of an OpenFileDialog object, OpenFileDialog1. The only types of file handling we've really seen so far are using the `FromFile` method of `Image` objects and the `LoadFile` and `SaveFile` methods of rich text boxes, so here's how we might load an image into a picture box. Note that the code checks to make sure that the OK button was clicked before doing anything and recovers the selected file's name from the `OpenFileDialog1.FileName` property:

```
Private Sub Button1_Click(ByVal sender As System.Object, _
    ByVal e As System.EventArgs) Handles Button1.Click
    If OpenFileDialog1.ShowDialog() = DialogResult.OK Then
        PictureBox1.Image = Image.FromFile(OpenFileDialog1.FileName)
    End If
End Sub
```

And that's it! Now you can let the user select what file to open and load into a picture box. If you've set the dialog's `Multiselect` property to `True`, the user can select multiple files. To get the names of those files, you can use the `FileNames` property, which returns an array of strings.

You can also use the `Filter` property to set possible file extensions. For example, you might set that property to this string: `JPEG files (*.jpg)|*.jpg|GIF files (*.gif)|*.gif|TIF files (*.tif)|*.tif|All files (*.*)|*.*`. This makes four possibilities appear in the Files of Type box in the dialog: JPEG files (*.jpg), GIF files (*.gif), TIF files (*.tif), and All files (*.*). The file extension following the upright bar (|) tells the application what file extension to use.

You can also set the `InitialDirectory` property, which sets the directory that the Open File dialog first shows. And if you set the `ShowHelp` property to `True`, a Help button will appear in the dialog. If that button is clicked, a `HelpRequest` event occurs, and you can display a help window.

Using Save File Dialogs

Save File dialogs are those dialogs that allow the users to give your program the name and/or location of the file they want their data saved to. You can see an example at work in the SaveFileDialogs example from the book's code in Figure 7.24.

Save File dialogs are based on the `SaveFileDialog` class, which has this class hierarchy:

```
System.Object
   System.MarshalByRefObject
      System.ComponentModel.Component
         System.Windows.Forms.CommonDialog
            System.Windows.Forms.FileDialog
               System.Windows.Forms.SaveFileDialog
```

7

FIGURE 7.24

A Save File dialog.

You can find the significant public properties of `SaveFileDialog` objects in Table 7.12, their significant public methods in Table 7.13, and their significant public events in Table 7.14.

TABLE 7.12 Significant Public Properties of `SaveFileDialog` Objects

Property	Means
AddExtension	Returns or sets whether the dialog will add an extension to a filename if the user doesn't give an extension.
CheckFileExists	Returns or sets whether the dialog shows a warning if the user indicates a file that does not exist.
CheckPathExists	Returns or sets whether the dialog shows a warning if the user indicates a path that does not exist.
CreatePrompt	Returns or sets whether the dialog prompts the user for permission to create a file if that file does not exist.
DefaultExt	Returns or sets the default file extension.
FileName	Returns or sets the filename selected in the file dialog.
FileNames	Returns the filenames of all selected files in the dialog.
Filter	Returns or sets the current filename filter string, which determines the choices that appear in the Save as File Type or Files of Type box in the dialog.
InitialDirectory	Returns or sets the starting directory displayed by the file dialog.
OverwritePrompt	Returns or sets whether to show a warning if the user indicates a filename that already exists.
RestoreDirectory	Returns or sets whether the dialog restores the current directory before the dialog closes.
ShowHelp	Returns or sets whether a Help button is displayed in the file dialog.
Title	Returns or sets the file dialog title.
ValidateNames	Returns or sets whether the dialog allows only valid Windows filenames.

TABLE 7.13   Significant Public Methods of `SaveFileDialog` Objects

Method	Means
OpenFile	Opens the file with read/write permission.
Reset	Resets all dialog options to their default values.
ShowDialog	Shows the dialog.

TABLE 7.14   Significant Public Events of `SaveFileDialog` Objects

Event	Means
FileOk	Occurs when the user clicks the Open or Save button.
HelpRequest	Occurs when the user clicks the Help button.

As with other Windows dialogs, you use the `ShowDialog` method to display the dialog. You can use the `FileName` property to get the file the user selected, open a file using the dialog's `OpenFile` method, and so on.

Creating Save File Dialogs

You can see an example of a Save File dialog in Figure 7.24 in the SaveFileDialogs example. That example allows the user to save the text in a rich text box to a file by using the rich text box's `SaveFile` method. Note that the code first makes sure that the OK button was clicked and, if so, recovers the name of the file to save with the `SaveFileDialog1.FileName` property:

```
Private Sub Button1_Click(ByVal sender As System.Object, _
    ByVal e As System.EventArgs) Handles Button1.Click
    If SaveFileDialog1.ShowDialog = DialogResult.OK Then
        RichTextBox1.SaveFile(SaveFileDialog1.FileName)
    End If
End Sub
```

As with Open File dialogs, you can use the `Filter` property to set possible file extensions as options.

 Tip

Here are some other handy properties: The `CheckFileExists` and `CheckPathExists` properties enable you to check whether a file or path already exists. You can use the `CreatePrompt` property to make the dialog display a prompt asking whether a file that does not exist should be created and the `OverwritePrompt` property to ask the user whether an existing file should be overwritten.

7

Using Font Dialogs

You use Font dialogs to allow the user to select a font, including the font itself, the font size, color, and more. For example, Figure 7.25 shows the FontDialogs example in the code for this book.

FIGURE 7.25

A Font dialog.

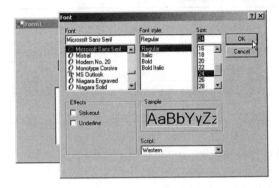

After the user selects a font and color and clicks the OK button, the new font is installed in a rich text box, as you see in Figure 7.26.

FIGURE 7.26

Setting a rich text box's font.

The Font dialog is especially useful because it actually returns a Font object with all the characteristics that the user has selected. The font color the user selected is returned as a Visual Basic .NET Color object (we'll see more on Color objects in Day 10).

Font dialogs are supported by the FontDialog class, and the class hierarchy for that class is as follows:

```
System.Object
   System.MarshalByRefObject
```

```
System.ComponentModel.Component
  System.Windows.Forms.CommonDialog
    System.Windows.Forms.FontDialog
```

You can find the significant public properties of `FontDialog` objects in Table 7.15, the significant public methods in Table 7.16, and the significant public events in Table 7.17.

TABLE 7.15   Significant Public Properties of `FontDialog` Objects

Property	Means
Color	Returns or sets the selected font color.
Font	Returns or sets the selected font.
MaxSize	Returns or sets the maximum point size a user can select.
MinSize	Returns or sets the minimum point size a user can select.
ShowApply	Returns or sets whether the dialog contains an Apply button.
ShowColor	Returns or sets whether the dialog displays the color choice.
ShowEffects	Returns or sets whether the dialog contains controls that allow the user to specify strikethrough, underline, and text color options.
ShowHelp	Returns or sets whether the dialog displays a Help button.

TABLE 7.16   Significant Public Methods of `FontDialog` Objects

Method	Means
Reset	Resets all dialog options to their default values.
ShowDialog	Shows the dialog.

TABLE 7.17   Significant Public Events of `FontDialog` Objects

Event	Means
Apply	Occurs when the user clicks the Apply button.
HelpRequest	Occurs when the user clicks the Help button.

Creating Font Dialogs

This next example, FontDialogs in the code for this book, shows how to use Font dialogs. If the user clicks the OK button, we can recover the font color the user has selected with the `FontDialog Color` property and make that the text color in a rich text box by using the rich text box's `ForeColor` property:

7

```
Private Sub Button1_Click(ByVal sender As System.Object, _
    ByVal e As System.EventArgs) Handles Button1.Click
    If FontDialog1.ShowDialog = DialogResult.OK Then
        RichTextBox1.ForeColor = FontDialog1.Color
            .
            .
            .
    End If
End Sub
```

You can also install the new font the user has selected, getting that font from the Font dialog's Font property like this:

```
Private Sub Button1_Click(ByVal sender As System.Object, _
    ByVal e As System.EventArgs) Handles Button1.Click
    If FontDialog1.ShowDialog = DialogResult.OK Then
        RichTextBox1.ForeColor = FontDialog1.Color
        RichTextBox1.Font = FontDialog1.Font
    End If
End Sub
```

As you can see, Font dialogs save you a lot of programming time and effort. If you had to dig out all available fonts in the system yourself, as well as their sizes and so on, and display all the font options to users, you would need a great deal of code. Not only does the Font dialog save you all that, but it also provides you with the same user interface that other Windows programs use.

Using Color Dialogs

Color dialogs, as you would expect, enable the user to select colors. You can find a Color dialog at work in Figure 7.27, in the ColorDialogs example in the code for this book.

FIGURE 7.27

Selecting a color.

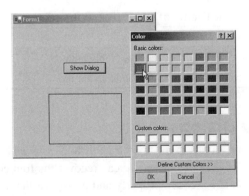

After the user selects a color and clicks the OK button, the new color appears in a picture box, as you see in Figure 7.28 (in this case, the new color is a brilliant red, which is hard to tell in these black-and-white figures, of course).

FIGURE 7.28

Setting a picture box's color.

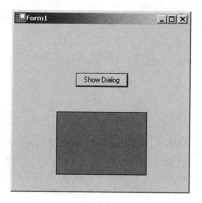

Color dialogs are supported by the ColorDialog class, and the class hierarchy for that class is as follows:

```
System.Object
    System.MarshalByRefObject
        System.ComponentModel.Component
            System.Windows.Forms.CommonDialog
                System.Windows.Forms.ColorDialog
```

You can find the significant public properties of ColorDialog objects in Table 7.18, the significant public methods in Table 7.19, and the significant public events in Table 7.20.

TABLE 7.18 Significant Public Properties of ColorDialog Objects

Property	Means
AllowFullOpen	Returns or sets whether the user can define custom colors.
AnyColor	Returns or sets whether the dialog displays all available colors in the set of basic colors.
Color	Returns or sets the color selected by the user.
CustomColors	Returns or sets the set of custom colors shown in the dialog.
FullOpen	Returns or sets whether the controls used to create custom colors are visible when the dialog is first opened.
ShowHelp	Returns or sets whether a Help button appears in the Color dialog.
SolidColorOnly	Returns or sets whether the dialog will allow only solid colors to be selected.

7

TABLE 7.19   Significant Public Methods of `ColorDialog` Objects

Method	Means
Reset	Resets all options to their default values.
ShowDialog	Shows the dialog.

TABLE 7.20   Significant Public Event of `ColorDialog` Objects

Event	Means
HelpRequest	Occurs when the user clicks the Help button.

If you click the Define Custom Colors button in a Color dialog, the dialog opens completely, as you see in Figure 7.29, and the user can make up his or her own color. If you want to allow the user to pick only from the predefined color set you see in Figure 7.27, set the `AllowFullOpen` property to `False`.

FIGURE 7.29

Defining custom colors.

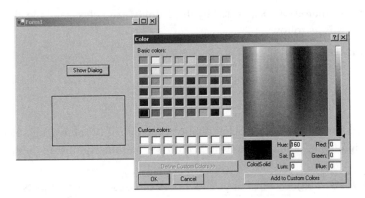

 Tip   NEW TERM   If you set the `SolidColorOnly` property to `True`, the user can select only solid colors, not mixed, called *dithered*, colors.

Creating Color Dialogs

In the ColorDialogs example, the code uses the Color dialog's `Color` property to get a `Color` object holding the user's selected color. That `Color` object is assigned to the `BackColor` property of a picture box to display the new color:

```
Private Sub Button1_Click(ByVal sender As System.Object, _
ByVal e As System.EventArgs) Handles Button1.Click
```

```
    If ColorDialog1.ShowDialog = DialogResult.OK Then
        PictureBox1.BackColor = ColorDialog1.Color
    End If
End Sub
```

That's all it takes! Now you're letting the user select colors.

Using Folder Browser Dialogs

You can use Folder Browser dialogs to let the user specify a path (not a filename). This dialog appears in Figure 7.30 and in the FolderDialogs example in the book's code.

FIGURE 7.30

Selecting a folder.

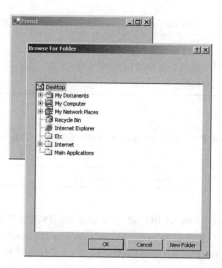

As you might expect, Folder Browser dialogs are supported by the FolderBrowserDialog class, which has this hierarchy:

```
System.Object
    System.MarshalByRefObject
        System.ComponentModel.Component
            System.Windows.Forms.CommonDialog
                System.Windows.Forms.FolderBrowserDialog
```

You can find the significant public properties of FolderBrowserDialog objects in Table 7.21, the significant public methods in Table 7.22, and the significant public events in Table 7.23.

7

TABLE 7.21　Significant Public Properties of `FolderBrowserDialog` Objects

Property	Means
AllowFullOpen	Returns or sets whether the user can use the dialog to define custom colors.
Description	Returns or sets the text displayed above the tree view control in the dialog.
RootFolder	Returns or sets the root folder where the browsing starts from.
SelectedPath	Returns or sets the path selected by the user.
ShowNewFolderButton	Returns or sets a value indicating whether the New Folder button appears in the Folder Browser dialog.

TABLE 7.22　Significant Public Methods of `FolderBrowserDialog` Objects

Method	Means
Reset	Resets all options to their default values.
ShowDialog	Shows the dialog.

TABLE 7.23　Significant Public Event of `FolderBrowserDialog` Objects

Event	Means
Disposed	Occurs when the dialog is disposed of.

Before displaying a Folder Browser dialog, you can set the `RootFolder` property to specify what folder to let the user start browsing from. When the user dismisses the dialog by clicking the OK button, you can get the folder the user selected in the `SelectedPath` property.

> **Tip**
>
> If you set the `SelectedPath` property before displaying a Folder Browser dialog, the dialog will appear with the corresponding directory already selected.

Creating Folder Browser Dialogs

Folder Browser dialogs are good in cases in which you know the name of the file you want to save (such as appconfig.ini or backup.sav) and only want to let the user indicate where to save that file. In the FolderBrowserDialogs example, the code allows the user to save the text in a rich text box in a file named schedule.txt in a user-designated folder like this:

```
Private Sub Button1_Click(ByVal sender As System.Object, _
    ByVal e As System.EventArgs) Handles Button1.Click
    If FolderBrowserDialog1.ShowDialog = DialogResult.OK Then
        RichTextBox1.SaveFile(FolderBrowserDialog1.SelectedPath & _
            "\schedule.txt")
    End If
End Sub
```

And that's all it takes! Using the SelectedPath property, you can determine which folder the user has designated.

Printing with the PrintDocument and PrintSettings Objects

Printing from a Visual Basic .NET application is not necessarily an easy operation. To see how to implement it, look at the Printer example in the code for this book, which you can see in Figure 7.31. This application is designed to print three ellipses (in red, green, and blue) on three different pages. You can see page 1 in Figure 7.31 in a Print Preview dialog. We'll look at how this application works in the remainder of today's work (and for the sake of reference, you can find this application's code at the end of today's text in Listing 7.2).

FIGURE 7.31

A Print Preview dialog.

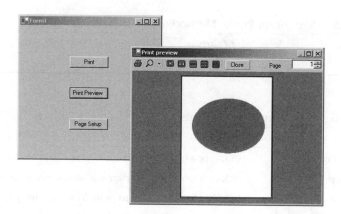

Besides the different dialogs you can use to print, you need a good command of two objects: PrintDocument and PrintSettings. The PrintDocument object is the one that really handles the printing. You are passed a Graphics object in the PrintDocument object's event handlers, and you can draw each page using that Graphics object (we'll

7

see all about the Graphics object in Day 10). For example, to draw text, you can use the DrawString method of the Graphics object. The PrintSettings object allows you to configure the printer you want to use.

Here is the hierarchy of the PrintDocument class:

```
System.Object
    System.MarshalByRefObject
        System.ComponentModel.Component
            System.Drawing.Printing.PrintDocument
```

You can find the significant public properties of PrintDocument objects in Table 7.24, the significant public methods in Table 7.25, and the significant public events in Table 7.26.

TABLE 7.24   Significant Public Properties of PrintDocument Objects

Property	Means
DefaultPageSettings	Returns or sets the default settings that apply to a single page of the document.
DocumentName	Returns or sets the document name to show in the printer queue while printing the document.
PrinterSettings	Returns or sets the printer to print the document.

TABLE 7.25   Significant Public Method of PrintDocument Objects

Method	Means
Print	Prints the document.

TABLE 7.26   Significant Public Events of PrintDocument Objects

Event	Means
BeginPrint	Occurs when the Print method is called to start a print job.
EndPrint	Occurs when the last page of the document has printed.
PrintPage	Occurs for each page to print. You draw the page in this event's handler.
QueryPageSettings	Occurs before each PrintPage event.

When you're using PrintDocument objects, you start the printing process with the Print method. First, a BeginPrint event occurs, followed by a PrintPage event for each page, followed by an EndPrint event when the whole job is complete. You are passed the Graphics object in the PrintPage event and draw what you want on the page using that object. If the document you're printing has more pages left to print, you set the HasMorePages property of the PrintPageEventArgs object passed to you to True, letting Visual Basic .NET know there's more coming.

You use the PrinterSettings class to configure how a document will be printed—on what printer, from what page to what page, and so forth. You can find the significant public properties of PrinterSettings objects in Table 7.27 and the significant public methods in Table 7.28.

TABLE 7.27 Significant Public Properties of PrinterSettings Objects

Property	Means
CanDuplex	True if the printer supports double-sided printing.
Collate	Returns or sets whether the document is collated.
Copies	Returns or sets the number of copies of the document to print.
DefaultPageSettings	Returns the default page settings for this printer.
Duplex	Returns or sets the printer setting for double-sided printing.
FromPage	Returns or sets the page number of the first page to print.
LandscapeAngle	Returns the angle, in degrees, that the page orientation is rotated to produce landscape orientation.
MaximumCopies	Returns the maximum number of copies that the printer allows you to print at a time.
MaximumPage	Returns or sets the maximum FromPage or ToPage that can be selected.
MinimumPage	Returns or sets the minimum FromPage or ToPage that can be selected.
PaperSizes	Returns the paper sizes supported by this printer.
PaperSources	Returns the paper source trays that are available.
PrinterName	Returns or sets the name of the printer to use.
PrinterResolutions	Gets all the resolutions that are supported by this printer.
PrintRange	Returns or sets the page numbers that the user has specified to be printed.
PrintToFile	Returns or sets whether the output is sent to a file instead of a port.
SupportsColor	Returns whether the printer supports color printing.
ToPage	Returns or sets the number of the last page to print.

TABLE 7.28 Significant Public Method of PrinterSettings Objects

Method	Means
CreateMeasurementGraphics	Returns a Graphics object that contains printer information.

7

Behind the scenes, you use PrintDocument and PrintSettings objects to manage your printing, as we'll see. You can create PrintDocument objects using the toolbox. There's a PrintDocument object in the Printer example, and the Print dialog we'll see next will return the PrintSettings object we'll need.

Using Print Dialogs

The Print dialog is what the user actually sees to start the printing process. You can see the Print dialog that appears when the user clicks the Print button in the Printer example in Figure 7.32.

FIGURE 7.32

Displaying a Print dialog.

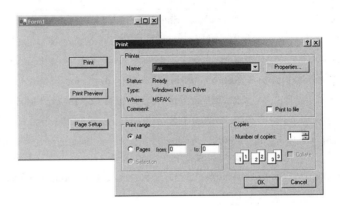

The Print dialog is supported by the PrintDialog class; here is the hierarchy of that class:

```
System.Object
    System.MarshalByRefObject
        System.ComponentModel.Component
            System.Windows.Forms.CommonDialog
                System.Windows.Forms.PrintDialog
```

You can find the significant public properties of PrintDialog objects in Table 7.29, the significant public methods in Table 7.30, and the significant events in Table 7.31.

TABLE 7.29 Significant Public Properties of PrintDialog Objects

Property	Means
AllowSelection	Returns or sets whether the Selection radio button is enabled.
AllowSomePages	Returns or sets whether the From... To... Page radio button is enabled.
Document	Returns or sets the PrintDocument object used to obtain PrinterSettings.

TABLE 7.29 continued

Property	Means
PrinterSettings	Returns or sets the PrinterSettings object the dialog will modify.
ShowHelp	Returns or sets whether the Help button is displayed.
ShowNetwork	Returns or sets whether the Network button is displayed.

TABLE 7.30 Significant Public Methods of PrintDialog Objects

Method	Means
Reset	Resets all options.
ShowDialog	Shows the dialog.

TABLE 7.31 Significant Public Event of PrintDialog Objects

Event	Means
HelpRequest	Occurs when the user clicks the Help button.

The usual printing operation goes like this: You add a PrintDocument object to your application, as well as a PrintDialog object to enable the user to print. Before actually showing the Print dialog, you assign the PrintDocument object to the PrintDialog object's Document property. Then you can use the ShowDialog method to show the dialog, and if the user clicks the OK button in the Print dialog, you call the PrintDocument object's Print method.

The following code shows how that looks in the Printer example. The code first assigns the PrintDocument object in the application to PrintDialog1.Document, and the current PrinterSettings object to PrintDialog1.PrinterSettings, as well as sets the PrintDialog1.AllowSomePages property to True to allow the user to print only a range of pages if he or she wants:

```
Private Sub Button1_Click(ByVal sender As System.Object, _
    ByVal e As System.EventArgs) Handles Button1.Click
    PrintDialog1.Document = PrintDocument1
    PrintDialog1.PrinterSettings = PrintDocument1.PrinterSettings
    PrintDialog1.AllowSomePages = True
        .
        .
        .
End Sub
```

7

If the user clicks the OK button in the Print dialog, we assign the Print dialog's
`PrinterSettings` object to `PrintDocument1` and print like this:

```
Private Sub Button1_Click(ByVal sender As System.Object, _
    ByVal e As System.EventArgs) Handles Button1.Click
    PrintDialog1.Document = PrintDocument1
    PrintDialog1.PrinterSettings = PrintDocument1.PrinterSettings
    PrintDialog1.AllowSomePages = True
    If PrintDialog1.ShowDialog = DialogResult.OK Then
        PrintDocument1.PrinterSettings = PrintDialog1.PrinterSettings
        PrintDocument1.Print()
    End If
End Sub
```

As soon as you call the `PrintDocument` object's `Print` method, the print job starts by
causing this object's `BeginPrint` event to occur, followed by a `PrintPage` event for each
page to print, followed by an `EndPrint` event at the end of the printing job. In the
`PrintPage` event, you're passed an object of the `PrintPageEventArgs` class, which has
these members:

- `Cancel`—Setting this value to `True` cancels the print job.
- `Graphics`—Specifies the `Graphics` object used to draw the page.
- `HasMorePages`—Returns or sets whether there are more pages to print.
- `MarginBounds`—Sets the rectangular area that represents the part of the page inside
  the margins.
- `PageBounds`—Sets the rectangular area representing the area of the page.
- `PageSettings`—Specifies the page settings of the current page.

For example, here's how we can print three pages of ellipses in the Printer example; note
that the code keeps track of the current page as `intPage` and increments that value for
each new page to print. If there are more pages to print, the code sets the `HasMorePages`
property to `True` to indicate that fact (more on `Graphics` object methods such as
`FillEllipse` in Day 10):

```
Dim intPage As Integer

Private Sub PrintDocument1_BeginPrint(ByVal sender As Object, _
    ByVal e As System.Drawing.Printing.PrintEventArgs) _
    Handles PrintDocument1.BeginPrint
    intPage = 0
End Sub
```

```
Private Sub PrintDocument1_PrintPage(ByVal sender As Object, _
    ByVal e As System.Drawing.Printing.PrintPageEventArgs) _
    Handles PrintDocument1.PrintPage
    intPage += 1
    Select Case intPage
        Case 1
            e.Graphics.FillEllipse(Brushes.Red, _
                100, 200, 680, 500)
            e.HasMorePages = True
        Case 2
            e.Graphics.FillEllipse(Brushes.Green, _
                100, 200, 680, 500)
            e.HasMorePages = True
        Case 3
            e.Graphics.FillEllipse(Brushes.Blue, _
                100, 200, 680, 500)
            e.HasMorePages = False
    End Select
End Sub
```

Tip

> The Printer example just prints all three pages, but you can determine the range of pages that the user has requested by using the PageSettings object's FromPage and ToPage properties. (You can get this object from the PageSetting property of the PrintPageEventArgs class passed to the PrintPage event handler.)

What about seeing what we're going to print before we actually do print? That's coming up with Print Preview dialogs.

Using Print Preview Dialogs

You use Print Preview dialogs to enable the user to see what a document will look like before it's printed. You can click the Print Preview button in the Printer example to see a preview of the three-page document that example prints, page by page, as you see in Figure 7.31.

The Print Preview dialog is supported by the PrintPreviewDialog class, which has this class hierarchy:

```
System.Object
    System.MarshalByRefObject
        System.ComponentModel.Component
            System.Windows.Forms.Control
```

7

```
System.Windows.Forms.ScrollableControl
   System.Windows.Forms.ContainerControl
      System.Windows.Forms.Form
         System.Windows.Forms.PrintPreviewDialog
```

You can find the significant public properties of `PrintPreviewDialog` objects in Table 7.32.

TABLE 7.32   Significant Public Properties of `PrintPreviewDialog` Objects

Property	Means
Document	Returns or sets the document to preview.
HelpButton	Returns or sets whether a help button should be displayed in the caption box of the form.

You use this dialog's `Document` property to hold the document to be previewed (the document must be a `PrintDocument` object). You can also set other properties such as the `Columns` and `Rows` properties, which set the number of pages displayed horizontally and vertically, with the `PrintPreviewDialog1.PrintPreviewControl.Columns` and `PrintPreviewDialog1.PrintPreviewControl.Rows` properties.

Creating Print Preview Dialogs

All you need to use a Print Preview dialog is a `PrintDocument` object you can assign to the dialog's `Document` property and to have implemented at least an event handler for the `PrintDocument` object's `PrintPage` event. Here's how it looks in the Printer example in this book's code:

```
Private Sub Button2_Click(ByVal sender As System.Object, _
ByVal e As System.EventArgs) Handles Button2.Click
    PrintPreviewDialog1.Document = PrintDocument1
    PrintPreviewDialog1.ShowDialog()
End Sub
```

And that's all you need! You can see the Print Preview dialog that appears when you click the Print Preview button in the Printer example in Figure 7.31.

Using Page Setup Dialogs

Another printing dialog available to you in Visual Basic .NET is the Page Setup dialog. This dialog allows the user to configure the printed page, setting margins, paper size, and page orientation. You can see the Page Setup dialog the `PageSetupDialog` control displays in the Printer example in Figure 7.33.

FIGURE 7.33

Displaying a Page Setup dialog.

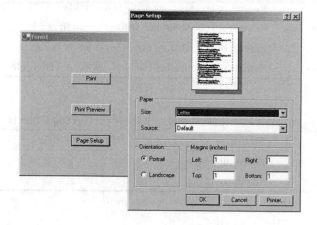

The `PageSetupDialog` class has this class hierarchy:

```
System.Object
    System.MarshalByRefObject
        System.ComponentModel.Component
            System.Windows.Forms.CommonDialog
                System.Windows.Forms.PageSetupDialog
```

You can find the significant properties of `PageSetupDialog` objects in Table 7.33, the significant methods in Table 7.34, and the significant events in Table 7.35.

TABLE 7.33 Significant Public Properties of `PageSetupDialog` Objects

Property	Means
AllowMargins	Returns or sets whether the margins section of the dialog is enabled.
AllowOrientation	Returns or sets whether the Orientation section of the dialog (landscape or portrait) is enabled.
AllowPaper	Returns or sets whether the Paper section of the dialog (paper size and paper source) is enabled.
AllowPrinter	Returns or sets whether the Printer button is enabled.
Document	Returns or sets the `PrintDocument` to get page settings from.
MinMargins	Returns or sets the minimum margins the user is allowed to select (measured in hundredths of an inch).

7

TABLE 7.33 continued

Property	Means
PageSettings	Returns or sets the page settings to modify.
PrinterSettings	Returns or sets the printer settings to modify.
ShowHelp	Returns or sets whether the Help button is visible.
ShowNetwork	Returns or sets whether the Network button is visible.

TABLE 7.34 Significant Public Methods of `PageSetupDialog` Objects

Method	Means
Reset	Resets all options.
ShowDialog	Shows the dialog.

TABLE 7.35 Significant Public Event of `PageSetupDialog` Objects

Event	Means
HelpRequest	Occurs when the user clicks the Help button.

Page Setup dialogs enable you to specify both page and printer properties. For example, you can specify the margins of each page in addition to what printer to use. This means that these dialogs can configure both the `PrinterSettings` objects we saw in Tables 7.27 and 7.28 and a new type of object: `PageSettings` objects. You can see the significant properties of `PageSettings` objects in Table 7.36. `PageSetupDialog` objects return the setup options the user has specified in both `PrinterSettings` and `PageSettings` objects (accessible using the `PageSetupDialog` object's `PrinterSettings` and `PageSettings` properties).

TABLE 7.36 Significant Public Properties of `PageSettings` Objects

Property	Means
Bounds	Gets the bounds of the page.
Color	Returns or sets whether the page should be printed in color.
Landscape	Returns or sets whether the page should be printed in landscape or portrait orientation.
Margins	Returns or sets the margins for this page.

TABLE 7.36   continued

Property	Means
PaperSize	Returns or sets the paper size for the page.
PrinterResolution	Returns or sets the printer resolution for the page.
PrinterSettings	Returns or sets the printer settings associated with the page.

Creating Page Setup Dialogs

Actually, using Page Setup dialogs is relatively easy, despite the fact that you work with both `PrinterSettings` and `PageSettings` objects. Here's how this procedure works in the Printer example: First, you assign the `PrintDocument` object that holds the document to print to the Page Setup dialog's `Document` property. Next, you assign the `PrinterSettings` object for the document (accessed through the document's `DefaultPageSettings` property) to the dialog's `PageSettings` property and assign the document's `PrinterSettings` object (accessed through the document's `PrinterSettings` property) to the dialog's `PrinterSettings` property:

```
Private Sub Button3_Click(ByVal sender As System.Object, _
    ByVal e As System.EventArgs) Handles Button3.Click
    PageSetupDialog1.Document = PrintDocument1
    PageSetupDialog1.PageSettings = PrintDocument1.DefaultPageSettings
    PageSetupDialog1.PrinterSettings = PrintDocument1.PrinterSettings
         .
         .
         .

End Sub
```

When the Page Setup dialog appears (you can see the Page Setup dialog in the Printing example in Figure 7.33), the user makes the changes he or she wants in the current page and printer settings and clicks OK. When the user does, we can simply re-install those settings in the main `PrintDocument` object this way:

```
Private Sub Button3_Click(ByVal sender As System.Object, _
    ByVal e As System.EventArgs) Handles Button3.Click
    PageSetupDialog1.Document = PrintDocument1
    PageSetupDialog1.PageSettings = PrintDocument1.DefaultPageSettings
    PageSetupDialog1.PrinterSettings = PrintDocument1.PrinterSettings
    If PageSetupDialog1.ShowDialog = DialogResult.OK Then
        PrintDocument1.DefaultPageSettings = PageSetupDialog1.PageSettings
        PrintDocument1.PrinterSettings = PageSetupDialog1.PrinterSettings
    End If
End Sub
```

7

That's all you need to do! The `PrintDocument` object's `Print` method will take it from here when you print the document. And that finishes our work with printing for today. For the sake of reference, Listing 7.2 presents the code for the Printer application.

LISTING 7.2 Printing in Visual Basic .NET (Printer project, Form1.vb)

```
Public Class Form1
    Inherits System.Windows.Forms.Form

' Windows Form Designer generated code

    Dim intPage As Integer

    Private Sub Button1_Click(ByVal sender As System.Object, _
        ByVal e As System.EventArgs) Handles Button1.Click
        PrintDialog1.Document = PrintDocument1
        PrintDialog1.PrinterSettings = PrintDocument1.PrinterSettings
        PrintDialog1.AllowSomePages = True
        If PrintDialog1.ShowDialog = DialogResult.OK Then
            PrintDocument1.PrinterSettings = PrintDialog1.PrinterSettings
            PrintDocument1.Print()
        End If
    End Sub

    Private Sub PrintDocument1_BeginPrint(ByVal sender As Object, _
        ByVal e As System.Drawing.Printing.PrintEventArgs) _
        Handles PrintDocument1.BeginPrint
        intPage = 0
    End Sub

    Private Sub PrintDocument1_PrintPage(ByVal sender As Object, _
        ByVal e As System.Drawing.Printing.PrintPageEventArgs) _
        Handles PrintDocument1.PrintPage
        intPage += 1
        Select Case intPage
            Case 1
                e.Graphics.FillEllipse(Brushes.Red, _
                    100, 200, 680, 500)
                e.HasMorePages = True
            Case 2
                e.Graphics.FillEllipse(Brushes.Green, _
                    100, 200, 680, 500)
                e.HasMorePages = True
            Case 3
                e.Graphics.FillEllipse(Brushes.Blue, _
                    100, 200, 680, 500)
                e.HasMorePages = False
        End Select
    End Sub
```

LISTING 7.2   continued

```
    Private Sub Button2_Click(ByVal sender As System.Object, _
        ByVal e As System.EventArgs) Handles Button2.Click
        PrintPreviewDialog1.Document = PrintDocument1
        PrintPreviewDialog1.ShowDialog()
    End Sub

    Private Sub Button3_Click(ByVal sender As System.Object, _
        ByVal e As System.EventArgs) Handles Button3.Click
        PageSetupDialog1.Document = PrintDocument1
        PageSetupDialog1.PageSettings = PrintDocument1.DefaultPageSettings
        PageSetupDialog1.PrinterSettings = PrintDocument1.PrinterSettings
        If PageSetupDialog1.ShowDialog = DialogResult.OK Then
            PrintDocument1.DefaultPageSettings = PageSetupDialog1.PageSettings
            PrintDocument1.PrinterSettings = PageSetupDialog1.PrinterSettings
        End If
    End Sub
End Class
```

Summary

Today, we saw a great deal of programming power in Windows controls. We began with menus, seeing how to create menus with a MainMenu control. After adding that control to a form, you simply type the menu and menu item captions you want into the control and add Click event handlers for the menu items. Using this control, you also can easily add submenus to menu items.

Menu items can also support check marks, and menu items can be checked at runtime. At runtime, you can work with a menu item's check mark using the Checked property. We also saw that it was easy to add both access keys and shortcuts to menus.

MDI applications can handle child window menus in a special way, letting you merge those menus with the menu system of the main MDI parent. We saw how that merging process works today.

We also saw how to create context menus and how to add them to controls and forms so that they'll appear when the user right-clicks the mouse.

Next, we turned to the built-in dialogs that Visual Basic .NET supports, starting with the Open File and Save File dialogs. These two dialogs gave us an introduction to file handling, letting the user specify what file to save data in and what file to open.

7

We saw that the Font dialog allows the user to select a font, and we saw how to install the user's selection in a rich text box. We also saw how to create Color dialogs to let the user specify colors and Folder Browser dialogs that enable the user to select a directory.

We finished off today's work by seeing how to print in Visual Basic .NET. The printing process is supported with the `PrintDocument` object, and we saw how to use this object's `Print` method to print documents. We also saw how to tailor the printing process with dialogs—the Print dialog, the Print Preview dialog, and the Page Setup dialog.

And that's it! We've come far today, augmenting our programming arsenal with a lot of power using the controls available in the toolbox. Tomorrow, we're going to see even more: image lists, tree views, list views, toolbars, status bars, and progress bars.

Q&A

Q I want to customize a menu item but don't want to draw it from scratch in code. Is there some way to display an image from an image file in a menu item?

A Yes, you can use the `FromFile` method of `Image` objects to load the image and the `Graphics` class's `DrawImage` method to draw the image in the menu item. (As we saw today in "Drawing Menu Items in Code," you're passed a `Graphics` object in `DrawItem` event handlers.) For more details on image handling and the `Graphics` class, see Day 10.

Q I'd like to display print previews as the user is working on a document. Is there any way to customize how my program displays print previews?

A There sure is. The `PrintPreviewControl` control (available in the toolbox) enables you to print previews at any time. You can customize this control to produce your own custom print preview windows. To get it to display a print preview, you assign the document to its `Document` property.

Workshop

This workshop tests whether you understand the concepts you saw today. It's a good idea to make sure you can answer these questions before pressing on to tomorrow's work.

Quiz

1. How do you give a menu item an access key?
2. How do you display a check mark in front of a menu item from code?

3. What property can you use to get the name of the file the user selected in a Open File dialog? What about when you're letting the user select multiple files?

4. How do you know when the user clicked the OK button in a dialog?

5. What events handle the printing process in `PrintDocument` objects?

Quiz Answers

1. You simply place an ampersand (&) in front of the character you want to use for the access key in the menu item's caption. When the user presses the Alt key, the available access keys will be underlined.

2. You set the menu item's `Checked` property to `True`. To toggle the check mark in front of a menu item, you can do something like this: `MenuItem2.Checked = Not MenuItem2.Checked`.

3. You use the `FileName` property to recover the name of the selected file. If you're allowing the user to make multiple selections, you use the `FileNames` property, which holds an array of names.

4. The `ShowDialog` method of the dialog will return a value of `DialogResult.OK`.

5. First, a `BeginPrint` event occurs. Next, a `PrintPage` event occurs for each page. Finally, an `EndPrint` event occurs when the print job is complete.

Exercises

1. Try creating a menu system in code where one menu item has a submenu of three items. When the user clicks one of these submenu items, have your code display a message box indicating which menu item was selected.

2. Create a small word processor application based on a rich text box. Let the user use an Open File dialog to open a text file, a Save As dialog to save the text, a Font dialog to set the font in the rich text box, and a Color dialog to let the user set the color of text. (**Extra credit:** Implement printing with printing dialogs as well.)

7

DAY 8

Windows Forms: Working with Image Lists, Tree Views, List Views, Toolbars, Status Bars, and Progress Bars

Today we're going to look at a set of more advanced Windows controls: image lists, tree views, list views, toolbars, status bars, and progress bars. These controls will finish off our main survey of Windows controls, although we'll see a few more later in the book when discussing data handling in Day 17, "Binding Visual Basic Controls to Databases." These controls pack a lot of power in them; here are today's topics:

- Creating image lists
- Using image lists with various Windows controls
- Creating tree views

- Handling tree view events
- Creating list views
- Selecting list views
- Creating toolbars
- Handling toolbar button clicks
- Connecting toolbar buttons to menu items
- Creating progress bars
- Creating status bars
- Adding panels to a status bar
- Handling status bar panel clicks
- Creating tab controls
- Creating multiple rows of tabs

The first controls we'll look at are image lists because these controls are designed to be used with the other controls we'll see today. You use image lists to store images—sort of a storehouse for images. You don't use image lists directly in a form (they go into the component tray, not on a form); instead, you use them to hold the images you use in other controls, as we'll see.

Using Image Lists

Many Windows controls are designed to work with image lists, such as list views, tree views, toolbars, tab controls, check boxes, buttons, radio buttons, and labels. (For some of these controls, using image lists is the only way you can display images.) All these controls have ImageList and ImageIndex properties. After you store images in an image list, you can connect that image list to another control by using the control's ImageList property. To display the various images in the image list, you only have to assign the (zero-based) index of the image in the image list to the control's ImageIndex property.

You can see an example in the ImageLists example in the code for this book, which appears in Figure 8.1. That's not the image list itself you're seeing in the figure; it's a Label control connected to an image list, and you can use the arrow buttons at the bottom to move through all three images in the image list.

Here is the class hierarchy of the ImageList control:

```
System.Object
    System.MarshalByRefObject
        System.ComponentModel.Component
            System.Windows.Forms.ImageList
```

FIGURE 8.1

Using an image list with a label.

You can find the significant public properties of ImageList objects in Table 8.1 and the significant methods in Table 8.2.

TABLE 8.1   Significant Public Properties of ImageList Objects

Property	Means
Images	Returns the collection of images in this image list.
ImageSize	Returns or sets the size of the images in the image list.

TABLE 8.2   Significant Public Method of ImageList Objects

Method	Means
Draw	Draws the indicated image.

The main property in an image list is the Images property, which holds the images in a collection (you can access the images like this: ImageList1.Images(1)). Let's see how to put image lists to work to make all this clear.

Creating Image Lists

To add an image list to a program, you just drag one from the toolbox. To load images into the new image list, select its Images property in the Properties window. This opens the Image Collection Editor you see in Figure 8.2, and you can add new images to the image list by clicking the Add button (which also lets you browse to various image files) or remove them by clicking the Remove button.

FIGURE 8.2

*The Image Collection
Editor.*

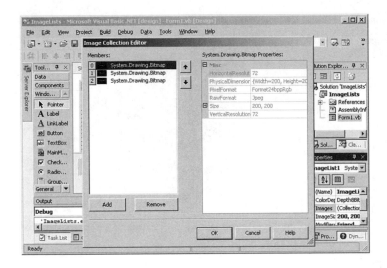

Note that the images in an image list aren't sized automatically to match the images you load into it. Instead, you set the `ImageSize` property (which has two subproperties, `Width` and `Height`) to the size you want the images to be. You can set the image size you want to use by clicking this property in the Properties window and entering a width and height, separated by a comma, like `200, 200` (all images in an image list have the same size).

Tip

The default image size is 16×16 pixels, so if your images appear very small at runtime, you know you still need to set the `ImageSize` property.

You can also load images into an image list at runtime by using the `Images` collection's `Add` method. For example, if you've let the user select a number of images using a File Open dialog, here's how you might add all those images to an image list:

```
For intLoopIndex As Integer = 0 To OpenFileDialog1.FileNames.Length - 1
    ImageList1.Images.Add( _
        Image.FromFile(OpenFileDialog1.FileNames(intLoopIndex)))
Next intLoopIndex
```

Using Image Lists with Windows Controls

Image lists are really designed to be used with controls that have both `ImageList` and `ImageIndex` properties. Those controls are list views, tree views, toolbars, tab controls, check boxes, buttons, radio buttons, and labels.

You connect an image list to the control by using the `ImageList` property at design time or runtime (for example, `Label1.ImageList = ImageList1`) and specify which image from that list is displayed in the control by using the zero-based `ImageIndex` property (for example, `Label1.ImageIndex = 0`).

Here's how that looks in the ImageLists example in the book's code, which uses two buttons to let the user cycle through the available images (note that you can use the `Count` property of an image list's `Images` collection to determine how many images are in the image list):

```
Private Sub Button1_Click(ByVal sender As System.Object, _
    ByVal e As System.EventArgs) Handles Button1.Click
    If Label1.ImageIndex < ImageList1.Images.Count - 1 Then
        Label1.ImageIndex += 1
    Else
        Label1.ImageIndex = 0
    End If
End Sub

Private Sub Button2_Click(ByVal sender As System.Object, _
    ByVal e As System.EventArgs) Handles Button2.Click
    If Label1.ImageIndex > 0 Then
        Label1.ImageIndex -= 1
    Else
        Label1.ImageIndex = ImageList1.Images.Count - 1
    End If
End Sub
```

You can see the results in Figure 8.1, where the user can display various images from an image list just by clicking the buttons.

Although image lists were intended to be used with controls that have `ImageList` and `ImageIndex` properties, you can also use image lists with controls that simply have `Image` or `BackGroundImage` properties if you access the images in the `Images` collection directly. Picture boxes have only `Image` properties, for example, so you can load an image from an image list into a picture box by using something like this: `PictureBox1.Image = ImageList1.Images(0)`. You can also cycle through the images in an image list if you keep track of the image's index in the image list yourself like this:

```
Dim intImageIndex As Integer = 0

Private Sub Button1_Click(ByVal sender As System.Object, _
    ByVal e As System.EventArgs) Handles Button1.Click
    If intImageIndex < ImageList1.Images.Count - 1 Then
        intImageIndex += 1
```

```
    Else
        intImageIndex = 0
    End If
    PictureBox1.Image = ImageList1.Images(intImageIndex)
End Sub
```

In fact, you can draw using an image list in any control, even if it doesn't support images at all. All you need to do is use the control's CreateGraphics method to get a Graphics object for the control and pass that object to the image list's Draw method, along with the point inside the control at which to start drawing (usually (0, 0)), and the index of the image to draw. You do that in the control's Paint event, which occurs when the control needs to be redrawn, or when you call the control's Refresh method. For example, here's how we might display images in a panel, which normally doesn't display images:

```
Dim intImageIndex = 0

Private Sub Panel1_Paint(ByVal sender As Object, _
    ByVal e As System.Windows.Forms.PaintEventArgs) Handles Panel1.Paint
    ImageList1.Draw(Panel1.CreateGraphics(), New Point(0, 0), intImageIndex)
End Sub

Private Sub Button3_Click(ByVal sender As System.Object, _
    ByVal e As System.EventArgs) Handles Button3.Click
    If intImageIndex < ImageList1.Images.Count - 1 Then
        intImageIndex += 1
    Else
        intImageIndex = 0
    End If
    Panel1.Refresh()
End Sub
```

That's it for our look at image lists for the moment; we'll look at tree views next.

Using Tree Views

NEW TERM   You can use a tree view to display a set of *nodes* in a hierarchy. The nodes are just items displaying text in a tree view, such as the items you see in the Windows Explorer (which is based on a tree view). For example, you can see a tree view at work in Figure 8.3, from the TreeViews example in the code for this book.

FIGURE 8.3

A tree view.

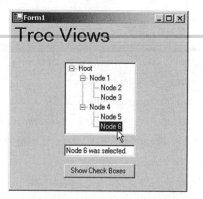

8

To expand or collapse parent nodes, you click the plus (+) or minus (–) sign in the boxes in front of each node (as you see in Figure 8.3). When a parent node is expanded, its child nodes are visible. You can also display images from an image list in each node, including different images for expanded and collapsed nodes, such as folders and documents.

Tip

> You can find images for open and closed folders, as well as for documents, in the Visual Basic Common7\Graphics\icons directory.

The class hierarchy of the `TreeView` class is as follows:

```
System.Object
    System.MarshalByRefObject
        System.ComponentModel.Component
            System.Windows.Forms.Control
                System.Windows.Forms.TreeView
```

You can find the significant public properties of `TreeView` objects in Table 8.3, the significant public methods in Table 8.4, and the significant public events in Table 8.5. (Note that these tables don't include properties, methods, and events `TreeView` objects inherit from the `Control` class; you can find them in Tables 5.1, 5.2, and 5.3.)

TABLE 8.3   Significant Public Properties of `TreeView` Objects

Property	Means
BorderStyle	Returns or sets the border style of the tree view.
CheckBoxes	Returns or sets whether check boxes are displayed in front of the nodes in the tree view.

TABLE 8.3   continued

Property	Means
HotTracking	Returns or sets whether a tree node's text should change appearance as the mouse pointer passes over it.
ImageIndex	Returns or sets the image list index of the default image in tree nodes.
ImageList	Returns or sets the image list that contains images used by tree nodes.
Indent	Returns or sets the distance to indent each level of nodes.
LabelEdit	Returns or sets whether text in the nodes may be edited at runtime.
Nodes	Returns the collection of nodes in the tree view.
Scrollable	Returns or sets whether the tree view should display scrollbars (when needed).
SelectedImageIndex	Returns or sets the image list index of the image displayed when a node is selected.
SelectedNode	Returns or sets the currently selected node in the tree view.
ShowLines	Returns or sets whether lines are drawn between nodes in the tree view.
ShowPlusMinus	Returns or sets whether plus (+) and minus (–) sign buttons are displayed in front of nodes that contain child tree nodes.
ShowRootLines	Returns or sets whether lines should be drawn between the nodes and the root of the tree view.
Sorted	Returns or sets whether the tree nodes in the tree view are sorted.
TopNode	Returns the first visible node in the tree view.
VisibleCount	Returns the number of nodes that can be seen in the tree view.

TABLE 8.4   Significant Public Methods of `TreeView` Objects

Method	Means
CollapseAll	Collapses all tree nodes.
ExpandAll	Expands all the tree nodes.
GetNodeAt	Returns the node at the given location.
GetNodeCount	Returns the number of nodes in the tree view.

TABLE 8.5   Significant Public Events of `TreeView` Objects

Event	Means
AfterCheck	Occurs when a tree node's check box is checked.
AfterCollapse	Occurs when a tree node is collapsed.

TABLE 8.5   continued

Event	Means
AfterExpand	Occurs when a tree node is expanded.
AfterLabelEdit	Occurs when a tree node's label text is edited.
AfterSelect	Occurs when a tree node is selected.
BeforeCheck	Occurs before a tree node check box is checked.
BeforeCollapse	Occurs before a tree node is collapsed.
BeforeExpand	Occurs before a tree node is expanded.
BeforeLabelEdit	Occurs before a tree node's label text is edited.
BeforeSelect	Occurs before a tree node is selected.

Each node in a tree view is a `TreeNode` object. Here is the class hierarchy of the `TreeNode` class:

```
System.Object
   System.MarshalByRefObject
      System.Windows.Forms.TreeNode
```

You can find the significant public properties of `TreeNode` objects in Table 8.6 and the significant public methods in Table 8.7.

TABLE 8.6   Significant Public Properties of `TreeNode` Objects

Property	Means
Checked	Returns or sets whether the tree node shows check boxes.
FirstNode	Returns the first child tree node.
FullPath	Returns the full path from the root node to the current node.
ImageIndex	Returns or sets the image list index of the image displayed when the node is not selected.
Index	Returns the position of the node in the node collection.
IsExpanded	Returns whether the node is expanded.
IsSelected	Returns whether the node is selected.
IsVisible	Returns whether the node is visible.
LastNode	Returns the last child node.
NextNode	Returns the next sibling node.
NextVisibleNode	Returns the next visible node.
NodeFont	Returns or sets the font for the node's text.

TABLE 8.6   continued

Property	Means
Nodes	Returns the collection of nodes (TreeNode objects) for the current node.
Parent	Returns the parent tree node of the current tree node.
PrevNode	Returns the previous sibling node.
PrevVisibleNode	Returns the previous visible node.
SelectedImageIndex	Returns or sets the image list index of the image displayed when the node is selected.
Text	Returns or sets the text in the label of the node.
TreeView	Returns the parent tree view of the node.

TABLE 8.7   Significant Public Methods of TreeNode Objects

Method	Means
Collapse	Collapses the node.
EnsureVisible	Ensures the node is visible, scrolling the tree view if needed.
Expand	Expands the node.
GetNodeCount	Returns the number of child nodes.
Remove	Removes the current node from the tree view.
Toggle	Toggles the node to the expanded or collapsed state.

The major properties of tree views are Nodes and SelectedNode. The Nodes property contains the list of nodes in the tree view, and the SelectedNode property holds the currently selected node. Nodes themselves are supported by the TreeNode class. The Nodes collection is important because it holds all the tree view's TreeNode objects. As with all collections, the Nodes collection has methods such as Add and Remove, and you can access items individually by index.

Each tree node can contain other nodes, and in code, that's reflected in expressions like this: TreeView1.Nodes(3).Nodes(7).Nodes(2). (You can also use the FullPath property to specify nodes in terms of their full paths.) You can also navigate through tree views with various properties: FirstNode, LastNode, NextNode, PrevNode, NextVisibleNode, PrevVisibleNode. To select a node from code, you just assign a node to the tree view's SelectedNode property.

The text for each node is held in the TreeNode Text property. You can also display an image in a tree node using an image list; you begin by assigning the image list control (such as ImageList1) to the tree view's ImageList property. Then you can set the ImageIndex property of various TreeNode objects to the index of the image you want the node to display. You can also assign an image index to the SelectedImageIndex property to set the image that should be displayed when the node is selected.

And you can expand or collapse nodes in code by using the Expand method to expand a single node, ExpandAll to expand all nodes, or the Collapse or CollapseAll methods to collapse nodes. Let's look at some of this in practice now as we see how to create tree views.

Creating Tree Views

To create a tree view at design time, just drag a tree view control onto a Windows form. To add nodes to it, you open the Nodes property in the Properties window, which displays the TreeNode editor you see in Figure 8.4.

FIGURE 8.4

The TreeNode editor.

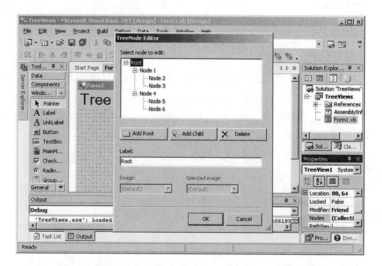

To start creating nodes in the TreeNode editor, you use the Add Root button, which adds a top-level node. To add children to that node, you select the node and use the Add Child button. You can add text to any node in the Label box in the TreeNode editor, or double-click the text next to any node directly to edit it.

If you've added an image list to the form and stored images in it, you can display those images in the tree view. Just connect an image and a selected image to each node by using the drop-down boxes in the TreeNode editor.

You can also create tree views entirely in code, of course, and we'll see how to do that in the section "Creating a Tree View in Code."

Handling Tree View Events

As you can see in Table 8.5, tree views support quite a few events. The default event is the AfterSelect event, which occurs when a node was selected. You can determine which node was selected by using the TreeViewEventArgs object that is passed to this event's handler because this object has a Node property that contains the selected node. For example, here's how the code in the TreeViews example displays the text of the selected node in a text box:

```
Private Sub TreeView1_AfterSelect(ByVal sender As System.Object, _
ByVal e As System.Windows.Forms.TreeViewEventArgs) _
Handles TreeView1.AfterSelect
    TextBox1.Text = e.Node.Text & " was selected."
End Sub
```

You can see how this works in Figure 8.3, where the user has clicked a node and the code is reporting which one was clicked.

Adding Check Boxes to Tree Views

You can also display check boxes in tree views. To do that, you set the tree view's CheckBoxes property to True. As with standard check boxes, you can check or uncheck nodes by setting the node's Checked property to True or False.

Here's how that works in the TreeViews example: When the user clicks the Show Check Boxes button, we turn on the check boxes in the tree view:

```
Private Sub Button1_Click(ByVal sender As System.Object, _
    ByVal e As System.EventArgs) Handles Button1.Click
    TreeView1.CheckBoxes = True
End Sub
```

You can determine which check box has been checked or unchecked in a tree view's AfterCheck event handler like this:

```
Private Sub TreeView1_AfterCheck(ByVal sender As Object, _
    ByVal e As System.Windows.Forms.TreeViewEventArgs) _
    Handles TreeView1.AfterCheck
        If e.Node.Checked Then
            TextBox1.Text = e.Node.Text & " is checked."
        Else
            TextBox1.Text = e.Node.Text & " is not checked."
        End If
    End If
End Sub
```

You can see how this works in Figure 8.5, where the user has checked a node, and the code is reporting which node was checked in the text box.

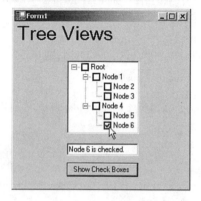

Creating a Tree View in Code

As with all the other controls, you can create tree views in code. To see how that works, look at the CodeTreeViews example in the code for this book, as shown in Listing 8.1. This example creates the same tree view as the TreeViews example but does it all in code. (You can add event handlers to the tree view as well if you want, using the AddHandler method we first saw in Day 4, "Creating Windows Forms.")

LISTING 8.1   Creating Tree Views in Code (CodeTreeViews project, Form1.vb)

```vb
Public Class Form1
    Inherits System.Windows.Forms.Form

' Windows Form Designer generated code

    Dim TreeView1 As TreeView

    Private Sub Button1_Click(ByVal sender As System.Object, _
        ByVal e As System.EventArgs) Handles Button1.Click
        TreeView1 = New TreeView
        TreeView1.Location = New Point(75, 100)
        TreeView1.Size = New Size(150, 150)
        Controls.Add(TreeView1)
        TreeView1.Nodes.Clear()

        Dim RootNode = New TreeNode("Root")
        TreeView1.Nodes.Add(RootNode)
        TreeView1.Nodes(0).Nodes.Add(New TreeNode("Node 1"))
```

LISTING 8.1   continued

```
For intLoopIndex As Integer = 2 To 3
    TreeView1.Nodes(0).Nodes(0).Nodes.Add(New _
        TreeNode("Node" & Str(intLoopIndex)))
Next intLoopIndex

TreeView1.Nodes(0).Nodes.Add(New TreeNode("Node 4"))

For intLoopIndex As Integer = 5 To 6
    TreeView1.Nodes(0).Nodes(1).Nodes.Add(New _
        TreeNode("Node" & Str(intLoopIndex)))
Next intLoopIndex

        End Sub

    End Class
```

You can see the results in Figure 8.6. When you click the Create Tree View button, the code creates the tree view you see in the figure.

FIGURE 8.6

Creating a tree view in code.

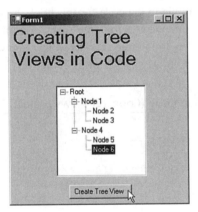

Using List Views

List views are all about displaying lists of items. For example, you can see a list view in the right pane in the Windows Explorer; the list view there shows what files are in a particular directory. You can also see a list view at work in Figure 8.7, which is in the ListViews example in the code for this book.

FIGURE 8.7

A list view.

 List views are versatile controls; they can display their items in four different *views*: View.LargeIcon, View.SmallIcon, View.List, and View.Details. You set the view by assigning one of those values to the list view's View property. Using the combo box in the ListViews example, you can select all these views so that you can see what they look like.

As you might expect, list views are supported by the ListView class, which has this class hierarchy:

```
System.Object
    System.MarshalByRefObject
        System.ComponentModel.Component
            System.Windows.Forms.Control
                System.Windows.Forms.ListView
```

You can find the significant public properties of ListView objects in Table 8.8, the significant public methods in Table 8.9, and the significant public events in Table 8.10. (Note that these tables don't include those properties, methods, and events ListView objects inherit from the Control class; you can find them in Tables 5.1, 5.2, and 5.3.)

TABLE 8.8   Significant Public Properties of ListView Objects

Property	Means
Activation	Returns or sets the action needed to activate an item.
AllowColumnReorder	Returns or sets whether the user can drag column headers.
CheckBoxes	Returns or sets whether check boxes appear in front of list items.
CheckedIndices	Returns the indices of the currently checked list items.
CheckedItems	Returns the currently checked list items.
Columns	Returns the collection of columns in the list view.

TABLE 8.8 continued

Property	Mean
FocusedItem	Returns the item that currently has the user focus.
HeaderStyle	Returns or sets the column header style.
HoverSelection	Returns or sets whether items can be selected by hovering with the mouse.
Items	Returns the list items.
LabelEdit	Returns or sets whether the user can edit the text of items in a list view.
LabelWrap	Returns or sets whether item labels wrap.
LargeImageList	Returns or sets the currently set ImageList for large icon views.
MultiSelect	Returns or sets whether multiple items can be selected.
Scrollable	Returns or sets whether scrollbars are visible.
SelectedIndices	Returns the indices of the currently selected items.
SelectedItems	Returns the currently selected items.
SmallImageList	Returns or sets the list view's small icon image list.
Sorting	Returns or sets the sort order of the items.
TopItem	Returns the item at the top of the list.
View	Returns or sets the current view.

TABLE 8.9 Significant Public Methods of ListView Objects

Method	Means
ArrangeIcons	Arranges items in large icon or small icon view.
Clear	Removes all items and columns from the list view.
EnsureVisible	Ensures that the item is visible, scrolling if needed.
GetItemAt	Returns the item corresponding to the given x,y coordinate.

TABLE 8.10 Significant Public Events of ListView Objects

Event	Means
AfterLabelEdit	Occurs when a label has been edited.
BeforeLabelEdit	Occurs before a label is edited.
ColumnClick	Occurs when the user clicks a column.
ItemActivate	Occurs when an item is activated.
ItemCheck	Occurs when an item is checked.
SelectedIndexChanged	Occurs when the selected index is changed.

The items in a list view are stored in the list view's `Items` collection, accessed with the `Items` property. Each list view item is an object of the `ListViewItem` class; here is the class hierarchy of the that class:

```
System.Object
    System.Windows.Forms.ListViewItem
```

You can find the significant public properties of `ListViewItem` objects in Table 8.11 and the significant public methods in Table 8.12.

TABLE 8.11 Significant Public Properties of `ListViewItem` Objects

Property	Means
Checked	Returns `True` if the item is checked, `False` otherwise.
Index	Returns the index of the item in the list view.
Selected	Returns or sets whether the item is selected.
Text	Returns or sets the text for this item.

TABLE 8.12 Significant Public Method of `ListViewItem` Objects

Method	Means
EnsureVisible	Ensures that the item is visible, scrolling the view as necessary.

The main properties in list views include `ListItems`, which contains the items displayed by the control, and `SelectedItems`, which contains a collection of the items currently selected in the control (the user can select multiple items if the `MultiSelect` property is set to `True`). Also, like tree views, list views can display check boxes next to the items if the `CheckBoxes` property is set to `True`.

You can use the `SelectedIndexChanged` event to handle item selections and `ItemCheck` events to handle check mark events. Also, you can sort the items in a list view with the `Sorting` property. Let's look at creating a list view now to make this all clear.

Creating List Views

After adding a list view from the toolbox to a form, you can add items to the list view by clicking the `Items` property to open the ListViewItem Collection Editor you see in Figure 8.8.

FIGURE 8.8

*The ListViewItem
Collection Editor.*

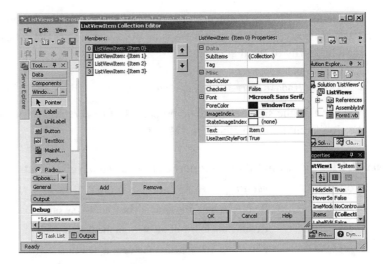

This editor is much like the TreeNode editor, and it works in the same way. To add a new list view item, click Add; to delete one, click Remove. Note that a new list item doesn't have any text by default; you can add text to an item in the Text entry in the ListViewItem Collection Editor (in the box at right).

List view items don't have an image by default either, and you need an image view to associate an image with a list view item. The ListViews example has an image list in it, and the image list includes one image, an icon from an icon file that comes with Visual Basic .NET: Common7\Graphics\icons\Writing\note12.ico. You can see this icon's image in the list view in Figure 8.7.

List views display their items with two different sized icons—small (16×16 pixel) images and large (32×32 pixel) images, depending on which view you select, so actually you need two different image lists (recall that the images in an image list must all be the same size). Each icon file already has a 16×16 and a 32×32 version of the icon in it, so you just need to add that icon to each image list (but make sure you set one image list's image size to 32×32 pixels, not the default 16×16). Next, assign the small icon's image list to the list view's SmallImageList property and the large icon's image list to the LargeImageList property. Then, in the ListViewItem Collection Editor (see Figure 8.8), assign the image index of the image you want to use in the image list (if you've added only one icon to each image list, that's item 0) to each item's ImageIndex property.

In Report View, a list view displays its items in columns, and you can set the number of columns you want in the ColumnHeader Collection Editor, which you open at design time with the list view's Columns property, as you see in Figure 8.9. You can add new columns with the Add button and give them text by entering that text in the box marked Text at right in the ColumnHeader Collection Editor.

FIGURE 8.9

The ColumnHeader Collection Editor.

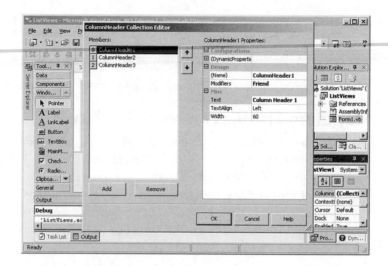

 Tip

If you set the list view's `AllowColumnReorder` property to `True`, the user can reorder the columns in a list view's Report mode by dragging them.

As you know, list views can present their items in four different views. Here are the possibilities, as given by the constants you can assign to the `View` property:

- `View.LargeIcon`—Large icon view displays large icons (32×32 pixels) next to the item's text.
- `View.SmallIcon`—Small icon view is the same as the large icon mode except that it displays small icons (16×16 pixels).
- `View.List`—List view displays small icons. Items are arranged in columns, but with no column headers.
- `View.Details`—Report view (also called the details mode) displays items in multiple columns, displaying column headers and fields.

To enable the user to select between views, the combo box in the ListViews example holds the items `Large Icon View`, `Report View`, `Small Icon View`, and `List View`. By design, the index of each combo box item matches the numeric value of each item in the `View` enumeration, so the code can simply assign the index of the combo box's selected item to the list view's `View` property when the user makes a selection in the combo box:

```
Private Sub ComboBox1_SelectedIndexChanged(ByVal sender As System.Object, _
    ByVal e As System.EventArgs) Handles ComboBox1.SelectedIndexChanged
    ListView1.View = ComboBox1.SelectedIndex
End Sub
```

That creates our list view. We'll look at how to handle item selections next.

Handling List View Item Selections

You can determine when the user has selected items in a list view by using the
SelectedIndexChanged event (the default event for list views). In this event's handler,
you can check the list view's SelectedIndices property to determine which items are
currently selected (the SelectedIndices property holds the indices of those items that
are selected if the list view's MultiSelect property is True, or of the single selected item
if MultiSelect is False). Here's what that code looks like in the ListViews example,
which displays the selected item in a text box:

```
Private Sub ListView1_SelectedIndexChanged(ByVal _
    sender As System.Object, ByVal e As System.EventArgs) _
    Handles ListView1.SelectedIndexChanged
    If ListView1.SelectedIndices.Count > 0 Then
        TextBox1.Text = "Item " & ListView1.SelectedIndices(0) & _
            " was clicked."
    End If
End Sub
```

You can see the results in Figure 8.7, where the code is indicating that Item 3 was
selected.

Tip

As in list boxes, you can also use a list view's SelectedItems property to get a collection of the selected items themselves. This capability is useful if you've made each item
an object, for example, and want to use that object's properties and methods.

Adding Check Boxes

As in menus, list views can also display a check mark in front of each item. The
ListViews example supports check boxes too. Just click the Show Check Boxes button,
which sets the CheckBoxes property of ListView1 to True:

```
Private Sub Button1_Click(ByVal sender As System.Object, _
    ByVal e As System.EventArgs) Handles Button1.Click
    ListView1.CheckBoxes = True
End Sub
```

You can handle check box events with the list view's `ItemCheck` event. In this event's handler, you can find the new setting of a check box by using the `NewValue` property of the `ItemCheckEventArgs` object passed to you. You can also get the list view index of the target item itself with the `Index` property. For example, here's how the ListViews example reports which item was checked or unchecked:

```
Private Sub ListView1_ItemCheck(ByVal sender As Object, _
    ByVal e As System.Windows.Forms.ItemCheckEventArgs) _
    Handles ListView1.ItemCheck
    If e.NewValue = CheckState.Checked Then
        TextBox1.Text = "Item " & e.Index() & " is checked."
    Else
        TextBox1.Text = "Item " & e.Index() & " is not checked."
    End If
End Sub
```

You can see this code at work in Figure 8.10, where the user has just checked the check box for item 1, and the code is reporting that.

FIGURE 8.10

Using check marks in a list view.

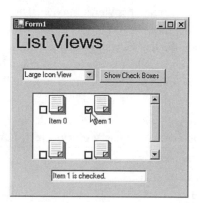

Handling Column Clicks

A list view can also display its items in columns, using report view (sometimes called details view). The user can click the column headers in report view because those headers are buttons. You use the `ColumnClick` event to handle column header clicks; here's how that code looks in the ListViews example, where the code reports what column header the user clicked:

```
Private Sub ListView1_ColumnClick(ByVal sender As Object, _
    ByVal e As System.Windows.Forms.ColumnClickEventArgs) _
    Handles ListView1.ColumnClick
    TextBox1.Text = "Column " & (e.Column + 1) & " was clicked."
End Sub
```

You can see this example at work in Figure 8.11.

FIGURE 8.11

*Clicking columns in a
list view.*

Creating List Views in Code

As with all other controls, you can create list views in code. The CodeListViews example
in the code for this book does just that. As you might expect, you can add items to a list
view by using the Add method of the list view's Items collection. You can also create
columns and column headers in code. When you create a column header, you give the
text for the column header, as well as the width of the column and the alignment of its
contained text, as you see in Listing 8.2.

LISTING 8.2   Creating List Views in Code (CodeListViews project, Form1.vb)

```
Public Class Form1
    Inherits System.Windows.Forms.Form

' Windows Form Designer generated code

    Dim ListView1 As ListView

    Private Sub Button1_Click(ByVal sender As System.Object, _
        ByVal e As System.EventArgs) Handles Button1.Click
        ListView1 = New ListView
        ListView1.Location = New Point(75, 90)
        ListView1.Size = New Size(150, 150)
        Controls.Add(ListView1)

        ListView1.Columns.Add("Column 1", ListView1.Width / 4, _
        HorizontalAlignment.Left)
        ListView1.Columns.Add("Column 2", ListView1.Width / 4, _
            HorizontalAlignment.Left)
        ListView1.Columns.Add("Column 3", ListView1.Width / 4, _
            HorizontalAlignment.Left)
```

LISTING 8.2 continued

```
        ListView1.Columns.Add("Column 4", ListView1.Width / 4, _
            HorizontalAlignment.Left)

        Dim ListItem1 As ListViewItem
        ListItem1 = ListView1.Items.Add("Item 1")
        ListItem1.ImageIndex = 0

        Dim ListItem2 As ListViewItem
        ListItem2 = ListView1.Items.Add("Item 2")
        ListItem2.ImageIndex = 0

        Dim ListItem3 As ListViewItem
        ListItem3 = ListView1.Items.Add("Item 3")
        ListItem3.ImageIndex = 0

        Dim ListItem4 As ListViewItem
        ListItem4 = ListView1.Items.Add("Item 4")
        ListItem4.ImageIndex = 0

        ListView1.SmallImageList = ImageList1
        ListView1.LargeImageList = ImageList2

        ListView1.View = View.SmallIcon
    End Sub
End Class
```

You can see the results in Figure 8.12, which shows the list view in small icon view.

FIGURE 8.12

Creating a list view in code.

Using Toolbars

Everyone who uses Windows knows about toolbars; they're those button bars that appear under menu bars. You can see a sample toolbar created in Visual Basic .NET in Figure 8.13, in the ToolBars example in the code for this book.

FIGURE 8.13

Using a toolbar.

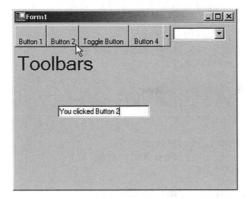

Toolbars are supported with the ToolBar class, which has the following hierarchy:

```
System.Object
   System.MarshalByRefObject
      System.ComponentModel.Component
         System.Windows.Forms.Control
            System.Windows.Forms.ToolBar
```

You can find the significant public properties of ToolBar objects in Table 8.13 and the significant public events in Table 8.14. (Note that these tables do not include the properties, methods, and events toolbars inherit from the Control class, which you can find in Tables 5.1, 5.2, and 5.3.)

TABLE 8.13   Significant Public Properties of ToolBar Objects

Property	Means
Appearance	Returns or sets the appearance of a toolbar and the contained buttons.
AutoSize	Returns or sets whether the toolbar adjusts its size automatically as needed.
BorderStyle	Returns or sets the border style of the toolbar.
Buttons	Returns the collection of buttons in the toolbar.
ButtonSize	Returns or sets the size of the buttons.
DropDownArrows	Returns or sets whether drop-down buttons in a toolbar display down arrows.
ImageList	Returns or sets the collection of images for the toolbar buttons.

TABLE 8.13 continued

Property	Means
ShowToolTips	Returns or sets whether the toolbar displays a tool tip for each button.
TextAlign	Returns or sets the alignment of text in buttons.
Wrappable	Returns or sets whether buttons wrap to the next line if needed.

TABLE 8.14 Significant Public Events of ToolBar Objects

Event	Means
ButtonClick	Occurs when a button is clicked.
ButtonDropDown	Occurs when a drop-down button or its down arrow is clicked.

The buttons in a toolbar are actually ToolBarButton objects. Here is the class hierarchy for the ToolBarButton class:

```
System.Object
   System.MarshalByRefObject
      System.ComponentModel.Component
         System.Windows.Forms.ToolBarButton
```

You can find the significant public properties of ToolBarButton objects in Table 8.15.

TABLE 8.15 Significant Public Properties of ToolBarButton Objects

Property	Means
DropDownMenu	Returns or sets the menu for a drop-down button.
Enabled	Returns or sets whether the button is enabled.
ImageIndex	Returns or sets the image list index of the image for the button.
Parent	Returns the toolbar that the toolbar button is part of.
Style	Returns or sets the style of the toolbar button.
Text	Returns or sets the text displayed in the button.
ToolTipText	Returns or sets the text that appears as a tool tip for the button.
Visible	Returns or sets whether the toolbar button is visible.

Toolbars support various kinds of buttons. You can have standard pushbuttons, toggle buttons (that can appear up or pressed), drop-down buttons that can display a drop-down menu, and buttons that display images. Buttons can also be converted into separators, which display empty horizontal space to separate other buttons.

Usually, the buttons in a toolbar correspond to the most popular menu items in the application. In such cases, the code for a toolbar button is easy to implement: You just use the corresponding `MenuItem` object's `PerformClick` method, which clicks the menu item just as though the user did.

Toolbars are usually docked along the top of their parent window, but in fact, they can be docked to any side of a form. (By default, the `Dock` property is set to `Top`, but you can set it to `Top`, `Bottom`, `Fill`, or whatever you prefer.) Note that toolbars can display tool tips when the mouse hovers over a button. (To display `tool tips`, you must set the `ShowToolTips` property to `True`.)

Creating Toolbars

When you add a toolbar to a form from the toolbox, the toolbar is docked to the top of the form by default. To add buttons to a toolbar at design time, you click the `Buttons` property in the Properties window, which opens the ToolBarButton Collection Editor you see in Figure 8.14. Just click the Add button to add a new button to the toolbar and Remove to remove a button.

FIGURE 8.14

Adding buttons to a toolbar.

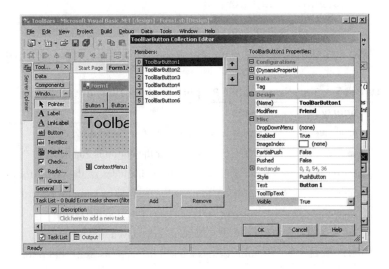

You can set the text in a button by using the `Text` property in the ToolBarButton Collection Editor, the image from an image list to use in a button by using the `ImageIndex` property, as well as the style of the button by using the `Style` property, which can take these values:

- PushButton—A normal button.

- ToggleButton—A toggle button that toggles between up and down (when you click it, it stays "clicked" until you click it again).

- Separator—A space between other buttons, used to divide and group buttons together.

- DropDownButton—A button that displays a drop-down menu.

To show images in a toolbar button, you add an image list to the form and set the ImageIndex property of the button in the ToolBarButton Collection Editor to the image you want to use.

As you might expect, you can also add buttons to a toolbar at runtime. Just create a new button and use the Add method of the toolbar's Buttons collection (you don't need to add a new event handler for the button, as we'll see in the next topic):

```
Private Sub Button1_Click(ByVal sender As System.Object, _
    ByVal e As System.EventArgs) Handles Button1.Click
    Dim ToolBarButton As New ToolBarButton("This is a new button")
    ToolBar1.Buttons.Add(ToolBarButton)
End Sub
```

That creates a new toolbar with various buttons in it. So how do you handle those buttons in code? That's coming up next.

Handling Button Clicks

When the user clicks a button in a toolbar, a ButtonClick event occurs, but it's a toolbar event, not a button event. The individual buttons in a toolbar do not generate their own events, which means you have only one ButtonClick event handler for a toolbar, no matter how many buttons it has. You can determine which button was clicked by using the Button property of the ToolBarButtonClickEventArgs object passed to the ButtonClick event handler. Here's how that works in the ToolBars example, which reports the text of the clicked button in a text box:

```
Private Sub ToolBar1_ButtonClick(ByVal _
    sender As System.Object, ByVal e As _
    System.Windows.Forms.ToolBarButtonClickEventArgs) _
    Handles ToolBar1.ButtonClick
    TextBox1.Text = "You clicked " & e.Button.Text
End Sub
```

If you want to check if a particular button was clicked, here's how you could do it:

```
If e.Button Is ToolBar1.Buttons(2) Then
    .
    .
    .
End If
```

As mentioned, toolbar buttons often correspond to menu items, and you can make a tool-bar button click a menu item like this:

```
Private Sub ToolBar1_ButtonClick(ByVal sender As System.Object, _
    ByVal e As System.Windows.Forms.ToolBarButtonClickEventArgs) _
    Handles ToolBar1.ButtonClick
    If e.Button Is ToolBar1.Buttons(2) Then
        MenuItem7.PerformClick()
    End If
End Sub
```

Creating Drop-Down Buttons

NEW TERM   Toolbars can display *drop-down buttons*, which can display a drop-down menu if you click their displayed arrow. To add a menu to a drop-down button, you can create a menu, such as a context menu, and assign that menu to the drop-down button's `DropDownMenu` property. To see how this works, look at the ToolBars example, which includes a context menu, `ContextMenu1`, with three menu items: Red, Blue, and Green. Here's how those menu items are handled in code:

```
Private Sub MenuItem1_Click(ByVal sender As System.Object, _
    ByVal e As System.EventArgs) Handles MenuItem1.Click
    TextBox1.Text = "You clicked the Red item."
End Sub

Private Sub MenuItem2_Click(ByVal sender As System.Object, _
    ByVal e As System.EventArgs) Handles MenuItem2.Click
    TextBox1.Text = "You clicked the Green item."
End Sub

Private Sub MenuItem3_Click(ByVal sender As System.Object, _
    ByVal e As System.EventArgs) Handles MenuItem3.Click
    TextBox1.Text = "You clicked the Blue item."
End Sub
```

To make the drop-down button active, you assign the context menu, `ContextMenu1`, to the `DropDownMenu` property of the drop-down button in the toolbar (you do that in the ToolBarButton Collection Editor). And that's it! You can see the active drop-down button at work in Figure 8.15.

FIGURE 8.15

A drop-down button in a toolbar.

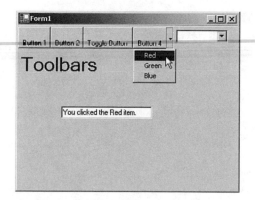

Adding Combo Boxes

Besides buttons, you'll sometimes see other controls, such as combo boxes, in toolbars. For example, combo boxes appear in the toolbars in the Visual Basic .NET IDE, as well as Microsoft Word, Microsoft Excel, and so on. Adding a combo box, or another control, to a toolbar is easy; you just leave some space for it in the toolbar and drag the combo box into place.

To leave space in a toolbar, you can add buttons and set their style to Separator. This style just adds a little horizontal space (no button) in a toolbar, allowing you to separate groups of buttons, much like separators in menus. This means that to add a combo bar between two toolbar buttons, you just insert a few separators to create a blank space and drag the combo box on top of that space. Then you can treat the combo box as a standard combo box in code. Here's what that looks like in the ToolBars example, which displays the item selected in the combo box in a text box:

```
Private Sub ComboBox1_SelectedIndexChanged(ByVal _
    sender As System.Object, ByVal e As System.EventArgs) _
    Handles ComboBox1.SelectedIndexChanged
    TextBox1.Text = "You selected item " & ComboBox1.SelectedIndex
End Sub
```

You can see the results of this code in Figure 8.16, where the combo box is in the toolbar.

FIGURE 8.16

*Using a combo box in
a toolbar.*

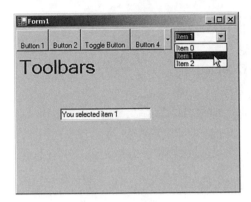

FIGURE 8.16

*Using a combo box in
a toolbar.*

Using Progress Bars

Progress bars are those bars that show the user the progress of a time-consuming operation by displaying rectangles in a horizontal bar. The idea is to give the user some visual feedback on how the operation is progressing and how long it will take. You can see a progress bar in Figure 8.17, in the ProgressBars example in the code for the book. (In this case, the progress bar is being drawn using timer events that start when you click the Go button.)

FIGURE 8.17

Using a progress bar.

Here's the class hierarchy of the ProgressBar class:

```
System.Object
    System.MarshalByRefObject
        System.ComponentModel.Component
            System.Windows.Forms.Control
                System.Windows.Forms.ProgressBar
```

You can find the significant public properties of `ProgressBar` objects in Table 8.16 and the significant public methods in Table 8.17. (Note that these tables don't include the properties, methods, and events progress bars inherit from the `Control` class, which you can find in Tables 5.1, 5.2, and 5.3.)

TABLE 8.16   Significant Public Properties of `ProgressBar` Objects

Property	Means
ForeColor	Returns or sets the foreground color of the progress bar.
Maximum	Returns or sets the maximum value of the progress bar.
Minimum	Returns or sets the minimum value of the progress bar.
Step	Returns or sets the amount that calling `PerformStep` increases the `Value` property.
Value	Returns or sets the current position of the progress bar.

TABLE 8.17   Significant Public Methods of `ProgressBar` Objects

Method	Means
Increment	Increments the `Value` property of the progress bar by the specified amount.
PerformStep	Increases the `Value` property of the progress bar by the amount of the `Step` property.

As in scrollbars and track bars, the main properties of a progress bar are `Value`, `Minimum`, and `Maximum`. You use the `Minimum` and `Maximum` properties to set the minimum and maximum values the progress bar can display. To change the display, you write code to set the `Value` property. For example, if the `Maximum` property is set to 100, the `Minimum` property is set to 10, and the `Value` property is set to 50, five rectangles will appear.

Creating Progress Bars

After adding a progress bar from the toolbox to a form, you set its `Minimum` (default = 1), `Maximum` (default = 100), and `Value` properties as you want. In the ProgressBars example in the code for this book, clicking the Go button starts a timer that steadily increments the `Value` property of the progress bar:

```
Private Sub Button1_Click(ByVal sender As System.Object, _
    ByVal e As System.EventArgs) Handles Button1.Click
    Timer1.Enabled = True
End Sub
```

In the timer's `Tick` event handler, we can increment the progress bar's `Value` property this way:

```
Private Sub Timer1_Tick(ByVal sender As System.Object, _
    ByVal e As System.EventArgs) Handles Timer1.Tick
    If ProgressBar1.Value <= ProgressBar1.Maximum - 1 Then
        ProgressBar1.Value += 1
    Else
        Timer1.Enabled = False
    End If
End Sub
```

And that's all you need! You can see this code at work in Figure 8.17.

Using Status Bars

Status bars appear at the bottom of a window and give the user some additional information, such as error information, whether the program is connected to the Internet, time of day, whether the Caps Lock key is down, and so on. In Visual Basic .NET, you support status bars by using the `StatusBar` control. This control can display panels, as you see in Figure 8.18, which is the StatusBars example in the code for this book.

FIGURE 8.18

Using a status bar.

This control is supported by the `StatusBar` class, and here is that class's hierarchy:

```
System.Object
    System.MarshalByRefObject
        System.ComponentModel.Component
            System.Windows.Forms.Control
                System.Windows.Forms.StatusBar
```

You can find the significant public properties of `StatusBar` objects in Table 8.18 and the significant public events in Table 8.19. (Note that these tables do not include the properties, methods, and events status bars inherit from the `Control` class, which you can find in Tables 5.1, 5.2, and 5.3.)

TABLE 8.18   Significant Public Properties of `StatusBar` Objects

Property	Means
BackgroundImage	Returns or sets the background image.
Dock	Returns or sets how the status bar docks.
Font	Returns or sets the font in the status bar.
Panels	Returns the collection of status bar panels.
ShowPanels	Returns or sets whether panels should be shown.
Text	Returns or sets the status bar text.

TABLE 8.19   Significant Public Event of `StatusBar` Objects

Event	Means
PanelClick	Occurs when a panel in the status bar is clicked.

Another class we need to know about here is the `StatusBarPanel` class, which supports status bar panels. The hierarchy of this class is as follows:

```
System.Object
    System.MarshalByRefObject
        System.ComponentModel.Component
            System.Windows.Forms.StatusBarPanel
```

You can find the significant public properties of `StatusBarPanel` objects in Table 8.20.

TABLE 8.20   Significant Public Properties of `StatusBarPanel` Objects

Property	Means
Alignment	Returns or sets the panel's alignment.
BorderStyle	Returns or sets the border style.
Icon	Returns or sets the icon for this panel.
MinWidth	Returns or sets the minimum width for the panel.
Parent	Returns the status bar that contains the panel.
Style	Returns or sets the style of the panel.
Text	Returns or sets the text of the panel.
ToolTipText	Returns or sets the panel's tool tip text.
Width	Returns or sets the width of the panel.

By default, when you create a status bar, it's a simple status bar. A simple status bar can display only one text item, and it does not support panels. You can also add panels to a status bar; each panel is a `StatusbarPanel` object, and each panel can display its own text.

Creating Simple Status Bars

NEW TERM   Adding a status bar to a form from the toolbox creates a *simple status bar*, without panels. Although it is docked to the bottom of a form by default, you can dock the status bar to any edge of the form by using its Dock property.

You can display text in a simple status bar just by using its Text property. Here's how that works in the StatusBars example, which displays some text when the user clicks a button:

```
Private Sub Button1_Click(ByVal sender As System.Object, _
    ByVal e As System.EventArgs) Handles Button1.Click
    StatusBar1.Text = "You clicked the button."
End Sub
```

You can see this code at work in Figure 8.18, where the simple status bar in the figure is reporting that the user clicked the button. The next step is to start adding panels to this status bar.

Adding Panels to a Status Bar

Most status bars display panels, and you can easily add them to a status bar. To do that, you select the status bar's Panels property in the Properties window, opening the StatusBarPanel Collection Editor you see in Figure 8.19. You can use this editor to add new panels to the status bar. Just click the Add button to add a new panel and fill in the properties of the panel you want. To remove a panel, use the Remove button. If you don't want any code to appear in a panel by default, clear its Text item in the StatusBarPanel Collection Editor. To allow the status bar to display panels, set its ShowPanels property to True.

To add panels to a status bar in code, you use the StatusBar.Panels.Add and StatusBar.Panels.AddRange methods; to remove panels, you use the StatusBar. Panels.Remove and StatusBar.Panels.RemoveAt methods. You can access the Text property of a status bar panel by using the Panels collection of a StatusBar object, as in the following code, which displays the text "Hello there!" in the second panel:

```
Private Sub Button1_Click(ByVal sender As System.Object, _
    ByVal e As System.EventArgs) Handles Button1.Click
    StatusBar1.Panels(1).Text = "Hello there!"
End Sub
```

You can see this code at work in Figure 8.20, in the second panel in the status bar of the StatusBars example.

FIGURE 8.19

The StatusBarPanel Collection Editor.

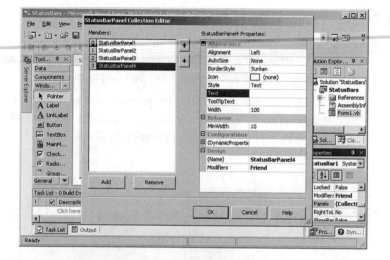

FIGURE 8.20

Displaying text in a status bar panel.

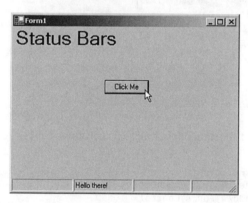

Handling Panel Clicks

You can use the PanelClick event to handle panel clicks. The panel that caused the event is passed to the PanelClick event handler in the StatusBarPanelClickEventArgs object's StatusBarPanel property. That means you can determine which panel was clicked and take the appropriate action like this:

```
Private Sub StatusBar1_PanelClick(ByVal sender As System.Object, _
    ByVal e As System.Windows.Forms.StatusBarPanelClickEventArgs) _
    Handles StatusBar1.PanelClick
    If e.StatusBarPanel Is StatusBar1.Panels(1) Then
        TextBox1.Text = "You clicked the date/time panel."
    End If
End Sub
```

Using Tab Controls

Another control that enables you to save space in Windows applications is the tab control. These controls are popular in dialogs, especially dialogs that let the user set program options, because they enable you to layer several pages on top of each other.

You can see a tab control with three tab pages in it in Figure 8.21, in the Tabs example in the code for this book. You access a tab page by clicking a tab in the tab control; each tab page in the Tabs example has a label covering it, displaying text to indicate which tab page you're viewing.

FIGURE 8.21

Tab controls.

The class hierarchy of the TabControl class is as follows:

```
System.Object
    System.MarshalByRefObject
        System.ComponentModel.Component
            System.Windows.Forms.Control
                System.Windows.Forms.TabControl
```

You can find the significant public properties of TabControl objects in Table 8.21 and the significant public events in Table 8.22. (Note that these tables do not include the properties, methods, and events tab controls inherit from the Control class, which you can find in Tables 5.1, 5.2, and 5.3.)

TABLE 8.21   Significant Public Properties of TabControl Objects

Property	Means
Alignment	Returns or sets where the tabs should appear (top, left, and so on).
Appearance	Returns or sets the appearance of the control's tabs.
HotTrack	Returns or sets whether the tabs' appearance changes when the mouse moves over them.

TABLE 8.21   continued

Property	Means
ImageList	Returns or sets the image list for the tabs.
Multiline	Returns or sets whether more than one row of tabs can be shown.
RowCount	Returns the number of displayed rows.
SelectedIndex	Returns or sets the index of the selected tab page.
SelectedTab	Returns or sets the selected tab page.
ShowToolTips	Returns or sets whether a tab's tool tip can be shown.
TabCount	Returns the number of tabs in the tab strip.
TabPages	Returns the collection of tab pages.

TABLE 8.22   Significant Public Event of `TabControl` Objects

Event	Means
SelectedIndexChanged	Occurs when the `SelectedIndex` property changes.

Tab controls contain tab pages, and tab pages are based on `Panel` controls (which means they can easily contain other controls). Here is the class hierarchy of `TabPage`:

```
System.Object
   System.MarshalByRefObject
      System.ComponentModel.Component
         System.Windows.Forms.Control
            System.Windows.Forms.ScrollableControl
               System.Windows.Forms.Panel
                  System.Windows.Forms.TabPage
```

You can find the significant public properties of `TabPage` objects in Table 8.23. (Note that this table does not include the properties, methods, and events tab pages inherit from the `Control` class, which you can find in Tables 5.1, 5.2, and 5.3—not to mention the properties they inherit from `Panel` controls, which you can find in Table 5.20.)

TABLE 8.23   Significant Public Properties of `TabPage` Objects

Property	Means
ImageIndex	Returns or sets the image list index of the image for this tab.
Text	Returns or sets the text in the tab.
ToolTipText	Returns or sets the tool tip text for this tab.

The tab control property `TabPages` contains the tab pages in the control (and each page is a `TabPage` object). At runtime, you can add new tab pages by using the `TabPages` collection's `Add` method, and you can remove them by using the `Remove` method. When the user clicks a tab, the corresponding tab page opens and a `Click` event for that `TabPage` object occurs. Let's put some of this into practice.

Creating Tab Controls

To create a new tab control, you just drag it from the toolbox onto a form. You can dock these controls with the `Dock` property, and, like most tab controls, the tab control in the Tabs example is docked to the bottom of the form. To add tab pages to the control, open the `TabPages` property in the Properties window, opening the TabPage Collection Editor you see in Figure 8.22. As with the other editors we've seen today, you can add new tab pages by clicking the Add button and remove them by clicking the Remove button. You can also use this editor to set various properties for each page, such as the text that appears in the tab.

FIGURE 8.22

The TabPage Collection Editor.

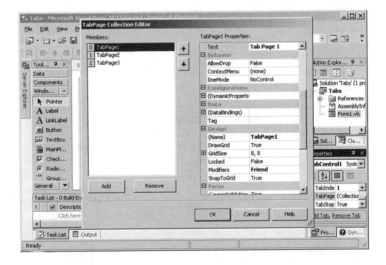

After you've set up the tab pages you want, you can drag the controls you want onto those pages. You can also add controls at runtime, as we'll see in a minute.

You can also display multiple rows of tabs in a tab control. To do that, set the control's `Multiline` property to `True`. Each `TabPage` object also has an `ImageIndex` property, which you can use as an index in an image list to display an image in the page's tab.

8

Tip If setting the Multiline property to True doesn't arrange the tabs in multiple rows, make the Width property of the control smaller than the width of all the tabs put together.

The Alignment property of tab controls specifies where the tabs should appear; you can set this property to Left, Right, Top, or Bottom. In fact, you can even make the tabs appear as buttons. To do that, set the Appearance property of the tab control to Buttons or FlatButtons.

Here's a little flash you can add to your programs: When you set a tab control's HotTrack property to True, the tab captions will turn from black to blue when the mouse moves over them (you can see this at work in the Tabs example, where the HotTrack property is set to True), and back to black after the mouse moves on.

Creating Tab Pages at Runtime

You can add new tab pages to a tab control at runtime; you just need to use the Add method of the TabPages collection. You can see such an example in the Tabs example. When the user clicks the Add New Tab button, a new tab page appears, as you see in Figure 8.23.

FIGURE 8.23

Adding a new tab page at runtime.

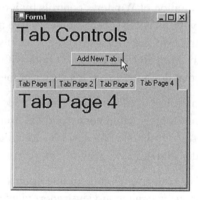

In code, when the user clicks a button, we create a new TabPage object and add it to the tab control's TabPages collection:

```
Dim tabPage4 As New TabPage

Private Sub Button1_Click(ByVal sender As System.Object, _
    ByVal e As System.EventArgs) Handles Button1.Click
    tabPage4.Text = "Tab Page 4"
```

```
        TabControl1.TabPages.Add(tabPage4)
            .
            .
            .
End Sub
```

Then we can add a new label to the new tab page by using the Add method of the tab page's Controls collection:

```
Dim tabPage4 As New TabPage
Dim lblLabel1 As New Label

Private Sub Button1_Click(ByVal sender As System.Object, _
    ByVal e As System.EventArgs) Handles Button1.Click
    tabPage4.Text = "Tab Page 4"
    TabControl1.TabPages.Add(tabPage4)
    lblLabel1.Dock = DockStyle.Fill
    lblLabel1.Text = "Tab Page 4"
    lblLabel1.Font = New Font("Microsoft San Serif", 24)
    TabControl1.TabPages(3).Controls.Add(lblLabel1)
End Sub
```

And that's all you need! Now the new tab page is added to the tab control.

Summary

Today, we rounded off our exploration of Windows controls by looking at a few advanced controls. We started with image lists because they serve as the image repositories that most of the other controls we saw today are designed to use. An image list can store a set of images of the same size, and you can use it both with controls that have an ImageList property and those that don't (although it's easier in the former case).

Tree views are sophisticated controls that can display a set of nodes in a hierarchical way. One node can be the parent of other, child nodes, and the user can expand a node, showing its children, or collapse it at runtime. We saw how to build tree views, including how to populate them with nodes at runtime.

List views display items in a list, even arranging them in columns. List views have four different view types: small icon view, large icon view, report view (using columns and column headers), and list view (using columns but no column headers).

Toolbars enable you to display buttons that usually correspond to menu items; clicking a button performs the same action as selecting the corresponding menu item. We saw how to create toolbars, stocking them with standard buttons, drop-down menu buttons, and toggle buttons. We also saw how to add other controls such as combo boxes to a toolbar.

Progress bars enable you to display the progress of a time-consuming operation by displaying a blue bar that grows, providing visual feedback to the user on the progress of the operation. As we saw, progress bars work much like scrollbars and track bars in code, with `Minimum`, `Maximum`, and `Value` properties.

Status bars allow you to display information to the user, usually in a bar docked to the bottom of a window. By default, status bars contain no panels and are called simple status bars. You can add panels to a status bar by using the `Panels` collection.

Finally, we also looked at tab controls today. These controls contain tab pages, which themselves are containers of other controls. Tab controls enable you to layer pages of controls on top of each other, saving space and cleaning up the user interface.

And that's it. Tomorrow, it's time to dig deeper into Visual Basic .NET as we tackle in-depth OOP, allowing us to master techniques that will really let us take control of Visual Basic .NET.

Q&A

Q Are there any special provisions for when I want to perform some action when the user double-clicks an item in a list view?

A Yes, this is called item *activation*, and it's handled in the `ItemActivate` event. The idea here is that you perform some action (launch an application, open a file, and so on) when an item is activated. You can set the `Activation` property of a list view to determine when the `ItemActivate` event occurs: `ItemActivation.Standard` (activation occurs on double-click), `ItemActivation.OneClick` (one-click activation, and the item's color changes as the mouse moves over it), or `ItemActivation.TwoClick` (two-click activation, and the item's color changes as the mouse moves over it).

Q Can I display icons in a status bar, such as a trash can to handle deleted items?

A You can easily add icons to panels in a status bar. At design time, just select the status bar, click the `Panels` property in the Properties window, to open the StatusBarPanel Collection Editor. Then select the panel, click the `Icon` property in the StatusBarPanel Collection Editor, and browse to the icon file you want to use.

Workshop

This workshop tests whether you understand the concepts you saw today. It's a good idea to make sure you can answer these questions before pressing on to tomorrow's work.

Quiz

1. How do you support multiple-sized images in an image control?

2. How do you expand all the nodes in a tree view at once? How about collapse them all at once?

3. What properties can you use to assign small and large icons to the items in a list view?

4. How do you connect a context menu to a drop-down button in a toolbar?

5. If a status bar has three panels, how do you display the text `"Status OK"` in the rightmost panel?

Quiz Answers

1. That's a trick question; you can't. All images in an image list must be the same size, which you set with the `ImageSize` property (the default is 16×16 pixels).

2. You can use the `ExpandAll` and `CollapseAll` methods. To work on individual nodes, use the `Expand` and `Collapse` methods.

3. You use the `SmallImageList` and `LargeImageList` properties to assign an image list to the list view and assign the image index of the image you want to use in the image list to each item's `ImageIndex` property.

4. You assign the context menu object (such as `ContextMenu1`) to the drop-down button's `DropDownMenu` property.

5. You could use this code: `StatusBar1.Panels(2).Text = "Status OK"`.

Exercises

1. Create a tree view that the user can customize. Let the user select a node (which you can find with the `SelectedNode` property), enter the text for a new child node in a text box, and click a button to add that child node to the tree view.

2. Create a status bar with multiple panels, one of which uses a timer control to display the time of day, updated once a second. **Hint:** As we did when we built our alarm clock in Day 6, "Windows Forms: Working with List Boxes, Combo Boxes, Picture Boxes, Scrollbars, Splitters, Tool Tips, and Timers," use the `TimeOfDay` function to get a string holding the current time that you can display in the panel. (**Extra credit:** Make it an alarm clock, letting the user set the alarm time and turn off the alarm with a dialog that appears when the user clicks the time panel.)

PART II

In Review

Creating Windows Applications in Visual Basic .NET

In Part II, we've covered a lot of ground, seeing how to create Windows applications, including multiple-window applications, owned forms, always-on-top forms, as well as how to communicate between windows, and much more.

We also spent time stocking our Windows applications with controls. As you've seen, a variety of controls is available, and they all are used in different ways—and supported in code in different ways. We saw text boxes, buttons, check boxes, radio buttons, tool tips, status bars, progress bars, tree views, splitters, times, picture boxes, and many more.

Let's spend a moment putting what we've learned into an application for the purposes of review—if you can master all that's in this application, you're ready to go on to the next part of this book. This example will be a text editor that will let you read in and save RTF files (which can then be opened by editors such as WordPad or word processors such as Microsoft Word). You can see this application, editor.exe, at work in Figure P2.1.

As you can see in the figure, this example hosts much of what we've been doing in the last few days—it has a menu system, a rich text box for editing text, a toolbar, and a status bar; it also uses Open File and Save File dialogs, as well as a timer. The code will also use a message box to query the user as needed. Let's take a look at the code for this example in overview—if you know what's going on, you've got a good handle on Windows applications in Visual Basic .NET 2003.

4

5

6

7

8

Figure P2.1

The editor example application.

To create this application, add a menu system to a Windows form, giving it two menus, File and Edit. The File menu should have the items Open, Save As, and Quit; the Edit menu should have the items Copy, Paste, and Cut. Also add a toolbar with the buttons Open, Save As, and Quit (as you see in Figure P2.1), a status bar, and dock a rich text box to the center of the form. Finally, create Open File and Save File dialog objects.

When the user clicks the File, Open menu item, we can open the .rtf file she requests in the Open File dialog, using the rich text box's `LoadFile` method, and display the message `"File opened."` in the status bar, like this:

```
Private Sub MenuItem2_Click(ByVal sender As System.Object, _
    ByVal e As System.EventArgs) Handles MenuItem2.Click
    OpenFileDialog1.DefaultExt = "*.rtf"
    OpenFileDialog1.Filter = "RTF Files|*.rtf"
    If OpenFileDialog1.ShowDialog() = DialogResult.OK Then
        RichTextBox1.LoadFile(OpenFileDialog1.FileName)
        StatusBar1.Text = "File opened."
    End If
End Sub
```

When the user selects the File, Save As menu item, we can use the rich text box's `SaveFile` method and the name we get from the Save File dialog to save the file, as well as displaying the message `"File saved."` in the status bar, like this:

```
Private Sub MenuItem3_Click(ByVal sender As System.Object, _
    ByVal e As System.EventArgs) Handles MenuItem3.Click
    If SaveFileDialog1.ShowDialog() = DialogResult.OK Then
        SaveFileDialog1.ShowDialog()
        RichTextBox1.SaveFile(SaveFileDialog1.FileName())
        StatusBar1.Text = "File saved."
    End If
End Sub
```

If the user selects the File, Quit menu item, we can just use the End method to quit:

```
Private Sub MenuItem4_Click(ByVal sender As System.Object, _
    ByVal e As System.EventArgs) Handles MenuItem4.Click
    End
End Sub
```

Using the ToolBarButton Collection Editor, you can give the Open, Save As, and Quit buttons tool tips, such as "Opens a file.", using each button's ToolTipText property. To make the toolbar active, all you've got to do is to activate the menu item that each button corresponds to, which you can do with the PerformClick method:

```
Private Sub ToolBar1_ButtonClick(ByVal sender As System.Object, _
    ByVal e As System.Windows.Forms.ToolBarButtonClickEventArgs) _
    Handles ToolBar1.ButtonClick

    If e.Button Is ToolBar1.Buttons(0) Then
        MenuItem2.PerformClick()
    End If

    If e.Button Is ToolBar1.Buttons(1) Then
        MenuItem3.PerformClick()
    End If

    If e.Button Is ToolBar1.Buttons(2) Then
        MenuItem4.PerformClick()
    End If

End Sub
```

It's also not difficult to implement the Edit menu's Copy, Paste, and Cut items, using the rich text box methods of the same name. Here's what that code looks like—note that we're careful to make sure that some text is actually selected before cutting it, and we're using a message box to ask the user if she wants to paste over the current selection if there is one:

```
Private Sub MenuItem6_Click(ByVal sender As System.Object, _
    ByVal e As System.EventArgs) Handles MenuItem6.Click
    If (RichTextBox1.SelectionLength > 0) Then
        RichTextBox1.Copy()
    End If
End Sub

Private Sub MenuItem7_Click(ByVal sender As System.Object, _
    ByVal e As System.EventArgs) Handles MenuItem7.Click
    If (RichTextBox1.SelectionLength > 0) Then
        If (MessageBox.Show("Do you want to paste over the current selection?", _
```

```
            "Editor", MessageBoxButtons.YesNo) = DialogResult.No) Then
            RichTextBox1.SelectionStart = RichTextBox1.SelectionStart +
                RichTextBox1.SelectionLength
        End If
        RichTextBox1.Paste()
    End If
End Sub

Private Sub MenuItem8_Click(ByVal sender As System.Object, _
    ByVal e As System.EventArgs) Handles MenuItem8.Click
    If (RichTextBox1.SelectedText <> "") Then
        RichTextBox1.Cut()
    End If
End Sub
```

Finally, we can let the timer clear the text in the status bar so that messages such as
"File saved." aren't displayed forever; first, we set the timer's Interval property to
5 seconds, and then we add code to the timer's Tick event handler to erase the status
bar text every five seconds and enable the timer in the form Load event handler:

```
Private Sub Timer1_Tick(ByVal sender As System.Object, _
    ByVal e As System.EventArgs) Handles Timer1.Tick
    StatusBar1.Text = ""
End Sub

Private Sub Form1_Load(ByVal sender As Object, _
    ByVal e As System.EventArgs) Handles MyBase.Load
    Timer1.Enabled = True
End Sub
```

And that's it—that creates the editor you can see in Figure P2.1. This is a fairly substantial Windows application; if you're up to speed on this code, you've gotten Windows
applications under your belt, and you're ready to turn to the next part of this book—
where we start doing some in-depth programming.

PART III

At a Glance

In-Depth Programming with Visual Basic .NET

In Part III, we're going to do some in-depth Visual Basic .NET programming as we take a look at object-oriented programming (OOP), creating classes and objects, class inheritance, abstract classes, overloading, and overriding. Visual Basic .NET is object oriented, so all these are essential skills to have.

We'll also take a look at working with files in this part, opening and creating files on disk, writing to and reading from them, copying files, as well as setting file modes, access levels, and sharing privileges. And we'll also see how to work with graphics, drawing figures and images, including putting together a mouse-driven drawing application.

DAY 9

Object-Oriented Programming

Everything you do in Visual Basic .NET involves objects in some way—even simple variables are based on the Visual Basic Object class. And all your code has to appear in a class of some sort (even if you're using a module or a structure, which are also OOP constructs in Visual Basic). OOP provides the framework on which Visual Basic programming is built, and we're going to examine OOP in depth today. In the previous few days, we've been concentrating on the visual side of things as we worked with the controls you can use in Windows forms. Today, we're going to turn back to the code side of Visual Basic programming as we take a look at an essential skill—object-oriented programming. Here are the topics you will see:

- Abstraction, encapsulation, inheritance, and polymorphism
- Creating constructors and destructors
- Using Is to compare objects
- Creating class (shared) data members and methods

- Creating events
- Overloading methods
- Using public, protected, and private inheritance
- Using Friend access
- Overriding base class members
- Inheriting constructors
- Creating interfaces
- Creating abstract classes
- Using MustOverride, Overridable, and NotOverridable
- Supporting shadowing
- Using the MyBase and MyClass keywords
- Using inheritance-based and interface-based polymorphism
- Early and late binding

You're already familiar with creating classes and objects in code. In Day 3, "Mastering the Visual Basic Language: Procedures, Error Handling, Classes, and Objects," you saw this example, which used the Class statement to create a new class with a data member, property, and method, and the Dim statement to create a new object of that class:

```
Module Module1

    Sub Main()
        Dim TheObject As New TheClass
        Console.WriteLine("ThePublicData holds """ &
        ➥TheObject.ThePublicData & """")
        Console.WriteLine("TheMethod returns """ & TheObject.TheMethod() & """")
        Console.WriteLine("TheProperty holds """ & TheObject.TheProperty & """")
        Console.WriteLine("Press Enter to continue...")
        Console.ReadLine()
    End Sub

End Module

Class TheClass
    Public ThePublicData = "Hello there!"
    Private TheInternalData As String = "Hello there!"

    Function TheMethod() As String
        Return "Hello there!"
    End Function
```

```
    Public Property TheProperty() As String
        Get
            Return TheInternalData
        End Get
        Set(ByVal Value As String)
            TheInternalData = Value
        End Set
    End Property
End Class
```

NEW TERM Data members such as TheInternalData and ThePublicData in the preceding code are called *fields* in OOP, and I'll start using that terminology here. In fact, getting the terminology down is a good way to get an overview of object-oriented programming; there are four essential terms to know—abstraction, encapsulation, inheritance, and polymorphism. You need to support them all if you want your language to be object oriented:

- *Abstraction*—The capability of creating an abstract representation of a concept in code (as an object named friend is an abstraction of a real friend).

- *Encapsulation*—When you encapsulate an object, you make its code and data *internal* and no longer accessible outside an object, except through a well-defined interface. This is also called *data hiding*.

- *Polymorphism*—The capability of enabling the same code to operate on objects of different types. For example, if both friend and enemy objects have a last_name property, polymorphic code can store either friend or enemy objects in the same variable and access the last_name property of that variable in either case.

- *Inheritance*—The capability of deriving new classes from other classes. For example, if you create a class and then derive a new class from it, the derived class will *inherit* all the base's class's functionality, even before you start adding code or customizing the new class.

You will see all these aspects of OOP at work today. In the first third of today's work, we're going to see the techniques you need to become a Visual Basic object-oriented programmer, and in the second two thirds, we're going to master the vital OOP technique of inheritance.

Let's begin the actual coding now. When you first create an object, you use its constructor, and that's a good place to start—understanding how to build constructors in code to initialize objects.

Constructors and Destructors

As you know, you create objects with the New keyword, like this:

```
Dim objData As New Data()
```

You can also customize your new object by passing data to the constructor, as in this case, where we're passing a value of 10 to store in the new object:

```
Dim objData As New Data(10)
```

You've seen constructors as long ago as Day 3, where you saw this example that creates a Size object that stores the screen size of 200×200 pixels:

```
Size = New Size(200, 200)
```

So how do you create a constructor in your own code? All you have to do is to add a Sub procedure named New to a class—that's all it takes. For example, here's how that might look for the Data class; in this case, the code stores the value passed to New in a private data member named intInternalData and adds a method named GetData to return that stored value as needed:

```
Public Class Data
    Private intInternalData As Integer

    Public Sub New(ByVal newValue As Integer)
        intInternalData = newValue
    End Sub

    Public Function GetData() As Integer
        Return intInternalData
    End Function
End Class
```

Now you can store the value 10 inside an object of the Data class simply by passing 10 to the constructor, and you can retrieve that value with the GetData method:

```
Dim objData As New Data(10)
TextBox1.Text = Str(objData.GetData())
```

A constructor begins the life cycle of an object. That life cycle ends when you assign the object the keyword Nothing, when the object goes out of scope, or when it is otherwise released by Visual Basic. For example, here's how you can delete an object:

```
Dim objData As New Data(10)
TextBox1.Text = Str(objData.GetData())
objData = Nothing
```

NEW TERM When all references to an object in your program are released in this way, the object's Finalize method is called, and you can create a *destructor* for the object by adding code to this method. The Finalize method allows you to clean up after the object, releasing resources, closing files, disconnecting from the Internet, and so on.

Here's an example. In this case, the code creates an object of the Data class and uses a Finalize method to display a message box when the object is destroyed:

```
Public Class Form1
    Inherits System.Windows.Forms.Form

    'Windows Form Designer generated code

    Dim objData As New Data(10)
    TextBox1.Text = Str(objData.GetData())
    objData = Nothing
End Class

Public Class Data
    Private intInternalData As Integer

    Public Sub New(ByVal newValue As Integer)
        intInternalData = newValue
    End Sub

    Public Function GetData() As Integer
        Return intInternalData
    End Function

    Protected Overrides Sub Finalize()
        MsgBox("Warning, data object about to be destroyed!")
    End Sub
End Class
```

You use the Overrides keyword in the destructor here because the Finalize method *replaces* the Finalize method already built into the Object class. (You're going to see more about overriding later today.)

NEW TERM It's important to realize that Finalize isn't called automatically when an object is destroyed; it's only called when Visual Basic decides that it has time to get rid of obsolete objects—a process called *garbage collection*.

Tip

> The Visual Basic .NET documentation says that you can't start the garbage collection process by yourself, but in fact you can. Just use this statement:
>
> ```
> System.GC.Collect().
> ```

Constructors and destructors give us our first insight into OOP today, and they even introduced us to the idea of overriding a method. Overriding methods has to do with inheritance—when you derive one class from another, you can override methods in the base class with new versions. But there's an allied OOP technique that is even simpler—*overloading* methods.

Overloading Methods

NEW TERM *Overloading* a method (including a property) means that you can define a method or property multiple times with different argument lists. For example, say that you can call a method named `Alert` to display a message box, passing it the text to display. But also say that in some circumstances, you want to specify the icon that the message box displays. You can do that by overloading `Alert`, as you can see in the Overloads example in the code for this book.

To do that in code, you just define the `Alert` method twice as shown in Listing 9.1, each time with a different argument list, as you can see in the code for the Overloads example in the code for this book.

LISTING 9.1   Supporting Overloading in Code (Overloads Project, Form1.vb)

```
Public Class Form1
    Inherits System.Windows.Forms.Form

' Windows Form Designer generated code

    Dim Alerter As New AlertClass

    Private Sub Button1_Click(ByVal sender As System.Object, _
        ByVal e As System.EventArgs) Handles Button1.Click
        Alerter.Alert("No Problems!", MsgBoxStyle.Exclamation)
    End Sub

    Public Class AlertClass
        Public Sub Alert(ByVal Text As String)
            MsgBox(Text)
        End Sub
        Public Sub Alert(ByVal Text As String, ByVal Icon As MsgBoxStyle)
            MsgBox(Text, Icon)
        End Sub
    End Class

End Class
```

How does Visual Basic know which overloaded version to use? All it has to do is check the argument list you're passing to the method and find the version of the method that has the same number and types of arguments, in the same order. And that's all it takes—you can see the results in Figure 9.1.

FIGURE 9.1

Overloading a method.

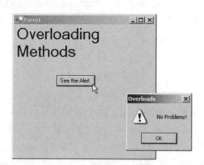

In this way, you can overload a method in OOP, and Visual Basic .NET will know which one to use based on the argument list—you don't have to use argument lists with different numbers of arguments; two argument lists with the same number of arguments, but with different argument *types*, are also valid.

Creating Class (Shared) Members

The fields, method, and properties you've seen so far have all been created to be used with objects. However, fields, methods, and properties can also be used simply with the classname—no object is needed. For example, say that you have a class named Constants with fields such as Pi, which holds 3.1415926535. To access that value, you could create an object of the Constants class, objConstants, and then use the Pi field like this: Dim dblPi As Double = objConstants.Pi. But if you make Pi a class field, you can access it using the class's name alone—no object is needed, like this: Dim dblPi As Double = Constants.Pi. Let's take a look at how this works.

Creating Shared Fields

You can use the Shared keyword to create class fields. You can use a class data member with the name of the class alone; no object is needed. For example, here's how to create a shared variable named Pi in the Constants class that holds the value of Pi:

```
Public Class Constants
    Public Shared Pi As Double = 3.1415926535
End Class
```

Now you can use `Pi` as a class variable with the `Constants` class directly; no object is needed:

```
dblPi = Constants.Pi
```

The value Pi is more naturally handled as a constant, of course; you can use `Const` instead of `Shared` to create a shared constant that works the same way (except, of course, that you can't assign values to it because it's a constant):

```
Public Class Constants
    Public Const Pi As Double = 3.1415926535
End Class
```

New Term Variables you declare with the `Shared` keyword are called *shared* because they're shared over all objects of that class. For example, take a look at the Shared example in the code for this book, which supports a class named counter whose `Count` method you can call to increment a running count. Here's how it works in code; there's a shared field named `Data` in the `Counter` class:

```
Public Class Counter
    Shared Data As Integer = 0
          .
          .
          .
End Class
```

When you call the `Count` method, that field is incremented:

```
Public Class Counter
    Shared Data As Integer = 0

    Public Function Count() As Integer
        Data += 1
        Return Data
    End Function
End Class
```

Because the `Data` field is shared, all objects of the `Counter` class will use the same value in this field. For example, if you create two different objects of the `Counter` class, `Counter1` and `Counter2`, you can call the `Count` method of both objects (as with the Shared example's two buttons), but you will be incrementing the same, shared value. You can see how this works in Listing 9.2.

LISTING 9.2   Sharing Data in Code (Shared Project, Form1.vb)

```
Dim Counter1 As New Counter
Dim Counter2 As New Counter

Private Sub Button1_Click(ByVal sender As System.Object, _
    ByVal e As System.EventArgs) Handles Button1.Click
    TextBox1.Text = "Total count = " & Counter1.Count()
End Sub

Private Sub Button2_Click(ByVal sender As System.Object, _
    ByVal e As System.EventArgs) Handles Button2.Click
    TextBox1.Text = "Total count = " & Counter2.Count()
End Sub
```

You can see the results in Figure 9.2—when you call Counter1.Count(), the Data variable is incremented to 1. When you call Counter2.Count(), the Data variable is incremented to 2, and so on. In this way, Data holds the *total* number of times both objects have been incremented because it's a shared field.

FIGURE 9.2

Using shared data.

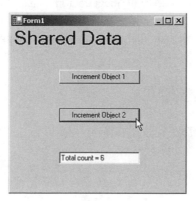

Creating Shared Methods

Besides shared fields, you can also create shared methods in OOP. A shared method, also called a class method, can be used with just the classname; no object is needed.

Here's an example. The Summer class in the following code has a class method named Sum, which returns the sum of two integers. You can call Summer.Sum directly—no object is needed. To make Sum a class method, you just have to declare it shared, like this:

```
Private Sub Button1_Click(ByVal sender As System.Object, _
    ByVal e As System.EventArgs) Handles Button1.Click
```

```
    TextBox3.Text = Str(Summer.Sum(Val(TextBox1.Text), Val(TextBox2.Text)))
End Sub

Public Class Summer
    Shared Function Sum(ByVal value1 As Integer, ByVal value2 As Integer) As
Long
        Return value1 + value2
    End Function
End Class
```

There's a restriction you should know about, however—you can't use local data (that is, variables declared in the method) in a shared method because no object allocated in memory could hold that data. On the other hand, you can use shared data in a shared method, as well as the values that are passed to you (as the Sum class method does in this example).

Creating Shared Properties

You can also make properties shared with the Shared keyword, which means that you can use them with the classname and don't need a specific object to work with. However, as in a shared method, you can't work with local data in a shared property, but you can work with shared data. Here's an example of a shared property, the Text property of the Book class, which just holds text (note that you can refer to this property as Book.Text, no object of the Book class is needed):

```
Public Class Book
    Shared internalText As String
    Shared Property Text()
        Get
            Return internalText
        End Get
        Set(ByVal Value)
            internalText = Value
        End Set
    End Property
End Class

Private Sub Button1_Click(ByVal sender As System.Object, _
    ByVal e As System.EventArgs) Handles Button1.Click
    Book.Text = "No problems!"
End Sub
```

That gives us a look at fields, methods, and properties, but classes in Visual Basic .NET can also support *events*. We'll take a look at creating your own events using OOP next.

Supporting Events with Objects

You can design and support your own events in Visual Basic using the Event statement:

```
[ <attrlist> ] [ Public | Private | Protected | Friend | Protected Friend ]
[ Shadows ] Event eventname[(arglist)]
[ Implements interfacename.interfaceeventname ]
```

Here are the various parts of this statement:

- *attrlist* – List of attributes that apply to this event. Separate multiple attributes by commas.

- Public – Events declared Public have public access, which means that there are no restrictions on their use.

- Private – Events declared Private have private access, which means that they are accessible only within their declaration context.

- Protected – Events declared Protected have protected access, which means that they are accessible only from within their own class or from a derived class.

- Friend – Events declared Friend have friend access, which means that they are accessible only within the program containing the its declaration.

- Protected Friend – Events declared Protected Friend have both protected and friend accessibility.

- Shadows – Indicates that this event shadows an identically named programming element in a base class.

- *eventname* – Name of the event.

- *interfacename* – The name of an interface.

- *interfaceeventname* – The name of the event being implemented.

Let's see an example; this one is named Events in the code for this book. As you know, Visual Basic .NET supports Click and DblClick events—but no triple click events. In this example, we'll create one, named TplClick. This event will take a text string message as an argument, like this:

```
Public Class TripleClicker

    Public Event TplClick(ByVal Text As String)
        .
        .
        .
End Class
```

NEW TERM   How do you actually make an event like this occur? You use the `RaiseEvent`
statement. For example, we might use a new method, `Click`, to keep track of
the number of times a button is clicked. When the button is clicked three times, we
can *raise* the `TplClick` event, passing it the message `"The button was triple`
`clicked."`:

```
Public Class TripleClicker

    Public Event TplClick(ByVal Text As String)

    Public Sub Click()
        Static intCount As Integer = 0
        intCount += 1
        If intCount >= 3 Then
            intCount = 0
            RaiseEvent TplClick("The button was triple clicked.")
        End If
    End Sub
End Class
```

To put this new event to work, the Events example creates an object named `Click3` that
uses the `WithEvents` keyword so that Visual Basic knows we want this object to be able
to handle events:

```
Dim WithEvents Click3 As New TripleClicker
```

Now when the user clicks the button, we can keep track of the number of clicks with the
`Click` method:

```
Dim WithEvents Click3 As New TripleClicker
```

```
Private Sub Button1_Click(ByVal sender As System.Object, _
    ByVal e As System.EventArgs) Handles Button1.Click
    Click3.Click()
End Sub
```

After the user clicks the button three times, the `TplClick` event occurs. To handle that
event, we need an event handler, which looks like this, where we display the event's message in a text box:

```
Private Sub Click3_TplClick(ByVal Text As String) Handles _
    Click3.TplClick
    TextBox1.Text = Text
End Sub
```

You can see the result in Figure 9.3. Now you're creating custom events using OOP!

FIGURE 9.3

Supporting events

Listing 9.3 shows the complete sample code.

LISTING 9.3   Supporting Events in Code (Events Project, Form1.vb)

```
Public Class Form1
    Inherits System.Windows.Forms.Form

' Windows Form Designer generated code

    Dim WithEvents Click3 As New TripleClicker

    Private Sub Button1_Click(ByVal sender As System.Object, _
        ByVal e As System.EventArgs) Handles Button1.Click
        Click3.Click()
    End Sub

    Private Sub Click3_TplClick(ByVal Text As String) Handles _
    Click3.TplClick
        TextBox1.Text = Text
    End Sub
End Class

Public Class TripleClicker

    Public Event TplClick(ByVal Text As String)

    Public Sub Click()
        Static intCount As Integer = 0
        intCount += 1
        If intCount >= 3 Then
            intCount = 0
            RaiseEvent TplClick("The button was triple clicked.")
```

LISTING 9.3   continued

```
        End If
    End Sub
End Class
```

Events can also be declared as Shared:

```
Public Shared Event TplClick(ByVal Text As String)
```

That's useful to know because if your code is in a shared method, you can only raise shared events.

Comparing Objects

A special keyword in Visual Basic .NET can be used to compare objects in If statements—the Is keyword. If the two objects you're checking are the same object, Is returns True. For example, say that you have a generic Click event handler for buttons, Button_Click. The actual button that caused the event is passed in the sender argument, so you can determine which button was clicked, even if the event handler handles multiple buttons, like this:

```
Private Sub Button_Click(ByVal sender As System.Object, _
    ByVal e As System.EventArgs)
    If sender Is Button1 Then
        TextBox1.Text = "Button 1 was clicked."
    Else
        TextBox1.Text = "Button 2 was clicked."
    End If
End Sub
```

OOP with Structures and Modules

You've seen a lot of work with classes so far, but it's also important to know that other programming constructs in Visual Basic—in particular, structures and modules—are also based on classes.

Structures were originally a half-way solution between variables and true objects, allowing you to create your own data types, much like adding fields to a class—that is, they were much like classes without methods. However, in Visual Basic .NET, structures can also support methods. In fact, you create them just as you would a class, except that you use the `Structure` keyword instead of `Class`. So what's the difference between structures and classes? Here's the list:

- Structure members cannot be declared as `Protected`.
- Structures cannot inherit from other structures.
- You cannot use the `Finalize` method.
- The declarations of data members in a structure cannot include initializers, the `New` keyword, or set initial sizes for arrays.
- You cannot define a constructor that takes no arguments for a structure unless you make the constructor shared.
- If you declare them with `Dim`, the default access of data members in structures is public (not private as in classes and modules).
- When you pass a data item created from a structure to a procedure, the entire structure is copied.

Modules in Visual Basic are designed primarily to hold code, but they can also now support members, just like classes. In fact, modules are just like classes, but with a few important distinctions:

- The members of a module are implicitly shared.
- Modules can never be instantiated, which means that you cannot create objects based on them.
- Modules do not support inheritance.
- Modules cannot implement interfaces.
- Modules cannot be nested in other types.

So far today, we've taken a look at a number of OOP techniques, but the biggest technique is yet to come—inheritance. One of the main rationales for OOP is that you can base one class on another, reusing your code. That's useful because Visual Basic .NET comes with thousands of classes that you can use as a base for your own classes, which means that your classes will have all the power of the base class already built in. This is a really big topic in OOP, and we're going to take it apart step by step now.

Using Inheritance

We're already familiar with the process of inheritance from our work with Windows forms because we derive our forms from `System.Windows.Forms.Form` and then customize them with buttons and event handlers like this:

```
Public Class Form1
    Inherits System.Windows.Forms.Form

    'Windows Form Designer generated code

    Private Sub Button1_Click(ByVal sender As System.Object, _
        ByVal e As System.EventArgs) Handles Button1.Click
        .
        .
        .
    End Sub

End Class
```

You use the `Inherits` statement here when you create a new class, called the derived class, from an already existing class called the base class. Derived classes inherit—which means that they can extend or restrict the fields, properties, methods, and events of the base class. (The exception here are constructors, which are *not* inherited.)

For example, if you have a class named `Person`, which has a method named `Walk`, and then derive a class named `Bob` from `Person`, `Bob` will already have the `Walk` method built in.

New Term In Visual Basic, any class can serve as a base class (unless you use the `NotInheritable` keyword, as you will see later today). You can only inherit from *one* base class, not more. However, Visual Basic allows you to implement multiple *interfaces*, which you will see in a few pages, and that can accomplish much that multiple inheritance could, but with more work on our part.

Let's take a look at an example, which is named Inheritance in the code for this book. This example implements the `Person` and `Bob` classes; in the `Person` class, the `Walk` method displays a message box with the text `"Walking..."`:

```
Class Person
    Sub Walk()
        MsgBox("Walking...")
    End Sub
End Class
```

The `Bob` class inherits the `Person` class, like this:

```
Class Bob
    Inherits Person
End Class
```

Now all `Bob` objects include the `Walk` method, just as all `Person` objects do. Listing 9.4 shows how you might create a `Bob` object and call the `Walk` method when the user clicks a button.

LISTING 9.4   Supporting Inheritance in Code (Inheritance Project, Form1.vb)

```
Public Class Form1
    Inherits System.Windows.Forms.Form

' Windows Form Designer generated code

    Private Sub Button1_Click(ByVal sender As System.Object, _
        ByVal e As System.EventArgs) Handles Button1.Click
        Dim objBob As New Bob
        objBob.Walk()
    End Sub
End Class

Public Class Person
    Public Sub Walk()
        MsgBox("Walking...")
    End Sub
End Class

Class Bob
    Inherits Person
End Class
```

You can see the results in Figure 9.4. When the user clicks the button, the code creates a new Bob object and calls its Walk method. Now we're using inheritance.

FIGURE 9.4

Supporting inheritance.

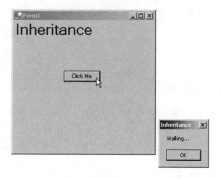

NEW TERM   And, as I've discussed as far back as Day 3, you can control the access derived classes have to base class members with *access modifiers* like Public, Private, and Protected.

Using Access Modifiers

Access modifiers are the `Public`, `Private`, and `Protected` keywords you've already seen in this book. You can use access modifiers at the class level (which includes structures and modules) to restrict the access of items in a base class from a derived class. Here are the various access modifiers:

- `Public` – Items declared `Public` have public access. No restrictions are on the accessibility of public items. You can use `Public` at module, namespace, or file level.

- `Protected` – Items declared `Protected` have protected access. They are accessible only from within their own class or from within a derived class. You can use `Protected` only at class level.

- `Friend` – Items declared `Friend` have friend access. They are accessible from within the program that contains their declaration and from anywhere else in the same assembly. You can use `Friend` at module, namespace, or file level.

- `Protected Friend` – Items declared `Protected Friend` have both protected and friend access. They can be used by code in the same assembly, as well as by code in derived classes. The rules for `Protected` and `Friend` apply to `Protected Friend` as well.

- `Private` – Items declared `Private` have private access. They are accessible only inside their *declaration context*, such as the class in which they are declared. You can use `Private` at module, namespace, or file level.

It's important to get these concepts straight, so we'll take a look at them in some detail here.

Using Public Inheritance

You make items public in a class with the `Public` keyword; when making a member of a class public, no restrictions are on its scope—it can be used by any part of your program. Public members in a base class become public members of a derived class by default.

Here's how we can make the `Walk` method public in the `Person` class, which means that it is accessible in the derived class `Bob`:

```
Public Class Form1
    Inherits System.Windows.Forms.Form

' Windows Form Designer generated code
```

```
        Private Sub Button1_Click(ByVal sender As System.Object,
            ByVal e As System.EventArgs) Handles Button1.Click
            Dim objBob As New Bob
            objBob.Walk()
        End Sub

    End Class

    Class Person
        Public Sub Walk()
            MsgBox("Walking...")
        End Sub
    End Class

    Class Bob
        Inherits Person
    End Class
```

You can also set the accessibility of the class by declaring the class (not just class members) with an access modifier like this:

```
Public Class Form1
    Inherits System.Windows.Forms.Form

' Windows Form Designer generated code
        .
        .
        .
```

Declaring classes with an access modifier this way lets you set the accessibility of that class. For example, say that you declare a class, A, inside another class, B. If class A is declared private, it's private to class B.

Using Protected Inheritance

You can use the Protected keyword to restrict access when an item is inherited. When you declare a member of a base class protected, it's available throughout that class and in any derived classes, but nowhere else.

For example, if you make Walk a protected method in the Person class, code in the derived Bob class can call it, but code outside those two classes can't. So if you want to be able to call Walk when the user clicks a button, you might create a new method, CallWalk, in the derived Bob class that calls the protected Walk in the base class like this:

```
Public Class Form1
    Inherits System.Windows.Forms.Form
```

```
' Windows Form Designer generated code

    Private Sub Button1_Click(ByVal sender As System.Object, _
        ByVal e As System.EventArgs) Handles Button1.Click
        Dim objBob As New Bob
        objBob.CallWalk()
    End Sub

End Class

Class Person
    Protected Sub Walk()
        MsgBox("Walking...")
    End Sub
End Class

Class Bob
    Inherits Person
    Public Sub CallWalk()
        Walk()
    End Sub
End Class
```

Using Private Inheritance

On the other hand, if you make a class member private, it's only available in the present class—not outside that class, and not in any class derived from that class. In other words, the Private keyword stops the inheritance process cold.

For example, if we made the Walk method private in the Person class, you can't call it in the derived Bob class, so this code won't work:

```
Public Class Form1
    Inherits System.Windows.Forms.Form

' Windows Form Designer generated code

    Private Sub Button1_Click(ByVal sender As System.Object, _
        ByVal e As System.EventArgs) Handles Button1.Click
        Dim objBob As New Bob
        objBob.CallWalk()
    End Sub

End Class

Class Person
    Private Sub Walk()
        MsgBox("Walking...")
    End Sub
End Class
```

```
Class Bob
    Inherits Person
    Public Sub CallWalk()
        Walk()                                  'Will not work!
    End Sub
End Class
```

Using Friend Access

You can also give items friend access. There is no restriction at all to the accessibility of public items, but friend scope restricts them to the current program (that is, the program that contains their declaration) and anywhere else in the same assembly. (Public members, by contrast, are available across assemblies.) You can use the Friend keyword in these statements:

- Class
- Const
- Declare
- Dim
- Enum
- Event
- Function
- Interface
- Module
- Property
- Structure
- Sub

You can use Friend just as any other access modifier; here's an example:

```
Private Sub Button1_Click(ByVal sender As System.Object, _
    ByVal e As System.EventArgs) Handles Button1.Click
    Dim objBob As New Bob
    objBob.Walk()
End Sub

Class Person
    Friend Sub Walk()
        MsgBox("Walking...")
    End Sub
End Class
```

```
Class Bob
    Inherits Person
End Class
```

Using Inheritance Modifiers

New Term   In Visual Basic .NET, all classes can serve as base classes by default. However, you can change that behavior using two class-level modifiers called *inheritance modifiers*:

- `MustInherit`—Objects of `MustInherit` classes cannot be created directly; they can only be used as a base class for a derived class. In other words, these classes are intended for use as base classes *only*.

- `NotInheritable`—Does not allow a class to be used as a base class.

Let's take a look at these two options briefly.

Using `MustInherit` to Create Abstract Classes

New Term   You use the `MustInherit` keyword to create a class that you can't create objects from directly. Instead, such a class, called an *abstract class*, is intended to be used only as a base class. For example, if you used `MustInherit` in `Person`, this code, which derives a `Bob` object from `Person`, is fine:

```
Private Sub Button1_Click(ByVal sender As System.Object, _
    ByVal e As System.EventArgs) Handles Button1.Click
    Dim objBob As New Bob
    objBob.Walk()
End Sub

Public MustInherit Class Person
    Public Sub Walk()
        MsgBox("Walking...")
    End Sub
End Class

Class Bob
    Inherits Person
End Class
```

However, trying the same thing by creating an object of the Person class will not work:

```
Private Sub Button1_Click(ByVal sender As System.Object, _
    ByVal e As System.EventArgs) Handles Button1.Click
    Dim objPerson As New Person                          'Will not work!
    objPerson.Walk()
```

```
End Sub

Public MustInherit Class Person
    Public Sub Walk()
        MsgBox("Walking...")
    End Sub
End Class

Class Bob
    Inherits Person
End Class
```

Using `NotInheritable` to Stop Inheritance

If you want to make sure that no one can derive a new class from a particular class, just declare that class with the `NotInheritable` keyword. This is useful when you want to make sure that no one can change the methods or fields in your class, for example. Here's how that might look in code—if you declare `Person NotInheritable`, you cannot derive `Bob` from it:

```
Public NotInheritable Class Person
    Public Sub Walk()
        MsgBox("Walking...")
    End Sub
End Class

Class Bob
    Inherits Person                              'Will not work!
End Class
```

Overloading, Overriding, and Shadowing with Inheritance

Three concepts are very important in Visual Basic .NET inheritance—overloading, overriding, and shadowing. I've already discussed overloading, which means creating more than one version of a method or property in which each version has a different argument list. Here's an overview of what all these terms mean:

- *Overloaded* members provide different versions of a property or method that have the same name, but that accept different number of parameters or parameters of different types.

- *Overridden* properties and methods are used to replace an inherited property or method. When you override a member from a base class, you replace it. Overridden members must accept the same data type and number of arguments.

- *Shadowed* members are used to create a local version of a member that has broader scope. You can also shadow a type with any other type. For example, you can declare a property that shadows an inherited method with the same name.

We'll take a look at these various techniques in action next.

Overloading and Inheritance

We already took a look at overloading earlier today, but it turns out that there's more to know when you overload a method or property while using inheritance. When you overload a method or property from a base class, you must use the Overloads keyword—that keyword isn't necessary when you're overloading a method or property in the same class, but it is when you're overloading a method or property from another class, such as a base class.

Listing 9.5 shows how this works—in this case, the code in the derived Bob class overloads the Walk method in the base Person class to let you pass the string the Walk method should display. That looks like this in the OverloadsInheritance example in the code for this book, where the Walk method displays the string "Now I'm walking...":

LISTING 9.5   Supporting Overloading and Inheritance in Code (OverloadsInheritance Project, Form1.vb)

```vb
Public Class Form1
    Inherits System.Windows.Forms.Form

' Windows Form Designer generated code

    Private Sub Button1_Click(ByVal sender As System.Object, _
        ByVal e As System.EventArgs) Handles Button1.Click
        Dim objBob As New Bob
        objBob.Walk("Now I'm walking...")
    End Sub
End Class

Public Class Person
    Public Sub Walk()
        MsgBox("Walking...")
    End Sub
End Class

Class Bob
    Inherits Person
```

LISTING 9.5   continued

```
    Public Overloads Sub Walk(ByVal Text As String)
        MsgBox(Text)
    End Sub
End Class
```

You can see the results in Figure 9.5. When the user clicks the button, the code creates a new Bob object and calls its overloaded Walk method.

FIGURE 9.5

Supporting overloading and inheritance.

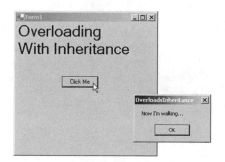

Overriding and Inheritance

NEW TERM   So what is overriding? If an inherited property or method needs to behave differently in the derived class, it can be *overridden*; that is, you can redefine the method or property in the derived class. You use these modifiers to control how properties and methods are overridden:

- Overridable – Allows a property or method in a class to be overridden.

- Overrides – Overrides an Overridable property or method.

- NotOverridable – Prevents a property or method from being overridden. (Public methods are NotOverridable by default.)

- MustOverride – Requires that a derived class override the property or method. MustOverride methods must be declared in MustInherit classes.

Let's see an example of overriding at work by creating a new Person-based object, Mary. Unlike Bob, Mary is a runner, so when we call Mary's Walk method, we should see a message that says "Running...", not "Walking...". This means that we must override the Walk method in the base class Person to display "Running...". You do that by using the

Overridable keyword to indicate that Walk may be overridden and using the Overrides keyword in the derived class to perform the overriding, like this:

```
Public Class Form1
    Inherits System.Windows.Forms.Form

' Windows Form Designer generated code

    Private Sub Button1_Click(ByVal sender As System.Object, _
        ByVal e As System.EventArgs) Handles Button1.Click
        Dim objMary As New Mary
        objMary.Walk()
    End Sub
End Class

Public Class Person
    Public Overridable Sub Walk()
        MsgBox("Walking...")
    End Sub
End Class

Class Mary
    Inherits Person
    Public Overrides Sub Walk()
        MsgBox("Running...")
    End Sub
End Class
```

You can see the results in Figure 9.6, as well as in the Overriding example in the code for this book. When the user clicks the button, the code creates a new Mary object and calls its overridden Walk method, displaying the "Running..." message shown in the figure.

FIGURE 9.6

Supporting overriding and inheritance.

Shadowing and Inheritance

NEW TERM   Besides overloading and overriding, you can also use *shadowing* in Visual Basic. What's shadowing about? When you want to have two items with the same name and overlapping scope, you can have one *shadow* the other. By default, Visual Basic will use the value of the item with the more local, more restricted scope.

Listing 9.6 shows an example, the Shadows project in the code for this book. Here, BaseClass defines a field named Value, and the class derived from this class, DerivedClass, defines a property named Value. These names conflict, so you have to use the Shadows keyword to declare the Value property in the derived class:

LISTING 9.6   Supporting Shadowing (Shadows Project, Form1.vb)

```
Public Class Form1
    Inherits System.Windows.Forms.Form

' Windows Form Designer generated code

    Private Sub Button1_Click(ByVal sender As System.Object, _
        ByVal e As System.EventArgs) Handles Button1.Click
        Dim objDerivedClass As New DerivedClass
        MsgBox(objDerivedClass.Value)
    End Sub
End Class

Class BaseClass
    Public Value As Double = 3.1415926535
End Class

Class DerivedClass
    Inherits BaseClass

    Public Shadows ReadOnly Property Value() As Double
        Get
            Return 2.718281828
        End Get
    End Property
End Class
```

Now when you use the Value member of an object of the DerivedClass class, Visual Basic will choose the member with the most local scope, which is the Value property. You can see this result in Figure 9.7 in the Shadows example.

FIGURE 9.7

Supporting shadowing.

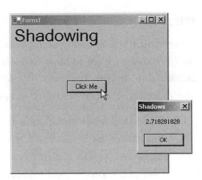

Using MyBase and MyClass with Inheritance

When you're working with inheritance, there are two important keywords to know—
MyBase and MyClass. You use MyBase when you want to access a method in a base class
that's been overridden. Using MyBase, you can access the original, base class version of
the method. For example, if you're defining a new constructor for a class that you're
deriving from a base class, you override the New method of base class in the derived
class:

```
Public Sub New(ByVal Text As String)
    .
    .
    .
End Sub
```

But what if you wanted to reach the constructor of the base class? For example, what if
that constructor took a string argument, and you had to pass that string back to it for the
code to work properly? You can specify that you're referring to a method in the base
class with the MyBase keyword this way:

```
Public Sub New(ByVal Text As String)
    MyBase.New(Text)
End Sub
```

In other words, MyBase gives you access to base class methods that have been overridden
in the current class.

Using the MyClass keyword in a derived class lets you work with all the methods in the
base class as if they were not overridable. The MyClass keyword actually represents the
current object, and it's the same as Me, except for that one difference—it treats all inherited methods as if they were not overridable.

Here's an example to make this clear and show how `MyClass` differs from `Me`; this is the MyClass example in the code for this book. Here, `BaseClass` has a method named Message that displays the message `"Base class here..."`. This class also has two other methods, `CallMe` and `CallMyClass`, which call the `Message` method using `Me` and `MyClass`, respectively:

```
Class BaseClass
    Public Overridable Sub Message()
        MsgBox("Base class here...")
    End Sub

    Public Sub CallMe()
        Me.Message()
    End Sub

    Public Sub CallMyClass()
        MyClass.Message()
    End Sub
End Class
```

Now say that you derive a class, `DerivedClass`, from `BaseClass` and that you override Message to display `"Derived class here..."`:

```
Class DerivedClass
    Inherits BaseClass
    Public Overrides Sub Message()
        MsgBox("Derived class here...")
    End Sub
End Class
```

Then, in an object of `DerivedClass`, calling `CallMe` will call `Me.Message()` in the base class, which will use the *overridden* version of message and display `"Derived class here..."`. Calling `CallMyClass`, on the other hand, will call `MyClass.Message()` in the base class, which will use the *original* version of message and display `"Base class here..."`. Listing 9.7 shows how this works in the MyClass example.

LISTING 9.7 Using the `MyClass` Keyword (MyClass Project, Form1.vb)

```
Public Class Form1
    Inherits System.Windows.Forms.Form

' Windows Form Designer generated code

    Private Sub Button1_Click(ByVal sender As System.Object, _
        ByVal e As System.EventArgs) Handles Button1.Click
```

LISTING 9.7   continued

```
        Dim objDerivedClass As DerivedClass = New DerivedClass
        objDerivedClass.CallMe()
        objDerivedClass.CallMyClass()
    End Sub
End Class

Class BaseClass
    Public Overridable Sub Message()
        MsgBox("Base class here...")
    End Sub

    Public Sub CallMe()
        Me.Message()
    End Sub

    Public Sub CallMyClass()
        MyClass.Message()
    End Sub
End Class

Class DerivedClass
    Inherits BaseClass
    Public Overrides Sub Message()
        MsgBox("Derived class here...")
    End Sub
End Class
```

You can see the MyClass example at work in Figure 9.8. When you click the button, you will first see "Derived class here..." as the Me keyword uses the overridden Message method, and then you will see "Base class here..." as the MyClass keyword uses the original Message method.

FIGURE 9.8

Using MyClass.

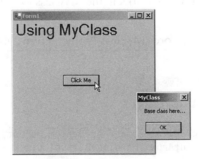

Inheriting Constructors

NEW TERM   I've been discussing inheriting methods from base classes, but here's one type of method you can't inherit—constructors. In fact, that isn't quite true—you can't inherit constructors that take *arguments*. If a base class has a constructor that takes no arguments—which is called a *default constructor*—that will be inherited in a derived class. In fact, even if the derived class doesn't have a constructor, the default constructor of the base class, if there is one, is called.

However, say that your base class has a constructor that takes arguments, but no default constructor. In that case, Visual Basic will not let you inherit the base class's constructor and will insist that you call that constructor explicitly in the derived class. (Visual Basic will require you to add a Sub New to the derived class and call the base class's constructor in that Sub procedure.)

Here's an example—the InheritingConstructors example in the code for this book, which shows how to use constructors with inheritance. In this case, you pass the Person class's constructor the text you want to display when the Walk method is called. A class named Ted is derived from the Person class, and you also pass its constructor the text you want to display in the Walk method—all you need to do to pass that text back to the base class's constructor is to call MyBase.New—see Listing 9.8.

LISTING 9.8   Inheriting Constructors (InheritingConstructors Project, Form1.vb)

```
Public Class Form1
    Inherits System.Windows.Forms.Form

' Windows Form Designer generated code

    Private Sub Button1_Click(ByVal sender As System.Object, _
        ByVal e As System.EventArgs) Handles Button1.Click
        Dim objTed As New Ted("Walking...")
        objTed.Walk()
    End Sub
End Class

Public Class Person
    Private Text As String

    Public Sub New(ByVal Message As String)
        Text = Message
    End Sub

    Public Sub Walk()
        MsgBox(Text)
    End Sub
End Class
```

LISTING 9.8   continued

```
Class Ted
    Inherits Person
    Public Sub New(ByVal Message As String)
        MyBase.New(Message)
    End Sub
End Class
```

You can see the results in Figure 9.9—when the user clicks the button, a new object of the Ted class is created by passing the text "Walking..." to that class's constructor, which passes the text back to the Person base class's constructor.

FIGURE 9.9

Inheriting constructors.

Creating Interfaces

Although a class can only inherit from one base class, it can *implement* multiple *interfaces*. An interface is a *specification* for a set of class members—not an implementation, just a specification. When you implement an interface, you write a definition for each class member.

An example in the code for this book named Interfaces shows how this works. This example makes Person into an interface, not a class, and adds two methods to it— SetName and GetName to store and return the name of the person:

```
Public Interface Person
    Sub SetName(ByVal Name As String)
    Function GetName() As String
End Interface
```

As you can see, there's no implementation of these methods here, just their declarations. When you implement an interface, you use the clause Implements Person and add the definitions for each of these methods. For example, here's how that looks in the Interfaces example, which creates a new class named Neighbor:

```
Public Class Neighbor
    Implements Person
    Dim InternalName As String

    Sub SetName(ByVal Name As String) Implements Person.SetName
        InternalName = Name
    End Sub

    Function GetName() As String Implements Person.GetName
        Return InternalName
    End Function
End Class
```

As you can see, you indicate which method implements which member of the interface with a clause such as `Implements Person.SetName`. Now you're free to create new objects of the `Neighbor` class this way:

```
Private Sub Button1_Click(ByVal sender As System.Object, _
    ByVal e As System.EventArgs) Handles Button1.Click
    Dim objNeighbor As New Neighbor
    objNeighbor.SetName("Jill")
    TextBox1.Text = "Your neighbor is " & objNeighbor.GetName()
End Sub
```

You can see the results in Figure 9.10, where the new `Neighbor` object, which implements the `Person` interface, has been created.

FIGURE 9.10

Implementing interfaces.

As their name implies, interfaces let you specify an interface of methods. When you implement an interface, you implement those methods. A class can't inherit from multiple base classes, but it can implement several interfaces.

Listing 9.9 shows how this works—in this case, say that you have a neighbor who is also an artist, so the `Neighbor` object will implement both the `Person` interface and a new interface named Artist. The Artist interface will let you specify an action (such as painting or sculpting) with the SetAction and GetAction methods. You can see what that looks like in the Interfaces example in the code for this book in Listing 9.9.

LISTING 9.9   Implementing Multiple Interfaces (Interfaces Project, Form1.vb)

```vb
Public Class Form1
    Inherits System.Windows.Forms.Form

' Windows Form Designer generated code
    Private Sub Button1_Click(ByVal sender As System.Object, _
        ByVal e As System.EventArgs) Handles Button1.Click
        Dim objNeighbor As New Neighbor
        objNeighbor.SetName("Jill")
        objNeighbor.SetAction("paint")
        TextBox1.Text = "Your neighbor " & objNeighbor.GetName() _
        & " likes to " & objNeighbor.GetAction()
    End Sub
End Class

Public Interface Person
    Sub SetName(ByVal Name As String)
    Function GetName() As String
End Interface

Public Interface Artist
    Sub SetAction(ByVal Name As String)
    Function GetAction() As String
End Interface

Public Class Neighbor
    Implements Person, Artist
    Dim InternalName, InternalAction As String

    Sub SetName(ByVal Name As String) Implements Person.SetName
        InternalName = Name
    End Sub

    Function GetName() As String Implements Person.GetName
        Return InternalName
    End Function

    Sub SetAction(ByVal Name As String) Implements Artist.SetAction
        InternalAction = Name
    End Sub

    Function GetAction() As String Implements Artist.GetAction
        Return InternalAction
    End Function
End Class
```

You can see the results in Figure 9.11, where the new `Neighbor` object, which implements both the `Person` and `Artist` interfaces, has been created.

FIGURE 9.11

Implementing multiple interfaces.

Working with Polymorphism

Polymorphism lets you assign objects of a derived class to variables of the class's base class. (Doesn't make a lot of sense yet? Don't worry; plenty of examples are coming up.) This is useful, for example, because you can use one procedure to handle objects of a base class and all classes derived from that base class.

There are two ways to handle polymorphism in Visual Basic—inheritance-based polymorphism and interface-based polymorphism. We'll take a look at them here to see how they work.

Inheritance-Based Polymorphism

In inheritance-based polymorphism, you first create a base class such as the `Person` class that you've already seen:

```
Class Person
    Public Sub Walk()
        MsgBox("Walking...")
    End Sub
End Class
```

Next, you derive a class, such as the `Bob` class, from `Person`:

```
Class Bob
    Inherits Person
    Public Sub Sleep()
        MsgBox("Sleeping...")
```

```
        End Sub
End Class
```

Now you can create a variable of the base class, Person, as with this code that is executed when the user clicks a button in the Polymorphism example in the code for this book:

```
Public Class Form1
    Inherits System.Windows.Forms.Form

' Windows Form Designer generated code

    Private Sub Button1_Click(ByVal sender As System.Object, _
        ByVal e As System.EventArgs) Handles Button1.Click
        Dim objPerson As Person
            .
            .
            .
    End Sub

End Class
```

You can assign an object of the Person class to this new variable, of course—but you can also assign it an object of the derived Bob class as well. And you can call the various methods of the Bob object, such as the Walk method:

```
Public Class Form1
    Inherits System.Windows.Forms.Form

' Windows Form Designer generated code

    Private Sub Button1_Click(ByVal sender As System.Object, _
        ByVal e As System.EventArgs) Handles Button1.Click
        Dim objPerson As Person
        objPerson = New Bob
        objPerson.Walk()
    End Sub

End Class
```

Now we've stored a Bob object (the derived class) in a Person variable (the base class), and there was no problem. You can see the results in Figure 9.12—when you click the Inheritance-Based Polymorphism button, a Bob object is stored in a Person variable, and we can call the Walk method of that object.

Note, however, that you cannot use any members that are not part of the Person class with objects you store in objPerson. For example, the Bob class includes a Sleep method:

```
Class Bob
    Inherits Person
    Public Sub Sleep()
        MsgBox("Sleeping...")
    End Sub
End Class
```

Because the Sleep method is not part of the Person class, you cannot call objPerson.Sleep() even if you store an object of the Bob class in objPerson.

FIGURE 9.12

Implementing polymorphism.

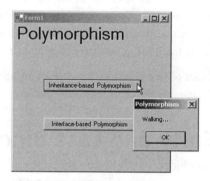

Interface-Based Polymorphism

Interfaces give you another way to implement polymorphism in Visual Basic.NET. Let's add another button, Interface-Based Polymorphism, to the previous Polymorphism example to see how this works. First, we create a new interface, PersonInterface, which has a Walk method:

```
Public Interface PersonInterface
    Sub Walk()
End Interface
```

Next, we implement this new interface in a class named BobInterface (to distinguish it from the inheritance-based Bob class):

```
Public Class BobInterface
    Implements PersonInterface
    Sub Walk() Implements PersonInterface.Walk
        MsgBox("Walking...")
    End Sub
End Class
```

When the user clicks the Interface-Based Polymorphism button, we can declare the objPerson variable to be of type PersonInterface—but we can actually store a BobInterface object in it:

```
Private Sub Button2_Click(ByVal sender As System.Object, _
    ByVal e As System.EventArgs) Handles Button2.Click
    Dim objPerson As PersonInterface
    objPerson = New BobInterface
    objPerson.Walk()
End Sub
```

Now when you call `objPerson.Walk`, the version of `Walk` in the `BobInterface` class is called, not the unimplemented version in `PersonInterface`. Clicking the Interface-Based Polymorphism button gives you the same result as in Figure 9.12—a message box appears with the message `"Walking..."`. As you can see, you can declare variables to be of an interface's type and fill them with objects that implement that interface (even if the implementation of the interfaces methods are entirely different in those objects).

And speaking of using an object of one type in a variable of another types, there's one more important topic to understand here—early and late binding.

Understanding Early and Late Binding

Normally, when you create an object, Visual Basic knows exactly what kind of object you're creating and can immediately check the syntax of what you're typing. For example, say that you create a new object of the `Jessica` class and try to use that object's `Walk` method—if the `Jessica` class doesn't support a `Walk` method, Visual Basic will give you a syntax error as you type this code:

```
Dim objJessica As New Jessica
objJessica.Walk()
```

NEW TERM   This is called *early binding* because an object is *bound* to its variable as soon as the variable is created. On the other hand, you can also use *late binding*. In late binding, you create an object of class `Object`, and you can use that object in a typeless way—Visual Basic won't check the object's type until runtime.

 Tip   If you use `Option Strict` in your code, late binding causes an error.

Let's take a look at how this works in the LateBinding example in the code for this book. There are two classes in this example—`Bob`, which has a `Walk` method, and `Jessica`, which doesn't:

```
Public Class Bob
    Public Sub Walk()
        MsgBox("Walking...")
```

```
        End Sub
End Class

Public Class Jessica
    Public Sub Run()
        MsgBox("Running...")
    End Sub
End Class
```

Now we can create two new variables of type Object and place an object of class Bob in one and an object of class Jessica in the other:

```
Private Sub Button1_Click(ByVal sender As System.Object, _
    ByVal e As System.EventArgs) Handles Button1.Click
    Dim objBob As Object
    Dim objJessica As Object
    objBob = New Bob
    objJessica = New Jessica
        .
        .
        .
End Sub
```

Visual Basic will treat these new variables, objBob and objJessica, as *typeless*. This means that we can invoke the Walk method of both objects—even though objJessica doesn't have a Walk method (we will catch this error at runtime with a Try/Catch block):

```
Private Sub Button1_Click(ByVal sender As System.Object, _
    ByVal e As System.EventArgs) Handles Button1.Click
    Dim objBob As Object
    Dim objJessica As Object
    objBob = New Bob
    objJessica = New Jessica

    Try
        objBob.Walk()
    Catch
        MsgBox("Sorry, no Walk method available in objBob.")
    End Try

    Try
        objJessica.Walk()
    Catch
        MsgBox("Sorry, no Walk method available in objJessica.")
    End Try
End Sub
```

Note that if it weren't for late binding, the expression objJessica.Walk() here would cause us problems before we even ran the code. As it is, however, Visual Basic doesn't object, and when the example runs, objJessica.Walk() simply causes an exception that we can handle, as you see in Figure 9.13.

FIGURE 9.13

Implementing late binding.

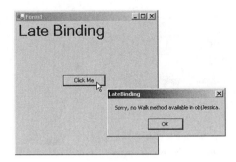

And that's all there is to it.

Summary

Today, you've seen a great deal about object-oriented programming in Visual Basic. You saw how to create your own classes and objects as long ago as Day 3, but today we dug deeply into the topic.

We started with an overview of the basic OOP concepts of abstraction, encapsulation, inheritance, and polymorphism. From there, you saw how to create both constructors and destructors, initializing and disposing of your objects as needed.

We also got in some basic OOP programming by seeing how to compare objects with the Is keyword and how to create shared class members. In particular, you saw that shared class fields hold the same data in all objects of that class and how you can use a shared method with simply the name of the class—no object is needed. You also saw how objects can support events.

You can overload the methods of a class simply by defining a method multiple times with the same name, but different arguments lists. That can mean different numbers or types of arguments, or both.

You also saw how to use public, protected, and private inheritance today, as well as friend access. You saw how public inheritance places no restriction on items, protected inheritance restricts them to a class and any derived classes, and private inheritance restricts them to the present class.

Besides overloading, you also saw how to override class members when you inherit them. Overriding means replacing, but you also saw that using keywords such as MyBase will access the original version of overridden class members.

Interfaces let you specify a set of class members creating, as the name implies, an interface. An interface is simply a specification of class members, and when you implement an interface, you must also implement those members (such as defining interface methods).

You saw that you can customize inheritance using the `MustOverride`, `Overridable`, and `NotOverridable` keywords and how you can get around overridden members using the `MyBase` and `MyClass` keywords. And we also took a look at inheritance-based and interface-based polymorphism, as well as early and late binding.

Tomorrow, we're going to take a look at more in-depth Visual Basic .NET programming as we take a look at two topics near and dear to many programmers' hearts—graphics and file handling.

9

Q&A

Q I know that I can use the `Is` keyword to check if a particular variable holds a specific object, but is there way to simply check an object's class?

A Yes. You can use the `TypeOf` keyword to get the type of an object. Here's an example: `If TypeOf sender Is Button Then....`

Q Why can't I inherit non-default constructors?

A You can't inherit a constructor because Visual Basic assumes that the way you initialize a derived object will differ from the way you initialize the derived class's base class.

Workshop

This workshop tests whether you understand the concepts you saw today. It's a good idea to make sure that you can answer these questions before pressing on to tomorrow's work.

Quiz

1. What method do you override to create a class destructor?
2. How do you make a custom event occur?
3. Where are items declared with the `Protected` keyword available?
4. How can you make sure that no one can derive a new class from one of your classes?
5. What's the difference between the `Me` and `MyClass` keywords?

Quiz Answers

1. You override the Finalize method, which is a method of the Object class.

2. You use the RaiseEvent method, passing it the name of the event and any arguments the event takes. For example, today we made the TplClick event occur with this statement: RaiseEvent TplClick("The button was triple clicked.").

3. Items declared with Protected are accessible only from within their own class (which includes structures and modules) or from within a derived class.

4. Declare it with the NotInheritable keyword, like this: Public NotInheritable Class TheClass.

5. Just like the Me keyword, the MyClass keyword represents the current object. It's the same as Me, except that it treats all inherited methods as if they were not overridable.

Exercises

1. Try creating your own event, the X event, whenever anyone types an X (uppercase or lowercase) into a text box (use the KeyChar argument passed to the text box's KeyPress event handler, as discussed in Day 4, "Creating Windows Forms," to determine when an X is pressed). Add an event handler to handle the X event and display a warning message box to the user indicating that they've just pressed the X key.

2. Create a class named Math2D with an *overloaded* method named Area. If you are passed a single argument to Area, assume that it's the radius of a circle and return the area of the circle (Πr^2); if you are passed two arguments to Area, assume that they are the base (b) and height (h) of a triangle and return the area of that triangle (bh/2). Next, derive a new class, Math3D, from Math2D, and *override* both versions of the Area method to work with 3D objects. If you are passed one argument to the Area method in Math3D, assume that it's the radius of a sphere and return the surface area of the sphere ($4\Pi r^2$). If you are passed two arguments to Area in Math3D, assume that they are the radius of the base (r) and length (l) of the side (apex to base) of a cone and return the surface area of the cone (Πrl).

DAY 10

Graphics and File Handling

Today, we're going to take a look at two programming topics that are very popular in Visual Basic .NET—drawing graphics and working with files. Both are essential skills for the Visual Basic .NET programmer—drawing graphics lets you display data in an easily recognized form and adds pizzazz to your program, and file handling is essential to store and retrieve program data. You're going to get a solid foundation in both these topics today. (But note that there is more to these topics than we have room for today—both file and graphics handling can get very involved if you get into advanced subjects.) Here's what's coming up:

- Using the `Graphics` class
- Drawing figures
- Handling images
- Drawing text
- Specifying drawing colors
- Working with files
- Using the `FileStream` class

- Setting file mode, access, and sharing
- Opening and creating files
- Writing to files and reading from them
- Using the `File` and `Directory` classes

We'll start today's work with graphics handling. This is a huge topic, so let's get started immediately.

Graphics Handling

In Visual Basic, graphics handling is based on GDI+ (GDI stands for Graphics Device Interface). Using the GDI+ methods, you can draw graphics without having to worry about the specific device those graphics are sent to—the drawing process is the same for drawing on the screen or in printer pages. The three major parts of GDI+ are as follows:

- 2D vector graphics
- Imaging
- Typography

We'll take a look at these parts in an overview here.

Working with 2D Vector Graphics

Vector graphics means drawing line-based shapes, including rectangles, ellipses, lines, curves, and so on. To draw figures such as these, you typically provide either a start and an end point or a rectangle bounding the figure you want to draw to the methods of the `Graphics` class.

The `Graphics` class is what our drawing operations will focus on. This huge Visual Basic class has all kinds of built-in methods such as `DrawRectangle`, which draws rectangles, `DrawEllipse`, which draws ellipses, and so on.

In 2D graphics, the drawing origin, (0, 0), is at upper left of the drawing surface. The positive X axis extends to the right, and the positive Y axis extends downward. (The axes are set up much as you'd read text on a page.) All measurements are in pixels.

Another important class that GDI+ supports is the `Pen` class, which lets you specify how you want to draw your figures. When you draw a figure such as an ellipse, you use a particular `Pen` object, and you can customize that object specifying such items as color, line width, and line style. You use the `Pen` class when you're drawing the outline of various figures, and you can use the `Brush` class to fill in those figures. You will see how to use both pens and brushes today.

Working with Images

Visual Basic is also good at handling images. GDI+ lets you handle bitmaps, which are arrays of points—each one of which corresponds to a pixel on the screen. Working with images is more complex than handling vector graphics, and GDI+ supports a `Bitmap` class that lets you work with bitmaps, stretching and copying them as you prefer.

Besides the `Bitmap` class, you can also work with the `Image` class in Visual Basic .NET. As you've already seen, the `Image` class lets you load images from files and display those images in controls similar to picture boxes. Today, we're going to see how to work with the `Graphics` class's `DrawImage` method to draw images.

Working with Typography

Typography means text handling, and GDI+ has a lot of built-in support for text. When you're working with graphics, you *draw* text—it's just another graphics figure. (That's very different from display text in controls such as text boxes.) Using GDI+ methods, you can display text using various different fonts, various sizes, and various styles (such as italic and bold), as well as using different colors.

That gives you an overview of what's coming up. Today's graphics work centers on the GDI+ `Graphics` class, and we'll start there.

Using the Graphics Class

Most of the drawing you do in Visual Basic .NET involves objects of the `Graphics` class. A `Graphics` object corresponds to the drawing surface of forms or controls. For example, you can use the `CreateGraphics` method of a form, as we'll do today, to get a `Graphics` object for a form. After you do, you can use the methods of that `Graphics` object, such as `DrawString` to draw text, `DrawRectangle`, `FillEllipse`, `DrawImage`, and so on to draw in that form.

Here's the class hierarchy of the `Graphics` class:

```
System.Object
   System.MarshalByRefObject
      System.Drawing.Graphics
```

You can find the significant public class methods of the `Graphics` class in Table 10.1, the significant public properties of `Graphics` objects in Table 10.2, and their significant public methods in Table 10.3.

TABLE 10.1   Significant Class Methods of the Graphics Class

Method	Means
FromHwnd	Returns a new Graphics object given a Windows handle (which you can get from the Control class's Handle runtime property)
FromImage	Returns a new Graphics object given an Image object.

TABLE 10.2   Significant Public Properties of Graphics Objects

Property	Means
DpiX	Contains the horizontal resolution of this Graphics object.
DpiY	Contains the vertical resolution of this Graphics object.
SmoothingMode	Sets the quality for drawing with this Graphics object.

TABLE 10.3   Significant Public Methods of Graphics Objects

Method	Means
Clear	Clears the drawing surface.
DrawArc	Draws an arc.
DrawBezier	Draws a Bézier curve.
DrawBeziers	Draws Bézier curves.
DrawClosedCurve	Draws a closed curve.
DrawCurve	Draws a curve.
DrawEllipse	Draws an ellipse.
DrawIcon	Draws an icon.
DrawIconUnstretched	Draws an icon without scaling the icon.
DrawImage	Draws an image.
DrawImageUnscaled	Draws an image without scaling the image.
DrawLine	Draws a line.
DrawLines	Draws lines.
DrawPath	Draws a graphics path.
DrawPie	Draws a pie section.
DrawPolygon	Draws a polygon.
DrawRectangle	Draws a rectangle.
DrawRectangles	Draws rectangles.
DrawString	Draws a text string.

TABLE 10.3   continued

Method	Means
FillClosedCurve	Fills a closed curve.
FillEllipse	Fills an ellipse.
FillPath	Fills the inside of a path.
FillPie	Fills a pie section.
FillPolygon	Fills a polygon.
FillRectangle	Fills a rectangle.
FillRectangles	Fills rectangles.
FillRegion	Fills the inside of a region.
GetNearestColor	Gets the nearest color to a given color.
MeasureString	Gets the length of a string to display.
Save	Saves this object as a GraphicsState object.

To actually draw in a Graphics object, you can Pen objects as we'll do today. For example, to draw a rectangle, you can call the DrawRectangle method like this:
Graphics.DrawRectangle(*Pen*, *Rectangle*), where *Pen* is a Pen object and *Rectangle* is a Rectangle object that lets you specify the rectangle to draw.

Using the Pen Class

Here is the class hierarchy of the Pen class:

```
System.Object
    System.MarshalByRefObject
        System.Drawing.Pen
```

You can find the significant public properties of Pen objects in Table 10.4 and their significant public method in Table 10.5.

TABLE 10.4   Significant Public Properties of Pen Objects

Property	Means
Brush	Returns or sets the Brush object of this Pen.
Color	Returns or sets the pen's color.
CompoundArray	Returns or sets an array of dashes and spaces to configure a pen.
CustomEndCap	Returns or sets the cap style used at the end of lines.
CustomStartCap	Returns or sets the cap style used at the beginning of lines.

10

TABLE 10.4   continued

Property	Means
DashCap	Returns or sets the cap style used at the beginning or end of dashed lines.
DashOffset	Returns or sets the length from the beginning of a line to the beginning of a dash pattern.
DashPattern	Returns or sets an array of dashes and spaces.
DashStyle	Returns or sets the style used for dashed lines.
EndCap	Returns or sets the cap style used at the end of lines.
LineJoin	Returns or sets the style used to join the ends of overlapping lines.
PenType	Returns the style of lines this pen draws.
StartCap	Returns or sets the cap style used at the beginning of lines.
Width	Returns or sets the width of this pen (in pixels).

TABLE 10.5   Significant Public Method of Pen Objects

Method	Means
SetLineCap	Sets the style of cap used to end lines.

Using Predefined Pens

When you're going to draw using a pen, you can create a Pen object from scratch by passing a drawing color to the Pen class's constructor. However, there are also many predefined pens for you to use; they all have a width of one pixel and a predefined color. To use them, you use a member of the Pens class. For example, to draw with a forest green pen, you can use Pens.ForestGreen like this:

Graphics.DrawRectangle(*Pens.ForestGreen, Rectangle*). The predefined pen colors appear in Table 10.6.

TABLE 10.6   Colors of the Pens and Brushes Classes

AliceBlue	GhostWhite	NavajoWhite
AntiqueWhite	Gold	Navy
Aqua	Goldenrod	OldLace
Aquamarine	Gray	Olive
Azure	Green	OliveDrab
Beige	GreenYellow	Orange
Bisque	Honeydew	OrangeRed

TABLE 10.6 continued

Black	HotPink	Orchid
BlanchedAlmond	IndianRed	PaleGoldenrod
Blue	Indigo	PaleGreen
BlueViolet	Ivory	PaleTurquoise
Brown	Khaki	PaleVioletRed
BurlyWood	Lavender	PapayaWhip
CadetBlue	LavenderBlush	PeachPuff
Chartreuse	LawnGreen	Peru
Chocolate	LemonChiffon	Pink
Coral	LightBlue	Plum
CornflowerBlue	LightCoral	PowderBlue
Cornsilk	LightCyan	Purple
Crimson	LightGoldenrodYellow	Red
Cyan	LightGray	RosyBrown
DarkBlue	LightGreen	RoyalBlue
DarkCyan	LightPink	SaddleBrown
DarkGoldenrod	LightSalmon	Salmon
DarkGray	LightSeaGreen	SandyBrown
DarkGreen	LightSkyBlue	SeaGreen
DarkKhaki	LightSlateGray	SeaShell
DarkMagenta	LightSteelBlue	Sienna
DarkOliveGreen	LightYellow	Silver
DarkOrange	Lime	SkyBlue
DarkOrchid	LimeGreen	SlateBlue
DarkRed	Linen	SlateGray
DarkSalmon	Magenta	Snow
DarkSeaGreen	Maroon	SpringGreen
DarkSlateBlue	MediumAquamarine	SteelBlue
DarkSlateGray	MediumBlue	Tan
DarkTurquoise	MediumOrchid	Teal
DarkViolet	MediumPurple	Thistle
DeepPink	MediumSeaGreen	Tomato
DeepSkyBlue	MediumSlateBlue	Transparent

10

TABLE 10.6   continued

DimGray	MediumSpringGreen	Turquoise
DodgerBlue	MediumTurquoise	Violet
Firebrick	MediumVioletRed	Wheat
FloralWhite	MidnightBlue	White
ForestGreen	MintCream	WhiteSmoke
Fuchsia	MistyRose	Yellow
Gainsboro	Moccasin	YellowGreen

Drawing With Graphics Objects

We're ready to start drawing. To see how drawing operations work from start to finish, we'll use the Artist example in the code for this book. This example lets you draw various graphics figures—all you do is to click a button with the caption Rectangle, Ellipse, and so on, and then use the mouse to draw your figures, as you can see in Figure 10.1.

FIGURE 10.1

The Artist application.

For reference, the code for the Artist example appears in Listing 10.1, and we're going to dissect that code over the next few pages.

LISTING 10.1   Drawing Graphics (Artist Project, Form1.vb)

```
Public Class Form1
    Inherits System.Windows.Forms.Form

' Windows Form Designer generated code

    Dim gphFormGraphics As Graphics
    Dim pt1, pt2 As Point
    Dim ptPointsArray() As Point
```

LISTING 10.1 continued

```
Dim intNumberOfPoints As Integer = 0
Dim recDrawingRectangle As Rectangle
Dim btnCurrentButton As Buttons
Enum Buttons
    Rectangle
    Ellipse
    Line
    Freehand
End Enum

Private Sub Form1_Load(ByVal sender As System.Object, _
    ByVal e As System.EventArgs) Handles MyBase.Load
    gphFormGraphics = Me.CreateGraphics()
End Sub

Private Sub Form1_MouseDown(ByVal sender As Object, _
    ByVal e As System.Windows.Forms.MouseEventArgs) Handles MyBase.MouseDown
    pt1 = New Point(e.X, e.Y)
End Sub

Private Sub Form1_MouseUp(ByVal sender As Object, _
    ByVal e As System.Windows.Forms.MouseEventArgs) Handles MyBase.MouseUp
    pt2 = New Point(e.X, e.Y)
    recDrawingRectangle = New Rectangle(Math.Min(pt2.X, pt1.X), _
        Math.Min(pt2.Y, pt1.Y), _
        Math.Abs(pt2.X - pt1.X), Math.Abs(pt2.Y - pt1.Y))

    Select Case btnCurrentButton
        Case Buttons.Rectangle
            gphFormGraphics.DrawRectangle(Pens.Navy, recDrawingRectangle)
        Case Buttons.Ellipse
            gphFormGraphics.DrawEllipse(Pens.Navy, recDrawingRectangle)
        Case Buttons.Line
            gphFormGraphics.DrawLine(Pens.Navy, pt2, pt1)
    End Select
End Sub

Private Sub Button1_Click(ByVal sender As System.Object, _
    ByVal e As System.EventArgs) Handles Button1.Click
    btnCurrentButton = Buttons.Rectangle
End Sub

Private Sub Button2_Click(ByVal sender As System.Object, _
    ByVal e As System.EventArgs) Handles Button2.Click
    btnCurrentButton = Buttons.Ellipse
End Sub

Private Sub Button3_Click(ByVal sender As System.Object, _
    ByVal e As System.EventArgs) Handles Button3.Click
```

10

LISTING **10.1**   continued

```
        btnCurrentButton = Buttons.Line
    End Sub

    Private Sub Button4_Click(ByVal sender As System.Object, _
        ByVal e As System.EventArgs) Handles Button4.Click
        btnCurrentButton = Buttons.Freehand
    End Sub

    Private Sub Form1_MouseMove(ByVal sender As Object, _
        ByVal e As System.Windows.Forms.MouseEventArgs) Handles MyBase.MouseMove
        If btnCurrentButton = Buttons.Freehand And e.Button = _
            MouseButtons.Left Then
            Dim ptNew As New Point(e.X, e.Y)

            ReDim Preserve ptPointsArray(intNumberOfPoints)

            ptPointsArray(intNumberOfPoints) = ptNew
            intNumberOfPoints += 1

            If intNumberOfPoints >= 2 Then
                gphFormGraphics.DrawLines(Pens.Navy, ptPointsArray)
            End If
        End If
    End Sub

    Private Sub Form1_Paint(ByVal sender As Object, _
        ByVal e As System.Windows.Forms.PaintEventArgs) Handles MyBase.Paint
        Select Case btnCurrentButton
            Case Buttons.Rectangle
                gphFormGraphics.DrawRectangle(Pens.Navy, recDrawingRectangle)
            Case Buttons.Ellipse
                gphFormGraphics.DrawEllipse(Pens.Navy, recDrawingRectangle)
            Case Buttons.Line
                gphFormGraphics.DrawLine(Pens.Navy, pt2, pt1)
            Case Buttons.Freehand
                If intNumberOfPoints >= 2 Then
                    gphFormGraphics.DrawLines(Pens.Navy, ptPointsArray)
                End If
        End Select
    End Sub
End Class
```

Getting a Graphics Object

There are two steps to drawing figures—getting a Graphics object and using that
object's drawing methods. You can get a Graphics object in several ways—by creating
one from scratch or by using one passed to you in an event handler.

You can create a Graphics object in a number of ways. For example, you can use the Control class's CreateGraphics method like this: Dim gphGraphics = Form1.CreateGraphics() to draw in a form or Dim gphGraphics = Button1.CreateGraphics() to draw in a button. In fact, that's how the Artist application gets a Graphics object for the form—it uses the CreateGraphics method in the form load event:

```
Dim gphFormGraphics As Graphics

Private Sub Form1_Load(ByVal sender As System.Object, _
    ByVal e As System.EventArgs) Handles MyBase.Load
    gphFormGraphics = Me.CreateGraphics()
End Sub
```

Control class objects, such as forms and controls, also have a Handle property that contains a Windows handle. That handle is an ID value that Windows uses to keep track of a window. If you pass that handle to the FromHwnd class method of the Graphics class, it will return a Graphics object for the form or control. You can also pass the Graphics class's FromImage method an Image object, and this method will return a Graphics object for the image, allowing you to draw offscreen in Image objects.

If you want to draw in a control or a form, you can get a Graphics object in the event handler for the control or form's Paint event. This event occurs when the form needs to be drawn (or redrawn) for any reason, as when it first appears or something that covers it is moved. You're passed a PaintEventArgs object in the control or form's Paint event handler, and you can get a Graphics object for the control or form using that object's Graphics property. Here's an example:

```
Private Sub Form1_Paint(ByVal sender As Object, _
    ByVal e As System.Windows.Forms.PaintEventArgs) Handles MyBase.Paint
    e.Graphics.DrawRectangle(Pens.Navy, New Rectangle(0, 0, 100, 100))
End Sub
```

It's important to realize that you can't draw graphics in a form from its Load event because the form's drawing surface hasn't been created yet. You must use the Paint event instead of the Load event. You can trigger a paint event for a form or control by calling the form or control's Invalidate method.

Now that we have a Graphics object to draw in, let's start drawing.

10

Drawing Figures

When the user clicks a mouse button in the Artist application, we store the location of
the mouse in a `Point` object named `pt1` in the `MouseDown` event handler:

```
Dim pt1 As Point

Private Sub Form1_MouseDown(ByVal sender As Object, _
    ByVal e As System.Windows.Forms.MouseEventArgs) _
    Handles MyBase.MouseDown
    pt1 = New Point(e.X, e.Y)
End Sub
```

This point, `pt1`, gives us the starting location of the figure to draw. The user then
moves the mouse to the other location that defines the figure to draw—a line, a rectangle, or whatever—and releases the mouse, causing a `MouseUp` event to occur. In the
`MouseUp` event handler, the code stores the location at which the mouse button was
released and creates a `Rectangle` object enclosing the figure. To create the rectangle,
you pass the `Rectangle` class's constructor the X and Y location of the upper left of the
rectangle, as well as the width and height of the rectangle (note the use of the `Math.Min`
and `Math.Abs` methods to find the upper-left corner, width, and height of the rectangle
here):

```
Dim pt1, pt2 As Point

Private Sub Form1_MouseUp(ByVal sender As Object, _
    ByVal e As System.Windows.Forms.MouseEventArgs) _
    Handles MyBase.MouseUp
    pt2 = New Point(e.X, e.Y)
    recDrawingRectangle = New Rectangle(Math.Min(pt2.X, pt1.X),
        Math.Min(pt2.Y, pt1.Y), _
        Math.Abs(pt2.X - pt1.X), Math.Abs(pt2.Y - pt1.Y))
        .
        .
        .
End Sub
```

Now we have the rectangle that we should draw the figure in, `recDrawingRectangle`—
but what figure should we draw? As you saw in Figure 10.1, the Artist application lets
the user click buttons marked Rectangle, Ellipse, Line, and Freehand to let him draw various figures. How do we know which button was clicked? We can keep track of that
using a variable named `btnCurrentButton`, which holds a member of the Buttons enumeration we'll create—`Buttons.Line`, `Buttons.Ellipse`, `Buttons.Line`, and
`Buttons.Freehand`. When the user clicks a button, such as the Ellipse button, we'll
assign the corresponding value to `btnCurrentButton` like this:

```
Dim btnCurrentButton As Buttons
Enum Buttons
    Rectangle
    Ellipse
    Line
    Freehand
End Enum

Private Sub Button1_Click(ByVal sender As System.Object, _
    ByVal e As System.EventArgs) Handles Button1.Click
    btnCurrentButton = Buttons.Rectangle
End Sub

Private Sub Button2_Click(ByVal sender As System.Object, _
    ByVal e As System.EventArgs) Handles Button2.Click
    btnCurrentButton = Buttons.Ellipse
End Sub

Private Sub Button3_Click(ByVal sender As System.Object, _
    ByVal e As System.EventArgs) Handles Button3.Click
    btnCurrentButton = Buttons.Line
End Sub

Private Sub Button4_Click(ByVal sender As System.Object, _
    ByVal e As System.EventArgs) Handles Button4.Click
    btnCurrentButton = Buttons.Freehand
End Sub
```

Now it's easy to know which figure to draw—we just check the value in the btnCurrentButton variable. If that variable holds Buttons.Rectangle, for example, we know that we have to draw a rectangle in the drawing rectangle we've set up. We can draw that rectangle by passing a Pen object—we'll use the predefined pen Pens.Navy in the Artist example—and the drawing rectangle to the Graphics object's DrawRectangle method:

```
Private Sub Form1_MouseUp(ByVal sender As Object, _
    ByVal e As System.Windows.Forms.MouseEventArgs) _
    Handles MyBase.MouseUp
    pt2 = New Point(e.X, e.Y)
    recDrawingRectangle = New Rectangle(Math.Min(pt2.X, pt1.X), _
        Math.Min(pt2.Y, pt1.Y), _
        Math.Abs(pt2.X - pt1.X), Math.Abs(pt2.Y - pt1.Y))

    Select Case btnCurrentButton
        Case Buttons.Rectangle
            gphFormGraphics.DrawRectangle(Pens.Navy, recDrawingRectangle)
        Case Buttons.Ellipse
            gphFormGraphics.DrawEllipse(Pens.Navy, recDrawingRectangle)
```

10

```
        Case Buttons.Line
            gphFormGraphics.DrawLine(Pens.Navy, pt2, pt1)
    End Select
End Sub
```

You can see the result in Figure 10.2, where the user is drawing a rectangle. The process works the same way for drawing ellipses, except that you pass the `DrawEllipse` method the rectangle to draw the ellipse in, and for drawing lines, except that you pass the two points to draw the line between to the `DrawLine` method. Now we're drawing with `Graphics` methods.

FIGURE 10.2

Drawing rectangles.

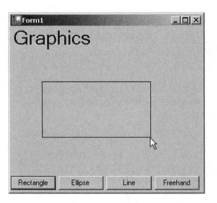

So far, we've used these graphics methods to draw rectangles and ellipses, where you pass a `Pen` and a `Rectangle` object holding the rectangle to draw in:

```
Graphics.DrawRectangle(Pen, Rectangle)
Graphics.DrawEllipse(Pen, Rectangle)
```

You create the `Rectangle` object like this: `Dim r as New Rectangle(x, y, width, height)`. In fact, you can also pass those *x*, *y*, *width*, and *height* values (all integers) to `DrawRectangle` and `DrawEllipse` directly, this way:

```
Graphics.DrawRectangle(Pen, x, y, width, height)
Graphics.DrawEllipse(Pen, x, y, width, height)
```

You might also note that there's also a button with the caption Freehand in the Artist application in Figure 10.1. To implement freehand drawing, you can add code to the `MouseMove` event handler and use the `Graphics` class's `DrawLines` method. You pass this method an array of the points to connect with lines, so all we need to do is to store the points passed to us in `MouseMove`. (A `MouseMove` event is not generated for every pixel the mouse passes over, but only so many times a second, so all we need to do is to connect the dots with short lines using `DrawLines`.)

The Artist application saves the points to connect with an array of `Point` objects named `ptPointsArray`—every time the mouse moves, we can add a new point to that array. All we have to do is to pass this array to the `DrawLines` method (note that the code doesn't invoke the `DrawLines` method unless at least two points are stored in the `ptPointsArray` array, which is the minimum that `DrawLines` requires):

```
Dim ptPointsArray() As Point
Dim intNumberOfPoints As Integer = 0

Private Sub Form1_MouseMove(ByVal sender As Object, _
    ByVal e As System.Windows.Forms.MouseEventArgs) _
    Handles MyBase.MouseMove
    If btnCurrentButton = Buttons.Freehand And e.Button = MouseButtons.Left Then
        Dim ptNew As New Point(e.X, e.Y)

        ReDim Preserve ptPointsArray(intNumberOfPoints)

        ptPointsArray(intNumberOfPoints) = ptNew
        intNumberOfPoints += 1

        If intNumberOfPoints >= 2 Then
            gphFormGraphics.DrawLines(Pens.Navy, ptPointsArray)
        End If
    End If
End Sub
```

You can see the results in Figure 10.3, where the user is drawing freehand with the mouse.

10

Figure 10.3

Drawing freehand.

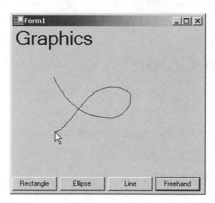

The Artist application looks good, but there's more to come. If you were to put another window on top of Artist and then move it, or minimize and then restore Artist's window, you'll note that the affected graphics would not automatically be redrawn. So how can you redraw a window when you need to?

Redrawing Windows on Demand

When a form or control, or part of a form or control, needs to be redrawn, a `Paint` event occurs. Currently when you minimize and then restore the Artist application, it reappears with a blank window. You can fix that by redrawing the figure(s) in it in the `Form_Paint` event. As an example, the Artist application redraws the most recent figure in that event's handler this way:

```
Private Sub Form1_Paint(ByVal sender As Object, _
    ByVal e As System.Windows.Forms.PaintEventArgs) Handles MyBase.Paint
    Select Case btnCurrentButton
        Case Buttons.Rectangle
            gphFormGraphics.DrawRectangle(Pens.Navy, recDrawingRectangle)
        Case Buttons.Ellipse
            gphFormGraphics.DrawEllipse(Pens.Navy, recDrawingRectangle)
        Case Buttons.Line
            gphFormGraphics.DrawLine(Pens.Navy, pt2, pt1)
        Case Buttons.Freehand
            If intNumberOfPoints >= 2 Then
                gphFormGraphics.DrawLines(Pens.Navy, ptPointsArray)
            End If
    End Select
End Sub
```

Give this a try—try drawing something in the Artist application and then minimize and restore the window. You'll see the most recent figure redrawn automatically.

Setting Drawing Colors

You've seen that you can use the predefined colors listed in Table 10.6 to draw figures as follows:

```
gphGraphics.DrawEllipse(Pens.Navy, recDrawingRectangle)
```

But what if you didn't want to use a predefined color—what if you wanted to use your own color? You can pass the `Pen` class's constructor a `Color` object to create a pen of the color you want.

You can get a `Color` object from a `Color` dialog, as you've seen in Day 7, "Windows Forms: Working with Menus, Built-in Dialogs, and Printing," which is great to let the user select the drawing color he wants. You can also create a `Color` object with the `Color` class's `FromArgb` method, passing it the red, green, and blue color values for the new color as bytes (with values ranging from 0 to 255). For example, white has the (*red*, *green*, *blue*) color values (255, 255, 255), bright red is (255, 0, 0), bright blue is (0, 0, 255), gray is (128, 128, 128), and so on. Here's how you can use the `FromArgb` method to create a bright blue pen and use it to draw an ellipse:

```
Dim clrColor As Color = Color.FromArgb(0, 0, 255)
Dim pnBluePen As New Pen(clrColor)
gphGraphics.DrawEllipse(pnBluePen, recDrawingRectangle)
```

You can also set the width, in pixels, of a pen when you create it. All you have to do is to pass that width to the `Pen` class's constructor as in this case, where the code uses a pen four pixels wide:

```
Dim clrColor As Color = Color.FromArgb(0, 0, 255)
Dim pnBluePen As New Pen(clrColor, 4)
gphGraphics.DrawEllipse(pnBluePen, recDrawingRectangle)
```

Like the `Pens` class, you can also use the predefined colors from Table 10.6 as predefined colors in `Color` objects. For example, some predefined colors are `Color.SkyBlue`, `Color.MediumSeaGreen`, `Color.LightSalmon`, `Color.LemonChiffon`, and so on.

10

Filling In Figures

So far, we've just draw figures in outline, but you can also fill them in. To do that, you use `Graphics` object methods such as `FillEllipse`, `FillRectangle`, and so on, as well as a `Brush` object. The `Brush` class is actually an abstract class, which means that you can't directly create objects from it. Instead, you use the classes derived from that class, and here they are:

```
System.Object
    System.MarshalByRefObject
        System.Drawing.Brush
            System.Drawing.Drawing2D.HatchBrush
            System.Drawing.Drawing2D.LinearGradientBrush
            System.Drawing.Drawing2D.PathGradientBrush
            System.Drawing.SolidBrush
            System.Drawing.TextureBrush
```

The various brush classes don't have many significant properties or methods in themselves—you simply create the brush you want and pass it to a `Graphics` method to use that brush. You can see an example in the Brushes application that comes in the code for this book. This example draws four rectangles and fills them in with the

FillRectangle method using various brushes—LinearGradientBrush, HatchBrush, SolidBrush, and TextureBrush as shown in Figure 10.4. (The other brush type, PathGradientBrush, is pretty involved to use and requires that you create graphics paths and other constructs.)

FIGURE 10.4

Filling in figures.

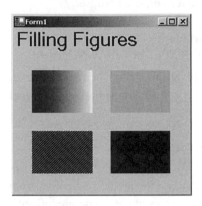

Let's take a look at the code that created the result you see in Figure 10.4. To use the LinearGradientBrush and HatchBrush classes, you must import the System.Drawing.Drawing2D namespace. You do that with the statement Imports System.Drawing.Drawing2D, which appears at the head of the code. Some namespaces, such as the System.Windows namespace, are imported automatically so that you can use classes such as System.Windows.Forms.Form. But that's not true for the System.Drawing.Drawing2D or the System.IO namespace we'll see when working with files today. (In general, if you use a built-in Visual Basic class and Visual Basic claims that it can't find that class, you probably need to import the class's namespace first—the built-in classes are divided into various namespaces, and to save resources such as memory, not all namespaces are automatically imported.)

Then you simply need to create the various brushes and pass them to the FillRectangle method, as you can see in Listing 10.2. (Note that the texture brush, which paints textures based on images, loads the Blue Lace 16.bmp file in here—this file comes with Windows 2000.)

LISTING 10.2   Filling in Rectangles (Brushes Project, Form1.vb)

```
Imports System.Drawing.Drawing2D

Public Class Form1
    Inherits System.Windows.Forms.Form
```

Listing 10.2 continued

```
' Windows Form Designer generated code

    Private Sub Form1_Paint(ByVal sender As Object, _
        ByVal e As System.Windows.Forms.PaintEventArgs) Handles MyBase.Paint
        Dim recDrawingRectangle As Rectangle

        recDrawingRectangle = New Rectangle(30, 70, 100, 70)
        Dim lgb As New LinearGradientBrush( _
            recDrawingRectangle, Color.Blue, Color.Yellow, _
            LinearGradientMode.Horizontal)
        e.Graphics.FillRectangle(lgb, recDrawingRectangle)

        recDrawingRectangle = New Rectangle(160, 70, 100, 70)
        Dim sb As New SolidBrush(Color.LightSalmon)
        e.Graphics.FillRectangle(sb, recDrawingRectangle)

        recDrawingRectangle = New Rectangle(30, 170, 100, 70)
        Dim hb As New HatchBrush(HatchStyle.LightUpwardDiagonal, _
            Color.Aquamarine)
        e.Graphics.FillRectangle(hb, recDrawingRectangle)

        recDrawingRectangle = New Rectangle(160, 170, 100, 70)
        Dim tb As New TextureBrush(Bitmap.FromFile("Blue Lace 16.bmp"))
        e.Graphics.FillRectangle(tb, recDrawingRectangle)

    End Sub
End Class
```

10

And that's all you need. Note that there are also predefined solid brushes in the Brushes class corresponding to the colors in Table 10.6. For example, you can use a "steel blue" solid brush like this: Graphics.FillRectangle(Brushes.SteelBlue, recDrawingRectangle).

Handling Images

You've already seen in this book that you can use various controls such as labels and picture boxes to handle images, assigning an Image object to the Image property or using an image list. However, you can also use the Graphics class's methods to directly draw an image in forms and controls. In particular, you can use the DrawImage method. To see how this works, take a look at the ImageHandler example in the code for this book, which you can see at work in Figure 10.5.

FIGURE **10.5**

Scrolling an image.

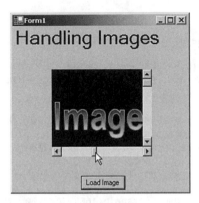

This example handles the graphics work itself; when you click the Load Image button, an Open File dialog appears, letting the user select an image file to load. The image is loaded into a picture box, as you see in Figure 10.5, and scrollbars appear if needed to let you scroll the image. The scrollbars in this example actually appear inside the picture box itself to avoid overlapping other controls nearby.

Because picture boxes don't support scrollbars by themselves, we're going to handle scrolling the image ourselves in code. We'll need to use Graphics methods to do that. That's what this example is all about—getting a Graphics object for the picture box and redrawing the image in the picture box each time it's scrolled, using the DrawImage method.

Here's how it all starts—when the user clicks the Load Image button, the code displays the Open File dialog, loads the image the user requested into an Image object, and assigns that image to the picture box's Image property to display it. We also check whether the vertical and horizontal scrollbars should be displayed in case the image won't fit entirely into the picture box (by default, both scrollbars' Visible property is False):

```
Private Sub Button1_Click(ByVal sender As System.Object, _
    ByVal e As System.EventArgs) Handles Button1.Click
    If OpenFileDialog1.ShowDialog() = DialogResult.OK Then
        PictureBox1.Image = Image.FromFile(OpenFileDialog1.FileName)
        HScrollBar1.Maximum = PictureBox1.Image.Width - _
            PictureBox1.Width + HScrollBar1.Height
        VScrollBar1.Maximum = PictureBox1.Image.Height - _
            PictureBox1.Height + VScrollBar1.Width

        VScrollBar1.Visible = True
        HScrollBar1.Visible = True
```

```
        If PictureBox1.Height > PictureBox1.Image.Height Then
            VScrollBar1.Visible = False
        End If

        If PictureBox1.Width > PictureBox1.Image.Width Then
            HScrollBar1.Visible = False
        End If
    End If
End Sub
```

Now the image and the scrollbars we need—horizontal, vertical, or both—have appeared. In this example, the actual action takes place when the user scrolls one of those scrollbars because the picture box isn't about to scroll that image automatically. We'll do that ourselves, using the Graphics class's DrawImage method to draw the image in the picture box according to the new scrollbar position.

We start by getting a Graphics object for the picture box, and then we use DrawImage to draw the image in the picture box. The basic version of DrawImage simply draws an image in a Graphics object starting at a particular point (the point will correspond to the upper left of the drawn image—recall that Point objects have two fields, X and Y, that let you specify a point):

```
Graphics.DrawImage(Image, Point)
```

You can also specify a rectangle in which to draw the image (Rectangle objects have X and Y fields, as well as Height and Width fields to let you specify the rectangle you want to draw in):

```
Graphics.DrawImage(Image, Rectangle)
```

There are other versions of DrawImage as well, such as the one we're going to use—this version lets you specify the image to draw, as well as a target rectangle in which to draw in the picture box and a source rectangle that lets you get a specific section of the image from the Image object (that's what we need because when the user scrolls the image, we want to display the new section of the image the user has scrolled to):

```
Graphics.DrawImage( _
    ByVal image As Image, _
    ByVal destRect As Rectangle, _
    ByVal srcRect As Rectangle, _
    ByVal srcUnit As GraphicsUnit _
)
```

This is the version of DrawImage that will let us scroll the image by selecting what rectangle from the image to draw in the picture box. Here's what it looks like in code—note

10

that you must also specify the graphics units with the GraphicsUnit enumeration, and we must use GraphicsUnit.Pixel here:

```
Private Sub HScrollBar1_Scroll(ByVal sender As System.Object, _
    ByVal e As System.Windows.Forms.ScrollEventArgs) Handles HScrollBar1.Scroll
    Dim gphPictureBox As Graphics = PictureBox1.CreateGraphics()
    gphPictureBox.DrawImage(PictureBox1.Image, New Rectangle(0, 0, _
        PictureBox1.Width - HScrollBar1.Height, _
        PictureBox1.Height - VScrollBar1.Width), _
        New Rectangle(HScrollBar1.Value, VScrollBar1.Value, _
        PictureBox1.Width - HScrollBar1.Height, _
        PictureBox1.Height - VScrollBar1.Width), GraphicsUnit.Pixel)
End Sub
```

And that's all the code we need—both the horizontal and vertical scrollbars in this example use this same code. Listing 10.3 presents the whole code.

LISTING 10.3   Scrolling Images (ImageHandler Project, Form1.vb)

```
Public Class Form1
    Inherits System.Windows.Forms.Form

' Windows Form Designer generated code

    Private Sub Button1_Click(ByVal sender As System.Object, _
        ByVal e As System.EventArgs) Handles Button1.Click
        If OpenFileDialog1.ShowDialog() = DialogResult.OK Then
            PictureBox1.Image = Image.FromFile(OpenFileDialog1.FileName)
            HScrollBar1.Maximum = PictureBox1.Image.Width - _
                PictureBox1.Width + HScrollBar1.Height
            VScrollBar1.Maximum = PictureBox1.Image.Height - _
                PictureBox1.Height + VScrollBar1.Width

            VScrollBar1.Visible = True
            HScrollBar1.Visible = True

            If PictureBox1.Height > PictureBox1.Image.Height Then
                VScrollBar1.Visible = False
            End If

            If PictureBox1.Width > PictureBox1.Image.Width Then
                HScrollBar1.Visible = False
            End If
        End If
    End Sub

    Private Sub HScrollBar1_Scroll(ByVal sender As System.Object, _
        ByVal e As System.Windows.Forms.ScrollEventArgs) _
```

LISTING **10.3**   continued

```
            Handles HScrollBar1.Scroll
            Dim gphPictureBox As Graphics = PictureBox1.CreateGraphics()
            gphPictureBox.DrawImage(PictureBox1.Image, New Rectangle(0, 0, _
                PictureBox1.Width - HScrollBar1.Height, _
                PictureBox1.Height - VScrollBar1.Width), _
                New Rectangle(HScrollBar1.Value, VScrollBar1.Value, _
                PictureBox1.Width - HScrollBar1.Height, _
                PictureBox1.Height - VScrollBar1.Width), GraphicsUnit.Pixel)
        End Sub

    Private Sub VScrollBar1_Scroll(ByVal sender As System.Object, _
        ByVal e As System.Windows.Forms.ScrollEventArgs) Handles _
            VScrollBar1.Scroll
        Dim gphPictureBox As Graphics = PictureBox1.CreateGraphics()
        gphPictureBox.DrawImage(PictureBox1.Image, New Rectangle(0, 0, _
            PictureBox1.Width - HScrollBar1.Height, _
            PictureBox1.Height - VScrollBar1.Width), _
            New Rectangle(HScrollBar1.Value, VScrollBar1.Value, _
            PictureBox1.Width - HScrollBar1.Height, _
            PictureBox1.Height - VScrollBar1.Width), GraphicsUnit.Pixel)
        End Sub
End Class
```

10

You can see the results of this example, the ImageHandler example, in Figure 10.5. Give it a try—just load an image and scroll it around. (The image displayed in the picture box in Figure 10.5, image.jpg, comes with the code for this book.)

Drawing Text

In graphics handling, text is simply drawn as graphics, and you can use the Graphics class's DrawString method to draw that text. As with other Graphics methods, there are various overloaded forms of the DrawString method; here's one that's probably the most popular:

Graphics.DrawString(*String, Font, Brush, Single, Single*)

To draw text, you pass this method the string to display, a Font object to use, a Brush to use to draw the text, and the X and Y positions of the upper-left location at which to draw the text. Getting a Brush object is easy—we can just use one of the predefined brushes, such as Brushes.Maroon.

To create a new Font object, you can use the Font class's constructor, which has a number of overloaded forms. For example, you can pass it the name of a font (such as "Arial") and the size you want that font to be (measured in points, 1/72nds of an inch):

```
Font.New(String, Single)
```

And you can also specify the font style using a member of the FontStyle enumeration:

```
Font.New(String, Single, FontStyle)
```

Here are the members of the FontStyle enumeration:

- FontStyle.Bold—Bold text
- FontStyle.Italic—Italic text
- FontStyle.Regular—Normal text
- FontStyle.Strikeout—Text with a line through the middle
- FontStyle.Underline—Underlined text

Here's an example—the DrawText example in the code for this book. In this case, we'll use maroon Times New Roman font (you can select any font installed in the computer), 48 points high and in italic to display the message "Hello there!" in the Form1_Paint event handler:

```
Private Sub Form1_Paint(ByVal sender As Object, _
    ByVal e As System.Windows.Forms.PaintEventArgs) Handles MyBase.Paint
    Dim fntText = New Font("Times New Roman", 48, FontStyle.Italic)
    e.Graphics.DrawString("Hello there!", fntText, Brushes.Maroon, 10, 100)
End Sub
```

You can see the results in Figure 10.6.

FIGURE 10.6

Drawing Text.

> **Tip**
>
> Want to figure out how many lines of text will fit into the `Graphics` object passed to you in a `Paint` event handler? You can use this expression: `Dim intNumberLines = e.MarginBounds.Height / Font.GetHeight(e.Graphics)`, where *Font* is the `Font` object you're using.

And that completes our work with graphics today. Now let's turn to today's other topic—file handling.

Handling Files

To store data in a permanent way, applications use files, and today we'll take a look at file handling. In Visual Basic.NET, file handling is based on the `System.IO` namespace, which includes a class library that supports string, character, and file manipulation. These classes include properties, methods, and events for creating, copying, moving, and deleting files. The most commonly used classes are `FileStream`, `BinaryReader`, `BinaryWriter`, `StreamReader`, and `StreamWriter`.

Using the `FileStream` Class

New Term The `FileStream` class is the foundation of the file handling you will see today. You use this class to open a file on disk, and then you can pass the `FileStream` object to the `BinaryReader`, `BinaryWriter`, `StreamReader`, and `StreamWriter` classes to work with the data in the file.

The `FileStream` class treats files as *streams* of data and acts as a sort of conduit for those streams, as you will see. This class is designed to give you access to files—you begin work with a file by opening it or creating it, and you can use the members of the `FileAccess`, `FileMode`, and `FileShare` enumerations with the constructors of the `FileStream` class to determine how the file is created, opened, and shared.

Here's the class hierarchy of the `FileStream` class (note that `FileStream` is in the `System.IO` namespace, which you must import explicitly, as you will see):

```
System.Object
    System.MarshalByRefObject
        System.IO.Stream
            System.IO.FileStream
```

10

You can find the more significant public properties of FileStream objects in Table 10.7, and the more significant public methods in Table 10.8.

TABLE 10.7   Significant Public Properties of FileStream Objects

Property	Means
CanRead	Indicates whether the file stream supports reading.
CanSeek	Indicates whether the file stream supports seeking.
CanWrite	Indicates whether the file stream supports writing.
Length	Gets the length of the file stream in bytes.
Name	Gets the name of the file passed to the constructor.
Position	Returns or sets the position in this stream.

TABLE 10.8   Significant Public Methods of FileStream Objects

Method	Means
Close	Closes a file, making it available to other programs.
Flush	Flushes all buffers for this stream, writing any buffered data out to its target (such as a disk file).
Lock	Prevents access to the file by other programs.
Read	Reads a block of bytes.
ReadByte	Reads a byte from the file.
Seek	Sets the current read/write position.
SetLength	Sets the length of the stream.
Unlock	Gives access to other processes to a file that had been locked.
Write	Writes a block of bytes to this stream.
WriteByte	Writes a byte to the current read/write position.

NEW TERM   When you use the FileStream class to open a file, you specify the *file mode* you want to use—for example, if you want to create a new file, you use the file mode FileMode.Create; if you want to append data to an existing file, you use FileMode.Append. The various possible file modes are part of the FileMode enumeration, and you can find the members of this enumeration in Table 10.9.

TABLE 10.9 Members of the `FileMode` Enumeration

Member	Means
`FileMode.Append`	Opens a file and moves to the end of the file (or creates a new file if the specified file doesn't exist). You can only use `FileMode.Append` with `FileAccess.Write`.
`FileMode.Create`	Creates a new file. (If the file already exists, it is overwritten.)
`FileMode.CreateNew`	Creates a new file. (If the file already exists, an `IOException` occurs.)
`FileMode.Open`	Opens an existing file.
`FileMode.OpenOrCreate`	Opens a file if it exists or creates a new file if it does not.
`FileMode.Truncate`	Opens an existing file and truncates it to zero length (letting you write over its current data).

NEW TERM You can also specify the *file access* when you open a file using the `FileStream` class. The file access indicates the way you're going to use the file—to read from, to write to, or both. To indicate the type of file access you want, you use members of the `FileAccess` enumeration. You can find the members of the `FileAccess` enumeration in Table 10.10.

TABLE 10.10 Members of the `FileAccess` Enumeration

Member	Means
`FileAccess.Read`	You can read data from the file.
`FileAccess.ReadWrite`	You can both read and write to and from a file.
`FileAccess.Write`	You can write to the file.

NEW TERM You can also specify the file *sharing mode* when you open a file. For example, if you want to allow other applications to read a file at the same time you're working with it, you use the file sharing mode `FileShare.Read`. To deny access to other applications, use `FileShare.None`. The various possible file sharing modes are part of the `FileShare` enumeration, and you can find the members of this enumeration in Table 10.11.

TABLE 10.11 Members of the `FileShare` Enumeration

Member	Means
`FileShare.None`	The file cannot be shared. Other processes cannot access it.
`FileShare.Read`	The file can also be opened by other processes for reading.
`FileShare.ReadWrite`	The file can also be opened by other processes for reading and writing.
`FileShare.Write`	The file can also be opened by other processes for writing.

10

Let's put the `FileStream` class to work now in an example. This example,
StreamReadWrite, in the code for this book, will let the user write text to a file and read
that text back. You can see this example at work in Figure 10.7, where the user can click
the Write File button to write text to a file named file.txt, and the Read File button to
read that text back in, displaying it in a multiline text box.

FIGURE 10.7

*Writing and reading
text to a file.*

We'll work on creating this example now; it all starts by using the `FileStream` class to
open and create new files.

Opening or Creating a File

The `FileStream` class has many constructors, and you use those constructors to open or
create a file. You can specify the file mode (for example, `FileMode.Open`), file access
(such as `FileAccess.Read`), or the file sharing mode (such as `FileShare.None`) in
`FileStream` constructors such as these:

```
Dim fs As New System.IO.FileStream(String, FileMode)
Dim fs As New System.IO.FileStream(String, FileMode, FileAccess)
Dim fs As New System.IO.FileStream(String, FileMode, FileAccess, FileShare)
```

When the user clicks the Write File button in the `StreamReadWrite` example in the
book's code, the code will create a file named file.txt using `FileMode.Create` (which
overwrites the file if it exists already) and sets the file access to `FileAccess.Write` to
indicate that we want to write to that file. Note that we have to also import the
`System.IO` namespace with an `Imports` statement to use the `FileStream` class:

```
Imports System.IO

Public Class Form1
    Inherits System.Windows.Forms.Form

    'Windows Form Designer generated code
```

```
Private Sub Button1_Click(ByVal sender As System.Object, _
    ByVal e As System.EventArgs) Handles Button1.Click
    Dim fsStream As New FileStream("filo.txt", _
        FileMode.Create, FileAccess.Write)
    .
    .
    .
```

Our next step is to write text to this newly created file. To do that, we'll use the `StreamWriter` class, coming up next.

Writing Text with the StreamWriter Class

To work with text data in files, you can use the `StreamReader` and `StreamWriter` classes. In the StreamReadWrite example, we've opened a file for writing using the `FileStream` class, and now we can create a `StreamWriter` object to write text to the file. Here is the class hierarchy of the `StreamWriter` class:

```
System.Object
    System.MarshalByRefObject
        System.IO.TextWriter
            System.IO.StreamWriter
```

You can find the more significant public properties of the `StreamWriter` class in Table 10.12 and the more significant methods in Table 10.13.

TABLE 10.12 Significant Public Properties of `StreamWriter` Objects

Property	Means
AutoFlush	Returns or sets whether the `StreamWriter` will flush (write out) its buffer after a `Write` or `WriteLine` operation.
BaseStream	Gets the base stream, such as the `FileStream` object, for this stream, giving you access to the base stream's properties and methods.
Encoding	Gets the character encoding for this stream.

TABLE 10.13 Significant Public Methods of `StreamWriter` Objects

Method	Means
Close	Closes the current stream, flushing out all data remaining in internal stream buffers, and making the associated file available to other processes.
Flush	Flushes all buffers for the stream writer, writing any buffered stream data to the base stream.
Write	Writes data to the stream.

Here's how we can create a `StreamWriter` object from the `FileStream` object we already have:

```
Imports System.IO

Public Class Form1
    Inherits System.Windows.Forms.Form

    'Windows Form Designer generated code

    Private Sub Button1_Click(ByVal sender As System.Object, _
        ByVal e As System.EventArgs) Handles Button1.Click
        Dim fsStream As New FileStream("file.txt", _
            FileMode.Create, FileAccess.Write)
        Dim swWriter As New StreamWriter(fsStream)
        .
        .
        .
End Class
```

We're set to write to our text file. For example, we can use the `WriteLine` method to write a line of text followed by a carriage-return linefeed pair to skip to the next line—note that you should enclose file operations, which are among the most error-prone of all programming operations, in a `Try`/`Catch` block—the exception file methods throw is `IOException`:

```
Private Sub Button1_Click(ByVal sender As System.Object, _
    ByVal e As System.EventArgs) Handles Button1.Click
    Dim fsStream As New FileStream("file.txt", FileMode.Create,
FileAccess.Write)
    Dim swWriter As New StreamWriter(fsStream)

    Try
        swWriter.WriteLine("Here is the text.")
        .
        .
        .
    Catch ex As IOException
        MsgBox(ex.Message)
    End Try
End Sub
```

You can also use the `StreamWriter` `Write` method to write text without an added carriage-return linefeed pair at the end of the line. You can add that carriage-return linefeed pair yourself with the `CrLf` member of the `ControlChars` enumeration. When you're done writing to a file, you use the Close method to close the file (which also writes any data to the file that was waiting in internal buffers and hadn't been written out yet):

```
Private Sub Button1_Click(ByVal sender As System.Object, _
    ByVal e As System.EventArgs) Handles Button1.Click
    Dim fsStream As New FileStream("file.txt", FileMode.Create, _
FileAccess.Write)
    Dim swWriter As New StreamWriter(fsStream)

    Try
        swWriter.WriteLine("Here is the text.")
        swWriter.Write("This text is stored in a file." & ControlChars.CrLf)
        swWriter.WriteLine("And now you can read it.")
        swWriter.Close()
        MsgBox("Wrote text data to the file.")
    Catch ex As IOException
        MsgBox(ex.Message)
    End Try
End Sub
```

That's it—you've written out text data to a file. So what about reading it back in? That's coming up next.

Reading Text with the StreamReader Class

You use the StreamReader class to read text data from files; here's the class hierarchy of this class:

```
System.Object
    System.MarshalByRefObject
        System.IO.TextReader
            System.IO.StreamReader
```

You can find the more significant public properties of the StreamReader class in Table 10.14 and the more significant methods of this class in Table 10.15.

TABLE 10.14   Significant Public Properties of StreamReader Objects

Property	Means
BaseStream	Holds the underlying stream, such as a FileStream object, giving you access to that stream's properties and methods.
CurrentEncoding	Gets the character encoding for the stream reader.

TABLE 10.15 Significant Public Methods of `StreamReader` Objects

Method	Means
Close	Closes the reader.
Peek	Peeks ahead and returns the next available character in the stream (but does not actually read that character as `Read` would, so does not advance the read/write position). Returns -1 if there is no more data waiting to be read.
Read	Reads the next character or characters.
ReadLine	Reads a line of text from the stream, returning that data as a string.
ReadToEnd	Reads from the current position in the stream to the end of the stream.

When the user clicks the Read File button in the StreamReadWrite example, we want to read the file that we just wrote back in. To do that, we can open the file we've written to, file.txt, with the `FileMode.Open` and `FileAccess.Read` items, and create a new `StreamReader` object corresponding to the file like this:

```
Private Sub Button2_Click(ByVal sender As System.Object, _
    ByVal e As System.EventArgs) Handles Button2.Click
    Dim fsStream As New FileStream("file.txt", FileMode.Open, FileAccess.Read)
    Dim srReader As New StreamReader(fsStream)
        .
        .
        .
End Sub
```

Now the file, represented by the `StreamReader` object `srReader`, is ready to be read from. We can read text from the file using the `StreamReader` `Read` method, which reads one character and returns that character.

There are also additional forms of the `Read` method. For example, you can also use an overloaded form of the `Read` method to read as many characters at once into an array of type `Char` like this: `Read(CharArray(), Index, Count)`, where *Index* indicates the character position at which to start reading, and *Count* is the number of characters you want to read. This form of the method returns the number of characters actually read.

You can also read a line of text at a time with the `StreamReader` `ReadLine` method, which is how we'll do it in the StreamReadWrite example. Here, we'll just keep reading lines of text until there are no more to read—something we can check with the `StreamReader` `Peek` method. This method returns the next character that will be read (but doesn't actually advance the position at which the next read operation will take place); if there's no more data to read, `Peek` will return -1. Here's how we can use `Peek` and `ReadLine` to read the data in file.txt and display it:

```
Private Sub Button2_Click(ByVal sender As System.Object, _
    ByVal e As System.EventArgs) Handles Button2.Click
    Dim fsStream As New FileStream("file.txt", FileMode.Open, FileAccess.Read)
    Dim srReader As New StreamReader(fsStream)

    Try
        While srReader.Peek() > -1
            TextBox1.Text &= srReader.ReadLine() & ControlChars.CrLf
        End While
        srReader.Close()
    Catch ex As IOException
        MsgBox(ex.Message)
    End Try
End Sub
```

And that's it—you can see the results in Figure 10.7, where the code reads in the text from the file we wrote and displays it in a text box. Now we're reading text data from a file. You can see the code for the StreamReadWrite example in Listing 10.4.

LISTING 10.4   Writing and Reading Text Files (StreamReadWrite Project, Form1.vb)

```
Imports System.IO
Public Class Form1
    Inherits System.Windows.Forms.Form

' Windows Form Designer generated code

    Private Sub Button1_Click(ByVal sender As System.Object, _
        ByVal e As System.EventArgs) Handles Button1.Click
        Dim fsStream As New FileStream("file.txt", _
            FileMode.Create, FileAccess.Write)
        Dim swWriter As New StreamWriter(fsStream)

        Try
            swWriter.WriteLine("Here is the text.")
            swWriter.Write("This text is stored in a file." & ControlChars.CrLf)
            swWriter.WriteLine("And now you can read it.")
            swWriter.Close()
            MsgBox("Wrote text data to the file.")
        Catch ex As IOException
            MsgBox(ex.Message)
        End Try
    End Sub

    Private Sub Button2_Click(ByVal sender As System.Object, _
        ByVal e As System.EventArgs) Handles Button2.Click
        Dim fsStream As New FileStream("file.txt", _
            FileMode.Open, FileAccess.Read)
```

Listing 10.4   continued

```
            Dim srReader As New StreamReader(fsStream)

            Try
                While srReader.Peek() > -1
                    TextBox1.Text &= srReader.ReadLine() & ControlChars.CrLf
                End While
                srReader.Close()
            Catch ex As IOException
                MsgBox(ex.Message)
            End Try
        End Sub
    End Class
```

New Term Here's something else to know about when you're writing to or reading from a file—you can use the `FileStream` `Seek` method to move to various locations in a file—this is called moving the read/write *position* or the read/write *pointer*. You can access the underlying `FileStream` object in a `StreamReader` or `StreamWriter` object with the `BaseStream` property, so to move to the beginning of a file, you can use this statement:

`srReader.BaseStream.Seek(0, SeekOrigin.Begin)`

You pass the `Seek` method a byte offset (which can be negative) and a member of the `SeekOrigin` enumeration to indicate where to measure the offset from:

- `SeekOrigin.Begin`—The beginning of the file
- `SeekOrigin.Current`—The current position (You can find the current position with the `FileStream` Position property.)
- `SeekOrigin.End`—The end of the file

New Term Using the `Seek` method allows you to break up a file into *records*, each of the same length. For example, if you're keeping track of 10,000 employees, you can create 10,000 records in a file, each with data on the corresponding employee. Because you know the length of each record, it's easy to move to the beginning of a specific record and read it in—or overwrite it with new data. This record-based way of doing things, in which you move around in a file and select the data you want, is called *random access*. The other form of file access, in which you must read or write data to a file one item after the other—and so much read through the first 2002 data items if you want to read the 2003th—is called *sequential access*.

Reading Binary Data with the `BinaryReader` Class

To work with binary (that is, the 0s and 1s that your data is stored as in your computer) files, you use the `BinaryReader` and `BinaryWriter` classes. Examples of binary files include image files, executable program files, database files, and so on—in fact, any file can be treated as a binary file. You can treat text files as binary files, of course, because they're made up of binary data just as any other files, but you would normally use the text handling streams already shown for text files because those streams offer methods to work with lines of text (such as `ReadLine`) that binary streams don't.

You can use the `BinaryWriter` class's `Write` method to write binary data to a file. To read it back, you can use the `BinaryReader` class's `Read` method. As before, you open a file with a `FileStream` object, and then pass that `FileStream` object to the `BinaryReader` or `BinaryWriter` class constructors.

We'll start by taking a look at the `BinaryReader` class. You can use this class to read binary data from files once you have a `FileStream` object; here's `BinaryReader`'s class hierarchy:

```
System.Object
   System.IO.BinaryReader
```

You can find the more significant public property of the `BinaryReader` class in Table 10.16 and the more significant methods in Table 10.17.

TABLE 10.16 Significant Public Property of `BinaryReader` Objects

Property	Means
BaseStream	Holds the underlying stream of the binary reader (such as a `FileStream` object), allowing you access to that stream's properties and methods.

TABLE 10.17 Significant Public Methods of `BinaryReader` Objects

Method	Means
Close	Closes the binary reader.
PeekChar	Peeks ahead and returns the next available character (but does not advance the read/write position).
Read	Reads characters from the stream and advances the current position of the stream.
ReadBoolean	Reads a Boolean from the stream.

TABLE 10.17 continued

Method	Means
ReadByte	Reads the next byte from the stream.
ReadBytes	Reads a number vof bytes from the stream into a byte array.
ReadChar	Reads the next character from the stream.
ReadChars	Reads a number of characters from the stream.
ReadDecimal	Reads a decimal value from the stream.
ReadDouble	Reads an 8-byte floating point value from the stream.
ReadInt16	Reads a 2-byte signed integer from the stream.
ReadInt32	Reads a 4-byte signed integer from the stream.
ReadInt64	Reads an 8-byte signed integer from the stream.
ReadSByte	Reads a signed byte from the stream.
ReadSingle	Reads a 4-byte floating point value from the stream.
ReadString	Reads a String from the current stream.
ReadUInt16	Reads a 2-byte unsigned integer from the stream.
ReadUInt32	Reads a 4-byte unsigned integer from the stream.
ReadUInt64	Reads an 8-byte unsigned integer from the stream.

Here's an example showing how to use the `BinaryReader` class—the BinaryStreamReadWrite example in the book's code. This example reads a binary file (such as the image.jpg file you've already seen in the ImageHandler example) and copies it, giving it the name "copied" and preserving the file's original extension. (For example, image.jpg will be copied to copied.jpg.)

You can see this example at work in Figure 10.8. There are two buttons—Read File, which displays an Open File dialog and reads the binary file's data into an array of bytes, and Write File, which writes that data back out to the copy of the original file.

FIGURE 10.8

Reading and writing a binary file.

Here's how the code works when you click the Read File button—the user specifies the name of a file to copy, and the code creates a new `FileStream` object for the selected file and uses that object to create a new `BinaryReader` object:

```
Imports System.IO

Public Class Form1
    Inherits System.Windows.Forms.Form

    'Windows Form Designer generated code

    Dim ByteArray() As Byte

    Private Sub Button1_Click(ByVal sender As System.Object, _
        ByVal e As System.EventArgs) Handles Button1.Click
        If OpenFileDialog1.ShowDialog = DialogResult.OK Then
            Try
                Dim fsStream As New FileStream(OpenFileDialog1.FileName, _
                    FileMode.Open, FileAccess.Read)
                Dim brReader As New BinaryReader(fsStream)
                .
                .
                .
            Catch ex As IOException
                MsgBox(ex.Message)
            End Try
        End If
    End Sub
```

Now you can use the `BinaryReader` `ReadBytes` method to read the entire binary file. How many bytes should you read? You can determine the length of the binary file with the `FileStream.Length` method, so here's how the code reads in the entire file and stores it in a byte array named `ByteArray`:

```
Dim ByteArray() As Byte

Private Sub Button1_Click(ByVal sender As System.Object, _
    ByVal e As System.EventArgs) Handles Button1.Click
    If OpenFileDialog1.ShowDialog = DialogResult.OK Then
        Try
            Dim fsStream As New FileStream(OpenFileDialog1.FileName, _
                FileMode.Open, FileAccess.Read)
            Dim brReader As New BinaryReader(fsStream)
            ByteArray = brReader.ReadBytes(fsStream.Length)
            brReader.Close()
            MsgBox("Read the file.")
```

10

```
        Catch ex As IOException
            MsgBox(ex.Message)
        End Try
    End If
End Sub
```

Now the entire binary file is stored in our byte array. The next step is to write that back out in a copy of the original file, and we'll do that with the `BinaryWriter` class.

Writing Binary Data with the `BinaryWriter` Class

When you have a `FileStream` object, you can use the `BinaryWriter` class to write binary data to a file. Here is the class hierarchy of the `BinaryWriter` class:

```
System.Object
    System.IO.BinaryWriter
```

You can find the more significant public property of the `BinaryWriter` class in Table 10.18 and the more significant methods of this class in Table 10.19.

TABLE 10.18   Significant Public Property of `BinaryWriter` Objects

Property	Means
BaseStream	Gets the underlying stream, such as a `FileStream` object, giving you access to that stream's properties and methods.

TABLE 10.19   Significant Public Methods of `BinaryWriter` Objects

Method	Means
Close	Closes the binary writer as well as the underlying stream.
Flush	Flushes the buffer of the binary writer and writes out any buffered data.
Seek	Sets the read/write position in the stream.
Write	Writes data to the stream.

When the user clicks the Write File button in the BinaryStreamReadWrite example, the code uses a `FileStream` object to create a new file named "copied" but with the same extension as the original file (so a .jpg file will remain a .jpg file and so on). Then it uses that object to create a new `BinaryWriter` object:

```
Private Sub Button2_Click(ByVal sender As System.Object, _
    ByVal e As System.EventArgs) Handles Button2.Click
    Try
        Dim strExtension As New String(OpenFileDialog1.FileName.Substring( _
            OpenFileDialog1.FileName.Length - 3, 3))
        Dim fsStream As FileStream = New FileStream("copied." & _
            strExtension, FileMode.Create)
        Dim bwWriter As BinaryWriter = New BinaryWriter(fsStream)
          .
          .
          .
    Catch ex As IOException
        MsgBox(ex.Message)
    End Try
End Sub
```

The code then uses the `BinaryWriter` `Write` method to write the entire byte array holding the copied data out to the file like this:

```
Private Sub Button2_Click(ByVal sender As System.Object, _
    ByVal e As System.EventArgs) Handles Button2.Click
    Try
        Dim strExtension As New String(OpenFileDialog1.FileName.Substring(
            OpenFileDialog1.FileName.Length - 3, 3))
        Dim fsStream As FileStream = New FileStream("copied." & _
            strExtension, FileMode.Create)
        Dim bwWriter As BinaryWriter = New BinaryWriter(fsStream)
        bwWriter.Write(ByteArray)
        bwWriter.Close()
        MsgBox("Wrote the copy.")
    Catch ex As IOException
        MsgBox(ex.Message)
    End Try
End Sub
```

And that's it; you've read a binary file and copied it. As you might recall, you can specify how many bytes to read with the `BinaryReader` `ReadBytes` method—and you can also specify how many bytes to write with the `BinaryWriter` `Write` method, as well as where to start writing from an array of bytes:

```
BinaryWriter.Write(buffer() As Byte, index As Integer, count As Integer)
```

Besides the `ReadBytes` method, the `BinaryReader` class also has a `Read` method. You can specify where in a byte array to start storing data, as well as how many bytes to read, as in this example:

```
Dim fs As FileStream = New FileStream("data.dat", FileMode.Open)
Dim brReader As BinaryReader = New BinaryReader(fs)
Dim buffer() As Byte
brReader.Read(buffer, 0, 1024)
```

10

In fact, the `BinaryReader` class also has other methods available—for example, you can declare integer variables as `Int32` (32-bit integers) in Visual Basic. And if you know you're reading in an `Int32` value, you can use the `BinaryReader` class's `ReadInt32` method. For `Double` values, you can use `ReadDouble`, for `Boolean` values, `ReadBoolean`, and so on. For example, here's how you can write three `Int32` values to a file and then read them back in with the `ReadInt32` method:

```
Dim fs As FileStream = New FileStream("data.dat", _
    FileMode.Create, FileAccess.Write)
Dim bwWriter As BinaryWriter = New BinaryWriter(fs)
Dim intArray() As Int32 = {1, 2, 3}

For intLoopIndex As Integer = 0 To 2
    bwWriter.Write(intArray(intLoopIndex))
Next

fs.Close()

Dim intArray2(2) As Int32

fs = New FileStream("data.dat", FileMode.Open, FileAccess.Read)
Dim brReader As BinaryReader = New BinaryReader(fs)
brReader.BaseStream.Seek(0, SeekOrigin.Begin)

For intLoopIndex As Integer = 0 To 2
    intArray(intLoopIndex) = brReader.ReadInt32()
Next

fs.Close()
```

Using the `File` and `Directory` Classes

The `File` and `Directory` classes let you work with files and directories in a simple way. For example, you've seen how to open a binary file and copy its contents into another binary file, but doing things byte by byte like that is the hard way. To copy a file, all you really need to do is use the `File` class's `Copy` method. The `File` class lets you work with files without even opening them, copying them, renaming them, and so on. The `Directory` class lets you work with directories, creating them, renaming them, and so on. And the methods you use with these two classes are class methods, which makes it even easier—you don't have to create a `File` or `Directory` object to work with these class's methods.

Here is the hierarchy for the `File` class (note that it's part of the `System.IO` namespace, which means that you have to use the `Imports System.IO` statement):

```
System.Object
    System.IO.File
```

You can find the significant public class methods of this class in Table 10.20.

TABLE 10.20 Significant Public Class Methods of the `File` Class

Method	Means
AppendText	Appends text to a file or creates the file if it does not exist.
Copy	Copies a file to a new file.
Create	Creates a file.
CreateText	Creates a `StreamWriter` object, which writes a new text file.
Delete	Deletes a file.
Exists	Determines whether a file exists.
GetAttributes	Gets the file attributes of a file.
GetCreationTime	Gets a file's date and time.
GetLastAccessTime	Gets the date and time a file was last accessed.
GetLastWriteTime	Gets the date and time a file was last written.
Move	Moves a file to a new location.
Open	Opens a `FileStream` object for the file.
OpenRead	Creates a read-only file.
OpenText	Creates a `StreamReader` object, which reads from a text file.
OpenWrite	Creates a read/write stream for a file.
SetAttributes	Sets file attributes for a file.
SetCreationTime	Sets a file's creation date and time.
SetLastAccessTime	Sets a file's last access date and time.
SetLastWriteTime	Sets a file's last written date and time.

10

The `Directory` class lets you create, edit, and delete folders, as well as maintain the drives on your system. Here is the hierarchy of this class:

```
System.Object
    System.IO.Directory
```

You can find the public class methods of this class in Table 10.21.

TABLE 10.21 Significant Public Class Methods of the `Directory` Class

Method	Means
CreateDirectory	Creates a directory.
Delete	Deletes a directory (and the directory's contents).
Exists	True if a directory exists.
GetCreationTime	Returns a directory's creation date and time.
GetCurrentDirectory	Returns the current directory (that is, the default directory).
GetDirectories	Returns the directories in the current directory.
GetDirectoryRoot	Returns the root part of a path.
GetFiles	Returns the files in a directory.
GetFileSystemEntries	Returns the file system entries for a path.
GetLastAccessTime	Returns the date and time a directory was last accessed.
GetLastWriteTime	Returns the date and time a directory was last written.
GetLogicalDrives	Returns the names of the computer's logical drives.
GetParent	Returns the parent directory.
Move	Moves a directory (including its contents).
SetCreationTime	Sets a directory's creation time.
SetCurrentDirectory	Sets the current directory.
SetLastAccessTime	Sets a directory's last accessed date and time.
SetLastWriteTime	Sets a directory's last written-to date and time.

For example, to create the new directory whose name the user has entered into a text box, you could use the `Directory` class's `CreateDirectory` method like this:

```
Imports System.IO
    .
    .
    .
Try
    Directory.CreateDirectory(TextBox1.Text)
Catch
    MsgBox("Could not create the directory.")
    End
End Try

MsgBox("Directory was created.")
```

You can find an example showing how to use the `File` class's `Copy` method to copy a file in the FileCopy example in the code for this book. When the user clicks the Copy a File button, an Open File dialog appears, and the user can select a file to copy. When he clicks OK, the code copies the file, giving it the name "copy" (instead of "copied", which the previous example used, to avoid file-name conflicts) and the same extension as the original had. You use the Copy method in code like this:

```
File.Copy(sourceFileName As String, _
targetFileName As String)
```

Note that this version of the Copy method can only create a new copy of a file if the target filename doesn't already exist. If it does, use this version and set the *overwrite* argument to True to allow overwriting of the target file:

```
File.Copy(sourceFileName As String, _
targetFileName As String, overwrite As Boolean)
```

Here's how this looks in code, in the FileCopy example, where we display an Open File dialog and let the user copy a file (the copy will be placed in the same directory as the original in this code):

```
Private Sub Button1_Click(ByVal sender As System.Object, _
    ByVal e As System.EventArgs) Handles Button1.Click
    Try
        If OpenFileDialog1.ShowDialog = DialogResult.OK Then
            Dim strExtension As New String(_
                OpenFileDialog1.FileName.Substring(_
                    OpenFileDialog1.FileName.Length - 3, 3))
            File.Copy(OpenFileDialog1.FileName, "copy." & strExtension)
        End If
    Catch
        MsgBox("Could not copy the file.")
        Exit Sub
    End Try
    MsgBox("Copied the file.")
End Sub
```

You can see this example at work in Figure 10.9, where it has just finished copying a file.

And that finished our file handling for today—more is coming up in Day 16, "Handling Databases with ADO.NET," when we start working with databases.

10

FIGURE 10.9

Copying a file.

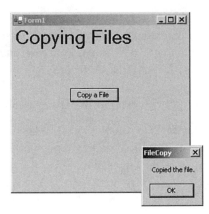

Summary

Today, you've seen a great deal about two topics—graphics and file handling. We started with graphics work based on the `Graphics` object, which corresponds to a drawing surface. You saw that there are several ways to get a `Graphics` object to draw in.

We used the Artist example application to let the user draw various figures using the mouse. You saw how to draw ellipses, rectangles, lines, even how to draw freehand.

You also saw how to handle images using `Image` objects and the `Graphics` `DrawImage` method. In particular, we took a look at drawing images in a picture box (although the same techniques apply to any object you can get a `Graphics` object for), scrolling an image as needed to display the whole image.

You can draw text with the `Graphics` `DrawText` method, and you saw how to do that today, creating `Font` objects and drawing text in various sizes and colors.

The second half of today's work was about working with files. Today, the basis of our file handling was the `FileStream` class, which lets you work with both text-oriented and binary files.

You saw that there are various ways to open a file with the `FileStream` constructor—you can set the file mode, file access, and sharing mode when you open or create files.

You saw how to use the `StreamReader` and `StreamWriter` classes to open, write to, read, and close text files. And you saw how to use the `BinaryReader` and `BinaryWriter` classes to work with binary files.

Finally, you saw that the `File` and `Directory` classes give you access to working with files and directories without even opening them, copying and renaming files, creating directories, and more.

Tomorrow, we're going to begin working with a big topic in Visual Basic .NET—Web forms.

Q&A

Q **How can I determine the red, green, and blue color values of a color as represented by a `Color` object?**

A In fact, there is a way—you can use the `Color` object's `R`, `G`, and `B` (read-only) members.

Q **How can I make sure that what I write to a file is written at the end of the file's current contents? And how can I open a file if it exists—but create it if it doesn't?**

A To append data to the end of a file's current contents, use the file mode `FileMode.Append` when opening the file. To open a file if it exists, or to create it otherwise, use `FileMode.OpenOrCreate`.

10

Workshop

This workshop tests whether you understand the concepts you saw today. It's a good idea to make sure that you can answer these questions before pressing on to tomorrow's work.

Quiz

1. Name the three major parts of GDI+.

2. List three ways to get a `Graphics` object in code.

3. How can you draw a red rectangle that extends from location (1, 1) to (31, 31) in a form?

4. How can you open an existing file and indicate that you want to write over its present contents?

5. After reading from a file and before closing it, how can you move back to the beginning of the file?

Quiz Answers

1. 2D vector graphics, imaging, and typography.

2. You can use the `Control` class's `CreateGraphics` method. You can get a `Graphics` object in the event handler for a control or form's `Paint` event. And you can pass a Windows handle (accessible from a form or control's `Handle` property) to the `FromHwnd` class method of the `Graphics` class.

3. After getting a `Graphics` object for the form, you can use the statement `Graphics.DrawRectangle(Pens.Red, 1, 1, 31 ,31)`. (The last two items are the rectangle's width and height.)

4. Open it with the file mode `FileMode.Truncate`.

5. You can use a statement such as `srReader.BaseStream.Seek(0, SeekOrigin.Begin)`.

Exercises

1. Augment the Artist application to let the user draw polygons with five vertices (points) when the user clicks five locations in the form. To do that, just add a new button, Polygon; keep track of the next five mouse clicks in an array of `Point` objects, `ptArray`; and then call the `Graphics` method `DrawPolygon(Pen, ptArray)`.

2. Write an application that checks a text file the user specifies for a text string that he also specifies—that is, let the user search text files for a match to a string. (**Extra credit**: Use an Open File dialog to let the user specify multiple text files to search.)

PART III

In Review

In-Depth Programming with Visual Basic .NET

In Part III, we took a look at some in-depth programming, covering object-oriented programming, graphics, and file handling. That's a lot to cover in two days work, and we packed in the topics.

In Day 9, we took a look at OOP in Visual Basic .NET, starting with an overview of the OOP concepts—abstraction, encapsulation, inheritance, and polymorphism. We saw how to create our own classes and how to create objects from those classes. We also took a look at using access modifiers, such as public, protected, and private.

To initialize the data in these objects, we took a look at writing constructors; in Visual Basic .NET, you give a constructor the name New and pass it data you want to store in a new object. We also took a look at creating destructors, which let you clean up after objects.

You saw how to create class (shared) data members and methods and how to use them, as well as how to create and support events. And you saw how to support public, protected, and private inheritance, overriding base class members, inheriting constructors, creating interfaces, using Friend access, as well as creating abstract classes.

You also got a good foundation in working with inheritance in Visual Basic .NET, seeing the extensive OOP support available, using keywords such as MustOverride, Overridable, MyBase, MyClass and NotOverridable, as well as supporting shadowing. And you saw how to support inheritance-based and interface-based polymorphism, as well as early and late binding.

In Day 10, we took a look at the `Graphics` class, the basis for graphics work in Visual Basic .NET, and you saw how to use it to draw figures, including lines, rectangles, ellipses, and so on, as well as how to draw text and handle images. We took a look at some advanced graphics work, and you saw how to scroll images in picture boxes.

We also took a look at working with files in Day 10, using the `FileStream` class, opening and closing files, setting file modes, access, and sharing options. You saw how to write to and read from files in various ways, as well as using the `File` and `Directory` classes to manipulate files without even opening them.

As you can see, we did indeed pack a lot into the previous two days. These days gave us a lot of the basic skills needed in the infrastructure of Visual Basic .NET programming. When you develop large-scale programs, for example, you should automatically think in terms of objects to compartmentalize your code.

Let's take a brief look at an example that sums up some of the programming you saw in Part III. If you can follow what's going on here without trouble, you're up to speed on Part III and ready to move on. In this example, we'll create a class named `Display` that will encapsulate an object of the `Graphics` class and draw lines as you direct it to do. You can see an object of this class at work in Figure P3.1; when the user clicks the button, an object of the `Display` class draws the line you see in that figure.

FIGURE P3.1

Using the `Display`
class.

Here's how you use the `Display` class—when the form first loads, we create a new object of that class. This new object will need to draw in the form, so we pass its constructor a `Graphics` object corresponding to the form:

```
Dim displayer As Display
```

```
Private Sub Form1_Load(ByVal sender As System.Object, _
    ByVal e As System.EventArgs) Handles MyBase.Load
    displayer = New Display(Me.CreateGraphics())
End Sub
```

You set the end points of the line to draw with the Display object's FromPoint and ToPoint properties. Then you draw the line by calling the Display object's DrawLine method:

```
Private Sub Button1_Click(ByVal sender As System.Object, _
    ByVal e As System.EventArgs) Handles Button1.Click
    displayer.FromPoint = New Point(50, 100)
    displayer.ToPoint = New Point(250, 100)
    displayer.DrawLine()
End Sub
```

And that's it for using the Display class—all that's left is to write this class itself. That's not difficult—all we need is a constructor that stores the Graphics object we've been passed, the FromPoint and ToPoint properties to store the end points of the line to draw, and the DrawLine method to actually draw the line. Here's the code we need:

```
Public Class Display
    Dim gphFormGraphics As Graphics
    Dim Point1, Point2 As Point

    Public Sub New(ByVal g As Graphics)
        gphFormGraphics = g
    End Sub

    Public Property FromPoint() As Point
        Get
            Return Point1
        End Get
        Set(ByVal Value As Point)
            Point1 = Value
        End Set
    End Property

    Public Property ToPoint() As Point
        Get
            Return Point2
        End Get
        Set(ByVal Value As Point)
            Point2 = Value
        End Set
    End Property
```

```
Public Sub DrawLine()
    gphFormGraphics.DrawLine(System.Drawing.Pens.Black, Point1, Point2)
End Sub
```

End Class

You can see the results in Figure P3.1—when you create an object of the Display class, you pass it the Graphics object it needs. Then all you need to do is to set the FromPoint and ToPoint properties and call DrawLine. In this way, you've encapsulated the drawing aspects of your program into an object, compartmentalizing your code. And the Display class is ready to base other classes on, such as one that might draw rectangles or cross-hatch shading, which can make use of the DrawLine method they inherit from the Display class.

This is a relatively simple example of what we've seen in the previous two days, but if you're up to speed on this code, you're ready to turn to the next part of this book. In that part, we're going to start some Web programming.

PART IV

At a Glance

Creating Web Applications in Visual Basic .NET

In Part IV, the Web will be our arena as we create Web applications. We'll see how to work with Web forms, how to understand special considerations needed to handle events, and how to preserve data across server round-trips. We'll see how to support all the Web server controls available in our Web forms—text boxes, labels, check boxes, radio buttons, list boxes, hyperlinks, link buttons, and many more. We'll also see how to validate the data the user enters into a Web form in a browser before sending it back to the server, and even how to use ad rotators to display banner ads in Web pages.

11

12

13

14

15

DAY 11

Creating Web Forms with ASP.NET

Today, we'll start our investigation of Web applications—Web applications make up one of the biggest parts of Visual Basic .NET, because they let you create distributed Web applications. We're going to take a look at the very core of Web applications today—Web forms—and in the following days, we'll put Web forms to work by adding and handling the various Web controls available to you in Visual Basic .NET. An amazing amount of programming power is coming up in the next few days; here are some of today's topics:

- Creating Web applications
- Using Web forms
- The `System.Web.UI.Page` class
- Using server and client controls
- Understanding event handling
- Saving program data across server round-trips
- Navigating to other forms

- Redirecting browsers
- Detecting browser type and capabilities
- Supporting client-side programming with JavaScript

We'll get started creating Web applications immediately.

Creating Web Applications

Web applications are based on the ASP.NET protocol. (ASP stands for Active Server Pages, Microsoft's software that runs on the server and lets you create HTML to send back to the browser.) You don't have to know a lot of ASP in order to create Web applications, and that's the beauty of it—Visual Basic .NET will handle the details for you. Even though you're creating an application on the Internet, the development process feels just as though you're writing a Windows application. Visual Basic .NET even handles the uploading of your code to the Web server for you.

To create Web applications, you'll need an accessible computer that has Microsoft Internet Information Services (IIS) version 5.0 or later installed. IIS must be running on a Windows machine with the .NET framework installed so that your Visual Basic code can run. For development purposes, you can use IIS locally if you install it on the same machine on which you develop programs (IIS comes preinstalled in some Windows operating systems such as Windows 2000 Server, and it comes on the CDs for other systems such as Windows 2000 Professional).

Web Forms

NEW TERM   Web applications are designed to run in browsers, not in the standard Windows forms you've seen up to this point. Web applications are based on *Web forms*, which are designed to appear in Web browsers. However, as far as the actual development in the IDE goes, Web forms look and act very much like Windows forms, as you will see.

> **Tip**   The Web forms you create don't have to run in Microsoft's Internet Explorer. (But if they don't, a number of features are usually disabled because they need the Internet Explorer to work.)

In fact, developing a Web application is very similar to developing a Windows application (and that was Microsoft's intent). You can still make use of all that the Visual Basic IDE already offers, such as drag-and-drop development, IntelliSense prompts, what-you-see-is-what-you-get visual interface, project management, and so on. When you create a new Web application, a default Web form is added to the project, just as a Windows form is added to Windows projects. And you can populate that Web form with various controls—Web controls, not Windows controls. You can add Web controls to Web forms just as you can with Windows controls in Windows applications, but Web controls take a little more understanding. In fact, there are different types of Web controls—those that run on the server, and those that run in the client (the browser).

Web Server Controls

Web server controls are designed to look and act similar to the Visual Basic controls you already know from Windows programming. They don't run in the browser, but in the server. This means that when an event occurs, the browser has to send the Web page back to the server. Your Visual Basic .NET code on the server will handle the event. Things work this way because Web browsers differ greatly in their capabilities and in order to give you a more controlled—and powerful—programming environment for Web applications; you can run your code back on the server.

However, sending the whole Web page back to the server slows down things, so Microsoft has restricted the number of type of events you can work with. Most Web server controls can only handle Click events, for example, and you'll find that Web forms don't handle mouse events such as MouseMove and so forth—the continual round-trips to the server would be just too time-consuming.

In fact, there's another compromise here—many controls, such as list boxes, don't even send their events back to the server automatically. Instead, their events are handled when the whole page is next sent back to the server. There is a way, however, to force these controls to send the whole Web page back to the server for event handling each time an event in them occurs—you can set the control's AutoPostBack property to True (more on this when we create our first Web application today).

To add Web controls to a Web form, you select the Web Forms tab in the toolbox. The advantage of Web server controls is that you can use Visual Basic code with them because their code runs on the server. This means that the Visual Basic programming you've already seen applies here too. To be able to run in Web browsers, Web server controls are actually made up of standard HTML controls (the type you see as you surf the Web). But because Visual Basic often demands more functionality from a control than HTML controls can give, Web server controls are sometimes made up of a combination of standard HTML controls.

11

You can find the Web server controls—many of which you'll recognize from Windows forms—in Table 11.1.

TABLE 11.1 Web Server Controls

Control	Action
Label	Creates a label control.
TextBox	Creates a text box control.
DropDownList	Allows users to select items from a list or enter text directly.
ListBox	Creates a list box control.
Image	Displays an image.
AdRotator	Displays ad banners.
CheckBox	Creates a check box control.
CheckBoxList	Supports a group of check boxes.
RadioButton	Creates a radio button control.
RadioButtonList	Supports a group of radio buttons.
Calendar	Displays a calendar for choosing dates.
Button	Creates a button control.
LinkButton	Creates a button that looks like a hyperlink.
ImageButton	Creates a button that displays an image.
HyperLink	Displays a hyperlink.
Table	Creates an HTML table.
TableCell	Creates a cell in an HTML table.
TableRow	Creates a row in an HTML table.
Panel	Creates a panel control.
Repeater	Creates a data control that displays information from a data set using HTML elements.
DataList	Displays data with more formatting options than a Repeater control.
DataGrid	Displays data in a table of columns.

You will become familiar with the Web server controls in Table 11.1 in the coming days—their names are the same as many Windows controls, but how they work and how you handle them in code is often quite different.

HTML Server Controls

Visual Basic .NET gives you a lot of power with the Web server controls, but Microsoft also realizes that Web surfing users might expect to find the standard HTML controls that they normally see in Web pages in your Web application. For that reason, Visual Basic .NET also supports the standard HTML controls such as HTML text fields (in HTML, text boxes are called *text fields*) and HTML buttons. When you want to add these controls to a Web form, you use the HTML tab in the toolbox.

NEW TERM You can turn standard HTML controls into *HTML server controls* whose events are handled back at the server. To do that, you right-click a control and select the Run As Server Control item. When you do, you can handle such HTML server controls in Visual Basic code in your program by connecting event handling code just as you would in Windows forms.

You can find the HTML server controls in Table 11.2.

TABLE 11.2   HTML Server Controls

Control	Action
HtmlForm	Creates an HTML form.
HtmlInputText	Creates an HTML text field. (You can also use this control to create password fields).
HtmlTextArea	Creates an HTML text area (two-dimensional text field).
HtmlAnchor	Creates an <a> element for navigation.
HtmlButton	Creates an HTML button using the <button> element.
HtmlInputButton	Creates an HTML button using the <input> element.
HtmlInputImage	Creates an HTML button that displays images.
HtmlSelect	Creates an HTML select control.
HtmlImage	Creates an HTML <img> element.
HtmlInputHidden	Creates an HTML hidden control.
HtmlInputCheckbox	Creates an HTML check box.
HtmlInputRadioButton	Creates an HTML radio button.
HtmlTable	Creates an HTML table.
HtmlTableRow	Creates an HTML row in a table.
HtmlTableCell	Creates an HTML cell in a table.
HtmlInputFile	Creates an HTML file upload control.
HtmlGenericControl	Creates a basic control for an HTML element.

11

HTML Client Controls

NEW TERM When you add an HTML control to a Web form from the HTML tab in the tool-box, that control is a standard HTML control, called an *HTML client control* in Visual Basic .NET, which means that its code runs in the browser, not on the server. If you right-click the control and select the Run As Server Control item, the control will be turned into an HTML server control and will be handled in the server. (And you can add Visual Basic code to handle the control's events as you would any other Visual Basic control.) If you don't turn the control into an HTML server control, however, it will remain an HTML client control.

HTML client controls are handled in the browser out of the reach of Visual Basic code. If you handle events in the Web client—the browser—instead of the server, the whole page doesn't have to make the round-trip to the server, which saves a lot of time. Because these controls run in the browser, just as any other such controls in a Web page, you have to program them with a language the browser understands, such as JavaScript.

You do that with the Visual Basic HTML editor, which allows you to edit the HTML of the Web page directly; you will see a quick example showing how this works today.

Validation Controls

NEW TERM Another type of control is available to you in addition to Web server controls, HTML server controls, and HTML client controls. You can also use *validation controls* in Web forms.

A validation control lets you test a user's input—for example, you can make sure that the user has entered text into a text field. You can also perform more complex tests, such as comparing what's been entered against a pattern of characters or numbers to make sure that things are in the right format. You can find the validation controls in Table 11.3.

TABLE 11.3   Validation Controls

Control	Action
RequiredFieldValidator	Makes sure that the user enters data in this field.
CompareValidator	Uses comparison operators to compare user entered data to a constant value.
RangeValidator	Makes sure that user entered data in a range between given lower and upper boundaries.
RegularExpressionValidator	Makes sure that user entered data matches a regular-expression pattern.
CustomValidator	Makes sure user entered data passes validation criteria that you set yourself.

Know Your HTML

Web applications run in Web browsers. Although Visual Basic lets you do a great deal with them using the Visual Basic techniques you've already learned, sooner or later, you'll probably want to work directly with the HTML in a Web application. You might want to customize a Web form, or you might want to add some client-side programming—after all, your application uses pure HTML to interact with the browser. If you're going to work with Web applications in the long run, you should know both HTML and some scripting language that can run in a browser, such as JavaScript.

You don't have to be an expert in these topics for the work we'll do today and in the next few days, but some knowledge of HTML will help. For example, you should know enough to realize that what follows is an HTML *element* made up of an opening *tag*, text content, and a closing tag that displays its text as an H1 header:

```
<H1>No Troubles!</H1>
```

You should also know a little about the standard HTML controls, such as this HTML text field named Text1 and sized to display 20 characters:

```
<INPUT TYPE= "TEXT" NAME = "Text1" SIZE = "20">
```

For reference, you'll find the HTML 4.01 (the current version of HTML) tags in Table 11.4. The formal definition of HTML 4.01 can be found at http://www.w3.org/TR/REC-html40/.

11

TABLE 11.4 HTML 4.01 Tags

Tag	Use For
<! -->	Indicating HTML comments.
<!doctype>	Starting an HTML page.
<a>	Creating a hyperlink or anchor.
<abbr>	Displaying abbreviations.
<acronym>	Displaying acronyms.
<address>	Displaying an address.
<applet>	Embedding applets in Web pages.
<area>	Creating clickable regions in image maps.
<b>	Creating bold text.
<base>	Setting a base for hyperlinks.
<basefont>	Setting a base font.
<bdo>	Overriding the bidirectional character algorithm.
<bgsound>	Adding background sounds.

TABLE 11.4 continued

Tag	Use For
<big>	Creating big text.
<blink>	Making text blink.
<blockquote>	Indenting quotations.
<body>	Creating a Web page's body.
 	Inserting line breaks.
<button>	Creating a customizable button.
<caption>	Creating a table caption.
<center>	Centering text.
<cite>	Creating a citation.
<code>	Displaying program code.
<col>	Defining a column.
<colgroup>	Grouping and formatting columns.
<dd>	Creating definition list definitions.
<del>	Displaying text as deleted.
<dfn>	Defining new terms.
<dir>	Deprecated list.
<div>	Formatting block text.
<dl>	Creating definition lists.
<dt>	Creating definition list terms.
<em>	Emphasizing text.
<embed>	Embedding multimedia and plug-ins in a Web page.
<fieldset>	Grouping form elements.
<font>	Specifying a font.
<form>	Creating HTML forms.
<frame>	Creating a frame.
<frameset>	Creating frames.
<h1> through <h6>	Creating Web page headings.
<head>	Creating a Web page's head.
<hr>	Creating horizontal rules.
<html>	Starting an HTML page.
<i>	Creating italic text.
<iframe>	Creating inline or floating frames.
<ilayer>	Creating inline layers.

TABLE 11.4   continued

Tag	Use For
`<img>`	Displaying an image in a Web page.
`<input type="button">`	Creating buttons.
`<input type="checkbox">`	Creating check boxes.
`<input type="file">`	Creating file input for a form.
`<input type="hidden">`	Creating hidden data.
`<input type="image">`	Creating image submit buttons.
`<input type="password">`	Creating password controls.
`<input type="radio">`	Creating radio buttons.
`<input type="reset">`	Creating reset buttons.
`<input type="submit">`	Creating submit buttons.
`<input type="text">`	Creating text fields.
`<ins>`	Displaying inserted text.
`<isindex>`	Using an index.
`<kbd>`	Displaying text the user is to type.
`<keygen>`	Processing secure transactions.
`<label>`	Labeling form elements.
`<layer>`	Arranging text in layers.
`<legend>`	Creating a legend for form elements.
`<li>`	Creating list items.
`<link>`	Setting link information.
`<map>`	Creating client-side image maps.
`<marquee>`	Displaying text in a scrolling marquee.
`<menu>`	Indicating a form of list.
`<meta>`	Including more information about your Web page.
`<multicol>`	Creating columns.
`<nobr>`	Avoiding line breaks.
`<noembed>`	Handling browsers that don't handle embedding.
`<nolayer>`	Handling browsers that don't handle layers.
`<noscript>`	Handling browsers that don't handle JavaScript.
`<object>`	Placing an object into a Web page.
`<ol>`	Creating ordered lists.
`<optgroup>`	Creating a Select control item group.
`<option>`	Creating a Select control item.

11

TABLE 11.4 continued

Tag	Use For
`<p>`	Creating paragraphs.
`<param>`	Specify a parameter.
`<pre>`	Displaying preformatted text.
`<q>`	Displaying short quotations.
`<rt>`	Creating ruby text.
`<ruby>`	Creating rubies (annotation).
`<s>` and `<strike>`	Striking out text.
`<samp>`	Displaying sample program output.
`<script>`	Creating a script.
`<select>`	Creating a `Select` control.
`<server>`	Running server-side JavaScript scripts.
`<small>`	Creating small text.
`<spacer>`	Controlling horizontal and vertical spacing.
`<span>`	Formatting inline text.
`<strong>`	Strongly emphasizing text.
`<style>`	Using embedded style sheets.
`<sub>`	Creating subscripts.
`<sup>`	Creating superscripts.
`<table>`	Creating a table.
`<tbody>`	Create a table body and grouping rows.
`<td>`	Creating table data.
`<textarea>`	Creating text areas.
`<tfoot>`	Creating a table foot when grouping rows.
`<th>`	Creating table headings.
`<thead>`	Creating a table head when grouping rows.
`<title>`	Giving a Web page a title.
`<tr>`	Creating a table row.
`<tt>`	Creating "teletype" text.
`<u>`	Underlining text.
`<ul>`	Creating unordered lists.
`<var>`	Displaying program variables and arguments.
`<wbr>`	Allowing word breaks.
`<xml>`	Accessing XML data with an XML data island.

Now let's put what you've learned to work as we create our first Web application.

Creating a Web Application

As discussed, you need more than Visual Studio to create a Web form—you need to be able to interact with an installation of Microsoft's Internet Information Server (IIS) running on the target server (which must also have the .NET framework installed). Visual Basic .NET will create the files you need and upload them directly on the server when you create the Web application (usually in the IIS directory named wwwroot).

Here's where things get familiar again. To create a new Web application, select the File, New menu item in Visual Basic, just as you would to create a new Windows application. This time, however, select the ASP.NET Web Application icon, as shown in Figure 11.1. This first application will be called FirstWeb (our first Windows application was called FirstWin) in the code for this book.

FIGURE 11.1

Creating a Web application.

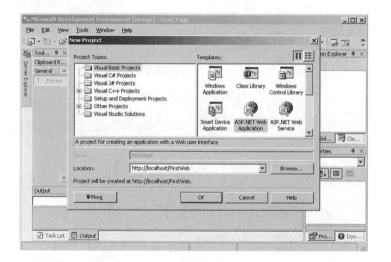

In the Location box you see in Figure 11.1, enter the location and name of the new application. In this case, FirstWeb will be developed locally, using IIS on the local computer. When you run IIS on the local computer, its URL is http://localhost. So the location of our new application, as you see entered into the Location box, is http://localhost/FirstWeb. For applications on the Internet, that URL might look something like this: http://www.starpowder.com/FirstWeb. (If you're unsure how to reach your server, click the Browse button next to the Location box as shown in Figure 11.1.) After filling in the Location box, create the new Web application by clicking the OK button.

Tip

> To open a Web application that you've already created, use the File, Open
> Project From Web menu item (not the File, Open menu item). Visual Basic will
> ask for the URL of the server to use, and then open the Open Project dialog.

By default, a new Web form is automatically added to the new Web application, and that
Web application opens in the Visual Basic IDE, as you see in Figure 11.2.

FIGURE 11.2

*A Web application
under design.*

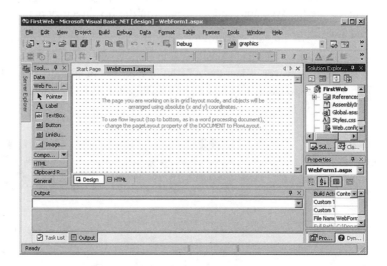

You'll also see some new files in the Solution Explorer; here's an overview of what
they do:

- *AssemblyInfo.vb*—Contains information about your assembly, such as assembly
  version.
- *Global.asax*—Handles application level ASP requests.
- *Styles.css*—Contains the Cascading Style Sheet (CSS) styles for the Web form.
  This is an important file when you want to start to customize your Web application's appearance in the browser because it sets the styles of all the HTML elements used. If you take a look at Styles.css, you'll see the style specification
  (including font, font weight, and so on) for many HTML elements. Before working
  with this file, you should have a good acquaintance with CSS. (You can find the
  official definition of CSS at http://www.w3.org/TR/REC-CSS1 and http://www.
  w3.org/TR/REC-CSS2/.)

- *Web.config*—Contains data on how the server will handle your project. You can set options for tracing, security, and permission here, including how to make sure that no one can download your code from the server. This file is written in XML (Extensible Markup Language), which is the language that handles much of the data transfer going on behind the scenes in Web applications. You will see more on XML in the days to come. (You can find the official definition of XML at `http://www.w3.org/TR/REC-xml`.)

- *Projectname.vsdisco*—A "discovery" file, which is an XML file that contains data about an ASP.NET Web application.

- *WebForm.aspx*—Supports Web form itself.

Working with Web Forms

NEW TERM   You can see the new Web form in the middle of Figure 11.2. The text in the Web form indicates that Web form is in *grid layout mode*, which means that you can position controls where you want them in the Web form, just as you would in a Windows form.

NEW TERM   You can set the Web form's layout yourself using the `pageLayout` property. Besides the grid layout mode, the other option is *flow layout*—the layout for controls that browsers normally use. With flow layout, the controls you add to a Web form "flow," much as the words in a word processor's page, changing position when the page changes size. To anchor your controls where you want them, use grid layout.

Now that you've got the Web form open in the Visual Basic IDE, you can customize it much as you'd customize a Windows form. For example, you can set the Web form's background color using the properties window—but this time, use the `bgColor` property, which is the HTML property you'll see in Web pages that corresponds to the `BackColor` property of Windows forms. When you're customizing a Web form, the Properties window will display the HTML properties of the form you can work with. You can also set the foreground color (that is, the default color of text) used in Web forms and HTML pages with the `text` property, mirroring the attribute of the same name in HTML pages.

Colors such as the ones you assign to the `bgColor` and `text` properties are HTML colors, which can be specified in two ways: by using a color name (such as "Red," "Blue," or "Magenta", using predefined color names supported by the browser), or by using numbers to denote an RGB color value. In HTML, an RGB color value is made up of three two-digit hexadecimal (base 16) numbers (range: 0 to 255, which is to say #00 to #FF in hexadecimal, where # indicates a hexadecimal number) specifying the intensity of the

11

corresponding color, in this form: "*#RRGGBB*," where *RR* is the red color value, *GG* is the green color value, and *BB* is the blue color value. For example, "#FFFFFF" is pure white, "#000000" pure black, "#FF0000" is pure red, magenta is "#FF00FF," maroon is "#800000," and so on. Note also that when you select a property that can be set to a color in the Properties window, a color picker dialog opens automatically, allowing you to easily set colors at design time.

You can also set the text in the browser's title bar when the Web form is being displayed using the `title` property. And you can set the size of the page margins surrounding the content in a Web form and other HTML pages with these properties (measured in pixels):

- `rightMargin`—Sets the right margin.
- `leftMargin`—Sets the left margin.
- `topMargin`—Sets the top margin.
- `bottomMargin`—Sets the bottom margin.

As in other Web pages, you can set the background image used in Web forms and HTML pages, using the `background` property. You can set this property to the URL of an image at runtime. Or, at design time, you can browse to an image file to assign to this property.

The Web form itself, WebForm1.aspx, stores the actual HTML that browsers will see. You can see that HTML directly if you click the HTML button at the bottom of the Web form designer (next to the Design button), as you see in Figure 11.3.

FIGURE 11.3

Using the HTML view.

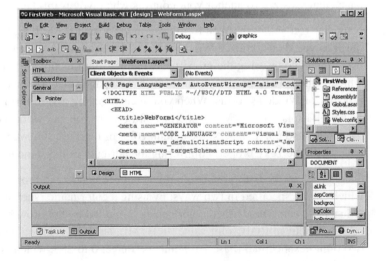

This is the HTML that a Web browser will see, and you can edit this HTML directly (which we'll do later in this chapter). Note the ASP directives in this document, which begin here with <%@ and <asp:. These ASP directives will be executed by IIS, which will create HTML from them; that's what is sent to the browser. That's how ASP works: ASP directives are executed in the server, creating the HTML corresponding to the various ASP commands. That HTML is what the browser actually sees.

You can see WebForm1.aspx looks like in Listing 11.1—as you can see, this is just standard HTML, with ASP directives embedded in it for IIS. (Note in particular the Codebehind attribute, which connects this code to the appropriate Visual Basic code.)

LISTING 11.1 WebForm1.aspx (FirstWeb Project)

```
<%@ Page Language="vb" AutoEventWireup="false" _
    Codebehind="WebForm1.aspx.vb" Inherits="FirstWeb.WebForm1"%>
<!DOCTYPE HTML PUBLIC "-//W3C//DTD HTML 4.0 Transitional//EN">
<HTML>
  <HEAD>
    <title>WebForm1</title>
    <meta name="GENERATOR" content="Microsoft Visual Studio .NET 7.1">
    <meta name="CODE_LANGUAGE" content="Visual Basic .NET 7.1">
    <meta name=vs_defaultClientScript content="JavaScript">
    <meta name=vs_targetSchema content=
        "http://schemas.microsoft.com/intellisense/ie5">
  </HEAD>
  <body MS_POSITIONING="GridLayout">

    <form id="Form1" method="post" runat="server">

    </form>

  </body>
</HTML>
```

This is the page that's sent to the browser, and it doesn't look much like the Visual Basic code we've been working with so far. That Visual Basic code will appear in the server-side "code-behind" file, WebForm1.aspx.vb, which is specifically designed to hold the Visual Basic code in Web applications.

Now that we've got a Web form, how about adding a few controls?

Adding Controls to a Web Form

You can add controls to a Web form just as you can with Windows forms. In this case, we'll use Web server controls, so click the Web Forms tab in the toolbox, making the Web server controls appear in the toolbox, as you see in Figure 11.4.

11

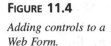

FIGURE 11.4

*Adding controls to a
Web Form.*

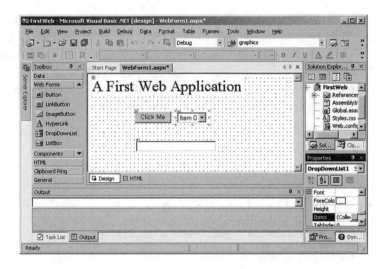

Just as if you were working with a Windows form, drag a button, a text box, and a
drop-down list box from the toolbox to the Web form, as you see in Figure 11.4. (This
example also adds a descriptive label to the Web form with the text A First Web
Application.) You can work with these controls as you would Windows controls—for
example, to add a few items to the list box, click the ellipsis (. . .) button in the list
box's Items entry in the Properties window, opening the ListItem Collection Editor dialog. Enter **"Item 0"** to **"Item 2"** in that dialog and click OK to insert those items into
the list box.

When you select server controls in a Web form, you'll see the normal Visual Basic
properties (such as Text and Visible) of those controls in the Properties window.
When you select client controls, on the other hand, you'll see HTML properties (such
as bgColor and title) because these controls are being treated as HTML. (HTML
properties correspond to the attributes in the HTML elements used to create the
controls.)

After you've added these Web server controls to the Web form, they're added to the
HTML <form> element in WebForm1.aspx. (You don't have to know how this ASP code
works—we'll be working with these controls in Visual Basic in a second.)

```
<form id="Form1" method="post" runat="server">
<asp:Label id=Label1 style="Z-INDEX: 101; LEFT: 8px;
    POSITION: absolute; TOP: 8px" runat="server" Font-Size="X-Large">
    A First Web Application</asp:Label>
<asp:Button id=Button1 style="Z-INDEX: 102; LEFT: 97px;
```

```
   POSITION: absolute; TOP: 78px" runat="server" Text="Click Me"></asp:Button>
<asp:TextBox id=TextBox1 style="Z-INDEX: 103; LEFT: 100px;
   POSITION: absolute; TOP: 138px" runat="server" Width="167px"></asp:TextBox>
<asp:DropDownList id=DropDownList1 style="Z-INDEX: 104; LEFT: 186px;
   POSITION: absolute; TOP: 80px" runat="server" AutoPostBack="True">
<asp:ListItem Value="Item 0">Item 0</asp:ListItem>
<asp:ListItem Value="Item 1">Item 1</asp:ListItem>
<asp:ListItem Value="Item 2">Item 2</asp:ListItem>
</asp:DropDownList>
</form>
```

Now that we've added these controls to a new Web form, let's start adding code to handle their events when the user works with them. As we'll see, when it's time to code these controls, it'll be pure Visual Basic.

Handling Events in Code

Working with events in Web forms is as easy as working with events in Windows forms. For example, to add code to the button's Click event, just double-click the button in the IDE now, opening the code designer that appears in Figure 11.5.

FIGURE 11.5

A Web form code designer.

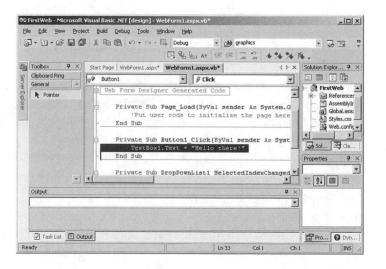

The code you write for this button, a Web server control, is Visual Basic code, and that code will run on the server. In fact, you're looking at the code in the server file WebForm1.aspx.vb (also called the code-behind file). It might be reassuring to see that

11

the button's `Click` event handler has exactly the same form and uses the same arguments
as in Windows programming:

```
Private Sub Button1_Click(ByVal sender As System.Object, _
    ByVal e As System.EventArgs) Handles Button1.Click
        .
        .
        .
End Sub
```

The code you add to this event handler is pure Visual Basic too. For example, you can
display the message `"Hello there!"` in the text box when the button is clicked with this
code:

```
Private Sub Button1_Click(ByVal sender As System.Object, _
    ByVal e As System.EventArgs) Handles Button1.Click
    TextBox1.Text = "Hello there!"
    End Sub
```

You can also add code to the drop-down list box's `SelectedIndexChanged` event handler
in the same way. For example, here's how the list box might display which item was
selected in the text box:

```
Private Sub ListBox1_SelectedIndexChanged(ByVal sender As _
    System.Object, ByVal e As System.EventArgs) Handles _
    ListBox1.SelectedIndexChanged
    TextBox1.Text = "Item " & sender.SelectedIndex & " was selected."
End Sub
```

As you can see, you use Visual Basic in the .aspx.vb file and HTML in the .aspx file. In
a Web application, the programming is divided into two distinct parts this way: the visual
component, which is the Web page that the browser will see, and the Visual Basic code
behind that page, which handles the controls in the page on the server. That there are two
files reflects the fact that part of your application is handled by the browser and part by
the server. Visual Basic will handle both files for us during the development process.

WebForm1.aspx.vb resembles the .vb file you'd see for a Windows form. Here's what it
looks like after you've added the preceding code. (Note that you use the `Page_Load` event
here to initialize the Web form, not `Form_Load` as in Windows forms.)

LISTING 11.2   WebForm1.aspx.vb (FirstWeb Project)

```
Public Class WebForm1
    Inherits System.Web.UI.Page

#Region " Web Form Designer Generated Code "
```

LISTING 11.2   continued

```
    'This call is required by the Web Form Designer.
    <System.Diagnostics.DebuggerStepThrough()> Private Sub InitializeComponent()

    End Sub
    Protected WithEvents Label1 As System.Web.UI.WebControls.Label
    Protected WithEvents Button1 As System.Web.UI.WebControls.Button
    Protected WithEvents TextBox1 As System.Web.UI.WebControls.TextBox
    Protected WithEvents DropDownList1 As System.Web.UI.WebControls.DropDownList

    'NOTE: The following placeholder declaration is required
    'by the Web Form Designer.
    'Do not delete or move it.
    Private designerPlaceholderDeclaration As System.Object

    Private Sub Page_Init(ByVal sender As System.Object, _
        ByVal e As System.EventArgs) Handles MyBase.Init
        'CODEGEN: This method call is required by the Web Form Designer
        'Do not modify it using the code editor.
        InitializeComponent()
    End Sub

#End Region

    Private Sub Page_Load(ByVal sender As System.Object, _
        ByVal e As System.EventArgs) Handles MyBase.Load
        'Put user code to initialize the page here
    End Sub

    Private Sub Button1_Click(ByVal sender As System.Object, _
        ByVal e As System.EventArgs) Handles Button1.Click
        TextBox1.Text = "Hello there!"
    End Sub

    Private Sub DropDownList1_SelectedIndexChanged(ByVal _
        sender As System.Object, ByVal e As System.EventArgs) _
        Handles DropDownList1.SelectedIndexChanged
        TextBox1.Text = "Item " & sender.SelectedIndex & " was selected."
    End Sub
End Class
```

As you can see in Listing 11.2, Web forms are based on the System.Web.UI.Page class:

```
Public Class WebForm1
    Inherits System.Web.UI.Page
        .
        .
        .
```

11

Here is the class hierarchy for the System.Web.UI.Page class—note that the Control class that Web forms are based on is the ASP.NET System.Web.UI.Control class, not the Windows form's System.Windows.Forms.Control class:

```
System.Object
    System.Web.UI.Control
        System.Web.UI.TemplateControl
            System.Web.UI.Page
```

You can find the significant public properties of System.Web.UI.Page objects in Table 11.5, the significant methods in Table 11.6, and the significant events in Table 11.7. (These tables do not include the properties, methods, and events that the System.Web.UI.Page class inherits from the System.Web.UI.Control class—you can find them in tomorrow's material, Tables 12.1, 12.2, and 12.3, which starts our work with Web form controls.)

TABLE 11.5   Significant Public Properties of Page Objects.

Property	Means
ErrorPage	Returns or sets an error page's URL in case there are unhandled page exceptions.
IsPostBack	Indicates whether a page was created after a client "postback," or whether it is being loaded for the first time.
IsValid	Indicates whether a page validation was successful.
Request	Returns the current HTTP Request object.
Response	Returns the current HTTP Response object.
Server	Returns the current Server object.
Session	Returns the current Session object.
Site	Returns Web site data.
User	Returns data about the user.
Validators	Returns a collection of the validation controls in the page.

TABLE 11.6   Significant Public Methods of Page Objects.

Method	Means
HasControls	True if the page has any child controls.
ResolveUrl	Converts a relative URL to an absolute URL.
Validate	Validates data using validation control in the page.

TABLE 11.7   Significant Public Events of Page Objects.

Event	Means
Disposed	Occurs when a Web form is disposed of.
Error	Occurs when an unhandled exception has occurred.
Init	Occurs when the Web form is initialized.
Load	Occurs when the Web form is loaded.
Unload	Occurs when the server control is unloaded.

Running a Web Application

At this point, we've completed our first Web application, FirstWeb, and it's ready to go.
To run this application, you can simply use the Visual Basic Debug, Start menu item, just
as you would in Windows. This starts the new application in a browser window, as you
see in Figure 11.6. Congratulations! Now you're programming on the Web.

FIGURE 11.6

*Running a Web
application.*

You don't need the Visual Basic IDE to run a Web application, of course—you can start
the application by navigating to its .aspx page with your browser. For example, if your
application were on a server named starpowder.com, you could also browse to a URL
something like http://www.starpowder.com/steve/FirstWeb/WebForm1.aspx.

Give the new Web application a try—click the button. When you do, the entire page is
sent back to the server for processing; the code-behind Visual Basic code is executed,
and the results are sent back to the browser. You can see the results in Figure 11.6—the
message "Hello there!" appears in the text box.

So far, so good. Now click an item in the list box. *Nothing happens.* Why? We saw the reason earlier—not every event that happens in a Web form triggers a round-trip to the server for processing. By default, a list box's SelectedIndexChanged event does not trigger a round-trip—instead, it's recorded, and the next time the page is sent back to the server, the event's handler is called. Click events cause an immediate trip back to the server for processing, but not events such as list box's SelectedIndexChanged event.

Storing events until the next server round-trip means fewer such trips to the server, which improves a program's performance. On the other hand, you need to wait for a round-trip to handle such events—in this case, that might mean adding a button the user can click after she has made selections in a few list boxes.

But there are times when you just want more control than that—you want your events handled *now*. You can force a program to handle a Web server control's events with automatic server round-trips if you set the control's AutoPostBack property to True.

To see how that works, set the list box's AutoPostBack property to True and try the application again. When you click a new selection in the list box now, a message displaying the item you clicked appears in the text box, as shown in Figure 11.7. There's no need to wait until some other event sends the form back to the server in this case.

FIGURE 11.7

Using AutoPostBack.

Now you've gotten a full Web application to work—very cool. To close the application, just close the Web browser or select the Debug, Stop Debugging menu item in the Visual Basic .NET IDE.

Customizing Web Page Appearance in HTML

When you're programming on the Web, the appearance of your Web pages is important—there's a lot of competition out there. You can use the items in the toolbox to add labels, images, and controls in a Web form, of course, but there might be times when you want more control over the actual HTML in your Web pages.

You can get that kind of control with the HTML editor, which gives you direct access to the HTML in your Web page. To bring up a Web page's HTML editor, just click the HTML tab at the bottom of the code designer for the page's .aspx file.

Tip

> Before you turn to the HTML editor to change the appearance of your Web pages, bear in mind that you can also set the values of many HTML properties in the properties window of the IDE, as you've already seen. And if you're familiar with CSS styles, you can also edit the styles used in your Web page in the project's Styles.css file.

When you click the HTML tab, you'll see the HTML for a Web form, including embedded ASP directives (which are converted to HTML by the ASP server before being sent to the Web browser), as you see in Figure 11.3. That HTML must be something that a Web browser can understand, so it must be in the form of a normal HTML document—with <HTML>, <HEAD>, and <BODY> elements—as you see here. Note that the Web server controls are supported with a <FORM> element. (The capitalization of these elements is inconsistent, but that's the way Visual Basic writes them, and it doesn't matter to the browser.)

```
<%@ Page Language="vb" AutoEventWireup="false"
    Codebehind="WebForm1.aspx.vb" Inherits="FirstWeb.WebForm1"%>
<!DOCTYPE HTML PUBLIC "-//W3C//DTD HTML 4.0 Transitional//EN">

<HTML>
  <HEAD>
    <title>WebForm1</title>
    <meta name="GENERATOR" content="Microsoft Visual Studio .NET 7.1">
    <meta name="CODE_LANGUAGE" content="Visual Basic .NET 7.1">
    <meta name=vs_defaultClientScript content="JavaScript">
    <meta name=vs_targetSchema content=
        "http://schemas.microsoft.com/intellisense/ie5">
  </HEAD>

  <body MS_POSITIONING="GridLayout">

    <form id="Form1" method="post" runat="server">
<asp:Label id=Label1 style="Z-INDEX: 101; LEFT: 8px;
POSITION: absolute; TOP: 8px" runat="server" Font-Size="X-Large">
A First Web Application</asp:Label>
<asp:Button id=Button1 style="Z-INDEX: 102; LEFT: 97px;
```

11

```
POSITION: absolute; TOP: 78px" runat="server" Text="Click Me"></asp:Button>
<asp:TextBox id=TextBox1 style="Z-INDEX: 103; LEFT: 100px;
POSITION: absolute; TOP: 138px" runat="server" Width="167px"></asp:TextBox>
<asp:DropDownList id=DropDownList1 style="Z-INDEX: 104; LEFT: 186px;
POSITION: absolute; TOP: 80px" runat="server" AutoPostBack="True">
<asp:ListItem Value="Item 0">Item 0</asp:ListItem>
<asp:ListItem Value="Item 1">Item 1</asp:ListItem>
<asp:ListItem Value="Item 2">Item 2</asp:ListItem>
</asp:DropDownList>

    </form>

  </body>
</HTML>
```

You can let Visual Basic edit this HTML as you work with the Web page in the IDE, or you can edit this HTML directly. When you edit the HTML directly, the IDE's IntelliSense feature helps out every step of the way. For example, say that you want to add some text to be displayed in your Web page, in a <H1> header. As soon as you start to edit the HTML—as soon as you type the opening angle bracket, <—IntelliSense gives you a list of the possible HTML tags, as you can see in Figure 11.8.

FIGURE 11.8

Adding a new element to a Web page.

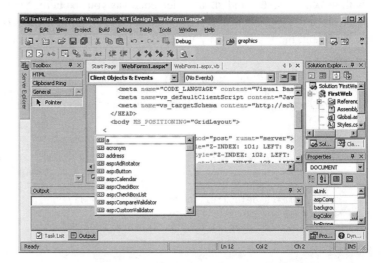

You can add the new <h1> element just by typing it. To set the style for this element, you can add a style attribute to the element by typing that, which makes IntelliSense display a button with the text Build Style, which, when you click it, brings up the Style Builder as you can see in Figure 11.9. This tool is a great one because it lets you build CSS styles for individual elements without having to know any CSS at all.

FIGURE 11.9

The Style Builder.

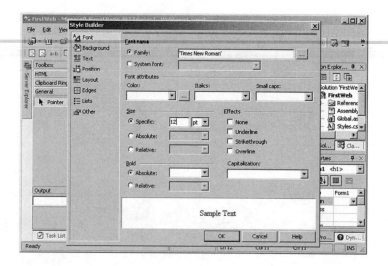

Using the HTML editor, you can add the HTML to WebForm1.aspx to display the text My New Web Page in an `<h1>` header with 12-point text (along with two `<br>` elements to position that text under the A First Web Application label) like this:

```
<HTML>
  <HEAD>
    <title>WebForm1</title>
    <meta name="GENERATOR" content="Microsoft Visual Studio .NET 7.1">
    <meta name="CODE_LANGUAGE" content="Visual Basic .NET 7.1">
    <meta name=vs_defaultClientScript content="JavaScript">
    <meta name=vs_targetSchema content=
        "http://schemas.microsoft.com/intellisense/ie5">
  </HEAD>

  <body MS_POSITIONING="GridLayout">
  <br>
  <br>
<h1 style="FONT-SIZE: 12pt; FONT-FAMILY: 'Times New Roman'">My New Web Page</h1>
    <form id="Form1" method="post" runat="server">
<asp:Label id=Label1 style="Z-INDEX: 101; LEFT: 8px;
POSITION: absolute; TOP: 8px" runat="server" Font-Size="X-Large">
A First Web Application</asp:Label>
          .
          .
          .
```

How will this new text appear in the Web page in the browser? You can see the results of your HTML edits immediately—just click the Design button to switch to design view, as you see in Figure 11.10.

FIGURE 11.10

A new HTML element in a Web form.

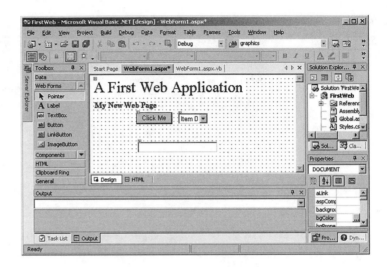

Now you've been able to directly edit the HTML for your Web form.

 Tip

> If you want to paste HTML into the HTML editor, use the Edit, Paste as HTML
> menu item, not the Edit, Paste item. The Edit, Paste item will convert ele-
> ments such as <h1> to "<h1>", but the Edit, Paste as HTML item will
> paste the HTML as HTML.

Preserving a Web Application's Data Between Server Accesses

One significant way in which Web applications differ from Windows applications is in saving the data in your application while the user works with that application. That's not really an issue in Windows programming because the program is running as the user works with it—all you have to know is that you can preserve the values of variables that go out of scope between procedure calls by making those variables static. But in a Web application, you're not directly connected to the server code—you're looking at a Web page in your browser on your own computer.

This means that your application might be storing data in two places—in the client (the browser) and on the server. This is an important issue because it turns out, for example, that the data in your application's code on the server is *not* preserved by default between round-trips. They're reset to their default value each time the page is sent on a round-trip to the server, so making sure that the data in your variables is preserved is up to you.

Preserving Data in the Client

By default, the data in the controls in a Web form is stored in an HTML hidden field (that is, in an HTML <input> element with the type attribute set to "hidden") when the page is sent back to the server, so you don't have to worry about it. When the page is sent to the server and then back, that data is automatically restored in the controls. Another method Visual Basic uses to store that kind of client control data is with cookies.

On the other hand, preserving the data in the variables in your code on the server is another story.

Preserving Data in the Server

Making sure that your data is stored in the variables in your code on the server between server round-trips is something you have to pay attention to. By default, all the data in your variables in the code on the server is set back to its default value between server accesses.

This means that if you increment a variable named counter each time the user clicks a button, that variable will be reset to 0 each time the code is accessed on the server, which is a problem. The issue here is that program execution is *asynchronous*—the application on the server starts anew each time the page is sent to it. So how do you address this issue and preserve the values in your variables in your server code? There are three ways to preserve those values, and we'll take a look at them here.

The first technique is a server-side technique. Here, you store data on the server, using the ASP.NET Session object. When the user starts working with your Web application, a Session object is created exactly for the purpose we'll put it to—to store your local data. You can store and retrieve values using the Session object in Visual Basic code; here's how that might look when the user clicks a button to increment the value in the variable named counter—you can store your data by giving it a name (such as "counter" here) and using the same name to retrieve that data:

```
Private Sub Button1_Click(ByVal sender As System.Object, _
    ByVal e As System.EventArgs) Handles Button1.Click
    Dim counter As Integer = Session("counter")
    counter += 1
    TextBox1.Text = "Counter value: " & counter
    Session("counter") = counter
End Sub
```

Session objects, which are maintained on the server, can time out after a while (typically 30 minutes) after no accesses from the client. To avoid timeouts, you can also save data in the Web page itself, not just on the server. To do that, you can use the Web form's `ViewState` property to store and retrieve your data across server round-trips. Here's how that might work when the user clicks a button to increment `counter`:

```
Private Sub Button1_Click(ByVal sender As System.Object, _
    ByVal e As System.EventArgs) Handles Button1.Click
    Dim counter As Integer = Me.ViewState("counter")
    counter += 1
    TextBox1.Text = "Counter value: " & counter
    Me.ViewState("counter") = counter
End Sub
```

Besides these two techniques, you can also create your own HTML hidden fields in a Web form and use them to store data. To add a hidden field to a Web form, you just click the HTML tab in the toolbox and double-click the Hidden tool. Note that you need to make this field into a server control so that its data will be preserved across server round-trips—right-click it and select the Run As Server Control item. Also, you must give it an ID value, using the `(id)` property in the properties window; in this case, we'll use the ID value `Hidden1`.

At this point, you can address the data in the hidden control as `Hidden1.Value` in your code. Here's how that might look in code, where you're using the hidden control to hold incremented data:

```
Private Sub Button1_Click(ByVal sender As System.Object, _
    ByVal e As System.EventArgs) Handles Button1.Click
    Hidden1.Value += 1
    TextBox1.Text = "Counter value: " & Hidden1.Value
End Sub
```

Creating a Multiform Web Application

We've come far today already, and there's more to come. In our second Web application, we will take a look at how to work with multiple Web forms. The example application here is called MultiForms in the code for this book, and it shows how to support and navigate between multiple forms in an application.

We're going to add two new pages to this example—one a new Web form and one a standard HTML page. To navigate to those documents, we'll use hyperlinks. So after creating this new application, add two hyperlink controls from the toolbox to the Web form, as you see in Figure 11.11. (You will learn about hyperlink controls in Day 14, "Web Forms: Working with Images, Image Buttons, List Boxes, Drop-Down Lists, Hyperlinks, and Link Buttons.") Change the Text property of the first hyperlink to Second Web Form and the Text property of the second hyperlink to HTML Page as you see in the figure.

11

FIGURE 11.11

Creating a multiform application.

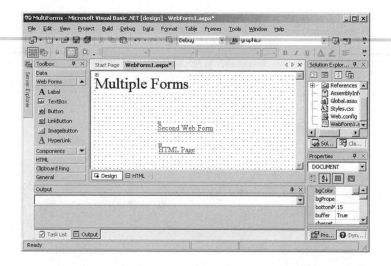

Add a new Web form to this application—just select the Project, Add Web Form menu item and click Open in the Add New Item dialog that appears. This creates and adds a new Web form, WebForm2, to the project. In the same way, we can add a simple HTML page, like any other Web page, to the project with the Project, Add HTML Page menu item—click the Open button to create HTMLPage1 and add it to the project. This new page is just a simple HTML page—you can't use Web server or HTML server controls in an HTML page, just HTML client controls. (The MultiForms example adds a label control to both the second Web form and the HTML page to label those pages for clarity.) You can switch between the various forms in your application at design time by using the tabs at the top of the visual designer in the IDE.

Now all you have to do is to make the hyperlinks active. To do that, go to the first Web form, select the first hyperlink, HyperLink1, and click the ellipsis (. . .) button corresponding to the NavigateURL property in the Properties window, opening the Select URL dialog you see in Figure 11.12. This dialog lists the other forms and pages in the project—select WebForm2.aspx and click OK to connect the hyperlink to WebForm2. Also, set the NavigateURL property for the second hyperlink, HyperLink2, to HTMLPage1.htm, connecting that hyperlink to the simple HTML page.

And that's it—when you run this code, you see the two hyperlinks, as shown in Figure 11.13.

FIGURE 11.12

Setting up a hyperlink.

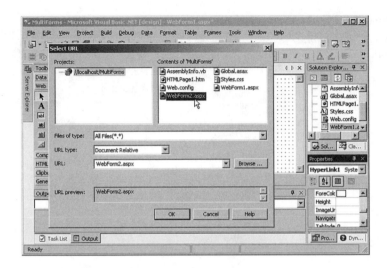

FIGURE 11.13

A multiform application.

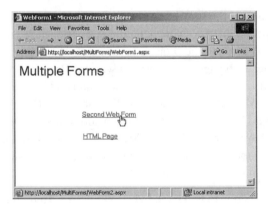

When you click a hyperlink, such as the one to the second Web Form, that new form appears in the browser, as you see in Figure 11.14. To move back to the first Web form, just click the browser's Back button. The same process works for navigating to the simple HTML page in the application—just click its hyperlink.

That's how to create a multiform Web application and how to support basic navigation between those forms.

Here's another thing to know—you can redirect users from one Web page to another in your application's code. To redirect users to another page, you can use the ASP.NET `Response` object's `Redirect` method. The `Response` object allows you to customize what you send back to the browser; for example, here's how the code might work in a

Page_Load event handler if you wanted the user's browser to be immediately redirected to another page:

```
Response.Redirect("http://www.starpowder.com/NewPage.html")
```

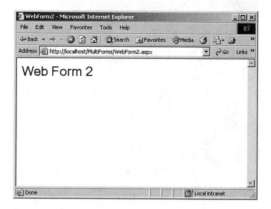

The Response object is also useful in other ways. For example, this object has a method, Write, that lets you write HTML directly to Web pages; to write an <h1> header with the text Dynamic HTML! in a Web form at runtime, you can use this Visual Basic code in the Page_Load event handler:

```
Response.Write("<h1>Dynamic HTML!</h1>")
```

11

Mobile Web Applications

As of Visual Basic .NET 2003, you can also create mobile Web applications targeted at Personal Data Assistants (PDAs). These applications support only a relatively small subset of the functionality of full Web applications. To create a mobile Web application, select the File, New, Project menu item, select the ASP.NET Mobile Web Application icon, give the new project a name—the example project in the code for this book is named MobileWeb—and click OK. This creates the new project, as shown in Figure 11.15.

You can add various controls to this new application, as you can see in Figure 11.15, and you can add code to the controls you see in that figure as usual:

```
Private Sub Command1_Click(ByVal sender As System.Object, _
    ByVal e As System.EventArgs) Handles Command1.Click
    TextBox1.Text = "Hello there!"
End Sub
```

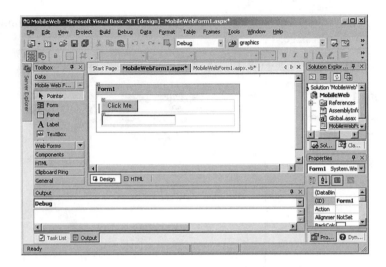

FIGURE 11.15

Creating a Mobile Web application.

This application can run in PDAs; you can also run it in the Internet Explorer, as you see in Figure 11.16.

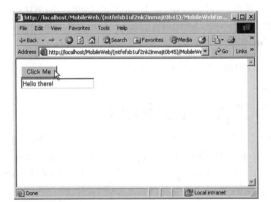

FIGURE 11.16

A Mobile Web application.

Handling Browser Programming in JavaScript

So far, we've been handling events in the server, not in the browser, but that way of doing things has some trade-offs—you can use Visual Basic code to handle events, but you need a server round-trip to do so. You can also handle events in the *browser* if you don't mind using a language that the browser understands, such as JavaScript. We'll take a look at that here, in the JavaScripting example in the code for this book. We'll also use client HTML controls in this case, not server controls that must be handled on the server.

To see how this works, create a new Web application now. This application displays a button, and when you click it, JavaScript will display a message in a text field—no Visual Basic is needed.

To add HTML button and text field controls to the Web form in this example, click the HTML tab in the toolbox, and then add those controls to the form. These HTML controls are not given names by default, so enter "Button1" for the button's (id) property in the properties window. This property corresponds to the id attribute of the <input> HTML element that will be used to create the button. (Because these are HTML controls, you'll see HTML attributes in the Properties window.) Similarly, set the (id) property of the text field to "TextField1". You can also give the button the caption Click Me by entering that text in the button's value property, which corresponds to the value attribute of the <input> HTML element that will be used to create the button.

The next step is to add the JavaScript code we'll use to handle the button click. To do that, first click the HTML button in the form designer so that you see the Web form's HTML. Next, select the button, which we've named Button1, in the left, drop-down list box above the code designer, and the onclick event (which is the HTML version of the Visual Basic Click event) in the right drop-down list, as you see in Figure 11.17.

11

FIGURE 11.17

Working with client events.

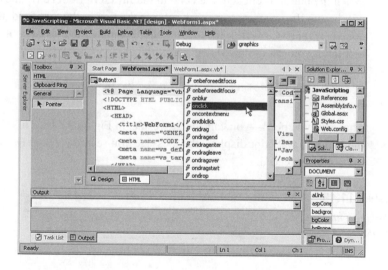

Doing so adds a new *JavaScript* event handler to the HTML for the button in our Web form like this:

```
<%@ Page Language="vb" AutoEventWireup="false"
    Codebehind="WebForm1.aspx.vb" Inherits="JavaScripting.WebForm1"%>
```

```
<!DOCTYPE HTML PUBLIC "-//W3C//DTD HTML 4.0 Transitional//EN">
<HTML>
  <HEAD>
    <title>WebForm1</title>
    <meta name="GENERATOR" content="Microsoft Visual Studio .NET 7.1">
    <meta name="CODE_LANGUAGE" content="Visual Basic .NET 7.1">
    <meta name=vs_defaultClientScript content="JavaScript">
    <meta name=vs_targetSchema content=
        "http://schemas.microsoft.com/intellisense/ie5">
  <script id=clientEventHandlersJS language=javascript>
<!—

function Button1_onclick() {

}
//—>
</script>
</HEAD>
     .
     .
     .
</HTML>
```

When the button is clicked, the code in the JavaScript `Button1_onclick` event handler
will be run. In JavaScript, you can refer to the text in the text field as
`document.Form1.TextField1.value`. So to display the message `"Hello there!"` in the
text field, you can use this JavaScript:

```
function Button1_onclick() {
    document.Form1.TextField1.value = "Hello there!"
}
```

That's all you need—you can see the results in Figure 11.18. This time when you click
the button, JavaScript displays the message you see, not Visual Basic. No round-trip to
the server is needed.

FIGURE 11.18

*Working with
JavaScript.*

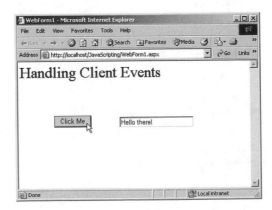

Detecting Browser Capabilities

You've already seen the Response object, which is the object that ASP.NET uses to create what it sends to the browser (usually HTML). There's another object that ASP.NET uses to handle the incoming data from the browser—the Request object—and it's useful to know as well. For example, to determine what kind of browser you're dealing with—and therefore how you can work with it—you can use the Request object's Browser property. This property returns an object which itself has various properties that tell you about the browser the user has. You can see these properties in Table 11.8—each property contains either text (such as the browser's name) or a Boolean value of True or False.

TABLE 11.8   Request.Browser Properties

To Determine...	Use This:
Browser Type (example: IE6)	Request.Browser.Type
Browser Name (example: IE)	Request.Browser.Browser
Version (example: 6.0b)	Request.Browser.Version
Major Version (example: 6)	Request.Browser.MajorVersion
Minor Version (example: 0)	Request.Browser.MinorVersion
Platform (example: WinNT)	Request.Browser.Platform
Is this a beta version?	Request.Browser.Beta
Is this an AOL browser?	Request.Browser.AOL
Is this Win16?	Request.Browser.Win16
Is this Win32?	Request.Browser.Win32
Supports Frames?	Request.Browser.Frames
Supports Tables?	Request.Browser.Tables
Supports Cookies?	Request.Browser.Cookies
Supports VB Script?	Request.Browser.VBScript
Supports JavaScript?	Request.Browser.JavaScript
Supports Java Applets?	Request.Browser.JavaApplets
Supports ActiveX Controls?	Request.Browser.ActiveXControls

11

Embedding Visual Basic Code in Web Pages

To round off today's discussion on Web forms, let's take a look at a somewhat advanced topic. So far, our Visual Basic code in Web applications has been stored in the .aspx.vb code-behind file, and that's the way it will be in the rest of the book. But it's interesting to know that you can store Visual Basic in the .aspx file itself (the file that is used to generate the HTML sent back to the browser). In other words, you can create Visual Basic–based Web applications that don't use a code-behind file to store Visual Basic code.

You can see how this works in the OneFile example in the code for this book, which you see in Figure 11.19. You can click the button in this example to display a message in the text box, even though there's no code-behind file.

FIGURE 11.19

Including Visual Basic code in the client.

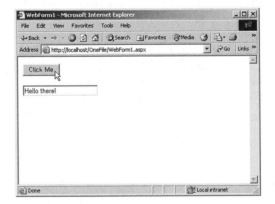

Here's how this works. First, you create a Web application, and then you add the controls you want to the default Web form by creating them yourself with ASP code. You can add two controls, a text box and button, by typing this ASP code directly into the Web application's .aspx file (note the `Page` directive's `Codebehind="WebForm1.aspx.vb"` attribute here—that attribute does nothing in this case, and you can remove it if you prefer):

```
<%@ Page Language="vb" AutoEventWireup="false"
    Codebehind="WebForm1.aspx.vb" Inherits="OneFile.WebForm1"%>
<!DOCTYPE HTML PUBLIC "-//W3C//DTD HTML 4.0 Transitional//EN">
<html>
  <head>
    <title>WebForm1</title>
    <meta name="GENERATOR" content="Microsoft Visual Studio .NET 7.1">
    <meta name="CODE_LANGUAGE" content="Visual Basic .NET 7.1">
    <meta name=vs_defaultClientScript content="JavaScript">
    <meta name=vs_targetSchema content=
        "http://schemas.microsoft.com/intellisense/ie5">
  </head>
  <body MS_POSITIONING="GridLayout">
```

```
    <form id="Form1" method="post" runat="server">
        <asp:Button id="Button1" Text="Click Me" OnClick="Button1_Click"
            runat="server"/>
        <P>
        <asp:TextBox id=TextBox1 runat="server"></asp:TextBox></P>
    </form>

    </body>
</html>
```

Note that the HTML onclick event handler is set to Button1_Click here. You can add that event handler yourself with a <script> element, where you set the language attribute to "VB" and the runat attribute to "server". This event handler is written in standard Visual Basic, like this:

```
<%@ Page Language="vb" AutoEventWireup="false"
    Codebehind="WebForm1.aspx.vb" Inherits="OneFile.WebForm1"%>
<!DOCTYPE HTML PUBLIC "-//W3C//DTD HTML 4.0 Transitional//EN">
<html>
  <head>
    <title>WebForm1</title>
    <meta name="GENERATOR" content="Microsoft Visual Studio .NET 7.1">
    <meta name="CODE_LANGUAGE" content="Visual Basic .NET 7.1">
    <meta name=vs_defaultClientScript content="JavaScript">
    <meta name=vs_targetSchema content=
        "http://schemas.microsoft.com/intellisense/ie5">
    <script language="VB" runat="server">
        Private Sub Button1_Click(ByVal sender As System.Object, _
            ByVal e As System.EventArgs)
            TextBox1.Text = "Hello there!"
        End Sub
    </script>
  </head>
  <body MS_POSITIONING="GridLayout">

    <form id="Form1" method="post" runat="server">
        <asp:Button id="Button1" Text="Click Me" OnClick="Button1_Click"
            runat="server"/>
        <P>
        <asp:TextBox id=TextBox1 runat="server"></asp:TextBox></P>
    </form>

    </body>
</html>
```

And that's all you need; you've embedded your Visual Basic code in the page that's sent to the browser. When you click the button in this application, that Visual Basic code will be sent back to the server with the rest of the page and executed, as you saw in Figure 11.19.

If you know ASP programming, you might even prefer to do things this way. Because this is a book on Visual Basic, however, we're going to stick to the standard Visual Basic way in the upcoming days, which means using standard Visual Basic code-behind files.

Summary

Today, we got our start with Web applications and Web forms. You saw how to create Web applications using IIS and ASP.NET. And we spent most of today's work looking at Web forms, which are the basis of what we'll be doing in the next several days.

Web forms are based on the `System.Web.UI.Page` class, and you saw that class today. You got an introduction to the code in a Web form and how it works. You saw that there are typically two code files that you work with—a .aspx file used by ASP.NET to create the HTML sent to the browser and a .aspx.vb code-behind file that holds the Visual Basic for your application that resides on the server.

You saw that the controls you use in a Web form can be either server or client (browser) controls. Server controls can either be Visual Basic Web server controls or HTML controls that are handled on the server. Client controls are made up of the standard HTML controls that you normally see in Web pages.

Events are handled in Web forms in a different way from Windows forms because Web forms appear in browsers, not in a window directly connected to your code. Some events, such as `Click` events, make the browser send the Web page back to the server for processing. But the handling of some events, such as a list box's `SelectedIndexChanged` event, do not cause the Web page to be sent back to the server by default. You can either handle the second type of event when the Web page is sent back to the server, or force them to be handled immediately in the server by setting the control's `AutoPostBack` property to `True`.

You saw how to create and work with multiple forms in a Web application—not just Web forms, but simple HTML pages as well. And you got an introduction to using hyperlink controls in Web applications to navigate between forms.

You also saw that the ASP.NET `Response` object lets you write HTML directly to a Web page, and the `Request` object can give you a great deal of information about the browser the user has.

In addition, we took a look at how to preserve program data across server round-trips. Because the code in a Web application starts anew each time a Web page is sent back to it, the values in the variables are reset to their default values. You saw various ways to preserve that data—both on the server and in the Web page itself sent to the browser.

That's it for today's work—tomorrow, we're going to start working with the many controls that Visual Basic supports for use in Web forms.

Q&A

Q **Is there some way to handle errors that occur in a Web form while it's in a browser?**

A You can use the `ErrorPage` attribute in the ASP.NET `Page` directive. You assign this attribute a URL the browser should jump to if there's been an error, like this: `<%@ Page Language="vb" AutoEventWireup="false" Inherits="Application.WebForm1" ErrorPage="http://www.starpowder.com/error.html"%>`. For more on this process, take a look at a book on ASP programming.

Q **Is there any reason to prefer code-behind files instead of embedding my Visual Basic code in .aspx files?**

A Yes, there is—Visual Basic maintains the code in code-behind .aspx.vb files for you, which it doesn't do if you embed Visual Basic in .aspx files. That also includes supporting IntelliSense, which makes it easier to develop your code. And if you embed a lot of Visual Basic code in the .aspx files that are sent to the browser, you can start to degrade performance simply by the sheer volume of text you're sending.

11

Workshop

This workshop tests whether you understand the concepts you saw today. It's a good idea to make sure that you can answer these questions before pressing on to tomorrow's work.

Quiz

1. What's the difference between Web server controls, HTML server controls, and HTML client controls?

2. What kinds of layouts can you use for controls in Web pages?

3. The list box you've added to a Web form doesn't seem to do anything at runtime in the browser even though you've added an event handler. What do you have to do to handle events as they occur?

4. How can you preserve the data in your Web application's variables between server round-trips?

5. How can you tell if the user's browser supports cookies?

Quiz Answers

1. Web server controls are controls made to look and work like Visual Basic Windows controls, HTML server controls are standard HTML controls that are handled on the server, and HTML client controls are standard HTML controls that are handled in the browser.

2. Grid layout (where controls stay where you put them) and flow layout (where controls "flow" as they do in standard Web pages). You use the pageLayout property to set the layout you want to use.

3. Set the list box's AutoPostBack property to True.

4. You saw three ways today—using the Session object, the ViewState property, and HTML hidden fields.

5. You can check the Request.Browser.Cookies property in your Visual Basic code—if it returns True, the browser supports cookies.

Exercises

1. Create a new Web application now and add code in the Page_Load event handler to tell the user about the browser she has, using the properties in Table 11.8. (Display your text in a text box.)

2. Implement one of the techniques discussed today for preserving data in variables between server round-trips. In this case, just increment a counter each time the user clicks a button, displaying the new count in a text box each time the button is clicked.

Day 12

Web Forms: Working with Buttons, Text Boxes, Labels, Literals, and Placeholders

Today, we'll start our examination of the Visual Basic .NET Web server controls. These controls are the ones that were designed to look and act most like standard Visual Basic controls. You first saw them yesterday—you will see them in the coming days as well.

We're going to start by taking a look at Web controls in general today—including showing and hiding Web controls, adding them at runtime, and so on, as well as taking an in-depth look at a specific set of Web server controls—buttons, text boxes, labels, literals, and placeholders. Here are today's topics:

- Enabling and disabling controls
- Making controls visible and invisible

- Giving controls tool tips
- Moving controls
- Setting control border styles
- Creating buttons
- Creating text boxes
- Creating multiline text boxes
- Creating password controls
- Creating read-only text boxes
- Creating labels
- Setting label text and style
- Creating literals
- Using placeholders
- Using XML controls
- Adding controls at runtime

The transition between Windows forms and Web forms is made easier by the fact that so many Web server controls resemble Windows controls. That fact makes the whole situation much more familiar. Not all the Windows controls we've been working with can be displayed in Web browsers, even using combinations of the standard HTML controls, but quite a few can.

You've gotten a basic introduction to the use of Web server controls yesterday—you saw that you can add a Web server control from the toolbox to a Web form, set its properties, and add code to handle its events. Today, we're going to work with Web server controls in more depth, starting by taking a look at the classes those controls are based on.

Web server controls are based on the `Control` class, but not the `System.Windows.Forms.Control` class we've seen in Windows programming—the `System.Web.UI.Control` class. This class is the base class for the controls you will be seeing over the next few days (as well as the Web form Page class you saw yesterday), and as such, we should take a closer look at it. This class is derived directly from the `Object` class like this:

```
System.Object
    System.Web.UI.Control
```

You can find the significant public properties of `System.Web.UI.Control` objects in Table 12.1, the significant methods in Table 12.2, and the significant events in Table 12.3.

TABLE 12.1   Significant Public Properties of `Control` Objects

Property	Means
Controls	Returns a collection of the control's child controls.
EnableViewState	Returns or sets whether the control maintains its state between server round-trips.
ID	Returns or sets the ID for the control.
Page	Returns the `Page` object that contains the control.
Parent	Returns the control's parent control.
Site	Returns the control's Web site.
UniqueID	Returns the unique ID for the control.
Visible	Returns or sets whether the control is visible.

TABLE 12.2   Significant Public Methods of `Control` Objects

Method	Means
DataBind	Binds a control to a data source.
FindControl	Searches a container for a control.
HasControls	True if the control contains child controls.
RenderControl	Draws the control using HTML.
ResolveUrl	Converts relative URLs into absolute URLs based on the location of the control's page.

TABLE 12.3   Significant Public Events of `Control` Objects

Event	Means
Disposed	Occurs when a control is disposed of.
Init	Occurs when a control is initialized.
Load	Occurs when a control is loaded into a `Page` object.
PreRender	Occurs when a control is about to be drawn.
Unload	Occurs when a control is unloaded.

Note in particular the `EnableViewState` property of Web controls, which specifies whether the control saves its state during round-trips to the server—the default setting for this property is `True`, which means that controls will retain their internal data (such as

12

the text in a text box) during server round-trips. As far as events go, take a look at the Init and Load events, which you can use to initialize your controls, as well as Web forms.

We should take a look at another class here as well because Web server controls aren't based directly on the System.Web.UI.Control class—they are based on the System.Web.UI.WebControls.WebControl class, which itself is based on the System.Web.UI.Control class. Here's the hierarchy of the System.Web.UI.WebControls.WebControl class:

```
System.Object
    System.Web.UI.Control
        System.Web.UI.WebControls.WebControl
```

You can find the significant public properties of System.Web.UI.WebControls.WebControl objects in Table 12.4, and the significant methods in Table 12.5. (Note that there's no table of events here—that's because System.Web.UI.WebControls.WebControl inherits all its events from the System.Web.UI.Control class.)

TABLE 12.4 Significant Public Properties of WebControl Objects

Property	Means
AccessKey	Returns or sets the access key for the control.
Attributes	Returns a collection of HTML attributes used to draw the control.
BackColor	Returns or sets the control's background color.
BorderColor	Returns or sets the control's border color.
BorderStyle	Returns or sets the control's border style.
BorderWidth	Returns or sets the control's border width.
ControlStyle	Returns the control's style.
CssClass	Returns or sets the control's CSS class.
Enabled	Returns or sets whether the control is enabled.
Font	Returns or sets font information for the control.
ForeColor	Returns or sets the control's foreground color.
Height	Returns or sets the control's height.
Style	Returns the HTML style of the control as a collection of text attributes.
TabIndex	Returns or sets the control's tab index.
ToolTip	Returns or sets the control's tool tip text.
Width	Returns or sets the control's width.

TABLE 12.5   Significant Public Methods of `WebControl` Objects

Method	Means
CopyBaseAttributes	Copies the base attributes (AccessKey, Enabled, ToolTip, TabIndex, and Attributes) from a source control to this control.
RenderBeginTag	Renders the HTML starting tag of the control.
RenderEndTag	Renders the HTML ending tag of the control.

Working with Web Server Controls

In today's work, we'll look at Web server controls in general, including enabling and disabling them, showing and hiding them, adding them at runtime, and so on. This overview of Web controls is illustrated by the WebControls example in the code for the book.

Enabling and Disabling Web Controls

You can see the WebControls example at work in Figure 12.1; this example lets you check out a number of ways of handling Web controls with just the click of a button.

FIGURE 12.1

The WebControls example.

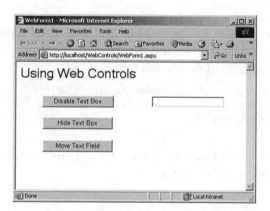

12

The first thing we'll take a look at with this example is how controls can be enabled and disabled. As in Windows forms, you use the `Enabled` property to enable or disable controls; when you click the Disable Text Box button, the code sets this property to `False` like this:

```
Private Sub Button1_Click(ByVal sender As System.Object, _
    ByVal e As System.EventArgs) Handles Button1.Click
    TextBox1.Enabled = False
End Sub
```

You can see the result in Figure 12.2, where the text in the text box has been disabled after the user clicks the Disable Text Box button—the text in the text box is grayed out and made inaccessible. The text box can no longer accept the keyboard focus when it's disabled, which means that the user can't change the text in the control.

FIGURE 12.2

Disabling a text box.

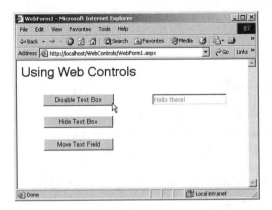

Showing and Hiding Web Controls

You can make Web server controls visible or invisible using their `Visible` property, which you can set to `True` or `False` and which all Web server controls support. For example, when you click the Hide Text Box button in the WebControls example, the code sets the `Visible` property of the text box to `False`:

```
Private Sub Button2_Click(ByVal sender As System.Object, _
    ByVal e As System.EventArgs) Handles Button2.Click
    TextBox1.Visible = False
End Sub
```

You can see the results in Figure 12.3, where the text box has disappeared after the user has clicked the Hide Text Box button.

FIGURE 12.3

Hiding a text box.

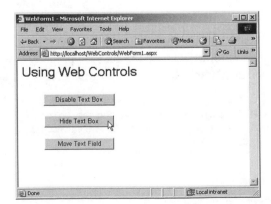

Moving Web Controls at Runtime

NEW TERM As you recall from Day 4, "Creating Windows Forms," there are a number of ways of moving around Windows controls. Unfortunately, Web server controls don't have handy properties such as `Top` or `Right` that let you position them at runtime. However, you can access properties like that as *CSS style properties*. Specifically, you can set the top and right location of a Web control by assigning values to the `Style("Top")` and `Style("Right")` properties and the bottom and left locations with the `Style("Bottom")` and `Style("Left")` properties.

You can see how this works in the WebControls example; when you click the Move Text box button, the code moves the text box down the page by assigning `TextBox1.Style("Top")` the value `200px` (that is, 200 pixels):

```
Private Sub Button3_Click(ByVal sender As System.Object, _
    ByVal e As System.EventArgs) Handles Button4.Click
    TextBox1.Style("Top") = "200px"
End Sub
```

You can see the result in Figure 12.4, where the text box has been moved downward. (Note that we're using grid layout for this to work, not flow layout—you can only position Web elements in an absolute way when you're using grid layout or when you set the control's `Style("Position")` property to `"Absolute"`.)

FIGURE 12.4

Moving a text box.

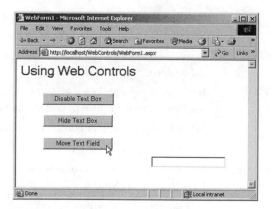

12

Plenty of CSS styles are available to use—you'll find the complete listing of CSS style properties, such as `Top` and `Bottom`, at `http://www.w3.org/TR/REC-CSS1/` for CSS level 1 (called CSS1) and `http://www.w3.org/TR/REC-CSS2/` for CSS level 2 (CSS2). These CSS specifications are maintained by the World Wide Web Consortium, W3C, who are the people responsible for standardizing HTML and XML. All of CSS1 and most of CSS2 is supported in Internet Explorer 6. If you want to learn about moving, coloring, and formatting your Web controls in a browser, these URLs are the place to look.

For example, you can access the background color of a control such as a text box this way: `TextBox1.Style("Background-Color")`, which means that you can set the text box's background color to cyan like this (this works because "cyan" is a predefined color in Internet Explorer—you can also assign any text string that holds an HTML color to this property, like this: "0000FF" to set the background color to blue):

```
TextBox1.Style("Background-Color") = "cyan"
```

To see all the CSS styles and what values you can set them to, go to `http://www.w3.org/TR/REC-CSS1/` and `http://www.w3.org/TR/REC-CSS2/`. Table 12.6 illustrates a sampling of these styles to give you an idea of what's available. For example, to underline text in a label control, you can use a statement like this:

```
Label1.Style("Text-Decoration") = "Underline"
```

TABLE 12.6 A Sampling of CSS Styles

Property	Means
background-attachment	Sets whether a background image is fixed or scrolls when the user scrolls the rest of the page.
background-color	Specifies the background color of an element.
background-image	Specifies the background image of an element.
background-position	If you are using a background image, this property specifies its initial position.
background-repeat	If you are using a background image, this property specifies whether the image is tiled (repeated), and if so, how.
border-color	Sets the color of the four borders of an element.
border-style	Specifies the style of the four borders of an element.
border-top, border-right, border-bottom, border-left	Sets the width, style, and color of the top, right, bottom, and left border of an element.
border-width	Sets the border-top-width, border-right-width, border-bottom-width, and border-left-width properties at the same time.
bottom, top, left, right	Indicates how far an element's bottom, top, left, or right content edge should be offset from the corresponding edge of the element's container.
color	Sets the foreground color of elements that display text.

TABLE 12.6 continued

Property	Means
font-family	Holds a list of font family names, separated by commas. Because not all fonts are available on all systems, this property allows you to specify a list of fonts—the browser will use the first one it can find, starting from the first item in the list.
font-size	This property describes the size of a font.
font-style	Specifies normal (also called Roman or upright), italic, and oblique font faces.
font-weight	Indicates the weight of a font, such as normal or bold.
height, width	Gives the content height or width of boxes.
margin-top, margin-right, margin-bottom, margin-left	Sets the top, right, bottom, and left margin of an element.
padding-top, padding-right, padding-bottom, padding-left	These properties specify the top, right, bottom, and left padding of an element.
text-align	Sets how the content of a block is aligned: left, right, or center.
text-decoration	Sets the decorations that are added to the text of an element, such as underlining, overlining, and line-through (strike-through).
text-indent	Sets the indentation of the first line of text.
vertical-align	Sets the vertical positioning of text in the element.
visibility	Indicates whether the element is displayed. Set to "visible" or "hidden".
z-index	Specifies the stacking level of the element for positioned boxes with regard to other elements (that is, what's on top of what).

12

Giving Web Controls Tool Tips and Access Keys

Another way that Web controls are like Windows controls is that you can give them tool tips and access keys. To give a Web control a tool tip, you can use its ToolTip property. Just set that property to a text string at runtime or design time—for example, the top button in the WebControls example has the tool tip Click this button!, as you see in Figure 12.5.

And, as with Windows forms controls, you can give Web form controls access keys. When you press Alt and the access key (such as Alt+X), the corresponding control gets the focus. You give a Web control an access key with its AccessKey property.

FIGURE 12.5

A tool tip.

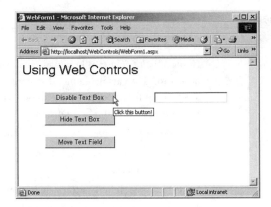

Web Control Fonts

The font that a Web server control uses must be one that is supported by the browser. There are two ways to set those fonts—with a control's Font property and by using the Style property.

You can set the font in a control (such as a label or a text box) to a standard HTML font with the Font property. Instead of assigning a Font object to that property, however, the Font holds a FontInfo object, which has these properties (note that not all properties will be supported by all browsers):

- Bold—Returns or sets whether the font is bold. Set to True or False.
- Italic—Returns or sets whether the font is italic. Set to True or False.
- Name—Returns or sets the main font name.
- Names—Returns or sets an array of font names.
- Overline—Returns or sets whether the font is overlined. Set to True or False.
- Size—Returns or sets the font size.
- Strikeout—Returns or sets whether the font has strike through. Set to True or False.
- Underline—Returns or sets whether the font is underlined. Set to True or False.

For example, to change the font in a label to italic, you can use code like this:

```
Private Sub Button1_Click(ByVal sender As System.Object,
    ByVal e As System.EventArgs) Handles Button1.Click
    Label1.Font.Italic = True
End Sub
```

The Size property specifies the HTML-based font sizes you can use in Web browsers, and can take these values from the FontUnit enumeration:

- FontUnit.Large—Font size is two sizes larger than the default font size.
- FontUnit.Larger—Font size is one size larger than in the parent element.
- FontUnit.Medium—Font size is one size larger than the default font size.
- FontUnit.Small—The default font size.
- FontUnit.Smaller—Font size is one size smaller than the parent element.
- FontUnit.XLarge—Font size is three sizes larger than the base font size.
- FontUnit.XSmall—Font size is one size smaller than the base font size.
- FontUnit.XXLarge—Font size is four sizes larger than the base font size.
- FontUnit.XXSmall—Font size is two sizes smaller than the base font size.

For example, here's how you might make text extra large:

```
Label1.Font.Size = FontUnit.XXLarge
```

The other way to set font attributes is using CSS styles, using CSS style attributes (such as the ones you see in Table 12.6) with a control's Style property. You actually have considerably more control over fonts using styles such as font-family, font-size, and font-weight than using the Font property—here's an example, where this code is setting a font face, size, and weight in a label control:

```
Label1.Style("font-family") = "Times New Roman"
Label1.Style("font-size") = "24pt"
Label1.Style("font-weight") = "Bold"
```

Note that these styles are not restricted to the types of font styling supported by HTML—here, you're picking your own font face, size in points (a point is 1/72nd of an inch), and weight. CSS styles were introduced over the years expressly to give you more control over your Web page's appearance than is possible with standard HTML.

Setting Web Control Border Style

Many Web server controls, including labels and text boxes, let you set their border styles (although not all border styles will be supported by all browsers). You can set the BorderStyle property to one of these values from the BorderStyle enumeration:

- BorderStyle.Dashed—A dashed line border
- BorderStyle.Dotted—A dotted line border
- BorderStyle.Double—A double solid line border
- BorderStyle.Groove—A grooved border

12

- `BorderStyle.Inset`—An inset border
- `BorderStyle.None`—No border
- `BorderStyle.NotSet`—No set border style
- `BorderStyle.Outset`—An outset border
- `BorderStyle.Ridge`—A ridged border
- `BorderStyle.Solid`—A solid line border

For example, you can make the text box in the WebControls example dotted, as you see in Figure 12.6.

FIGURE 12.6

Dotting a text box's border.

Adding Controls at Runtime

As with Windows controls, you can add Web controls to a form at runtime, although it takes a little more work. Controls based on the `System.Web.UI.Control` class support a `Controls` collection that holds the controls contained in the control, and you can use the `Add` method of that collection to add new controls to a container control. You can see how this works in the CreateControls example in the code for this book. When you click the button in this example, an additional button is added to the Web form, and when you click that new button, it displays a message in a text box.

It's easiest to add new controls to a Web form by adding them to a container control, not the Web form itself. One popular container control is the `Panel` control, and there's a `Panel` control, `Panel1`, in the CreateControls example, as you see in the middle of the Web form at design time in Figure 12.7. We'll get all the details on panels tomorrow; you can think of them much like the `Panel` controls in Windows programming (see Day 5, "Windows Forms: Working with Text Boxes, Buttons, Labels, Check Boxes, and Radio Buttons").

FIGURE 12.7

The CreateControls example.

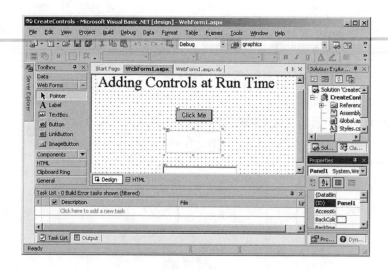

When you run this example, you start by clicking the Click Me button as you see in Figure 12.8.

FIGURE 12.8

Using the CreateControls example.

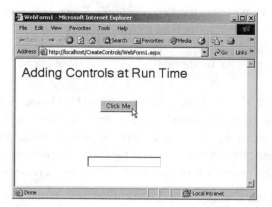

When you click the Click Me button, a new button, Click Me Too, appears as you see in Figure 12.9. Clicking this new button displays a message in the text box, as you also see in Figure 12.9.

Here's how this example works—we create a new button, Button2, in code, configure it (adding an event handler and setting its caption) and add it to the Panel1 control's Controls collection when the user clicks the Click Me button:

```
Dim Button2 As New _
    System.Web.UI.WebControls.Button
```

12

```
Private Sub Button1_Click(ByVal sender As System.Object, _
    ByVal e As System.EventArgs) Handles Button1.Click
    AddHandler Button2.Click, AddressOf Button2_Click
    Button2.Text = "Click Me Too"
    Panel1.Controls.Add(Button2)
End Sub
```

FIGURE 12.9

Adding a new button.

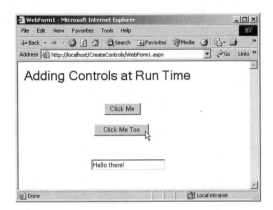

Here's the new button's event handler, which just displays the text `"Hello there!"` in the example's text box when this button is clicked:

```
Private Sub Button2_Click(ByVal sender As Object, ByVal e As System.EventArgs)
    TextBox1.Text = "Hello there!"
End Sub
```

However, although this new button, `Button2`, was added to the `Panel1.Controls` collection, that collection is *not* preserved between server round-trips. Nor can you explicitly save and restore the `Panel1.Controls` collection yourself (using the Web form's `ViewState` property, for example) because the `Controls` property is read-only. This means that the new button will disappear when the page is refreshed.

One way around this is to explicitly add the new button to the `Panel1.Controls` collection each time the page is loaded. However, we only want to do that after the first button, `Button1`, is clicked, so we'll set up a Boolean variable, `blnShowButton`, to indicate if we should show `Button2` when the page loads. When we click `Button1`, that sets `blnShowButton` to `True` like this (note that we must also preserve the value in `blnShowButton` between server round-trips, which we do with the form's `ViewState` property here):

```
Dim Button2 As New _
    System.Web.UI.WebControls.Button
Dim blnShowButton As Boolean = False
```

```
Private Sub Button1_Click(ByVal sender As System.Object, _
    ByVal e As System.EventArgs) Handles Button1.Click
    blnShowButton = True
    Me.ViewState("button") = blnShowButton
    AddHandler Button2.Click, AddressOf Button2_Click
    Button2.Text = "Click Me Too"
    Panel1.Controls.Add(Button2)
End Sub
```

Now we can test the blnShowButton variable in the Page_Load event handler, and if that variable is True, we can add the new button to Panel1.Controls when the page loads:

```
Private Sub Page_Load(ByVal sender As System.Object, _
    ByVal e As System.EventArgs) Handles MyBase.Load
    'Put user code to initialize the page here
    blnShowButton = Me.ViewState("button")
    If blnShowButton Then
        AddHandler Button2.Click, AddressOf Button2_Click
        Button2.Text = "Click Me Too"
        Panel1.Controls.Add(Button2)
    End If
    Me.ViewState("button") = blnShowButton
End Sub
```

And that's all you need. You can see the results in Figure 12.8 and 12.9. You can see the code for this example in Listing 12.1.

LISTING 12.1   WebForm1.aspx (AddControls Project)

```
Public Class WebForm1
    Inherits System.Web.UI.Page

' Web Form Designer Generated Code

    Dim Button2 As New _
        System.Web.UI.WebControls.Button
    Dim blnShowButton As Boolean = False

    Private Sub Page_Load(ByVal sender As System.Object, _
        ByVal e As System.EventArgs) Handles MyBase.Load
        'Put user code to initialize the page here
        blnShowButton = Me.ViewState("button")
        If blnShowButton Then
            AddHandler Button2.Click, AddressOf Button2_Click
            Button2.Text = "Click Me Too"
            Panel1.Controls.Add(Button2)
        End If
        Me.ViewState("button") = blnShowButton
    End Sub
```

12

LISTING 12.1 continued

```
        Private Sub Button1_Click(ByVal sender As System.Object, _
            ByVal e As System.EventArgs) Handles Button1.Click
            blnShowButton = True
            Me.ViewState("button") = blnShowButton
            AddHandler Button2.Click, AddressOf Button2_Click
            Button2.Text = "Click Me Too"
            Panel1.Controls.Add(Button2)
        End Sub

        Private Sub Button2_Click(ByVal sender As Object, _
            ByVal e As System.EventArgs)
            TextBox1.Text = "Hello there!"
        End Sub

    End Class
```

That completes our look at Web server controls in overview. It's time to start working on a control-by-control basis to see what these controls have to offer us, starting with buttons.

Using Buttons

As you've already seen, you use the Button control to create a button in a Web page. Web server button controls send their data back to the server when they're clicked, so they're made into Submit buttons in HTML. (Submit buttons are the ones you click to send the data in an HTML form back to the server.) Here's what a typical Web server button looks like after it has been converted into the HTML that is sent to the browser:

```
<input type="submit" name="Button1" value="Click me" id="Button1"
style="height:24px;width:125px;Z-INDEX: 101; LEFT: 100px;
POSITION: absolute; TOP: 100px" />
```

That's the HTML representation of the button, but in code, you can stick to Visual Basic if you prefer—in fact, the Click event handler for buttons looks exactly as it would in a Windows forms project, with the same two arguments passed to this Sub procedure:

```
Private Sub Button1_Click(ByVal sender As System.Object, _
    ByVal e As System.EventArgs) Handles Button1.Click
    TextBox1.Text = "Thanks for clicking me."
End Sub
```

Buttons can also be *command buttons* in Visual Basic. A command button is just like a standard button—it's also turned into a Submit button in HTML, but it also supports two additional properties, CommandName and CommandArgument, as well as a Command event. These properties can hold text values, letting you know which button was clicked, which is useful if you only want to have one event handler for all the buttons in your application.

The big event in buttons is the Click event, which we've already put to work. When a button's Click event occurs, the page is sent back to the server for processing. And it's the same for the Command event, which occurs if you've given a button a CommandName value.

Here is the hierarchy of the System.Web.UI.WebControls.Button class:

```
System.Object
    System.Web.UI.Control
        System.Web.UI.WebControls.WebControl
            System.Web.UI.WebControls.Button
```

You can find the significant public properties of Button objects in Table 12.7, and the significant events in Table 12.8. (Note that there's no table of methods here—Button inherits all its methods from the WebControl class.) As with other Web server controls, these tables do not list the significant properties, methods, and events this class inherits from the Control and WebControl classes—you can find them in Tables 12.1 to 12.5.

TABLE 12.7   Significant Public Properties of Button Objects

Property	Means
CausesValidation	Returns or sets whether the button causes data validation.
CommandArgument	Returns or sets the command argument, which is passed to the Command event handler.
CommandName	Returns or sets the command name, which is passed to the Command event handler.
Text	Returns or sets the caption in the button.

TABLE 12.8   Significant Public Events of Button Objects

Event	Means
Click	Occurs when a button is clicked.
Command	Occurs when a command button is clicked.

12

Creating Standard Buttons

Standard buttons are the simplest control in Visual Basic .NET Web programming. Handling buttons in Web forms is similar to using buttons in Windows forms, as you can see in the Button example in the code for this book. You can see this example at work in Figure 12.10; when you click the button labeled Click Me, the text `You clicked the button.` appears in a text box.

FIGURE 12.10

Buttons at work.

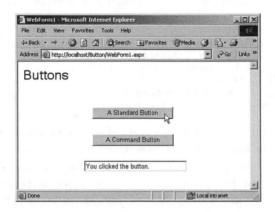

To add a new button to a Web form, you just drag it from the toolbox, as we have in Windows programming. You can also work with a button's `Click` event just as we did in Windows programming—just double-click a button to bring up this code in a code designer:

```
Private Sub Button1_Click(ByVal sender As System.Object, ByVal e As _
    System.EventArgs) Handles Button1.Click
    .
    .
    .
End Sub
```

This is exactly the same as we've seen in Windows programming. To display text in the text box in this example, `TextBox1`, we can use code like this:

```
Private Sub Button1_Click(ByVal sender As System.Object, ByVal e As _
    System.EventArgs) Handles Button1.Click
    TextBox1.Text = "You clicked the button."
End Sub
```

Creating Command Buttons

You can also turn Web server buttons into command buttons. You turn a button into a command button simply by assigning text to its `CommandName` property. Besides

CommandName, you can also assign an object, usually text, to a button's CommandArgument property. When you click a command button, the button's Click event fires as well as its Command event.

You can see how this works in the Button example. In that example, the bottom button is a command button, with its CommandName property set to "Command1" and its CommandArgument property set to You clicked the command button. Because text is assigned to this button's CommandName property, a Command event will occur when the button is clicked:

```
Private Sub Button2_Command(ByVal sender As Object, ByVal e As _
    System.Web.UI.WebControls.CommandEventArgs) Handles Button2.Command
        .
        .
        .
End Sub
```

The CommandEventArgs object passed to this event handler has both a CommandName and CommandArgument property, and you can recover the text in those properties using this object. For example, here's how you can make sure that the command button Command1 was the button that was clicked, and if so, display this button's CommandArgument text:

```
Private Sub Button2_Command(ByVal sender As Object, ByVal e As _
    System.Web.UI.WebControls.CommandEventArgs) Handles Button2.Command
        If e.CommandName = "Command1" Then
            TextBox1.Text = e.CommandArgument
        End If
End Sub
```

You can see the result in Figure 12.11, where the user has clicked the command button, the bottom button, in the Button example.

FIGURE 12.11

A command button at work.

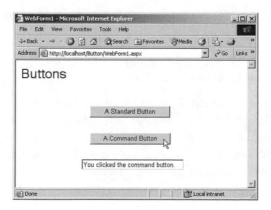

Using Text Boxes

We already know all about buttons, and we already know a lot about text box Web server controls. In Web programming, text boxes are like a stripped-down version of Windows text boxes. When sent to the browser, these controls are turned into standard HTML text fields, which don't have as much functionality as Visual Basic Windows text boxes. Here's what a typical Web server text box looks like in the HTML that is actually sent to the browser—it's just an HTML `<input>` element with the `type` attribute set to `"text"`:

```
<input name="TextBox1" type="text" id="TextBox1"
style="Z-INDEX: 104; LEFT: 100px; POSITION: absolute; TOP: 100px" />
```

Here's another way that Web server text boxes differ from Windows text boxes— although you can create multiline and password controls using text boxes, you don't do so with `MultiLine` and `PasswordChar` properties—you use the `TextMode` property. By default, the `TextMode` property is set to `SingleLine` to create a single-line HTML text field, but it can be also be set to `MultiLine` for a multiline text box or `Password` to create a password control.

Password controls are turned into HTML `<input>` controls controls> with the `type` attribute set to `"password"` like this:

```
<input name="TextBox1" type="password" id="TextBox1"
style="Z-INDEX: 104; LEFT: 182px; POSITION: absolute; TOP: 209px" />
```

A multiline text box is actually an HTML text area control—here's what one looks like in the HTML that ASP.NET sends to the browser:

```
<textarea name="TextBox1" id="TextBox1"
style="height:74px;width:157px;Z-INDEX: 103; LEFT: 100px;
POSITION: absolute; TOP: 100px"></textarea>
```

Here is the hierarchy of the `System.Web.UI.WebControls.TextBox` class:

```
System.Object
   System.Web.UI.Control
      System.Web.UI.WebControls.WebControl
         System.Web.UI.WebControls.TextBox
```

You can find the significant public properties of `TextBox` objects in Table 12.9 and the significant event in Table 12.10. (Note that there's no table of methods here—`TextBox` inherits all its methods from the `WebControl` class.) Note that as with other Web server controls, these tables do not list the significant properties, methods, and events this class inherits from the `Control` and `WebControl` classes—you can find them in Tables 12.1 to 12.5.

TABLE 12.9 Significant Public Properties of `TextBox` Objects

Property	Means
AutoPostBack	Returns or sets whether events will be automatically sent back to the server when they occur.
Columns	Returns or sets the text box's width (in characters).
MaxLength	Returns or sets the maximum number of characters that may be displayed in the text box.
ReadOnly	Returns or sets whether the text box is read-only.
Rows	Returns or sets a multiline text box's display height.
Text	Returns or sets the text in a text box.
TextMode	Returns or sets whether a text box should be single line, multiline, or a password control.
Wrap	Returns or sets whether text wraps in the text box.

TABLE 12.10 Significant Public Event of `TextBox` Objects

Events	Means
TextChanged	Occurs when the text in the text box is changed.

To recover the text in a text box, you can use its `Text` property in Visual Basic code, and it has a `TextChanged` event to handle events when the user edits the text in the text box. You can set the display width of a text box with its `Columns` property. And, if it's a multiline text box, you can set the display height with the `Rows` property. You can also make text boxes read-only, where the user can't change the text in the control, by setting their `ReadOnly` property to `True`.

The Textbox example in the code for this book shows several ways to work with text boxes, as you see in Figure 12.12. In this example, you can see how to work with single line text boxes, multiline text boxes, and password controls.

Text boxes are pretty simple controls; in most applications, you just use the `Text` property to display text or read the text the user has entered—we've already seen that in the Button example today, which uses code like this:

```
Private Sub Button1_Click(ByVal sender As System.Object, ByVal e As _
    System.EventArgs) Handles Button1.Click
    TextBox1.Text = "You clicked the button."
End Sub
```

12

FIGURE 12.12

Text boxes at work.

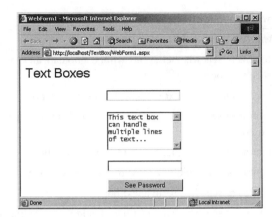

But there's more power available here—for example, you can create multiline text boxes using the `TextMode` property.

Creating Multiline Text Boxes

When you set the `TextMode` property of a Web server text box to `MultiLine`, you create a multiline text box capable of handling several lines of text. You can size the multiline text box at design time by stretching it into place or with the `Rows` and `Columns` properties at runtime.

The fact that multiline text boxes are really text areas—supported with the `<textarea>` HTML element, not the `<input>` element—gives you an idea of how Visual Basic takes care of the details for you behind the scenes. Working with the text in a text area is completely different from working with the text in an HTML text field—in a text field, you assign the text to the `<input>` element's `value` HTML attribute:

```
<input name="TextBox1" type="text" value="No worries."
id="TextBox1" style="Z-INDEX: 102; LEFT: 180px;
POSITION: absolute; TOP: 64px" />
```

But in a text area, you enclose the text between the `<textarea>` and `</textarea>` tags like this:

```
<textarea name="TextBox2" id="TextBox2"
style="height:79px;width:156px;Z-INDEX: 103;
LEFT: 181px; POSITION: absolute; TOP: 109px">
    This text box can handle multiple lines of text...
</textarea>
```

Visual Basic hides those details—all you have to do is to use the `Text` property of a multiline text box to work with its text, just as you would with a single line text box. For example, to assign the text "No worries." to a multiline text box when the user clicks a button, you use code like this:

```
Private Sub Button1_Click(ByVal sender As System.Object, _
    ByVal e As System.EventArgs) Handles Button1.Click
    TextBox2.Text = "No worries."
        .
        .
        .
End Sub
```

Creating Password Controls

In Windows programming, you convert a text box to a password control by assigning a character to the text box's PasswordChar property; the password character is the masking character that will appear when the user types a character into the control. In Web programming, on the other hand, you convert a text box to a password control by assigning a text box's TextMode property the value Password. You don't have any choice for the password character here—it's always an asterisk (*).

You can see a password control at the bottom of the Textbox example in this book's code. In HTML, a password control like that becomes an <input> element with the type attribute set to "password" like this:

```
<input name="TextBox3" type="password" id="TextBox3"
style="height:24px;width:118px;Z-INDEX: 104; LEFT: 100px;
POSITION: absolute; TOP: 100px" />
```

In code, you can read the text in the password control using the control's Text property, as the code does in the Textbox example. When you click the See Password button, the text in the password control is copied (unmasked) to the top text box like this:

```
Private Sub Button1_Click(ByVal sender As System.Object,
    ByVal e As System.EventArgs) Handles Button1.Click
    TextBox1.Text = TextBox3.Text
End Sub
```

You can see the result in Figure 12.13.

Note that HTML password controls, like the Windows password controls discussed in Day 5, don't let the user copy his text and paste that text somewhere else to read the password. And when a page is refreshed, Web server password controls don't redisplay their text, which means that no one can gain access to that text by taking a look at the page's source HTML.

12

FIGURE **12.13**

A password control at work.

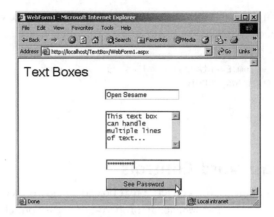

Handling Text Box Events

Most of the work you do with a text box revolves around the Text property. As with Windows text boxes, you can catch changes to the text in a text box with the TextChanged event. For example, if you change the text in the multiline text box in the TextBox example and then click somewhere else so that the multiline text box loses the focus, a TextChanged event occurs, and the message "Text was changed!" will appear in the single-line text box at the top of the example. Here's how that works in code, in a TextChanged event handler:

```
Private Sub TextBox2_TextChanged(ByVal sender As System.Object, _
    ByVal e As System.EventArgs) Handles TextBox2.TextChanged
    TextBox1.Text = "Text was changed!"
End Sub
```

Although the TextChanged event occurs as soon as the text in the text box is changed and the text box loses the focus (which indicates that the edit is complete), text box events are not automatically posted back to the server when they occur. If you want that to happen, set the text box's AutoPostBack property to True.

As with any other Web control, you can create new text boxes at runtime. For example, this code adds a new text box to a panel control when the user clicks a button:

```
Dim TextBox2 As New _
    System.Web.UI.WebControls.TextBox2

Private Sub Button1_Click(ByVal sender As System.Object, _
    ByVal e As System.EventArgs) Handles Button1.Click
    AddHandler TextBox2.TextChanged, AddressOf TextBox_TextChanged
    TextBox2.Text = "No worries."
```

```
        Panel1.Controls.Add(TextBox2)
    End Sub
```

```
Private Sub TextBox_TextChanged(ByVal sender As System.Object,
    ByVal e As System.EventArgs)
        TextBox1.Text = "Text was changed!"
End Sub
```

Besides text boxes, there are other ways of displaying text, of course, especially if you don't want to allow that text to be edited interactively—for example, you can use label controls, coming up next.

Using Labels

Text boxes display text that the user can edit; labels display text that the user can't edit, although you can change that text in your code at runtime. Labels in Visual Basic Web programming work much as labels in Windows programming, except that there's not as much functionality here because you're restricted to using the HTML that browsers can support.

You can change the displayed text in a label with the Text property in code as you can in Windows forms. (Bear in mind, however, that it takes a round-trip to the server to change that text.) In HTML, Web server labels become <span> elements that enclose text. Here's an example—this label displays the text "No Worries.", surrounded by a dashed border:

```
<span id="Label1" style="border-style:Dashed;font-size:XX-Large;
height:118px;width:203px;Z-INDEX: 101; LEFT: 250px;
POSITION: absolute; TOP: 79px">No worries.</span>
```

Here's the hierarchy of the System.Web.UI.WebControls.Label class:

```
System.Object
   System.Web.UI.Control
      System.Web.UI.WebControls.WebControl
         System.Web.UI.WebControls.Label
```

The only significant noninherited property of this class is the Text property, which gets and sets the text in the label. (This control has no noninherited methods or events.) And as with other Web server controls, labels inherit the significant properties, methods, and events of the Control and WebControl classes, which you can find in Tables 12.1 to 12.5.

Working with Labels

You can see a number of label options at work in the Label example, which appears in Figure 12.14.

12

FIGURE **12.14**

Using labels.

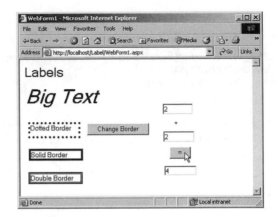

Among other things, the Label application illustrates how to use labels to display text that the user can't change in a Web page. You can enter two numbers to add in the text boxes at the right in this example, and click the button marked =. When you do, the code in this example reads the numbers entered into the two text boxes and displays their sum in the label control at the bottom, as you see in Figure 12.14; because the sum is displayed in a label, the user can't edit that value. Here's the code:

```
Private Sub Button1_Click(ByVal sender As System.Object, _
    ByVal e As System.EventArgs) Handles Button1.Click
    Label7.Text = Str(Val(TextBox1.Text) + Val(TextBox2.Text))
End Sub
```

Note that the `BorderStyle` property of the label in which the sum appears is set to `BorderStyle.Inset`, and the `BorderWidth` property is set to two pixels, which makes the label look like a text box. Another option is to make it obvious that the label in which the sum appears is *not* a text box and so cannot be edited, which you can do with another border style instead, such as `BorderStyle.Solid`. All of which brings up the next topic—setting label borders and styles.

Tip

> Don't forget that you can also use a text box to display read-only text by setting the text box's `ReadOnly` property to `True`.

Setting Label Borders and Styles

You can see a variety of border styles in the labels in Figure 12.14. As with other Web server controls, you set the border style of labels using the `BorderStyle` property, which you can assign the values `BorderStyle.Dashed`, `BorderStyle.Dotted`, `BorderStyle.Double`, `BorderStyle.Groove`, `BorderStyle.Inset`, `BorderStyle.None`, `BorderStyle.NotSet`, `BorderStyle.Outset`, `BorderStyle.Ridge`, or `BorderStyle.Solid`. You can also set the width of the border with the `BorderWidth` property to different values (in pixels).

You can change the `BorderStyle` and `BorderWidth` properties at design time or at runtime. For example, the button in the Label program sets the `BorderStyle` property of the label next to it to `BorderStyle.Dashed` when you click it (and changes the label's text from "Dotted Border" to "Dashed Border"):

```
Private Sub Button2_Click(ByVal sender As System.Object, _
    ByVal e As System.EventArgs) Handles Button2.Click
    Label3.BorderStyle = BorderStyle.Dashed
    Label3.Text = "Dashed Border"
End Sub
```

You can see how this works in Figure 12.15, where the border of the label next to the button has been changed to a dashed border when the user clicks the Change Border button.

FIGURE 12.15

Setting label borders.

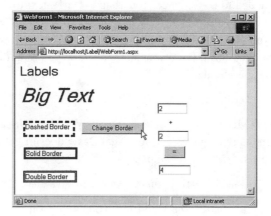

Note also the label that displays `Big Text` in the Label example. You can style text like that in various ways using a label's `Font` property. The values you can assign to this property match what's available in Web browsers. The `Font` holds a `FontInfo` object, which has these properties as you saw earlier today: `Bold`, `Italic`, `Name`, `Names`, `Overline`, `Size`, `Strikeout`, and `Underline`. Setting properties such as `Bold`, `Italic`, or `Underline` to `True` makes the font bold, italic, and underlined to match. The `Size` property lets you set the size of text you can use in Web browsers and can take these values: `FontUnit.Large`, `FontUnit.Larger`, `FontUnit.Medium`, `FontUnit.Small`,

FontUnit.Smaller, FontUnit.XLarge, FontUnit.XSmall, FontUnit.XXLarge, and
FontUnit.XXSmall.

And as we know, you have even more control if you use the Style property, which most
modern browsers will support. For example, here's how you can set the font in Label1 to
48 point, bold, underlined Arial font:

```
Label1.Style("text-decoration") = "Underline"
Label1.Style("font-family") = "Arial"
Label1.Style("font-size") = "48pt"
Label1.Style("font-weight") = "Bold"
```

Using Literals

As you saw yesterday, you can click the HTML button in a Web form designer and start
working with the HTML in a Web page. Isn't there some way to work with the HTML in
a Web page while sticking to the Visual Basic interface?

NEW TERM   There is—you can use *literals*. A literal is a control that simply holds HTML,
which is added to a Web page. You assign HTML text to a literal control's Text
property, and that text is inserted directly into the Web form. This control doesn't appear
in a Web page—you just set the Text property to the HTML you want, and that HTML
is inserted into the Web form. For example, here's how you might insert the HTML for
some bold text using a literal:

```
Literal1.Text = "<b>This text is bold.</b>"
```

When you quote HTML that itself contains quotes, you should make sure that you make
the inner quotes into single quotes ('), so Visual Basic doesn't get confused about where
your quoted text ends. Here's an example:

```
Literal1.Text = "He said, 'Hello there, young programmer.'"
```

When you add a literal control to a Web form, you can't position that literal in the form;
Visual Basic places it at upper left in the form. There's no need to position this control in
any case because it doesn't have any runtime appearance; it simply inserts HTML into a
Web page.

Here is the hierarchy of the System.Web.UI.WebControls.Literal class:

```
System.Object
   System.Web.UI.Control
      System.Web.UI.WebControls.Literal
```

This class's only significant property is the Text property, which you assign the text you want to insert into a Web form's HTML—it has no methods or events that are not inherited from the WebControl class. Note that as with other Web server controls, this class also inherits the significant properties, methods, and events from the Control and WebControl classes you see in Tables 12.1 to 12.5.

You can see the Literal class at work in the Literal example in the code for this book. When you click the button in this example, the code inserts the HTML needed to display the word Literals in a left-aligned HTML <h1> header. Here's what that code looks like:

```
Private Sub Button1_Click(ByVal sender As System.Object, _
    ByVal e As System.EventArgs) Handles Button1.Click
    Literal1.Text = "<div align='left'><h1>Literals</h1></div>"
End Sub
```

You can see the results in Figure 12.16. When the user clicks the button in this example, the label Literals appears at upper left in an <h1> HTML header (instead of in a label control as in the other Web examples you've seen so far).

FIGURE 12.16

Using literals.

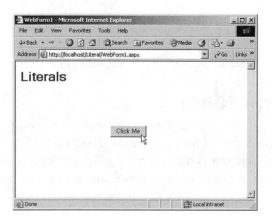

The HTML we've assigned to Literal1 is simply inserted into the Web page, replacing the literal control. For example, say that you put a button, a literal control, and a text box into a Web form in that order; those controls will all be placed in a <form> element, which encloses all the controls in a Web page. Now say that you assign HTML to the literal control. In that case, the <form> element will contain the button, followed by the HTML you assigned to the literal control, followed by the text box.

If you want to create an HTML element using a literal control and position that element, the positioning is up to you. Here's how that might look in an example that inserts a <h1> header into a Web page and positions that header to start at (200, 200) in the page using the style HTML attribute of an HTML <div> element:

```
Literal1.Text = "<div align='left' " & _
"style='POSITION: absolute; TOP: 200px; LEFT: 200px'>" & _
"<h1>Literals</h1></div>"
```

You can see the results of this code in Figure 12.17.

FIGURE 12.17

Positioning text in a Web page.

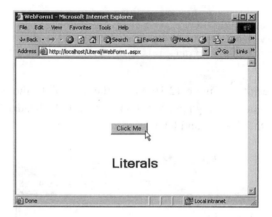

Using Placeholders

Earlier today, you saw how to add Web controls to a Web page at runtime, using a panel control as a container control for a new button. There's actually a control specially designed to let you add new controls at runtime—placeholder controls. Like the literal control you just saw, the PlaceHolder control does not produce any visible output. This control is used only as a container for other controls on the Web page, especially when you add new controls.

Here's the hierarchy of the System.Web.UI.WebControls.PlaceHolder class:

```
System.Object
    System.Web.UI.Control
        System.Web.UI.WebControls.PlaceHolder
```

This class doesn't have any noninherited members—to add controls to a placeholder, you just use its Controls collection's Add member. Note that as with other Web server controls, this class inherits properties and methods from the Control and WebControl classes—you can find them in Tables 12.1 to 12.5.

The difference between adding controls to a panel and adding controls to a placeholder is that placeholders are not positioned controls. You can position a panel where you want it in a Web page, and when you add controls to it, they'll appear in the panel. On the other hand, Visual Basic positions placeholders at the upper left in Web form, and when you add controls to a placeholder, they'll appear at the upper left. However, you can position those new controls as you want them.

For example, if we were to modify the AddControls example from earlier today to use a placeholder instead of a panel control, you'd have to explicitly position the new button after displaying it, which you can do like this:

```
Private Sub Button1_Click(ByVal sender As System.Object, _
    ByVal e As System.EventArgs) Handles Button1.Click
    blnShowButton = True
    Me.ViewState("button") = blnShowButton
    AddHandler Button2.Click, AddressOf Button2_Click
    Button2.Text = "Click Me Too"
    PlaceHolder1.Controls.Add(Button2)
    Button2.Style("Position") = "Absolute"
    Button2.Style("Top") = "130px"
    Button2.Style("Left") = "170px"
End Sub
```

You can see this new version of the AddControls example, called PlaceHolder in the code for this book, at work in Figure 12.18. This version works just like the AddControls example—when you click the Click Me button, a new button, Click Me Too, appears, as you see in Figure 12.18. When you click the Click Me Too button, a message appears in the text box, as you also see in Figure 12.18.

12

FIGURE 12.18

Using placeholders.

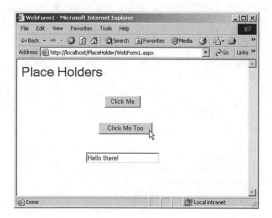

You can see the code for the PlaceHolder example in Listing 12.2. Note that, as with panels, the Controls collection in a placeholder is not preserved between server round-trips, so you have to add the new button to the placeholder every time the page is loaded.

LISTING 12.2   WebForm1.aspx (PlaceHolder Project)

```
Public Class WebForm1
    Inherits System.Web.UI.Page

' Web Form Designer Generated Code

    Dim Button2 As New _
        System.Web.UI.WebControls.Button
    Dim blnShowButton As Boolean = False

    Private Sub Page_Load(ByVal sender As System.Object, _
        ByVal e As System.EventArgs) Handles MyBase.Load
        'Put user code to initialize the page here
        blnShowButton = Me.ViewState("button")
        If blnShowButton Then
            AddHandler Button2.Click, AddressOf Button2_Click
            Button2.Text = "Click Me Too"
            PlaceHolder1.Controls.Add(Button2)
            Button2.Style("Position") = "Absolute"
            Button2.Style("Top") = "130px"
            Button2.Style("Left") = "170px"
        End If
        Me.ViewState("button") = blnShowButton
    End Sub

    Private Sub Button1_Click(ByVal sender As System.Object, _
        ByVal e As System.EventArgs) Handles Button1.Click
        blnShowButton = True
        Me.ViewState("button") = blnShowButton
        AddHandler Button2.Click, AddressOf Button2_Click
        Button2.Text = "Click Me Too"
        PlaceHolder1.Controls.Add(Button2)
        Button2.Style("Position") = "Absolute"
        Button2.Style("Top") = "130px"
        Button2.Style("Left") = "170px"
    End Sub

    Private Sub Button2_Click(ByVal sender As Object, _
        ByVal e As System.EventArgs)
        TextBox1.Text = "Hello there!"
    End Sub

End Class
```

Using XML Controls

The final Web server control we'll take a look at today is the XML control. You can use this control to display XML or formatted XML in a Web page—it's the XML equivalent of the Literal control for HTML.

Extensible Markup Language, XML, is all about holding data in text form in documents, and it plays a huge part in the behind-the-scenes Web programming that goes on in Visual Basic Web programming because the data transfer that goes on between components uses XML. You probably have some familiarity with XML already; XML is much like HTML, except that you make up your own tags. For example, the XML document we'll use here, planets.xml, stores data about various planets. It starts with an `<?xml?>` tag, indicating the version of XML we're using (1.0), and an element named `<PLANETS>` that will contain all the other elements in this XML document (XML documents require such an element, the root element, which contains all other elements):

```
<?xml version="1.0"?>
<PLANETS>
        .
        .
        .
</PLANETS>
```

We'll put three `<PLANET>` elements into the `<PLANETS>` element, and each `<PLANET>` element will contain other elements such as `<NAME>` for the name of the planet, `<MASS>` for the mass of the planet, and so on—in this way, you're free to make up your own tag names in XML:

```
<?xml version="1.0"?>
<PLANETS>

    <PLANET>
        <NAME>Mercury</NAME>
        <MASS UNITS="(Earth = 1)">.0553</MASS>
        <DAY UNITS="days">58.65</DAY>
        <RADIUS UNITS="miles">1516</RADIUS>
        <DENSITY UNITS="(Earth = 1)">.983</DENSITY>
        <DISTANCE UNITS="million miles">43.4</DISTANCE><!—At perihelion—>
    </PLANET>
        .
        .
        .
</PLANETS>
```

You can see the whole XML document, planets.xml, in Listing 12.3. If you're not already familiar with XML, you might want to take a look at the official XML specification at

12

www.w3.org/TR/REC-xml, which describes XML and how to construct it, as well as how
to create legal tag names, nest elements, and much more.

LISTING 12.3   planets.xml (XML Project)

```
<?xml version="1.0"?>
<PLANETS>

    <PLANET>
        <NAME>Mercury</NAME>
        <MASS UNITS="(Earth = 1)">.0553</MASS>
        <DAY UNITS="days">58.65</DAY>
        <RADIUS UNITS="miles">1516</RADIUS>
        <DENSITY UNITS="(Earth = 1)">.983</DENSITY>
        <DISTANCE UNITS="million miles">43.4</DISTANCE><!—At perihelion—>
    </PLANET>

    <PLANET>
        <NAME>Venus</NAME>
        <MASS UNITS="(Earth = 1)">.815</MASS>
        <DAY UNITS="days">116.75</DAY>
        <RADIUS UNITS="miles">3716</RADIUS>
        <DENSITY UNITS="(Earth = 1)">.943</DENSITY>
        <DISTANCE UNITS="million miles">66.8</DISTANCE><!—At perihelion—>
    </PLANET>

    <PLANET>
        <NAME>Earth</NAME>
        <MASS UNITS="(Earth = 1)">1</MASS>
        <DAY UNITS="days">1</DAY>
        <RADIUS UNITS="miles">2107</RADIUS>
        <DENSITY UNITS="(Earth = 1)">1</DENSITY>
        <DISTANCE UNITS="million miles">128.4</DISTANCE><!—At perihelion—>
    </PLANET>

</PLANETS>
```

The XML control lets you directly display XML documents, such as planets.xml, in a
Web page; you can use these properties of the control to display XML documents:

- Document—Returns or sets the System.Xml.XmlDocument object to display in the
  XML control.

- DocumentContent—Sets a string that contains the XML document to display in the
  XML control.

- DocumentSource—Returns or sets the path to an XML document to display in the
  XML control.

The XML control also lets you use Extensible Stylesheet Language Transformations, XSLT, to format the XML as you want it. XSLT can transform an XML document by working with its data into an XML document of another type or into an HTML document, plain text, or any other text-based format, even including rich text, RTF, format.

NEW TERM Rather than displaying XML directly, you normally use the XML control with an XSLT *stylesheet* to transform an XML document into HTML to be displayed in a Web page. You'll find an XSLT stylesheet, planets.xsl, in Listing 12.4 that extracts the data in planets.xml and formats it into an HTML table. We can use that stylesheet with an XML control in the XML example in the code for this book. Like XML, XSLT is also a specification of the World Wide Web Consortium; you can read all about XSLT at http://www.w3.org/TR/xslt.

LISTING 12.4 planets.xsl (XML Project)

```
<?xml version="1.0"?>
<xsl:stylesheet version="1.1"
xmlns:xsl="http://www.w3.org/1999/XSL/Transform">

    <!— This template matches all PLANETS elements —>
    <xsl:template match="/PLANETS">
        <HTML>
            <HEAD>
                <TITLE>
                    The Planets Table
                </TITLE>
            </HEAD>
            <BODY>
                <H1>
                    The Planets Table
                </H1>
                <TABLE BORDER="2">
                    <TR>
                        <TD>Name</TD>
                        <TD>Mass</TD>
                        <TD>Radius</TD>
                        <TD>Day</TD>
                    </TR>
                    <xsl:apply-templates/>
                </TABLE>
            </BODY>
        </HTML>
    </xsl:template>

    <xsl:template match="PLANET">
        <TR>
```

12

LISTING 12.4   continued

```
            <TD><xsl:value-of select="NAME"/></TD>
            <TD><xsl:apply-templates select="MASS"/></TD>
            <TD><xsl:apply-templates select="RADIUS"/></TD>
            <TD><xsl:apply-templates select="DAY"/></TD>
        </TR>
    </xsl:template>

    <xsl:template match="MASS">
        <xsl:value-of select="."/>
        <xsl:text> </xsl:text>
        <xsl:value-of select="@UNITS"/>
    </xsl:template>

    <xsl:template match="RADIUS">
        <xsl:value-of select="."/>
        <xsl:text> </xsl:text>
        <xsl:value-of select="@UNITS"/>
    </xsl:template>

    <xsl:template match="DAY">
        <xsl:value-of select="."/>
        <xsl:text> </xsl:text>
        <xsl:value-of select="@UNITS"/>
    </xsl:template>

</xsl:stylesheet>
```

To transform planets.xml using planets.xsl into HTML that you can see in a Web page, we'll use an XML control. Here's the hierarchy of the `System.Web.UI.WebControls.Xml` class that supports XML controls:

```
System.Object
   System.Web.UI.Control
      System.Web.UI.WebControls.Xml
```

You can find the significant public properties of `System.Web.UI.WebControls.Xml` objects in Table 12.11. (There's no table of methods or events here—`System.Web.UI.WebControls.Xml` inherits all its methods and events from the `WebControl` class.) Note that as with other Web server controls, this table does not list the significant properties, methods, and events this class inherits from the `Control` and `WebControl` classes—you can find them in Tables 12.1 to 12.5.

TABLE 12.11   Significant Public Events of XML Controls

Events	Means
Document	Returns or sets the `System.Xml.XmlDocument` object to display in the XML control.
DocumentContent	Sets a string that contains the XML document to display in the XML control.
DocumentSource	Returns or sets the path to an XML document to display in the control.
Transform	Returns or sets the `System.Xml.Xsl.XslTransform` object that formats the XML document.
TransformSource	Returns or sets the path to an XSLT style sheet that formats the XML document.

All we have to do is to assign a new XML control's `DocumentSource` property the name of our XML document, and the `TransformSource` property the name of XSLT style sheet. (You can browse to these documents at design time.) When you run the XML example, you'll see the data in planets.xml formatted using the XSLT style sheet in planets.xsl into an HTML table, as you see in Figure 12.19. (To position the HTML table below the label displaying the text `XML Controls`, all that was necessary was to add a few HTML `<br>` elements to the HTML page using the Visual Basic HTML editor.)

FIGURE 12.19

Using XML controls.

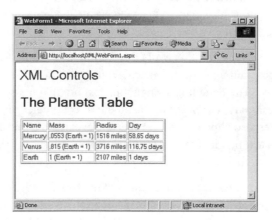

And that's it—now you're transforming XML into HTML using XSLT and the XML control.

Summary

Today, we started working in depth with Web server controls. We started with an overview of Web server controls, getting an idea of what properties, methods, and events these controls support. You saw that although these controls are much like Windows controls, they only support a subset of the properties, methods, and events of Windows controls. And you saw that there are some differences even in the functionality both types of controls support—for example, you convert Windows text boxes to a password control with the `PasswordChar` property, but in a Web server text box, you set the `TextMode` property to `Password`.

We also took a look at how to handle Web server controls in general, including how to enable and disable controls, how to make controls visible and invisible at runtime, how to set a control's style, and how to add tool tips. You saw how to move Web server controls at runtime, how to set the border style of controls, and how to set the fonts used in a control. And we also took a look at how to add Web server controls to a Web page at runtime.

Then we moved on to working with specific Web server controls, starting with buttons. There are two types of buttons—standard buttons and command buttons. As you saw, both types of buttons cause a server round-trip when clicked. In addition to a `Click` event, command buttons also cause a `Command` event, and you can read the button's `CommandName` and `CommandArgument` properties in that event's handler.

The text box Web server control is really three different controls—a single-line text box, a multiline text box, and a password control. You specify which of these to use with the `TextMode` property. (The default is a single-line text box.) You also saw that text boxes could be made read-only, which means that the user can't enter text into them. And we saw that text boxes also support the `TextChanged` event, which occurs when the user edits the text in a text box and then moves to another control, causing the text box to lose the focus.

Labels display text that the user is not supposed to change, at least not directly. (The text in labels can be changed under programmatic control.) We saw that labels can display text in various fonts, using various styles such as bold and italic, and can display various types of borders as well.

Literal controls let you insert HTML into a Web page. Literals are treated as controls like any other when they're inserted into a Web page, but you can assign HTML to their `Text` property, and that HTML will be inserted into the Web page at the location of the Literal control (which is in the Web page's `<form>` element, between the controls that surround the Literal control, if any).

Placeholders are designed to let you add controls to a Web form at runtime. As we've seen, placeholders are not positioned controls—Visual Basic places them at the upper left in a Web form, and when you add controls to them using their `Controls` collection, it's up to you to position the control where you want it.

XML controls let you display raw XML in a Web page or XML formatted with an XSL style sheet. That's great to create hybrid XML/HTML pages that display your data in formatted form.

That's it for today's work—tomorrow, we're going to continue working with Web server controls as we turn to check boxes, radio buttons, tables, and panels.

Q&A

Q I need to initialize the text in a control dynamically, at runtime, first thing. How does that work?

A The earliest event you can use for controls is the `Init` event. Note, however, that the appearance of some controls won't be set at that point, so drawing in the control (as with a `Graphics` object) might not be successful.

Q Isn't there any way to handle mouse events in a Web form?

A Although Web forms don't support mouse events directly, there are still one or two options here. You can support mouse events in JavaScript, although you'll have to add your own JavaScript code (you saw how to do that yesterday) to support mouse events. Another way is to use a Web server image button, which you will see in Day 14, "Web Forms: Working with Images, Image Buttons." Image buttons let you create image maps, and the location at which the mouse was clicked is passed to a Visual Basic event handler in your code.

12

Workshop

This workshop tests whether you understand the concepts you saw today. It's a good idea to make sure that you can answer these questions before pressing on to tomorrow's work.

Quiz

1. How can you move a Web server control in a Web form at runtime?
2. What is the largest and smallest settings for a Web server control's `Font.Size` property?

3. Into what type of HTML buttons are Web server buttons converted?

4. Is `AutoPostBack` enabled for text box `TextChanged` events by default?

5. What's the difference between adding controls to a panel and adding controls to a placeholder?

Quiz Answers

1. You can set the top, right, bottom, and left position of a Web control by assigning values to the `Style("Top")`, `Style("Right")`, `Style("Bottom")`, and `Style("Left")` properties.

2. `FontUnit.XXLarge` and `FontUnit.XXSmall`. (Don't forget that you can't assign `Font` objects to a Web server control's `Font` property.)

3. Web server buttons are converted into Submit buttons (`<input type="submit"...>`)before being sent to the browser.

4. No, `AutoPostBack` is set to `False` by default for text boxes. If you want `TextChanged` events to be handled on the server when those events occur (as opposed to waiting for the next server round-trip), set `AutoPostBack` to `True`.

5. Placeholders are not positioned controls, but panels are. When you add a control to a placeholder, you also need to set its position (unless you want the control to appear at (0, 0—that is, at upper left—in the Web form). When you add a control to a panel, the control appears at the location of the panel in the Web form.

Exercises

1. Create a new Web application that uses the `TextChanged` event in a password control to check the password the user has entered. If the password matches one you've chosen, display the text `"Pass!"` in a label control—otherwise, display the text `"Sorry!"`.

2. Create a tic-tac-toe game for two players using a grid of 3×3 buttons with X and O captions. When the game starts, each button should be blank. When a button is clicked, change the caption of that button to an X or an O as appropriate. (But don't change it if it already displays an X or an O.) (**Extra credit**: Determine in code when one player wins, and display `"X Wins"` or `"O Wins"` in a label control.)

DAY **13**

Web Forms: Working with Check Boxes, Radio Buttons, Tables, and Panels

Today, we're going to get all the details on a number of popular Web server controls: check boxes, check box lists, radio buttons, radio button lists, tables, and panels. These are all basic controls that you find yourself using frequently, and we're going to add them to our programming toolbox today. Here's an overview of today's topics:

- Creating check boxes
- Creating check box lists
- Creating radio buttons
- Creating radio button lists
- Handling check box and radio button events in lists

- Creating a table
- Creating tables in code
- Creating panels
- Organizing controls using panels

Check boxes and radio buttons are familiar to Windows users; new in Web programming for us are check box lists and radio button lists, which let you handle multiple check boxes or radio buttons in a single control. We'll also take a look at the Table control today, which lets you create and display HTML tables. Finally, panels let you organize other controls, and because they're often used to display sets of check boxes and radio buttons, we'll include them in today's work. Panels can have a visual appearance in a Web page—you can give them a border, for example—but they need not have any such appearance; their main function is as control containers, containing other controls such as check boxes and radio buttons.

That's what's coming up today, so let's get started immediately, digging into check boxes, followed by check box lists.

Using Check Boxes

NEW TERM   Windows users know all about check boxes—they're those square boxes that toggle a check mark when clicked and can display caption text. For instance, you can see check boxes in the CheckBox example in the code for this book in Figure 13.1. On the left, you see four individual check boxes. When you check or uncheck one of these check boxes, the program tells you what you've done in the text box you see under those check boxes. On the left, however, you see four check boxes that are actually part of a *check box list*. A check box list displays a collection of check boxes, and it's set up to handle those check boxes together, as part of a single control. If you check or uncheck a check box in the check box list, the program will display which check boxes are checked and which are unchecked in the multiline text box you see in Figure 13.1.

Web server check boxes look very much like the ones we've seen in Windows forms, but of course, there are quite a few differences. As usual with Web server controls, you're restricted to what HTML will let you do in a Web browser. In particular, check boxes are converted to `<input type="checkbox">` HTML controls when sent to the Web browser, like this:

```
<span style="Z-INDEX: 102; LEFT: 52px; POSITION: absolute; TOP: 65px">
<input id="CheckBox1" type="checkbox" name="CheckBox1"
onclick="__doPostBack('CheckBox1','')" language="javascript" />
<label for="CheckBox1">Check Box 1</label></span>
```

FIGURE 13.1

The CheckBox example.

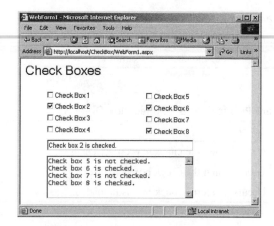

This means that Web forms check boxes are more restricted than Windows forms check boxes. For example, Web server check boxes cannot be made three-state; they do not have a `Select` method; they do not have `Show` or `Hide` methods; they cannot display images; and you need to set their `AutoPostBack` property to `True` if you want to handle their events back on the server when they happen. If you set `AutoPostBack` to `True`, Visual Basic will add JavaScript to the HTML page to send the whole page back to the server when you check or uncheck a check box.

Here is the class hierarchy of the `System.Web.UI.WebControls.CheckBox` class:

```
System.Object
    System.Web.UI.Control
        System.Web.UI.WebControls.WebControl
            System.Web.UI.WebControls.CheckBox
```

You can find the significant public properties of `System.Web.UI.WebControls.CheckBox` objects in Table 13.1, the significant public method in Table 13.2, and the significant public events in Table 13.3. (Note that as with other Web server controls, these tables do not list the significant properties, methods, and events this class inherits from the `Control` and `WebControl` classes—you can find them in Tables 12.1 to 12.5.

13

TABLE 13.1   Significant Public Properties of `CheckBox` Objects

Property	Means
AutoPostBack	Returns or sets whether the check box automatically sends the page back to the server.
Checked	Returns or sets whether the check box displays a check mark.
Text	Returns or sets the text caption for the check box.
TextAlign	Returns or sets the alignment of the text caption.

TABLE 13.2 Significant Public Method of CheckBox Objects

Method	Means
Dispose	Disposes of the check box control.

TABLE 13.3 Significant Public Events of CheckBox Objects

Event	Means
CheckedChanged	Occurs when the Checked property changes.
Load	Occurs when the check box is loaded.
Unload	Occurs when the check box is unloaded.

As you can see by comparing, for instance, Table 13.1 with Table 5.16, Web server check boxes don't have as much functionality as Windows check boxes—they can't display images, align their check marks, become toggle buttons, and so on. However, they can still perform as you'd expect check boxes to perform in Web pages, and we're going to take a look at how to handle them in code now.

Working with Check Boxes

If you take a look at the CheckBox example application, you'll see that the check boxes at the left are set up to handle the CheckChanged event in code. When you check or uncheck a check box, this event occurs, and you can use the check box's Checked property to determine its new setting. Here's what the code looks like for these check boxes—all you have to do is to look at the Checked property to determine whether a check box is checked, and display that information in the text box (don't forget to set the check box's AutoPostBack property to True if you want the CheckChanged event to be handled immediately; otherwise, it'll be handled the next time the page is sent back to the server, such as when the user clicks a button):

```
Private Sub CheckBox1_CheckedChanged(ByVal sender As System.Object,
    ByVal e As System.EventArgs) Handles CheckBox1.CheckedChanged
    If CheckBox1.Checked Then
        TextBox1.Text = "Check box 1 is checked."
    Else
        TextBox1.Text = "Check box 1 is not checked."
    End If
End Sub

Private Sub CheckBox2_CheckedChanged(ByVal sender As System.Object,
    ByVal e As System.EventArgs) Handles CheckBox2.CheckedChanged
```

```
    If CheckBox2.Checked Then
        TextBox1.Text = "Check box 2 is checked."
    Else
        TextBox1.Text = "Check box 2 is not checked."
    End If
End Sub

Private Sub CheckBox3_CheckedChanged(ByVal sender As System.Object,
    ByVal e As System.EventArgs) Handles CheckBox3.CheckedChanged
    If CheckBox3.Checked Then
        TextBox1.Text = "Check box 3 is checked."
    Else
        TextBox1.Text = "Check box 3 is not checked."
    End If
End Sub

Private Sub CheckBox4_CheckedChanged(ByVal sender As System.Object,
    ByVal e As System.EventArgs) Handles CheckBox4.CheckedChanged
    If CheckBox4.Checked Then
        TextBox1.Text = "Check box 4 is checked."
    Else
        TextBox1.Text = "Check box 4 is not checked."
    End If
End Sub
```

What if you wanted to check or uncheck a check box in code? You can set the check box's Checked property to True or False, as in this code, which checks a check box when the user clicks a button:

```
Private Sub Button1_Click(ByVal sender As System.Object,
    ByVal e As System.EventArgs)
    CheckBox1.Checked = True
End Sub
```

You can also set a check box's checked property to True at design time (the default is False), and if you do, the check box will appear checked initially when the application first starts. And you can add check boxes to a Web form at runtime too, using the techniques you saw for adding Web server controls to Web forms in Day 12, "Web Forms: Working with Buttons, Text Boxes, Labels, Literals, and Placeholders." And that's about it for Web server check boxes—as you can see, they're quite simple controls.

On the other hand, the other check boxes, at right in the CheckBox example, are part of a check box list control, and we're going to take a look at check box lists next.

13

Using Check Box Lists

A check box list is a single control that can display a number of check boxes at once—in other words, they create check box *groups*. This is useful in some circumstances, as where you might want to loop over a set of check boxes that are part of a set, such as check boxes that let the user select items for a sandwich. They're most useful, however, when you want to vary the number of check boxes you display at runtime. For example, if you want to add a new check box with the caption, say, Spell Checking, to the other check boxes already present, you only have to use the Add method of a check box list's Items collection. (You will see how to do this in a page or two.)

> **Tip**
>
> Check box lists are often connected to the data in database records because the number of check boxes can vary automatically depending on the number of Boolean fields in a record (this happens when you *bind* a check box list to a data source—for more on data binding, see Day 17, "Binding Visual Basic Controls to Databases"), and the Boolean values of True and False easily translate into checked and unchecked.

Check box lists have an Items collection, inherited from the ListControl class, with members corresponding to check boxes in the list. The main event here is the SelectedIndexChanged (not CheckChanged) event, which occurs when the user clicks a check box. Each item in the Items collection is an object of the ListItem class, and you can use the ListItem class's Value, Text, and Selected properties to work with the individual check boxes. To find out which check boxes are checked, you can loop through the list and test the Selected property of each item (for example, If CheckBoxList1.Items(19).Selected Then...).

Check box lists also support SelectedItem or SelectedIndex properties, but these are less useful than you might think—because check box lists can support multiple selections, the SelectedItem and SelectedIndex properties hold only the selected item with the lowest index value, and the index value of the selected item with the lowest index value—which tells you nothing about the other selected items.

> **Tip**
>
> You usually use the SelectedItem or SelectedIndex properties with radio button lists, coming up later today, which only support a single selected item.

Here's the hierarchy of the `System.Web.UI.WebControls.CheckBoxList` class:

```
System.Object
    System.Web.UI.Control
        System.Web.UI.WebControls.WebControl
            System.Web.UI.WebControls.ListControl
                System.Web.UI.WebControls.CheckBoxList
```

As you can see, the `System.Web.UI.WebControls.CheckBoxList` class is based on the `System.Web.UI.WebControls.ListControl` class. In fact, most of its functionality comes from the `ListControl` class, so we'll take a look at the `ListControl` class first.

The `ListControl` Class

The `ListControl` class is an abstract base class that supports the properties, methods, and events common for all list-type controls, including ones you will see today—check box lists and radio button lists. Here's the hierarchy of this class:

```
System.Object
    System.Web.UI.Control
        System.Web.UI.WebControls.WebControl
            System.Web.UI.WebControls.ListControl
```

You can find the significant public properties of `System.Web.UI.WebControls.ListControl` objects in Table 13.4 and their significant public event in Table 13.5. (This class has no non-inherited methods.) Note that as with other Web server controls, these tables do not list the significant properties, methods, and events this class inherits from the `Control` and `WebControl` classes—you can find them in Tables 12.1 to 12.5.

TABLE 13.4 Significant Public Properties of `ListControl` Objects

Property	Means
Items	Returns the collection of items that are in this list control.
SelectedIndex	Returns or sets the index of the selected item in the list. If more than one item is selected, this value holds the lowest selected index.
SelectedItem	Returns the selected item in the list control. If more than one item is selected, this property holds the item with the lowest index.

TABLE 13.5 Significant Public Event of `ListControl` Objects

Event	Means
SelectedIndexChanged	Occurs when the list selection changes.

13

The `ListControl` control's `Items` property holds a collection of `ListItem` objects, and each `ListItem` object corresponds to a check box in the list; to add check boxes to a check box list, you use the `Items` collection's `Add` method. Because you handle the check boxes in a check box list as `ListItem` objects (*not* as `CheckBox` objects), we'll also take a quick look at the `ListItem` class here.

The `ListItem` Class

A `ListItem` object represents an individual item in a list control, such as a check box in a check box list. Here is the hierarchy of this class:

```
System.Object
    System.Web.UI.WebControls.ListItem
```

You can find the significant public properties of `System.Web.UI.WebControls.ListItem` objects in Table 13.6. (This class has no noninherited methods or events.)

TABLE 13.6   Significant Public Properties of `ListItem` Objects

Properties	Means
Selected	True if the item is selected.
Text	Returns or sets the text list item's displayed text.
Value	Returns or sets the list item's value.

Now, with the `ListControl` and `ListItem` classes under your belts, you're ready to take a look at the `CheckBoxList` class itself.

The `CheckBoxList` Class

The `System.Web.UI.WebControls.ListControl` class is based on the `System.Web.UI.WebControls.WebControl` class:

```
System.Object
    System.Web.UI.Control
        System.Web.UI.WebControls.WebControl
            System.Web.UI.WebControls.ListControl
                System.Web.UI.WebControls.CheckBoxList
```

You can find the significant public properties of `System.Web.UI.WebControls.CheckBoxList` objects in Table 13.7, the significant method in Table 13.8, and the significant public events in Table 13.9. Note that as with other Web server controls, these tables do not list the significant properties, methods, and events this class inherits from the `Control` and `WebControl` classes—you can find them in Tables 12.1 to 12.5—not to mention the properties and events this class inherits from the `ListControl` class—you can find them in Tables 13.4 and 13.5.

TABLE 13.7 Significant Public Properties of `CheckBoxList` Objects

Properties	Means
CellPadding	Returns or sets the distance between the check box and the table cell that contains it (measured in pixels).
CellSpacing	Returns or sets the distance between the table cells the check boxes are displayed in (measured in pixels).
RepeatColumns	Returns or sets the number of columns in the check box list.
RepeatDirection	Returns or sets whether check boxes are arranged vertically or horizontally.
RepeatLayout	Returns or sets the check box layout.
TextAlign	Returns or sets the alignment of the caption text for the check boxes.

TABLE 13.8 Significant Public Method of `CheckBoxList` Objects

Method	Means
Dispose	Disposes of the check box list.

TABLE 13.9 Significant Public Events of `CheckBoxList` Objects

Event	Means
Load	Occurs when the check box list is loaded.
Unload	Occurs when the check box list is unloaded.

When working with check box lists, you can set the way the list is displayed by using the `RepeatLayout` and `RepeatDirection` properties. For example, if `RepeatLayout` is set to `RepeatLayout.Table` (the default), the list is drawn in an HTML table. However, if it is set to `RepeatLayout.Flow`, the list is drawn without a table. By default, the `RepeatDirection` property is set to `RepeatDirection.Vertical`, which draws the list vertically, as you saw in Figure 13.1. On the other hand, setting this property to `RepeatDirection.Horizontal` draws the list horizontally.

Check box lists are one of the composite controls that Visual Basic puts together with several HTML controls. Here's what a default check box list control looks like in the HTML that is actually sent to the browser—note that this HTML uses an HTML table to align the check boxes vertically:

```
<table id="CheckBoxList1" border="0"
style="width:127px;Z-INDEX: 106; LEFT: 257px; POSITION: absolute; TOP: 64px">
<tr>
```

13

```
<td><input id="CheckBoxList1_0" type="checkbox" name="CheckBoxList1:0"
    onclick="__doPostBack('CheckBoxList1$0','')" language="javascript" />
<label for="CheckBoxList1_0">Check Box 5</label></td>
  </tr><tr>
    <td><input id="CheckBoxList1_1" type="checkbox" name="CheckBoxList1:1"
    checked="checked" onclick="__doPostBack('CheckBoxList1$1','')"
    language="javascript" />
<label for="CheckBoxList1_1">Check Box 6</label></td>
  </tr><tr>
    <td><input id="CheckBoxList1_2" type="checkbox" name="CheckBoxList1:2"
onclick="__doPostBack('CheckBoxList1$2','')" language="javascript" />
<label for="CheckBoxList1_2">Check Box 7</label></td>
  </tr><tr>
    <td><input id="CheckBoxList1_3" type="checkbox" name="CheckBoxList1:3"
checked="checked" onclick="__doPostBack('CheckBoxList1$3','')"
language="javascript" /><label for="CheckBoxList1_3">Check Box 8</label></td>
  </tr>
</table>
```

Working with Check Box Lists

If you take a look at Figure 13.1, you'll see a check box list at right in the CheckBox example (check boxes 5 to 8). When you click a check box list, the program loops over all check boxes in the list and indicates whether they're checked, as you can see in the multiline text box at the bottom of the example.

To add items to a check box list at design time, click the ellipsis (...) button in the Items property in the Properties window. Doing so opens the ListItem Collection editor, as you see in Figure 13.2.

FIGURE 13.2

The ListItem Collection editor.

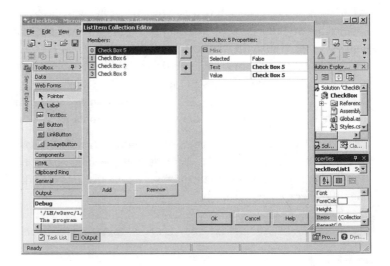

The ListItem Collection editor works much like other collection editors we've seen—to add a new item to the check box list control, click the Add button, and fill in its Text (the check box's caption), Value (holds optional text associated with the check box), and Selected (set this to True to make the corresponding check box appear selected initially) properties. You can also add check boxes to a check box list at runtime using the Add method of the control's Items collection like this:

```
CheckBoxList1.Items.Add(New ListItem("Tuesday"))
```

When the user clicks a check box in a check box list, a SelectedIndex event occurs. You can loop over all the check boxes in the list by looping from 0 to CheckBoxList1.Items.Count - 1 like this:

```
Private Sub CheckBoxList1_SelectedIndexChanged(ByVal _
    sender As System.Object, ByVal e As System.EventArgs) _
    Handles CheckBoxList1.SelectedIndexChanged
    For intLoopIndex As Integer = 0 To CheckBoxList1.Items.Count - 1
        .
        .
        .
    Next
End Sub
```

To determine which items in a check box list are checked, you can loop over the items in the control and examine their Selected properties. Here's how that works in the CheckBox example, which indicates which check boxes are checked and which are not in a multiline text box (note the use of ControlChars.CrLf to insert a carriage-return linefeed pair in the text to skip to the next line in the text box):

```
Private Sub CheckBoxList1_SelectedIndexChanged(ByVal _
    sender As System.Object, ByVal e As System.EventArgs) _
    Handles CheckBoxList1.SelectedIndexChanged
    TextBox2.Text = ""
    For intLoopIndex As Integer = 0 To CheckBoxList1.Items.Count - 1
        If CheckBoxList1.Items(intLoopIndex).Selected Then
            TextBox2.Text &= "Check box " & intLoopIndex + 5 & _
                " is checked." & ControlChars.CrLf
        Else
            TextBox2.Text &= "Check box " & intLoopIndex + 5 & _
                " is not checked." & ControlChars.CrLf
        End If
    Next
End Sub
```

And that's all you need. That's the way check box lists were intended to be used—you don't usually determine which check box in the list just had its check mark changed; you

13

loop over the whole list at once. Note that you can also set the `Selected` property in the `ListItem` Collection editor at design time for each check box in the list so that it will appear checked or not initially as you want it to be.

You can also add check box lists and radio button lists to a Web form at runtime, of course. Here's how you can create a check box list with seven check boxes in it (corresponding to the seven days of the week), add it to a Panel control in a Web form, and attach an event handler to the `SelectedIndexChanged` event when the user clicks a button:

```
Dim CheckBoxList1 As New CheckBoxList
Dim blnCheckBoxList As Boolean = False

Private Sub Page_Load(ByVal sender As System.Object, _
    ByVal e As System.EventArgs) Handles MyBase.Load
    blnCheckBoxList = Me.ViewState("blnCheckBoxList")
    If blnCheckBoxList Then
        CheckBoxList1.Items.Add("Monday")
        CheckBoxList1.Items.Add("Tuesday")
        CheckBoxList1.Items.Add("Wednesday")
        CheckBoxList1.Items.Add("Thursday")
        CheckBoxList1.Items.Add("Friday")
        CheckBoxList1.Items.Add("Saturday")
        CheckBoxList1.Items.Add("Sunday")
        AddHandler CheckBoxList1.SelectedIndexChanged, _
            AddressOf CheckBoxList1_SelectedIndexChanged
        CheckBoxList1.AutoPostBack = True
        Panel1.Controls.Add(CheckBoxList1)
    End If
End Sub

Private Sub Button1_Click(ByVal sender As System.Object, _
    ByVal e As System.EventArgs) Handles Button1.Click
    blnCheckBoxList = True
    Me.ViewState("blnCheckBoxList") = blnCheckBoxList
    CheckBoxList1.Items.Add("Monday")
    CheckBoxList1.Items.Add("Tuesday")
    CheckBoxList1.Items.Add("Wednesday")
    CheckBoxList1.Items.Add("Thursday")
    CheckBoxList1.Items.Add("Friday")
    CheckBoxList1.Items.Add("Saturday")
    CheckBoxList1.Items.Add("Sunday")
    AddHandler CheckBoxList1.SelectedIndexChanged, AddressOf _
        CheckBoxList1_SelectedIndexChanged
    CheckBoxList1.AutoPostBack = True
    Panel1.Controls.Add(CheckBoxList1)
End Sub
```

```
Private Sub CheckBoxList1_SelectedIndexChanged(ByVal _
    sender As System.Object, ByVal e As System.EventArgs)
    TextBox1.Text = ""
    For intLoopIndex As Integer = 0 To CheckBoxList1.Items.Count - 1
        If CheckBoxList1.Items(intLoopIndex).Selected Then
            TextBox1.Text &= CheckBoxList1.Items(intLoopIndex).Text & _
                " is checked." & ControlChars.CrLf
        Else
            TextBox1.Text &= CheckBoxList1.Items(intLoopIndex).Text & _
                " is not checked." & ControlChars.CrLf
        End If
    Next
End Sub
```

Using Radio Buttons

Radio buttons are as familiar as check boxes; they're those round controls that you can check or uncheck with a round dot. Whereas check boxes let the user select from a set of nonexclusive items, radio buttons let the user select from a set of exclusive items, such as the current month of the year. You can see a set of radio buttons at work in the RadioButton example in Figure 13.3.

FIGURE 13.3

The RadioButton example.

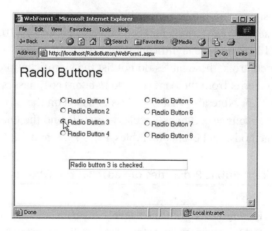

As we know from Day 5, "Windows Forms: Working with Text Boxes, Buttons, Labels, Check Boxes, and Radio Buttons," radio buttons usually operate in groups, where only one radio button at a time can be checked. When you add radio buttons to a Windows form, they're automatically placed into a single group. That's not true in Web forms—in this case, you must set the GroupName property of every radio button you want to be in a group to the same name as the others in the group. And if you want a radio button's events to be handled when they occur rather than waiting for the next server round-trip,

13

you must set the radio button's `AutoPostback` property to `True`. Radio buttons are supported in the Web browser with the HTML `<input type="radio">` element like this:

```
<span style="Z-INDEX: 102; LEFT: 88px; POSITION: absolute; TOP: 73px">
<input id="RadioButton1" type="radio" name="RadioButtons"
value="RadioButton1" onclick="__doPostBack('RadioButton1','')"
language="javascript" />
<label for="RadioButton1">Radio Button 1</label></span>
```

In addition to individual radio buttons, you can also use radio button lists, which work much like check box lists. The radio buttons in a radio button list control are automatically part of the same group. A radio button list looks just like a set of standard radio buttons at runtime—the radio buttons at right in the RadioButton example (radio buttons 5 to 8) are part of a radio button list.

We'll take a look at radio button controls first, and then radio button lists. Here is the hierarchy of the `System.Web.UI.WebControls.RadioButton` class:

```
System.Object
   System.Web.UI.Control
      System.Web.UI.WebControls.WebControl
         System.Web.UI.WebControls.CheckBox
            System.Web.UI.WebControls.RadioButton
```

You can find the significant public properties of `System.Web.UI.WebControls.RadioButton` objects in Table 13.10, the significant public method in Table 13.11, and the significant public event in Table 13.12. Note that as with other Web server controls, these tables do not list the significant properties, methods, and events this class inherits from the `Control` and `WebControl` classes—you can find them in Tables 12.1 to 12.5. Note also that this class is based on the `System.Web.UI.WebControls.CheckBox` class—you'll find the `CheckBox` class's significant properties, methods, and events in Tables 13.1, 13.2, and 13.3.

TABLE 13.10   Significant Public Properties of `RadioButton` Objects

Property	Means
GroupName	Returns or sets the radio button's group name. A radio button will act in concert with other radio buttons that have the same group name.
Text	Returns or sets the text caption for with the radio button.

TABLE 13.11   Significant Public Method of `RadioButton` Objects

Method	Means
Dispose	Disposes of the radio button.

TABLE 13.12   Significant Public Event of `RadioButton` Objects

Event	Means
CheckedChanged	Occurs when the Checked property changes.

When you click a radio button, a `CheckChanged` event occurs, and you can determine whether the radio button is checked with the `Checked` property. You can also check a radio button by setting this property to `True`.

Working with Radio Buttons

You can add radio buttons to a Web form at design time just as you do with Windows forms—just drag or double-click one using the toolbox. However, to group a number of radio buttons so that they act in concert, you must set their `GroupName` property to the same name—the radio buttons in the RadioButton example in the code for this book simply uses the name "RadioButtons" for this purpose. When you group radio buttons with the same `GroupName` value, they don't have to be next to each other or arranged in groups—they can be anywhere you want in the page.

The RadioButton example you saw in Figure 13.3 uses four radio buttons on the left in a single radio button group. When the user clicks one of these radio buttons, a `CheckChanged` event occurs. Because the `AutoPostBack` property of each of these controls has been set to `True`, the `CheckChanged` event is handed back on the server in an event handler like this:

```
Private Sub RadioButton1_CheckedChanged(ByVal sender As System.Object, _
    ByVal e As System.EventArgs) Handles RadioButton1.CheckedChanged
        .
        .
        .
End Sub
```

Because there's a separate event handler for each radio button, it's no problem to check whether the radio button is checked using the `Checked` property, as well as to indicate its new status in a text box. Here's what that looks like for the radio buttons in the RadioButton example:

```
Private Sub RadioButton1_CheckedChanged(ByVal sender As System.Object, _
    ByVal e As System.EventArgs) Handles RadioButton1.CheckedChanged
    If RadioButton1.Checked Then
        TextBox1.Text = "Radio button 1 is checked."
    Else
        TextBox1.Text = "Radio button 1 is not checked."
    End If
End Sub
```

13

```
Private Sub RadioButton2_CheckedChanged(ByVal sender As System.Object, _
    ByVal e As System.EventArgs) Handles RadioButton2.CheckedChanged
    If RadioButton2.Checked Then
        TextBox1.Text = "Radio button 2 is checked."
    Else
        TextBox1.Text = "Radio button 2 is not checked."
    End If
End Sub

Private Sub RadioButton3_CheckedChanged(ByVal sender As System.Object, _
    ByVal e As System.EventArgs) Handles RadioButton3.CheckedChanged
    If RadioButton3.Checked Then
        TextBox1.Text = "Radio button 3 is checked."
    Else
        TextBox1.Text = "Radio button 3 is not checked."
    End If
End Sub

Private Sub RadioButton4_CheckedChanged(ByVal sender As System.Object, _
    ByVal e As System.EventArgs) Handles RadioButton4.CheckedChanged
    If RadioButton4.Checked Then
        TextBox1.Text = "Radio button 4 is checked."
    Else
        TextBox1.Text = "Radio button 4 is not checked."
    End If
End Sub
```

That's all it takes—you can see the results in Figure 13.3. Besides checking whether a radio button is checked with the Checked property, you can also check or uncheck it, as in this code, which checks a radio button when the user clicks a button:

```
Private Sub Button1_Click(ByVal sender As System.Object, _
    ByVal e As System.EventArgs) Handles Button1.Click
    RadioButton1.Checked = True
End Sub
```

You can also set a radio button's Checked property to True (the default is False) at design time to make it appear selected when it's first displayed. And as with check boxes, you can add radio buttons to a Web form at runtime, using the techniques you saw for adding Web server controls to Web forms in Day 12.

The radio buttons you see at the right in the RadioButton example are part of a radio button list, and that list functions much like a check box list except that instead of check boxes, you're displaying radio buttons. We'll take a look at radio button lists next.

Using Radio Button Lists

Radio button lists let you display a number of radio buttons using a single control. In this way, they give you an easy way to display a single-selection radio button group. One useful aspect of this control is that lists of radio buttons can be generated at runtime using data binding, just as lists of check boxes can be generated at runtime by binding check box lists to data sources.

Like check box lists, these controls are useful when you want to change the number of radio buttons in a list in code. This control has an `Items` collection that holds the individual radio buttons in the list, and you can add new radio buttons with this collection's `Add` method. Each item in the `Items` collection is an object of the `ListItem` class, and you can use the `ListItem` class's `Value`, `Text`, and `Selected` properties to work with the individual radio buttons in the list. To determine which item is selected, you can test the `SelectedIndex` and `SelectedItem` properties of the list; you don't need to loop over each item individually. The `SelectedIndex` property holds the index of the selected radio button, and the `SelectedItem` property holds the selected `ListItem` object itself. If you do want to loop over the radio buttons in the list, however, each radio button in a radio button list has a `Selected` property, which is `True` if the radio button is checked. Radio button lists are composite controls in HTML, just as check box lists are, except radio button lists are made up of tables filled with `<input type="radio">` elements instead of `<input type="checkbox">` elements.

Here is the inheritance hierarchy of the `System.Web.UI.WebControls.RadioButtonList` class:

```
System.Object
   System.Web.UI.Control
      System.Web.UI.WebControls.WebControl
         System.Web.UI.WebControls.ListControl
            System.Web.UI.WebControls.RadioButtonList
```

You can find the significant public properties of `System.Web.UI.WebControls.RadioButtonList` objects in Table 13.13, the significant method in Table 13.14, and the significant public event in Table 13.15. Note that as with other Web server controls, these tables do not list the significant properties, methods, and events this class inherits from the `Control` and `WebControl` classes—you can find them in Tables 12.1 to 12.5. This class is also based on the `ListControl` class—you can find the significant public properties of `ListControl` objects in Table 13.4, and their significant public event in Table 13.5.

13

TABLE 13.13   Significant Public Properties of `RadioButtonList` Objects

Property	Means
CellPadding	Returns or sets the distance between the radio button and the table cell that contains it, in pixels.
CellSpacing	Returns or sets the distance between the table cells the radio buttons are displayed in, in pixels.
RepeatColumns	Returns or sets the number of displayed columns in the radio button list.
RepeatDirection	Returns or sets the display direction of radio buttons.
RepeatLayout	Returns or sets the radio button layout.
TextAlign	Returns or sets the radio button's caption text alignment.

TABLE 13.14   Significant Public Method of `RadioButtonList` Objects

Methods	Means
Dispose	Disposes of the radio button list control.

TABLE 13.15   Significant Public Event of `RadioButtonList` Objects

Events	Means
SelectedIndexChanged	Occurs when the selection in the radio button list changes.

As with check box lists, you can customize how a radio button list is displayed using the `RepeatLayout` and `RepeatDirection` properties. If `RepeatLayout` is set to `RepeatLayout.Table` (the default), the list is drawn using an HTML table. If it is set to `RepeatLayout.Flow`, on the other hand, the list is drawn without using a table, and the radio buttons flow like other controls in the Web page. And by default, `RepeatDirection` is set to `RepeatDirection.Vertical`; setting this property to `RepeatDirection.Horizontal` draws the list horizontally.

Working with Radio Button Lists

You can add radio buttons to a radio button list at design time or at runtime. At design time, you add items to a radio button list by clicking the `Items` property in the properties window, opening the ListItem Collection Editor you see in Figure 13.4.

FIGURE 13.4

Adding items to a radio button list.

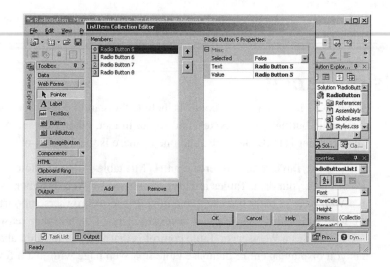

As you'd expect, this collection editor works much like other collection editors. In order to add a new item to the radio button list control, you click the Add button, and fill in the Text (the radio button's caption), Value (holds optional text associated with the radio button), and Selected (set this to True to make the corresponding radio button appear selected when it first appears) properties. You can also add radio buttons to a radio button list at runtime using the Add method of the radio button list's Items collection.

To work with events in a radio button list (don't forget to set AutoPostBack to True if you want to handle this control's events when they occur), you typically work with the default event, the SelectedIndexChanged event. You can use the radio button list's SelectedIndex and SelectedItem properties to get the selected index and item, respectively. You can see this in the code for the RadioButton example. In this case, the code displays which radio button in the list is checked, using the SelectedIndex property:

```
Private Sub RadioButtonList1_SelectedIndexChanged(ByVal sender As System.Object, _
    ByVal e As System.EventArgs) Handles RadioButtonList1.SelectedIndexChanged
    TextBox1.Text = "Radio button " & RadioButtonList1.SelectedIndex + 5 _
        & " is checked."
End Sub
```

You can see the results in Figure 13.3. Besides the SelectedIndex property, you can use the SelectedItem property to get the currently selected item's ListItem object, and you can use the Value property to get the text associated with the selected item in this property if you've assigned text to this property. You can also add a radio button list to a Web form at runtime, of course; the process is just like adding a check box list to a Web form at runtime, which we did a few pages ago.

13

Next, we'll take a look at working with and creating tables using the Table Web server control.

Using Tables

As you've seen, Web server controls include the standard browser controls such as buttons, radio buttons, check boxes, and so on. In fact, other Web server controls let you support other HTML elements, and one of these is the Table control.

You use the Table control to create an HTML table—a good choice to organize the presentation of your data. Tables are also often used by Web designers to position elements in a Web page in older browsers, but now that most browsers support absolute positioning with styles, that's usually not necessary. One of the primary reasons Visual Basic .NET includes a Web server Table control is that you can bind databases to tables, which lets you display an entire database table in a Web page with just a few lines of code. (For more on data binding, see Day 17.)

Using Table controls, you can create HTML tables at design time or at runtime, and you will see both of those techniques today. You can see a table designed and created at design time in the Table example in the code for this book, which is illustrated in Figure 13.5.

FIGURE 13.5

The Table example.

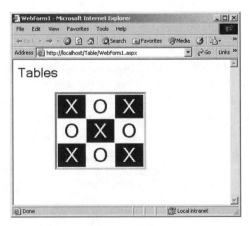

To create a table in HTML, you use a `<table>` element, and in Visual Basic .NET code, you use an object of the `Table` class. You add rows to the table in HTML with `<tr>` (table row) elements and in Visual Basic .NET code with objects of the `TableRow` class in Visual Basic. And you add the cells in an HTML table with the `<td>` (table data) element and in Visual Basic .NET code with `TableCell` objects.

Here is the hierarchy of the `System.Web.UI.WebControls.Table` class—note that it's based on the `System.Web.UI.WebControls.WebControl` class:

```
System.Object
   System.Web.UI.Control
      System.Web.UI.WebControls.WebControl
         System.Web.UI.WebControls.Table
```

You can find the significant public properties of `Table` objects in Table 13.16. (This class has no noninherited methods or properties.) Note that as with other Web server controls, this table does not list the significant properties, methods, and events this class inherits from the `Control` and `WebControl` classes—you can find them in Tables 12.1 to 12.5.

TABLE 13.16   Significant Public Properties of `Table` Objects

Property	Means
BackImageUrl	Holds the URL of the background image to display behind the table.
CellPadding	Returns or sets the distance (in pixels) between the border and the contents of the table cell.
CellSpacing	Returns or sets the distance (in pixels) between table cells.
HorizontalAlign	Returns or sets the horizontal alignment of the table within the page.
Rows	Returns the collection of rows within the table.

After creating a `Table` object, you can use the `TableRow` class to add table rows to that `Table` object. Here's the hierarchy for the `TableRow` class:

```
System.Object
   System.Web.UI.Control
      System.Web.UI.WebControls.WebControl
         System.Web.UI.WebControls.TableRow
```

You can find the significant public properties of `TableRow` objects in Table 13.17 (this class has no noninherited methods or events). Note that as with other Web server controls, this table does not list the significant properties, methods, and events this class inherits from the `Control` and `WebControl` classes—you can find them in Tables 12.1 to 12.5.

13

TABLE 13.17   Significant Public Properties of `TableRow` Objects

Property	Means
Cells	Returns a collection of the table cells for this table row (each of which is a `TableCell` object).
HorizontalAlign	Returns or sets the horizontal alignment of the row contents.
VerticalAlign	Returns or sets the vertical alignment of the row contents.

You can use the `TableRow` class to specify how the contents of a table row are displayed. For example, you can set the font used in an entire row with the table row's `Font.Size` property, and the alignment of the contents in the row can be specified by setting the row's `HorizontalAlign` and `VerticalAlign` properties. You can manage the cells in the row in code by using the `Cells` collection. In addition, the `Cells` collection in a `TableRow` object holds a collection of `TableCell` objects that represent the cells in the row.

Here is the hierarchy of the `TableCell` class:

```
System.Object
    System.Web.UI.Control
        System.Web.UI.WebControls.WebControl
            System.Web.UI.WebControls.TableCell
```

You can find the significant public properties of `TableCell` objects in Table 13.18. (This class has no noninherited methods or events.) Note that as with other Web server controls, this table does not list the significant properties, methods, and events this class inherits from the `Control` and `WebControl` classes—you can find them in Tables 12.1 to 12.5.

TABLE 13.18   Significant Public Properties of `TableCell` Objects

Property	Means
ColumnSpan	Returns or sets the number of columns the cell spans.
HorizontalAlign	Returns or sets the cell content's horizontal alignment.
RowSpan	Returns or sets the number of rows the cell spans.
Text	Returns or sets the text in the cell.
VerticalAlign	Returns or sets the cell content's vertical alignment.
Wrap	Returns or sets whether the cell content wraps.

When working with `TableCell` objects, you can use the `Text` property to get or set the text in the cell. You can align the contents in the cell with the `HorizontalAlign` and `VerticalAlign` properties, set the font used in an individual cell with the Font property (with subproperties such as `Font.Size`, `Font.Italic`, `Font.Bold`, and so on), and use the `Wrap` property to specify whether the contents of the cell wrap in the cell. You can also specify how many rows or columns in the `Table` control are occupied by one single cell with the `RowSpan` and `ColumnSpan` properties, which set how may rows and columns, respectively, should be spanned by the cell.

Working with Tables

To see how to create tables at design time, we can take a look at the Tables example in the code for this book. As you saw in Figure 13.5, the Table example displays a table that formats its contents—a tic-tac-toe board of Xs and Os, cell by cell.

At design time, you create a table with a Table control from the toolbox. To create the `TableRow` and `TableCell` objects you need in a table, the Visual Basic IDE uses collection editors, as you might expect.

After you've added a `Table` control to a Web form, you can click its `Rows` property in the Properties window to open a TableRow Collection Editor, as you see in Figure 13.6. This editor lets you add new rows (not individual cells) to a table. You add new table rows to the table by clicking the Add button, as in other collection editors, and you set the properties of each row in on the right side of the editor.

FIGURE 13.6

The TableRow Collection.

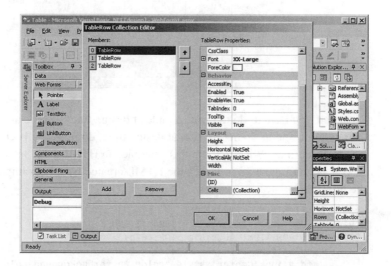

To add table cells to a table row, click the `Cells` property's ellipsis (...) button in the TableRow Collection Editor, opening the TableCell Collection Editor you see in Figure 13.7. As you'd add items to any collection, you can add cells to a row by clicking the Add button, and you can set the properties of the various cells, such as font properties, in the editor as well. For instance, in the Table example, the `ForeColor` and `BackColor` properties of each cell are set to give you the results from Figure 13.5. You can also set the `Font` property for your text for each row or each cell as you prefer.

13

Note

There is also a `TableHeaderCell` class, which corresponds to the `<th>` element, that you use for table headers. (This element displays its text in bold.) However, the TableRow Collection and TableCell Collection editors don't support this class.

FIGURE 13.7

*The TableCell
Collection.*

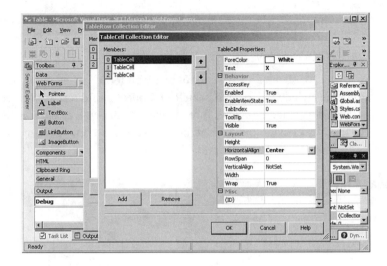

That's all you have to do to create a table at design time—you can also stretch the table as you like using its sizing handles at design time; doing so will set the table's width and height at runtime. When you run this example, an HTML table appears in your browser, as you saw in Figure 13.5. Here's the HTML created by this example and displayed in the browser:

```html
<table id="Table1" border="0"
style="border-style:Inset;width:189px;Z-INDEX: 102;
LEFT: 86px; POSITION: absolute; TOP: 67px">
    <tr style="font-size:XX-Large;">
        <td align="Center" style="color:White;background-color:Black;">X</td>
        <td align="Center" style="color:Black;">O</td>
        <td align="Center" style="color:White;background-color:Black;">X</td>
    </tr>
    <tr style="color:White;background-color:White;font-size:XX-Large;">
        <td align="Center" style="color:Black;background-color:White;">O</td>
        <td align="Center" style="color:White;background-color:Black;">X</td>
        <td align="Center" style="color:Black;background-color:White;">O</td>
    </tr>
    <tr style="font-size:XX-Large;">
        <td align="Center" style="color:White;background-color:Black;">X</td>
        <td align="Center" style="color:Black;background-color:White;">O</td>
        <td align="Center" style="color:White;background-color:Black;">X</td>
    </tr>
</table>
```

You can also create a Table object in code, of course. You can see how this works in the CreateTable example in the code for this book, which you see at work in Figure 13.8. This example creates the same table you see in the Table example in Figure 13.5, but uses code from start to finish. You just click the Create Table button to create and display this table, as you can see in Figure 13.8—this example adds a table to a panel control.

FIGURE 13.8

Creating a table in code.

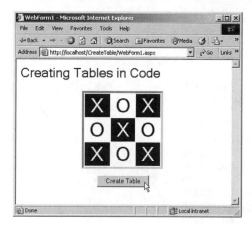

You can see how the CreateTable example works in Listing 13.1. You first just create the `Table`, `TableRow`, and `TableCell` objects you need:

```
Dim Table1 As New Table

Dim TableRow1 As New TableRow
Dim TableRow2 As New TableRow
Dim TableRow3 As New TableRow

Dim TableCell1 As New TableCell
Dim TableCell2 As New TableCell
Dim TableCell3 As New TableCell
Dim TableCell4 As New TableCell
Dim TableCell5 As New TableCell
Dim TableCell6 As New TableCell
Dim TableCell7 As New TableCell
Dim TableCell8 As New TableCell
Dim TableCell9 As New TableCell
        .
        .
        .
```

Then you configure the table rows and cells as you want them, such as putting the needed Xs and Os into the table cells:

```
TableCell1.Text = "X"
TableCell2.Text = "O"
TableCell3.Text = "X"
TableCell4.Text = "O"
```

13

```
TableCell5.Text = "X"
TableCell6.Text = "O"
TableCell7.Text = "X"
TableCell8.Text = "O"
TableCell9.Text = "X"
        .
        .
        .
```

Then you add the table cells to the rows, the rows to the table, and the table to the panel control:

```
TableRow1.Cells.Add(TableCell1)
TableRow1.Cells.Add(TableCell2)
TableRow1.Cells.Add(TableCell3)
TableRow2.Cells.Add(TableCell4)
TableRow2.Cells.Add(TableCell5)
TableRow2.Cells.Add(TableCell6)
TableRow3.Cells.Add(TableCell7)
TableRow3.Cells.Add(TableCell8)
TableRow3.Cells.Add(TableCell9)

Table1.Rows.Add(TableRow1)
Table1.Rows.Add(TableRow2)
Table1.Rows.Add(TableRow3)

Panel1.Controls.Add(Table1)
        .
        .
        .
```

You can see the entire code in Listing 13.1. The only other unusual part here is when the code sets the width of the table, using the Table control's Width property. In Windows programming, you can set a control's dimension properties such as Width simply by assigning it a pixel value (such as CheckBox1.Width = 170). In Web programming, however, you assign properties such as Width a System.Web.UI.WebControls.Unit object, which you can do like this to make the width of the table 170 pixels:

```
Table1.Width = New Unit("170px")
```

LISTING 13.1   WebForm1.aspx (CreateTable Project)

```
Public Class WebForm1
    Inherits System.Web.UI.Page

' Web Form Designer Generated Code

    Private Sub Page_Load(ByVal sender As System.Object, _
        ByVal e As System.EventArgs) Handles MyBase.Load
```

LISTING 13.1   continued

```
        'Put user code to initialize the page here
    End Sub

    Private Sub Button1_Click(ByVal sender As System.Object, _
        ByVal e As System.EventArgs) Handles Button1.Click
        Dim Table1 As New Table
        Dim TableRow1 As New TableRow
        Dim TableRow2 As New TableRow
        Dim TableRow3 As New TableRow

        Table1.BorderStyle = BorderStyle.Inset
        Table1.Width = New Unit("170px")

        Dim TableCell1 As New TableCell
        Dim TableCell2 As New TableCell
        Dim TableCell3 As New TableCell
        Dim TableCell4 As New TableCell
        Dim TableCell5 As New TableCell
        Dim TableCell6 As New TableCell
        Dim TableCell7 As New TableCell
        Dim TableCell8 As New TableCell
        Dim TableCell9 As New TableCell

        TableRow1.Font.Size = FontUnit.XXLarge
        TableRow2.Font.Size = FontUnit.XXLarge
        TableRow3.Font.Size = FontUnit.XXLarge

        TableCell1.Text = "X"
        TableCell2.Text = "O"
        TableCell3.Text = "X"
        TableCell4.Text = "O"
        TableCell5.Text = "X"
        TableCell6.Text = "O"
        TableCell7.Text = "X"
        TableCell8.Text = "O"
        TableCell9.Text = "X"

        TableCell1.BackColor = Color.Black
        TableCell2.BackColor = Color.White
        TableCell3.BackColor = Color.Black
        TableCell4.BackColor = Color.White
        TableCell5.BackColor = Color.Black
        TableCell6.BackColor = Color.White
        TableCell7.BackColor = Color.Black
        TableCell8.BackColor = Color.White
        TableCell9.BackColor = Color.Black

        TableCell1.ForeColor = Color.White
        TableCell2.ForeColor = Color.Black
```

13

LISTING 13.1   continued

```
            TableCell3.ForeColor = Color.White
            TableCell4.ForeColor = Color.Black
            TableCell5.ForeColor = Color.White
            TableCell6.ForeColor = Color.Black
            TableCell7.ForeColor = Color.White
            TableCell8.ForeColor = Color.Black
            TableCell9.ForeColor = Color.White

            TableCell1.HorizontalAlign = HorizontalAlign.Center
            TableCell2.HorizontalAlign = HorizontalAlign.Center
            TableCell3.HorizontalAlign = HorizontalAlign.Center
            TableCell4.HorizontalAlign = HorizontalAlign.Center
            TableCell5.HorizontalAlign = HorizontalAlign.Center
            TableCell6.HorizontalAlign = HorizontalAlign.Center
            TableCell7.HorizontalAlign = HorizontalAlign.Center
            TableCell8.HorizontalAlign = HorizontalAlign.Center
            TableCell9.HorizontalAlign = HorizontalAlign.Center

            TableRow1.Cells.Add(TableCell1)
            TableRow1.Cells.Add(TableCell2)
            TableRow1.Cells.Add(TableCell3)
            TableRow2.Cells.Add(TableCell4)
            TableRow2.Cells.Add(TableCell5)
            TableRow2.Cells.Add(TableCell6)
            TableRow3.Cells.Add(TableCell7)
            TableRow3.Cells.Add(TableCell8)
            TableRow3.Cells.Add(TableCell9)

            Table1.Rows.Add(TableRow1)
            Table1.Rows.Add(TableRow2)
            Table1.Rows.Add(TableRow3)

            Panel1.Controls.Add(Table1)
        End Sub
    End Class
```

Using Panels

You've seen that panel controls, just like their Windows counterparts, are used to contain other controls. At runtime, panels can or cannot display a border, as you prefer. You've already seen how to add controls to a panel in code—take a look at "Adding Controls at Runtime" in Day 12 or the CreateTable example you just saw in the previous topic. You can also add controls to a panel at design time, of course; and you can see an example in the Panel application in the code for this book, which you see at work in Figure 13.9.

FIGURE 13.9

The Panel example.

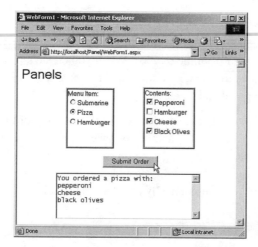

This example lets the user order various menu items—submarine sandwiches, pizza, and hamburgers—using radio buttons in the panel you see at the left. (To make these panels visible, both panels in this example have been given borders.) The user can also customize what he wants on an item with the check boxes in the panel at left.

The radio buttons and check boxes in this example have been added to the panels at design time, and their `AutoPostBack` property has been left `False` so that the user can make his selection and then click the Submit Order button to send the order back to the server. The code on the server determines what the user has ordered and displays that order as you saw in Figure 13.9. You will see how to create this example using panels.

Here is the hierarchy of the `Panel` class:

```
System.Object
    System.Web.UI.Control
        System.Web.UI.WebControls.WebControl
            System.Web.UI.WebControls.Panel
```

You can find the significant public properties of `Panel` objects in Table 13.19. (This class has no noninherited methods or events.) Note that as with other Web server controls, this table does not list the significant properties, methods, and events this class inherits from the `Control` and `WebControl` classes—you can find them in Tables 12.1 to 12.5.

13

TABLE 13.19   Significant Public Properties of `Panel` Objects

Property	Means
BackImageUrl	Returns or sets the background image's URL for the panel.
HorizontalAlign	Returns or sets the horizontal alignment of the panel's contents.
Wrap	Returns or sets whether the panel's content wraps.

Working with Panels

You can add a panel to a Web application as you would any other Web server control—just add a panel to a Web from the toolbox. When you create a panel, the text Panel appears in it; to remove this text, you don't use the Text property (there isn't one)—select the text in the panel and delete it.

You can add controls to a panel just by dragging them on top of the panel. You can also set the Wrap property to True (the default) to make the contents of the panel wrap as needed or False to prevent wrapping. As you can see in Figure 13.10, the Panel example has various radio buttons and check boxes added to two panel controls—when you drag a control onto a panel, it's automatically added to the panel.

FIGURE 13.10

Populating panel controls.

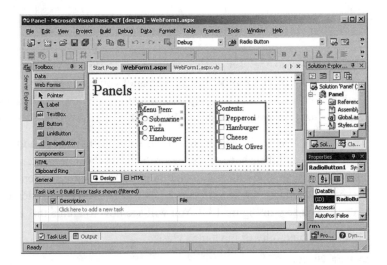

When the user selects a radio button, we just display the menu item he has ordered in the text box:

```
Private Sub RadioButton1_CheckedChanged(ByVal sender As System.Object, _
    ByVal e As System.EventArgs) Handles RadioButton1.CheckedChanged
    TextBox1.Text = "You ordered a " & _
        New String(RadioButton1.Text).ToLower() & " with: " & _
        ControlChars.CrLf
    CheckBoxes()
End Sub
```

The CheckBoxes Sub procedure called when the user clicks a radio button examines what contents the user has ordered for his menu item, and adds that to the text box:

```
Private Sub CheckBoxes()
```

```
            If CheckBox1.Checked Then
                TextBox1.Text &= New String(CheckBox1.Text).ToLower() & _
                    ControlChars.CrLf
            End If
            If CheckBox2.Checked Then
                TextBox1.Text &= New String(CheckBox2.Text).ToLower() & _
                    ControlChars.CrLf
            End If
            If CheckBox3.Checked Then
                TextBox1.Text &= New String(CheckBox3.Text).ToLower() & _
                    ControlChars.CrLf
            End If
            If CheckBox4.Checked Then
                TextBox1.Text &= New String(CheckBox4.Text).ToLower() & _
                    ControlChars.CrLf
            End If
    End Sub
```

That's all it takes; now the user can make his order using the radio buttons and check boxes as organized using the panels in this example. You can see the whole code in Listing 13.2.

LISTING 13.2　WebForm1.aspx (Panel Project)

```
Public Class WebForm1
    Inherits System.Web.UI.Page

' Web Form Designer Generated Code

    Private Sub Page_Load(ByVal sender As System.Object, _
        ByVal e As System.EventArgs) Handles MyBase.Load
        'Put user code to initialize the page here
    End Sub

    Private Sub RadioButton1_CheckedChanged(ByVal sender As System.Object, _
        ByVal e As System.EventArgs) Handles RadioButton1.CheckedChanged
        TextBox1.Text = "You ordered a " & _
            New String(RadioButton1.Text).ToLower() & " with: " & _
            ControlChars.CrLf
        CheckBoxes()
    End Sub

    Private Sub RadioButton2_CheckedChanged(ByVal sender As System.Object, _
        ByVal e As System.EventArgs) Handles RadioButton2.CheckedChanged
        TextBox1.Text = "You ordered a " & _
            New String(RadioButton2.Text).ToLower() & " with: " & _
            ControlChars.CrLf
        CheckBoxes()
    End Sub
```

13

LISTING 13.2   continued

```
    Private Sub RadioButton3_CheckedChanged(ByVal sender As System.Object, _
        ByVal e As System.EventArgs) Handles RadioButton3.CheckedChanged
        TextBox1.Text = "You ordered a " & _
            New String(RadioButton3.Text).ToLower() & " with: " & _
            ControlChars.CrLf
        CheckBoxes()
    End Sub

    Private Sub CheckBoxes()
        If CheckBox1.Checked Then
            TextBox1.Text &= New String(CheckBox1.Text).ToLower() & _
                ControlChars.CrLf
        End If
        If CheckBox2.Checked Then
            TextBox1.Text &= New String(CheckBox2.Text).ToLower() & _
                ControlChars.CrLf
        End If
        If CheckBox3.Checked Then
            TextBox1.Text &= New String(CheckBox3.Text).ToLower() & _
                ControlChars.CrLf
        End If
        If CheckBox4.Checked Then
            TextBox1.Text &= New String(CheckBox4.Text).ToLower() & _
                ControlChars.CrLf
        End If
    End Sub
End Class
```

And that's it for panels. As you see, these controls are good for containing other controls—both in Windows and Web programming.

Summary

Today, you got a good look at a number of crucial Web server controls—check boxes, radio buttons, tables, and panels. Three of these controls—check boxes, radio buttons, and panels—have counterparts in Windows Visual Basic .NET programming. As you've seen today, and as we expected from our previous Web server work, the Web server versions of these controls don't offer as much in the way of properties, methods, and events as the Windows versions because we're limited to what browsers will support. For that reason, working with these controls in Web programming is different from working with them in Windows programming—check boxes can't be three-state, for example, and you need to set AutoPostBack to True if you want to handle these controls' events as they happen.

On the other hand, both check boxes and radio buttons share a lot of functionality with their Windows counterparts—you use the CheckedChanged event to handle check events, and you can use the Checked property to check or uncheck these controls. You can use their Text properties to given them captions.

Check box and radio button lists give you the opportunity to support multiple check boxes and radio buttons in a single control. These controls are often bound to data sources. (We'll take a look at the process of binding data sources to controls in Day 17.) When the check box list or radio button list SelectedIndexChanged event occurs, you can loop over the check boxes or radio buttons in the control's Items collection, checking the Selected property to determine which check boxes or radio buttons are selected.

Table Web server controls let you create HTML tables. You've seen that the HTML <table>, <tr>, and <td> elements are handled by the classes Table, TableRow, and TableCell. We were able to build HTML tables at design time, and using various OOP methods, we were also able to build HTML tables in code.

The last control we took a look at today was panels. Panels work very much as they do in Windows (largely because they're very simple controls). You use panels to group and organize other controls, and you saw yesterday how to add Web server controls to panels. Today, you saw how to add controls to panels at design time, using panels to organize a set of radio buttons and check boxes.

That's it for today's work—tomorrow, we're going to get more Web server power as we turn to images, image buttons, list boxes, drop-down lists, hyperlinks, and link buttons.

Q&A

Q Is there some way to determine exactly which check box or radio button in a check box or radio button list caused the SelectedIndexChanged event?

A Not in a check box list (although you can determine which check boxes are checked using the Selected ListItem property). In a radio button list, however, the radio button that was clicked to cause the SelectedIndexChanged event will be the only radio button selected because only one radio button can be selected at a time, and you can determine it with the SelectedIndex or SelectedItem property.

Q What's the difference between using the Table control and inserting a table using the IDE's Table menu?

A When you insert a Table control, you're using a Web server control with properties, methods, and events. The Table menu, on the other hand, lets you insert an HTML table directly into a Web form or Web page—no Visual Basic code-behind is involved. If you use the Table menu, you'll be creating a <table> element with <tr> and <td> elements.

13

Workshop

This workshop tests whether you understand the concepts you saw today. It's a good idea to make sure that you can answer these questions before pressing on to tomorrow's work.

Quiz

1. What event occurs when a single check box or radio button (not part of a list) is clicked?

2. What event occurs when a check box or radio button that *is* part of a list is clicked?

3. How can you determine how many check boxes or radio buttons are in a check box or radio button list?

4. How can you add a `TableRow` object to the rows in a `Table` control at runtime?

5. How do you insert text into a Panel control at design time?

Quiz Answers

1. The `CheckChanged` event.

2. The `SelectedIndexChanged` event.

3. You can use the Items collection's Count property like this: `CheckBoxList1.Items.Count` or `RadioButtonList1.Items.Count`.

4. You use the `Add` method, like this: `Table1.Rows.Add(TableRow1)`.

5. There's no `Text` property—you just select the `Panel` control in the Web form and click it a second time to make a blinking cursor appear in the panel. Then type the text you want in the panel.

Exercises

1. Create a new Web application that lets the user add check boxes to a check box list by typing the text for the new check box in a text box and clicking a button. (**Extra credit**: Let the user remove a check box as well, using the `Remove` or `RemoveAt` methods.)

2. This exercise points out another use for panels—let the user select a new color with a Color dialog and display the new color in a `Panel` control, using that control's `BackColor` property, to give the user some visual feedback on the color he has selected.

DAY 14

Web Forms: Working with Images, Image Buttons, List Boxes, Drop-Down Lists, Hyperlinks, and Link Buttons

Today, we're going to dig into another set of Web server controls in our coverage of all the Web server controls in Visual Basic .NET. Here, we're going to be working with image controls, image buttons, list boxes, hyperlinks, and link buttons—all fundamental parts of Web programming in Visual Basic .NET. Here's an overview of today's topics:

- Creating image controls
- Creating image buttons
- Using image buttons as image maps

- Creating single-selection list boxes
- Creating multiple-selection list boxes
- Adding items to list boxes at runtime
- Creating drop-down lists
- Creating hyperlinks
- Creating link buttons
- Executing code when a link button is clicked

Some of these controls, such as image controls and list controls, have counterparts in Windows programming—some, such as image buttons and link buttons, don't. As you'd expect, even those controls that handle tasks similar to their Windows counterparts are nonetheless different in Web programming code. Because all these Visual Basic .NET controls have to run in browsers, they're all based on HTML controls even though Visual Basic .NET handles them back on the server. This means that they're not as complex or feature rich as standard Visual Basic Windows controls.

We'll get started immediately with image controls.

Using Image Controls

Web server image controls are the Web counterpart of Windows picture boxes. As their name indicates, you use these controls to display images in Web applications. In fact, that's really all they do—display passive images.

Not that much is going on in image controls—they're simply translated to HTML `<img>` elements, and they don't support events such as the `Click` event. (For that, see the image button control, coming up next.) You just use them to display images. Here's the inheritance hierarchy for the `System.Web.UI.WebControls.Image` class:

```
System.Object
    System.Web.UI.Control
        System.Web.UI.WebControls.WebControl
            System.Web.UI.WebControls.Image
```

You can find the significant public properties of `System.Web.UI.WebControls.Image` objects in Table 14.1. (This class has no noninherited methods or events.) Note that as with other Web server controls, this table does not list the significant properties, methods, and events this class inherits from the `Control` and `WebControl` classes—you can find them in Tables 12.1 to 12.5.

TABLE 14.1   Significant Public Properties of `Image` Objects

Property	Means
AlternateText	Returns or sets the text to display in an image control when the image it's supposed to display is not available. Also, in browsers that display tool tips, this text will become the tool tip text.
Font	Returns or sets the font for the alternate text used by this control.
ImageAlign	Returns or sets the image alignment of the image control. See the upcoming text for all the possible options.
ImageUrl	Returns or sets the URL of the image you want to display. This property can be changed at runtime to make the image control display a different image.

You can see an image control at work in Figure 14.1. The Image example is in the code for this book. This example simply displays the image from the image file image.jpg, also included in the code for this book.

FIGURE 14.1

The Image example.

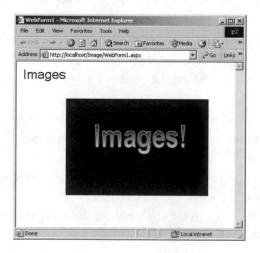

Here's the HTML used in the browser to display the image you see in Figure 14.1 (note that the full local URL for image.jpg, `file:///C:\inetpub\wwwroot\Image\image.jpg`, is used here, so if the URL of the image you want to display is different, you'll have to change this URL in the Image example's WebForm1.aspx file):

```
<img id="Image1" src="file:///C:\inetpub\wwwroot\Image\image.jpg"
border="0" style="Z-INDEX: 102; LEFT: 103px; POSITION: absolute; TOP: 77px" />
```

To connect an image to an image control, you just assign the image's URL to the image control's `ImageUrl` property. At design time, you can browse to the image you want to

14

use by clicking this property in the Properties window. Of course, you can also set the `ImageUrl` property at runtime to the URL of an image, whether local (such as `file:///C:\inetpub\wwwroot\Image\image.jpg`) or on the Web (such as `http://www.starpowder.com/images/etheldreda.jpg`).

You can specify the alignment of the image in relation to other elements in the page by setting the `ImageAlign` property, which can take these values from the `ImageAlign` enumeration:

- `ImageAlign.AbsBottom` — Aligns the lower edge of the image with the lower edge of the largest element on the same line.
- `ImageAlign.AbsMiddle` — Aligns the middle of the image with the middle of the largest element on the same line.
- `ImageAlign.Baseline` — Aligns the lower edge of the image with the lower edge of the first line of text.
- `ImageAlign.Bottom` — Aligns the lower edge of the image with the lower edge of the first line of text.
- `ImageAlign.Left` — Aligns the image on the left edge of the Web page with text wrapping on the right.
- `ImageAlign.Middle` — Aligns the middle of the image with the lower edge of the first line of text.
- `ImageAlign.NotSet` — Indicates that the alignment is not set.
- `ImageAlign.Right` — Aligns the image on the right edge of the Web page with text wrapping on the left.
- `ImageAlign.TextTop` — Aligns the upper edge of the image with the upper edge of the highest text on the same line.
- `ImageAlign.Top` — Aligns the upper edge of the image with the upper edge of the highest element on the same line.

You can also specify the text to display in place of image if the image is not available by setting the `AlternateText` property. And you can position an image with its `Top` and `Left` style properties like this:

```
Private Sub Page_Load(ByVal sender As System.Object, _
    ByVal e As System.EventArgs) Handles MyBase.Load
    Image1.Style("Top") = "200px"
    Image1.Style("Left") = "200px"
End Sub
```

Like other Web server controls, you can set the height and width of image controls with the Height and Width properties:

```
Image1.Height = New Unit("200px")
Image1.Width = New Unit("200px")
```

Image controls such as these only display images—if you want to handle Click events, you'll need to use image button controls, coming up next, instead.

Using Image Buttons

Image controls let you display static images, but not all images are static in Web pages; some are interactive. For example, Web pages can support image maps—those clickable images with "hotspots" that, when clicked, will cause something to happen, as well as images that act like buttons when you click them. You can support those kinds of interactive images with image buttons.

Image controls are supported in HTML with HTML <img> elements, but image buttons use HTML <input> elements where the type attribute is set to "image" (in other words, an HTML image map). As with other Web server controls, image buttons support both Click and Command events. You can see an image button at work in Figure 14.2, where the ImageButton example in the code for this book is displaying the location of the mouse when you click the image.

FIGURE 14.2

The ImageButton example.

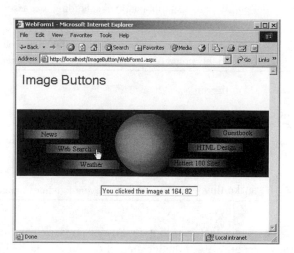

Here's the HTML created to support the image button you see in Figure 14.2; the image here is stored in the file map.jpg, which also comes with the code for this book:

14

```
<input type="image" name="ImageButton1" id="ImageButton1"
src="file:///C:\inetpub\wwwroot\ImageButton\map.jpg" border="0"
style="Z-INDEX: 102; LEFT: 2px; POSITION: absolute; TOP: 90px" />
```

Image buttons are supported with the System.Web.UI.WebControls.ImageButton class;
here is the hierarchy of this class:

```
System.Object
   System.Web.UI.Control
      System.Web.UI.WebControls.WebControl
         System.Web.UI.WebControls.Image
            System.Web.UI.WebControls.ImageButton
```

You can find the significant public properties of
System.Web.UI.WebControls.ImageButton objects in Table 14.2 and the significant
public events in Table 14.3. (This class has no non-inherited methods.) Note that as with
other Web server controls, these tables do not list the significant properties, methods, and
events this class inherits from the Control and WebControl classes—you can find them
in Tables 12.1 to 12.5. Note also that this class inherits from the
System.Web.UI.WebControls.Image class as well; you can find the public properties of
that class in Table 14.1.

TABLE 14.2   Significant Public Properties of ImageButton Objects

Property	Means
CommandArgument	Returns or sets an (optional) value holding text associated with the command given by the CommandName property.
CommandName	Returns or sets the command name for this image button. If you assign a value to this property, the Command event occurs when the button is clicked.

TABLE 14.3   Significant Public Events of ImageButton Objects

Method	Means
Click	Occurs when the image button was clicked.
Command	Occurs when the image button was clicked and the CommandName property holds some text—use a Command event handler to handle this one.

Image buttons are images that also support Click events. When you handle Click events
in image buttons, you are passed the location of the mouse in the image in an
ImageClickEventArgs object; that location is what you need when you want to create an
image map that the user can click to perform some action.

The position of the mouse is stored in pixels; the origin, (0, 0), is at the upper-left corner of the image. Here's how the ImageButton example displays the coordinates in the image at which the user clicked the mouse:

```
Private Sub ImageButton1_Click(ByVal sender As System.Object, _
    ByVal e As System.Web.UI.ImageClickEventArgs) Handles _
    ImageButton1.Click
    TextBox1.Text = "You clicked the image at " & e.X & ", " & e.Y
End Sub
```

You can see the results in Figure 14.2. Image maps often let the user navigate to a new URL when you click a "hotspot" in them, and you can handle that with the Response object's Redirect method. (See "Creating a Multiform Web Application" in Day 11, "Creating Web Forms with ASP.NET," for more on the Redirect method.) Here's an example that makes the browser navigate to http://www.microsoft.com when the user clicks a region of the image—the rectangle stretching from (100, 50) to (200, 150)—which we'll treat as a hotspot:

```
Private Sub ImageButton1_Click(ByVal sender As System.Object, _
    ByVal e As System.Web.UI.ImageClickEventArgs) Handles _
    ImageButton1.Click
    If (e.X >= 100 And e.X <= 200) And (e.Y >= 50 And e.Y <= 150) Then
        Response.Redirect("http://www.microsoft.com")
    End If
End Sub
```

You can also use the Command event handler to make the ImageButton control work like command buttons. In particular, you can connect a command name to the image button with the CommandName property, and the CommandArgument property can also be used to pass additional information about the command. Here's how you might put that to work in code:

```
Private Sub ImageButton1_Command(ByVal sender As Object, _
    ByVal e As System.Web.UI.WebControls.CommandEventArgs) _
    Handles ImageButton1.Command
    If e.CommandName = "NavigateButton" Then
        TextBox1.Text = e.CommandArgument
    End If
End Sub
```

As with image controls, you can set the URL of the image to be used to the ImageUrl property. To set the ImageUrl property at design time, click this property in the Properties window and browse to the image you want to use. You can also set the ImageUrl property at runtime; just assign it a string containing the URL of the image

14

you want to use. You can also set the image's width and height with the Width and Height properties.

That's it for image controls and buttons. There are only a few ways to display images in Web pages that browsers will understand, and we've covered them now—the background property of Web forms that let you set background images, image controls that translate into HTML <img> elements, and image buttons that translate into HTML <input type = "image"> elements. Next, we'll take a look at Web server list controls.

Using List Boxes

As when working with Windows forms, you use list boxes to create a control that allows single or multiple selection of items from a list. For example, you can see a single-selection list box in Figure 14.3 in the ListBox example in the code for this book. When the user clicks an item in the list box, that item appears in the text box at the bottom of the application, as you see in the figure.

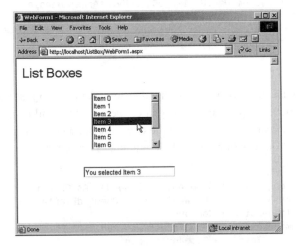

In HTML, list boxes are supported with the HTML <select> control, and the items in the list box are supported with HTML <option> elements. For example, here's the HTML that creates the single-selection list box you see in Figure 14.3:

```
<select name="ListBox1" size="4" onchange="__doPostBack('ListBox1','')"
language="javascript" id="ListBox1"
style="height:128px;width:145px;Z-INDEX: 102;
LEFT: 156px; POSITION: absolute; TOP: 72px">
```

```
        <option value="Item 0">Item 0</option>
        <option value="Item 1">Item 1</option>
        <option value="Item 2">Item 2</option>
        <option value="Item 3">Item 3</option>
        <option value="Item 4">Item 4</option>
        <option value="Item 5">Item 5</option>
        <option value="Item 6">Item 6</option>
        <option value="Item 7">Item 7</option>
        <option value="Item 8">Item 8</option>
        <option value="Item 9">Item 9</option>
</select>
```

Web server list boxes are supported by the `System.Web.UI.WebControls.ListBox` class; here's the hierarchy for that class (note that this class inherits the `System.Web.UI.WebControls.ListControl` class, as check box lists and radio button lists do):

```
System.Object
    System.Web.UI.Control
        System.Web.UI.WebControls.WebControl
            System.Web.UI.WebControls.ListControl
                System.Web.UI.WebControls.ListBox
```

You can find the significant public properties of `System.Web.UI.WebControls.ListBox` objects in Table 14.4. (This class has no non-inherited methods or events.) Note that as with other Web server controls, this table does not list the significant properties, methods, and events this class inherits from the `Control` and `WebControl` classes—you can find them in Tables 12.1 to 12.5. Note that this class also inherits the `ListControl` class, and you can find the significant public properties of the `ListControl` objects in Table 13.4, and their significant public event in Table 13.5. (The `ListControl` class has no non-inherited methods.)

TABLE 14.4   Significant Public Properties of `ListBox` Objects

Property	Means
Items	Returns the collection of items (as `ListItem` objects) in the control.
Rows	Returns or sets the number of rows in the list box.
SelectedIndex	Returns or sets the selected item's index.
SelectedItem	Returns the `ListItem` object corresponding to the selected item.
SelectionMode	Returns or sets the list box's selection mode, single or multiple.
SelectedValue	Returns the value of the `Value` property of the selected item.
ToolTip	Returns or sets the tool tip text for this list box.

14

The major event in Web server list boxes is the `SelectedIndexChanged` event, which occurs when the selected item in the list box is changed. Note also, as you saw in Day 11, that if you want to handle a list box's events immediately, you must set its `AutoPostBack` property to `True`.

Here's an overview of list boxes in code. You use the `Rows` property to specify the height of the control. To enable multiple item selection, you set the `SelectionMode` property to `ListSelectionMode.Multiple`. You can determine the selected item in a single-selection list box using the `SelectedItem` and `SelectedIndex` properties. The `SelectedItem` property returns the selected item as a `ListItem` object, which supports `Text`, `Value`, and `Selected` properties. The `ListControl` class's `Items` property holds a collection of `ListItem` objects that you can use to access any item in a list box. (You saw the `ListItem` class in Day 13, "Web Forms: Working with Check Boxes, Radio Buttons, Tables, and Panels"; you can find the significant public properties of `ListItem` objects in Table 13.6.)

Creating Single-Selection List Boxes

At design time, you can add a list box to a Web form as you can any other Web server control; just drag one from the toolbox. To add items to a list box at design time, you can click the `Items` property in the list box to open the ListItem Collection Editor you see in Figure 14.4.

FIGURE 14.4

Adding items to a list box at design time.

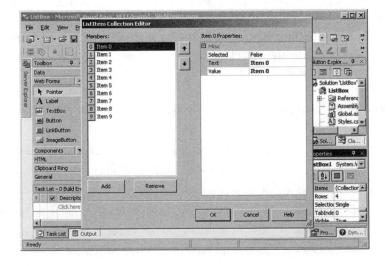

Tip   You can make an item appear initially selected in a list box by setting its
Selected property to True (the default is False) in the ListItem Collection
Editor at design time.

How do you handle single-selection Web server list boxes in code? When the user makes
a selection by clicking an item in the control, a SelectedIndexChanged event occurs.
Here's how we handle that in the ListBox example, which displays the currently selected
item when the user changes the selection in the list box:

```
Private Sub ListBox1_SelectedIndexChanged(ByVal sender As System.Object, _
    ByVal e As System.EventArgs) Handles ListBox1.SelectedIndexChanged
    TextBox1.Text = "You selected " & ListBox1.SelectedItem.Text
End Sub
```

You can see the results in Figure 14.3. In single-selection list boxes, you can determine
which item is selected with the list box's SelectedItem property and the index of the
item in the list with the SelectedIndex property.

The ListBox example sets the list box's AutoPostBack property to True so that its events
are handled on the server when they occur. It's more usual, however, to leave
AutoPostBack set to False (the default) and read what item the user has selected in the
list box when the page is sent back after the user clicks a Submit button. For example,
the user might work with several list boxes, selecting names, dates, colors, and so on,
and then click the Submit button to apply those selections. In the code that handles the
button's click, you can read the current selection in the various list boxes all at once,
something like this:

```
Private Sub Button1_Click(ByVal sender As System.Object, _
    ByVal e As System.EventArgs) Handles Button1.Click
    TextBox1.Text = ListBox1.SelectedItem.Text & _
        " is currently selected in list box 1."
    TextBox2.Text = ListBox2.SelectedItem.Text & _
        " is currently selected in list box 2."
    TextBox3.Text = ListBox3.SelectedItem.Text & _
        " is currently selected in list box 3."
End Sub
```

On the other hand, what if a list box can support multiple selections? Handling more
than one selection at a time takes a little more thought.

14

Creating Multiple-Selection List Boxes

Standard Web server list boxes only let the user select one item at a time. However, if you set the list box's `SelectionMode` property to `Multiple`, the list box will support multiple selections. You can make multiple selections in list boxes the same way as in other Web controls—you can use the Shift key with the mouse to select a range of items or the Ctrl key to select multiple items, clicking one after the other.

You can see a multiple selection list box in the MultiSelectListBox example in the code for the book in Figure 14.5. The user can select multiple items in the list box, click the Submit button, and the program will display her selections in a multiline text box, as you see in the figure.

FIGURE 14.5

The MultiSelectListBox example.

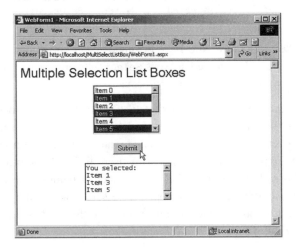

The HTML for the multiple-selection list box in Figure 14.5 is almost the same as for the single-selection list box you saw earlier, except for the addition of the `multiple` attribute. This attribute is a standalone HTML attribute, which means that you don't have to assign it a value—but, following the lead of the W3C XHTML specification, Visual Basic assigns it the value "multiple" to make the HTML more compatible with XML, which does not support standalone attributes:

```
<select name="ListBox1" size="4" multiple="multiple"
id="ListBox1" style="height:113px;width:141px;Z-INDEX:
103; LEFT: 158px; POSITION: absolute; TOP: 49px">
    <option value="Item 0">Item 0</option>
    <option value="Item 1">Item 1</option>
    <option value="Item 2">Item 2</option>
    <option value="Item 3">Item 3</option>
```

```
    <option value="Item 4">Item 4</option>
    <option value="Item 5">Item 5</option>
    <option value="Item 6">Item 6</option>
    <option value="Item 7">Item 7</option>
    <option value="Item 8">Item 8</option>
    <option value="Item 9">Item 9</option>
</select>
```

> **Tip** XHTML is a reformulation of HTML 4 in XML 1.0. We're not going to work with XHTML much in this book, but if you're interested, take a look at the XHTML specification at http://www.w3.org/TR/xhtml1/.

When the user makes a new selection in a multiple-selection list box, a SelectedIndexChanged event occurs. You don't usually send the page back to the server each time the user selects a new item in a multiple selection list box, however; instead, you normally use a Submit button and read the list box selections in the button's Click event handler.

To determine which items are selected in a multiple selection list box, you can loop over the Items collection of ListItem objects, checking each item's Selected property to see if that item is selected. Here's how that works in MultiSelectListBoxes example:

```
Private Sub Button1_Click(ByVal sender As System.Object, _
    ByVal e As System.EventArgs) Handles Button1.Click
    TextBox1.Text = "You selected: " & ControlChars.CrLf
    For intLoopIndex As Integer = 0 To ListBox1.Items.Count - 1
        If ListBox1.Items(intLoopIndex).Selected Then
            TextBox1.Text &= ListBox1.Items(intLoopIndex).Text & _
                ControlChars.CrLf
        End If
    Next
End Sub
```

That's all you need to handle multiple selections in Web server list boxes.

Adding New Items to List Boxes at Runtime

When you use any Web server control based on the ListControl class, you can use the Items collection's Add method to add items to it, which works for Web server list boxes as well. The Items collection is a collection of ListItem objects, and you can either pass a ListItem object to the Add method or the text you want to give to the new item. To see how this works, take a look at the AddItems example in the code for this book. You can

14

see this example at work in Figure 14.6—when you click the Add New Item button, a new item is added to the list box (Item 3 is new in this figure).

FIGURE **14.6**

Adding new items to a
list box at runtime.

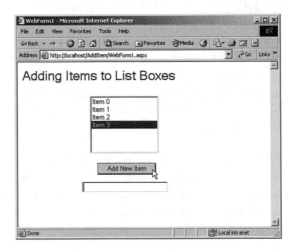

To add a new item to the list box, you can use the Add method like this, which adds a new item and set the correct caption using the Count property of the list box's Items collection:

```
Private Sub Button1_Click(ByVal sender As System.Object, _
    ByVal e As System.EventArgs) Handles Button1.Click
    ListBox1.Items.Add("Item " & ListBox1.Items.Count)
End Sub
```

When the list box appears the first time, the list box has three items in it:

```
<select name="ListBox1" size="4" onchange="__
    doPostBack('ListBox1','')" language="javascript"
    id="ListBox1" style="height:123px;width:142px;Z-INDEX:
    102; LEFT: 153px; POSITION: absolute; TOP: 70px">
    <option value="Item 0">Item 0</option>
    <option value="Item 1">Item 1</option>
    <option value="Item 2">Item 2</option>
</select>
```

After you click the Add New Item button, the list box will come back from the server with four items in it:

```
<select name="ListBox1" size="4" onchange="__
    doPostBack('ListBox1','')" language="javascript"
    id="ListBox1" style="height:123px;width:142px;Z-INDEX:
    102; LEFT: 153px; POSITION: absolute; TOP: 70px">
```

```
    <option value="Item 0">Item 0</option>
    <option value="Item 1">Item 1</option>
    <option value="Item 2">Item 2</option>
    <option value="Item 3">Item 3</option>
</select>
```

That's all there is to it; the next time you click the Add New Item button, another item will be added, and so on.

This example also adds code to the list box's `SelectedIndexChanged` event handler to display the selection the user makes in a text box, like this:

```
Private Sub ListBox1_SelectedIndexChanged(ByVal _
    sender As System.Object, ByVal e As System.EventArgs) _
    Handles ListBox1.SelectedIndexChanged
    TextBox1.Text = "You selected " & ListBox1.SelectedItem.Text
End Sub
```

As you can see, it's fairly easy to work with standard Web server list box controls. Another type of HTML control functions very similar to list controls—drop-down list controls—and they're coming up next.

Using Drop-Down Lists

Drop-down lists hide the lists of items the users can select from until the users click the control's down-arrow button. Clicking that button makes the control display its drop-down list, and the user can select an item in that list—she can't select multiple items because the list closes as soon as a selection is made.

You can see a drop-down list in the DropDownList example in the code for this book, which appears in Figure 14.7.

When you've selected an item in a drop-down list, you can use the control's `SelectedIndex` and `SelectedItem` properties in code to determine what selection was made. The `SelectedIndex` property gives you the index in the list of the selected item, and the `SelectedItem` property gives you the actual `ListItem` object that corresponds to the selected item. You can use the `ListItem` class's `Value`, `Text`, and `Selected` properties to get more information about the selection.

The DropDownList example in the code for this book uses the `SelectedItem` property to get the selected `ListItem` object and displays that item's text, as you see in Figure 14.8.

14

FIGURE **14.7**

*The DropDownList
example.*

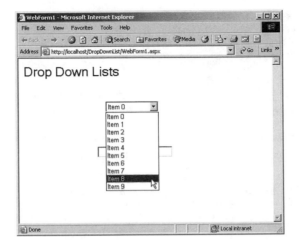

FIGURE **14.8**

*Selecting an item in
a drop-down list
example.*

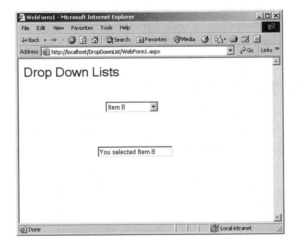

Similar to Web server list boxes, drop-down lists are supported with `<select>` controls.
In this case, the `<select>` controls are created without a `size` attribute, which means that
the browser will create a drop-down list instead of a list box. (The `size` attribute indicates how many items in the list to display at one time, and if you omit it, the browser
displays a drop-down list.) Here's the HTML that creates the drop-down list you see in
Figure 14.7:

```
<select name="DropDownList1" onchange="__
    doPostBack('DropDownList1','')" language="javascript"
    id="DropDownList1" style="width:110px;Z-INDEX: 102; LEFT: 182px;
    POSITION: absolute; TOP: 90px">
    <option value="Item 0">Item 0</option>
```

```
        <option value="Item 1">Item 1</option>
        <option value="Item 2">Item 2</option>
        <option value="Item 3">Item 3</option>
        <option value="Item 4">Item 4</option>
        <option value="Item 5">Item 5</option>
        <option value="Item 6">Item 6</option>
        <option value="Item 7">Item 7</option>
        <option value="Item 8">Item 8</option>
        <option value="Item 9">Item 9</option>
    </select>
```

This control is supported with the System.Web.UI.WebControls.DropDownList class, and here is the hierarchy of that class:

```
System.Object
    System.Web.UI.Control
        System.Web.UI.WebControls.WebControl
            System.Web.UI.WebControls.ListControl
                System.Web.UI.WebControls.DropDownList
```

You can find the significant public properties of System.Web.UI.WebControls. DropDownList objects in Table 14.5. (This control has no non-inherited methods or events.) Note that as with other Web server controls, this table does not list the significant properties, methods, and events this class inherits from the Control and WebControl classes—you can find them in Tables 12.1 to 12.5. This class inherits the ListControl class, and you can find the significant public properties of ListControl objects in Table 13.4 and their significant public event in Table 13.5 (the ListControl class has no non-inherited methods).

TABLE 14.5   Significant Public Properties of DropDownList Objects

Property	Means
Items	Returns the collection of items (as ListItem objects) in the control.
SelectedIndex	Returns or sets the selected item's index.
SelectedItem	Returns the ListItem object corresponding to the selected item.
SelectedValue	Returns the value of the Value property of the selected item.

Note that the ListControl class's Items property returns a collection of ListItem objects, which you can use to access an item in a list box. You can find the significant public properties of ListItem objects in Table 13.6. (The ListItem class has no non-inherited methods or events.)

As with list boxes, you need to set this control's AutoPostBack property to True if you want events handled on the server as soon as they happen. Determining the selection the

14

user has made in a drop-down list is easy—because you can only select one item at a time in a drop-down list, you use the SelectedItem and SelectedIndex properties of this control. Here's how that works in the DropDownLists example:

```
Private Sub DropDownList1_SelectedIndexChanged(ByVal _
    sender As System.Object, ByVal e As System.EventArgs) _
    Handles DropDownList1.SelectedIndexChanged
    TextBox1.Text = "You selected " & DropDownList1.SelectedItem.Text
End Sub
```

There's another property worth looking at both here and in standard list boxes—the Value property.

Using the Value Property

Controls that hold ListItem objects, such as check box lists, radio button lists, list boxes, and drop-down list boxes, let you add text to each item using the Value property (which is of type String). That's useful if you want to store more text in each item than is displayed in the control itself.

For example, in the DropDownListValues example in the code for the book, the drop-down list displays the abbreviations of various states, CA, MA, NY, and so on—but behind the scenes, each item in the list has the full text of each state's name, California, Massachusetts, New York, and so on, stored in its Value property. That text is retrieved when the user makes a selection, as you can see in Figure 14.9.

FIGURE 14.9

Using the Value *property.*

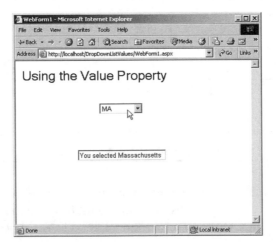

You can set a ListItem object's Value property at runtime in code or at design time using the ListItem Collection editor, as you see at right in Figure 14.10.

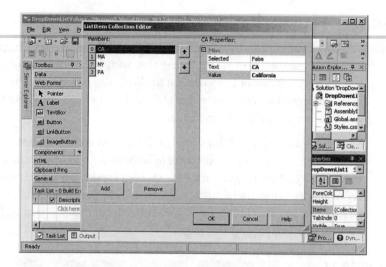

To work with the current selection in list-oriented controls, you can use the
SelectedIndex, SelectedItem, and SelectedValue properties. The SelectedValue
property holds the value in the Value property of the currently selected item. This means
that you can display the full name of the selected state in the DropDownListValues
example like this:

```
Private Sub DropDownList1_SelectedIndexChanged(ByVal _
    sender As System.Object, ByVal e As System.EventArgs) _
    Handles DropDownList1.SelectedIndexChanged
    TextBox1.Text = "You selected " & DropDownList1.SelectedValue
End Sub
```

As you can see, the Value property is useful to store additional text in each item in a list.

 Tip

> You might want to store even more information in list items by deriving a
> new class from the System.Web.UI.WebControls.ListItem class, adding a
> few properties and methods of your own and storing objects of the new
> class in a list control. Unfortunately, the ListItem class is declared
> NonInheritable, which means that you can't derive your own classes from it.

That takes care of list controls for the moment—next, we'll take a look at two other controls that are specifically targeted for Web use: hyperlinks and link buttons.

14

Using Hyperlinks

Web pages can contain hyperlinks, and in Visual Basic .NET Web applications, you use the HyperLink control to create hyperlinks. Such hyperlinks can link to another page in your Web application or anywhere on the Web. You can specify the location of the linked page in an absolute way, where you use the linked page's complete URL, or in a relative way, with respect to the current page.

You can see both types of links in Figure 14.11, in the HyperLink example in the code for this book—this example supports hyperlinks both to Microsoft's Web site (using an absolute URL: `"http://www.microsoft.com"`) and to an HTML page in the same project (using a relative URL: `"HTMLPage1.htm"`). In that figure, the link to the other page in the same project (an HTML page, HTMLPage1.htm, that's been added to the project) has been clicked, bringing up that page.

FIGURE 14.11

The HyperLink example.

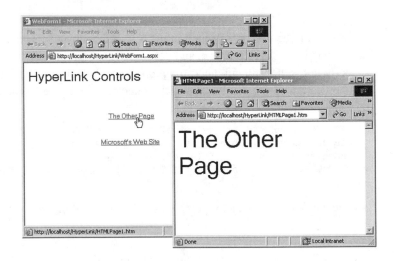

The HTML used to support hyperlinks is, of course, the <a> element; here's the HTML generated for the two hyperlinks you see in Figure 14.11:

```
<a id="HyperLink1" href="HTMLPage1.htm" target="_blank"
style="Z-INDEX: 102; LEFT: 174px; POSITION: absolute; TOP: 103px">
The Other Page</a>

<a id="HyperLink2" href="http://www.microsoft.com"
style="Z-INDEX: 103; LEFT: 158px; POSITION: absolute; TOP: 157px">
Microsoft's Web Site</a>
```

You use the `System.Web.UI.WebControls.HyperLink` class to create hyperlinks in Web applications. Here is the hierarchy of that class:

```
System.Object
   System.Web.UI.Control
      System.Web.UI.WebControls.WebControl
         System.Web.UI.WebControls.HyperLink
```

You can find the significant public properties of the `System.Web.UI.WebControls.HyperLink` objects in Table 14.6. (This class has no non-inherited methods or events.) Note that as with other Web server controls, this table does not list the significant properties, methods, and events this class inherits from the `Control` and `WebControl` classes—you can find them in Tables 12.1 to 12.5.

TABLE 14.6   Significant Public Properties of `HyperLink` Objects

Property	Means
ImageUrl	Returns or sets the URL of an image for use in the hyperlink.
NavigateUrl	Returns or sets the URL to navigate to when the hyperlink is clicked.
Target	Returns or sets the target window or frame to display the linked-to content in when the hyperlink is clicked.
Text	Returns or sets the clickable text displayed in the Web page for the hyperlink.

You create hyperlink controls by dragging them from the toolbox at design time, and, as with any other control, you can also create them in code.

When you create a hyperlink, you need to set the text it displays, as well as the URL it links to. The text in the hyperlink control is specified with the `Text` property. You can also display an image, which you specify with the `ImageUrl` property. You set the URL that the link navigates to with the `NavigateUrl` property.

Tip

> If both the `Text` and `ImageUrl` properties are set, the `ImageUrl` property is used. If the image to display is not available, the text in the `Text` property is displayed instead.

You can set the `Text` property at design time simply by entering the hyperlink's text into the `Text` property in the Properties window. When you click the `NavigateUrl` property's ellipsis (...) button in the Properties window, the Select URL dialog opens, as you see in Figure 14.12. You can select the type of URL you want to specify with the URL Type drop-down list box; the various types are Absolute, Document Relative, or Root Relative.

14

In Figure 14.12, we're setting a hyperlink to a relative URL to the HTML page added to the project, HTMLPage1.htm. To connect to an absolute URL on the Internet, set the URL Type to absolute and type the URL into the URL text box.

FIGURE **14.12**

The Select URL dialog.

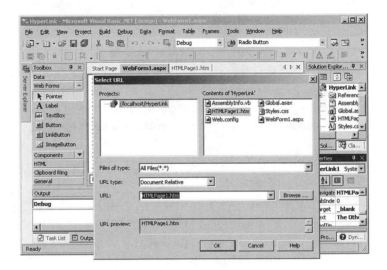

There's more to this story—you can also specify how you want to display the new page when its URL is clicked, using the Target property. The target specifies where the linked-to content will be displayed. By default, when you click a hyperlink control, the linked-to content replaces the current page in the browser, and no new browser window is opened. However, you can open a new window if you prefer by setting the Target property to the name of a window or frame or one of these HTML values:

- _blank—Will display the linked-to content in a new window, without frames.
- _parent—Will display the linked-to content in the frameset parent of the current window.
- _self—Will display the linked-to content in the frame with focus.
- _top—Will display the linked-to content in the top window without frames.

You can also create hyperlinks in code, of course, as you see in the CreateHyperLink example in the code for the book. You can see this example at work in Figure 14.13; when you click the Create HyperLink button, a new HyperLink control is created and added to a panel control.

FIGURE 14.13

The CreateHyperLink example.

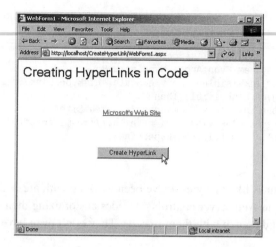

You can create a new hyperlink control as we've created other Web server controls; here, we'll use the Dim statement to create the control in code, customize its properties, and add it to a panel using the panel's Controls collection's Add method:

```
Dim HyperLink1 As New HyperLink

Private Sub Button1_Click(ByVal sender As System.Object, _
    ByVal e As System.EventArgs) Handles Button1.Click
    HyperLink1.Text = "Microsoft's Web Site"
    HyperLink1.NavigateUrl = "http://www.microsoft.com"
    Panel1.Controls.Add(HyperLink1)
End Sub
```

To make sure that the new control reappears each time the page is reloaded, you can add the control to the panel in the Page_Load event handler. First, we create a new Boolean variable, blnHyperLinkVisible, and set it to True after the button has been clicked:

```
Dim HyperLink1 As New HyperLink
Dim blnHyperLinkVisible As Boolean = False

Private Sub Button1_Click(ByVal sender As System.Object, _
    ByVal e As System.EventArgs) Handles Button1.Click
    HyperLink1.Text = "Microsoft's Web Site"
    HyperLink1.NavigateUrl = "http://www.microsoft.com"
    Panel1.Controls.Add(HyperLink1)
    blnHyperLinkVisible = True
End Sub
```

14

In the `Page_Load` event handler, all you have to do is to check `blnHyperLinkVisible` and display the hyperlink if it's `True`:

```
Private Sub Page_Load(ByVal sender As System.Object, _
    ByVal e As System.EventArgs) Handles MyBase.Load
        blnHyperLinkVisible = Me.ViewState("blnHyperLinkVisible")
        If blnHyperLinkVisible Then
            HyperLink1.Text = "Microsoft's Web Site"
            HyperLink1.NavigateUrl = "http://www.microsoft.com"
            Panel1.Controls.Add(HyperLink1)
        End If
End Sub
```

Note that hyperlinks like the ones we've been working with are really just HTML `<a>` controls made into Web server controls—besides customizing their text, targets, and URLs, you can't do much with them in code. They don't even have a `Click` event. But link *buttons* do.

Using Link Buttons

As a programmer, you have little control over what happens when the user clicks a hyperlink because the browser takes over. But what if you need to set a hyperlink's target on-the-fly when it's clicked, or if you want to ask the user to confirm that she wants to navigate to a new URL or execute some Visual Basic code when a link is clicked? For that, you use link buttons.

Link buttons look just like hyperlinks, but act like buttons, with both `Click` and `Command` events. When the corresponding hyperlink is clicked, you can take some action in code, not just let the browser automatically navigate to a new page. For example, the LinkButton example in the code for this book makes a message appear in a label with a dashed border when you click the link button, as you see in Figure 14.14.

FIGURE 14.14

The LinkButton example.

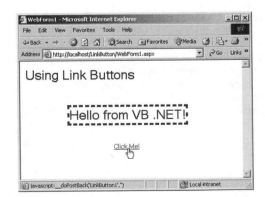

Like hyperlink controls, link buttons are supported with HTML <a> elements, but the code for link buttons is processed back at the server. Here's what the HTML for the link button you see in Figure 14.13 looks like:

```
<a id="LinkButton1" href="javascript:__doPostBack('LinkButton1','')"
style="Z-INDEX: 101; LEFT: 193px; POSITION: absolute; TOP: 169px">
Click Me!</a>
```

Link buttons are supported with the System.Web.UI.WebControls.LinkButton class; here's the hierarchy for this class:

```
System.Object
   System.Web.UI.Control
      System.Web.UI.WebControls.WebControl
         System.Web.UI.WebControls.LinkButton
```

You can find the significant public properties of System.Web.UI.WebControls.LinkButton objects in Table 14.7 and their significant public events in Table 14.8. (This class has no noninherited methods.) Note that as with other Web server controls, these tables do not list the significant properties, methods, and events this class inherits from the Control and WebControl classes—you can find them in Tables 12.1 to 12.5.

TABLE 14.7   Significant Public Properties of LinkButton Objects

Property	Means
CommandArgument	Returns or sets an (optional) argument holding text associated with the command specified with the CommandName property.
CommandName	Returns or sets the command name for this link button.
Text	Returns or sets the text displayed in the link button.

TABLE 14.8   Significant Public Events of LinkButton Objects

Event	Means
Click	Occurs when the link button was clicked.
Command	Occurs when the link button was clicked and you've assigned text to the CommandName property.

The whole point of link buttons is that you can handle hyperlink events in code. In particular, you can add code to the Click and Command event handlers for link buttons, which you can't do for hyperlink controls. Like hyperlink controls, you set the text in a

14

link button with the `Text` property. Unlike hyperlink controls, however, link buttons don't have a `NavigateUrl` property—instead, you use code in the `Click` and `Command` events to handle link button events.

You can see a link button at work in the LinkButton example in Figure 14.14. When the user clicks the hyperlink, a label with the text `"Hello from VB .NET!"` and a dashed border becomes visible, as you see in the figure. To make that label visible, all you need to do is to add code to the link button's `Click` event like this:

```
Private Sub LinkButton1_Click(ByVal _
    sender As System.Object, ByVal e As System.EventArgs) _
    Handles LinkButton1.Click
    Label1.Visible = True
End Sub
```

Here's another example; when the user clicks a link button in this case, the code displays a button with the caption `"Navigate to Microsoft's Web Site?"`. If the user confirms her choice by clicking this button, the code navigates the browser to `http://www.microsoft.com`:

```
Private Sub Page_Load(ByVal sender As _
    System.Object, ByVal e As System.EventArgs) _
    Handles MyBase.Load
    Button1.Visible = False
End Sub

Private Sub LinkButton1_Click(ByVal sender As System.Object, _
    ByVal e As System.EventArgs) Handles LinkButton1.Click
    Button1.Text = "Navigate to Microsoft's Web Site?"
    Button1.Visible = True
End Sub

Private Sub Button1_Click(ByVal _
    sender As System.Object, ByVal e As System.EventArgs) _
    Handles Button1.Click
    Response.Redirect("http://www.microsoft.com")
End Sub
```

Here's one more example, which sets the target of a link button on-the-fly, depending on the current time of day (which you can find with the `Month`, `Hour`, `Minute`, and `Day` functions if you pass them the current time, contained in the Visual Basic `Now` property). When the user clicks this link button, she will see a breakfast, lunch, or dinner menu, as appropriate (the `Hour` function returns the current hour of the day in 0–23 format):

```
Private Sub LinkButton1_Click(ByVal _
    sender As System.Object, ByVal e As System.EventArgs) _
    Handles LinkButton1.Click
    If Hour(Now) > 0 And Hour(Now) <= 11 Then
        Response.Redirect("BreakfastMenu.html")
```

```
        ElseIf Hour(Now) > 11 And Hour(Now) <= 17 Then
            Response.Redirect("LunchMenu.html")
        Else
            Response.Redirect("DinnerMenu.html")
        End If
End Sub
```

That's the whole idea behind link buttons—when the user clicks them, you can execute code, not just automatically jump to a new URL. And that's it for our look at Web server hyperlink and link button controls.

Summary

Today, continuing our coverage of all the Web server controls in Visual Basic .NET, we got a look at a number of important Web server controls—image controls, image buttons, list boxes, drop-down lists, hyperlinks, and link buttons.

Image controls are designed simply to display images, which is more or less it. They correspond to HTML <img> elements and don't support events such as the Click event. Image buttons, on the other hand, do support Click events, and you can use them to create clickable image maps. When an image button is clicked, the exact location of the mouse in the image is recorded and sent to the Click event's handler, allowing you to take the action you want in response to "hotspot" clicks.

Today, we also took a look at Web server list boxes today. By default, Web server list boxes support only single selections, and you can determine which item in a list was selected using the SelectedIndex property, which returns the index of the selected item; the SelectedItem property, which returns the ListItem object corresponding to the selected item; and the SelectedValue property, which returns the value of the selected item's Value property.

You can support multiple selections in list boxes (but not drop-down list boxes) by setting the SelectionMode property to ListSelectionMode.Multiple. To determine which items are selected in a multiple selection list box, you can loop over the Items collection of ListItem objects, checking each item's Selected property to see if that item is selected.

You can add items to list controls at design time using the ListItem Collection editor, or at runtime using the list control's Items collection's Add method. We saw how to do both today.

We also took a look at drop-down lists here. These controls are similar to list boxes, except that they omit the size HTML attribute, which makes the browser display the

14

control as a drop-down list. Drop-down lists display an arrow button that, when clicked, opens a list from which the user can make a selection. The user can only make single selections from drop-down lists, however, because when you make a selection, the drop-down list closes immediately.

Similar to list boxes, you can make sure drop-down list box events, such as the SelectedIndexChanged event, are sent back to the server as soon as they occur by setting the AutoPostback property to True, but you usually let the user make selections in list boxes and handle those selections only after the user clicks a Submit button to send the page back to the server.

Today, we also took a look at working with hyperlink controls. These controls are handled by HTML <a> elements, and we saw that you can customize hyperlink controls with the Text, NavigateUrl, ImageUrl, and Target properties. However, hyperlink controls don't support the Click event—for that, you need to use link buttons.

Link buttons appear at runtime just like hyperlinks, but in Visual Basic code they function just like Web server buttons. Specifically, you can handle Click and Command events for link buttons just as you can with Web server buttons. You use link buttons when you want to execute code when the user clicks a hyperlink, not just let the browser automatically navigate to a new URL. You saw several examples showing how link buttons can be useful, including setting URL targets on-the-fly, according to the time of day, or making other controls, such as labels, visible when a hyperlink is clicked.

That's it for today's work—tomorrow, we're going to get more Web server power as we round off our Web application work by covering the final Web server controls—validation controls, calendars, and ad rotators.

Q&A

Q Is there some way to customize the appearance of hyperlinks in a Web form as you might in a standard Web page?

A You can customize the appearance of hyperlinks in a Web form by setting that form's link (the color of a hyperlink before it has been clicked), alink (the color of a hyperlink as it has being clicked), and vlink (the color of a hyperlink the user has already visited) properties in the Properties window.

Q Can I add code to change a hyperlink's color when the mouse moves over it as you see in many pages on the Web?

A Yes, you can by adding JavaScript to handle the hyperlink's OnMouseOver and OnMouseOut events. You can't do that by adding onmouseover and onmouseout JavaScript attributes directly to the <asp:HyperLink> element in the .aspx file because `<asp:HyperLink>` creates a Web server control and Visual Basic will complain if you try to modify it. But you can attach JavaScript to handle these events using `for` and `event` HTML attributes in a `<script>` element in the Web form's `<head>` section. The `for` attribute, which is crucial here, is supported only in Internet Explorer; using this attribute, you can specify which HTML element a script is for, and that lets you use JavaScript to handle events for any HTML element, even Web server controls. For example, to make the text in `HyperLink1` change to red when the mouse is over the link and back to blue (the default color for links in Web forms) when the mouse moves on, you can add this HTML and JavaScript to a Web form's `<head>` element in the .aspx file:

```
<head>
    .
    .
    .
    <style>
        .red {color:red}
        .blue {color:blue}
    </style>
    <script for = "HyperLink1" event = "onmouseover">
        HyperLink1.className = "red"
    </script>
    <script for = "HyperLink1" event = "onmouseout">
        HyperLink1.className = "blue"
    </script>
    .
    .
    .
</head>
```

Workshop

This workshop tests whether you understand the concepts you saw today. It's a good idea to make sure that you can answer these questions before pressing on to tomorrow's work.

Quiz

1. What property do you use to store the text an image control should display if the image is unavailable?

2. What is the type of the object passed to you in an image button's `Click` event handler that contains the mouse location?

3. What's the major event for a list box control—the one that lets you determine what item was most recently selected?

14

4. How do you make a drop-down list box support multiple selections?

5. What properties do you use to set a hyperlink control's text, URL, target, and image?

Quiz Answers

1. The `AlternateText` property.

2. It's an `ImageClickEventArgs` object. You use the `X` and `Y` properties of this object to get the mouse position.

3. The `SelectedIndexChanged` event, which occurs when the selected item is changed. To handle this event when it occurs, you need to set the `AutoPostBack` property to `True`.

4. That's a trick question—you can't make a drop-down list box support multiple selections.

5. You use the `Text`, `NavigateUrl`, `Target`, and `ImageUrl` properties.

Exercises

1. Create a new Web application with an image map that supports four hotspots and lets the user navigate to four of your favorite Web sites. If the user clicks the image map outside any hotspot, display a prompt in a label suggesting that the user try again.

2. When the user clicks a hyperlink with the text `"Select URL"` as displayed using a link button, display a drop-down list box full of Web site names from which the user can select. Store the URL for each Web site in the corresponding list item's `Value` property. After the user has made her selection, recover that URL from the `SelectedValue` property and navigate to it.

DAY 15

Web Forms: Working with Validation Controls, Calendars, and Ad Rotators

Today, we're going to finish our work with the Web server controls available in Visual Basic .NET. Today's work centers on controls mostly designed for the Web: validation controls, calendar controls, and ad rotators. You use validation controls to check data the user has entered into a Web page, calendar controls to enable the user to select dates, and ad rotators to display banner ads in your Web pages. (You may not be happy to hear that Visual Basic .NET supports banner ads in Web applications—lots of people hate those ads—but that's exactly what ad rotators let you do—display advertising in your applications). Here are today's topics:

- Using validators to check data the user enters
- Creating required field validators

- Creating comparison validators
- Creating range validators
- Creating regular expression validators
- Creating custom validators
- Creating a validation summary
- Creating calendars to enable users to select dates
- Creating ad rotators to display banner ads
- Assigning banner ads to ad rotators

Validators are useful controls in Web applications because they allow you to check data the user has entered before that data is sent back to the server. And that's a powerful technique in Web applications because it saves you a lot of time on the server.

Using Validation Controls

Round-trips to the server take a lot of time, and validation controls were invented to help you avoid losing some of that valuable time. These controls work with the client browser, as long as the client browser supports JavaScript and some simple dynamic HTML (DHTML is used to make an error message visible without a server roundtrip), checking the data that the user has entered before sending it to the server. This is common practice in Web pages, and you've probably seen warnings like "You must enter an e-mail address" in Web pages.

> **Tip**
>
> In fact, validation controls still work even if the browser does not support JavaScript and DHTML, but the validation will be done back in the server. And note also that you can turn off validation by setting a validation control's Enabled property to False.

You can see all the validation controls in the Validators example, which you see at work in Figure 15.1. This example simulates what you might see from a wine store on the Web, where the user wants to order a number of bottles of wine. As you can see in Figure 15.1, however, the user has not filled in any fields in the order form and has merely clicked the Submit My Order! button. The required field validator next to the top text box objects to this action and displays its message, which we've set to "You must indicate the number of bottles." Required field validators like this one ensure that the user has entered data into a control you select. If no date is entered, the validator will

15

display an error message when the control you want to validate loses the focus, or the user clicks a Submit button. The same error message appears in the Validation Summary control we've placed at the bottom of the page; this control displays all the validation errors that occur in a page when the Submit button is clicked and allows you to group all the error messages. Although you can't see color in the figure, these error messages are in red; you can set the text color for error messages yourself by using a validation control's ForeColor property.

FIGURE 15.1

The Validators example.

A different validation control is used for each text box you see in Figure 15.1. When you add a validation control to a Web form, you indicate what control's data you want to check by setting the validator's ControlToValidate property. (If the validator allows you to compare data in that control to another control, you can also set the ControlToCompare property; in fact, you can assign more than one control to validate to the same validator at one time.) The actual error message in a validation control is stored in the ErrorMessage property. If any errors occur when the control to validate loses the focus or a Submit button is clicked, the validator displays its error message, which is hidden until that point. When the user fixes the problem and tries again, the error message disappears if the new data is okay.

At design time, you can place validators where you want them; you can see the various validators in the Validators example at design time in Figure 15.2, one of a different type next to each text box. At design time, each validator displays its error message, as you see in the figure.

FIGURE 15.2

*The Validators example
at design time.*

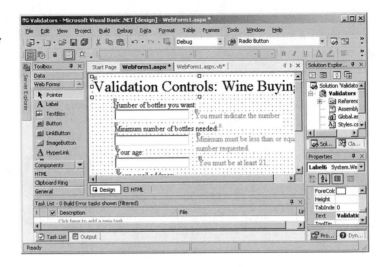

You can find the validation controls, and what they do, in Table 15.1. We'll go through them all, control by control, today.

TABLE 15.1   Validation Controls

Validator	Does This
RequiredFieldValidator	Ensures the user enters data in a data-entry control you specify.
CompareValidator	Uses comparison operators to compare user-entered data to either constant data or the data in another data-entry control.
RangeValidator	Ensures that user-entered data is in a range between given lower and upper bounds.
RegularExpressionValidator	Ensures that user-entered data matches a regular-expression pattern successfully.
CustomValidator	Ensures user-entered data passes validation criteria that you implement in a script function.

The BaseValidator class, which is the base class for validation controls, is based on the Label class:

```
System.Object
   System.Web.UI.Control
      System.Web.UI.WebControls.WebControl
         System.Web.UI.WebControls.Label
            System.Web.UI.WebControls.BaseValidator
```

You can find the significant public properties of `BaseValidator` objects in Table 15.2 and their significant public method in Table 15.3 (this class has no noninherited events). Note that as with other Web server controls, these tables do not list the significant properties, methods, and events this class inherits from the `Control` and `WebControl` classes; you can find them in Tables 12.1 to 12.5.

TABLE 15.2   Significant Public Properties of `BaseValidator` Objects

Property	Means
ControlToValidate	Returns or sets the data-entry control you want to validate.
Display	Returns or sets how error messages should be displayed.
EnableClientScript	Returns or sets whether validation is enabled.
Enabled	Returns or sets whether the validator control is enabled.
ErrorMessage	Returns or sets the text of the error message.
ForeColor	Returns or sets the color of the error message text.
IsValid	Returns or sets whether the data in the associated data-entry control is validated.

TABLE 15.3   Significant Public Method of `BaseValidator` Objects

Method	Means
Validate	Checks the associated data-entry control and updates the `IsValid` property.

The first validator we'll look at in depth is the required field validator, which is the one you see at work in Figure 15.1, checking the number of bottles of wine the user is ordering.

Using Required Field Validators

Required field validators are the simplest validators; they just make sure that the user has entered data into a specific control. If the user hasn't entered data, they'll display an error message.

These validators have a property called `InitialValue`, which holds an empty string (`""`) by default. If the data in the control has not changed from the value in `InitialValue` when the required field validator does its work, it will display its error message.

Tip

> Here's something that's important to know: If a data-entry control is empty, *no* validation is performed by any of the validation controls, except for required field validators. In other words, by default, all validation operations will appear to succeed if a data-entry control is empty, except for required field validations. That means it's a good idea to use a required field validator (in addition to any other validators) to make sure the user enters data into a data-entry control before checking that data.

Required field validators are supported by the `RequiredFieldValidator` class, and the hierarchy of that class is as follows:

```
System.Object
   System.Web.UI.Control
      System.Web.UI.WebControls.WebControl
         System.Web.UI.WebControls.Label
            System.Web.UI.WebControls.BaseValidator
               System.Web.UI.WebControls.RequiredFieldValidator
```

You can find the significant public property of `RequiredFieldValidator` objects in Table 15.4 (this class has no noninherited methods or events). Note that as with other Web server controls, this table does not list the significant properties, methods, and events this class inherits from the `Control` and `WebControl` classes; you can find them in Tables 12.1 to 12.5. This class inherits the `BaseValidator` class, which you can see in Tables 15.2 and 15.3.

TABLE 15.4 Significant Public Property of `RequiredFieldValidator` Objects

Property	Means
InitialValue	Returns or sets the initial value in the associated data-entry control.

Here's the HTML for the required field validator in the Validators example; note that it's just an HTML `<SPAN>` element whose text (the error message) is hidden when the page first loads:

```
<span id="RequiredFieldValidator1" controltovalidate="TextBox1"
errormessage="You must indicate the number of bottles."
evaluationfunction="RequiredFieldValidatorEvaluateIsValid"
initialvalue="" style="color:Red;Z-INDEX:101;LEFT:221px;POSITION:absolute;
TOP:81px;visibility:hidden;">
You must indicate the number of bottles.</span>
```

That's all you need to know to use required field validators! Just add one to a Web page, set the `ControlToValidate` property to the control whose data you want to validate, set the InitialValue property to the initial value of that data, and set the ErrorMessage property to the error message you want to display if a problem occurs. That's it.

Using Comparison Validators

A comparison validator, like the one connected to the second text box in Figure 15.3, allows you to compare the values in two controls, or the data in one control with a constant value. In the figure, the comparison validator is comparing the number of bottles the user has requested against the minimum number he or she will settle for in case there is not enough in stock. The minimum number of bottles must be less than or equal to the number requested, and if it's not—as is the case in Figure 15.3—the comparison validator displays its error message.

FIGURE 15.3

Using a comparison operator.

The comparison validator is based on the BaseCompareValidator class, which is an abstract base class for a number of validation controls that perform comparisons, such as the comparison validator. Here is the hierarchy for the BaseCompareValidator class:

```
System.Object
    System.Web.UI.Control
        System.Web.UI.WebControls.WebControl
            System.Web.UI.WebControls.Label
                System.Web.UI.WebControls.BaseValidator
                    System.Web.UI.WebControls.BaseCompareValidator
```

You can find the significant public property of BaseCompareValidator objects in Table 15.5 (this class has no noninherited methods or events). Note that as with other Web server controls, this table does not list the significant properties, methods, and events this class inherits from the `Control` and `WebControl` classes; you can find them in Tables 12.1 to 12.5. This class inherits the `BaseValidator` class, which you can find in Tables 15.2 and 15.3.

TABLE 15.5 Significant Public Property of `BaseCompareValidator` Objects

Property	Means
Type	Returns or sets the type of the data that is being compared.

Comparison validators are supported by the `CompareValidator` class, and the hierarchy for this class is as follows:

```
System.Object
    System.Web.UI.Control
        System.Web.UI.WebControls.WebControl
            System.Web.UI.WebControls.Label
                System.Web.UI.WebControls.BaseValidator
                    System.Web.UI.WebControls.BaseCompareValidator
                        System.Web.UI.WebControls.CompareValidator
```

You can find the significant public properties of `CompareValidator` objects in Table 15.6 (this class has no noninherited methods or events). Note that as with other Web server controls, this table does not list the significant properties, methods, and events this class inherits from the `Control` and `WebControl` classes; you can find them in Tables 12.1 to 12.5. This class inherits the `BaseValidator` class, which you can find in Tables 15.2 and 15.3, and the `BaseCompareValidator` class, which you can find in Table 15.5.

TABLE 15.6 Significant Public Properties of `CompareValidator` Objects

Property	Means
ControlToCompare	Returns or sets the data-entry control whose data you want to compare to the data in the data-entry control to validate.
Operator	Returns or sets the comparison operation you want to use in the comparison.
ValueToCompare	Returns or sets the constant value you want to compare with the value in the data-entry control to validate.

To set up a comparison validator, you specify the data-entry control to validate by setting the `ControlToValidate` property. If you want to compare a specific data-entry control with another data-entry control, set the `ControlToCompare` property to specify the control to compare with.

Instead of comparing the value of a data-entry control with another data-entry control, you can also compare the value of a data-entry control to a constant value. In this case, you specify the constant value to compare with by setting the ValueToCompare property.

Caution   Don't set both the ControlToCompare and ValueToCompare properties at the same time because they conflict. If you set them both, the ControlToCompare property is used.

You can also use the Operator property to specify the type of comparison to perform. Here are the possibilities:

- DataTypeCheck—Compares the data types of the value in the data-entry control being validated to the data type specified by the Type property.
- Equal—Determines whether the compared values are equal.
- GreaterThan—Determines for a greater than relationship.
- GreaterThanEqual—Determines for a greater than or equal to relationship.
- LessThan—Determines for a less than relationship.
- LessThanEqual—Determines for a greater than or equal to relationship.
- NotEqual—Determines whether the compared values are not equal.

You can use the Type property to specify the data type of both comparison values. This type is String by default, so don't forget to set this property yourself if you're comparing numbers (in string comparisons, a value of 120 is less than 15, for example). Both values are automatically converted to this data type before the comparison operation is performed. You can use the following data types:

- String—String data type.
- Integer—Integer data type.
- Double—Double data type.
- Date—Date data type.
- Currency—Currency data type.

In the Validators example you see at work in Figure 15.3, the comparison validator's ControlToValidate property is set to TextBox2, and its ControlToCompare property is set to TextBox1. The Type property is set to Integer and the Operator property to LessThanEqual. The error message is stored in the ErrorMessage property. You can see the result in Figure 15.3, where the comparison validator is checking the value in the top text box to the value in the text box beneath it.

Here's the HTML for the compare validator in the Validators example; as with other validators, it's based on an HTML <SPAN> element whose text is initially hidden:

```
<span id="CompareValidator1" controltovalidate="TextBox2"
errormessage="Minimum must be less than or equal to number requested."
type="Integer" evaluationfunction="CompareValidatorEvaluateIsValid"
controltocompare="TextBox1" controlhookup="TextBox1"
operator="LessThanEqual" style="color:Red;height:26px;width:239px;
Z-INDEX:102;LEFT:224px;POSITION:absolute;TOP:129px;visibility:hidden;">
Minimum must be less than or equal to number requested.</span>
```

Using Range Validators

You can use range validators to test whether the data in a particular control is inside a specific range. The properties you set here are the ControlToValidate property and the MinimumValue and MaximumValue properties to hold the minimum and maximum values of the range of data you want to accept. You also must set the Type property to the data type of the values to compare; the possible values are the same as for comparison validators, and the default value is String.

You can see a range validator at work in Figure 15.4 in the Validators example. Here, the range validator is making sure that the age the user enters is over 21.

FIGURE 15.4

Using a range operator.

Range validators are supported by the RangeValidator class, and the hierarchy for that class is as follows:

```
System.Object
   System.Web.UI.Control
```

```
System.Web.UI.WebControls.WebControl
  System.Web.UI.WebControls.Label
    System.Web.UI.WebControls.BaseValidator
      System.Web.UI.WebControls.BaseCompareValidator
        System.Web.UI.WebControls.RangeValidator
```

You can find the significant public properties of `RangeValidator` objects in Table 15.7 (this class has no noninherited methods or events). Note that as with other Web server controls, this table does not list the significant properties, methods, and events this class inherits from the `Control` and `WebControl` classes; you can find them in Tables 12.1 to 12.5. This class inherits the `BaseValidator` class, which you can find in Tables 15.2 and 15.3, and the `BaseCompareValidator` class, which you can see in Table 15.5.

TABLE 15.7   Significant Public Properties of `RangeValidator` Objects

Property	Means
ControlToCompare	Returns or sets the data-entry control you want to compare to the data-entry control you want to validate.
MaximumValue	Returns or sets the allowed range's maximum value.
MinimumValue	Returns or sets the allowed range's minimum value.

You can see the Validators range validator at work in Figure 15.4. Here's the HTML for the range validator in the Validators example; like the other validators, it's based on the HTML <SPAN> element, and it hides its red-colored text until an error occurs:

```
<span id="RangeValidator1" controltovalidate="TextBox3"
errormessage="You must be at least 21."
type="Integer" evaluationfunction="RangeValidatorEvaluateIsValid"
maximumvalue="150" minimumvalue="21" style="color:Red;
Z-INDEX:103;LEFT:228px;POSITION:absolute;TOP:178px;visibility:hidden;">
You must be at least 21.</span>
```

As you can see, range validators are useful for checking all kinds of ranges, from temperatures to the number of items in stock, allowing you, for example, to make sure that the number of items in a purchase order is greater than zero or that the user is of an appropriate age for age-restricted products.

Using Regular Expression Validators

NEW TERM   Regular expression validators enable you to check the text in a control against a *regular expression*. Regular expressions are made up of *patterns*, and when you check a pattern against text, you can determine whether the text matches that pattern, allowing you to handle and check all kinds of text in your code. Patterns are made up of text and various regular expression codes (which can act like wildcards) to match specific text or character sequences.

> **Tip** For more details on regular expressions and how to create them, search for "Regular Expression Syntax" in the Visual Basic .NET documentation or look at `http://www.perldoc.com/perl5.8.0/pod/perlre.html`.

NEW TERM Let's look at an example to make this topic clearer. Regular expression codes start with a backslash (\). For example, the code for the beginning or ending of a word, called a *word boundary*, is \b. That means that this regular expression pattern will match the word `"Hello"`:

`\bHello\b`

NEW TERM Here's another example. This regular expression matches any word made up of lowercase or uppercase characters using a *character class*, `[A-Za-z]`, which matches any lowercase or uppercase character, and a plus sign (+), which means "one or more of" in regular expressions:

`\b([A-Za-z]+)\b`

You can also use the \w word character code, which matches any alphanumeric character, so this regular expression even matches any word that contains digits:

`\b\w+\b`

These examples barely suggest what's possible with regular expressions, however; the complete syntax is reasonably involved and very powerful. But even if you know nothing about regular expressions, you can still use the regular expressions that come with Visual Basic .NET. To do that, add a regular expression validator to a Web form and click the ellipsis (...) button for the `ValidationExpression` property in the Properties window to open the Regular Expression Editor you see in Figure 15.5.

Using the Regular Expression Editor, you can select from a number of prewritten regular expressions. For example, the following is the regular expression Visual Basic .NET uses to determine whether text matches a valid email address; \w is for a word character, and the asterisk (*) means "zero or more of":

`\w+([-+.]\w+)*@\w+([-.]\w+)*\.\w+([-.]\w+)*`

FIGURE 15.5

Regular expressions built into Visual Basic .NET.

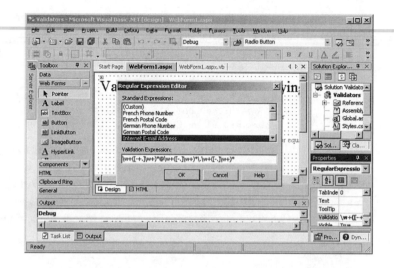

You can see the results in Figure 15.6, where the regular expression validator is checking the e-mail address entered in the text box it's supposed to validate, as set with the ControlToValidate property. In this case, it finds that steve is not a valid e-mail address and informs the user of that fact.

FIGURE 15.6

Using a regular expression validator.

The regular expression validator is supported by the `RegularExpressionValidator`
class, and the hierarchy of that class is as follows:

```
System.Object
   System.Web.UI.Control
      System.Web.UI.WebControls.WebControl
         System.Web.UI.WebControls.Label
            System.Web.UI.WebControls.BaseValidator
               System.Web.UI.WebControls.RegularExpressionValidator
```

You can find the significant public property of `RegularExpressionValidator` objects in
Table 15.8 (this class has no noninherited methods or events). Note that as with other
Web server controls, this table does not list the significant properties, methods, and
events this class inherits from the `Control` and `WebControl` classes; you can find them in
Tables 12.1 to 12.5. This class inherits the `BaseValidator` class, which you can find in
Tables 15.2 and 15.3.

TABLE 15.8   Significant Public Property of `RegularExpressionValidator` Objects

Property	Means
ValidationExpression	Returns or sets the regular expression you want to use to match against text for the validation operation.

That, then, is how to use a regular expression validator: You just assign the regular
expression you want to use to the `RegularExpression` property, assign the control whose
data you want to validate to the `ControlToValidate` property, enter an error message in
the `ErrorMessage` property, and you're set.

Creating regular expressions yourself is not the easiest task, but you will become accus-
tomed to working with them in time. And until then, you can always turn to the Regular
Expression Editor to use the prewritten regular expressions that come with Visual Basic
.NET.

Here's the HTML for the regular expression validator in the Validators example; you can
see the regular expression this validator uses in the `validationexpression` attribute:

```
<span id="RegularExpressionValidator1" controltovalidate="TextBox4"
errormessage="Please enter a vaild email address."
evaluationfunction="RegularExpressionValidatorEvaluateIsValid"
validationexpression="\w+([-+.]\w+)*@\w+([-.]\w+)*\.\w+([-.]\w+)*"
style="color:Red;Z-INDEX:104;LEFT:228px;POSITION:absolute;
TOP:225px;visibility:hidden;">
Please enter a vaild email address.</span>
```

Using Custom Validators

We've already seen most of the validation controls Visual Basic .NET offers today, and as we've seen, they can perform various validation tasks. But sometimes what they have to offer isn't enough. What if, for example, you wanted to accept only numbers ending in .5? Or what if you wanted only numbers that are multiples of 27? You can't use the validators we've seen for those kinds of tests—but you can use a custom validator.

For example, you can see a custom validator at work in Figure 15.7. In this case, the user has offered $10 per bottle, but we're willing to accept only a minimum of $20, so the validator is displaying an error. (Note that this is just a simple example; you don't need a custom validator to check data this way. You could use a range validator.)

FIGURE 15.7

Using a custom validator.

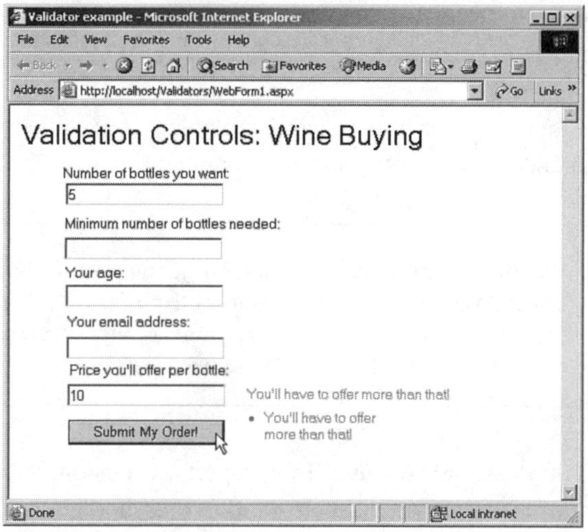

The custom validator control is supported by the `CustomValidator` class, and the hierarchy of this class is as follows:

```
System.Object
   System.Web.UI.Control
      System.Web.UI.WebControls.WebControl
         System.Web.UI.WebControls.Label
            System.Web.UI.WebControls.BaseValidator
               System.Web.UI.WebControls.CustomValidator
```

You can find the significant public property of `CustomValidator` objects in Table 15.9 and their significant event in Table 15.10. Note that as with other Web server controls, these tables do not list the significant properties, methods, and events this class inherits from the Control and WebControl classes; you can find them in Tables 12.1 to 12.5. This class also inherits the BaseValidator class, which you can find in Tables 15.2 and 15.3.

TABLE 15.9 Significant Public Property of CustomValidator Objects

Property	Means
ClientValidationFunction	Returns or sets the name of the script function you've added to the Web page for validation.

TABLE 15.10 Significant Public Event of CustomValidator Objects

Event	Means
ServerValidate	Occurs if and when validation takes place on the server.

The code a custom validator uses to validate its data is executed in the browser, so you must write that code in a browser scripting language such as JavaScript or VBScript.

> **Tip**
>
> VBScript is a Microsoft scripting language that supports a tiny subset of Visual Basic .NET for use in Internet Explorer only. For details on VBScript, see http://msdn.microsoft.com/library/default.asp?url=/library/en-us/script56/html/vtoriVBScript.asp.

You set the ClientValidationFunction property of custom validators to hold the name of this function. This function will be passed two arguments: source, which gives the source control to validate, and arguments, which holds the data to validate as arguments.Value. If you validate the data, you set arguments.IsValid to true; otherwise, you set it to false. (This code uses the JavaScript constants true and false, which are lowercase, not the standard Visual Basic .NET True and False constants.) And as with other validation controls, you set the ControlToValidate property to set the control whose data you want to validate and place the error message in the ErrorMessage property.

You add the validation function, which we will simply call Validate in this example, to the HTML in the Web form's .aspx file by clicking the HTML tab at the bottom of the code window and entering your script directly. This function goes inside a <script> element that you can add to the Web form's <head> element. Here's what that looks like in code:

```
<head>
    .
    .
    .
    <script language="javascript">
        function Validate(source, arguments)
        {
            if (arguments.Value > 20) {
                arguments.IsValid = true
            } else {
                arguments.IsValid = false
            }
        }
    </script>
    .
    .
    .
</head>
```

The `Validate` function just checks to make sure that the value the user has entered is greater than 20. To connect this function to the custom validator in the Validators example, you set the validator's `ClientValidationFunction` property to the name of the JavaScript function, `Validate`. Then you just enter the control whose data you want to check in the custom validator's `ControlToValidate` property and the error message you want to display if needed in the `ErrorMessage` property.

And that's all we need! Because the value the user has entered is less than 20 in the text box the custom validator is checking in Figure 15.7, the custom validator is displaying its error message. Now we're using custom validators in the client.

The HTML for the custom validator in the Validators example looks like the following. You can see the name of the JavaScript Validate function we've created here stored in the `clientvalidationfunction` attribute, which corresponds to the control's `ClientValidationFunction` property:

```
<span id="CustomValidator1" controltovalidate="TextBox5"
errormessage="You'll have to offer more than that!"
evaluationfunction="CustomValidatorEvaluateIsValid"
clientvalidationfunction="Validate" style="color:Red;
Z-INDEX:105;LEFT:233px;POSITION:absolute;TOP:273px;visibility:hidden;">
You'll have to offer more than that!</span>
```

Using Validation Summaries

The validation controls we've seen so far are tied to individual controls, but you can also display a summary of all the validation errors in a Web form by using a validation summary control. This control combines all the error messages from the various validation controls in the form of a bulleted list or just a paragraph of text, as you see at the bottom in Figure 15.8. (As with other validation controls, you can position the validation summary control anywhere you want in a Web form; it need not appear at the bottom.)

FIGURE 15.8

Using a validation summary.

This control is supported by the `System.Web.UI.WebControls.ValidationSummary` class; the hierarchy of this class is as follows:

```
System.Object
    System.Web.UI.Control
        System.Web.UI.WebControls.WebControl
            System.Web.UI.WebControls.ValidationSummary
```

You can find the significant public properties of `System.Web.UI.WebControls.ValidationSummary` objects in Table 15.11 (this class has no noninherited methods or events). Note that as with other Web server controls, this table does not list the significant properties, methods, and events this class inherits from the `Control` and `WebControl` classes; you can find them in Tables 12.1 to 12.5.

TABLE 15.11   Significant Public Properties of `ValidationSummary` Objects

Property	Means
DisplayMode	Returns or sets the summary's display mode (list, bulleted list, or paragraph).
EnableClientScript	Returns or sets whether validation should be performed in the browser.
HeaderText	Returns or sets the text displayed at the top of the summary.
ShowMessageBox	Returns or sets whether a message box displays the validation summary.
ShowSummary	Returns or sets whether the summary is displayed in the Web page.

The error summary that appears in this control can be displayed as a list, bulleted list, or single paragraph, based on the `DisplayMode` property, which you can set to `ValidationSummaryDisplayMode.List`, `ValidationSummaryDisplayMode.BulletList`, or `ValidationSummaryDisplayMode.SingleParagraph`. You can also specify whether the summary should be displayed in the Web page or in a message box by setting the `ShowSummary` and `ShowMessageBox` properties, respectively.

The validation summary is displayed using an HTML `<DIV>` element, instead of a `<SPAN>` element, because `<DIV>` elements can handle multiline text:

```
<div id="ValidationSummary1" style="color:Red;height:49px;width:149px;
Z-INDEX:106;LEFT:210px;POSITION:absolute;TOP:296px;display:none;">
```

And that's it for validation controls. If you have data input controls in your Web application, consider using these controls. They're easy to use, and they can save wear and tear on the server.

Using Calendars

Calendar controls are relatively simple controls, but we'll include them here for completeness. You just use the `Calendar` control to display a single month of a calendar in a Web form. This control allows you to select dates and move to the next or previous month. You can see a calendar control at work in the Calendar example in the code for this book, which you see at work in Figure 15.9. When the user selects a date, a `SelectionChanged` event occurs, and you can handle that event to find the dates the user selected.

FIGURE 15.9

The Calendar example.

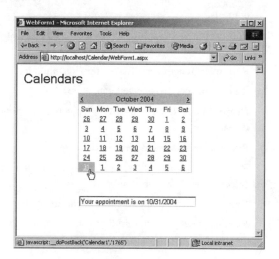

The hierarchy for the `System.Web.UI.WebControls.Calendar` class is as follows:

```
System.Object
   System.Web.UI.Control
      System.Web.UI.WebControls.WebControl
         System.Web.UI.WebControls.Calendar
```

You can find the significant public properties of `System.Web.UI.WebControls.Calendar` objects in Table 15.12 and their significant public events in Table 15.13 (this class has no noninherited methods). Note that as with other Web server controls, these tables do not list the significant properties, methods, and events this class inherits from the `Control` and `WebControl` classes; you can find them in Tables 12.1 to 12.5.

TABLE 15.12   Significant Public Properties of `Calendar` Objects

Property	Means
CellPadding	Returns or sets the space used for cell padding in the calendar control.
CellSpacing	Returns or sets the space between cells in the calendar control.
DayHeaderStyle	Returns the style used for the day of the week.
DayNameFormat	Returns or sets the format used for the day of the week's name.
DayStyle	Returns the style used for days.
FirstDayOfWeek	Returns or sets the day of the week you want displayed in the first column.
NextMonthText	Returns or sets the text for the next month's navigation control.
NextPrevFormat	Returns or sets the format of both the next and previous months' navigation controls.
NextPrevStyle	Returns or sets the style for the next and previous months' navigation controls.
OtherMonthDayStyle	Returns the style for the days other than those displayed in the current month.
PrevMonthText	Returns or sets the text for the previous month's navigation control.
SelectedDate	Returns or sets the selected date.
SelectedDates	Returns a collection of `DateTime` objects corresponding to the selected dates.
SelectedDayStyle	Returns the style used for selected dates.
SelectionMode	Returns or sets the date selection mode, which determines if the user can select a day, week, or month.
ShowDayHeader	Returns or sets whether the day of the week header should be shown.
ShowGridLines	Returns or sets whether gridlines should appear between days.

TABLE 15.12 continued

Property	Mean
ShowNextPrevMonth	Returns or sets whether to display next and previous months' navigation controls.
ShowTitle	Returns or sets whether the title should be displayed.
TitleFormat	Returns or sets the format for the title.
TitleStyle	Returns the style of the title.
TodayDayStyle	Returns the style for today's date.
TodaysDate	Returns or sets today's date.
VisibleDate	Returns or sets a date and makes sure that date is visible.
WeekendDayStyle	Returns the style used for weekend dates.

TABLE 15.13 Significant Public Events of `Calendar` Objects

Event	Means
DayRender	Occurs when each day is displayed.
SelectionChanged	Occurs when the user selects a date.
VisibleMonthChanged	Occurs when the user moves to a different month than the one currently displayed.

Calendar controls display the days of the month, day headings for the days of the week, a title with the month name, and arrow characters for navigating to the next and previous month. You can further customize what a `Calendar` control looks like by setting these properties:

- `DayHeaderStyle` — Sets the style for the days of the week.
- `DayStyle` — Sets the style for the dates in a month.
- `NextPrevStyle` — Sets the style for the navigation controls.
- `OtherMonthStyle` — Sets the style for dates not in the displayed month.
- `SelectedDayStyle` — Sets the style for the selected dates.
- `SelectorStyle` — Sets the style for the week and month selection column.
- `ShowDayHeader` — Shows or hides the days of the week.
- `ShowGridLines` — Shows or hides gridlines (displayed between the days of the month).

- ShowNextPrevMonth—Shows or hides the navigation controls to the next or previous month.
- ShowTitle—Shows or hides the title.
- TitleStyle—Sets the style for titles.
- TodayDayStyle—Sets the style for today's date.
- WeekendDayStyle—Sets the style for weekend dates.

When the user selects a date, a SelectionChanged event occurs, and you can use the control's SelectedDate property to determine the selection. You can have the control return dates in various formats; the default format, *mm/dd/yyyy* (such as 10/31/2004), appears in Figure 15.9. Here's the code that displays the selected date in the Calendar example:

```
Private Sub Calendar1_SelectionChanged(ByVal _
    sender As System.Object, ByVal e As System.EventArgs) _
    Handles Calendar1.SelectionChanged
    TextBox1.Text = "Your appointment is on " & Calendar1.SelectedDate
End Sub
```

You can specify whether the Calendar control allows users to select a single day, week, or month by setting the SelectionMode property, which can take these values:

- CalendarSelectionMode.Day—Specifies that a single date can be selected in the calendar.
- CalendarSelectionMode.DayWeek—Specifies that a single date or entire week can be selected in the calendar.
- CalendarSelectionMode.DayWeekMonth—Specifies that a single date, week, or entire month can be selected in the calendar.
- CalendarSelectionMode.None—Specifies that no dates can be selected in the calendar.

For example, setting a calendar control's SelectionMode property to CalendarSelectionMode.DayWeek allows the user to select an entire week if necessary, as you see in Figure 15.10.

As you see in the text box in Figure 15.10, the SelectedDate property returns only the first selected day, even if the user selects an entire week. To get all selected days, you use the SelectedDates property instead, which returns a collection of System.DateTime objects that represent the selected dates.

FIGURE 15.10

Selecting a week at a time.

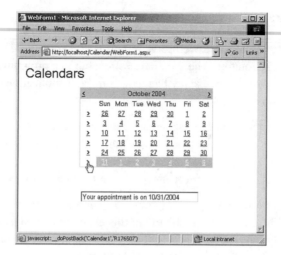

15

As you might expect from their appearance, Visual Basic .NET uses HTML tables to create calendar controls. Here's what the HTML for the calendar control looks like. Note that this code has an <a> element for each date in the control, which sends the page back to the server when it's clicked, but we're showing only a few of those elements for brevity:

```
<table id="Calendar1" cellspacing="0" cellpadding="2" border="0"
style="border-width:1px;border-style:solid;
border-collapse:collapse;Z-INDEX: 102; LEFT:
128px; POSITION: absolute; TOP: 59px">
    <tr><td colspan="8" style="background-color:Silver;">
<table cellspacing="0" border="0" style="width:100%;
border-collapse:collapse;">
    <tr><td style="width:15%;"><a href=
"javascript:__doPostBack('Calendar1','V1035')"
style="color:Black">&lt;</a></td><td align="Center"
style="width:70%;">December 2002</td><td align="Right"
style="width:15%;"><a href="javascript:__doPostBack('Calendar1','V1096')"
style="color:Black">&gt;</a></td></tr>
    </table></td></tr><tr><td align="Center"></td><td align="Center">
Sun</td><td align="Center">Mon</td><td align="Center">Tue</td>
<td align="Center">Wed</td><td align="Center">Thu</td><td align="Center">
Fri</td><td align="Center">Sat</td></tr><tr><td align="Center"
style="width:12%;">
<a href="javascript:__doPostBack('Calendar1','R105807')"
style="color:Black">&gt;</a></td><td align="Center" style="width:12%;">
<a href="javascript:__doPostBack('Calendar1','1058')"
style="color:Black">24</a></td><td align="Center" style="width:12%;">
                .
                .
                .
</td></tr>
</table>
```

Using Ad Rotators

Now we come to one of those Web server controls that some programmers consider a little questionable: ad rotators. They're not questionable in a programming sense because they work just fine, but they display banner ads in Web applications, and plenty of Web programmers dislike those ads.

To create an ad banner, you can use any type of image file that a browser can display, even animated GIF files. Ad rotators "rotate" through a set of banner ads by selecting which one to display randomly; you can also "weight" ads to appear more frequently than others. In fact, you can write your own code to cycle through the ad banners.

You can see an ad rotator at work in Figure 15.11 in the AdRotator example in the code for this book. When you click the button in this example, the page reloads and displays another randomly selected ad banner. When you click the ad banner itself, the browser navigates to a URL you've associated with that banner.

FIGURE 15.11

The AdRotator example.

Ad banners can also display customized tool tips, as you see in Figure 15.12.

This control is supported with the System.Web.UI.WebControls.AdRotator class, and the hierarchy of that class is as follows:

```
System.Object
   System.Web.UI.Control
      System.Web.UI.WebControls.WebControl
         System.Web.UI.WebControls.AdRotator
```

FIGURE 15.12

The AdRotator example displaying a tool tip.

You can find the significant public properties of System.Web.UI.WebControls. AdRotator objects in Table 15.14 and their event in Table 15.15 (this class has no noninherited methods). Note that as with other Web server controls, these tables do not list the significant properties, methods, and events this class inherits from the Control and WebControl classes; you can find them in Tables 12.1 to 12.5.

TABLE 15.14 Significant Public Properties of AdRotator Objects

Property	Means
AdvertisementFile	Returns or sets the XML file that contains information on the ads and ad banners.
KeywordFilter	Returns or sets a keyword to filter the ads that will be displayed.
Target	Returns or sets the name of the browser window or frame that displays linked-to Web pages when an ad banner is clicked.

TABLE 15.15 Significant Public Event of AdRotator Objects

Event	Means
AdCreated	Occurs before the Web page is displayed, allowing you to customize ad displays.

Putting an ad rotator to work is not very difficult; you just add this control to a Web form and set up the banners you want to show. You can set up your ads in the `AdCreated` event or, more usually, with an XML file.

In the `AdCreated` event, which occurs before an ad is displayed, you are passed an object of the `System.Web.UI.WebControls.AdCreatedEventArgs` class, which holds information about an ad banner:

```
Private Sub AdRotator1_AdCreated(ByVal sender As System.Object, ByVal e As _
    System.Web.UI.WebControls.AdCreatedEventArgs) _
    Handles AdRotator1.AdCreated
    .
    .
    .
End Sub
```

Using the `ImageUrl` property of the `AdCreatedEventArgs` object, you can set the URL of the image to display. The `NavigateUrl` property allows you to set the URL the browser should navigate to if the user clicks the ad. You can use these properties in the `AdCreatedEventArgs` object:

- `AdProperties`—Returns a `System.Collections.IDictionary` object that contains all the advertisement properties for an ad.

- `AlternateText`—Returns or sets the text displayed in the ad rotator control when the ad banner is unavailable. Browsers that support tool tips display this text as a tool tip for the ad.

- `ImageUrl`—Returns or sets the URL of the banner ad to display.

- `NavigateUrl`—Returns or sets the Web page to display when the banner ad is clicked.

It's more usual, however, to store ad information in an XML file, which is easily edited, updated, and maintained. Even though this file is written in XML, you don't need any special knowledge to adapt it for yourself; adapting it or adding other ads is simple.

Listing 15.1 shows the XML file, rotation.xml, for the AdRotator example in the code for this book. For each ad, the data in this file specifies the URL of the banner ad image, the URL to navigate to if the user clicks the ad, the alternate text to display if the ad banner isn't available (this text is also used as the tool tip), the number of impressions for each ad (this is a numeric value holding the relative probability of how often the ad should be shown, enabling you to weight ad banner appearances as you like), and a keyword to use in selecting ads (you use the `KeyWordFilter` property to filter ads for target audiences if you want to).

LISTING 15.1   rotation.xml (AdRotator project, Form1.vb)

```xml
<Advertisements>
    <Ad>
        <ImageUrl>banner1.jpg</ImageUrl>
        <NavigateUrl>http://www.starpowder.com/product1.html</NavigateUrl>
        <AlternateText>You can't get any better than Product 1!
        </AlternateText>
        <Impressions>80</Impressions>
        <Keyword>Candy</Keyword>
    </Ad>

    <Ad>
        <ImageUrl>banner2.jpg</ImageUrl>
        <NavigateUrl>http://www.starpowder.com/product2.html</NavigateUrl>
        <AlternateText>Product 2 is the favorite of millions!</AlternateText>
        <Impressions>80</Impressions>
        <Keyword>Candy</Keyword>
    </Ad>

    <Ad>
        <ImageUrl>banner3.jpg</ImageUrl>
        <NavigateUrl>http://www.starpowder.com/product3.html</NavigateUrl>
        <AlternateText>Product 3 beats them all!</AlternateText>
        <Impressions>80</Impressions>
        <Keyword>Hardware</Keyword>
    </Ad>
</Advertisements>
```

The rotation.xml document is stored in the main IIS folder for the AdRotator application, which is wwwroot\AdRotator. You assign the location of this XML file to the AdvertisementFile property of the ad rotator control, and the control reads it and uses the data in it by itself. The keyword for the first two ads is Candy, and for the last ad, it's Hardware. If you're targeting an audience interested only in candy, set the ad rotator's KeyWordFilter property to Candy and only those ads will appear.

The banner ads themselves—banner1.jpg, banner2.jpg, and banner3.jpg—are also stored in the main folder for the AdRotator application, wwwroot\AdRotator. Each banner ad is a JPG image here; by default, banner ads (such as banner1.jpg, banner2.jpg, and banner3.jpg) are 468×60 pixels, although you can set their sizes in the ad rotator control's Height and Width properties.

And that's how to use ad rotators. As you might expect, in the HTML sent to the browser, ad rotators appear as <a> hyperlink elements surrounding an <img> image element:

```
<a id="AdRotator1" href="http://www.starpowder.com/product1.html"
target="_top" style="Z-INDEX: 101; LEFT: 15px; POSITION:
absolute; TOP: 65px">
```

15

```
<img src="/AdRotator/banner1.jpg"
alt="You can't get any better than Product 1!" border="0"
style="height:60px;width:468px;" /></a>
```

As you can see, ad rotators are powerful controls. If you want to display banner ads in your Web applications, just add one of these controls to a Web form, position and size it as you want in the form, create your banner ads, connect them to the control, and you're set.

And that's it! With the ad rotator, we've completed our coverage of all the Web server controls, except for a few we'll see when working with databases in Day 19, "Using Databases in Web Applications." We'll start working with database applications tomorrow.

Summary

Today we completed our coverage of the Web server controls for use in Web forms in Visual Basic .NET, except for the database controls coming up in Day 19. We saw how to work with validators, calendar controls, and ad rotators.

Validation controls, also called validators, are used to check the data the user enters before that data is sent back to the Web server. Visual Basic .NET supports several different validators. You associate a validator with a data-entry control or controls by using the validator's `ControlToValidate` property and set the error message it should display by using the `ErrorMessage` property. If a validation error occurs when the control being validated loses the focus or a Submit button is clicked, the validation control—which is based on the label control—displays its error message at the location you've placed it (usually next to the control it's supposed to validate). After the user fixes the problem, he or she can try again.

Required field validators are the easiest to use. These validators just make sure the user has entered data into a control before submitting the page to Web server. You set the `InitialValue` to the value the control shows when it first appears, and if the value in the control to validate hasn't changed when that control loses the focus or the Submit button is clicked, the required field validator will display its error message.

Comparison validators allow you to compare the values in two different controls, which you set with the `ControlToValidate` and `ControlToCompare` properties. You can select various types of comparisons to perform by setting the `Operator` property to values such as `Equal`, `GreaterThan`, `LessThanEqual`, and so on.

Range validators test whether the data in a particular control is inside a specific range. The properties you set here are the `ControlToValidate` property and the `MinimumValue` and `MaximumValue` properties to hold the minimum and maximum values of the range of data you want to accept. You also must set the `Type` property to the data type of the values to compare.

Regular expression validators allow you to check text in a data-entry control using a regular expression. You enter the regular expression you want to use in the ValidationExpression property, and this control compares it against the data in the control to validate.

You can also create custom validators if the other validators can't do the job you need done. In a custom validator, the data in the control to validate is sent to a script function you write (whose name you assign to the ClientValidationFunction property), and you can indicate whether the data validates correctly.

Finally, validation summaries enable you to collect the errors from various validators and display them in one place when a Submit button is clicked. You can display the error messages in a variety of formats, including lists, bulleted lists, and paragraphs.

We also looked at the calendar control today. This control enables the user to select dates from a calendar that displays months. You can customize the calendar control in many ways, such as letting the user select weeks instead of just days.

The last control we looked at today was the ad rotator control. This control allows you to display banner ads in a Web form. You can handle ads in the control's AdCreated event or with an XML file. You specify the URL of a banner ad with the ImageUrl property of the AdCreatedEventArgs object passed to you in the AdCreated event or in the XML file, the URL to navigate to if the user clicks the ad with the NavigateUrl property, and the alternate text to display if the image isn't available in the AlternateText property.

And that's it for today's work. Tomorrow, we're going to start working with data in depth as we turn to databases.

Q&A

Q I want to work with the validation controls in a Web page myself in client-side script. How's that possible?

A You can loop through the page's Validators collection to work with each validation control in the page, checking their IsValid property to see whether their validation test was successful. And you can use the whole page's IsValid property to see whether all validation tests were successful. You can also force any validation control to check its data by using the control's Validate method.

Q Can I track which ads users are clicking by using an ad rotator?

A Unfortunately, the ad rotator control doesn't have any provision for tracking banner click-throughs, but you can add your own tracking code to the AdCreated event. Or you can set the NavigationUrl property to a page that tracks hits and immediately redirects the browser to the actual advertisement page.

Workshop

This workshop tests whether you understand the concepts you saw today. It's a good idea to make sure you can answer these questions before pressing on to tomorrow's work.

Quiz

1. You want to make sure the user types in the name of the product he or she is ordering. Which validator would be a good choice to use?

2. You want to make sure the user enters a phone number in a control. Which validator should you use?

3. What two properties do you use in a comparison validator to specify two data-entry controls you want to work with?

4. What event occurs in calendar controls when the user selects a date?

5. In an ad rotator, what properties do you use to specify an ad banner's URL and the URL the browser should navigate to when the ad banner is clicked?

Quiz Answers

1. A required field validator.

2. A regular expression validator. And it's a good idea to use a required field validator if the phone number is required information.

3. The `ControlToValidate` and `ControlToCompare` properties.

4. The `SelectionChanged` event handles date selections.

5. You use the `ImageUrl` and `NavigateUrl` properties.

Exercises

1. Create a new guest book application that accepts the reader's name, email address, and comments, using validators to make sure all required information is filled in. Store the information in a file on the server. (**Extra credit:** Make your guest book available on the Web by making the file where you store users' comments an HTML file accessible from the Web. Note that displaying users' email addresses is not a good idea in this case, both for security reasons and because some programs scan the Internet for email addresses to send spam to.)

2. Add banner ads to your guest book application (see Exercise 1), advertising the benefits of Visual Basic .NET. Tie those ads to various Web pages at the Microsoft Visual Basic .NET Web site, `http://msdn.microsoft.com/vbasic/`.

PART IV

In Review

Creating Web Applications in Visual Basic .NET

In Part IV, we worked with ASP.NET creating Web applications. We started by getting the details on Web forms, creating multi-window Web applications, adding Web server controls at runtime, preserving data across server round-trips, handling client-side programming, and more.

The following days focused on working with the controls available for use in Web applications as we built more powerful applications. We've seen and used all the Web server controls there are, from buttons to text boxes, from check boxes to radio buttons, from list boxes to hyperlinks, and from link buttons to ad rotators.

We also placed emphasis on working with the validation controls. These controls are useful because they let you check user-entered data on the client side before wasting time with possible errors on the server side.

To make sure that you've got these skills under your belt, take a look at the review project we'll create here that ties together much of what we've seen; this review project is a Web-based guest book application. It's quite a simple application, but if you can follow all that's going on without any problems, you're ready to move on to Part V. This application is a multi-window Web application that uses hyperlinks, buttons, text boxes, files on the server; navigates to new Web pages; and more. You can see it at work in Figure P4.1, where it's displaying a comment someone has entered.

11

12

13

14

15

The guest book.

To add another comment, you click the Add a New Comment hyperlink, which opens the new Web page you see in Figure P4.2. The user can type his name and comments, and then press the Submit button to add his name and comments to the guest book.

FIGURE P4.2

Adding a new comment to the guest book.

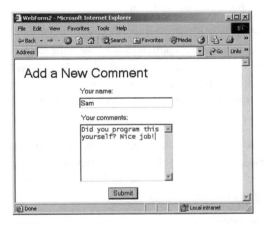

After the user's data has been stored, the code automatically navigates back to the first page where the new comment appears, as you see in Figure P4.3.

Figure P4.3

The guest book after a new comment was added.

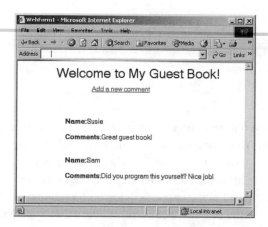

The first window, WebForm1, which you see in Figure P4.1, displays a label that says "Welcome to My Guest Book" and has a hyperlink containing the text "Add a new comment". The hyperlink is linked to a second window, WebForm2 (set the hyperlink's NavigateUrl property to WebForm2.aspx), which the user can use to enter his text in to the guest book. The guest book's text will be displayed in a literal using a <DIV> element, which can be positioned where we want it, so add that literal to WebForm1 now.

The guest book's text will be stored in a file named log.txt (be sure to update the path to this file for your installation of IIS in the code); if that file exists, we open it with a FileStream object and display its contents in the literal control like this:

```
Imports System.IO
Public Class WebForm1
    Inherits System.Web.UI.Page

' Web Form Designer Generated Code

    Private Sub Page_Load(ByVal sender As System.Object, _
    ByVal e As System.EventArgs) Handles MyBase.Load
        If (File.Exists("c:\inetpub\wwwroot\GuestBook\log.txt")) Then
            Dim fsStream As New FileStream(_
                "c:\inetpub\wwwroot\GuestBook\log.txt", _
                FileMode.Open, FileAccess.Read)
            Dim srReader As New StreamReader(fsStream)
            Literal1.Text = "<div align='left' " & _
            "style='POSITION: absolute; TOP: 100px; LEFT: 100px'>"
            Try
                While srReader.Peek() > -1
                    Literal1.Text &= srReader.ReadLine() & "<BR>"
                End While
                srReader.Close()
            Catch ex As IOException
```

```
                'Catch file error here
            End Try
            Literal1.Text &= "</div>"
        End If
    End Sub

End Class
```

We'll need a new Web form to accept user comments, so add that form, WebForm2, with the Project, Add the Web Form menu item and give it a label with the text "Add a New Comment", as well as two text boxes and a Submit button as you see in Figure P4.2. When the user enters his name and comments and clicks the Submit button, we can append his text to the end of the contents in log.txt (creating that file if necessary), and then navigate back to the original Web form, WebForm1 with the Response.Redirect method like this:

```
Imports System.IO
Public Class WebForm2
    Inherits System.Web.UI.Page

' Web Form Designer Generated Code

    Private Sub Button1_Click(ByVal sender As System.Object, _
        ByVal e As System.EventArgs) Handles Button1.Click
        Dim fsStream As New FileStream(_
            "c:\inetpub\wwwroot\GuestBook\log.txt", FileMode.Append, _
            FileAccess.Write)
        Dim swWriter As New StreamWriter(fsStream)

        Try
            swWriter.WriteLine("<B>Name:</B>" & TextBox1.Text & "<BR>")
            swWriter.WriteLine("<B>Comments</B>:" & TextBox2.Text & "<BR><BR>")
            swWriter.Close()
        Catch ex As IOException
            'Catch file errors
        End Try
        Response.Redirect("WebForm1.aspx")
    End Sub
End Class
```

When WebForm1 reopens, the user's new comments will be displayed, along with the previous comments added by other users. (If there is more text than can be displayed on one page, the browser's scrollbars will appear.) That's it; the guest book is operative (only in a very basic form, of course; in a real guest book, you'd add considerable embellishment, such as blocking the user from entering HTML in his text). If you can follow all this without any trouble, you're ready to move on to Part V.

PART V

At a Glance

Working with Databases in Visual Basic .NET

In Part V, we're going to spend four days working with a very popular Visual Basic .NET topic—handling databases. We'll connect to data sources, read and write data, bind data sources to data grids, list boxes, text boxes, and other controls, as well as master the objects provided in ADO.NET.

You'll see how to use the many visual tools that come with Visual Basic .NET to make working with databases easy, and we'll also see how to handle everything in code, without the use of those databases. You're going to see how to create data entry forms, update databases in code, create your own data tables, use SQL to extract data, and a great deal more in this part.

DAY 16

Handling Databases with ADO.NET

Today is our first day working with databases, one of the biggest topics in Visual Basic .NET programming. From a programmer's perspective, there are two main ways of working with databases in Visual Basic .NET: using the built-in visual tools and using code (where you work with database objects). Today and tomorrow, we'll see how to work with databases using visual tools, and the following day, Day 18, "Handling Databases in Code," will be about handling databases exclusively in code. Here are today's topics:

- Using the Server Explorer to explore data sources
- Creating data connections
- Dragging tables from the Server Explorer to a form
- Creating a dataset
- Populating a dataset
- Displaying data in a data grid
- Examining dataset data, properties, and schema
- Understanding basic SQL

- Handling relational databases
- Adding multiple tables to a single dataset
- Using data views for data snapshots
- Connecting to an MS Jet database

There's a lot to learn when it comes to working with databases in Visual Basic .NET, and at first, this topic might seem very complex. We're going to have to master a lot of objects. However, as we'll see, when we get the procedure down, it's not as hard as it first seems because the tools that come with Visual Basic .NET do a lot of the work for us. After you get your routine set and understand a few basic steps, things will become much easier.

What's a Database?

We'll start our database work with an overview of just what databases are and how they work. You may well already know all about databases, and so might want to skip this brief introduction; this overview is to make sure everyone understands the basic database concepts we'll use in the coming days.

Working with databases has become more complex over the years, but that's because it's become more popular, and people are always searching for ways to add more power to databases. Despite their complexity, the basic concepts here are simple ones, and when we have them under our belt, the rest will be much easier.

Say, for example, that you are in charge of some data; you might be teaching a class on Visual Basic .NET and want to store a grade for each of your students. You might write down a table of grades something like this:

```
-------------------
|Name    | Grade  |
|--------|--------|
|Ted     |   A-   |
|--------|--------|
|Frank   |   C+   |
|--------|--------|
|Mary    |   A    |
|--------|--------|
|Nancy   |   A+   |
|--------|--------|
|Wally   |   B-   |
|--------|--------|
|Bert    |   A    |
-------------------
```

NEW TERM   And that's it! You've already created a database—actually, a database *table*. This table is divided into *rows* and *columns*, and database tables are constructed the same way, dividing data into rows and columns. The benefit of storing your data in databases rather than on paper is that computers can search, replace, sort, and otherwise work with your data for you. You just have to tell them what you want to do, and that's what we'll be doing over the next few days.

NEW TERM Each item in this table goes into its own cell in the table, called a *field*. That is, the string `"Nancy"` is stored in one field, and her grade, `"A+"`, in another. Each cell in this table is a field, and each column of data usually has the same data type. The data types you can use for fields in Visual Basic .NET are as follows: `Boolean`, `Byte`, `Char`, `DateTime`, `Decimal`, `Double`, `Int16` (16-bit integer), `Int32` (32-bit integer), `Int64` (32-bit integer), `SByte` (signed byte), `Single`, and `String`.

NEW TERM Each row in the table is made up of several fields, such as the Name and Grade fields here. A row is called a *record* in a database. In other words, a collection of fields makes up a record, and a collection of records makes up a table. So what's a database? In its most common form, a *database* is just a collection of one or more tables. For example, if you have five classes of students, you would have five tables of data, and you could store them in a single database.

The tables in a database can also be related. For example, if some students take multiple classes from you, they would appear in several records. You might even have additional tables that store not only grades, but also contact information for each student. Now that some students appear in multiple tables, you can tie together their data between those tables.

NEW TERM For example, what if you want to warn all students who currently have a failing grade that they're in danger of failing? You could have your code search for all failing students and display their contact information. To do that, you treat the database as a *relational database* because you're relying on the relations between various tables. You might make your job easier by giving the students a special field that identifies them uniquely, such as their student ID:

```
- - - - - - - - - - - - - - - - - - - - - - - - - - -
|Name    |  Grade  |   ID   |
|- - - - -|- - - - - - |- - - - - - - - |
|Ted     |   A-    |  10221  |
|- - - - -|- - - - - - |- - - - - - - - |
|Frank   |   C+    |  10339  |
|- - - - -|- - - - - - |- - - - - - - - |
|Mary    |   A     |  10455  |
|- - - - -|- - - - - - |- - - - - - - - |
|Nancy   |   A+    |  10778  |
|- - - - -|- - - - - - |- - - - - - - - |
|Wally   |   B-    |  10331  |
|- - - - -|- - - - - - |- - - - - - - - |
|Bert    |   A     |  10667  |
- - - - - - - - - - - - - - - - - - - - - - - - - - -
```

16

Knowing a student's ID, you can look up his or her contact phone number in another table, say the contactinfo table, like this:

```
- - - - - - - - - - - - - - - - - - - -
|ID       |  Phone  |
|- - - - - - - -|- - - - - - - -|
|10221    |499.1010 |
|- - - - - - - -|- - - - - - - -|
|10339    |499.1210 |
|- - - - - - - -|- - - - - - - -|
|10455    |499.1020 |
|- - - - - - - -|- - - - - - - -|
|10778    |499.1012 |
|- - - - - - - -|- - - - - - - -|
|10331    |499.1230 |
|- - - - - - - -|- - - - - - - -|
|10667    |499.1014 |
- - - - - - - - - - - - - - - - - - - -
```

NEW TERM In this way, the ID value for each student ties together these tables. Using the ID value, you can move easily from working with the data in one table to the data in another table. In database terms, the ID value is the *key* you're using with these tables. The *primary key* you use for a table is the field that's the most important, such as the one on which you want to sort. You can also have a *foreign key* for each record, which represents the primary key in another table. In this example, the ID field is the foreign key in the Name/Grade/ID table because it represents a student's record in the other table, the ID/Phone Number table, that we want to work with.

NEW TERM As you can imagine, you can perform all kinds of operations with databases like this: You can sort records, extract records meeting specific criteria (such as failing students), combine the data for a specific record across several tables (as when you want to print both a student's grade and contact information), and so on. To do all that and more, you would need a whole programming language that works with databases, and that's exactly what *Structured Query Language (SQL)* is.

In Visual Basic .NET code, you use SQL statements to interact with a database, which means you have to know some SQL. We're going to get a basic introduction to SQL today, so even if you don't know any, don't panic. And as we'll see, a visual tool, the Query Builder, in Visual Basic .NET enables you to create SQL, and we're going to use this tool today. In the long run, however, if you're going to be doing a lot of database work, you have to learn the ins and outs of SQL in depth.

> You can get the actual documents that define SQL, as standardized by the
> International Organization for Standardization (ISO). See www.iso.org/iso/
> en/prods-services/catalogue/intstandards/CatalogueListPage.
> CatalogueList?ICS1=35&ICS2=60. The page at this URL lists the ISO's catalog
> for SQL documents, but these documents are not free. (If this URL has
> changed by the time you read this, go to the ISO site, www.iso.org, click the
> link for Information Technology, followed by the link for Languages Used in
> Information Technology.)

16

NEW TERM An SQL *statement*, also called an SQL *query*, can be applied to a database table
or set of tables, and when it is, some action is performed. For example, you
might want to delete a record or update it with new data in one of the fields, such as
changing the grade for one student. Or you might want to find all the students who have
failing grades, in which case the SQL statement would return a set of records, called a
dataset. A dataset holds the records that match the criteria you've set, and when you
want to work with the data in a database, you typically use SQL to create a dataset of the
records you want to use.

Now we're turning from the abstract to the concrete. So how do you actually connect to a
database and execute SQL statements in a database to get a dataset you can work with in
code? You do that by using three different types of objects in Visual Basic .NET: connection objects, data adapters, and dataset objects. And to work with databases in Visual
Basic .NET, you have to master all three.

Connections, Data Adapters, and Datasets

Connection objects, data adapters, and dataset objects are the objects you need to know
about to work with databases, and we'll spend some time introducing them before moving on to the actual code. These three objects make up the basis of ActiveX Data Objects
.NET, more commonly called ADO.NET, which is the primary data access protocol in
Visual Basic .NET.

Say, for example, that you have a database you want to work with in your code. How do
you get access to the data in that database? You start by getting a connection object for
the database.

Using Connections

NEW TERM To work with data, you first connect to a *data source* (such as a database made
accessible by a database server, like Microsoft's SQL Server), and to do that, you

use a *connection object*. What kind of connection object you use depends on what database system you're working with. The four types of connection objects in Visual Basic .NET 2003 are as follows:

- `SqlConnection` objects are supported by the .NET Framework Data Provider for SQL Server and are recommended for applications using Microsoft SQL Server 7.0 or higher.

- `OleDbConnection` objects are supported by the .NET Framework Data Provider for Object Linking and Embedding Database protocol (OLE DB) and are recommended for applications using Microsoft SQL Server 6.5 or earlier, or any OLE DB provider that supports the OLE DB interfaces.

- `OdbcConnection` objects are supported by the .NET Framework Data Provider for Open Database Connectivity (ODBC, which is a data protocol supported in earlier versions of Visual Basic); it is recommended for applications using ODBC data sources.

- `OracleConnection` objects are supported by the .NET Framework Data Provider for Oracle and are recommended for applications using Oracle data sources.

The default data provider that Visual Basic .NET works with is Microsoft's SQL Server, version 7.0 or higher. We'll use SQL Server 2000 in this book, but don't despair if you don't have a high-end database system to work with databases in Visual Basic .NET; you can create databases that Visual Basic .NET can access even if you use MS Access, which comes with MS Office (see "Working with MS Jet Databases" at the end of today's discussion). Visual Basic .NET can also work with any data source that can support ODBC, OLE DB, or Oracle. We'll see how to create connection objects such as these visually in a few pages.

Using Data Adapters

NEW TERM   After you have a connection object for a data source, you create a *data adapter* to work with that data. You need a data adapter because datasets do not maintain any active connection to the database; they are *disconnected* from the database and connect only as needed (this allows you, for example, to work with databases on the Internet).

Why do you need a data adapter? The data adapter is in charge of managing your connection to the data source. You're not connected to the data source by default, and it's the data adapter that connects you when you need to be connected. The data adapter is the place where you store the SQL statement that will be executed on the data in the database. The data adapter applies your SQL to the database when you need to connect to that database, and it fills your datasets with data. The types of data adapter object you use depend on the type of your data source; the possibilities are SqlDataAdapter, OleDbDataAdapter, OdbcDataAdapter, and OracleDataAdapter objects.

Using Datasets

NEW TERM When you have a data adapter object, you can generate a *dataset object* using that data adapter. Datasets are what you actually work with in your code when you want to handle data from databases.

For example, if you want to get access to the data in the students table we discussed earlier, you would first create a connection to the database where the table was stored and then create an adapter with the appropriate SQL statement to retrieve that table. For example, if the table was named students, that SQL might be "SELECT * FROM students", which retrieves all the records from the students table. Then you would fill a DataSet object using that adapter. Then you can use the methods of the DataSet object to read the data from individual records.

Those, then, are the three objects that you need to know about to work with databases using ADO.NET: data connections to connect to the database, data adapters to connect when needed and execute SQL, and datasets to store the actual data that your code will actually work on. That's how the process works in overview (and it's a simplified view—there are many other ADO.NET objects too—but this overview is a good foundation for most database handling). In Figure 16.1, you can see an overview of these and a few other data objects that we'll put to work.

FIGURE 16.1

Overview of ADO.NET objects.

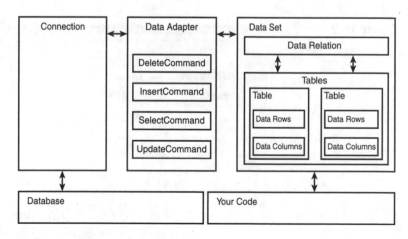

As always, the best way to understand this kind of discussion is by example, and now that we understand the preparation, we'll look at an example. Visual Basic .NET gives you a relatively easy way of working with the objects we've seen so far: simply using

visual tools. The easiest way to gain access to a database's data is to use the Server
Explorer, and we'll use that tool first to display the data in a database table. This example is called QuickDB in the code for this book.

Connecting to Databases with the Server Explorer

Our object in the QuickDB example is to get the data in a table from a database and display that data. In this case, we'll use the Microsoft SQL Server and work with a sample
database that comes with SQL Server, the pubs database. This database contains information about various publishers, authors, and books, and in this example, we'll see how
to display the authors table, which holds the records for various authors, in a Windows
form. And we'll do it the easiest way possible.

To work with a database, such as the pubs sample database, you first need a connection
to that database. In Visual Basic .NET, the Server Explorer is a tool that you use to establish connections to databases.

You can see the Server Explorer at left in Figure 16.2 in the Visual Basic .NET IDE.
Usually, the Server Explorer is docked to the left edge of the IDE, and you can open it
by letting the mouse pointer move over the Server Explorer tab. To display the Server
Explorer if it's not already visible, select the View, Server Explorer menu item or press
Ctrl+Alt+S.

FIGURE 16.2

The Server Explorer.

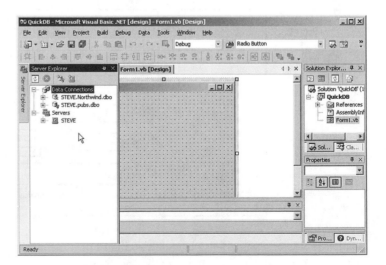

Tip

When you install Visual Basic .NET, it automatically searches your computer for database servers and adds them to the Server Explorer. To add additional servers to the Server Explorer, you select the Tools, Connect to Server menu item (or you can also right-click the Servers node that appears at the bottom of the Server Explorer and select the Add Server menu item). This opens the Add Server dialog, in which you can enter new database servers by computer name or IP address on the Internet.

NEW TERM The Server Explorer enables you to create and examine *data connections*, including connections to Web servers. A *data connection* is not the same as a *connection object*. To work with a data source, you need a data connection, and those data connections are managed by the Server Explorer. However, a data connection is not specific to any application; you can use such connections with any application, and they're always available in the Server Explorer no matter what application you're working on. Using those data connections, you can create connection objects, and those connection objects *are* specific to one particular application (they appear in the component tray of a form). The whole connection process, then, starts by creating a data connection to a data source, and that's what we'll do now.

In the QuickDB example, we're going to display the data from the authors table in the Microsoft SQL Server's pubs sample database, so we'll need a data connection to that database. To create that data connection, right-click the Data Connections icon in the Server Explorer and select the Add Connection item, or select the Tools, Connect to Database menu item. Doing so opens the Data Link Properties dialog you see in Figure 16.3.

FIGURE 16.3

The Data Link Properties dialog.

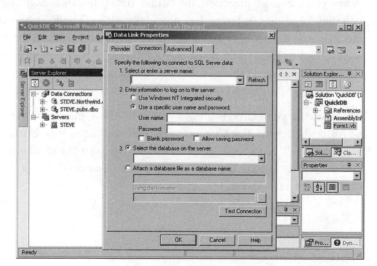

In the Data Link Properties dialog, you can enter the name of the server you want to work with, as well as your login name and password, if applicable. In this example, we'll use Windows NT integrated security to connect to the database because SQL Server is on the same machine as Visual Basic .NET here, but you can choose a server name and enter a username and password in the Data Link Properties dialog if you prefer. You can choose a database already on the server with the Select the Database on the Server option, or another database file with the Attach a Database File as a Database Name option. In this case, we'll use the pubs sample database that comes with SQL Server, so select the first option here and choose the pubs database, as you see in Figure 16.4.

FIGURE 16.4

Connecting to the pubs database.

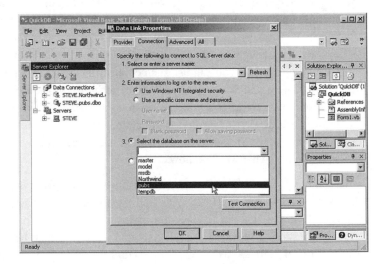

When you create a connection, the default data provider is SQL Server, but of course you may be using a different data provider such as Oracle. To specify a data provider other than SQL Server, click the Provider tab in the Data Link Properties dialog, as you seen in Figure 16.5. You can select from the list of data providers available and then click the Connection tab and select the database you want to work with. We'll discuss this topic more at the end of today's discussion when we connect to an MS Jet database.

The new data connection is almost ready. To test it, make sure the Connection tab is active, and click the Test Connection button you see in Figure 16.6. If the connection is working, you'll see a message box with the message "Test connection succeeded", as you see in Figure 16.6. If the connection wasn't successful, you'll see a message box explaining what's wrong.

FIGURE 16.5

Selecting a data provider.

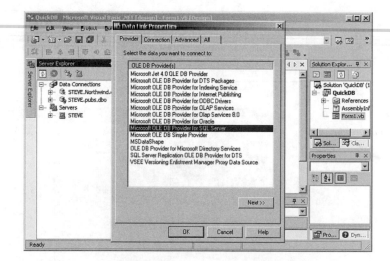

FIGURE 16.6

Testing a data connection.

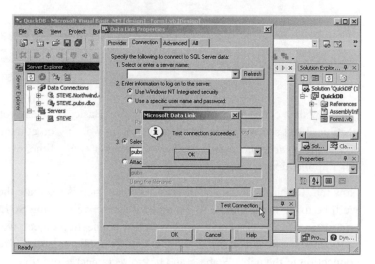

If the connection test is successful, click the OK button in the Data Link Properties dialog now to create the new data connection. The SQL Server on the machine where this example is located is named STEVE, so the connection to the pubs database is named STEVE.pubs.dbo, as you see in the Server Explorer in Figure 16.7. You can open the new connection using the plus (+) icon in front of the connection in the Server Explorer, which displays the tables in the pubs database, as you see in the figure. You can see the target table, authors, in the figure. Now that table is accessible to us.

Tip

Besides adding connections to data sources, you can also delete a data connection. You simply right-click the connection in the Server Explorer and select the Delete menu item.

FIGURE 16.7

Examining the pubs database.

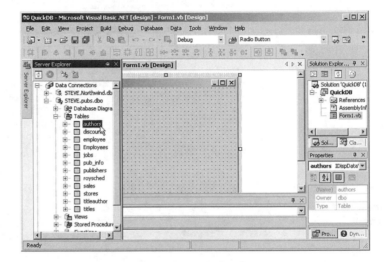

This new data connection is part of your Visual Basic .NET environment; it's not a connection object specific to the application you're working on at the moment. You can access this data connection in the Server Explorer at any time, even when working on other applications.

Now that we have our data connection, the next step is to create the connection object we'll be using in the QuickDB example. Because we're using SQL Server, we'll be using an SqlConnection object. To work with that connection object, we'll also need an SqlDataAdapter object; because the QuickDB application doesn't maintain an active connection to the pubs database and has to reconnect every time it wants to access that database, you use a data adapter object. The data adapter object's purpose is to connect to the database using the connection object, when needed, and execute the SQL, which is stored in the data adapter, in the database.

Here's where Visual Basic .NET makes life easier for us. To create both the SqlConnection and SqlDataAdapter objects we need, just drag the authors table from the Server Explorer to Form1 in the QuickDB example. That's all you need to do. Visual Basic .NET will automatically create the SqlConnection1 and SqlDataAdapter1 objects you see in the component tray in Figure 16.8. Usually, you should customize the SQL stored in the data adapter to fetch data from the database, but when you drag an entire table to a form, Visual Basic .NET automatically creates the SQL needed to fetch the entire table from the database for you.

FIGURE 16.8

Creating the SqlConnection1 *and* SqlDataAdapter1 *objects.*

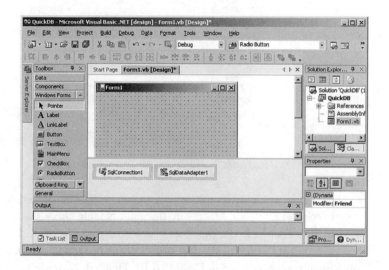

16

Now we have the SqlConnection and SqlDataAdapter objects we need. The next step is to create a DataSet object to hold the data the data adapter will fill. The DataSet object in this example will hold the entire authors table from the pubs database, making that data accessible to your code; that is, data adapters fetch your data and store them in datasets, and you actually work on the data in the dataset from your code. Datasets are expressly designed to hold data from databases.

To create a new DataSet object to hold the data passed to us from the data adapter, select the Data, Generate Dataset menu item, or right-click SqlDataAdapter1 and select the Generate Dataset menu item. This displays the Generate Dataset dialog you see in Figure 16.9.

Tip

If you don't see the Data menu in the IDE, click the main form in the application to give that form the focus. The Data menu appears only when an object that can contain data objects has the focus in a designer.

FIGURE 16.9

The Generate Dataset dialog.

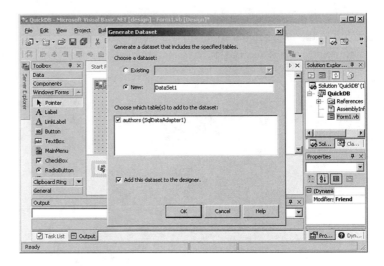

In this case, we'll stick with the default name given to this new dataset object, DataSet1, as you see in Figure 16.9. Make sure the authors table check box is checked, as well as the Add This Dataset to the Designer check box; then click OK. Doing so adds a new dataset, DataSet11 (that is, the first object of the DataSet1 class), to the form designer's component tray, as you see in Figure 16.10. That's it. Now we've created a new dataset holding the data from the authors table in the pubs database.

FIGURE 16.10

A new dataset object.

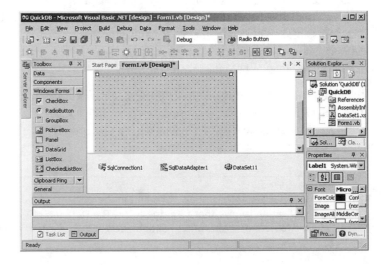

NEW TERM   So now we have a dataset object that holds the data in the authors table. How can we display that data in a Windows form, which is what we set out to do? To do that, we can *bind* the data in the dataset to a *data grid* control. As we're going to see tomorrow, most Visual Basic .NET controls can be bound to data sources, which means they'll automatically display data from those data sources. A data grid (which we'll also see in more detail tomorrow) is especially powerful because you can use it to display an entire database table at once.

To make this work, find the `DataGrid` tool in the Window Forms tab in the toolbox and drag a new data grid to the main form, sizing it to fit the form (you can use its `Dock` property to make that sizing easy). To bind the data grid to `DataSet11`, set the data grid's `DataSource` property to `Data11` (not `DataSet11.authors`, which will also be displayed as an option in the Properties window), and its `DataMember`property to `authors`. This connects the data in the dataset to the data grid. That binds the data in `DataSet11` to the data grid, `DataGrid1`.

There's one last step. As you recall, our application is not actually connected to the data source until we connect it. Because ADO.NET is also designed to be used with Internet data sources, we have to explicitly connect to a data source when we want to get data from that data source. You can make this connection in the `Form1_Load` event handler, for example. In this case, we'll use the `Clear` method of the `DataSet11` object to clear any data that might be in it and then use the `Fill` method of the `SqlDataAdapter1` object to fill `DataSet11` with data like this:

```
Private Sub Form1_Load(ByVal sender As System.Object, _
    ByVal e As System.EventArgs) Handles MyBase.Load
    DataSet11.Clear()
    SqlDataAdapter1.Fill(DataSet11)
End Sub
```

That's it. Now we've used an `SqlConnection` object and `SqlDataAdapter` object to fill a `DataSet` object and bound that dataset object to a data grid.

When you run the QuickDB application, you can see the results as they appear in Figure 16.11. That's the data from the authors table in the pubs database you see in the figure. You can see the rows and columns of this table in that figure. You can also see the name of each field, such as `au_id` (author ID), `au_lname` (author's last name), and so on.

FIGURE 16.11

Displaying data from a database.

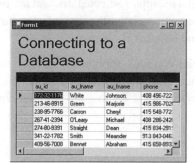

16

To reach this point, we did the following:

1. Created a data connection to the authors table.
2. Dragged the authors table from the Server Explorer onto `Form1`, automatically creating a data connection object and a data adapter object.
3. Generated a dataset using the data adapter.
4. Bound the dataset to a data grid.
5. Filled the dataset from the data adapter, which displays our data in the bound data grid.

If you're new to this process, it might seem a little involved, but actually, it was just about the easiest introduction to database handling in Visual Basic .NET possible. All we did was grab the data from a database table and display it—and Visual Basic .NET handled most of the details, from letting us simply drag a table onto a form to generating the SQL statement we would need behind the scenes.

But what we did was only a very special case because we displayed the entire contents of a table at once. What if we want to display data only from some select fields, or select records, from the authors table? In that case, we'll have to specify the SQL statement the data adapter uses instead of letting Visual Basic .NET create that statement for us automatically behind the scenes.

Because it's far more common to write our own SQL in a data adapter than it is to display entire tables at once, we'll look at the next step with a new example. In this example, we're going to explicitly create our own data adapter and configure the SQL in it to give us more control. In particular, in this example, which is called SelectedDB in the code for this book, we're going to display all records from the authors table, but only few selected fields for each record.

Working with Data Adapters

The main difference between this example, SelectedDB, and the previous example is that, here, we're going to create and configure the data adapter ourselves so we can specify the SQL statement to use and do what we want.

To see how this works, create the Windows application named SelectedDB now. There's a whole tab in the toolbox dedicated to data objects: the Data tab. Because we'll be working with a data adapter object here, click that tab now and drag an `SqlDataAdapter` object from the toolbox to Form1 in the SelectedDB application. Doing so opens the Data Adapter Configuration Wizard that you see in Figure 16.12. This wizard enables you to customize your data adapter as you want, which usually means creating the SQL statement this adapter will use.

| Tip | You can always right-click a data adapter and select the Configure Data Adapter menu item to change an adapter's configuration, including its SQL. |

FIGURE 16.12

The Data Adapter Configuration Wizard.

Click the Next button in the Data Adapter Configuration Wizard to choose the data connection you want to use, as you see in Figure 16.13. You can use an existing data connection of the type we've already created or click the New Connection button to create a new data connection. (Clicking this button opens the Data Link Properties dialog that we've already used to create a new connection; you can see this dialog in Figure 16.3.) In this case, we can use the connection we've already made to the pubs database, as you see in Figure 16.13.

Click Next to choose a query type for the new data adapter, as you see in Figure 16.14. In this case, we're going to create an SQL statement as seen in the figure, but notice that you can either create new or use existing stored SQL procedures. Stored SQL procedures allow you to store SQL in a database, and in addition to holding the SQL you want to use, they are stored in the database and can be used over and over by many different applications.

FIGURE 16.13

Selecting a data connection.

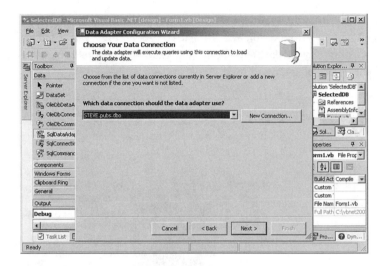

FIGURE 16.14

Choosing a query type.

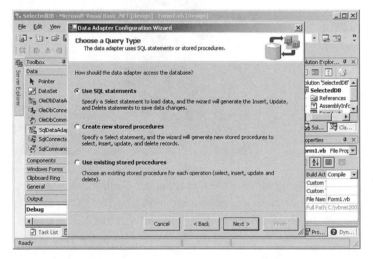

Click Next again to display the dialog you see in Figure 16.15, where we'll generate the SQL statement we'll use in this data adapter.

To make writing the SQL easy, click the Query Builder button you see in Figure 16.15 now. This displays the Add Table dialog that you see in Figure 16.16. An SQL statement can work with several tables at the same time (as when you join them), so here you select the tables you want to work with and click the Add button. After you've selected all the tables you want to work with in this way, you click the Close button. In this example, we're going to display a few fields from the authors table, so just select that table and click Add in the Add Table dialog; then click Close to close the Add Table dialog.

FIGURE 16.15

Generating an SQL statement.

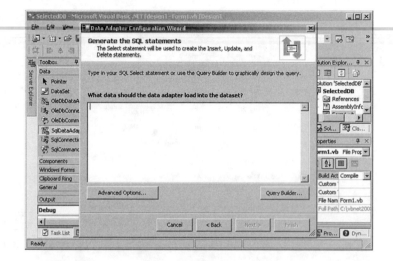

FIGURE 16.16

The Add Table dialog.

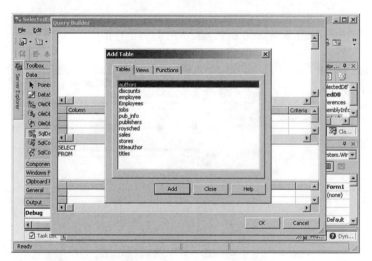

This action opens the Query Builder itself, as you see in Figure 16.17.

At the top of Figure 16.17, you can see a window displaying the fields in the authors table. You add a field to the generated SQL statement by clicking the field's check box in a table's window. In Figure 16.17, for example, we've checked the au_id, au_lname, and au_fname fields. You can also select all fields in a table by checking the check box labeled with an asterisk (*), which specifies all fields in SQL. Note that you must select at least one field when creating the SQL for a data adapter; otherwise, the Query Builder won't be able to create working SQL for you.

16

FIGURE 16.17

The Query Builder.

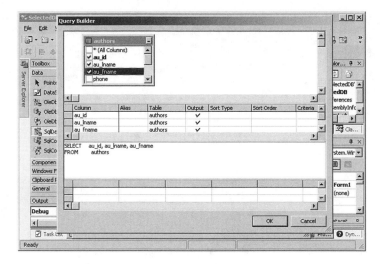

Now click the OK button, creating the SQL statement you see in the Data Adapter Configuration Wizard in Figure 16.18.

FIGURE 16.18

A created SQL statement.

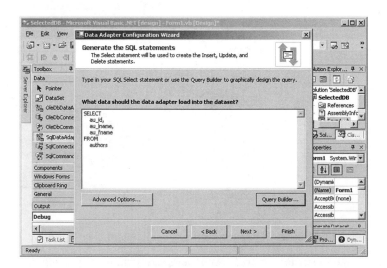

Here's what that SQL statement looks like; note that we're selecting the au_id, au_lname, and au_fname fields of records in the authors table:

```
SELECT
    au_id,
    au_lname,
    au_fname
FROM
    authors
```

This is the SQL this adapter will use to retrieve data from the database. When you click Next in the Data Adapter Configuration Wizard, the wizard configures the data adapter and reports on the results, as you see in Figure 16.19. In this case, the Data Adapter Configuration Wizard has seen what data we want to work with and has generated an SQL SELECT statement to fetch that data for us. It's also generated SQL INSERT, UPDATE, and DELETE statements to manipulate that data as needed (more on these statements in a few pages). We're done. Just click the Finish button to dismiss the Data Adapter Configuration Wizard.

FIGURE 16.19

Configuring a data adapter.

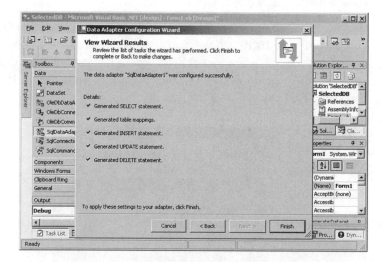

That creates the data adapter we'll need, SqlDataAdapter1. Now create a new dataset using this data adapter, as we've done before (for example, select the Data, Generate Dataset menu item), and connect the new dataset to a data grid by using the DataSource and DataMember properties, also as before.

In our previous example, QuickDB, we filled the data grid with data from the data adapter in the form's load event, but it's more usual to load data only when requested. For that reason, we'll add a Load Data button here, using this code:

```
Private Sub btnLoad_Click(ByVal sender As System.Object, _
    ByVal e As System.EventArgs) Handles btnLoad.Click
    DataSet11.Clear()
    SqlDataAdapter1.Fill(DataSet11)
End Sub
```

Now the user can load data into the data grid when he or she wants to just by clicking the Load Data button. The user can also edit the data in the data grid. To update the data stored back in the database, you use the data adapter's Update method. You can do that with a new button with the caption Save Data, using this code:

```
Private Sub btnUpdate_Click(ByVal sender As System.Object, _
    ByVal e As System.EventArgs) Handles btnUpdate.Click
    SqlDataAdapter1.Update(DataSet11)
End Sub
```

When the user edits the data in the data grid control, that control automatically updates the dataset. To send the new data back to the database, you can use the data adapter's Update method, as we're doing here.

And that's it. Now we have two buttons in our application—Load Data and Save Data, as you see in Figure 16.20—to load and save data on demand. To implement these buttons, we've used the data adapter's Fill and Update methods (we'll see all the methods supported in data adapters in Day 18). And as you can see in Figure 16.20, each record displays only the fields we want to display.

FIGURE 16.20

The SelectedDB example.

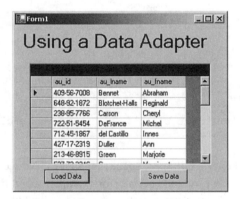

Let's review the steps we took here. We did the following:

1. Created a data connection (you can also use an existing data connection).
2. Dragged an SqlDataAdapter object onto a form, creating both SqlConnection and SqlDataAdapter objects.
3. Used the Data Adapter Configuration Wizard and the Query Builder to configure the data adapter and create the SQL we wanted to use.
4. Generated a dataset using the Data, Generate Dataset menu item.
5. Bound the dataset to a data grid.
6. Filled the dataset in code from the data adapter.

Now we've seen a few examples and so have some direct experience with database work. Because we know what we're talking about in the programming here, we can take a step back to see the bigger picture without getting lost in theory. We've seen some database objects and put them to work, but there are more available, so let's look at what's going on.

Understanding ADO.NET

The main data access system in Visual Basic .NET is ADO.NET, which supports the objects we've been using today. ADO.NET differs from its predecessor, ADO, used in earlier versions of Visual Basic, because ADO.NET relies on a disconnected data architecture. That means the data you're actually working with is just a copy of the data in the database. A data adapter fetches that copy for you, and when you want to update the data in the database, the data adapter will also do that for you, as we've seen.

ADO.NET was designed to enable you to work with databases on the Internet because you can see that maintaining a full-time connection to a database on the Internet would be difficult. However, ADO.NET's disconnected data architecture can help even in traditional client/server database applications because not requiring a full-time connection to a database frees up the server.

The local copy of the data you're working with is contained in a dataset, which works like a local cache of the records you're interested in. You work with the data in the dataset much as if it were data in the database, even though you're actually disconnected from the database. When it's time to update the data in the database, the data adapter will do the work for you with its Update method. Because datasets are really just passive data containers, the role of the data adapter is crucial: Each data adapter holds the SQL for working with your data in a database and updating it as needed.

The disconnected data architecture ADO.NET uses means you have to keep in mind that the data in your dataset might not be the most recent available. If other applications are working with the same data you're working with at the same time, you should probably refresh your dataset frequently. You can do that, as we've seen, by using the data adapter's Fill method.

How do data adapters communicate with databases? ADO.NET needs a protocol that will work both locally and on the Web, so it uses XML. You don't have to be an expert in XML to read this book or to use Visual Basic .NET because Visual Basic .NET does its XML work behind the scenes. However, it's interesting to know what's going on, and if you are proficient with XML, you can do a lot in Visual Basic .NET that can't be done any other way. The actual XML that holds the dataset in our SelectedDB example looks

like the following as used internally by Visual Basic .NET; note that each record has only
three fields: au_id, au_lname, and au_fname.

```xml
<?xml version="1.0" standalone="yes"?>
<DataSet1 xmlns="http://www.tempuri.org/DataSet1.xsd">
  <authors>
    <au_id>409-56-7008</au_id>
    <au_lname>Bennet</au_lname>
    <au_fname>Abraham</au_fname>
  </authors>
  <authors>
    <au_id>648-92-1872</au_id>
    <au_lname>Blotchet-Halls</au_lname>
    <au_fname>Reginald</au_fname>
  </authors>
  <authors>
    <au_id>238-95-7766</au_id>
    <au_lname>Carson</au_lname>
    <au_fname>Cheryl</au_fname>
  </authors>
        .
        .
        .
```

Tip

For the formal definition of XML documents and how they work in detail,
look at the W3C specification for XML, at www.w3.org/TR/REC-xml.

NEW TERM   Besides this XML to hold the data, the details of how the dataset are set up—that
is, what fields should be in what records and so on—are handled with an *XML
schema*, and you can see the name of the schema, DataSet1.xsd, in the preceding XML.
An XML schema is used to describe the structure of an XML document so that document's data can be checked to make sure it's in the correct form and make sure the data
in the document is valid. We'll take a brief look at the XML schemas used with database
XML documents later today.

Tip

XML schemas are also standardized by the W3C. You can see a primer on
XML schemas at http://www.w3.org/TR/xmlschema-0/.

We've already seen that ADO.NET relies on a set of objects, and we've gotten a good
handle on connection objects, data adapters, and datasets. They are the principal objects
in ADO.NET, but there are more objects you should know about. And now that we've

gotten an overview of ADO.NET itself, let's look at ADO.NET from a programmer's perspective as we get an overview of the ADO.NET objects.

ADO.NET Objects in Overview

There are plenty of objects to work with in ADO.NET, as we're going to see in Day 18. Here's a list of the most common ADO.NET objects you'll come across and what they're all about:

- Connection objects—To start working with a database, you must have a connection object. A data adapter needs a connection object to a data source to read and write data, and it uses connection objects, such as the `SqlConnection`, `OleDbConnection`, `OdbcConnection`, and `OracleConnection` objects, to communicate with a data source.

- Data Adapters—You use data adapters to communicate between a data source and a dataset. You typically configure a data adapter with SQL to execute on the data in the data source. The types of data adapters available are `SqlDataAdapter`, `OleDbDataAdapter`, `OdbcDataAdapter`, and `OracleDataAdapter`.

- Command objects—Data adapters can read, add, update, and delete records in a data source. To allow you to specify how each operation works, a data adapter contains command objects for each of them. Data adapters support four properties that give you access to these command objects: `SelectCommand`, `InsertCommand`, `UpdateCommand`, and `DeleteCommand`.

- Datasets—As you know, datasets store data in a disconnected cache. The structure of a dataset is similar to that of a relational database; it gives you access to an object model of tables, rows, and columns defined for the dataset. Datasets are supported with `DataSet` objects.

- `DataTable` objects—`DataTable` objects hold a data table from a data source. Data tables contain two important properties: `Columns`, which is a collection of the `DataColumn` objects that represent the columns of data in a table, and `Rows`, which is a collection of `DataRow` objects that represent the rows of data in a table.

- Data Readers—`DataReader` objects hold a read-only, forward-only (that is, you can move only from one record to the next record, not backward) set of data from a database. Using a data reader can increase speed because only one row of data is in memory at a time.

- Data Views—Data views represent a customized view of a single table that can be filtered, searched, or sorted. In other words, a data view, supported by the `DataView` class, is a data "snapshot" that takes up few resources.

16

NEW TERM • Constraint objects—Datasets can support *constraints* to check data integrity. Constraints are supported by the `Constraint` class, and a constraint is a rule that can be checked when rows are inserted, updated, or deleted. There are two types of constraints: unique constraints, which check that the new values in a column are unique throughout the table, and foreign-key constraints, which specify how related records should be updated when a record in another table is updated.

• `DataRelation` objects—`DataRelation` objects specify a relationship between parent and child tables. The relation is based on a specific field, called a key, that appears in both tables and relates those tables together.

• `DataRow` objects—`DataRow` objects correspond to a row in a data table. You use the `Item` property to get or set a value in a particular field in the row.

• `DataColumn` objects—`DataColumn` objects correspond to the columns in a table. Each object has a `DataType` property that specifies the kind of data each column contains, such as integers or string values.

We'll see these objects today and over the next several days.

Let's turn now from ADO.NET to SQL. You don't have to be an expert in SQL to read this book, but some familiarity will help, and will also go a long way when you're working with databases in Visual Basic .NET. For that reason, we'll look at some basic SQL now. This discussion will be useful, but not essential, for the upcoming database work. (If you're already an SQL pro, just skip over the following section unless you want a brush-up.)

 Tip   Bear in mind that you can also use the Visual Basic Query Builder to build many SQL statements automatically, as we'll do throughout today's work.

An SQL Primer

As we've seen, you can use Structured Query Language (SQL) in data adapters to configure what you want a database to do. When you create a data adapter using the Data Adapter Configuration Wizard, you can enter the SQL you want the adapter to use directly into the Generate the SQL Statements page in the wizard, as you see in Figure 16.17. You can also click the Query Builder button at that point to use the Query Builder to write the SQL for you.

Although a complete discussion of SQL is out of the scope of this book, it's a good idea to understand some basic SQL. There's not all that much to SQL, and a little understanding turns out to go a long way, so in our preparation for database handling, we'll get an introduction to the topic here.

We'll use the pubs database table that we've already seen as an example here, concentrating on the fields in that table, such as au_id (author ID), au_fname (author first name), au_lname (author last name), city, phone, address, state, zip, and so on. The foundation of SQL is the SELECT statement, and that's where we'll start.

Note Note that the case of SQL doesn't matter. You can use Select, SELECT, select, or even SeLeCt for the SELECT command, for example.

16

Working with the SELECT Statement

In SQL, you use the SELECT statement to get fields from a table; the statement returns records that contain the fields you specify. For example, here's how you can get all the records in the authors table, using the wildcard character *:

SELECT * FROM authors

This statement returns a dataset that holds all the records in the authors table. You can also use the SELECT statement to select specific fields from a table like this, which selects the au_id, phone, and city fields of all the records in the authors table:

SELECT au_id, phone, city FROM authors

This statement returns a dataset that holds as many records as there are in the authors table, and each record will have only a au_id, phone, and city field.

Working with WHERE Clauses

You can use the WHERE clause to specify criteria that you want records to match. For example, to select all the records in the authors table where the city field holds "Singapore", you can use this statement:

SELECT * FROM authors WHERE City = "Singapore"

You also can use the following operators instead of an equal sign:

- > (greater than)
- >= (greater than or equal to)
- < (less than)
- <= (less than or equal to)
- BETWEEN
- IN
- LIKE

Everyone knows about the logical operators such as < and >, of course, but what about BETWEEN, LIKE, and IN? See the next several topics.

Working with the BETWEEN Clause

You use the BETWEEN clause to specify a range of values you will accept. For example, here's how to select all the records from the authors table where the au_lname field starts with S:

```
SELECT * FROM authors WHERE au_lname BETWEEN "S*" AND "T*"
```

Note the use of wildcard characters: "S*" and "T*". Using these wildcards, you can specify that you want all the au_lname values that start with S here.

Working with the LIKE Clause

The LIKE clause enables you to match strings, including using wildcards. This example selects all the records from the authors table where the city field matches the wildcard string "San*":

```
SELECT * FROM authors WHERE city LIKE "San*"
```

This clause creates a dataset from the authors table with records whose city fields match names "San*", such as San Francisco, Sante Fe, and Santa Cruz.

Working with the IN Clause

You can use the IN clause to specify a set of values that fields can match. For example, here's how you can get records where the author lives in Singapore or Penang:

```
SELECT * FROM authors WHERE city IN ("Singapore", "Penang")
```

Working with Logical Operations

You can also use logical operations with the clauses in your SQL statements. This next example imposes two criteria: In this case, the city field cannot be either Singapore or Penang, *and* the author must have a phone number in the phone field (SQL uses the NULL keyword much like the Visual Basic .NET Nothing keyword to test whether there's anything in a field):

```
SELECT * FROM authors WHERE City NOT IN ("Singapore", "Penang")
AND phone IS NOT NULL
```

In logical expressions, you can use these logical operators: AND, OR, and NOT. These operators have the same meaning as in Visual Basic .NET. AND specifies that both clauses must be true for the overall expression to be true, OR specifies that either one can be true for the overall expression to be true, and NOT toggles the value of a clause from true to false or from false to true.

Working with the DISTINCT Clause

Let's look at another SQL clause: the DISTINCT clause. Say that you want to look at all the unique cities in the authors table. Several authors might come from the same city, so they would have the same value in the city field. You can use the DISTINCT clause to find the unique cities like this:

```
SELECT DISTINCT city FROM authors
```

Now the returned dataset will contain a dataset of records, and each record will have only a city field, and all city values will be unique.

Working with the ORDER BY Clause

Using SQL, you can order the records in the dataset. For example, here's how you can order the records in the authors table by au_lname:

```
SELECT * FROM authors ORDER BY au_lname
```

And note that you can also sort in descending order with the DESC keyword:

```
SELECT * FROM authors ORDER BY au_lname DESC
```

Working with SQL Functions

SQL also comes with some built-in functions that enable you to work with the records in a dataset, such as AVG, COUNT, MAX, MIN, and SUM. These functions work as follows:

- AVG—Returns the average value of a set of records.
- COUNT—Returns a count of records.
- MAX—Returns the maximum value of a set of records.
- MIN—Returns the minimum value of a set of records.
- SUM—Adds values over records.

Working with the GROUP BY Clause

Using SQL, you can group records with the GROUP BY clause like this example, which groups records by city:

```
SELECT * FROM authors GROUP BY city
```

This SQL statement will return the authors in the authors table grouped by city; that is, the authors in Pittsburgh will follow those in Philadelphia, and so on.

You can also use the SQL HAVING clause with GROUP BY. This clause is like the WHERE clause (but is used only with GROUP BY); it allows you to specify additional criteria that records must meet, like this SQL statement, which specifies that you want only records with cities that begin with "San":

```
SELECT * FROM authors GROUP BY city HAVING city LIKE "San*"
```

Working with the UPDATE Statement

Not all SQL statements are designed to return datasets. For example, you can use the UPDATE statement to update a database with data that has been changed. The following example changes the city field to Singapore in all records where it's Penang now:

```
UPDATE authors SET city = "Singapore" WHERE city = "Penang"
```

Or say that an author has gotten married and changed his or her last name. You could select the author by ID (the au_id field in the pubs database holds Social Security numbers) and change the name in the au_lname field like this:

```
UPDATE authors SET au_lame = "Grant" WHERE au_id = "151-33-0055"
```

Working with the DELETE Statement

In SQL, you can use the DELETE statement to delete records. Here's an example which deletes every record in the authors table that has city values that are not Singapore or Penang:

```
DELETE * FROM authors WHERE city NOT IN ("Singapore", "Penang")
```

This statement deletes all records in the authors table where the author is not from Singapore or Penang (something you might not want to do because no authors in that table come from these cities).

Working with the AS Clause

By default, the names of the fields in a dataset are the same as the original names they had in the original table. But you might want to change those names in the dataset; for example, you might want to rename the au_lname field simply name in a dataset. You can rename a field by using the AS clause like this, where the SQL changes au_lname to just name in the returned dataset:

```
SELECT au_lname AS name FROM authors
```

Now in the newly created dataset, the au_lname field will be called name.

NEW TERM   We'll look at another powerful SQL technique next: working with relational databases. This technique allows us to retrieve data from two different tables, using an SQL *inner join* to join the records of those tables together.

Handling Relational Databases

As mentioned in the beginning of today's discussion, relational databases are powerful databases that connect the data in various tables. And using SQL, you can perform many operations in relational databases.

Say that you want to display all the books that various authors have written. That's not as easy as it sounds because in the pubs database, the names of the authors are stored in the authors table, but the books that they've written are stored in the titleauthor table, which is a completely separate table. So how do you join the data you want from the authors table with the data you want from the titleauthor table into one dataset? You can use an SQL inner join. And you can see how this works in the RelationalDB example in the code for this book.

To follow along, create an application named RelationalDB now and drag a data adapter onto the main form, opening the Data Adapter Configuration Wizard. To configure the adapter's SQL statement, click the Query Builder button and use the Add Table dialog to add *both* tables we'll need from the SQL Server pubs database, authors and titleauthor, as you see in Figure 16.21.

FIGURE 16.21

Selecting two tables.

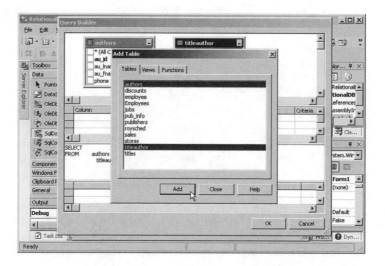

These two tables share the author ID field, au_id, which in this case is the key that relates the records of one table to the records of the other table. The Query Builder realizes that this is a shared field and displays this relation graphically, as you see in Figure 16.22.

FIGURE **16.22**

A relation between tables in the Query Builder.

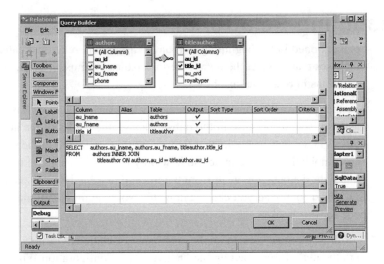

In the Query Builder, select the au_lname and au_fname fields from the authors table and the title_id field from the titleauthor table (the titleauthor table doesn't hold the actual title of each book, but rather an ID value such as "BU1032"). Then click OK to close the Query Builder. This generates the SQL you see in Figure 16.23 (keep in mind that you can always edit the SQL generated by the Query Builder by hand):

```
SELECT
    authors.au_lname,
    authors.au_fname,
    titleauthor.title_id
FROM
    authors INNER
JOIN
    titleauthor ON
        authors.au_id = titleauthor.au_id
```

Tip

If at any time you want to change the SQL used in a data adapter, you can right-click the data adapter object in the component tray and select the Configure Data Adapter item, or you can select the Configure Data Adapter item in the Data menu, to open the Data Adapter Configuration Wizard again.

Because we're working with *two* tables, not just one, the Data Adapter Configuration Wizard can't generate SQL statements for updating that data because doing so would involve updating parts of records in multiple tables. Therefore, you need to click the Advanced Options button in the Data Adapter Configuration Wizard you see in

Figure 16.23 and deselect the Generate Insert, Update, and Delete Statements check box (unless you do so, the Data Adapter Configuration Wizard will give you an error when you try to proceed at this point). Now click the Next button you see in Figure 16.23 and follow through to the end of the process as before to finish configuring the data adapter.

FIGURE 16.23

The SelectedDB example.

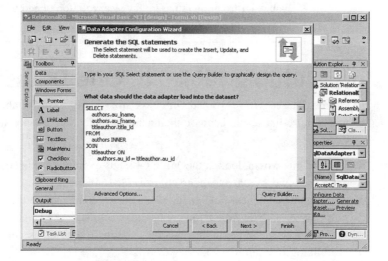

After you've configured the data adapter, generate a dataset as before and connect it to the data grid as we've also done before. You can see the results in Figure 16.24, where we've combined data from two tables in a relational database. Some authors in the authors table have multiple entries in the titleauthor table, so, for example, you can see that Green has two different `title_id` entries, as does Locksley, and so on. In this way, the authors and titleauthor tables have been *joined*, using their common key, au_id.

FIGURE 16.24

The SelectedDB example.

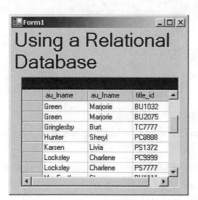

> **Tip**
>
> This example uses an SQL statement to join two related tables, but there's another way of working with related tables: You can create a data relation object to make the relationship explicit, while still leaving the two tables independent. In other words, the data relation object will combine the data you want from the tables in this case; you don't need to join them. We'll discuss this topic more tomorrow.

Using Multiple Tables in One Dataset

So far, the datasets we've worked with have stored only a single table of data, but a dataset is more like a full database than a single table, and it can contain several tables at once.

To see how this works, look at the MultiTableDB example in the code for this book. This example uses two `SqlDataAdapter` controls: `SqlDataAdapter1`, connected to the authors table in the pubs database, and `SqlDataAdapter2`, connected to the titleauthors table in the pubs database. Now when you create a dataset using the Data, Generate Dataset menu item, you can add both those tables to a single dataset, as you see in the Generate Dataset dialog in Figure 16.25.

FIGURE 16.25

Adding multiple tables to a dataset.

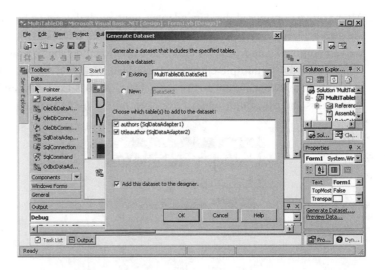

At this point, we've added both tables to the same dataset. Next, add two data grids to the main form and set the `DataSource` property of both to the new dataset object, `DataSet11`. Set the `DataMember` property of the first data grid to authors and the

`DataMember` property of the second data grid to titleauthors. All that's left is to use the adapters to fill `DataSet11` like this, which we can do when the form loads:

```
Private Sub Form1_Load(ByVal sender As System.Object, _
    ByVal e As System.EventArgs) Handles MyBase.Load
    SqlDataAdapter1.Fill(DataSet11)
    SqlDataAdapter2.Fill(DataSet11)
End Sub
```

And that's it! We've stored two tables in one dataset. You can see the result in Figure 16.26, where both data grids use the same dataset but are displaying different tables.

FIGURE 16.26

Retrieving multiple tables from a dataset.

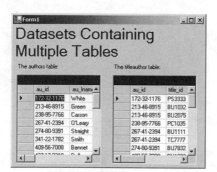

While we're discussing datasets, it's also useful to know that you can get an immediate look at the data in the dataset by selecting the dataset object, `DataSet11`; selecting the Data, Preview Data menu item; and then clicking the Fill DataSet button. This will display all the data in the table(s) in a dataset in a dialog box, as you see in Figure 16.27. This data preview feature is great; among other things, it helps remind you what fields are in each record in a table.

You can also look at a dataset's *properties*, such as how every field is formatted, for a dataset by selecting the dataset object and then selecting the Data, Dataset Properties menu item, or by right-clicking a dataset and selecting the Dataset Properties item. This opens the Dataset Properties dialog you see in Figure 16.28.

Using the Dataset Properties dialog, you can look at which tables are in which datasets, as well as which fields are in which tables, and how those fields are formatted. This capability is useful if you ever want to remind yourself of the detailed format of each field in a table.

Another way to examine the format of each field in a table is to look at the table's XML schema. As already discussed today, ADO.NET uses XML to transfer data and uses XML schema to validate that data. If you know what you're doing in XML, you might want to edit or check the schema that Visual Basic .NET is using for your data.

FIGURE 16.27

Previewing dataset data.

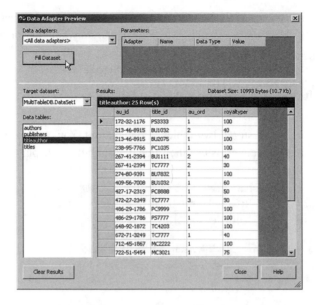

FIGURE 16.28

Previewing dataset properties.

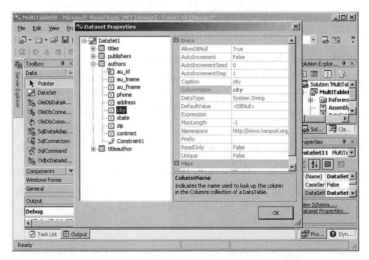

To look at the XML schema Visual Basic .NET uses for a particular dataset, select the Data, View Dataset Schema menu item, or right-click a dataset and select the View Schema menu item. This opens the dataset's schema in a Visual Basic .NET designer, as you see in Figure 16.29. Here, you can see all the data types used for the various fields in the tables of a dataset.

FIGURE 16.29

The XML schema for a dataset.

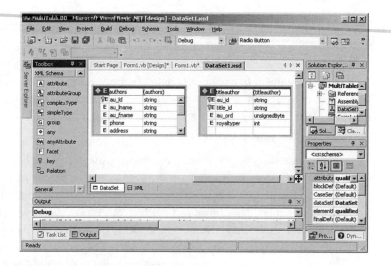

16

In addition, you can toggle between XML and Dataset views by clicking the buttons at the bottom of the designer. In Dataset view, you see the data types, field by field, for the dataset as you see in Figure 16.29. In XML view, you can see the XML of the schema, as shown in Figure 16.30.

FIGURE 16.30

The XML schema for a dataset, in XML view.

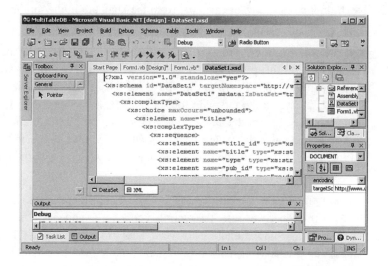

NEW TERM We've worked with datasets quite a bit today, but there's actually another way of holding data in Visual Basic .NET applications: You can use a *data view*.

Working with Data Views

We've put in a lot of work with datasets today because they're the containers you usually use for data from a database. However, another container can be very useful: data views. Data views are much like read-only datasets. Because they're read-only, they work like snapshots of your data, and they provide you with faster access to that data than datasets can. The term *data view* means just that—a view of your data—and they're usually used as containers for a subset of your data.

You can use the date view's RowFilter property to specify the SQL you want records to match before those records appear in the data view. For example, you might want to see which authors in the authors table have the last name Green, and you can use a data view to filter them out and hold those records for you. When you're working with a dataset, data views can provident convenient, temporary containers for data you want to filter out of the dataset this way. When you have the subset of data you're looking at, you can loop over the records in the data view. (Accessing individual records in code is discussed more thoroughly in Day 18.)

The DataViewDB example in the code for this book uses data views. To follow along, create a Windows application named DataViewDB now and connect to the authors table in the pubs database as we've seen before, using a dataset, DataSet11, to hold that table. Next, drag a data view, DataView1, from the Data tab in the toolbox and drop it onto the main form; the data view will appear in the component tray.

You connect a data view to a specific data table, not an entire database, with its Table property, so set that property to DataSet11.authors now. (When you click the Table property in the Properties window, you'll see a list of the available tables to work with.) Then add a data grid to the main form and set its DataSource property to DataView1. (You don't need to set the data grid's DataMember property here because we're dealing with only one particular table.) By doing all this, you've connected the data grid to the authors table, but you could have done that just by connecting the data grid to the dataset object directly.

The way this example is different is that you can also specify a value for the data view's RowFilter property to filter the records you want to appear in the data view. For example, to get only those authors whose last name is Green, assign this value to the RowFilter property: au_lname = 'Green'. (Note the single quotation marks here; Visual Basic .NET won't accept au_lname = "Green" as the value of this property because Visual Basic .NET will surround the text with double quotation marks before passing it on to the SQL processor, and the string "au_lname = "Green"" won't work with the SQL processor, which will assume the string terminates after the second double quotation mark.)

All we need now, as usual, is some code to populate the dataset from the data adapter, like this:

```
Private Sub Form1_Load(ByVal sender As System.Object, _
    ByVal e As System.EventArgs) Handles MyBase.Load
    SqlDataAdapter1.Fill(DataSet11)
End Sub
```

And that's it. You can see the results in Figure 16.31, where the only author whose last name is Green is displayed. In this way, you've been able to store a filtered snapshot of your data in a data view and bind it to a data grid.

FIGURE 16.31

Using data views.

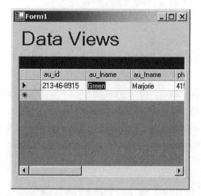

Here's another way to filter the records stored in a data view. Besides the **NEW TERM** RowFilter property, you can also use a data view's DataViewRowState property to store rows in a data view depending on their *state*. For example, you can place rows that have been deleted or are new in a data view by using this property. The following are the possible state values you can use, and the types of rows they match, from the DataRowState enumeration:

- DataRowState.Added—Specifies added rows.
- DataRowState.CurrentRows—Specifies current rows (including unchanged, new, and modified rows).
- DataRowState.Deleted—Specifies deleted rows.

- `DataRowState.ModifiedCurrent`—Specifies current rows (even if they are a modified version of the original data).

- `DataRowState.ModifiedOriginal`—Specifies the original rows before they are modified.

- `DataRowState.None`—Specifies no rows.

- `DataRowState.OriginalRows`—Specifies the original rows, including unchanged and deleted rows.

- `DataRowState.Unchanged`—Specifies the unchanged rows.

For example, here's how you might look at the rows that have been marked as deleted (before you call the `Update` method to actually delete them in the database) in a data view:

```
Private Sub Form1_Load(ByVal sender As System.Object, _
    ByVal e As System.EventArgs) Handles MyBase.Load
    DataSet11.Clear()
    SqlDataAdapter1.Fill(DataSet11)
    DataView1.RowStateFilter = DataViewRowState.Deleted
End Sub
```

Data views work something like temporary variables in your code: When you want to work with only a subset of the data in a table, you can stash those records in a data view and work with them there. They're particularly useful when you want to apply SQL to your local data without having to keep going back to the database.

Working with MS Jet Databases

So far today, we've used SQL data adapters with SQL Server, but as we know, other types of data adapters are available. To round off today's work, we'll look at how to use the OLE DB data adapter to work with MS Jet databases, which you can create with MS Access (which comes with MS Office). This capability is of particular interest because you don't need a standalone database server such as SQL Server or Oracle to work with MS Jet databases; the MS Jet database engine is already built into Visual Basic .NET.

All you need to do is create a database with Access, and you can open it with Visual Basic .NET—no special database server needed. (In fact, Visual Basic's data access system was originally built to work exclusively with Jet databases.) Plenty of people still use Jet databases because they use MS Access, so let's look at ways to connect a Jet database to your Visual Basic code now.

For example, you might remember the students table from the beginning of today's discussion:

```
.....................
|Name    |  Grade  |
|--------|---------|
|Ted     |   A-    |
|--------|---------|
|Frank   |   C+    |
|--------|---------|
|Mary    |   A     |
|--------|---------|
|Nancy   |   A+    |
|--------|---------|
|Wally   |   B-    |
|--------|---------|
|Bert    |   A     |
.....................
```

Let's create a new example that displays this data in a data grid using a Jet database created with MS Access. Using MS Access, you can easily enter this data into a table named students and store that table in a database named students.mdb, as you see in Figure 16.32 (and which you can find in the code for this book).

FIGURE 16.32

Using MS Access to create students.mdb.

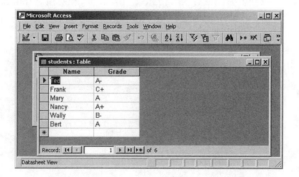

We'll connect the data in students.mdb to a data grid in a Visual Basic .NET application named JetDB. Start this example by dragging an OleDbDataAdapter object to the main form, which opens the Data Adapter Configuration Wizard. This time, don't use the connection we've already made to the pubs database; instead, click the New Connection button you see in the second window of the Data Adapter Configuration Wizard, opening the Data Link Properties dialog you see in Figure 16.33, where you can select the MS Jet OLE DB data provider after clicking the Provider tab. Doing so means that Visual Basic .NET will use its built-in Jet database engine to access your data.

Figure 16.33

The Provider tab of the Data Link Properties dialog.

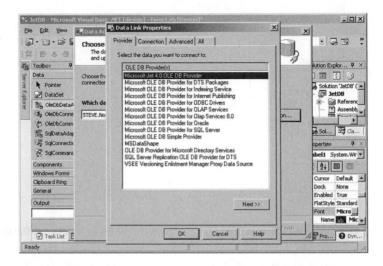

Now click the Next button in the Data Link Properties dialog to display the Connection tab, as you see in Figure 16.34. Navigate to the students.mdb database and click OK to close this dialog and return to the Data Adapter Configuration Wizard.

Figure 16.34

The Connection tab of the Data Link Properties dialog.

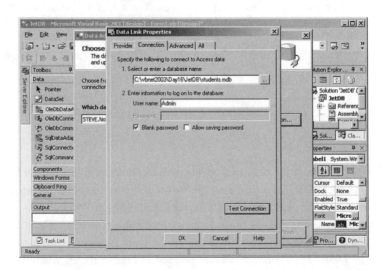

Back in the Data Adapter Configuration Wizard, select the Name and Grade fields of the students table, in much the same way as we did earlier today, as you see in Figure 16.35. Then keep clicking the Next button in the Data Adapter Configuration Wizard, followed by the Finish button to create the new OleDbDataAdapter and OleDbDataConnection objects we'll need.

FIGURE 16.35

Selecting the Name *and*
Grade *fields.*

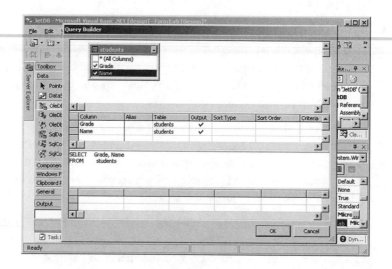

We're familiar with the following steps as well. Using the new data adapter, generate a new dataset using the students table with the Data, Generate Dataset menu item, thus creating a new dataset, DataSet11, and connect the new dataset to a data grid. The last step is to fill the dataset from the data adapter when the main form loads as follows:

```
Private Sub Form1_Load(ByVal sender As System.Object, _
    ByVal e As System.EventArgs) Handles MyBase.Load
    OleDbDataAdapter1.Fill(DataSet11)
End Sub
```

And that's all it takes! You can see the result in Figure 16.36, where the JetDB example is displaying the data from the students table.

FIGURE 16.36

Using an MS Jet
database.

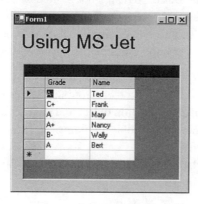

Now you've been able to connect to a database file using Visual Basic .NET's built-in Jet database engine.

Summary

Today, we got our introduction to working with databases, and we've come far. We emphasized the visual tools needed to work with databases (we'll see how to work with databases entirely in code in Day 18). We also saw the objects available in ADO.NET and put them to work.

Today's work started with an overview of what databases are. We were introduced to the terminology we need to work with databases: tables, rows, columns, relational databases, keys, and so on. We saw that databases are usually founded on the simple concept of tables, which are divided into records. Each record is in turn divided into fields, and each field corresponds to a column in a table.

We also became familiar with ADO.NET and the objects in it. We started with the three primary objects: data connection objects, which enable you to connect to data sources; data adapter objects, which store SQL statements and are responsible for fetching and storing data; and dataset objects, which hold a copy of your data locally. We saw that ADO.NET supports a disconnected data architecture, where no continuous connection to the data source is maintained. Instead, connections are made when you need to fetch more data or update the data in the data source. This disconnected data architecture allows you to take the strain off database servers locally and also makes it possible to connect to database servers on the Internet.

We saw that several visual tools in Visual Basic .NET enable you to work with databases. The first of these is the Server Explorer, which lets you examine not only what database providers you can connect to, but also what data connections you've made, and we've seen how to create data connections as well. A data connection is available to the various applications you create in Visual Basic .NET; it's not limited to a specific application (as discussed, data connections are not the same as connection objects, which *are* specific to a particular application). The Server Explorer also allows you to open a data connection to examine it, and you can see what tables are returned by various connections, as well as what fields there are in each table.

In our first database example, we dragged a table from the Server Explorer onto a form, which automatically creates a data connection object and data adapter object. We used the data adapter to generate a new dataset object holding the authors table from the SQL Server's pubs database. After making provisions to fill the dataset with data from the data adapter when the application started, we connected that dataset to a data grid, displaying the authors table in the data grid.

That was the easiest type of database use in Visual Basic .NET, but because you usually want more control over your data instead of simply displaying an entire table at once, our next example allowed us to configure a data adapter to display only the data we wanted. In particular, we dragged an SqlDataAdapter object onto a form, which opened the Data Adapter Configuration Wizard. Using that wizard, we were able to specify what data connection we wanted to use, and we were able to use the Query Builder to visually create the SQL statement we needed to select certain fields from the authors table to display. The data grid in this new example displayed those fields of each record in the authors table.

After getting our feet wet with these examples, we looked at the available ADO.NET objects in more depth and also got an introduction to SQL. Although you can use the Query Builder to create many SQL statements, there's no substitute for knowing SQL yourself as you go deeper into database handling.

We also looked at working with relational databases today. In particular, we used the au_id field as a key to connect the data from two different database tables: the authors table and the titleauthor table. After connecting those tables together with an SQL inner join, we were able to fill a dataset with data from fields in both tables as we required, displaying the result in a data grid. And we saw how to use multiple data adapters to add multiple tables to the same dataset—and how to access those tables in separate data grids.

We saw that data views can work as read-only snapshots of your data, and that you can use the RowFilter property to apply SQL to that data before storing it in the data view. And we finished today's work by looking at how to connect to MS Jet databases because the MS Jet database engine is built into Visual Basic .NET; no external database server is needed.

We used the data grid control a great deal today, and we saw how handy it is to connect to a data source. In fact, nearly all controls in Visual Basic .NET are built to connect to data sources, and that's the focus of tomorrow's work. As we'll see, some controls, such as list controls, have quite advanced data-binding capabilities, enabling you to bind to multiple tables at once. Binding data sources to controls is such a big topic because it lets you display and edit your data with a lot of power, as we'll see tomorrow.

Q&A

Q **Given that I can use OLE DB connections to most data sources, is there some reason that I should use connections specially designed for my database server, such as SqlConnection or OracleConnection objects?**

A Visual Basic .NET is up to 70% faster with dedicated connection objects such as SqlConnection or OracleConnection objects instead of simple OLE DB connections.

Q I know all about the disconnected database architecture in ADO.NET, but my database is in frequent use by other users, and I really want to make sure I'm using the most recent data. Is there really no way to maintain a continuous connection to a database in Visual Basic .NET?

A Actually, there is. If you really need a continuous connection to a database, you can use traditional ADO (instead of ADO.NET) objects. To work with these objects, you select the Project, Add Reference menu item, click the COM tab in the Add Reference dialog, and select one of the ADO libraries. Then you can use ADO objects in your code.

Workshop

This workshop tests whether you understand the concepts you saw today. It's a good idea to make sure you can answer these questions before pressing on to tomorrow's work.

Quiz

1. Name the three primary ADO.NET objects we used in today's examples and what their purposes are.
2. How can you create a data connection?
3. You've generated a dataset from a data adapter and connected that dataset to a data grid. But when you run the application, no data shows up in the data grid. What's wrong?
4. After editing data in a data grid, how can you send the new data back to the database?
5. Using SQL, how can you change the city data for the author with ID 274-80-9391 to Orlando in the authors table?

Quiz Answers

1. Connection objects are responsible for the actual connection to a data source, data adapter objects are responsible for fetching or updating data as needed from the data source, and datasets are objects that hold the records from the data source you want to work on.

2. To create that connection, right-click the Data Connections icon in the Server Explorer and select the Add Connection item, or select the Tools, Connect to Database menu item. Doing so opens the Data Link Properties dialog, which you use to create the connection.

3. You may have forgotten to fill the dataset with data using the data adapter's Fill method. Remember, datasets are disconnected from their data sources; what you're working with is a local copy of your data.

4. You can use the data adapter's `Update` method (assuming that the Data Adapter Configuration Wizard was successful in creating an update command for the data adapter).

5. `UPDATE authors SET city = "Orlando" WHERE au_id = "274-80-9391"`

Exercises

1. Using your connection to the pubs database, display the publishers table from that database in a data grid by dragging that table from the Server Explorer to a Windows form. (If you don't have SQL Server, use a table from any sample database in your database system.)

2. Redo the example in Exercise 1, this time dragging a data adapter object to the application's main form to open the Data Adapter Configuration Wizard. Now display only the `pub_id`, `pub_name`, and `city`.

DAY 17

Binding Visual Basic Controls to Databases

Today, we're going to get more database-handling experience as we take a look at binding controls to data sources. For example, you might bind the `au_lname` field from the authors table to a text box and, at runtime, the current author's last name will appear in that text box. You might bind the `au_id` field to a list box, which will make all the author IDs appear in the list box. Or you might bind the whole authors table to a data grid.

These days, all Visual Basic controls are data-enabled, and you can bind just about any property in them to a database. We're going to see how that works here, and lots more. For example, after binding a data source to controls in a form, we'll see how to navigate through the data in the data source, automatically updating the data in the bound controls as we move from record to record. We'll also take a look at other powerful database-handling techniques today, such as using SQL parameters, data relation objects, automatically created data forms, and more. Here's an overview of today's topics:

- Supporting simple and complex data binding
- Binding text boxes, buttons, check boxes, radio buttons, combo boxes, list boxes, and labels

- Binding and using data grids
- Using the (DataBindings) property for data binding
- Using the DataSource and DataMember properties
- Using the DisplayMember and ValueMember properties
- Working with binding contexts
- Navigating through the records in datasets
- Creating data forms using the Data Form Wizard
- Performing data validation in Windows controls
- Handling parameterized SQL queries
- Connecting tables with data relation objects

There's a lot coming up as we start exploring what's possible with Windows controls and databases. We'll start with today's biggest topic: data binding.

Using Data Binding

Data binding is all about connecting a data source to one or more Visual Basic controls. Here are some common uses for data binding:

- **Data entry**—Using bound controls, you can create data-entry forms, letting the user enter data, which can then be sent to a database to update that database.
- **Navigation**—When you bind a data source to controls, you can display the data in that source and allow the user to move through that data, record by record. Using navigation buttons is a great way to give the user easy access to your data.
- **Master/detail database handling**—Using bound controls, you can display, say, the names of the publishers from the publishers table in the pubs database in a list box (the *master* part). When the user clicks a publisher's name, you can list that publisher's books (the *detail* part) in a data grid. That's a good way to let users get all the details in your data simply by choosing items in an overview of that data.
- **Data lookups**—A list box can display the names of various authors from the authors table by using the DisplayMember property, and when the user clicks an author's name, the list box can display the selected author's ID in a text box using the ValueMember property. Using the ValueMember and DisplayMember properties, you can create user-friendly displays in controls while having those controls return code-friendly values to your program.

We're going to see all of these techniques at work today, with examples. For example, take a look at the BoundDB example from the code for this book at work in Figure 17.1.

This example binds various controls to the authors table in the SQL Server pubs database; you can use the buttons at the bottom to navigate through the authors table. We'll take a look at what makes this example tick today.

FIGURE 17.1

The BoundDB example.

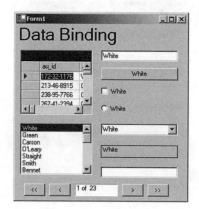

The first thing to realize about data binding is that there are actually two different types of data binding: simple and complex binding. We'll begin by taking a look at the difference.

Creating Simple Data Binding

Simple data binding is all about binding *one* data field to a control. To see an example, take a look at the BoundDB example in the code for this book, which you see at work in Figure 17.1. At upper right in this example, you can see a text box whose Text property is bound to the au_lname field in the authors table.

This example, BoundDB, has a dataset object, DataSet11, connected to the authors table from the pubs database; we've seen how to create such dataset objects yesterday (in this case, BoundDB uses an SqlDataAdapter to fill the DataSet11 object). So, how do you bind a text box to DataSet11? In particular, how do you bind a text box's Text property to the au_lname field?

If you open a text box's (DataBindings) property in the Properties window, you'll see a list of the most commonly bound properties, such as the Tag and Text properties for a text box, as shown in Figure 17.2. You can select a field in a dataset to bind to just by clicking a property and selecting a table from the drop-down list that appears, as you see in Figure 17.2.

17

FIGURE 17.2

Binding a text box.

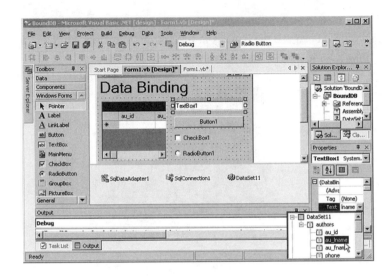

That's how you bind the Text property of a text box to a dataset object: You expand the text box's (DataBindings) property in the Properties window and use the drop-down list box to select the field in a data source you want to bind the Text property to. In this way, you can bind the most commonly bound properties of various controls, such as the Text property of a text box, to a field in a dataset, as long as that property is of the same data type as that field.

You can actually bind any property of a control like a text box to fields in a dataset. Only the most commonly bound properties of a control are listed in the (DataBindings) property in the Properties window, but you can access any property for data binding. To do so, click the ellipsis button that appears when you click the (Advanced) entry in the (DataBindings) property, which opens the Advanced Data Binding dialog you see in Figure 17.3.

When you use the Advanced Data Binding dialog, you can bind just about any property of a control to a data source. For example, as you see in Figure 17.3, you can tie such unlikely text box properties as PasswordChar, ScrollBars, and Multiline to a database. (Although the PasswordChar property can be bound to a text field in a data source, ScrollBars and Multiline have to be bound to a Boolean field in the data source; if you want to see how that works, you can use the contract field in the authors table, which holds a Boolean value.)

When you use simple binding, the simple-bound control will display the value in a single field of the *current record*. When you bind data to a data source, the form's *binding context* keeps track of where you are in that data source, and the record whose data is displayed in simple-bound controls at a particular time is called the current record. We'll see in a few pages how to use the binding context to navigate through a dataset, moving from record to record, back and forth, as the user clicks the arrow buttons you see at the bottom of the BoundDB example. As the current record changes, the data in all the bound controls will change the display the data in the bound field in the new record. When you use the navigation buttons at the bottom of the BoundDB example, you can move through the dataset and watch the data in all the simple-bound (single-item) controls change automatically to match the data in the new record.

FIGURE 17.3

The Advanced Data Binding dialog.

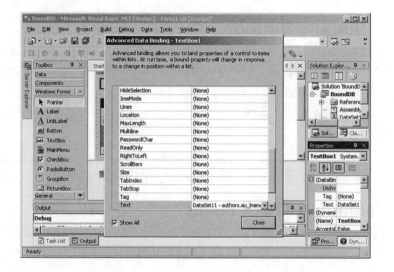

Because simple-bound controls can show data from only the current record, it's usual to include some sort of navigation controls, such as the buttons in the BoundDB example, to let the user move from record to record. That's not such a problem in a complex-bound control like a data grid because you can see data from multiple records at the same time. Nonetheless, the current record's data is automatically highlighted in complex-bound controls as you move from record to record, as you see in the data grid at upper left in Figure 17.1.

You can see several simple-bound controls displaying data from a single field from the data source in Figure 17.1. Let's take a look at the simple-bound controls in that figure in a little more depth now.

Binding Text Boxes

Text boxes are simple data-binding controls. Here are the commonly bound properties displayed when you expand the (DataBindings) property of a text box:

- Tag
- Text

When you click either of these properties, you can connect it to a database field by selecting from the choices offered in a drop-down list. And don't forget that you can bind just about any text box property—and just about any property of the other simple-bound controls coming up—to any data source field of the same data type; just click the (Advanced) entry in the (DataBindings) property to open the Advanced Data Binding dialog you see in Figure 17.3.

Binding Buttons

Like text boxes, buttons are simple data-binding controls. Here are the commonly bound properties displayed when you expand the (DataBindings) property—the same as those for text boxes:

- Tag
- Text

As with other simple-bound controls, to bind any property of a button, click the (Advanced) entry in the (DataBindings) entry in the Properties window.

Binding Check Boxes

Check boxes are also simple data-binding controls. Here are the commonly bound properties displayed when you expand the (DataBindings) property:

- CheckAlign
- Checked
- CheckState
- Tag
- Text

Note that you have to ensure that the data type of the field you bind properties like these to matches the data type of the property. For example, the Checked property of the check box must be bound to a Boolean field, like the contract field in the authors table.

As with other simple-bound controls, to bind any property of a check box, click the (Advanced) entry in the (DataBindings) entry in the Properties window.

Binding Radio Buttons

Radio buttons are also simple data-binding controls. Here are the commonly bound properties displayed when you expand the (DataBindings) property:

- CheckAlign
- Tag
- Text

For other simple-bound controls, don't forget that to bind any property of a radio button, you can click the (Advanced) entry in the (DataBindings) entry in the Properties window.

Binding Labels

Labels are also simple data-binding controls like the ones we've seen earlier. Here are the commonly bound properties displayed when you expand the (DataBindings) property:

- Tag
- Text

And that's it. At design time, you can use the Properties window to bind both commonly bound properties to a data source and, using the (Advanced) entry in the (DataBindings) property, you can also bind not-so-commonly bound properties to a data source. That gives us a good introduction to simple binding, where you bind a single field from a data source to a control, and at runtime, that control displays the field's data for the current record (more on how to set the current record after we discuss complex data binding).

As you'd expect, you can also perform simple binding in code, and that's coming up next.

Performing Simple Binding in Code

You can create simple bindings in code as well, working with various Binding objects. We'll take a look at how this works in overview here; if you're going to connect to different data sources as requested by the user on-the-fly, you'll have to set up your data bindings on-the-fly.

In code, you perform simple binding using a control's (DataBindings) property, which holds a collection of Binding objects corresponding to the bindings for that control. Here's an example where we'll bind a text box to the au_lname field. In code, you use the DataBindings collection's Add method to add a data binding, passing this method the property to bind, the data source to use, and the specific field you want to bind in the table you want to use. In this case, we might bind the au_lname field of the authors table to the Text property of a text box like this:

```
TextBox1.DataBindings.Add("Text", DataSet11, "authors.au_lname")
```

There's another form of the Add method that enables you to pass a Binding object directly. Here's what that looks like—this code binds the same text box to the au_lname field:

```
TextBox1.DataBindings.Add _
    (New Binding("Text", DataSet11, "authors.au_lname"))
```

In fact, data binding has become so advanced in Visual Basic .NET that you can actually bind a property of a control to a property of another control (which is still a little-known fact among Visual Basic .NET programmers). Here's an example that binds the Text property of TextBox1 to the Text property of TextBox2. When you change the text in TextBox2, the text in TextBox1 changes automatically to match:

```
TextBox1.DataBindings.Add("Text", TextBox2, "Text")
```

Let's take a look at some of the objects we're working with here in more depth. Formally speaking, the (DataBindings) property returns an object of the ControlBindingsCollection class, and the ControlBindingsCollection class holds a collection of Binding objects for a control. Here's the hierarchy for the ControlBindingsCollection class:

```
System.Object
    System.MarshalByRefObject
        System.Windows.Forms.BaseCollection
            System.Windows.Forms.BindingsCollection
                System.Windows.Forms.ControlBindingsCollection
```

You can find the significant public properties of ControlBindingsCollection objects in Table 17.1, their significant methods in Table 17.2, and their significant events in Table 17.3.

TABLE 17.1   Significant Public Properties of ControlBindingsCollection Objects

Property	Means
Control	Returns the collection's control.
Count	Returns the number of items in the collection.
Item	Returns a data binding.

TABLE 17.2   Significant Public Methods of `ControlBindingsCollection` Objects

Method	Means
Add	Adds a data binding.
Remove	Removes a data binding.
RemoveAt	Removes a specific data binding.

TABLE 17.3   Significant Public Event of `ControlBindingsCollection` Objects

Event	Means
CollectionChanged	Occurs when collection changes.

The `ControlBindingsCollection` class, in turn, is based on the `BindingsCollection` class, which has this hierarchy:

```
System.Object
    System.MarshalByRefObject
        System.Windows.Forms.BaseCollection
            System.Windows.Forms.BindingsCollection
```

You can find the significant public properties of `BindingsCollection` objects in Table 17.4, and their significant events in Table 17.5 (this class has no noninherited methods)

TABLE 17.4   Significant Public Properties of `BindingsCollection` Objects

Property	Means
Count	Contains the count of items in the collection.
Item	Returns the binding at the specified index.

TABLE 17.5   Significant Public Event of `BindingsCollection` Objects

Event	Means
CollectionChanged	Occurs when the collection changes.

The `ControlBindingsCollection` class holds a collection of `Binding` objects, and the `Binding` class represents the simple binding between the property value of an object and the property value of a control. Here's the hierarchy for this class:

```
System.Object
    System.Windows.Forms.Binding
```

You can find the significant public properties of `Binding` objects in Table 17.6, and their significant events in Table 17.7 (this class has no noninherited methods).

TABLE 17.6   Significant Public Properties of `Binding` Objects

Property	Means
BindingMemberInfo	Returns data binding information.
Control	Returns the control for this data binding.
DataSource	Returns the binding's data source.
IsBinding	True if the binding is active.
PropertyName	Returns or sets the control's data-bound property.

TABLE 17.7   Significant Event Properties of `Binding` Objects

Event	Means
Format	Occurs when a property is bound to a data value.
Parse	Occurs when a data-bound control's value changes.

That gives us a good foundation in simple data binding; we'll take a look at complex data binding next.

Creating Complex Binding

Simple data binding binds a control to one field in the current record, and you use it with controls that can display only one data item at a time, such as labels or text boxes. However, some controls, such as list boxes and data grids, can display multiple data items at the same time, and you use complex data binding with those controls.

In fact, we've already seen complex binding at work yesterday when we worked with data grids. As you recall, you set the `DataSource` property of a data grid to a database object, and the `DataMember` property to a table in that dataset. The data grid will then display that entire table. Complex binding centers on properties such as `DataSource` and `DataMember`. Here are the properties you use with complex binding; we'll put them all to work today:

- `DataSource`—The data source, typically a dataset such as `DataSet11`.
- `DataMember`—The data member you want to work with in the data source; typically a table in a dataset, such as the authors table in the pubs database. Data grids use this property to determine which table they should display.

- DisplayMember—The field whose data you want a control to display, such as the author's last name, au_lname. List boxes use the DisplayMember and ValueMember properties instead of a DataMember property. See the "Using the DisplayMember and ValueMember Properties" section later today.

- ValueMember—The field, such as au_id, you want the control to return in a value-oriented property such as SelectedValue. List boxes use the DisplayMember and ValueMember properties instead of a DataMember property.

We've seen the DataSource and DataMember properties already, but what are DisplayMember and ValueMember? These properties let some controls, such as list boxes, display data from one field but return data from another field using properties such as SelectedValue. For example, you might want to work with the ID of various authors in your code, behind the scenes, but a value such as 141-67-0225 won't mean much to the user when displayed in a list box. Instead, you can set the DisplayMember property of the list box to the au_lname property so that the list box will display authors' last names, and the ValueMember property to au_id so that the SelectedValue property of the list box will return the same author's ID value. In this way, a control can display user-friendly data from one field, while passing code-friendly data on to your program. We'll see how this works in an example later today; see the "Using the DisplayMember and ValueMember Properties" section.

You can see a number of controls that use complex binding (most controls in Visual Basic .NET support only simple binding) in the BoundDB example in the code for this book, which you can see at work in Figure 17.1. The combo box, list box, and data grid in that example are all complex-bound controls (and the list box uses both the DisplayMember and SelectedValue properties so that when you click an author's last name, the author's ID value appears in the text box at lower right). Let's take a look at complex binding these controls now.

Binding Combo Boxes

Combo boxes are complex-bound controls. Here are the properties you use to bind this control to a data source:

- DataSource
- DisplayMember
- ValueMember

The combo box you see in the BoundDB example shown in Figure 17.1 has its DataSource property set to DataSet11, which is connected to the authors table. Its DisplayMember property is set to the au_lname field, making the combo box display the current record's au_lname value, as you see in Figure 17.1.

17

Binding List Boxes

Like combo boxes, list boxes are complex data-binding controls. Here are the properties you use to bind this control to a data source—they're the same as for combo boxes:

- DataSource
- DisplayMember
- ValueMember

Like the combo box, the list box in the BoundDB example is bound to the au_lname field in the authors table using the DataSource and DisplayMember properties. However, there's more going on here—the list box also uses the ValueMember property. If you make a selection in the list box, you'll see the selected author's ID value in the text box at lower right, as shown in Figure 17.4. We'll cover how this works later today in the "Using the DisplayMember and ValueMember Properties" section.

FIGURE 17.4

Displaying an author's ID.

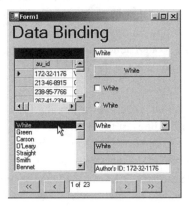

Binding Data Grids

The data grid control has already become a favorite control; we've seen it at work yesterday, and you can see it at upper left in today's BoundDB example in Figure 17.1, showing the authors table from the pubs database.

We didn't start using the data grid control until yesterday. Because this control is specifically for use with databases, we didn't cover it when discussing the other Windows controls in Days 5 through 8. For that reason, we'll take a moment here to list the properties, methods, and events of this control, as we've done earlier for other Windows controls. This control is the ultimate data-bound control, so it's worth taking a look at in more depth. The data grid is supported by the DataGrid class, and here is the hierarchy of that class:

```
System.Object
  System.MarshalByRefObject
    System.ComponentModel.Component
      System.Windows.Forms.Control
        System.Windows.Forms.DataGrid
```

You can find the significant public properties of DataGrid objects in Table 17.8, their significant methods in Table 17.9, and their significant events in Table 17.10. Note that as with other Windows controls, these tables do not list the significant properties, methods, and events that data grids inherit from the Control class, such as the Click event—you can find that information in Tables 5.1, 5.2, and 5.3.

TABLE 17.8 Significant Public Properties of DataGrid Objects

Property	Means
AllowNavigation	Returns or sets whether navigation is allowed in the data grid.
AllowSorting	Returns or sets whether the grid can be sorted when the user clicks a column header.
AlternatingBackColor	Returns or sets the background color used in alternating rows.
BackColor	Returns or sets the background color of the data grid.
BackgroundColor	Returns or sets the color of the nondata sections of the data grid.
BorderStyle	Returns or sets the data grid's style of border.
CaptionBackColor	Returns or sets the caption's background color.
CaptionFont	Returns or sets the caption's font.
CaptionForeColor	Returns or sets the caption's foreground color.
CaptionText	Returns or sets the caption's text.
CaptionVisible	Returns or sets whether the caption is visible.
ColumnHeadersVisible	Returns or sets whether the parent rows of a table are visible.
CurrentCell	Returns or sets which cell has the focus.
CurrentRowIndex	Returns or sets the index of the selected row.
DataMember	Returns or sets the table or list of data the data grid should display.
DataSource	Returns or sets the data grid's data source, such as a dataset.
FirstVisibleColumn	Returns the index of the first column visible in the grid.
FlatMode	Returns or sets whether the data grid should be shown flat.
ForeColor	Returns or sets the foreground color used in the data grid.
GridLineColor	Returns or sets the color of grid lines.
GridLineStyle	Returns or sets the grid line style.
HeaderBackColor	Returns or sets the background color of headers.

17

TABLE 17.8   continued

Property	Means
HeaderFont	Returns or sets the font used for headers.
HeaderForeColor	Returns or sets the foreground color of headers.
Item	Returns or sets the value in a particular cell.
LinkColor	Returns or sets the color of links to child tables.
LinkHoverColor	Returns or sets the color of links to child tables when the mouse moves over it.
ParentRowsBackColor	Returns or sets the background color of parent rows.
ParentRowsForeColor	Returns or sets the foreground color of parent rows.
ParentRowsLabelStyle	Returns or sets the style for parent row labels.
ParentRowsVisible	Returns or sets whether parent rows are visible.
PreferredColumnWidth	Returns or sets the width of the grid columns (measured in pixels).
PreferredRowHeight	Returns or sets the preferred row height.
ReadOnly	Returns or sets whether the grid is read-only.
RowHeadersVisible	Returns or sets whether row headers are visible.
RowHeaderWidth	Returns or sets the width of row headers.
SelectionBackColor	Returns or sets selected cell's background color.
SelectionForeColor	Returns or sets selected cell's foreground color.
TableStyles	Returns the table styles in the data grid.
VisibleColumnCount	Returns the number of visible columns.
VisibleRowCount	Returns the number of visible rows.

TABLE 17.9   Significant Public Methods of `DataGrid` Objects

Method	Means
BeginEdit	Makes the data grid allow editing.
Collapse	Collapses child table relations.
EndEdit	Ends editing operations.
Expand	Displays child relations.
HitTest	Coordinates the mouse position with points in the data grid.
IsExpanded	Returns whether a row is expanded or collapsed.
IsSelected	Returns whether a row is selected.

TABLE 17.9   continued

Method	Means
NavigateBack	Navigates to the previous table that was shown in the grid.
NavigateTo	Navigates to a specific table.
Select	Makes a selection.
SetDataBinding	Sets both the DataSource and DataMember properties; used at runtime.
UnSelect	Unselects a row.

TABLE 17.10   Significant Public Events of DataGrid Objects

Event	Means
AllowNavigationChanged	Occurs when the AllowNavigation property changes.
CurrentCellChanged	Occurs when the CurrentCell property changes.
DataSourceChanged	Occurs when the DataSource property value changes.
FlatModeChanged	Occurs when the FlatMode changes.
Navigate	Occurs when the user navigates to a new table.
ParentRowsVisibleChanged	Occurs when the ParentRowsVisible property value changes.
ReadOnlyChanged	Occurs when the ReadOnly property value changes.
Scroll	Occurs when the data grid is scrolled.

17

Here are the properties you use to bind this control to a data source:

- DataSource
- DisplayMember

To bind a data grid to a table, you can set the data grid's DataSource property (to an object like a dataset, such as DataSet11) and DataMember property (usually to text naming a table, such as "authors"). You can use these data sources with the data grid's DataSource property:

- DataTable objects
- DataView objects
- DataSet objects
- DataViewManager objects
- Single-dimension arrays

You can use the `CurrentCellChanged` event to determine when the user selects another cell. As the user moves around in a data grid using the keyboard, the `Navigate` event occurs, and you can determine which cell was selected by using the `CurrentCell` property. You can access and change the value of any cell using the `Item` property, which can take either the row or column indexes of the cell.

Data grids are the only Windows forms control designed exclusively to be bound to data sources. As we saw yesterday and in the BoundDB example in Figure 17.1, they display entire database tables at once. This is one of the more enjoyable controls to work with because you've got to set only a few properties, and the control does all the work—and a lot of it—behind the scenes.

Using the `DisplayMember` and `ValueMember` Properties

As you see in Figure 17.4, when you click the name of an author in the list box in the BoundDB example, the author's ID value appears in the text box at lower right.

The way this works is by using the list box's `DisplayMember` and `ValueMember` properties to bind to a specific data field. In the BoundDB example, the list box's `DisplayMember` property is bound to the `au_lname` field, and the `ValueMember` property is bound to the `au_id` field. That means the list box will show the author's last name in the list box, but when the user clicks an author, the list box's `SelectedValue` property will hold the author's ID value. Here's how that ID value is displayed in the text box:

```
Private Sub ListBox1_SelectedIndexChanged(ByVal _
    sender As System.Object, ByVal e As System.EventArgs) _
    Handles ListBox1.SelectedIndexChanged
    TextBox2.Text = "Author's ID: " & ListBox1.SelectedValue
End Sub
```

In this way, the list box can display user-friendly names, while actually returning code-friendly ID values.

Performing Complex Binding in Code

Despite its name, it's easier to handle complex binding in code than simple binding because complex binding is based on just four properties: `DataSource`, `DataMember`,

DisplayMember, and ValueMember. For example, here's how you can bind a data grid to a dataset in code:

```
DataGrid1.DataSource = DataSet11
DataGrid1.DataMember = "authors"
```

That's easy enough. You can also use the data grid method SetDataBinding like this (this is a handy method that's supported only by data grids):

```
DataGrid1.SetDataBinding(DataSet11, "authors")
```

Here's how you can bind other complex-bound controls to a dataset at runtime. This example binds a list box:

```
ListBox1.DataSource = DataSet11
ListBox1.DisplayMember = "authors.au_lname"
ListBox1.ValueMember = "authors.au_id"
```

As you can see, complex binding is easy in code; you just assign values to the complex-binding properties the control you're working with normally uses. That's all it takes.

We've spent some time understanding how to bind a data source to controls now, but as far as simple-bound controls go—which make up the majority of Visual Basic .NET controls—we've seen only half the story. When you bind a data source to a simple-bound control such as a text box, that control displays only a single field from the current record in the data source. If that were the end of the story, it would be pretty disappointing. How can you make the control show data from the other records in the data source? You do so by working with the binding context, which we'll take a look at next as we see how to navigate through data sources.

Navigating in Data Sources

When you work with simple-bound controls, you usually display navigation controls to let the user move from record to record in the data source. Take a look at the BoundDB example, for instance. You can see its navigation buttons at the bottom of Figure 17.5. When we click the << button, the first record in the dataset is displayed, and when the < button is clicked, we move back one record. The > button moves us forward one record, and the >> button moves us to the last record in the dataset. There are two more things to note in Figure 17.5: The current location in the dataset is displayed in the label in the middle of the buttons, and even the complex-bound controls in this example highlight or indicate with an arrow the current record as we navigate through the dataset. We'll see how all this works next.

FIGURE 17.5

Navigating through records.

In the old days, the current record was maintained in the data source, but in the days of disconnected data sources, that's changed. Today, you use local copies of data and the current record is also maintained locally. In a Windows form, you use the form's BindingContext property (part of the Control class), which holds a collection of BindingManagerBase objects, to set the current record for all controls in the form. That's how you get access to the binding context in a form—using an object of the BindingManagerBase class as returned by the BindingContext property. Here's the hierarchy of the BindingManagerBase class (note because data bindings are stored for the entire form at once, the BindingManagerBase is in the Forms namespace):

```
System.Object
    System.Windows.Forms.BindingManagerBase
```

The important properties of the BindingManagerBase class are the Position property, which returns or sets the current position in the binding context, and Count, which returns the number of records in the binding context.

You can find the significant public properties of BindingManagerBase objects in Table 17.11, their significant methods in Table 17.12, and their significant events in Table 17.13.

TABLE 17.11 Significant Public Properties of BindingManagerBase Objects

Property	Means
Bindings	Returns the collection of bindings being managed.
Count	Returns the number of rows managed by the BindingManagerBase.
Current	Returns the current object.
Position	Returns or sets the position in the list that controls bound to this data source point to.

TABLE 17.12 Significant Public Methods of `BindingManagerBase` Objects

Method	Means
AddNew	Adds a new item to the underlying list.
CancelCurrentEdit	Cancels the current edit.
EndCurrentEdit	Ends the current edit.
RemoveAt	Deletes the row at the specified index from the underlying list.
ResumeBinding	Resumes data binding (see also `SuspendBinding`).
SuspendBinding	Suspends data binding (see also `ResumeBinding`).

TABLE 17.13 Significant Public Events of `BindingManagerBase` Objects

Event	Means
CurrentChanged	Occurs when the bound value changes.
PositionChanged	Occurs when the `Position` property changes.

17

The next step is to dissect the code in the BoundDB example to understand how it works, starting with understanding how to determine what record is the current record.

Displaying the Current Record

The label in between the navigation buttons you see in Figure 17.5 displays the current location in the binding context with text like "2 of 23," meaning you're viewing record number 2 of 23 records. The code determines the current location using the form's `BindingContext` property. A form's `BindingContext` property holds a collection of `BindingManagerBase` objects, and when you pass arguments specifying which data source you want to work with (that's `DataSet11` here) and which table in that data source you're interested in (because datasets and other data objects can hold multiple tables), the collection will return a `BindingManagerBase` object for that binding. We can use the `BindingManagerBase` object's `Position` and `Count` properties to determine where we are in the binding context. And that's all we need—we can convert that data into a string and display it in the label:

```
Private Sub Form1_Load(ByVal sender As System.Object, _
    ByVal e As System.EventArgs) Handles MyBase.Load
    SqlDataAdapter1.Fill(DataSet11)
    Label2.Text = (((Me.BindingContext(DataSet11, "authors").Position _
        + 1).ToString + " of  ") & Me.BindingContext(DataSet11, _
        "authors").Count.ToString)
End Sub
```

That's how we can display the current location in the binding context. But what about moving around in the dataset?

Navigating to the Next Record

When the user clicks the > button, the code moves to the next record (if there is one), making that record the new current record in the binding context. To do that, the code simply increments the `Position` property in the form's `BindingManagerBase` object:

```
Private Sub Button4_Click(ByVal sender As System.Object, _
    ByVal e As System.EventArgs) Handles Button4.Click
    Me.BindingContext(DataSet11, "authors").Position = _
        (Me.BindingContext(DataSet11, "authors").Position + 1)
        .
        .
        .
End Sub
```

If you try to move beyond the end of the recordset, the `Position` property will not be incremented. All that's left is to display the new position in the label between the buttons, which we can do like this:

```
Private Sub Button4_Click(ByVal sender As System.Object, _
    ByVal e As System.EventArgs) Handles Button4.Click
    Me.BindingContext(DataSet11, "authors").Position = _
        (Me.BindingContext(DataSet11, "authors").Position + 1)
    Label2.Text = (((Me.BindingContext(DataSet11, "authors").Position _
        + 1).ToString + " of  ") & Me.BindingContext(DataSet11, _
        "authors").Count.ToString)
End Sub
```

And that's all you need. Now when you move to the new record, all the simple-bound controls in the form will display data from the new current record, and the complex-bound controls will display the new current record highlighted.

Navigating to the Previous Record

You move to the previous record when you click the < button. To do that, the code just decrements the `Position` property and then displays the new location:

```
Private Sub Button3_Click(ByVal sender As System.Object, _
    ByVal e As System.EventArgs) Handles Button3.Click
    Me.BindingContext(DataSet11, "authors").Position = _
        (Me.BindingContext(DataSet11, "authors").Position - 1)
    Label2.Text = (((Me.BindingContext(DataSet11, "authors").Position _
        + 1).ToString + " of  ") & Me.BindingContext(DataSet11, _
        "authors").Count.ToString)
End Sub
```

As when we incremented the `Position` property, if we attempt to decrement the `Position` property to a location before the beginning of the dataset, the `Position` property won't be decremented.

Navigating to the First Record

When the user clicks the << button, the code makes the first record the current record in the binding context. To do that, all we need to do is to set the `Position` property to 0 and display the new location, like this:

```
Private Sub Button2_Click(ByVal sender As System.Object, _
    ByVal e As System.EventArgs) Handles Button2.Click
    Me.BindingContext(DataSet11, "authors").Position = 0
    Label2.Text = (((Me.BindingContext(DataSet11, "authors").Position _
        + 1).ToString + " of  ") & Me.BindingContext(DataSet11, _
        "authors").Count.ToString)
End Sub
```

Navigating to the Last Record

Similarly, we can easily navigate to the last record in a binding context—all we have to do is to set the `Position` property to `Count` - 1 (we subtract 1 because `Position` is zero-based):

```
Private Sub Button5_Click(ByVal sender As System.Object, _
    ByVal e As System.EventArgs) Handles Button5.Click
    Me.BindingContext(DataSet11, "authors").Position = _
        Me.BindingContext(DataSet11, "authors").Count - 1
    Label2.Text = (((Me.BindingContext(DataSet11, "authors").Position _
        + 1).ToString + " of  ") & Me.BindingContext(DataSet11, _
        "authors").Count.ToString)
End Sub
```

That's all it takes. Using the `BindingContext` collection, you can get the `BindingManagerBase` object for the binding you're interested in, and the `BindingManagerBase` object's `Position` and `Location` properties give you what you need to navigate through records.

We've written our own navigation code here, but in fact, Visual Basic .NET will write that kind of code for you if you prefer, using the Data Form Wizard. We'll take a look at how that works next.

17

Creating Data Forms with the Data Form Wizard

A data form lets the user enter and edit data easily and update a data source as needed. The Data Form Wizard will create the code you need, as you'll see here. Data forms are an important database tool in Visual Basic .NET, so they're worth some of our time today.

This example is called DataFormDB in the code for this book. Data forms are made up of separate forms that you add to a project. In this example, we'll create a simple data form that enables the user to navigate and edit the authors table. You can do all that in code yourself, of course, but the Data Form Wizard will do all the hard work for you if you prefer (and you can customize and move the controls around as you like in the data form it creates).

To see how data forms work, create a new Windows application called DataFormDB. To create a new data form, DataForm1.vb, use the Project, Add New Item menu item. Select the Data Form Wizard icon in the Templates box and click OK. This opens the Data Form Wizard you see in Figure 17.6.

FIGURE 17.6

The Data Form Wizard, first pane.

Click the Next button in the Data Form Wizard to move to the pane you see in Figure 17.7, where the wizard is asking for the name of a dataset to create (or you can use an existing dataset). In this example, we'll name the new dataset dsAuthors, as you see in the figure.

FIGURE 17.7

*The Data Form Wizard,
second pane.*

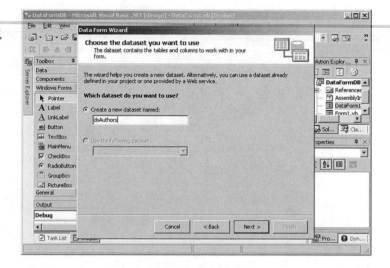

In the next pane, the wizard asks what data connection to use (or enables you to create a
new connection). We'll use a connection to the pubs database, as you see in Figure 17.8.

FIGURE 17.8

*The Data Form Wizard,
third pane.*

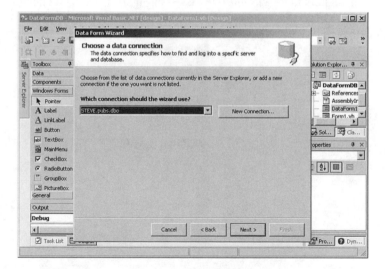

In the following pane, you can choose which table(s) to add to the data form. In this
case, we'll add only the authors table, as you see in Figure 17.9.

17

FIGURE 17.9

The Data Form Wizard, fourth pane.

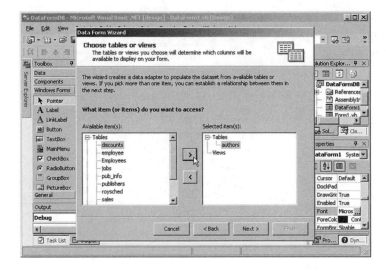

The following pane of the Data Form Wizard enables you to specify what tables and columns you want to display in the data form. In this case, we'll just leave all columns in the authors table selected, as you see in Figure 17.10, and click the Next button.

FIGURE 17.10

The Data Form Wizard, fifth pane.

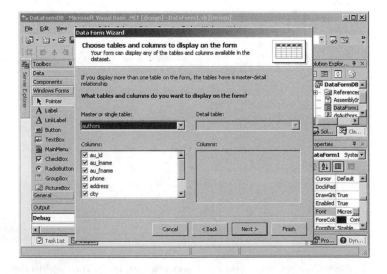

In the next pane, you select the display style—whether the data form will use a data grid or separate, simple-bound controls. To make things more interesting, we'll select separate controls, as you can see in Figure 17.11. That also means the data form will contain Add, Delete, and other editing controls.

FIGURE 17.11

The Data Form Wizard, sixth pane.

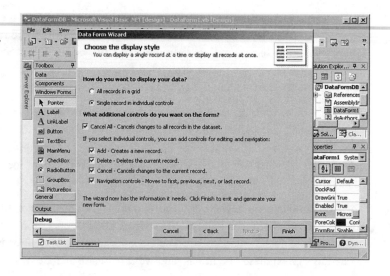

Now click the Finish button to create the data form, DataForm1.vb, and add it to the project. That creates the new data form. We can also add code to the main form to make a data form—an object of the DataForm1 class—visible when the user clicks a button:

```
Private Sub Button1_Click(ByVal sender As System.Object, _
    ByVal e As System.EventArgs) Handles Button1.Click
    Dim frmDataForm1 As New DataForm1
    frmDataForm1.Show()
End Sub
```

That completes the data form. What does this new data form look like? You can see it in Figure 17.12, where the user has clicked the Load button to load the authors table's data.

FIGURE 17.12

A new data form.

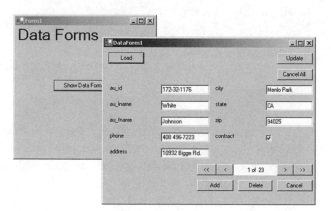

If you take a look at this new data form, you'll see it's much like the BoundDB example we created, with a few extra buttons. You can navigate through the records in the authors table as we did in the BoundDB example, using the <<, <, >, and >> buttons. As you see, the various fields of each record are bound to controls in the data form (note that the contract field, which is a Boolean field, is bound to a check box).

The user can also edit the data in the authors table by using the data form—note the Add, Delete, Cancel, and Update buttons. When the user changes the data in the bound controls, the changed data is sent to the dataset immediately, starting an edit operation in the dataset. But note that any changes to the dataset are sent back to the underlying database (that's the pubs database in SQL Server here) *only* when the user clicks the Update button.

The Add button adds a new empty record to the end of the dataset, the Delete button deletes a record, and the Cancel button cancels any edit operation in the dataset that hasn't been sent back to the database yet. The Data Form Wizard has already written the code needed to support these operations, and we'll dissect that code to see what's going on.

Creating New Records

When you click the Add button in the data form, the data form creates a new record, making it the last record in the dataset. (Bear in mind that, as with all editing operations, the underlying database—the authors table in the pubs database itself—isn't changed until the user clicks the Update button.) To add a new record to a dataset, you use the AddNew method of the BindingManagerBase connected to that dataset. Here's how the data form does it:

```
Private Sub btnAdd_Click(ByVal sender As System.Object, _
    ByVal e As System.EventArgs) Handles btnAdd.Click
    Try
        'Clear out the current edits
        Me.BindingContext(objdsAuthors, "authors").EndCurrentEdit()
        Me.BindingContext(objdsAuthors, "authors").AddNew()
    Catch eEndEdit As System.Exception
        System.Windows.Forms.MessageBox.Show(eEndEdit.Message)
    End Try
    Me.objdsAuthors_PositionChanged()
End Sub
```

That's all you need to add a new, blank record to a dataset; just use the AddNew method. Note also the call to the objdsAuthors_PositionChanged procedure here, which updates the label between the navigation buttons with the new position in the binding context, as we did in the BoundDB example.

Deleting Records

To delete a record, you can use the RemoveAt method. Here's how that works in the data form when the user clicks the Delete button, which deletes the current record (note that no changes are made to the underlying database until the Update button is clicked):

```
Private Sub btnDelete_Click(ByVal sender As System.Object, _
    ByVal e As System.EventArgs) Handles btnDelete.Click
    If (Me.BindingContext(objdsAuthors, "authors").Count > 0) Then
        Me.BindingContext(objdsAuthors, "authors").RemoveAt(_
            Me.BindingContext(objdsAuthors, "authors").Position)
        Me.objdsAuthors_PositionChanged()
    End If
End Sub
```

Canceling Edits

When you add new records, delete records, or edit the data in bound controls directly, you change the data in the dataset the controls are bound to. The data in the underlying database (the pubs database in SQL Server in this example) isn't changed until you click the Update button. If you want to cancel the current edit operation instead of updating the underlying database, you can use the CancelCurrentEdit method. Here's what that looks like in the data form's code:

```
Private Sub btnCancel_Click(ByVal sender As System.Object, _
    ByVal e As System.EventArgs) Handles btnCancel.Click
    Me.BindingContext(objdsAuthors, "authors").CancelCurrentEdit()
    Me.objdsAuthors_PositionChanged()
End Sub
```

When you click the Cancel button, the current edit operation is cancelled and the data from before the operation started is restored in the dataset.

Updating the Data Source

When you've finished an edit operation and want to send your changes back to the underlying database, you can use a data adapter's Update method, as we did yesterday. Here's what that looks like in the data form's code (note that the data form is using an OleDbConnection and OleDbDataAdapter despite the fact that we're connecting to a database using SQL Server):

```
Public Sub UpdateDataSource(ByVal ChangedRows As DataFormDB.dsAuthors)
    Try
        'The data source only needs to be updated if there are changes pending.
        If (Not (ChangedRows) Is Nothing) Then
            'Open the connection.
```

17

```
            Me.OleDbConnection1.Open()
            'Attempt to update the data source.
            OleDbDataAdapter1.Update(ChangedRows)
        End If
    Catch updateException As System.Exception
        'Add your error handling code here.
        Throw updateException
    Finally
        'Close the connection whether or not the exception was thrown.
        Me.OleDbConnection1.Close()
    End Try
End Sub
```

That completes our overview of the code for data forms. Using that form, the user can edit data, add records, delete records, and update the data source. Data forms use bound controls of the type we're working with today to give you all that you normally need in a data-entry form.

Now that we're creating data-entry forms, it's worth taking a look at another topic: validating data that the user has entered into data-entry forms.

Data Validation in Data-Entry Forms

In Day 15, "Web Forms: Working with Validation Controls, Calendars, and Ad Rotators," we saw how to validate data the user entered into Web application controls. It's useful to know that you can validate the data the user enters into data-entry controls in Windows forms as well. If a control contains data that you think invalid, you can use an *error provider*—a special Windows control to display error icons and text—to indicate what the error is.

You can see how this works in the Validating example in the code for this book. That example displays two text boxes, and its code insists that the user enter data into each text box. If the user hasn't entered data into a text box and clicks the other text box (making the current text box lose the focus), the error provider in this example displays an icon with a tool tip indicating what the error was, as you see in Figure 17.13.

FIGURE 17.13

Performing data validation in Windows controls.

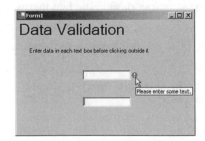

Data validation in Windows data-entry forms is based on the ErrorProvider class. Here's the hierarchy for this class:

```
System.Object
    System.MarshalByRefObject
        System.ComponentModel.Component
            System.Windows.Forms.ErrorProvider
```

You can find the significant public properties of ErrorProvider objects in Table 17.14, and their significant methods in Table 17.15 (this class has no noninherited events).

TABLE 17.14 Significant Public Properties of ErrorProvider Objects

Property	Means
BlinkRate	Returns or sets the error icon blink rate.
BlinkStyle	Returns or sets whether the error icon flashes.
ContainerControl	Returns or sets the parent control for this error provider.
DataMember	Returns or sets the data table to watch.
DataSource	Returns or sets the dataset to watch.
Icon	Returns or sets the icon to be displayed next to a control when you've assigned a nonempty string to the error provider.

TABLE 17.15 Significant Public Methods of ErrorProvider Objects

Method	Means
BindToDataAndErrors	Sets both the DataSource and DataMember properties at runtime.
GetError	Returns the error description string.
GetIconAlignment	Returns the position of the error icon with respect to the control.
GetIconPadding	Returns the space to leave next to the icon.
SetError	Sets the error text.
SetIconAlignment	Sets the position of the error icon with respect to the control.
SetIconPadding	Sets the space to leave next to the icon.

To validate a control's data, you add code to the control's Validating event, which occurs when the control loses the focus and the CausesValidation property of the control or form that gets the focus is True. True is the default for this property—if the CausesValidation property is False, validation is not performed in the control that lost the focus.

We'll see how this works in the Validating example in the code for this book. To follow along, add two text boxes to a project's main form, and make sure that the CausesValidation property of each is set to True, which means that when either text box receives the focus, it'll cause the Validating event of all the other controls in the form to occur. Also, add an error provider object, ErrorProvider1, from the toolbox to the form. The error provider will appear in the component tray below the form.

In the Validating event for TextBox1, you can check to see whether the user has entered data into that text box. If not, use the SetError method of the error provider to display a flashing error icon next to the text box; the icon's tool tip will hold an error message: "Please enter some text."

```
Private Sub TextBox1_Validating(ByVal sender As Object, _
    ByVal e As System.ComponentModel.CancelEventArgs) Handles
TextBox1.Validating
    If TextBox1.Text.Length = 0 Then
        ErrorProvider1.SetError(TextBox1, "Please enter some text.")
        .
        .
        .
    End If
End Sub
```

If the data is okay, you can set the error provider's text to "", which hides the error provider if it's currently visible:

```
Private Sub TextBox1_Validating(ByVal sender As Object, _
    ByVal e As System.ComponentModel.CancelEventArgs) _
    Handles TextBox1.Validating
    If TextBox1.Text.Length = 0 Then
        ErrorProvider1.SetError(TextBox1, "Please enter some text.")
    Else
        ErrorProvider1.SetError(TextBox1, "")
    End If
End Sub
```

You can add error handling for the second text box, TextBox2, in the same way:

```
Private Sub TextBox2_Validating(ByVal sender As Object, _
    ByVal e As System.ComponentModel.CancelEventArgs) _
    Handles TextBox2.Validating
    If TextBox2.Text.Length = 0 Then
        ErrorProvider1.SetError(TextBox2, "Please enter some text.")
    Else
        ErrorProvider1.SetError(TextBox2, "")
    End If
End Sub
```

Now you're validating the data the user enters into controls, as you see in Figure 17.13. If either text box loses the focus and there's no data in it, you'll see the flashing error icon.

Next we'll take a look at another example that uses bound controls: the SqlParametersDB example in the code for this book.

Working with SQL Parameters

The SqlParametersDB example will give us more insight into working with SQL in data adapters. In this case, we'll see how to use SQL parameters, which work much like variables that you can assign values to at runtime without changing the SQL in the data adapter.

Tip

> As we'll see tomorrow, we can change the SQL in a data adapter at runtime by creating new Command objects and assigning that object to data adapter properties such as SelectCommand.

The SqlParametersDB example shows how this works by letting the user select a state from a combo box. When the user clicks the Get Authors button, it makes the code display all the authors from that state in the authors table, as you see in Figure 17.14.

FIGURE 17.14

The SqlParametersDB example.

To make this work, this example uses an SQL parameter named state to hold the state the user has selected. Here's the SQL used in the SQL data adapter:

```
SELECT au_id, au_lname, state FROM authors WHERE (state = ?)
```

Note the state = ? part. This declares an SQL parameter named state, which we can assign data to at runtime. When we do, the data in the bound controls you see in

Figure 17.13 will be updated automatically. For example, if we set this parameter to "CA", this is the SQL that will be executed:

```
SELECT au_id, au_lname, state FROM authors WHERE (state = 'CA')
```

Let's take a look at how this works in code. The first step is to load the available states from the authors table into the combo box in this example. To do so, create a new `SqlDataAdapter` object, `SqlDataAdapter1`, and give it this SQL, using the SQL `DISTINCT` keyword to select every *unique* state from the authors table (this means no state will appear more than once):

```
SELECT DISTINCT state FROM authors
```

Next, generate a dataset object, `DataSet11`, from `SqlDataAdapter1`, and bind the state field to the combo box in this example. So far, then, all the distinct states in the authors table will appear in the combo box at runtime.

Now create a new data adapter, `SqlDataAdapter2`, that will hold the parameterized SQL that enables us to specify which state to use at runtime. In this case, we'll select the `au_id`, `au_lname`, `au_fname`, and `state` fields from the authors table. To parameterize the `state` field, add the text "= ?" to the Criteria item for that field in the Data Adapter Configuration Wizard's Query Builder, as you see in Figure 17.15.

FIGURE 17.15

Creating an SQL parameter.

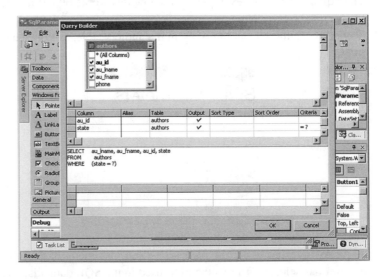

As you can see in Figure 17.16, the Query Builder generates this SQL:

```
SELECT
    au_lname,
    au_fname,
```

```
        au_id,
        state
FROM
        authors
WHERE
        (state = ?)
```

FIGURE 17.16

SQL using an SQL parameter.

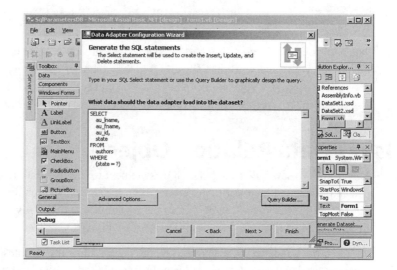

When you've finished creating SqlDataAdapter1, generate a new dataset object from the data adapter, DataSet21, and bind the au_fname and au_lname fields to text boxes, as you saw in Figure 17.14.

All that's left is to set our SQL parameter in code when the user clicks the Get Authors button. We can refer to the new parameter as @param1 in our code (a second parameter would be accessible as @param2, a third as @param3, and so on). In this case, we simply set that parameter's value to the selected state from the combo box, like this:

```
Private Sub Button1_Click(ByVal sender As System.Object, _
    ByVal e As System.EventArgs) Handles Button1.Click
    SqlDataAdapter2.SelectCommand.Parameters("@Param1").Value = _
        ComboBox1.Text
        .
        .
        .

End Sub
```

This customizes the SQL in SqlDataAdapter2. Now we're free to fill the dataset bound to the text boxes, DataSet21, from this data adapter (note that we also update the label between the navigation button to show where we are in the dataset):

```
Private Sub Button1_Click(ByVal sender As System.Object, _
    ByVal e As System.EventArgs) Handles Button1.Click
    SqlDataAdapter2.SelectCommand.Parameters("@Param1").Value = _
        ComboBox1.Text
    SqlDataAdapter2.Fill(DataSet21)
    Label3.Text = (((Me.BindingContext(DataSet21, _
        "authors").Position + 1).ToString + " of  ") _
        & Me.BindingContext(DataSet21, "authors").Count.ToString)
End Sub
```

The addition of the navigation button code we've already seen today, finishes the example, which we saw at work in Figure 17.14. Now the user can select a state and he'll see the authors from that state immediately. As you can see, you can set the value of an SQL parameter in an SQL statement at runtime, without rewriting your SQL at all.

Using Data Relation Objects

Yesterday, we saw how to use one SQL statement to join the data from two related tables (the authors and titleauthor tables from the pubs database, which are related using the au_id field). This joined the data from the two tables, and you saw the results in Figure 16.24 of Day 16, "Handling Databases with ADO.NET."

On the other hand, you don't have to merge the data from two tables into one dataset to work with related tables; you can keep the two tables separate, and use a data relation object to relate them. For example, you might want to set up a master/detail relationship, also called a *parent/child* relationship, between two tables, as you see in the DataRelationDB example that appears in Figure 17.17. When you select a publisher in the list box, that publisher's books appear in the data grid.

FIGURE 17.17

The DataRelationDB example.

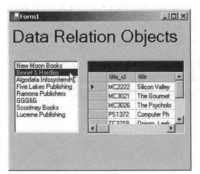

The DataRelationDB example relates the publishers and titles tables in the pubs database through the pub_id key (the publishers table contains publishers, and the titles table lists their books). The code first displays the pub_name field in the list box (this is the *master* part). When the user clicks a publisher in the list box, the code displays that publisher's books in the data grid (this is the *detail* part). Although the list box is bound to the pub_name field, the data grid is bound to a data relation object, `publisherstitles`, which we're going to create.

To see how this works, create a new Windows Forms project and drag an SQL data adapter, `SqlDataAdapter1`, to the main form in this project. In the Data Adapter Configuration Wizard, connect this data adapter to all fields in the pubs database's publishers table with the SQL statement **SELECT * FROM publishers**.

Next, create a second SQL data adapter, `SqlDataAdapter2`, and connect it to the titles table with the SQL statement **SELECT * FROM titles**. Then create a dataset using the Data, Generate Dataset menu item using both data adapters, as you see in Figure 17.18. This creates the `DataSet1` class, and an object of that class, `DataSet11`.

FIGURE 17.18

Creating the new dataset.

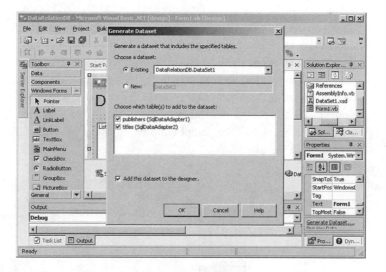

The new dataset doesn't know anything about the relationship between the publishers and titles tables. In fact, both tables share a common field, pub_id, the publisher ID. To tie together these tables, we'll add a data relation object to make this relationship explicit.

In particular, we'll create a data relation object named `publisherstitles` relating the publishers table and titles table. To create this object, right-click `DataSet11` and select the View Schema item. You'll see the XML schema for the two tables, publishers and titles, in an XML designer, as shown in Figure 17.19.

FIGURE 17.19

An XML designer.

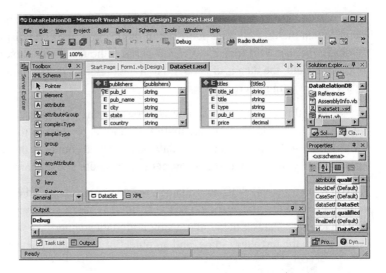

When you open the XML schema for `DataSet1`, the toolbox displays and opens an XML Schema tab. Drag a `Relation` object from the toolbox onto the child table, the titles table. Doing so opens the Edit Relation dialog you see in Figure 17.20; this dialog will create the data relation object we're going to use. The Edit Relation dialog has already given this relation a default name, `publisherstitles`, which we'll keep. As you see in Figure 17.20, the parent element is the publishers table and the child element is the titles table, which establishes the parent/child relationship we want. Click the OK button to close the Edit Relation dialog.

FIGURE 17.20

The Edit Relation dialog.

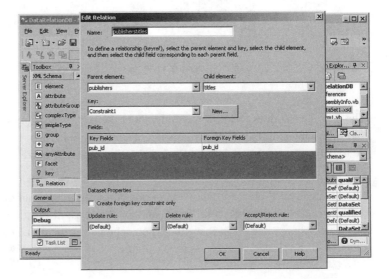

After closing the Edit Relation dialog, you can see a data relation object connecting the two tables in Figure 17.21. We've now added a relation between the two tables in the dataset we've created. Save DataSet1.xsd to disk to make the `publisherstitles` object available to the rest of your code.

FIGURE 17.21

A new data relation.

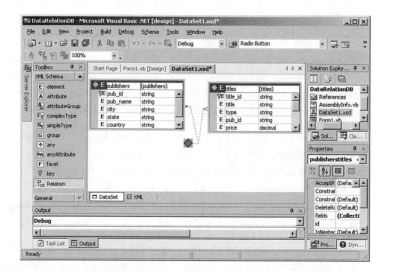

Next, create a list box and set its `DataSource` property to `DataSet11`, and its `DisplayMember` property to `pub_name` to display the names of publishers. Then create a data grid and set its `DataSource` property to `DataSet11`. In addition, set its `DataMember` property to the data relation object we created, `publisherstitles` (not to the titles table as you might expect), by selecting the `DataMember` property and clicking the plus sign, +, next to the publishers table in the drop-down list to display the `publisherstitles` item.

Finally, we need code to load the two tables into the dataset from the two data adapters, so add this code to the `Form1_Load` event:

```
Private Sub Form1_Load(ByVal sender As System.Object, _
    ByVal e As System.EventArgs) Handles MyBase.Load
    SqlDataAdapter1.Fill(DataSet11)
    SqlDataAdapter2.Fill(DataSet11)
End Sub
```

Now you've connected the list box and data grid using the data relation object, and you can see the results in Figure 17.17. When the user selects a publisher in the list box, the program responds by displaying all the publisher's titles in the data grid—all without the use of any extra SQL.

Summary

Today was a big day in database handling. We worked with databases using Windows controls today, and there was a great deal of ground to cover. We started with the BoundDB example, which illustrated the use of data-bound controls.

Simple-bound controls are those controls that display data from a single field in a record, such as text boxes, check boxes, radio buttons, labels, and buttons. To bind these kinds of controls, you can use the (DataBindings) property at design time. This property lists a few commonly bound properties for each control, such as the Text property for text boxes and labels. You can bind those properties to a data source by selecting a database table and field in that table from the drop-down list that appears.

You can also select the (Advanced) property in the (DataBindings) property entry to bind nearly all properties of a simple-bound control to a data source. This gives you a great deal of control over the behavior of controls using a database, although sometimes it's hard to see why you'd want to bind properties such as TextAlign, WordWrap, and Multiline to data sources. Note that the data type of the property must be the same as the field you're binding to in a data source.

In code, you can set up simple binding using a control's (DataBindings) property, which holds a collection of Binding objects corresponding to the bindings for the control.

Complex-bound controls, on the other hand, can display data from multiple fields at the same time. These controls include combo boxes, list boxes, and data grids, all of which we saw in the BoundDB example.

Complex binding centers on four properties: DataSource (the data source), DataMember (the member you want to work with in a data source; usually a database table), DisplayMember (the field whose data you want the control to display), and ValueMember (the field whose data the control will return in properties such as SelectedValue). We took a close look at using the DisplayMember and ValueMember properties in a list box, displaying the last name of authors in the list box, but passing on the author's ID in code when the user clicked one of those names.

Simple-bound controls can display data from only a single field in a single record at a time, so allowing the user some way to navigate through records becomes important. You let the user navigate through data with methods of the binding context in a Windows form. In particular, you use the form's BindingContext property, which returns an object of the BindingManagerBase class, to set the current record for all controls in the form. The current record in the binding context is the record whose data is displayed in simple-bound controls, and whose data is highlighted in a complex-bound control. You can use the Position property of a BindingManagerBase object to set the current record, and the Count property to determine the total number of records.

We also took a closer look at data grids today. These controls, which excel at data binding, were introduced yesterday, but covered in depth today.

Next, we got acquainted with the Data Form Wizard, which is the tool that Visual Basic uses to create data-entry forms automatically. Using the wizard, we created a data-entry form and dissected its code, seeing how it adds new records, deletes records, cancels edits, and updates the underlying data source.

While working with data-entry forms, we also took a look at validating data in controls in Windows forms by using error providers. An error provider can display a flashing icon next to a control whose data you consider problematic. When the control loses the focus to a control or form whose CausesValidation property is set to True (which is the default), that control's Validating event occurs, and you can check the data in the control in that event's handler. To display an error, you use the error provider's SetError method. Setting the error to an empty string, "", removes the flashing icon. When an error icon is displayed, the icon's tool tip displays the error message you've specified.

We also saw how to work with SQL parameters today. SQL parameters work much like variables in SQL statements, letting you assign values to them without having to rewrite the SQL itself. We saw how to create an SQL parameter, how to assign a value to it at runtime, and how to use the resulting SQL statement with the data in a data source.

Finally, we took a look at establishing connections between tables using data relation objects. Yesterday, we saw how to perform SQL inner joins on tables to create new datasets with records from both tables. Today, we saw how you can use data relation objects to connect the data in tables without using SQL.

That's it for today's work. Tomorrow, we're going to start working databases purely in code, without visual tools.

Q&A

Q I understand that data grids are good for displaying simple tables, but what about hierarchical tables, where each cell can itself contain a table?

A You can also display hierarchical tables in data grids. When you display a hierarchical table in a data grid, fields themselves can display Web-like links to child tables. You can click a link to navigate to a child table (and when a child table is displayed, a back button appears in the caption that can be clicked to navigate back to the parent table).

Q **The tool tip an error icon displays isn't doing it for me—users aren't seeing it, and are only confused by the flashing error icon. Isn't there a better way?**

A It's true that displaying an error's error message in a tool tip might be too subtle for some users. A better option might be to add code to the error provider's `Validating` event handler to display the error message in a message box, or in a label in the form itself, next to the error icon.

Workshop

This workshop tests whether you understand the concepts you saw today. It's a good idea to make sure that you can answer these questions before pressing on to tomorrow's work.

Quiz

1. How do you simple-bind controls at design time?
2. How do you complex-bind controls at design time?
3. What's the difference between a complex-bound control's `DisplayMember` and `ValueMember` properties?
4. How do you navigate to the next record in a dataset bound to controls in a Windows form?
5. How can you create a new, blank record in a dataset bound to the controls in a Windows form?

Quiz Answers

1. You use the `(DataBindings)` property in the Properties window. To bind just about any property to a data source, use the `(Advanced)` property in the `(DataBindings)` entry in the Properties window.
2. You use four properties in complex data binding: `DataSource`, `DataMember`, `DisplayMember`, and `ValueMember`.
3. The `DisplayMember` property is bound to the field you want the control to display, whereas the `ValueMember` property is bound to the field you want the control to return in code using properties such as the `SelectedValue` property. In this way, a complex-bound control can display user-friendly data while passing along code-friendly data after the user makes a selection.
4. You increment the `Position` property of the `BindingManagerBase` object returned by the form's `BindingContext` property. If you try to increment past the last record, the `Position` property will not be incremented.

5. You can use the form's `BindingContext` property, which returns an object of the `BindingManagerBase` class, and call the `AddNew` method of the `BindingManagerBase` object.

Exercises

1. If you have access to the SQL Server pubs database, bind a number of simple-bound controls to the `title` field in the titles table of that database. Also bind some complex-bound controls to that table as well. Finally, add the standard navigation buttons we used today to let the user navigate through the records in that table. If you don't have access to the pubs database, perform the same exercise with another database table.

2. Using the Data Form Wizard, create a data-entry form for the titles table of the pubs database. Rearrange the bound controls in the created data form as you prefer, and use the form to change the data in one record of the titles table to confirm everything is working as it should. If you don't have access to the pubs database, perform the same exercise with another database table.

17

DAY **18**

Handling Databases in Code

There are two main ways of working with databases in Visual Basic .NET. The first way is to use visual tools such as the Server Explorer, Data Adapter Configuration Wizard, and the Query Builder. The second way is to use code. We've taken a look at working with the visual tools already, and today you're going to see how working with databases in code works. The visual tools are great if you're going to be setting everything up at design time, but if you're going to connect to various databases at runtime, you have to do things in code. Some things, such as working with data readers as we'll do today, can't be done with visual tools.

To work with databases in code, you'll have to become familiar with many ADO.NET objects, and we're going to have to wade through them before actually working with databases in our code. Here are the topics we're going to be working with today:

- Connection objects
- Command objects

- Data adapter objects
- Dataset objects
- Data reader objects
- Data table objects
- Data row and column objects
- Data relation objects
- Creating datasets in code
- Creating data connections in code
- Creating command objects in code
- Creating data adapters in code
- Creating data tables in code
- Creating data relation objects in code
- Accessing the data in a table's cells from code
- Using data readers in code

Today's plan is to work directly with ADO.NET objects in Visual Basic code, creating connections, data adapters, data tables, datasets, and more. You'll see how to construct tables from scratch and how to place those tables in datasets. You'll see how to connect to a database by creating our own connection objects, how to place SQL statements in data adapters, and how to execute that SQL in the database.

All this depends on a good knowledge of ADO.NET objects, and we'll cover the objects we'll be using first, taking a look at their properties, methods, and events. For example, the most basic way of working with a database is to load some of its data into a dataset; doing so in code demands a knowledge of connection objects, command objects, and data adapter objects. In particular, to retrieve data from a database, you connect to the database with a connection object, assign that connection object to a command object's `Connection` property, assign the command object to a data adapter object's `SelectCommand` property, and then use the data adapter's `Fill` method to fill a dataset. (That's just an overview, and it skips a few steps such as calling the connection object's `Open` method.) We'll start with an understanding of all those objects, beginning with connection objects.

Using Connection Objects

To move data between a database and your application, you must first have a connection to the database. In ADO.NET, you can create and manage connections using these connection objects:

- OleDbConnection—An object that manages a connection to any data source accessible with the OLE DB protocol.

- SqlConnection—An object that manages a connection to a SQL Server version 7.0 or later. This object is optimized for use with SQL Server 7.0 or later.

- OdbcConnection—An object that manages a connection to a data source created by using an ODBC connection string or ODBC data source name (DSN).

- OracleConnection—An object that manages a connection to Oracle databases.

We'll begin our overview of connection objects with the OleDbConnection class.

Using the OleDbConnection Class

OleDbConnection objects support a connection to an OLE DB data provider. You can use OLE DB connections with many data providers (although note that, depending on the provider, not all properties of an OleDbConnection object can be supported).

Here's how you can establish a connection to a database. You start with a connection string, which holds a string full of attribute/value pairs that hold data needed to log on to a data provider and choose a specific database. These attribute/value pairs are specific to the data provider you're using, and they make up a list of items separated by semicolons. You can either assign a connection string to the connection's ConnectionString property, or you can pass the connection string to the connection object's constructor, like this:

```
Dim ConnectionString As String = "Provider=SQLOLEDB.1;Integrated " & _
"Security=SSPI;Persist Security Info=False;Initial " & _
"Catalog=pubs;Packet Size=4096;Workstation ID=STEVE;" & _
"Use Encryption for Data=False"
Dim Connection1 As OleDbConnection = New OleDbConnection(ConnectionString)
```

That connection string looks pretty arcane. If you have no idea how to create a connection string for a specific data provider, how would you construct one? All you need to do is use the visual tools built in to Visual Basic to build a few sample strings to that data provider, which you can either use directly in code or modify as you need. To do that, you drag a data adapter to a project's main form, which creates both data connection and data adapter objects. After configuring the data adapter using the Data Adapter Configuration Wizard, take a look at the connection object's ConnectionString property in the Properties window.

After you've created a connection object, you can open it with the Open method and assign it to the Connection property of a command object. (To specify the SQL you want to use, you can pass that SQL to the command object's constructor.) Then you can use

18

the command object with a data adapter—for example, you might assign the command object to the SelectCommand property of a data adapter, and you can use the data adapter's Fill method execute that command and fill a dataset. When done with the connection, use its Close method to close it. (The connection won't be closed otherwise, even if the connection object goes out of scope.)

The OleDbDataConnection class represents a connection to an OLE DB data source. Here is the hierarchy of the OleDbDataConnection class:

```
System.Object
    System.MarshalByRefObject
        System.ComponentModel.Component
            System.Data.OleDb.OleDbConnection
```

You can find the significant public properties of OleDbConnection objects in Table 18.1, their significant methods in Table 18.2, and their significant events in Table 18.3.

TABLE 18.1   Significant Public Properties of OleDbConnection Objects

Property	Means
ConnectionString	Returns or sets the connection string to open a database.
ConnectionTimeout	Returns the time to wait trying to make a connection (in seconds).
Database	Returns the name of the database you want to open.
DataSource	Returns the data source (usually the location and file name to open).
Provider	Returns the OLE DB provider's name.
ServerVersion	Returns the version of the of the server.
State	Returns the connection's current state.

TABLE 18.2   Significant Public Methods of OleDbConnection Objects

Method	Means
BeginTransaction	Starts a database transaction.
ChangeDatabase	Changes the current database.
Close	Closes the connection to the data provider.
CreateCommand	Creates an OleDbCommand object for this connection.
GetOleDbSchemaTable	Returns the current schema table.
Open	Opens a database connection.

TABLE 18.3 Significant Public Events of OleDbConnection Objects

Event	Means
InfoMessage	Occurs if the provider sends a message (including warnings).
StateChange	Occurs when a connection's state changes.

Using the SqlConnection Class

SqlConnection objects support a connection to SQL Server databases; these connections are optimized for use with SQL Server. For the most part, the difference between SqlConnection and OleDbConnection objects takes place behind the scenes, and the programming interface of these two types of objects is very similar—although the connection strings will be different. Here's how you might create an SqlConnection object:

```
Dim ConnectionString As String = "workstation id=STEVE;" & _
"packet size=4096;integrated security=SSPI;initial" & _
"catalog=pubs;persist security info=False"
Dim Connection1 As SqlConnection = New SqlConnection(ConnectionString)
```

As far as your code is concerned, the main difference is one of performance—SQL connections to the Microsoft SQL Server are up to 70% faster than OLE DB connections, so if you're using SQL Server, consider using SQL connections for all your connections.

Here is the hierarchy of the SqlConnection class:

```
System.Object
   System.MarshalByRefObject
      System.ComponentModel.Component
         System.Data.SqlClient.SqlConnection
```

The significant public properties, methods, and events of the SqlConnection class are the same as for the OleDbConnection class, except that the SqlConnection class doesn't support the GetOleDbSchema method, but it does support the additional methods you see in Table 18.4.

TABLE 18.4 Additional Significant Public Properties of SqlConnection Objects

Property	Means
PacketSize	Returns the size of communication packets to use (in bytes).
WorkstationId	Returns the database client ID.

Using the OdbcConnection Class

To connect to ODBC databases, you use the ObdcConnection class. ODBC connections are managed by using built-in ODBC drivers in Windows. To create and manage these

18

data sources, you use the OBDC Data Source administrator. (How you open this tool varies by operating system—for example, in Windows 2000, you select the Administrative Tools icon in the control panel, and then open the Data Sources [ODBC] icon.) You can see the OBDC Data Source administrator in Figure 18.1.

FIGURE 18.1

The OBDC Data Source administrator.

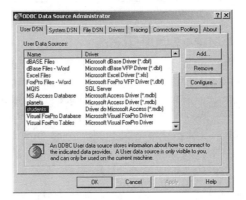

Using the OBDC Data Source administrator, you associate a data source with a data source name, or DSN. The connection strings you use with `ObdcConnection` connection objects specify the DSN name—for example, if you create an ODBC name named students for the students.mdb MS Access database from Day 16, "Handling Databases with ADO.NET," your connection string might look like this (as before, if you need help creating working connection strings, create some connections using the Visual Basic visual tools and take a look at the connection's `ConnectionString` property):

```
Dim ConnectionString As String = "MaxBufferSize=2048;FIL=MSAccess;" & _
"DSN=students;PageTimeout=5;UID=admin;DBQ=C:\students.mdb;DriverId=25" & _
"OdbcConnection1 = New System.Data.Odbc.OdbcConnection(ConnectionString)"
```

Here is the hierarchy for the `ObdcConnection` class:

```
System.Object
   System.MarshalByRefObject
      System.ComponentModel.Component
         System.Data.Odbc.OdbcConnection
```

The significant public properties, methods, and events of the `ObdcConnection` class are the same as for the `OleDbConnection` class, except that the `ObdcConnection` class doesn't support the `GetOleDbSchema` method, and it also supports the additional property you see in Table 18.5.

TABLE 18.5   An Additional Significant Public Property of `OdbcConnection` Objects

Property	Means
Driver	Returns the name of the ODBC driver for the current connection.

Using the `OracleConnection` Class

You can connect to Oracle data sources using `OleDbConnection` objects or `OracleConnection` objects. `OracleConnection` objects are optimized for use with the Oracle data provider. Here's how you might create an `OracleConnection` object and assign a connection string to its `ConnectionString` property:

```
Dim ConnectionString As String = "Provider=SQLOLEDB.1;" & _
Integrated Security=SSPI;Persist Security Info=False;Initial " & _
Catalog=pubs;Packet Size=4096;Workstation " & _
ID=STEVE;Use Encryption for Data=False"
Dim Connection1 As OleDbConnection = New OleDbConnection(ConnectionString)
```

Here is the hierarchy of `OracleConnection` class:

```
System.Object
    System.MarshalByRefObject
        System.ComponentModel.Component
            System.Data.OracleClient.OracleConnection
```

The significant public properties, methods, and events of `OracleConnection` class are the same as for the `OleDbConnection` class, except that the `OracleConnection` class doesn't support the `GetOleDbSchema` method.

Using Command Objects

To work with connection objects, you use command objects because command objects hold the actual SQL you'll use to extract data from a database. To retrieve data from a database, you can create a connection object, open the connection with its `Open` method, and then assign the open connection object to the `Connection` property of a command object.

You can then assign the command object to a command property of a data adapter, such as the `SelectCommand` property (which lets you retrieve rows of data from the database when you call the data adapter's `Fill` method). Besides the `SelectCommand` property, data adapters also support `UpdateCommand`, `InsertCommand`, and `DeleteCommand` properties—each of which take connection objects that perform these various functions.

How do you place the SQL you want to use in a command object? You can either assign that text to the command object's `CommandText` property, or you can pass it to the command object's constructor like this, which selects all the records in the pubs database's authors table:

```
Dim Command1 As OleDbCommand = _
New OleDbCommand("SELECT * FROM authors")
```

18

Now you can set the type of the command—which, for SQL statements, is
`CommandType.Text` (this is the default)—and assign an open connection to the command's `Connection` property to make this `Command` object active:

```
Dim Command1 As OleDbCommand = _
New OleDbCommand("SELECT * FROM authors")

Command1.CommandType = CommandType.Text

Connection1.Open()
Command1.Connection = Connection1
```

Now this command object is ready to go—for example, you can assign it to a data
adapter's `SelectCommand` property so that its SQL will be executed when you call the
data adapter's `Fill` method.

You can also use a command object's built-in methods to execute commands in a database; no data adapter is needed:

- `ExecuteNonQuery`—Executes SQL statements that do not return data rows (such as SQL `INSERT`, `DELELE`, `UPDATE`, and `SET` statements).

- `ExecuteReader`—Executes SQL commands that return rows—but note that this method does *not* return a dataset, it creates a data reader, which is much less powerful. More on data readers later today.

- `ExecuteScalar`—Calculates and returns a single value, such as a sum over various records, from a database.

That provides us with an overview of command objects; let's get familiar with the various command classes available.

Using the `OleDbCommand` Class

The `OleDbCommand` class contains an SQL statement or stored procedure that is executed
in a database supported by an OLE DB data provider. Here is the hierarchy of this class:

```
System.Object
    System.MarshalByRefObject
        System.ComponentModel.Component
            System.Data.OleDb.OleDbCommand
```

You can find the significant public properties of `OleDbCommand` objects in Table 18.6 and
their significant methods in Table 18.7. (This class has no noninherited events.)

TABLE 18.6 Significant Public Properties of `OleDbCommand` Objects

Property	Means
CommandText	Returns or sets the SQL statement or stored procedure for this command to execute.
CommandTimeout	Returns the amount of time to wait trying to execute a command (in seconds).
CommandType	Returns or sets the data type of the `CommandText` property (typically set to `CommandType.Text` for SQL).
Connection	Returns or sets the connection object to use.
DesignTimeVisible	Returns or sets whether the command object should be visible at design time.
Parameters	Returns the command parameters.
Transaction	Returns or sets the transaction that contains the command.
UpdatedRowSource	Returns or sets how results are used in a data row when you use the `Update` method.

TABLE 18.7 Significant Public Methods of `OleDbCommand` Objects

Method	Means
Cancel	Cancels a command.
CreateParameter	Creates a new parameter.
ExecuteNonQuery	Executes a non-row returning SQL statement, returning the number of affected rows.
ExecuteReader	Creates a data reader using the command.
ExecuteScalar	Executes the command and returns the value in the first column in the first row of the result.
Prepare	Creates a compiled version of the command.
ResetCommandTimeout	Resets the timeout value to the default value.

18

Using the `SqlCommand` Class

`SqlCommand` objects are very nearly the same as `OleDbCommand` objects, except that they're designed to be used with SQL connections instead. Here is the hierarchy of he `SqlCommand` class:

```
System.Object
    System.MarshalByRefObject
        System.ComponentModel.Component
            System.Data.SqlClient.SqlCommand
```

The significant public properties and methods of SqlCommand objects are the same as for OleDbCommand objects.

Using the OdbcCommand Class

OdbcCommand objects are also like OleDbCommand objects, but you use them with SQL connections, not OLE DB connections. Here is the hierarchy of the OdbcCommand class:

```
System.Object
   System.MarshalByRefObject
      System.ComponentModel.Component
         System.Data.Odbc.OdbcConnection
```

The significant public properties, methods, and events of OdbcCommand objects are the same as OleDbCommand objects.

Using the OracleCommand Class

In programming terms, OracleCommand objects are just like the other command objects, except that you use them with OracleConnection objects. Here is the hierarchy of the OracleCommand class:

```
System.Object
   System.MarshalByRefObject
      System.ComponentModel.Component
         System.Data.OracleClient.OracleCommand
```

The significant properties, methods, and events of the OracleCommand class are the same as for OleDbCommand objects, except that there is no CommandTimeout property and the OracleCommand class supports the additional methods you see in Table 18.8.

TABLE 18.8 Additional Significant Public Methods of OracleCommand Objects

Method	Means
ExecuteOracleNonQuery	Executes an SQL statement and returns the number of rows affected.
ExecuteOracleScalar	Executes the query and returns the first column of the first row in the result returned by the query as an Oracle-specific data type.

Using Data Adapters

Data adapters work much like bridges between datasets and data sources. As you know, datasets are really just caches of data; they don't maintain a direct connection to a database. OleDbDataAdapter objects connect datasets and data sources by supporting the Fill method to load data from the data source into the dataset and the Update method to send dataset changes you've made back to the data source.

After you've created a data connection and used it to create a command object, you can assign the command object to one of the command properties of the data adapter—`SelectCommand`, `InsertCommand`, `DeleteCommand`, and `UpdateCommand`. (All these command objects are created automatically when you use the Data Adapter Configuration Wizard.) These commands are used as needed by the data adapter; if you only plan to retrieve data from the data source, you only need to assign a command object to the `SelectCommand`.

NEW TERM You can also specify a *table mapping* when creating a data adapter object. By default, the names of the tables in a dataset are the same as they were in the data source. But they can be different from those in the data source, depending on how you've named them in the dataset. A table mapping relates the table names in the data source to the names in the dataset. For example, here's how you might connect the tables in the database to names you've given them in the dataset, where the table named authors will be stored in the table named writers in the dataset:

```
Dim Table1Mappings As New DataTableMappingCollection()
OleDbDataAdapter1.Table1Mappings.Add("authors", "writers")
```

We'll see all this at work in examples later today. Now, let's get familiar with the data adapter classes themselves. Data adapters are based on the `DataAdapter` class, and we'll start there.

Using the `DataAdapter` Class

The `DataAdapter` class is the base class for data adapters, which represent a bridge between a dataset and a database in a data provider. Here is the hierarchy of this class:

```
System.Object
   System.MarshalByRefObject
      System.ComponentModel.Component
         System.Data.Common.DataAdapter
```

You can find the significant public properties of the `DataAdapter` class in Table 18.9 and their significant methods in Table 18.10. (This class has no noninherited events.)

TABLE 18.9   Significant Public Properties of `DataAdapter` Objects

Property	Means
`AcceptChangesDuringFill`	Returns or sets whether the data row's `AcceptChanges` method is called after it is added to a table.
`TableMappings`	Returns the mapping between source tables and data tables.

18

TABLE 18.10   Significant Public Methods of DataAdapter Objects

Method	Means
Fill	Adds or updates rows in a data set to match those in the data source. Creates a table named "Table" by default.
FillSchema	Adds a table named "Table" to the specified DataSet object, making the table's schema match that in the data source.
GetFillParameters	Returns the parameters to use when executing a SELECT statement in SQL.
Update	Updates the data source by calling the INSERT, UPDATE, or DELETE statements for each inserted, updated, or deleted row in the given dataset.

Using the DbDataAdapter Class

The DbDataAdapter class is the base class for the OleDbDataAdapter and SqlDataAdapter classes. Here is the hierarchy of this class:

```
System.Object
    System.MarshalByRefObject
        System.ComponentModel.Component
            System.Data.Common.DataAdapter
                System.Data.Common.DbDataAdapter
```

You can find the significant public methods of DbDataAdapter objects in Table 18.11 and their significant event in Table 18.12. (This class has no noninherited properties.)

TABLE 18.11   Significant Public Methods of DbDataAdapter Objects

Property	Means
Fill	Adds or updates rows in a data set to match those in the data source.
GetFillParameters	Returns the parameters to use when executing an SQL SELECT statement.
Update	Updates the data store by calling the INSERT, UPDATE, or DELETE statements for each inserted, updated, or deleted row in the dataset.

TABLE 18.12   Significant Public Event of DbDataAdapter Objects

Event	Means
FillError	Occurs when an error happens while performing a fill operation.

That's it for the DataAdapter and DbDataAdapter classes; now let's take a look at the data adapter classes you actually use in code, starting with the OleDbDataAdapter class.

Using the `OleDbDataAdapter` Class

The `OleDbDataAdapter` class represents a bridge between a dataset and an OLE DB database. Here is the hierarchy of this class:

```
System.Object
    System.MarshalByRefObject
        System.ComponentModel.Component
            System.Data.Common.DataAdapter
                System.Data.Common.DbDataAdapter
                    System.Data.OleDb.OleDbDataAdapter
```

You can find the significant public properties of `OleDbDataAdapter` objects in Table 18.13, their significant method in Table 18.14, and their significant events in Table 18.15.

TABLE 18.13 Significant Public Properties of `OleDbDataAdapter` Objects

Property	Means
DeleteCommand	Returns or sets the SQL for deleting records.
InsertCommand	Returns or sets the SQL for inserting new records.
SelectCommand	Returns or sets the SQL for selecting records.
UpdateCommand	Returns or sets the SQL for updating records.

TABLE 18.14 Significant Public Method of `OleDbDataAdapter` Objects

Method	Means
Fill	Adds or refreshes rows to a dataset to make them match the rows in a data store.

TABLE 18.15 Significant Public Events of `OleDbDataAdapter` Objects

Event	Means
RowUpdated	Occurs when a row is updated.
RowUpdating	Occurs when a row is being updated.

18

Using the `SqlDataAdapter` Class

The `SqlDataAdapter` class is the data adapter designed especially for use with the SQL Server. Like the `OleDbDataAdapter` class, the `SqlDataAdapter` class includes the `SelectCommand`, `InsertCommand`, `DeleteCommand`, and `UpdateCommand` properties you use for loading and updating data. Here is the hierarchy of this class:

```
System.Object
   System.MarshalByRefObject
      System.ComponentModel.Component
         System.Data.Common.DataAdapter
            System.Data.Common.DbDataAdapter
               System.Data.SqlClient.SqlDataAdapter
```

The significant properties, methods, and events of the `SqlDataAdapter` class are the same as for the `OleDbDataAdapter` class.

Using the `OdbcDataAdapter` Class

You use the `OdbcDataAdapter` class with ODBC connections and command objects. Here is the hierarchy of this class:

```
System.Object
   System.MarshalByRefObject
      System.ComponentModel.Component
         System.Data.Common.DataAdapter
            System.Data.Common.DbDataAdapter
               System.Data.Odbc.OdbcDataAdapter
```

The significant properties, methods, and events of the `SqlDataAdapter` class are the same as for the `OdbcDataAdapter` class.

Using the `OracleDataAdapter` Class

As you might expect, you use the `OracleDataAdapter` class with the Oracle data provider. Here is the hierarchy of this class:

```
System.Object
   System.MarshalByRefObject
      System.ComponentModel.Component
         System.Data.Common.DataAdapter
            System.Data.Common.DbDataAdapter
               System.Data.OracleClient.OracleDataAdapter
```

Like the other data adapters, the significant properties, methods, and events of the `OracleDataAdapter` class are the same as for the `OdbcDataAdapter` class.

Now we've gotten an introduction to connection objects, command objects, and data adapter objects. These objects get the data to our program, but before we can create a working example and display that data, we need somewhere to store it. And that's what datasets are all about.

Using the DataSet Class

As we know, datasets are the caches you can use to store records from a database in ADO.NET. We've worked with datasets in the previous two days, but now it's time to look at them from a programming point of view. Here is the hierarchy of the DataSet class:

```
System.Object
    System.ComponentModel.MarshalByValueComponent
        System.Data.DataSet
```

You can find the significant public properties of DataSet objects in Table 18.16, their significant methods in Table 18.17, and their significant event in Table 18.18.

TABLE 18.16   Significant Public Properties of DataSet Objects

Property	Means
DataSetName	Returns or sets the name of the dataset.
EnforceConstraints	Returns or sets whether constraint rules are enforced.
HasErrors	Indicates if there are errors in any row in any of table.
Relations	Gets relation objects that link tables.
Tables	Returns tables in the dataset.

18

TABLE 18.17   Significant Public Methods of DataSet Objects

Method	Means
AcceptChanges	Accepts (commits) the changes made to the dataset.
Clear	Clears the dataset by removing all rows in all tables.
Copy	Copies the dataset.
GetChanges	Returns a dataset containing all changes made to the current dataset.
GetXml	Returns the data in the dataset in XML.
GetXmlSchema	Returns the XSD schema for the dataset.
HasChanges	Indicates whether the dataset has changes that have not yet been accepted.
Merge	Merges this dataset with another dataset.
ReadXml	Reads data into a dataset from XML.
ReadXmlSchema	Reads an XML schema into a dataset.
RejectChanges	Rolls back the changes made to the dataset since it was created or since the AcceptChanges method was last called.
Reset	Resets the dataset to the original state.
WriteXml	Writes the dataset's schema and data to XML.
WriteXmlSchema	Writes the dataset schema to XML.

TABLE **18.18**   Significant Public Event of `DataSet` Objects

Event	Means
MergeFailed	Occurs when a merge operation fails.

`DataSet` objects can hold a number of database tables, and, accordingly, each `DataSet` object is made up of a collection of DataTable objects, which you can connect to each other with `DataRelation` objects.

As you saw yesterday, you can use a binding context to navigate through the records in a dataset. In particular, you can use a `BindingManagerBase` object's `Position` and `Count` properties to get or set your location in a dataset and the total number of records in the dataset.

If you have bound a dataset to controls in your application, the user can edit the data that appears in those controls. When the user does that, the data in the dataset is also changed—but not the data in the underlying database that the data was originally fetched from. You can determine which rows have been changed with the dataset's `GetChanges` method, and when you use the data adapter's `Update` method, those changes are sent back to the underlying database in the data provider you're working with. That data provider might make some additional changes itself, such as updating fields that hold calculated values, and return a new dataset. If it does, you can merge those new fields into your dataset using the dataset's `Merge` method. Then you can use the `AcceptChanges` method in the dataset to accept the changes or the `RejectChanges` method to cancel the changes.

NEW TERM   In addition, datasets can be *typed* or *untyped*—if they're typed, as they usually are, Visual Basic will keep track of the data type of each field very carefully (and will object if you try to put the wrong type of data in to a field). Typed datasets hold their type information in XML schemas, as you've already seen. XML is the protocol datasets use to transport data, which makes them easy to use on the Internet. To see what a dataset looks like in XML, you can use the dataset `WriteXmlSchema` method to write out the XML schema for a dataset or the `WriteXml` method to write out both the XML schema and the data in the dataset in XML format. You can also use the `ReadXml` method to read data in XML format back into a dataset.

At this point, we've gotten an introduction to all the objects we need to start being able to work with databases in code—and as you can see, there are plenty of objects, properties, methods, and events to get acquainted with. Let's put them to work now in an example that creates its own connection, command, and data adapter objects and creates a dataset in code.

Creating Datasets in Code

The CreateDataSet example in the code for this book creates a connection, data adapter, and dataset, and then binds that dataset to a data grid. This example uses the authors table in the pubs database, and displays that table, as you can see in Figure 18.2.

FIGURE 18.2

The CreateDataSet example.

In this example, we're going to connect to the pubs database to retrieve our data. (In fact, you can also create datasets entirely in code—no outside connection is needed. We'll do that later today when we start creating data tables in our applications.)

18

When the user clicks the Load the Authors Table button you see in Figure 18.2, the code in this example creates a new dataset object named `dataset1` and passes that name to the `DataSet` constructor (passing the name to the constructor means, for example, that Visual Basic will use `"dataset1"` as the name of the XML document element when it converts the dataset into XML):

```
Private Sub Button1_Click(ByVal sender As System.Object, _
    ByVal e As System.EventArgs) Handles Button1.Click
    Dim dataset1 As New DataSet()
    dataset1 = New DataSet("dataset1")
        .
        .
        .
```

Now we'll need a connection object to connect to the authors table. Here's the connection string and connection object in this example (which you'll have to modify if you want to run this example yourself):

```
Private Sub Button1_Click(ByVal sender As System.Object, _
    ByVal e As System.EventArgs) Handles Button1.Click
    Dim dataset1 As New DataSet()
    dataset1 = New DataSet("dataset1")
```

```
Dim ConnectionString As String = "Provider=SQLOLEDB.1;Integrated " & _
    "Security=SSPI;Persist Security Info=False;Initial " & _
    "Catalog=pubs;Packet Size=4096;Workstation ID=STEVE;" & _
    "Use Encryption for Data=False"

Dim Connection1 As OleDbConnection = New OleDbConnection(ConnectionString)
    .
    .
    .
```

Now we have a connection object, and we're working our way up to creating a data adapter to fetch data from the database. First, we have to use the connection object to create a command object, and then we can assign that command object to a data adapter's SelectCommand property to set the SQL that the data adapter will use to fetch data from the database.

Here's how we can create an OleDbCommand object, give it the SQL "SELECT * FROM authors" command and set the command's type to CommandType.Text (which is the value you use for SQL—and which is also the default). Finally, after opening our new connection object, we can assign that connection object to the command object's Connection property:

```
Private Sub Button1_Click(ByVal sender As System.Object, _
    ByVal e As System.EventArgs) Handles Button1.Click
    Dim dataset1 As New DataSet()
    dataset1 = New DataSet("dataset1")

    Dim ConnectionString As String = "Provider=SQLOLEDB.1;Integrated " & _
        "Security=SSPI;Persist Security Info=False;Initial " & _
        "Catalog=pubs;Packet Size=4096;Workstation ID=STEVE;" & _
        "Use Encryption for Data=False"

    Dim Connection1 As OleDbConnection = New OleDbConnection(ConnectionString)

    Dim Command1 As OleDbCommand = _
        New OleDbCommand("SELECT * FROM authors")
    Command1.CommandType = CommandType.Text

    Connection1.Open()
    Command1.Connection = Connection1
        .
        .
        .
```

That's how it works in Visual Basic—you assign a Connection object to a command's Connection property before you use that command. Now we're ready to create our data adapter.

To get the authors table from the database, we can create an `OleDbDataAdapter` object and assign our command object to that adapter's `SelectCommand` property. This will execute the SQL in that command object when you call the data adapter's `Fill` method. Because we haven't created any tables in the new dataset object yet, and because we haven't set up any particular table mappings for the data adapter to use, we must specify what table in the dataset we want to store data in. We do that by passing the name `"authors"` to the `Fill` method. The last step is to bind the filled dataset to the data grid you see in Figure 18.2:

```
Private Sub Button1_Click(ByVal sender As System.Object, _
    ByVal e As System.EventArgs) Handles Button1.Click
    Dim dataset1 As New DataSet()
    dataset1 = New DataSet("dataset1")

    Dim ConnectionString As String = "Provider=SQLOLEDB.1;Integrated " & _
        "Security=SSPI;Persist Security Info=False;Initial " & _
        "Catalog=pubs;Packet Size=4096;Workstation ID=STEVE;" & _
        "Use Encryption for Data=False"

    Dim Connection1 As OleDbConnection = New OleDbConnection(ConnectionString)

    Dim Command1 As OleDbCommand = _
        New OleDbCommand("SELECT * FROM authors")
    Command1.CommandType = CommandType.Text

    Connection1.Open()
    Command1.Connection = Connection1

    Dim OleDbDataAdapter1 As OleDbDataAdapter = New OleDbDataAdapter()

    OleDbDataAdapter1.SelectCommand = Command1
    OleDbDataAdapter1.Fill(dataset1, "authors")

    DataGrid1.SetDataBinding(dataset1, "authors")
End Sub
```

18

And that's it—now we've connected to a database. You can see the results in Figure 18.2, where the authors table appears in the data grid.

Filling a DataSet with Your Own Data (No Data Source Needed)

On the other hand, you don't need to connect to any external data source, as we've done here, to create a dataset. You can create your own data tables and fill them with your own data instead of fetching them from a data provider. To do that, we'll start by getting introduced to the `DataTable` class. After we get the `DataTable` class under our belts, we'll be able to create our own data table, fill it with our own data in code, and store it in a dataset in the CreateDataTable example, which you can see at work in Figure 18.3.

FIGURE 18.3

The CreateDataTable example.

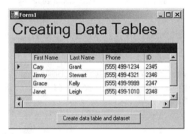

Using the `DataTable` Class

The `DataTable` class represents a table of data, and datasets are made up of collections of such tables. Here is the hierarchy of the `DataTable` class:

```
System.Object
    System.ComponentModel.MarshalByValueComponent
        System.Data.DataTable
```

You can find the significant public properties of `DataTable` objects in Table 18.19, their significant methods in Table 18.20, and their significant events in Table 18.21.

TABLE 18.19   Significant Public Properties of `DataTable` Objects

Property	Means
ChildRelations	Returns the child relations for this table.
Columns	Returns columns in this table.
Constraints	Returns constraints for this table.
DataSet	Returns the dataset this table belongs to.
HasErrors	Indicates if there are errors in any of the rows in the table.
MinimumCapacity	Returns or sets the table's starting size.
ParentRelations	Returns the parent relations for this table.
PrimaryKey	Returns or sets the columns that act as primary keys.
Rows	Returns the rows in this table.
TableName	Returns or sets the name of the table.

TABLE 18.20   Significant Public Methods of `DataTable` Objects

Method	Means
AcceptChanges	Accepts (commits) the changes made to the table.
Clear	Clears the data in the table.
Copy	Copies the table.
GetChanges	Returns a copy of the table with all changes made to it since the `AcceptChanges` method was last called.
GetErrors	Returns the rows that contain errors.
ImportRow	Copies a row into a table.
LoadDataRow	Finds and updates a row; if the row can't be found, a new row is created.
NewRow	Creates a new, empty row, with all the fields that each row in the table has.
RejectChanges	Rolls back the changes made to the table since it was created or since the `AcceptChanges` method was called.
Select	Returns an array of rows.

TABLE 18.21   Significant Public Events of `DataTable` Objects

Event	Means
ColumnChanged	Occurs after a value in a column was changed.
ColumnChanging	Occurs when a column's value is being changed.
RowChanged	Occurs after a row has been changed.
RowChanging	Occurs when a row is being changed.
RowDeleted	Occurs after a row was deleted.
RowDeleting	Occurs when a row is about to be deleted.

18

In the CreateDataTable example in the code for this book, we'll create our own data table and install it in a dataset. We begin by creating a new `DataTable` object when the user clicks the Create Data Table and Dataset button you see in Figure 18.3—note also that we pass the name of this new table, `"Customers"`, to the `DataTable` constructor:

```
Private Sub Button1_Click(ByVal sender As System.Object, _
    ByVal e As System.EventArgs) Handles Button1.Click
    Dim Table1 As DataTable
    Table1 = New DataTable("Customers")
    .
    .
    .
```

The next step in constructing our data table is to set up the columns in the table, which sets the fields in each record. In this case, we'll add first name, last name, phone number, and ID fields to each customer's record. To do that, we'll need to create objects of the DataColumn class.

Using the DataColumn Class

DataColumn objects represent the columns—that is, the fields—in a data table. Here is the hierarchy of the DataColumn class:

```
System.Object
    System.ComponentModel.MarshalByValueComponent
        System.Data.DataColumn
```

You can find the significant public properties of DataColumn objects in Table 18.22. (This class has no significant noninherited methods or events.)

TABLE 18.22 Significant Public Properties of DataColumn Objects

Property	Means
AllowDBNull	Returns or sets whether null values are allowed.
AutoIncrement	Returns or sets whether the column automatically increments the column's value when new rows are added to the table.
AutoIncrementSeed	Returns or sets the starting value for an autoincrement column.
AutoIncrementStep	Returns or sets the increment for an autoincrement column.
Caption	Returns or sets the caption for the column.
ColumnName	Returns or sets the name of the column.
DataType	Returns or sets the type of data in the column.
DefaultValue	Returns or sets the default value for the column (used in new rows).
Expression	Returns or sets an expression used to calculate values, create aggregate values, and so on.
MaxLength	Returns or sets the maximum length of a text column.
Ordinal	Returns the position of the column in the Columns collection.
ReadOnly	Returns or sets whether the column is read-only.
Table	Returns the table to which the column belongs.
Unique	Returns or sets whether the values in this column must be unique.

When you create a column in a data table, you give that column a name (you can do that by passing the name to the DataColumn constructor) and set the column's data type (you can do that with the DataType property). After creating a column, we can add it to our data table's Columns collection. In the CreateDataTable example, we'll add first name, last name, phone number, and ID fields to each customer's record like this:

```
Private Sub Button1_Click(ByVal sender As System.Object, _
    ByVal e As System.EventArgs) Handles Button1.Click
    Dim Table1 As DataTable
    Table1 = New DataTable("Customers")

    Dim FirstName As DataColumn = New DataColumn("First Name")
    FirstName.DataType = System.Type.GetType("System.String")
    Table1.Columns.Add(FirstName)

    Dim LastName As DataColumn = New DataColumn("Last Name")
    LastName.DataType = System.Type.GetType("System.String")
    Table1.Columns.Add(LastName)

    Dim Phone As DataColumn = New DataColumn("Phone")
    Phone.DataType = System.Type.GetType("System.String")
    Table1.Columns.Add(Phone)

    Dim ID As DataColumn = New DataColumn("ID")
    ID.DataType = System.Type.GetType("System.Int32")
    Table1.Columns.Add(ID)
    .
    .
    .
```

The next step is to create the actual rows of data that will go into our data table, and you do that with objects of the DataRow class.

Using the DataRow Class

You use DataRow objects to get access to, insert, delete, and update the records in a table. Here is the hierarchy of this class:

```
System.Object
    System.Data.DataRow
```

You can find the significant public properties of DataRow objects in Table 18.23, and their significant methods in Table 18.24. (This class has no noninherited events.)

TABLE 18.23 Significant Public Properties of DataRow Objects

Property	Means
HasErrors	Indicates whether there are errors in the row.
Item	Returns or sets data in a specified column.
ItemArray	Returns or sets all the data in a row.
RowError	Returns or sets a row's error description.
RowState	Returns the current state of a row.
Table	Returns the table that contains this row.

18

TABLE 18.24   Significant Public Methods of `DataRow` Objects

Method	Means
AcceptChanges	Accepts (commits) the changes made to the row.
BeginEdit	Begins an edit operation.
CancelEdit	Cancels the current edit operation.
ClearErrors	Clears the errors in the row.
Delete	Deletes the row.
EndEdit	Ends the current edit operation.
GetChildRows	Returns the row's child rows.
GetColumnError	Returns a column's error description.
GetColumnsInError	Returns the columns that have errors.
GetParentRow	Returns the parent row of a row.
GetParentRows	Returns the parent rows of a row.
IsNull	Indicates whether a column contains a null value.
RejectChanges	Rolls back the changes made to the table since it was created or since the `AcceptChanges` method was called.
SetColumnError	Sets a column's error description.
SetParentRow	Sets the parent row of a row.

To create `DataRow` objects, you can use the `NewRow` method of a `DataTable` object, which creates rows with all the fields you've already set up for that table. After you've stored the data you want in the row, you can add it to a data table with the `Add` method of the table's `Rows` collection.

Here's how we create the four new records you see in Figure 18.3 in the CreateDataTable example and add data to them:

```
Private Sub Button1_Click(ByVal sender As System.Object, _
    ByVal e As System.EventArgs) Handles Button1.Click
    Dim Table1 As DataTable
    Dim Row1, Row2, Row3, Row4 As DataRow
    Table1 = New DataTable("Customers")

    Dim FirstName As DataColumn = New DataColumn("First Name")
    FirstName.DataType = System.Type.GetType("System.String")
    Table1.Columns.Add(FirstName)

    Dim LastName As DataColumn = New DataColumn("Last Name")
    LastName.DataType = System.Type.GetType("System.String")
    Table1.Columns.Add(LastName)
```

```
Dim Phone As DataColumn = New DataColumn("Phone")
Phone.DataType = System.Type.GetType("System.String")
Table1.Columns.Add(Phone)

Dim ID As DataColumn = New DataColumn("ID")
ID.DataType = System.Type.GetType("System.Int32")
Table1.Columns.Add(ID)

Row1 = Table1.NewRow()

Row1("First Name") = "Cary"
Row1("Last Name") = "Grant"
Row1("Phone") = "(555) 499-1234"
Row1("ID") = 2345

Table1.Rows.Add(Row1)

Row2 = Table1.NewRow()

Row2("First Name") = "Jimmy"
Row2("Last Name") = "Stewart"
Row2("Phone") = "(555) 499-4321"
Row2("ID") = 2346

Table1.Rows.Add(Row2)

Row3 = Table1.NewRow()

Row3("First Name") = "Grace"
Row3("Last Name") = "Kelly"
Row3("Phone") = "(555) 499-9999"
Row3("ID") = 2347

Table1.Rows.Add(Row3)

Row4 = Table1.NewRow()

Row4("First Name") = "Janet"
Row4("Last Name") = "Leigh"
Row4("Phone") = "(555) 499-1010"
Row4("ID") = 2348

Table1.Rows.Add(Row4)

Dim dataset1 As New DataSet
dataset1 = New DataSet
dataset1.Tables.Add(Table1)
DataGrid1.SetDataBinding(dataset1, "Customers")
End Sub
```

18

Note that at the end of this code, we create a new dataset and use the Add method of the dataset's Tables collection to add the new table to the dataset. Then we bind the new dataset to a data grid, as you see in Figure 18.3. And that's it—you've created a new data table, filled it with your own data, and displayed that data in a data grid.

At this point, we've created our own data tables. How about taking the next step and relating tables by creating data relation objects in code? That's coming up next.

Creating a Data Relation in Code

Yesterday, the DataRelationDB example used the publishers and titles tables in the pubs database and related them through the pub_id key in a master/child relationship. The code displayed publishers' names in the list box you saw in Figure 17.17 (the "master" part), and when the user selected a publisher, the program displayed that publisher's books were displayed in a data grid (the "detail" part). To create that example, we visually created a data relation object using the XML schema for the dataset in the example. Today, we'll see how to get the same result by creating a DataRelation object in code, in the CreateDataRelation example that you see at work in Figure 18.4 (compare that figure to Figure 17.17).

FIGURE **18.4**

The
CreateDataRelation
example.

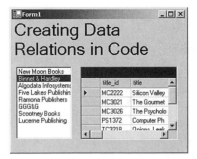

As they stand, datasets just hold your data in tables—they don't know anything about the relations between those tables. To set up those relations, you use DataRelation objects, which relate tables together using DataColumn objects. You can access the DataRelation objects in a dataset with the dataset's Relations property. Here is the hierarchy of the DataRelation class:

```
System.Object
    System.Data.DataRelation
```

You can find the significant public properties of DataRelation objects in Table 18.25. (This class has no significant noninherited methods or events.)

TABLE 18.25 Significant Public Properties of `DataRelation` Objects

Property	Means
ChildColumns	Returns the child column objects for the relation.
ChildTable	Returns the child table of this relation.
DataSet	Returns the dataset the relation is contained in.
ParentColumns	Returns the parent column objects for the relation.
ParentTable	Returns the parent table for the relation.
RelationName	Returns or sets the name of the relation.

To create the CreateDataRelation example you see at work in Figure 18.4, first add an
SQL data adapter, `SqlDataAdapter1`, to a Windows application's main form that will
return the pubs database's publishers table, and another data adapter, `SqlDataAdapter2`,
that will return the titles table. Then generate a new dataset, `DataSet11`, containing both
tables. When the main form loads, we can fill the dataset from the data adapters like this:

```
Private Sub Form1_Load(ByVal sender As System.Object, _
    ByVal e As System.EventArgs) Handles MyBase.Load
    DataSet11.Clear()
    SqlDataAdapter1.Fill(DataSet11)
    SqlDataAdapter2.Fill(DataSet11)
    .
    .
    .
```

18

Now add the list box and data grid we'll need and bind the list box to the `pub_name` field
in the publishers table in `DataSet11`. We'll need two `DataColumn` objects to create our
data relation and relate the publishers and titles tables. These `DataColumn` objects correspond to the `pub_id` column from both those tables, and here's how we create those
objects in code:

```
Private Sub Form1_Load(ByVal sender As System.Object, _
    ByVal e As System.EventArgs) Handles MyBase.Load
    DataSet11.Clear()
    SqlDataAdapter1.Fill(DataSet11)
    SqlDataAdapter2.Fill(DataSet11)

    Dim colPublishers As DataColumn
    Dim colTitles As DataColumn

    colPublishers = DataSet11.Tables("publishers").Columns("pub_id")
    colTitles = DataSet11.Tables("titles").Columns("pub_id")
    .
    .
    .
```

Finally, we can create the new data relation by passing the name of the data relation—we'll use the name `publisherstitles` as we did yesterday—and the two column objects to the `DataRelation` constructor. Then, to install this new data relation in the dataset, we will use the `Add` method of the dataset's `Relations` collection, and finally we bind the new data relation to the data grid like this:

```
Private Sub Form1_Load(ByVal sender As System.Object, _
    ByVal e As System.EventArgs) Handles MyBase.Load
    DataSet11.Clear()
    SqlDataAdapter1.Fill(DataSet11)
    SqlDataAdapter2.Fill(DataSet11)

    Dim colPublishers As DataColumn
    Dim colTitles As DataColumn

    colPublishers = DataSet11.Tables("publishers").Columns("pub_id")
    colTitles = DataSet11.Tables("titles").Columns("pub_id")

    Dim publisherstitles As DataRelation
    publisherstitles = New DataRelation("publisherstitles", colPublishers, _
        colTitles)

    DataSet11.Relations.Add(publisherstitles)
    DataGrid1.SetDataBinding(DataSet11, "publishers.publisherstitles")
End Sub
```

And that's all it takes to create and use a data relation in code. You can see the results in Figure 18.4, where our new data relation object has connected the data in the list box to the data grid—when the user clicks the name of a publisher, that publisher's titles appear in the data grid.

We're now considerably fluent with databases, but there's one crucial topic that we have yet to cover—how to read the data in the individual cells of a table.

Reading the Data in a Table's Cells in Code

To work with the data in a table in code, you must be able to access the data in the table's cells. We'll see how that works in the ReadFields example in the code for this book, which you see at work in Figure 18.5. This example reads the entire authors table, including the name of each column, and displays it in the multiline text boxes you see in the figure.

To follow along, create a new Windows application named ReadFields and create an SQL data adapter connected to the authors table in the pubs database. Then generate a new dataset, `DataSet11`, that holds the authors table as supplied by that data adapter.

FIGURE 18.5

The ReadFields example.

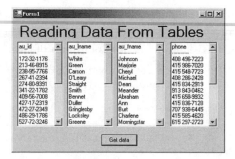

Next, add the multiline text boxes—TextBox1 to TextBox4 that we'll use to display data from the first four fields (au_id, au_lname, au_fname, and phone) in the authors table—and the Get Data button as you see in Figure 18.5.

When the user clicks the Get Data button, we can fill the dataset from the data adapter. Then the next step is to display the name of each column in the multiline text boxes, as you see in Figure 18.5. How do you get that name? We can access the authors table in the dataset as DataSet11.Tables("authors"). This table has a Columns collection that holds the columns in this table, and we can use the ColumnName property to get the name of each column and display those names in the text boxes like this:

```
Private Sub Button1_Click(ByVal sender As System.Object, _
    ByVal e As System.EventArgs) Handles Button1.Click
    DataSet11.Clear()
    SqlDataAdapter1.Fill(DataSet11)

    TextBox1.Text &= DataSet11.Tables("authors").Columns(0).ColumnName & _
        ControlChars.CrLf
    TextBox2.Text &= DataSet11.Tables("authors").Columns(1).ColumnName & _
        ControlChars.CrLf
    TextBox3.Text &= DataSet11.Tables("authors").Columns(2).ColumnName & _
        ControlChars.CrLf
    TextBox4.Text &= DataSet11.Tables("authors").Columns(3).ColumnName & _
        ControlChars.CrLf

    TextBox1.Text &= "------------" & ControlChars.CrLf
    TextBox2.Text &= "------------" & ControlChars.CrLf
    TextBox3.Text &= "------------" & ControlChars.CrLf
    TextBox4.Text &= "------------" & ControlChars.CrLf
        .
        .
        .
```

Now let's get the actual data from the cells in the table. To do that, we can access the individual rows in the table using the table's Rows collection. To access an item in a column in a row, you use the Item property like this:

18

DataSet11.Tables("authors").Rows(0).Item(0), which returns the value of the first field in the first row in the authors table. Here's how we can loop over the records in the authors table, displaying the data from the first four fields of each record:

```
Private Sub Button1_Click(ByVal sender As System.Object, _
    ByVal e As System.EventArgs) Handles Button1.Click
    DataSet11.Clear()
    SqlDataAdapter1.Fill(DataSet11)

    TextBox1.Text &= DataSet11.Tables("authors").Columns(0).ColumnName & _
        ControlChars.CrLf
    TextBox2.Text &= DataSet11.Tables("authors").Columns(1).ColumnName & _
        ControlChars.CrLf          '
    TextBox3.Text &= DataSet11.Tables("authors").Columns(2).ColumnName & _
        ControlChars.CrLf
    TextBox4.Text &= DataSet11.Tables("authors").Columns(3).ColumnName & _
        ControlChars.CrLf

    TextBox1.Text &= "------------" & ControlChars.CrLf
    TextBox2.Text &= "------------" & ControlChars.CrLf
    TextBox3.Text &= "------------" & ControlChars.CrLf
    TextBox4.Text &= "------------" & ControlChars.CrLf

    For RowLoopIndex As Integer = 0 To _
        (DataSet11.Tables("authors").Rows.Count - 1)
        TextBox1.Text &= DataSet11.Tables("authors").Rows( _
            RowLoopIndex).Item(0) & ControlChars.CrLf
    Next RowLoopIndex

    For RowLoopIndex As Integer = 0 To _
        (DataSet11.Tables("authors").Rows.Count - 1)
        TextBox2.Text &= DataSet11.Tables("authors").Rows(_
            RowLoopIndex).Item(1) & ControlChars.CrLf
    Next RowLoopIndex

    For RowLoopIndex As Integer = 0 To _
        (DataSet11.Tables("authors").Rows.Count - 1)
        TextBox3.Text &= DataSet11.Tables("authors").Rows(_
            RowLoopIndex).Item(2) & ControlChars.CrLf
    Next RowLoopIndex

    For RowLoopIndex As Integer = 0 To _
        (DataSet11.Tables("authors").Rows.Count - 1)
        TextBox4.Text &= DataSet11.Tables("authors").Rows(_
            RowLoopIndex).Item(3) & ControlChars.CrLf
    Next RowLoopIndex
End Sub
```

And that's what it takes to create the display you see in Figure 18.5. Now we're accessing the data from the individual cells in a data table.

Here's something else to know—you can access the data in the fields of a data row either by numeric index or by name, and you can abbreviate expressions by eliminating the keyword Item. For example, if you're working with a row of data named Row1, and the au_fname field is the third field in the row, all these statements are equivalent:

```
Dim strFirstName As String = Row1.Item("au_fname")
Dim strFirstName As String = Row1("au_fname")
Dim strFirstName As String = Row1.Item(2)
Dim strFirstName As String = Row1(2)
```

ADO.NET also supports data readers, and they're the last topic we'll take a look at today.

Using Data Readers

Data readers are designed to give you fast, low-level access to data. They let you read record after record, going forward in the database only. To see how to use data readers, take a look at the CreateDataReader example in the code for this book. When the user clicks the Get Data button in that example, the program uses a data reader to read the data in the authors table in the pubs database, as you see in Figure 18.6.

FIGURE 18.6

The CreateDataReader example.

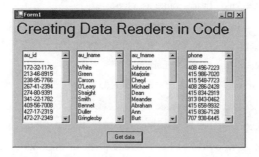

To work with data readers, we'll start by getting an introduction to the available data reader classes—OleDbDataReader, SqlDataReader, OdbcDataReader, and OracleDataReader.

Using the **OleDbDataReader** Class

The OleDbDataReader class creates a data reader for use with an OLE DB data provider. Here is the hierarchy of the OleDbDataReader class:

```
System.Object
   System.MarshalByRefObject
      System.Data.OleDb.OleDbDataReader
```

You can find the significant public properties of OleDbDataReader objects in Table 18.26 and their significant methods in Table 18.27. (This class has no noninherited events.)

TABLE 18.26   Significant Public Properties of OleDbDataReader Objects

Property	Means
Depth	Returns the current row's nesting depth.
FieldCount	Returns the number of columns in the current row.
IsClosed	Indicates whether a data reader is closed.
Item	Returns the value in a field.
RecordsAffected	Returns the number of rows changed, inserted, or deleted by an SQL statement.

TABLE 18.27   Significant Public Methods of OleDbDataReader Objects

Method	Means
Close	Closes the data reader.
GetBoolean	Returns a field's value as a Boolean.
GetByte	Returns a field's value as a byte.
GetBytes	Reads a stream of bytes.
GetChar	Returns a field's value as a character.
GetChars	Reads a stream of characters.
GetDataTypeName	Returns the name of the source data type.
GetDateTime	Returns a field's value as a DateTime object.
GetDecimal	Returns a field's value as a Decimal object.
GetDouble	Returns a field's value as a double-precision floating point number.
GetFieldType	Returns the Type that is the data type of the object.
GetFloat	Returns a field's value as a single-precision floating point number.
GetGuid	Returns a field's value as a globally-unique identifier (GUID).
GetInt16	Returns a field's value as a 16-bit signed integer.
GetInt32	Returns a field's value as a 32-bit signed integer.
GetInt64	Returns a field's value as a 64-bit signed integer.
GetName	Returns the name of the specified column.
GetOrdinal	Returns the column ordinal, given the name of the column.
GetSchemaTable	Returns a schema.
GetString	Returns a field's value as a string.

TABLE 18.27   continued

Method	Means
GetValue	Returns the value of the column in its original format.
GetValues	Returns all the attribute columns in the current row.
IsDBNull	Indicates whether a column contains nonexistent (or missing) values.
Read	Advances the data reader to the next record and reads that record.

Using the `SqlDataReader` Class

The `SqlDataReader` class creates a data reader for use with the SQL Server. Here is the hierarchy of this class:

```
System.Object
    System.MarshalByRefObject
        System.Data.SqlClient.SqlDataReader
```

The `SqlDataReader` class has the same significant public properties and methods as the `OleDbDataReader` class, with the additional significant methods you see in Table 18.28.

TABLE 18.28   Additional Significant Public Methods of `SqlDataReader` Objects

Method	Means
GetSqlBinary	Returns a field's value as a `SqlBinary`.
GetSqlByte	Returns a field's value as a `SqlByte`.
GetSqlDateTime	Returns a field's value as a `SqlDateTime`.
GetSqlDecimal	Returns a field's value as a `SqlDecimal`.
GetSqlDouble	Returns a field's value as a `SqlDouble`.
GetSqlGuid	Returns a field's value as a `SqlGuid`.
GetSqlInt16	Returns a field's value as a `SqlInt16`.
GetSqlInt32	Returns a field's value as a `SqlInt32`.
GetSqlInt64	Returns a field's value as a `SqlInt64`.
GetSqlMoney	Returns a field's value as a `SqlMoney`.
GetSqlSingle	Returns a field's value as a `SqlSingle`.
GetSqlString	Returns a field's value as a `SqlString`.
GetSqlValue	Returns an object of `SqlDbType` Variant.
GetSqlValues	Returns all the attribute columns in the current row.

18

Using the `OdbcDataReader` Class

The `OdbcDataReader` class lets you create a data reader for use with an ODBC data provider. Here's the hierarchy of this class:

```
System.Object
   System.MarshalByRefObject
      System.Data.Odbc.OdbcDataReader
```

The `OdbcDataReader` class has the same significant public properties and methods as the `OleDbDataReader` class.

Using the `OracleDataReader` Class

The `OracleDataReader` class lets you create a data reader for use with the Oracle data provider. Here's the hierarchy of this class:

```
System.Object
   System.MarshalByRefObject
      System.Data.OracleClient.OracleDataReader
```

The `OracleDataReader` class has the same significant public properties and methods as the `OleDbDataReader` class, with the additional significant methods you see in Table 18.29.

TABLE 18.29   Additional Significant Public Methods of `OracleDataReader` Objects

Method	Means
GetOracleBFile	Returns the value of the given column as an `OracleBFile` object.
GetOracleBinary	Returns the value of the given column as an `OracleBinary` object.
GetOracleDateTime	Returns the value of the given column as an `OracleDateTime` object.
GetOracleLob	Returns the value of the given column as an `OracleLob` object.
GetOracleMonthSpan	Returns the value of the given column as an `OracleMonthSpan` object.
GetOracleNumber	Returns the value of the given column as an `OracleNumber` object.
GetOracleString	Returns the value of the given column as an `OracleString` object.
GetOracleTimeSpan	Returns the value of the given column as an `OracleTimeSpan` object.
GetOracleValue	Returns the value of a column at the given location in Oracle format.
GetOracleValues	Returns all the attribute columns in the current row in Oracle format.

Creating Data Readers in Code

There is no data reader control in the Visual Basic toolbox—you can only create data readers in code. To create a data reader, you can use the `ExecuteReader` method of a command object. Here's how the CreateDataReader example creates an OLE DB data reader for the authors table when the user clicks the Get Data button you see in Figure 18.6:

```
Private Sub Button1_Click(ByVal sender As System.Object, _
    ByVal e As System.EventArgs) Handles Button1.Click
    Dim Connection1String As New String( _
        "Provider=SQLOLEDB;Data Source=;User ID=sa;Initial Catalog=pubs;")
    Dim Connection1 As New OleDbConnection(Connection1String)

    Dim Command1 As New OleDbCommand("SELECT * FROM authors", Connection1)

    Connection1.Open()

    Dim Reader1 As OleDbDataReader = _
        Command1.ExecuteReader(CommandBehavior.CloseConnection)
        .
        .
        .
```

To determine the names of the columns of the authors table, you can use the data reader's `GetSchemaTable` method, and you can recover and display the name of each column this way:

```
Private Sub Button1_Click(ByVal sender As System.Object, _
    ByVal e As System.EventArgs) Handles Button1.Click
    Dim Connection1String As New String( _
        "Provider=SQLOLEDB;Data Source=;User ID=sa;Initial Catalog=pubs;")
    Dim Connection1 As New OleDbConnection(Connection1String)

    Dim Command1 As New OleDbCommand("SELECT * from AUTHORS", Connection1)

    Connection1.Open()

    Dim Reader1 As OleDbDataReader = _
        Command1.ExecuteReader(CommandBehavior.CloseConnection)

    Dim schemaTable As DataTable = Reader1.GetSchemaTable()

    TextBox1.Text &= schemaTable.Rows(0).Item(0).ToString() & ControlChars.CrLf
    TextBox2.Text &= schemaTable.Rows(1).Item(0).ToString() & ControlChars.CrLf
    TextBox3.Text &= schemaTable.Rows(2).Item(0).ToString() & ControlChars.CrLf
    TextBox4.Text &= schemaTable.Rows(3).Item(0).ToString() & ControlChars.CrLf

    TextBox1.Text &= "--------------" & ControlChars.CrLf
    TextBox2.Text &= "--------------" & ControlChars.CrLf
    TextBox3.Text &= "--------------" & ControlChars.CrLf
    TextBox4.Text &= "--------------" & ControlChars.CrLf
        .
        .
        .
```

18

All that's left is to recover the actual data from the various records. Data readers just return the fields of a record, one after the next, and you use methods such as

GetBoolean, GetString, and GetDouble to read the actual data from a data reader. If you don't know the data type of the fields in the table you're working with in advance, you can use the XML schema for the table to determine those data types so that you know what data-reading method to use. Here's what that looks like in code, where we're checking for both string and boolean values:

```
Private Sub Button1_Click(ByVal sender As System.Object, _
    ByVal e As System.EventArgs) Handles Button1.Click
    Dim Connection1String As New String( _
        "Provider=SQLOLEDB;Data Source=;User ID=sa;Initial Catalog=pubs;")
    Dim Connection1 As New OleDbConnection(Connection1String)

    Dim Command1 As New OleDbCommand("select * from authors", Connection1)

    Connection1.Open()

    Dim Reader1 As OleDbDataReader = _
        Command1.ExecuteReader(CommandBehavior.CloseConnection)

    Dim schemaTable As DataTable = Reader1.GetSchemaTable()

    TextBox1.Text &= schemaTable.Rows(0).Item(0).ToString() & ControlChars.CrLf
    TextBox2.Text &= schemaTable.Rows(1).Item(0).ToString() & ControlChars.CrLf
    TextBox3.Text &= schemaTable.Rows(2).Item(0).ToString() & ControlChars.CrLf
    TextBox4.Text &= schemaTable.Rows(3).Item(0).ToString() & ControlChars.CrLf

    TextBox1.Text &= "--------------" & ControlChars.CrLf
    TextBox2.Text &= "--------------" & ControlChars.CrLf
    TextBox3.Text &= "--------------" & ControlChars.CrLf
    TextBox4.Text &= "--------------" & ControlChars.CrLf

    While Reader1.Read()
        If schemaTable.Rows(0).Item(5).ToString() = "System.String" Then
            TextBox1.Text &= Reader1.GetString(0) & ControlChars.Tab
        End If
        If schemaTable.Rows(0).Item(5).ToString() = "System.Boolean" Then
            TextBox1.Text &= Reader1.GetBoolean(0).ToString() & ControlChars.Tab
        End If

        If schemaTable.Rows(1).Item(5).ToString() = "System.String" Then
            TextBox2.Text &= Reader1.GetString(1) & ControlChars.Tab
        End If
        If schemaTable.Rows(1).Item(5).ToString() = "System.Boolean" Then
            TextBox2.Text &= Reader1.GetBoolean(1).ToString() & ControlChars.Tab
        End If

        If schemaTable.Rows(2).Item(5).ToString() = "System.String" Then
            TextBox3.Text &= Reader1.GetString(2) & ControlChars.Tab
        End If
```

```
        If schemaTable.Rows(2).Item(5).ToString() = "System.Boolean" Then
            TextBox3.Text &= Reader1.GetBoolean(2).ToString() & ControlChars.Tab
        End If

        If schemaTable.Rows(3).Item(5).ToString() = "System.String" Then
            TextBox4.Text &= Reader1.GetString(3) & ControlChars.Tab
        End If
        If schemaTable.Rows(3).Item(5).ToString() = "System.Boolean" Then
            TextBox4.Text &= Reader1.GetBoolean(3).ToString() & ControlChars.Tab
        End If

        TextBox1.Text &= ControlChars.CrLf
        TextBox2.Text &= ControlChars.CrLf
        TextBox3.Text &= ControlChars.CrLf
        TextBox4.Text &= ControlChars.CrLf
    End While

    Reader1.Close()
    Connection1.Close()

End Sub
```

And that's all it takes—now you're using data readers. You can see the result in Figure 18.6, where the data from the first four fields from the authors table are displayed. And that completes today's work—as you can see, it takes quite a bit of programming to work with databases in code, but when you know how to do it, it's worth the effort.

Summary

Today was another big day in the database-handling world. We took a look at working with databases in code today instead of using the visual tools we used in the previous two days. We went deep into database-handling here, working with the various ADO.NET objects available to us. There are many such objects, and getting an introduction to them was a large part of today's work.

Connection objects support the actual connections to data sources in ADO.NET. You need a Connection object—such as an OleDbConnection, SqlConnection, OdbcConnection or OracleConnection object—to connect to a database. To create a Connection object, you usually use a connection string, which you can pass to the Connection object's constructor or the ConnectionString property. To determine what the connection string should look like for a particular data source, you can use the visual tools in Visual Basic .NET, such as the Data Adapter Configuration Wizard.

Once you have a Connection object, you can use that object's Open method to open the connection and assign that object to the Connection property of a Command object, such as an OleDbCommand, SqlCommand, OdbcCommand, or OracleCommand object. Command objects are where you store the SQL you want to execute in the database, and you can create Command objects that will select data from the data source, insert new records, delete records, and update the database. Each Command object can have a Connection object associated with it. You can set up the SQL in a Command object by passing it to the Command object's constructor or with the Command object's CommandText property. You should also set the Command object's CommandType property to CommandType.Text if you're going to be using an SQL command.

You use the Command objects you've created with data adapter objects. Data adapters are responsible for maintaining your connection to the data source, and you can assign Command objects to a data adapter object's SelectCommand, DeleteCommand, UpdateCommand, and InsertCommand properties. If you just want to use the data adapter to fetch data for you, you only need to use the SelectCommand property.

Once you have a data adapter object, you can use its Fill method to fill a dataset object with data. And once you have a dataset filled with data, you can bind controls such as data grids to them.

You also saw today that you can create DataTable objects yourself to create data tables in datasets—which is also how you create your own datasets entirely in code; no connection to a data source is needed. You pass the name of the table to the DataTable object's constructor, and then use DataColumn objects to configure the fields in the each record.

When you create a data column, you pass the name of the new field to the DataColumn object's constructor and set the data type of the field with the DataColumn object's DataType property. Finally, you add the new column to the DataTable object's Columns collection using the Add method.

To create records in the new table, you use DataRow objects. You can create new rows with all the fields presently in the table using the table object's NewRow method. You can then assign values to the new row's fields by name like this: Row1("Last Name") = "Grant" and Row1("ID") = 2345, making sure that the data you're assigning a field in a row matches that field's data type. After you've configured the data in the new DataRow object, you add it to the table with the table object's Add method of its Rows collection. And you can add the newly created table to a dataset with the Add method of the dataset object's Tables collection.

You also saw how to create data relations in code using a DataRelation object. You pass the name of the data relation you want to create and the two key columns in the tables you want to relate to the DataRelation object's constructor. Then you add the new data relation to the dataset's Relations collection with the Add method. After that, you're free to bind controls to the data relation object, which lets you create master/detail applications as we've seen.

We also took a look at how to access individual data items in the cells of a table from your code today. You saw that you can use a DataRow object's Item property to access the value in a field in a row like this: Row1.Item("au_fname"). And you also saw that the Item property is the default, which means that you can also access the same data as Row1("au_fname").

The final topic we took a look at today concerns data readers. You saw that a data reader simply reads through your data in a forward-only way, supplying you with the data in record after record. We used a data reader to read and display the data in the authors table today.

And that's it for today's work—tomorrow, we're going to start working with data handling on the Web.

Q&A

Q Things are going slow because I need multiple connections to a data source and have to refer back to the original data often. Isn't there some way to improve performance?

A If your application uses a number of connections, you can use *connection pooling* to improve performance. Connection pooling lets you keep a cache of connections without having to create new ones all the time. When you use OLE DB or SQL Server data providers, connection pooling is usually enabled automatically. With SQL Server, make sure that the Pooling attribute in the connection string is set to 'true'.

Q I understand how to loop over all the rows in a single table to display that table's data, as we've done today, but what if I want to display all the data in *all* tables in a dataset?

A You can access all the tables in a dataset with its Tables property, so here's how to display all the data in an entire dataset, table by table, row by row, and column by column:

```
For Each TableObject in DataSet11.Tables
    For Each RowObject In TableObject.Rows
        For Each ColumnObject In TableObject.Columns
            TextBox1.Text &= RowObject(ColumnObject) & ControlChars.Tab _
        Next ColumnObject
        TextBox1.Text &= ControlChars.CrLf
    Next RowObject
Next TableObject
```

By the way, if you're interested, the maximum number of rows a table can have is 16,777,216.

18

Workshop

This workshop tests whether you understand the concepts you saw today. It's a good idea to make sure that you can answer these questions before pressing on to tomorrow's work.

Quiz

1. How do you indicate what data source you want to connect to using a `Connection` object?

2. How do you assign an SQL statement to a `Command` object?

3. How do you associate a `Connection` object with a `Command` object?

4. What four properties do data adapter objects support that you can assign `Command` objects to?

5. How do you add a `DataRow` object to a `DataTable` object?

Quiz Answers

1. You use a connection string specific to the data provider you're using.

2. You can pass the SQL to the `Command` object's constructor or assign it to the `Command` object's `CommandText` property. Don't forget to also set the `Command` object's `CommandType` property to `CommandType.Text`.

3. You assign the `Connection` object to the `Command` object's `Connection` property. Don't forget to call the `Connection` object's `Open` method as well.

4. The `SelectCommand`, `InsertCommand`, `DeleteCommand`, and `UpdateCommand` properties. If you're just getting data from the data source, you only have to use the `SelectCommand` property.

5. You can add a `DataRow` object to a `DataTable` object with the `Add` method of the `DataTable` object's `Rows` collection.

Exercises

1. Create a new Windows application that connects to the publishers table in the pubs database when the user clicks a button and display the data in the publishers table using a data grid. If you don't have access to the pubs database, perform the same exercise with another database table.

2. Create a new Windows application that lets the user enter data in text boxes for a phone book application. Store the data in a dataset (in other words, create your own `DataTable` object and add it to the `Tables` collection in a `DataSet` object) and let the user navigate through those records with navigation buttons. (**Extra credit**: To save the user's data to disk, use the `DataSet` method `WriteXml`, and then use the `ReadXml`.

DAY 19

Using Databases in Web Applications

Today, we're going to finish off our database work by taking a look at handling databases in Web applications. There are many similarities here to working with databases in Windows applications—when you connect to a database in a Web application, the connection is made in your Visual Basic code in the server, so much of what we've seen in the previous three days applies here too.

On the other hand, we're going to see that there are plenty of differences from Windows database handling here. For example, the controls in Web applications work in the browser, which means that they don't maintain a continual connection to a dataset. This means that you're responsible for refreshing that binding each time the Web page is sent back to the server. And Web forms don't maintain a binding context, which is going to make it trickier to do things such as navigate through a set of records.

Other differences exist as well—there are special data-oriented Web server controls that have no Windows counterpart, for example, and even the properties you use for complex binding are different. Even so, we're going to master all these issues today, allowing us to work with databases in Web applications as proficiently as in Windows applications. Here's an overview of our topics:

- Connecting to databases in Web applications
- Supporting simple and complex data binding
- Binding standard Web controls
- Navigating in datasets in Web applications
- Creating data grids
- Creating data lists
- Creating repeaters
- Creating master-detail Web data forms
- Binding to databases locally in Internet Explorer

One of the differences we're going to encounter today is that logging into a database provider such as SQL Server is a little different in Web applications than it is in Windows applications. In the Windows applications we've been using up to this point, we've been using Windows integrated security to connect to SQL Server, where the security credentials of the user are automatically sent to the data provider.

By default, however, that's not going to work in Web applications. You actually can set up Web applications so that the user's Windows credentials are passed to your Web applications. But even if you do, it means that all users must be have the same domain name, which isn't going to work if you're granting public access to a Web application. And it also means that you must edit the Web.config file for every one of your applications, as well as reconfigure IIS and SQL Server internally.

One way of getting around this issue is to ask the user for her credentials—that is, a username and password to be passed to the data provider—and include that information in the connection string you send to the data provider. That's not going to be a viable solution when you give general access to the public, however, because they're not going to have such credentials. And it's usually not a good idea to hard-code usernames and passwords into your code.

In other words, the problem is that if you grant general public access on the Web to your data-enabled Web applications, you lack a qualified user to log in to the data provider. One way to solve this problem is to treat the Web application *itself* as a qualified user. Web applications operate with the username "ASPNET" when they run, and if you can treat ASPNET as a qualified user and maintain your security, you've solved this problem.

Treating ASPNET as a qualified user means creating an account for ASPNET in the data provider. If the data provider and IIS are on the same machine, you can even use

Windows integrated security to log ASPNET into the data provider, which is how we'll do things today. In SQL Server, you simply create a login name of *computername*\ASP-NET, where *computername* is the name of your computer.

Tip

> There are a number of ways—supporting varying levels of security—to connect to SQL Server from ASP.NET applications, including connecting to SQL Server on remote servers, using real-time passwords, and so on. To get more details, search for "Accessing SQL Server from a Web Application" in the Visual Basic .NET help system.

How you create a new SQL Server login depends on the version of SQL Server you're using. For example, in SQL Server 2000, you can open the SQL Enterprise Manager, open the Security folder, right-click the Logins node, and select the New Login item to open the SQL Server Login Properties dialog you see in Figure 19.1. You enter the name of the new user (that's STEVE\ASPNET in the figure because the computer here is named STEVE), and click the Windows Authentication radio button to enable Windows integrated security. (Note that you don't have to use Windows integrated security if you prefer not to—you can click the SQL Server Authentication radio button and enter a password to use an SQL Server login.) Make sure that the Grant Access radio button is clicked, and then click the OK button to add this new user.

FIGURE 19.1

The SQL Server Login Properties dialog.

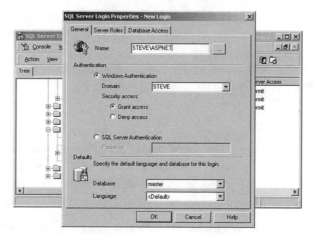

Now you've created a new SQL Server user, *computername*\ASPNET, which will allow your Web applications to log in to SQL Server automatically using Windows integrated security, the same type of security we used for Windows applications in the previous three days. If IIS is on the same machine as SQL Server, and you've added the *computer-name*\ASPNET login to SQL Server, you can use the same data connections you've already set up in the Server Explorer in your Web applications.

> **Caution**
>
> Before using this or any other login technique, make sure that the resulting security will be as tight as you require—in Web applications, security is always an important consideration. For example, you might not want to create new SQL users in your SQL Server installation; you might want to stick with and require specific usernames and passwords instead.

Here's another difference between Windows and Web database access—because no direct connection is maintained between a dataset and controls bound to that dataset, you're responsible for refreshing the data binding to controls in a Web form each time the page loads. In a Windows application, you don't need to do that—when the form loads, all you have to do is clear the dataset and use a data adapter to fill a dataset; the data bindings in the form are automatically updated:

```
Private Sub Form1_Load(ByVal sender As System.Object, _
    ByVal e As System.EventArgs) Handles MyBase.Load
    DataSet11.Clear()
    SqlDataAdapter1.Fill(DataSet11)
End Sub
```

In Web applications, the process is similar, but now you also have to explicitly run the DataBind method of any controls bound to the dataset to refresh the data binding:

```
Private Sub Page_Load(ByVal sender As System.Object, _
    ByVal e As System.EventArgs) Handles MyBase.Load
    DataSet11.Clear()
    SqlDataAdapter1.Fill(DataSet11)
    TextBox1.DataBind()
End Sub
```

This refreshes the data in the bound control each time the page loads—which you don't have to do in Windows applications because there that connection is "live." Calling DataBind to refresh data bindings is something you get used to doing in data-aware Web applications, and we'll see how to do it in almost all of today's examples.

Besides having to use DataBind to maintain data bindings, and besides the obvious fact that Web server controls have fewer properties than Windows forms controls, working with databases in Web applications is pretty similar to working with databases in Windows applications. For example, as with Windows database programming, there are two types of data binding—simple and complex. We'll take a look at simple binding first.

Using Simple Data Binding

You can use data connections with your Web applications just as you would with a Windows application. That is, you can drag a data adapter onto the Web form from the Data tab of the toolbox, use the Data Adapter Configuration Wizard to configure the data adapter to use the specific database you have in mind, and select the fields in the various tables you want from that database, as we have done before. Then you can use the Data, Generate Dataset menu item to create the dataset to use. That's all it takes to get a dataset ready to use binding controls in a Web form, and we haven't done anything we wouldn't have done in a Windows form.

And as in Windows applications, you can bind any property of any Web server control in a Web application to a data source. To do that, you click the ellipsis (...) button that appears when you select the control's (DataBindings) property. Doing so opens the DataBindings dialog box you see in Figure 19.2.

FIGURE 19.2

Simple binding a control.

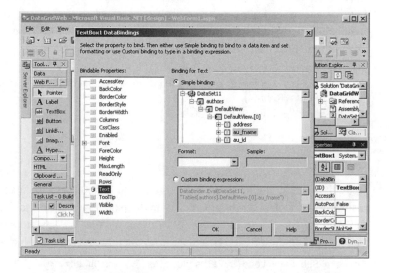

In Figure 19.2, you can see how to bind the Text property of a text box Web server control to the au_fname field in the pubs database's authors table—that is, to the author's first name. That's all it takes to support simple data binding—you just use a Web server control's (DataBindings). You can see a number of common Web server controls bound to a data source in the SimpleBindingWeb example in the code for this book, which you see at work in Figure 19.3.

19

FIGURE 19.3

The SimpleBindingWeb example.

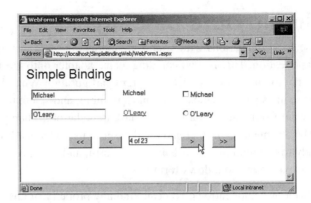

The controls in Figure 19.3 are all simple-bound Web server controls—text boxes, check boxes, link buttons, labels, and so on. You can use the (DataBindings) property to connect the Text property of these controls to a field in the pubs database's authors table. As you can see in the figure, these controls are connected to the authors' first and last names. As in a Windows application, you must add code to fill the dataset from the data adapter when the page loads:

```
Private Sub Page_Load(ByVal sender As System.Object, _
    ByVal e As System.EventArgs) Handles MyBase.Load
    DataSet11.Clear()
    SqlDataAdapter1.Fill(DataSet11)
        .
        .
        .
End Sub
```

In addition to setting up the data bindings with the (DataBindings) property, you must also refresh the data bindings every time the page loads (because they're broken when the Web page is sent to the browser). This means that we have to add code to call the DataBind method for each bound control when the page loads, like this:

```
Private Sub Page_Load(ByVal sender As System.Object, _
    ByVal e As System.EventArgs) Handles MyBase.Load
    DataSet11.Clear()
    SqlDataAdapter1.Fill(DataSet11)
    TextBox1.DataBind()
    TextBox2.DataBind()
    Label2.DataBind()
    LinkButton1.DataBind()
    CheckBox1.DataBind()
    RadioButton1.DataBind()
End Sub
```

That's okay as far as it goes, but that isn't actually very far—as things stand, this code only binds to the first record in the authors table. How do you move to other records?

Navigating Through Your Data

In Windows applications, you can move from record to record using a form's `BindingsContext` property, which maintains the current data bindings in the form and the position of the current record. On the other hand because Web forms are disconnected from your code until you send them back to the server, you shouldn't be surprised to learn that Web forms do not have a `BindingsContext` property and don't maintain any information about which record should be considered the current record.

That's a problem for us—how can we change the record a control is bound to unless we have a `BindingManagerBase` object whose `Position` and `Count` properties we can use to move through the records in a dataset? To solve this problem, you have to be a little clever—in this case, we'll use a data view (introduced in Day 16, "Handling Databases with ADO.NET") to hold a single record, bind our controls to that data view, and use the data view's `RowFilter` property to change the record in the data view as the user navigates through the dataset.

You can see how this works in the SimpleBindingWeb example in Figure 19.3, where the user is clicking the > button to move through the records in the authors table.

Note

This example is *not* intended to suggest that navigation buttons are a good idea in Web database applications because each time you click them, you need a server round-trip. This example just indicates how to implement simple binding and lets you select the record Web server that controls are bound to. For an example showing how to use navigation buttons to move through database records entirely in the browser (no server round-trip needed), see the topic "Using Datasets Locally With Internet Explorer" later today.

19

To follow along in this example, create the Web application named SimpleBindingWeb now, drag an SQL data adapter to the main Web form in that application, connect the data adapter to the authors table in the pubs database, and create a dataset, `DataSet11`, using that data adapter. In this example, we'll use a data view as a cache for a single data record whose data will be displayed in the simple-bound controls, so click the Data tab in the toolbox and drag a `DataView` object onto the main form. Next, set the `Table` property of the data view to `DataSet11.authors`.

Now add the Web server controls you see in Figure 19.3 to display authors' first and last names. Bind them to the au_fname and au_lname fields of the data view, `DataView1` (*not* the dataset). The next step is to implement the actual navigation, so add the <<, <, >, and >> buttons you see in Figure 19.3, as well as the label you see in the middle of these buttons to indicate the user's present location. To indicate that we are at the first record when the page first loads, add this code to the Page_Load event handler:

```
Private Sub Page_Load(ByVal sender As System.Object, _
    ByVal e As System.EventArgs) Handles MyBase.Load
    DataSet11.Clear()
    SqlDataAdapter1.Fill(DataSet11)
    TextBox1.DataBind()
    TextBox2.DataBind()
    Label2.DataBind()
    LinkButton1.DataBind()
    CheckBox1.DataBind()
    RadioButton1.DataBind()
    Label3.Text = 1 & " of " & DataSet11.Tables(0).Rows.Count
End Sub
```

The next step is to add the code for the navigation buttons. Let's start with the << button, which moves us back to the beginning of the dataset. To store our position in the dataset, we can use a variable named Position, which we set to 0 here to navigate to the first record. To make sure that Position persists across server round-trips, we can save it like this when the << button is clicked:

```
Private Sub Button1_Click(ByVal sender As System.Object, _
    ByVal e As System.EventArgs) Handles Button1.Click
    Dim Position As Integer
    Position = 0
    Me.ViewState("Position") = Position          .
        .
        .
        .
End Sub
```

Now we know what position we want to navigate to—how do we get there? We can use the RowFilter property of the data view to indicate what record from the dataset it should use (and therefore what record the bound controls in this example are bound to). You set this property to a string such as "au_id='141-99-0000'" to specify that the record(s) you want in the data view must all have the author ID field, au_id, set to "141-99-0000". Because we know the position in the dataset where we want to move, it's easy to get the au_id value for that particular record and store it in a variable named ID using this code in the << button handler:

```
Private Sub Button1_Click(ByVal sender As System.Object, _
    ByVal e As System.EventArgs) Handles Button1.Click
    Dim ID As String
    Dim Position As Integer
    Position = 0
    Me.ViewState("Position") = Position
```

```
    ID = DataSet11.Tables(0).Rows(Position).Item("au_id")
    .
    .
    .
End Sub
```

Now we've got the author ID for the record we want in the data view, and we can get that record into the data view with the `RowFilter` property this way. Note also that we also use the `DataBind` method of the bound controls to refresh the data binding and display our new location in the label between the navigation buttons:

```
Private Sub Button1_Click(ByVal sender As System.Object, _
    ByVal e As System.EventArgs) Handles Button1.Click
    Dim ID As String
    Dim Position As Integer
    Position = 0
    Me.ViewState("Position") = Position

    ID = DataSet11.Tables(0).Rows(Position).Item("au_id")
    DataView1.RowFilter = "au_id = '" & ID & "'"
    TextBox1.DataBind()
    TextBox2.DataBind()
    Label2.DataBind()
    LinkButton1.DataBind()
    CheckBox1.DataBind()
    RadioButton1.DataBind()
    Label3.Text = Position + 1 & " of " & DataSet11.Tables(0).Rows.Count
End Sub
```

And that's all we need—now when the user clicks the << button, `Position` is set to 0. We find the au_id field's value for that location in the dataset and load the corresponding record into the data view, which makes the record's data appear in the controls that are bound to that data view.

Now you know how to do it. Here's what the code for the other navigation buttons—<, >, and >>—looks like:

```
Private Sub Button2_Click(ByVal sender As System.Object, _
    ByVal e As System.EventArgs) Handles Button2.Click
    Dim ID As String
    Dim Position As Integer
    Position = Me.ViewState("Position")
    Position -= 1
    If Position < 0 Then
        Position = 0
    End If
    Me.ViewState("Position") = Position

    ID = DataSet11.Tables(0).Rows(Position).Item("au_id")
    DataView1.RowFilter = "au_id = '" & ID & "'"
```

19

```
        TextBox1.DataBind()
        TextBox2.DataBind()
        Label2.DataBind()
        LinkButton1.DataBind()
        CheckBox1.DataBind()
        RadioButton1.DataBind()
        Label3.Text = Position + 1 & " of " & DataSet11.Tables(0).Rows.Count
    End Sub

    Private Sub Button3_Click(ByVal sender As System.Object, _
        ByVal e As System.EventArgs) Handles Button3.Click
        Dim ID As String
        Dim Position As Integer
        Position = Me.ViewState("Position")
        Position += 1
        If Position > DataSet11.Tables(0).Rows.Count - 1 Then
            Position = DataSet11.Tables(0).Rows.Count - 1
        End If
        Me.ViewState("Position") = Position

        ID = DataSet11.Tables(0).Rows(Position).Item("au_id")
        DataView1.RowFilter = "au_id = '" & ID & "'"
        TextBox1.DataBind()
        TextBox2.DataBind()
        Label2.DataBind()
        LinkButton1.DataBind()
        CheckBox1.DataBind()
        RadioButton1.DataBind()
        Label3.Text = Position + 1 & " of " & DataSet11.Tables(0).Rows.Count
    End Sub

    Private Sub Button4_Click(ByVal sender As System.Object, _
        ByVal e As System.EventArgs) Handles Button4.Click
        Dim ID As String
        Dim Position As Integer
        Position = DataSet11.Tables(0).Rows.Count - 1
        Me.ViewState("Position") = Position

        ID = DataSet11.Tables(0).Rows(Position).Item("au_id")
        DataView1.RowFilter = "au_id = '" & ID & "'"
        TextBox1.DataBind()
        TextBox2.DataBind()
        Label2.DataBind()
        LinkButton1.DataBind()
        CheckBox1.DataBind()
        RadioButton1.DataBind()
        Label3.Text = Position + 1 & " of " & DataSet11.Tables(0).Rows.Count
    End Sub
```

In this way, you're able to implement data binding navigation yourself, despite the lack of a binding context. Now the user can select which record the controls in a Web form are bound to.

That gives us the simple-binding story in Web applications, but that's just the beginning. Next we'll take a look at complex data binding, where you can display data from multiple records at once.

Using Complex Data Binding

As with some Windows controls, some Web server controls support complex data binding, such as the Web server data grid control (other complex-bound controls include list boxes, data lists, and so on). In complex binding, a control can display multiple fields at once, as in a data grid, which can display an entire table. Here are the properties you use to support complex data binding in Web applications (not all complex-bound controls will support all these properties):

- `DataSource`—Returns or sets the source of data values, such as a dataset.
- `DataMember`—Returns or sets the data member in a data source you want to bind to.
- `DataKeyField`—Returns or sets the primary key field in the data source in the `DataSource` property.
- `DataTextField`—Returns or sets the field name from a data source a bound control should display.
- `DataTextFormatString`—Returns or sets the string specifying a data display format.
- `DataValueField`—Returns or sets the data field to use for the value of items, which is the value the bound control will return when selections are made (much like the `ValueMember` property in Windows controls).

 Tip
Even with complex-bound controls, you can also use the (DataBindings) property in addition to those listed here to bind every property of the control to a data source.

The `DataTextFormatString` property bears a little more discussion; you use this property to create a custom format indicating how to display data items. To do that, you use a data format string made up of two parts separated by a colon in curly braces like this {X:Ynn}. The value before the colon (that's X here) holds the location of the item you want to display; in Visual Basic .NET, this value is always zero because data fields can

19

only hold one value. The character after the colon (that's Y here) specifies the format to display the value with, and nn specifies format options. Here are the possible formats for the Y parameter:

- C—Uses currency format.
- D—Uses decimal format.
- E—Uses scientific (exponential) format.
- F—Uses fixed format.
- G—Uses general format.
- N—Uses number format.
- X—Uses hexadecimal format.

For example, if you wanted to display data items with six decimal places, you would set Y to "D" and nn to "6," making the formatting string you assign to the DataTextFormatString property "{0:D6}".

That's how complex binding works in overview; the next step is to take a look at a complex data binding example in code to make this concrete. This example is named ComplexBindingWeb in the code for this book, and you can see it at work in Figure 19.4. This example displays, from left to right, a Web server list box, a check box list, a data grid, and a data list control—all bound to the authors table in the SQL Server pubs sample database.

FIGURE 19.4

The ComplexBindingWeb example.

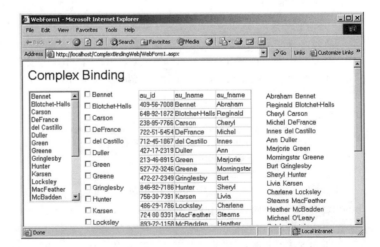

The first control we'll take a look at in the ComplexBindingWeb is the list box at left. Binding Web server list boxes is much like binding Windows list boxes; to display authors' last names, the list box has its `DataSource` property set to `DataSet11`, its `DataMember` property set to authors, and its `DataTextField` property set to `au_lname`.

As with Windows list boxes, you can make the list box return data from a different field than the one whose data is displayed. Here, however, you use the `DataValueField` property, not the `ValueMember` property, for this purpose. In addition, like the other complex-bound controls in this example, don't forget to use the `DataBind` method of this control to refresh the data binding in the `Page_Load` event:

```
Private Sub Page_Load(ByVal sender As System.Object, _
    ByVal e As System.EventArgs) Handles MyBase.Load
    DataSet11.Clear()
    SqlDataAdapter1.Fill(DataSet11)
    ListBox1.DataBind()
        .
        .
        .
End Sub
```

To the right of the list box, you can see a check box list. Like list boxes, both Web server check box lists and radio button lists will display one item for each record in the table they're bound to. The check box list in Figure 19.4 has its `DataSource` property set to `DataSet11`, its `DataMember` property set to authors, and its `DataTextField` property set to `au_lname`. Like other Web server controls, you must also call this control's `DataBind` method to refresh the data binding.

To the right of the check box list, you can see a data grid control bound to three fields (`au_id`, `au_fname`, and `au_lname`) of the authors table. Web server data grids are one of three Web server controls that are specifically designed to be used with data sources. The other two are data lists and repeaters; here's an overview of these controls:

- `DataGrid`—Creates a tabular display of an entire table or selected columns. Data grids can support edit, update, deletion operations.

- `DataList`—Creates a (non-tabular) list that you can customize. Data lists can support single selection of items. And you can edit the contents if you display text boxes in the list.

- `Repeater`—Creates a simple, read-only display. Repeaters only let you iterate over the records they're bound to—they have no default appearance at all. You're responsible for adding any HTML you want to use to display data, as we're going to see.

We'll take a look at these three controls in more detail now.

19

Binding Data Grids

The data grid you see in the ComplexBindingWeb example in Figure 19.4 has its
`DataSource` property set to `DataSet11` and its `DataMember` property set to authors. To
refresh the data binding, you call the `DataBind` method as with all data bound Web server
controls:

```
Private Sub Page_Load(ByVal sender As System.Object, _
    ByVal e As System.EventArgs) Handles MyBase.Load
    DataSet11.Clear()
    SqlDataAdapter1.Fill(DataSet11)
    CheckBoxList1.DataBind()
    ListBox1.DataBind()
    DataGrid1.DataBind()
        .
        .
        .

End Sub
```

The data grid you see in Figure 19.4 looks pretty plain, and it's obviously modeled on
the HTML `<table>` element. You can easily customize a data grid—just right-click the
data grid at design time and select the Auto Format item, opening the Auto Format dialog
you see in Figure 19.5. This dialog lets you select from a number of prebuilt styles for
the data grid, setting header color, border width, and so on.

FIGURE 19.5

*The Auto Format
dialog.*

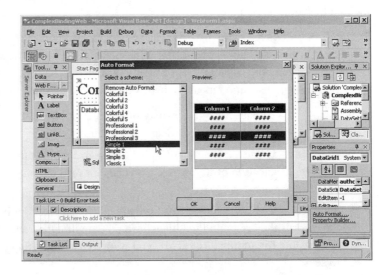

New Term   You can also customize the data grid with the Property Builder tool—just right-
click the data grid and select the Property Builder item, opening that tool as you
see in Figure 19.6. For example, in the Property Builder, you can select which columns

the data grid should display, what borders to use, and whether or not to use *paging* (which lets you display a table in pages, showing only a few records in the data grid at a time—the user clicks hyperlinks to see additional pages).

FIGURE 19.6

The Property Builder.

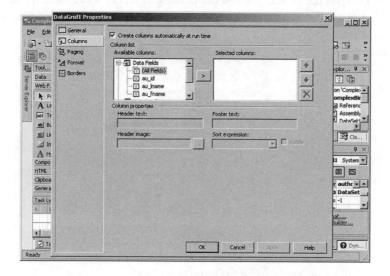

In a Web server data grid, different column types set the behavior of the columns in the control, even allowing you to edit the data in the data grid. Here are the different column types that you can use:

- BoundColumn—Shows a column bound to a field in a data source. (This is the default column type.)
- ButtonColumn—Shows a button for each item in the column.
- EditCommandColumn—Shows a column with editing commands for each item.
- HyperLinkColumn—Shows a hyperlink for each item.
- TemplateColumn—Shows each item using a given template.

At design time, you can install these column types in a data grid using the Property Builder—just click the Columns item you see in Figure 19.6, deselect the Create Columns Automatically at Run Time" item, and then select the column types you want to place in the data grid from the Available Columns box, which will list button columns, hyperlink columns, and so on. Click the > button to install those columns into the data grid.

For example, if you wanted to display only the au_fname and au_lname fields from the authors table, as well as a column of Delete "buttons" (represented by hyperlinks), you could use the Auto Format dialog to select an appearance you like for the data grid, and

19

then use the Property Builder to add only the au_fname and au_lname fields (turning off automatic creation of columns at runtime) and a Delete button column, as you see in Figure 19.7. When the Delete button is clicked, a DeleteCommand event occurs in the code on the server, and you can delete that record and rebind the data grid to the updated dataset. Besides Delete buttons, you can have Update buttons, Edit buttons, and so on.

FIGURE 19.7

A customized data grid.

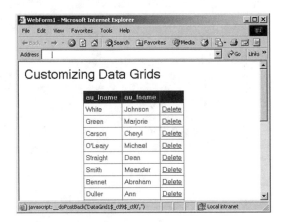

Here is the hierarchy of the DataGrid class:

```
System.Object
    System.Web.UI.Control
        System.Web.UI.WebControls.WebControl
            System.Web.UI.WebControls.BaseDataList
                System.Web.UI.WebControls.DataGrid
```

You can find the significant public properties of DataGrid objects in Table 19.1 and their significant events in Table 19.2. (These objects have no noninherited methods.) Note that as with other Web server controls, these tables do not list the significant properties, methods, and events this class inherits from the Control and WebControl classes—you can find them in Tables 12.1 to 12.5.

TABLE 19.1 Significant Public Properties of DataGrid Objects

Property	Means
AllowCustomPaging	Returns or sets whether custom paging is allowed.
AllowPaging	Returns or sets whether paging is enabled.
AllowSorting	Returns or sets whether sorting is enabled.
AlternatingItemStyle	Gets the style properties for alternating items.
AutoGenerateColumns	Returns or sets whether columns are automatically created for every field.

TABLE 19.1 continued

Property	Means
BackImageUrl	Returns or sets the URL of an image for the data grid's background.
Columns	Gets the columns of the data grid.
EditItemIndex	Returns or sets the index of an item to be edited.
EditItemStyle	Gets the style properties of edited items.
FooterStyle	Gets the footer style properties.
HeaderStyle	Gets the header style properties.
Items	Gets the items in the data grid.
ItemStyle	Gets the item style properties.
PageCount	Gets the number of pages in the data grid.
PagerStyle	Gets the paging section style properties.
PageSize	Returns or sets the number of items in a page.
SelectedIndex	Returns or sets the index of the selected item.
SelectedItem	Gets the currently selected item.
SelectedItemStyle	Gets the style of the currently selected item.
ShowFooter	Returns or sets whether the footer should be displayed.
ShowHeader	Returns or sets whether the header should be displayed.

TABLE 19.2 Significant Public Events of DataGrid Objects

Event	Means
CancelCommand	Occurs when the Cancel button for an item in the data grid is clicked.
DeleteCommand	Occurs when the Delete button for an item in the data grid is clicked.
EditCommand	Occurs when the Edit button for an item in the data grid is clicked.
ItemCommand	Occurs when any button is clicked.
ItemCreated	Occurs when an item is created.
ItemDataBound	Occurs when an item is data bound to the data grid.
PageIndexChanged	Occurs when a page selection element is clicked.
SortCommand	Occurs when a column is sorted.
UpdateCommand	Occurs when the Update button for an item in the data grid is clicked.

19

The next controls we'll take a look at are data lists.

Binding Data Lists

There's a data list control on the right in the ComplexBindingWeb example you see in Figure 19.4. Data lists aren't like other controls we've seen; you format the display in a data list using *templates*. In particular, each row in a data list is formatted using a template.

To create this data list, you start by adding a data list to a Web form, binding the DataSource property to `DataSet11` and the `DataMember` property to the authors table. Now the data list will provide data from that property to its internal items—the next step is to set up those items. To do that, right-click the data list and open the Edit Templates item displaying three menu subitems: Header and Footer Templates, Item Templates, and Separator Template. The item template is responsible for displaying the data items in each row, so select that item now, making the data list control display `ItemTemplate` (the default row template), `AlternatingItemTemplate` (the template for alternate rows), `SelectedItemTemplate` (the template for selected items), and `EditItemTemplate` (the template for items being edited) entries, as you see in Figure 19.8.

FIGURE 19.8

Editing item templates.

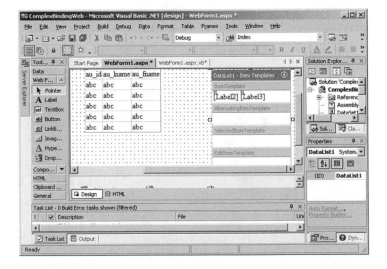

In the Item Template line, place a label control, followed by a space, and another label control, as you see in Figure 19.8. That creates an item template, which is used to display data items. To bind the labels to the `au_fname` and `au_lname` fields, start by selecting the first label's (DataBindings) property in the Properties window, opening the DataBindings dialog you see in Figure 19.9.

FIGURE **19.9**

The DataBindings dialog.

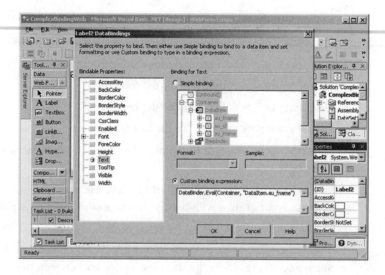

In the DataBindings dialog for the first label, click the Custom Binding Expression radio button and enter this custom binding expression:

DataBinder.Eval(Container, "DataItem.au_fname")

This binds the label to the au_fname field. Next, bind the second label to the au_lname field with this custom binding expression:

DataBinder.Eval(Container, "DataItem.au_lname")

To stop editing the item template in the data list, right-click the data list and select the End Template Editing menu item. And that's all you need—now when you run the program, you'll see the display in Figure 19.4. We've seen the Item Template now, which is the only template that you're required to create in order to display a data list, but there are others. Here are all the supported templates for data lists:

- AlternatingItemTemplate—Sets the layout for alternating items.
- EditItemTemplate—Sets the layout for the item being edited.
- FooterTemplate—Sets the layout for the footer.
- HeaderTemplate—Sets the layout for the header.
- ItemTemplate—Required template that sets the layout for displayed items.
- SelectedItemTemplate—Sets the layout for selected items.
- SeparatorTemplate—Sets the layout for separators between items.

19

You can also customize the appearance of a data list with various style properties

- `AlternatingItemStyle` — Sets the style for alternating items.
- `EditItemStyle` — Sets the style for the item being edited.
- `FooterStyle` — Sets the style for the footer.
- `HeaderStyle` — Sets the style for the header.
- `ItemStyle` — Sets the style for the displayed items.
- `RepeatDirection` — Sets the display direction of a data list; can be vertical or horizontal.
- `RepeatLayout` — Sets the layout of the data list; setting this property to `RepeatLayout.Table` will display data in a table format; `RepeatLayout.Flow` displays data without a table.
- `SelectedItemStyle` — Sets the style for selected items.
- `SeparatorStyle` — Sets the style for separators between items.

In addition, data lists support several events:

- `ItemCreated` — Gives you a way to customize the item-creation process at runtime.
- `ItemDataBound` — Gives you the ability to customize the DataList control, but after the data is available for examination.

If you display Web server button controls in a data list, certain events are automatically connected to those buttons based on the buttons' `CommandName` properties. For example, if the `CommandName` of a button is "edit," clicking that button will cause the data list's `EditCommand` event to occur; if the `CommandName` of a button is "delete," clicking that button will cause the data list's `DeleteCommand` event to occur. Here are the possible events:

- `EditCommand` — Occurs when a button with the `CommandName` "edit" is clicked.
- `DeleteCommand` — Occurs when a button with the `CommandName` "delete" is clicked.
- `UpdateCommand` — Occurs when a button with the `CommandName` "update" is clicked.
- `CancelCommand` — Occurs when a button with the `CommandName` "cancel" is clicked.

An `ItemCommand` event also occurs when a user clicks a button that doesn't have a predefined command.

The `DataList` class is based on the `BaseDataList`, and here is the hierarchy of the `BaseDataList` class:

```
System.Object
    System.Web.UI.Control
        System.Web.UI.WebControls.WebControl
            System.Web.UI.WebControls.BaseDataList
```

You can find the significant public properties of `BaseDataList` objects in Table 19.3, their significant method in Table 19.4, and their significant event in Table 19.5. Note that as with other Web server controls, this table does not list the significant properties, methods, and events this class inherits from the `Control` and `WebControl` classes—you can find them in Tables 12.1 to 12.5.

TABLE 19.3   Significant Public Properties of `BaseDataList` Objects

Property	Means
CellPadding	Returns or sets the cell padding used in the display table.
CellSpacing	Returns or sets the cell spacing used in the display table.
DataKeyField	Returns or sets the primary key field in the data source.
DataMember	Returns or sets the data member you want to bind to.
DataSource	Returns or sets the data source to use.
GridLines	Returns or sets grid line styles in the data list.
HorizontalAlign	Returns or sets the horizontal alignment of the control.

TABLE 19.4   Significant Public Method of `BaseDataList` Objects

Method	Means
DataBind	Binds the control to the data source.

TABLE 19.5   Significant Public Event of `BaseDataList` Objects

Event	Means
SelectedIndexChanged	Occurs when an item is selected.

19

Data list controls themselves are supported with the `DataList` class; here is the hierarchy of that class:

```
System.Object
   System.Web.UI.Control
      System.Web.UI.WebControls.WebControl
         System.Web.UI.WebControls.BaseDataList
            System.Web.UI.WebControls.DataList
```

You can find the significant public properties of `DataList` objects in Table 19.6, and their significant events in Table 19.7. (This class has no noninherited methods.) Note that as with other Web server controls, this table does not list the significant properties, methods, and events this class inherits from the `Control` and `WebControl` classes—you can find them in Tables 12.1 to 12.5.

TABLE 19.6   Significant Public Properties of DataList Objects

Property	Means
AlternatingItemStyle	Returns the style for alternating items.
AlternatingItemTemplate	Returns or sets the template for alternating items.
EditItemIndex	Returns or sets the index number of the selected item to edit.
EditItemStyle	Returns the style for the item selected for editing.
EditItemTemplate	Returns or sets the template for the item selected for editing.
FooterStyle	Returns the style for the footer.
FooterTemplate	Returns or sets the template for the footer.
GridLines	Returns or sets the grid line style.
HeaderStyle	Returns the style of the header.
HeaderTemplate	Returns or sets the template for the header.
Items	Returns the items in the list.
ItemStyle	Returns the style for the items in the list.
ItemTemplate	Returns or sets the template for items.
RepeatColumns	Returns or sets the number of columns to display.
RepeatDirection	Returns or sets whether data is displayed horizontally or vertically.
RepeatLayout	Returns or sets whether the control is displayed as a table or with a flow layout.
SelectedIndex	Returns or sets the selected item's index.
SelectedItem	Returns the selected item.
SelectedItemStyle	Returns the style properties for selected items.
SelectedItemTemplate	Returns or sets the template for selected items.
SeparatorStyle	Returns the style of separators.
SeparatorTemplate	Returns or sets the template for separators.
ShowFooter	Returns or sets whether the footer is displayed.
ShowHeader	Returns or sets whether the header is displayed.

TABLE 19.7   Significant Public Events of DataList Objects

Event	Means
CancelCommand	Occurs when a button with the CommandName "cancel" is clicked.
DeleteCommand	Occurs when a button with the CommandName "delete" is clicked.
EditCommand	Occurs when a button with the CommandName "edit" is clicked.

TABLE 19.7 continued

Event	Means
ItemCommand	Occurs when a button without a CommandName is clicked.
ItemCreated	Occurs when an item is created.
UpdateCommand	Occurs when a button with the CommandName "update" is clicked.

The next Web server controls we'll take a look at are data repeaters.

Binding Repeaters

Repeaters feel like Web server controls that aren't quite finished. For example, to configure them, you don't use an IDE tool; instead, you edit their HTML directly. Let's take a look to see how this works.

Tip

> Another way that repeaters feel like unfinished controls is that the way you configure a repeater in HTML—the way suggested by Microsoft—will often give you errors in the HTML editor. Microsoft calls them warnings, not errors, and says "You can safely ignore these warnings. The HTML elements will be displayed correctly when the application is run." In fact, these errors are the reason you must use HTML view instead of design view—the design view editor treats errors like these more seriously and won't let you launch your application.

19

Repeaters are template-driven controls, letting you display data by using templates repeatedly as they handle all the data in a data source, row by row. Like data lists and check box lists, repeaters are ideal for work with datasets because they'll automatically loop over all your data, displaying as many entries as there are items in your dataset. However, repeaters are even more free-form than data lists; they have no intrinsic appearance at all—it's up to you to write all their HTML. The repeater can be bound to a data source and data member, and you can access that bound data in the templates you configure, but that's it; the rest is up to you.

You can see an example in Figure 19.10, which is the RepeaterWeb example in the code for this book. This example uses a template with a header, a footer, an item template, and an alternating item template. (The alternating item template is what gives the display in Figure 19.10 a striped appearance—although you can't see it in the figure, the table's header and footer are colored light blue and the stripes are colored coral.)

FIGURE **19.10**

Using a data repeater.

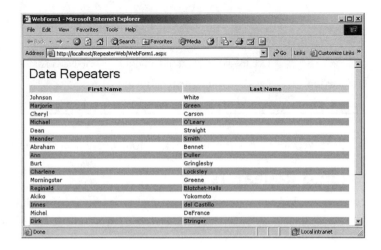

To develop this example, create a new Web application named RepeaterWeb now and add an SQL data adapter to it connected to the authors table. Next, generate a dataset, `DataSet11`, from the data adapter, and add a `Repeater` control to the Web form in this application. (`Repeater` controls are in the Web Forms tab of the toolbox, not in the Data tab.) Bind the repeater's `DataSource` property to `DataSet11` and its `DataMember` property to the authors table.

When you add a repeater control to a Web form, an `<asp:Repeater>` element appears in that Web form's HTML. You can see that element if you switch to HTML view by clicking the HTML tab at the bottom of the designer:

```
<form id="Form1" method="post" runat="server">

<asp:Repeater id=Repeater1 runat="server" DataSource="<%# DataSet11 %>"
    DataMember="authors">

</asp:Repeater>

</form>
```

We'll display our data in this example using an HTML table, so we will enclose the repeater in an HTML `<TABLE>` element. You can then create the elements in the various repeater templates using HTML `<TH>` elements to create HTML table headers and `<TR>` elements to create HTML table rows. For example, to create the header template that will generate the "First Name" and "Last Name" text you see in Figure 19.10, you can use this HTML:

```
<form id="Form1" method="post" runat="server">

<table width="100%" style="font: 8pt verdana"
    style="POSITION: absolute; TOP: 50px">
```

```
<asp:Repeater id=Repeater1 runat="server" DataSource="<%# DataSet11 %>"
    DataMember="authors">
  <HeaderTemplate>
  <tr style="background-color:lightblue">
     <th>First Name</th>
     <th>Last Name</th>
  </tr>
   </HeaderTemplate>
      .
      .
</asp:Repeater>
</table>
```

The repeater's usefulness comes in the item template, which you create with an
<ItemTemplate> element. This template will be automatically repeated for each data row
in DataSet11.

The repeater is already bound to the authors table. In the repeater's HTML, you can
access the data in a field of the authors table with an expression like this: <%#
DataBinder.Eval(Container, "DataItem.au_fname") %>, which retrieves the data in
the au_fname field for the current row in the repeater. To display both an author's first and
last name, then, all we have to do is to use this HTML in the repeater's item template:

```
<form id="Form1" method="post" runat="server">

<table width="100%" style="font: 8pt verdana"
    style="POSITION: absolute; TOP: 50px">
<asp:Repeater id=Repeater1 runat="server" DataSource="<%# DataSet11 %>"
    DataMember="authors">
  <HeaderTemplate>
  <tr style="background-color:lightblue">
     <th>First Name</th>
     <th>Last Name</th>
  </tr>
   </HeaderTemplate>
   <ItemTemplate>
   <tr>
     <td><%# DataBinder.Eval(Container, "DataItem.au_fname") %>
     </td>
     <td><%# DataBinder.Eval(Container,"DataItem.au_lname") %>
     </td>
  </tr>
   </ItemTemplate>
      .
      .
      .
</asp:Repeater>
</table>
```

19

You can also create a different template for alternate rows if you add an
`<AlternatingItemTemplate>` element. To see how that works, we can just add this
HTML, which gives alternating rows a coral background color (this works because
browsers such as Internet Explorer have built-in color constants named `"lightblue"`
and `"coral"`—you can always substitute an HTML color triplet such as `"ff22ee"` to
specify colors):

```
<form id="Form1" method="post" runat="server">

<table width="100%" style="font: 8pt verdana"
    style="POSITION: absolute; TOP: 50px">
<asp:Repeater id=Repeater1 runat="server" DataSource="<%# DataSet11 %>"
    DataMember="authors">
  <HeaderTemplate>
<tr style="background-color:lightblue">
    <th>First Name</th>
    <th>Last Name</th>
  </tr>
  </HeaderTemplate>
  <ItemTemplate>
  <tr>
    <td><%# DataBinder.Eval(Container, "DataItem.au_fname") %>
    </td>
    <td><%# DataBinder.Eval(Container,"DataItem.au_lname") %>
    </td>
  </tr>
  </ItemTemplate>
  <AlternatingItemTemplate>
  <tr>
    <td bgcolor="coral">
    <%# DataBinder.Eval(Container, "DataItem.au_fname") %> </td>
    <td bgcolor="coral">
    <%# DataBinder.Eval(Container,"DataItem.au_lname") %> </td>
  </tr>
  </AlternatingItemTemplate>
      .
      .
      .
</asp:Repeater>
</table>
```

Finally, we'll add a footer to round off the repeater's display. This footer will just mirror
the header, displaying the text "First Name" and "Last Name" on a light blue background:

```
<table width="100%" style="font: 8pt verdana"
    style="POSITION: absolute; TOP: 50px">
<asp:Repeater id=Repeater1 runat="server" DataSource="<%# DataSet11 %>"
    DataMember="authors">
  <HeaderTemplate>
```

```
<tr style="background-color:lightblue">
    <th>First Name</th>
    <th>Last Name</th>
  </tr>
  </HeaderTemplate>
  <ItemTemplate>
  <tr>
    <td><%# DataBinder.Eval(Container, "DataItem.au_fname") %>
    </td>
    <td><%# DataBinder.Eval(Container,"DataItem.au_lname") %>
    </td>
  </tr>
  </ItemTemplate>
  <AlternatingItemTemplate>
  <tr>
    <td bgcolor="coral">
    <%# DataBinder.Eval(Container, "DataItem.au_fname") %> </td>
    <td bgcolor="coral">
    <%# DataBinder.Eval(Container,"DataItem.au_lname") %> </td>
  </tr>
  </AlternatingItemTemplate>
  <FooterTemplate>
  <tr style="background-color:lightblue">
    <th>First Name</th>
    <th>Last Name</th>
  </tr>
  </FooterTemplate>

</asp:Repeater>
</table>
```

That completes the HTML for the repeater; to complete the RepeaterWeb example, you still need to fill the dataset in the example from the SQL data adapter and refresh the data binding to the repeater when the page loads, so add this Visual Basic .NET code to the Web form:

```
Private Sub Page_Load(ByVal sender As System.Object, _
    ByVal e As System.EventArgs) Handles MyBase.Load
    DataSet11.Clear()
    SqlDataAdapter1.Fill(DataSet11)
    Repeater1.DataBind()
End Sub
```

And that's all we need; you can see this repeater at work in Figure 19.10, where the repeater works as we want it to.

As you might expect, the most important template is the item template in a repeater, and every repeater must have an item template. The other templates are optional—here are all the possible templates you can use:

- `ItemTemplate`—Required template that sets the layout of displayed items.
- `AlternatingItemTemplate`—Sets the layout of alternating items.
- `SeparatorTemplate`—Sets the separator between items.
- `HeaderTemplate`—Sets the layout of the header.
- `FooterTemplate`—Sets the layout of the footer.

Repeaters are supported with the `System.Web.UI.WebControls.Repeater` class, and here is the hierarchy for that class:

```
System.Object
    System.Web.UI.Control
        System.Web.UI.WebControls.Repeater
```

You can find the significant public properties of `Repeater` objects in Table 19.8 and their significant events in Table 19.9. (This class has no noninherited methods.) Note that as with other Web server controls, this table does not list the significant properties, methods, and events this class inherits from the `Control` and `WebControl` classes—you can find them in Tables 12.1 to 12.5.

TABLE 19.8   Significant Public Properties of `Repeater` Objects

Property	Means
AlternatingItemTemplate	Returns or sets the template for alternating items.
DataMember	Returns or sets the specific table to bind to.
DataSource	Returns or sets the data source to bind to.
FooterTemplate	Returns or sets the template for the footer.
HeaderTemplate	Returns or sets the template for the header.
Items	Gets the items in the repeater.
ItemTemplate	Returns or sets the template for items.
SeparatorTemplate	Returns or sets the template for separators.

TABLE 19.9   Significant Public Events of `Repeater` Objects

Event	Means
ItemCommand	Occurs when any button is clicked.
ItemCreated	Occurs when an item is created.
ItemDataBound	Occurs when an item is data bound to the repeater.

That completes our look at both simple and complex data binding in Web applications. Next, we'll take a look at a database handling in more depth with a master-detail example.

Creating Master-Detail Data Forms

In Day 17, "Binding Visual Basic Controls to Databases," you saw how to create master-detail data forms—when the user clicked a single item in a Windows list box, the application displayed data from multiple fields for that item. You can see such an example using Web forms, the MasterDetailWeb example in the code for this book, in Figure 19.11. When the user clicks the last name of an author in the list box, more information about the author appears in the bound text boxes at right, as you see in the figure. (This is a simpler example than the one we saw in Day 17 because it just uses the authors table and doesn't tie together records from different tables with a data relation object—the big issue here is how to implement the data binding.)

FIGURE 19.11

A Master Detail data form.

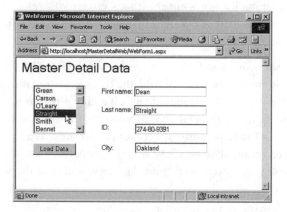

To follow along, create a Web application named MasterDetailWeb now, and add the controls you see in Figure 19.11. Also add an SQL data adapter for the authors table and generate a dataset, DataSet11, for that table. When the page loads, we can fill the dataset using the SQL data adapter this way:

```
Private Sub Page_Load(ByVal sender As System.Object, _
    ByVal e As System.EventArgs) Handles MyBase.Load
    SqlDataAdapter1.Fill(DataSet11)
End Sub
```

Now bind the list box to the authors table's au_lname field by setting its DataSource property to DataSet11, its DataMember property to "authors", and its DataTextField property to au_lname, which will make the list box display the authors' last names when

19

we call its `DataBind` method. In code, we'll use the `au_id` field to identify authors, so also set the list box's `DataValueField` to `au_id`. Doing so means that when the user clicks an author's last name, we'll be able to read that author's ID value from the list box's `SelectedValue` property.

Instead of automatically loading data into the list box when the Web form loads, this example uses a Load Data button (as you see in Figure 19.11) to load data into the list box. (We do things this way so that the user's selection in the list box will not be lost during server round-trips, as it would be if data were automatically reloaded into the list box.) To implement the Load Data button, add this code to the application:

```
Private Sub Button1_Click(ByVal sender As System.Object, _
    ByVal e As System.EventArgs) Handles Button1.Click
    ListBox1.DataBind()
End Sub
```

When the user clicks the Load Data button, the list box will display the authors' last names. Finally, set the list box's `AutoPostBack` property to `True` so that when the user makes a selection, the list box's `SelectedIndexChanged` event will occur in the code on the server.

How can we display the data for the author the user selected? As before, we can use a data view to hold the author's record from the dataset, setting the data view's `RowFilter` property with the author's ID to indicate which author's record we want. Drag a `DataView` object from the Data tab in the toolbox to the application's Web form now, and set the data view's `Table` property to `DataSet11.authors`. When the user makes her selection, we can set the data view's `RowFilter` property in the list box's `SelectedIndexChanged` event so that the data view will hold the selected author's full record:

```
Private Sub ListBox1_SelectedIndexChanged(ByVal sender _
    As System.Object, ByVal e As System.EventArgs) _
    Handles ListBox1.SelectedIndexChanged
    DataView1.RowFilter = "au_id = '" & ListBox1.SelectedValue & "'"
        .
        .
        .
End Sub
```

Finally, bind the four text boxes in the application to the data view using their (DataBindings) property—the top text box to the `au_fname` field in the data view to display the author's first name, the next text box to the `au_lname` field to display their last name, and so on. We also must refresh that binding after the user has loaded a new record into the data view, like this:

```
Private Sub ListBox1_SelectedIndexChanged(ByVal sender _
    As System.Object, ByVal e As System.EventArgs) _
```

```
   Handles ListBox1.SelectedIndexChanged
   DataView1.RowFilter = "au_id = '" & ListBox1.SelectedValue & "'"
   TextBox1.DataBind()
   TextBox2.DataBind()
   TextBox3.DataBind()
   TextBox4.DataBind()
End Sub
```

And that completes the code we need here. Now the user can click an author's last name in the list box shown in Figure 19.11, and the author's full details will appear in the bound text boxes, as you can also see in the figure.

Using Datasets Locally with Internet Explorer

Earlier today, we created an example that supported navigation buttons, letting the user navigate through a dataset. However, as also mentioned earlier, each time you click one of those buttons, you need a complete server round-trip to move to the next record. If you just want to navigate through a set of records, there's another option you should be aware of—a local option, which runs entirely in Internet Explorer. This option doesn't involve .NET programming, but it's a useful skill to know about.

Using Internet Explorer, you can bind controls in a Web page to an XML document using Internet Explorer's XML data source object (DSO). Internally, the XML DSO uses ADO (not ADO.NET) recordsets (not datasets) to bind to controls such as HTML text fields. You can see this at work in the LocalData example in the code for this book in Figure 19.12, where the Web page LocalData.html is displaying the authors table from the pubs database, and the user can use the navigation buttons to move through the records in that table. To use the example, you only need to open LocalData.html in the Internet Explorer.

19

FIGURE 19.12

The LocalData example.

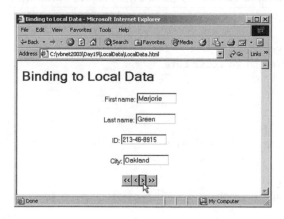

What's happening in this example is that the XML DSO is reading in an XML document named dataset.xml. You can create that document with the Visual Basic .NET `DataSet` class's `WriteXml` method, using that method to write out the complete authors table in XML in dataset.xml:

```
<?xml version="1.0" standalone="yes"?>
<DataSet1 xmlns="http://www.tempuri.org/DataSet1.xsd">
  <authors>
    <au_id>172-32-1176</au_id>
    <au_lname>White</au_lname>
    <au_fname>Johnson</au_fname>
    <phone>408 496-7223</phone>
    <address>10932 Bigge Rd.</address>
    <city>Menlo Park</city>
    <state>CA</state>
    <zip>94025</zip>
    <contract>true</contract>
  </authors>
  <authors>
    <au_id>213-46-8915</au_id>
    <au_lname>Green</au_lname>
    <au_fname>Marjorie</au_fname>
    <phone>415 986-7020</phone>
          .
          .
          .
```

You can read in the dataset.xml file using an object of the `com.ms.xml.dso.XMLDSO.class`, which comes with Internet Explorer. All you have to do is to pass the URL of that file to the `com.ms.xml.dso.XMLDSO.class` object. Listing 19.1 shows how it looks in code, in LocalData.html.

LISTING 19.1   Binding to Local Data (LocalData Project, LocalData.html)

```
<HTML>
    <HEAD>
        <TITLE>
            Binding to Local Data
        </TITLE>
    </HEAD>

    <BODY>
        <H1>
            Binding to Local Data
        </H1>

        <CENTER>
            <APPLET CODE="com.ms.xml.dso.XMLDSO.class"
```

LISTING 19.1   continued

```
                    ID="RecordSet1" WIDTH=0 HEIGHT=0 MAYSCRIPT=true>
                    <PARAM NAME="URL" VALUE="dataset.xml">
                </APPLET>

                First name: <INPUT TYPE="TEXT" DATASRC="#RecordSet1"
                    DATAFLD="au_fname" SIZE=10><P>
                Last name: <INPUT TYPE="TEXT" DATASRC="#RecordSet1"
                    DATAFLD="au_lname" SIZE=10><P>
                ID: <INPUT TYPE="TEXT" DATASRC="#RecordSet1"
                    DATAFLD="au_id" SIZE=12><P>
                City: <INPUT TYPE="TEXT" DATASRC="#RecordSet1"
                    DATAFLD="city" SIZE=12><P>

                <BUTTON ONCLICK="RecordSet1.recordset.MoveFirst()" >
                    &lt;&lt;
                </BUTTON>
                <BUTTON ONCLICK="if (!RecordSet1.recordset.BOF)
                    RecordSet1.recordset.MovePrevious()" >
                    &lt;
                </BUTTON>
                <BUTTON ONCLICK="if (!RecordSet1.recordset.EOF)
                    RecordSet1.recordset.MoveNext()" >
                    &gt;
                </BUTTON>
                <BUTTON ONCLICK="RecordSet1.recordset.MoveLast()">
                    &gt;&gt;
                </BUTTON>
            </CENTER>
        </BODY>
    </HTML>
```

You can see the results in Figure 19.12—the XML DSO reads in dataset.xml, and then we use the DATASRC and DATAFLD attributes of the XML DSO to bind to the text fields you see in the figure. That's a useful technique to know if you want to bind data locally in the client instead of relying on server round-trips.

Summary

Today, we took our database work to the Web, seeing how to create data-handling Web applications. We've found that although creating data-aware Web applications is similar to creating data-aware Windows applications, there are some significant differences—for example, you're much more responsible for maintaining data bindings yourself, from using the DataBind method for refreshing data bindings to working around the lack of BindingManagerBase objects that support handy Position and Count properties in Windows applications.

19

We started today's work with an overview of simple and complex data binding in Web applications. We saw that like data binding in Windows applications, you can use the (`DataBindings`) property of controls to bind many properties of simple-bound controls to a data source.

Navigating through records when using simple binding presents a challenge because Web forms do not maintain data bindings between round-trips to the server. You saw that a viable option is to use data views to store single records and to simple-bind controls such as text boxes to that data view.

We also took a look at complex binding in Web applications, which revolves around the `DataSource`, `DataMember`, `DataKeyField`, `DataTextField`, `DataTextFormatString`, and `DataValueField` properties. Using these properties, we were able to bind complex-bound controls such as list boxes and check box lists to data sources.

Three Web server controls are specially designed for use with data sources—data grids, data lists, and repeaters. Data grids work much like data grids in Windows applications— they display a table of data—except that these data grids use HTML tables to display data with. Data lists display lists that you can customize. You can create your own templates using Visual Basic controls to display items in data lists. Repeaters are even more free-form than data lists—you're responsible for creating their templates entirely in HTML, using HTML elements.

We also took a look at how to create master-detail Web data forms today, using a list box and several bound text boxes. In this case, the user could select an author's last name from the list box, and that author's first name, last name, ID, and city were displayed in the text boxes.

Today's final topic was about using datasets locally in Internet Explorer to avoid server round-trips, and we took a look at binding a dataset as stored in an XML document to Internet Explorer's XML DSO. We were also able to bind data from XML DSO to HTML text fields, and we created HTML buttons to let the user navigate through that data locally; no server round-trip was needed.

And that's it for today's work—tomorrow, we're going to start working user controls, Web user controls, and multithreading.

Q&A

Q How can I customize the HTML used between rows in a data list?

A Use a `SeparatorTemplate` template, which holds the HTML element(s) used between each row. For example, you might use an `<HR>` element here.

Q Can I use data readers in Web applications?

A Yes, you can create a data reader that will work in Web applications using the ExecuteReader method of a command object. Here's an example:

```
Private Sub Page_Load(ByVal sender As System.Object, _
    ByVal e As System.EventArgs) Handles MyBase.Load
    Dim Reader1 As System.Data.SqlClient.SqlDataReader
    DataReader1 = SqlCommand1.ExecuteReader()
    DataGrid1.DataSource = DataReader1
    DataGrid1.DataBind()
    DataReader1.Close()
End Sub
```

Workshop

This workshop tests whether you understand the concepts you saw today. It's a good idea to make sure that you can answer these questions before pressing on to tomorrow's work.

Quiz

1. You've bound a text box to a field in a dataset in a Web application, but when you run the application, the text box is blank. What could be wrong?

2. What property in the Properties window do you use to bind a simple-bound control to a data source?

3. What properties do you use to support complex data binding in Web applications?

4. Suppose that you have a data list bound to the authors table. What custom binding expression can you assign to a label in the data list's item template to bind the label to the au_fname field?

5. What element do you use to format alternate lines in a repeater?

Quiz Answers

1. There are two possible problems—you still might need to use the data adapter's Fill method to fill the dataset, and you might need to use the text box's DataBind method to refresh the data binding.

2. You use the (DataBindings) property.

3. Complex data binding in Web applications uses the DataSource, DataMember, DataKeyField, DataTextField, DataTextFormatString, and DataValueField properties.

4. You can use this custom binding expression: DataBinder.Eval(Container, "DataItem.au_fname").

5. You use the <AlternatingItemTemplate> element.

19

Exercises

1. Create a new Web application that binds text boxes to fields in the publishers table of the pubs database. Implement navigation buttons as well, letting the user navigate through the records in this table. If you don't have access to the pubs database, perform the same exercise with another database table.

2. Create a new Web application that lets the user search the authors table for a specific author by entering the author's last name in a text field and clicking a button labeled Find. If you find a match, display the author's information in bound text boxes. One way to do this is to use a data view and set its `RowFilter` property to find the author you're looking for. If you don't have access to the pubs database, perform the same kind of exercise with another database table. (**Extra credit**: allow for multiple authors with the same last name.)

PART V

In Review

Working with Databases in Visual Basic .NET

In Part V, we took an in-depth look at database programming. This is a complex topic that can cause a great deal of confusion, and we'll take a minute to review this topic here. As you saw, ADO.NET work centers around connection objects, data adapters, and dataset objects. These three objects make up the basis of ADO.NET, and a good knowledge of what these objects do is essential.

To connect to a data source in code, you use a *connection object*. In Visual Basic .NET 2003, there are four types of connection objects:

- SqlConnection objects for SQL Server (for applications using Microsoft SQL Server 7.0 or later)
- OleDbConnection objects for object linking and embedding Database protocol (OLE DB) (for applications using Microsoft SQL Server 6.5 or earlier or any OLE DB provider that supports the OLE DB interfaces)
- OdbcConnection for Open Database Connectivity (ODBC)
- OracleConnection for applications using Oracle data sources

You provide a connection string to connect using a Connection object; as you've seen, you can use the visual tools in the IDE to create sample connection strings. Here's how you might use such a string in code to create a connection object:

```
Dim ConnectionString As String = "Provider=SQLOLEDB.1;Integrated " & _
"Security=SSPI;Persist Security Info=False;Initial " & _
"Catalog=pubs;Packet Size=4096;Workstation ID=STEVE;" & _
"Use Encryption for Data=False"

Dim Connection1 As OleDbConnection = New OleDbConnection(ConnectionString)
        .
        .
        .
```

After you've created a Connection object, you can open it with its Open method, and assign it to the Connection property of a Command object. To do that, you first create a new Command object by passing the SQL you want to use to the Command class's constructor. Then you set the type of the command, such as CommandType.Text, and assign the open connection to the command's Connection property to make this Command object active:

```
Dim ConnectionString As String = "Provider=SQLOLEDB.1;Integrated " & _
"Security=SSPI;Persist Security Info=False;Initial " & _
"Catalog=pubs;Packet Size=4096;Workstation ID=STEVE;" & _
"Use Encryption for Data=False"

Dim Connection1 As OleDbConnection = New OleDbConnection(ConnectionString)

Dim Command1 As OleDbCommand = _
New OleDbCommand("SELECT * FROM authors")

Command1.CommandType = CommandType.Text

Connection1.Open()
Command1.Connection = Connection1
        .
        .
        .
```

Now you've got a working Connection object, and you can assign it to a data adapter's SelectCommand property so that its SQL will be executed when you call the data adapter's Fill method. Here's how you can create a new data adapter and assign our Command object to its SelectCommand property:

```
Dim Command1 As OleDbCommand = _
New OleDbCommand("SELECT * FROM authors")
Command1.CommandType = CommandType.Text

Connection1.Open()
Command1.Connection = Connection1
```

```
Dim OleDbDataAdapter1 As OleDbDataAdapter = New OleDbDataAdapter()

OleDbDataAdapter1.SelectCommand = Command1
            .
            .
            .
```

Now we can use the data adapter's `Fill` method to fill a dataset, and then we're free to use that dataset, as here, where we bind it to a data grid:

```
Dim Command1 As OleDbCommand = _
New OleDbCommand("SELECT * FROM authors")
Command1.CommandType = CommandType.Text

Connection1.Open()
Command1.Connection = Connection1

Dim OleDbDataAdapter1 As OleDbDataAdapter = New OleDbDataAdapter()

OleDbDataAdapter1.SelectCommand = Command1

OleDbDataAdapter1.Fill(dataset1, "authors")

DataGrid1.SetDataBinding(dataset1, "authors")
```

And that's it—we've connected to a data source with a `Connection` object, assigned that connection to a `Command` object, assigned that `Command` object to a data adapter's `SelectCommand` property, and then we used the data adapter to fill a dataset and bound that dataset to a data grid. Working with the various ADO.NET objects such as this takes some practice. If you feel you've gotten a good grasp on this topic, you're ready to move on to Part VI.

PART VI

20

At a Glance

21

Advanced Topics

In Part VI, we're going to take a look at some advanced topics, including creating your own Windows controls—called user controls—that you can use in your Windows applications. You can embed standard Windows controls such as text boxes, buttons, and list boxes in user controls, or you can create entirely new user controls from scratch, as you're going to see.

You'll also see how to create Web user controls to create our own controls for use in Web applications. And you'll see how to use multithreading to make your applications support multiple threads of execution so you can do two or more things at once.

You'll be shown how to create Windows services, which run in the background in Windows, and how to connect to those services from other applications, as well as how to create Web services, which enable your Windows applications to connect to code on the Web. Our final topic, appropriately enough, will be how to deploy your applications in the field. You'll see how to package your finished applications as files that the Windows installer can use to install your applications on other computers.

DAY 20

Creating User Controls, Web User Controls, and Multithreading

Today, we're going to work with three key topics: creating user controls, Web user controls, and multithreading. You can build user controls yourself for use in Windows forms; for example, you might want to create an alarm clock or a calculator built in to a control. Web user controls are the same for Web forms.

NEW TERM   Multithreading allows your programs to perform several tasks at once; each stream of execution is called a *thread*. When you create new threads in a program, those threads can execute code you give them in the background, no matter what the user is doing with the user interface. You can use multithreading for time-consuming tasks that would otherwise make your program seem to hang; for example, your program may use a thread to sort a huge number of records in the background while allowing the user to move on with other work.

Here's an overview of the topics we'll look at today:

- Creating user controls
- Adding properties to user controls
- Adding methods to user controls
- Adding events to user controls
- Testing user controls
- Creating Web user controls
- Adding properties to Web user controls
- Adding methods to Web user controls
- Adding events to Web user controls
- Testing Web user controls
- Creating threads
- Starting threads
- Suspending threads
- Resuming threads
- Stopping threads
- Making threads sleep
- Setting thread priority
- Synchronizing threads
- Using SyncLock to synchronize threads
- Joining threads

Let's begin today's work by looking at how to create user controls for use in Windows applications.

Creating User Controls

User controls are much like miniature Windows forms, and you can add the Windows controls you want to a user control at design time to put together your own composite control. Or you can draw the appearance of a user control yourself and use the events of that control, such as the Click event, to create a totally new control. To see how this works, look at the UserControl example in the code for this book.

To follow along in this example, select the File, New Project menu item to open the New Project dialog that you see in Figure 20.1. Select the Windows Control Library item and give this new project the name UserControl, as you see in the figure. (You can also add a new user control to an existing application by selecting the Project, Add User Control menu item.)

FIGURE 20.1

The New Project dialog.

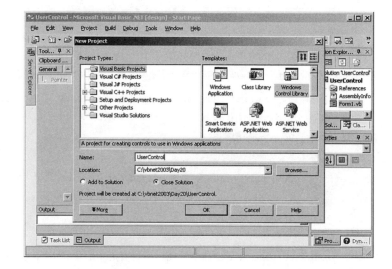

When you click the OK button in the New Project dialog, the new user control is created, and you can see it at design time in Figure 20.2. As you can see, the user control looks like a tiny Windows form, and it acts like one too—you can add your own controls to the user control or give it a custom appearance in code. In this example, we've added a label control to the user control and sized it so that it covers most of the control, as you can see in Figure 20.2.

FIGURE 20.2

A user control at design time.

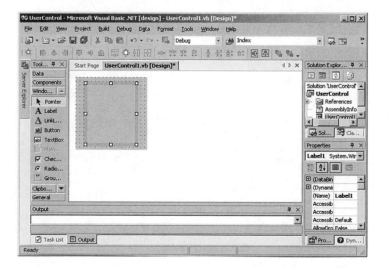

20

As with any other Windows control, user controls can support properties, methods, and events, so let's look at how to implement these items in our control.

Adding Properties to User Controls

As an example, we might give this new user control a property named `CenterColor` that sets the color of the label in the center of the control. When you assign a color to this property, that color will be assigned to the `BackColor` property of the label.

To add this property to the user control, open the user control's code now; you'll see that it's based on the `System.Windows.Forms.UserControl` class:

```
Public Class UserControl1
    Inherits System.Windows.Forms.UserControl

#Region " Windows Form Designer generated code "
        .
        .
        .
End Class
```

We can implement the `CenterColor` property using a `Property` statement, which we saw in Day 3, "Mastering the Visual Basic Language: Data, Operators, Conditionals, and Loops." Here's what that looks like; note that we store the new color in a private internal `Color` object named `InternalColor`, and implement the `Get` and `Set` methods to return and store that color to make this property function as you would expect:

```
Public Class UserControl1
    Inherits System.Windows.Forms.UserControl

#Region " Windows Form Designer generated code "

    Private InternalColor As Color

    Property CenterColor() As Color
        Get
            Return InternalColor
        End Get

        Set(ByVal ColorValue As Color)
            InternalColor = ColorValue
            Label1.BackColor = InternalColor
        End Set
    End Property

End Class
```

Now that we've added the `CenterColor` property to our user control, what about adding a method?

Adding Methods to User Controls

Adding methods to user controls is as easy as adding properties. You just need to add the new method to the user control's code; if you want the method to be accessible outside the control, make it a public method. For example, we can add a public method named SetText to our user control to set the text displayed in the label in the center of the control. Here's what that method looks like in the user control's code:

```
Public Class UserControl1
    Inherits System.Windows.Forms.UserControl

#Region " Windows Form Designer generated code "

    Private InternalColor As Color

    Property CenterColor() As Color
        Get
            Return InternalColor
        End Get

        Set(ByVal ColorValue As Color)
            InternalColor = ColorValue
            Label1.BackColor = InternalColor
        End Set
    End Property

    Public Sub SetText(ByVal LabelText As String)
        Label1.Text = LabelText
    End Sub

End Class
```

And, as you might expect, besides properties and methods, you can also add custom events to user controls.

Adding Events to User Controls

Adding events means using the Event statement, as we saw in Day 9, "Object-Oriented Programming." In this example, we'll add an event named TextChange (not TextChanged, which would interfere with the event of the same name built into the UserControl class) that will occur when the text in the label in our user control changes. We can create that event by using the Event statement and make it occur when the text changes by using the RaiseEvent statement like this:

```
Public Class UserControl1
    Inherits System.Windows.Forms.UserControl

#Region " Windows Form Designer generated code "
```

20

```
Private InternalColor As Color
Public Event TextChange(ByVal LabelText As String)

Property CenterColor() As Color
    Get
        Return InternalColor
    End Get

    Set(ByVal ColorValue As Color)
        InternalColor = ColorValue
        Label1.BackColor = InternalColor
    End Set
End Property

Public Sub SetText(ByVal LabelText As String)
    Label1.Text = LabelText
    RaiseEvent TextChange(LabelText)
End Sub
```

```
End Class
```

We've now completed our user control with a built-in custom property, method, and event. It's time to put this control to work.

Putting the User Control to Work

To make this control available to other projects, you must compile it into a dynamic link library (.dll) form, so select the Build, Build Solution menu item, which builds the control's .dll file. To use this control in another project, you have to add a reference to the control in the other project.

To see how that works, create a new project and add it to the current solution. Select the File, Add Project, New Project menu item to add a new Windows application, naming that application ControlTester, as you see in Figure 20.3.

Because you can't run user controls directly, you should make the new Windows application the startup project for the whole solution by selecting that project in the Solution Explorer, right-clicking it, and selecting the Project, Set as Startup Project menu item (or select the project and select the Project, Set as Startup Project menu item in the IDE's main menu system).

The next step is to add the user control to the new project's toolbox so we can add that control to the project's main form. To do that, we'll need a reference to the user control's project, so right-click the test application's References item in the Solution Explorer and choose the Add Reference menu item, opening the Add Reference dialog you see in Figure 20.4. To add a reference to the UserControls project, click the Projects tab and double-click the UserControls item, adding that item to the Selected Components box at the bottom of the dialog, and click OK.

FIGURE 20.3

Adding a new project to test the user control.

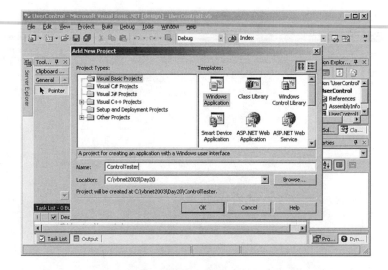

FIGURE 20.4

The Add Reference dialog.

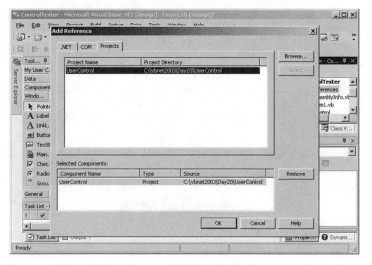

This step adds the user control to the text application's toolbox, as you see in Figure 20.5. You can now add a new user control, UserControl11 (that is, the first control of the UserControl1 class), to the test application's main form, as you would any other control. You can see this new user control in Figure 20.5. You can also see the custom property, CenterColor, in the Properties window. Because we've declared this property as type Color, Visual Basic .NET will display a drop-down list of palette colors you can select from if you select this property in the Properties window. In this example, we've selected Lime as the background color for use in our user control, and you can see that color (in glorious black and white) in the user control in the test application's main form in Figure 20.5.

FIGURE 20.5

Adding a user control to a Windows application.

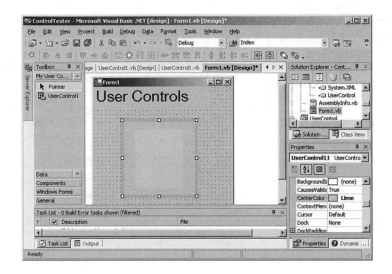

Besides setting the CenterColor property, you can also use the new control's SetText method in code. To do that, add a new button to the Windows application's main form with the caption "Click Me". In that button's Click event handler, you can set the text in the user control to "Hello from this User Control!" like this:

```
Private Sub Button1_Click(ByVal sender As System.Object, _
    ByVal e As System.EventArgs) Handles Button1.Click
    UserControl11.SetText("Hello from this User Control!")
End Sub
```

You can see the results in Figure 20.6. When the user clicks the Click Me button, the hello message appears in the control.

FIGURE 20.6

Using the SetText method.

Recall that when the text in the user control is changed with the SetText method, a TextChange event will occur. You can add code to this event's handler just as you would for any other Visual Basic .NET event, using the drop-down list boxes in the IDE's code designer. For example, the following event handler will display the new text in a text box we add to the Windows application when the `TextChange` event occurs:

```
Private Sub UserControl11_TextChange(ByVal _
    LabelText As String) Handles UserControl11.TextChange
    TextBox1.Text = "Text: " & LabelText
End Sub
```

When you run the Windows application and click the Click Me button, the `TextChange` event occurs and that event's handler displays the new text in the text box we've added to the Windows application, as you see in Figure 20.7.

FIGURE 20.7

Handling the
`TextChange` *event.*

And that's it! We've created a new user control, complete with a working property, method, and event. Now that we have a working example, we'll look at the properties, methods, and events in the class on which user controls are based: the `UserControl` class. That class inherits from the Windows `Control` class, through the `ScrollableControl` and `ContainerControl` classes. We saw the `Control` class in Day 5, "Windows Forms: Working with Text Boxes, Buttons, Labels, Check Boxes, and Radio Buttons," and we'll look at the others here, starting with the `ScrollableControl` class.

20

Working with the `ScrollableControl` Class

The `ScrollableControl` class is a base class for controls that support scrolling. This class is the base class for the `ContainerControl` class, which in turn is the base class for the `UserControl` class. The hierarchy of this class is as follows:

```
System.Object
    System.MarshalByRefObject
        System.ComponentModel.Component
            System.Windows.Forms.Control
                System.Windows.Forms.ScrollableControl
```

You can find the significant public properties of the `ScrollableControl` class in Table 20.1 and the significant method in Table 20.2 (this class has no noninherited events). Note that as with other Windows controls, these tables do not list the significant properties, methods, and events `ScrollableControl` inherits from the `System.Windows.Forms.Control` class, such as the `Click` event; you can see them in Tables 5.1, 5.2, and 5.3.

TABLE 20.1   Significant Public Properties of `ScrollableControl` Objects

Property	Means
AutoScroll	Returns or sets whether the control can scroll (allowing the user to control outside the control's visible boundaries).
AutoScrollMargin	Returns or sets the autoscroll margin's size.
AutoScrollMinSize	Returns or sets the autoscroll's minimum size.
AutoScrollPosition	Returns or sets the autoscroll's position.

TABLE 20.2   Significant Public Method of `ScrollableControl` Objects

Method	Means
SetAutoScrollMargin	Sets the margin size of the autoscroll.

Working with the `ContainerControl` Class

The `ContainerControl` class is the base class of the `UserControl` class, and the hierarchy for this class is as follows:

```
System.Object
   System.MarshalByRefObject
      System.ComponentModel.Component
         System.Windows.Forms.Control
            System.Windows.Forms.ScrollableControl
               System.Windows.Forms.ContainerControl
```

You can find the significant public properties of the `ContainerControl` class in Table 20.3 and the significant method in Table 20.4 (this class has no noninherited events). Note that as with other Windows controls, these tables do not list the significant properties, methods, and events `ContainerControl` inherits from the `System.Windows.Forms.Control` class, such as the `Click` event; you can see them in Tables 5.1, 5.2, and 5.3.

TABLE 20.3 Significant Public Properties of `ContainerControl` Objects

Property	Means
ActiveControl	Returns or sets the active control in this control.
ParentForm	Returns or sets the parent form of this control.

TABLE 20.4 Significant Public Method of `ContainerControl` Objects

Method	Means
Validate	Validates the last invalidated control.

Working with the `System.Windows.Forms.UserControl` Class

Formally speaking, the `UserControl` class, which is the basis for user controls, is actually the `System.Windows.Forms.UserControl` class. Keeping its full name in mind is helpful in distinguishing it from the other `UserControl` class we'll see today: the `System.Web.UI.UserControl` class. The hierarchy for the `System.Windows.Forms.UserControl` class is as follows:

```
System.Object
    System.MarshalByRefObject
        System.ComponentModel.Component
            System.Windows.Forms.Control
                System.Windows.Forms.ScrollableControl
                    System.Windows.Forms.ContainerControl
                        System.Windows.Forms.UserControl
```

You can find the significant public event of the `System.Windows.Forms.UserControl` class in Table 20.5 (this class has no noninherited properties or methods). Note that as with other Windows controls, this table does not list the significant properties, methods, and events `UserControl` inherits from the `System.Windows.Forms.Control` class, such as the `Click` event; you can see them in Tables 5.1, 5.2, and 5.3.

TABLE 20.5 Significant Public Event of `System.Windows.Forms.UserControl` Objects

Event	Means
Load	Occurs when the control is loaded (and before the control becomes visible).

We've completed our look at user controls; coming up next is our examination of Web user controls.

20

Creating Web User Controls

Web user controls are very much like Windows user controls, with the obvious difference that you use Web user controls in Web applications. The programming is similar, however, and to show how similar, we'll duplicate the same example we just created for user controls as a Web user control. This example will be called WebUserControl in the code for this book.

To follow along, create a new Web application called WebUserControl and then add a Web user control to this application by selecting the Project, Add Web User Control menu item. When you select this menu item, the Add New Item dialog opens, as you see in Figure 20.8. Accept the default name for the new Web user control, WebUserControl1, by clicking Open.

FIGURE 20.8

The Add New Item dialog.

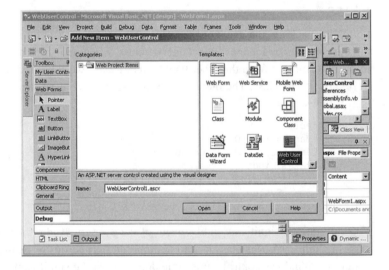

This action creates a new Web user control, as you see in Figure 20.9. The new Web user control's class is WebUserControl1, and at design time, it just looks like a standard Web page. We've already added the label we'll use to the Web control, as you also see in Figure 20.9.

Actually, programming a Web user control is so similar to programming a standard user control in Windows that you can use the same code. In this case, we'll just borrow the code we created to support the CenterColor property, the SetText method, and the TextChange event from the Windows user control we created earlier. All we have to do is drop that code into the code for our Web user control:

```
Public Class WebUserControl1
    Inherits System.Web.UI.UserControl

#Region " Web Form Designer Generated Code "

    Private InternalColor As Color
    Public Event TextChange(ByVal LabelText As String)

    Property CenterColor() As Color
        Get
            Return InternalColor
        End Get

        Set(ByVal ColorValue As Color)
            InternalColor = ColorValue
            Label1.BackColor = InternalColor
        End Set
    End Property

    Public Sub SetText(ByVal LabelText As String)
        Label1.Text = LabelText
        RaiseEvent TextChange(LabelText)
    End Sub

End Class
```

FIGURE 20.9

The new Web user control.

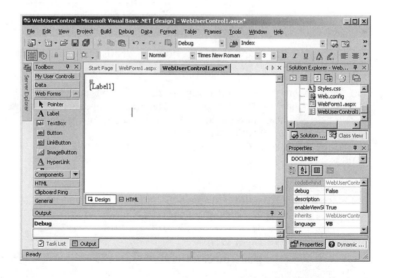

That's fine as far as the code goes, but at this point, things start to differ from creating user controls in Windows. To put our user control to work in Windows, we compiled that control, making it available to other projects. However, the IDE isn't designed to work that closely with the Web server, so for Web user controls, you open the Web application's main form in a form designer and then *drag* the WebUserControl1.ascx entry from the Solution Explorer onto that form, adding the Web user control, `WebUserControl11`, to the form as you see in Figure 20.10. Because the Web user control has not been compiled, Visual Basic .NET doesn't know what it will look like at runtime, so it gives the control a generic appearance at design time, as you see in the figure.

FIGURE 20.10

Adding a Web user control to a Web application.

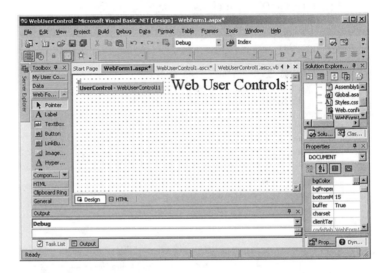

This action creates a new Web user control, `WebUserControl11`, in WebForm1.aspx like this:

```
<%@ Page Language="vb" AutoEventWireup="false"
    Codebehind="WebForm1.aspx.vb" Inherits="WebUserControl.WebForm1"%>
<%@ Register TagPrefix="uc1" TagName="WebUserControl1"
    Src="WebUserControl1.ascx" %>
<!DOCTYPE HTML PUBLIC "-//W3C//DTD HTML 4.0 Transitional//EN">
<HTML>
  <HEAD>
    <title>WebForm1</title>
    <meta name="GENERATOR" content="Microsoft Visual Studio .NET 7.1">
    <meta name="CODE_LANGUAGE" content="Visual Basic .NET 7.1">
    <meta name=vs_defaultClientScript content="JavaScript">
    <meta name=vs_targetSchema
        content="http://schemas.microsoft.com/intellisense/ie5">
  </HEAD>
  <body MS_POSITIONING="GridLayout">

    <form id="Form1" method="post" runat="server">
    <uc1:WebUserControl1 id=WebUserControl11 runat="server">
    </uc1:WebUserControl1>
```

```
            .
            .
            .
        </form>

    </body>
</HTML>
```

Because this control will not actually be compiled until runtime, Visual Basic .NET does not automatically add the user control, WebUserControl11, to the "code-behind" file for our Web application, WebForm1.aspx.vb. To use this control in code, you have to declare it in WebForm1.aspx.vb yourself, so add this code to that file:

```
Public Class WebForm1
    Inherits System.Web.UI.Page

#Region " Web Form Designer Generated Code "

    'This call is required by the Web Form Designer.
    <System.Diagnostics.DebuggerStepThrough()>
    Private Sub InitializeComponent()

    End Sub

    Protected WithEvents WebUserControl11 As WebUserControl1
        .
        .
        .
```

This code adds the Web user control to the code designer, which means you can work with the control's properties, methods, and events in code. Note that because the control hasn't been compiled, you can't work with its properties in the Properties window at design time. You can, however, set properties; for example, you can set the CenterColor property to Color.Lime when the Web form containing the control loads, as we do in the WebUserControl example:

```
Private Sub Page_Load(ByVal sender As System.Object, _
    ByVal e As System.EventArgs) Handles MyBase.Load
    WebUserControl11.CenterColor = Color.Lime
End Sub
```

As in the UserControl example we saw earlier today, we can also add a button with the caption "Click Me" and a text box to the Web application. And we can use the Web user control's SetText method and TextChange event just as we did in the UserControls example by adding the following code, except that this time, we'll use the text "Hello from this Web User Control!":

```
Private Sub Page_Load(ByVal sender As System.Object, _
    ByVal e As System.EventArgs) Handles MyBase.Load
```

20

```
        WebUserControl11.CenterColor = Color.Lime
End Sub

Private Sub Button1_Click(ByVal sender As System.Object, _
    ByVal e As System.EventArgs) Handles Button1.Click
    WebUserControl11.SetText("Hello from this Web User Control!")
End Sub

Private Sub WebUserControl11_TextChange(ByVal _
    LabelText As String) Handles WebUserControl11.TextChange
    TextBox1.Text = "Text: " & LabelText
End Sub
```

And that's all we need! In this way, we've been able to duplicate the work we did with the UserControls example earlier, but this time we're using a Web user control. You can see this example at work in Figure 20.11. When you click the Click Me button, the new text is displayed in the Web user control and the text box, as you see in the figure.

FIGURE 20.11

The Web user control at work.

Now that we have a working Web user control example, we'll look at the available properties, methods, and events built into Web user controls, starting with their base class, the `TemplateControl` class.

Working with the `TemplateControl` Class

The `TemplateControl` class is the class on which the `System.Web.UI.UserControl` class is built. The hierarchy of this class is as follows:

```
System.Object
    System.Web.UI.Control
        System.Web.UI.TemplateControl
```

You can find the significant public methods of `TemplateControl` objects in Table 20.6 and their significant public events in Table 20.7 (this class has no noninherited properties). Note that as with other Web controls, these tables do not list the significant properties, methods, and events `TemplateControl` inherits from the `System.Web.UI.Control` class, such as the `Click` event; you can see them in Tables 12.1, 12.2, and 12.3.

TABLE 20.6   Significant Public Methods of `TemplateControl` Objects

Method	Means
LoadControl	Loads the Web user control.
ParseControl	Parses an input string.

TABLE 20.7   Significant Public Events of `TemplateControl` Objects

Event	Means
AbortTransaction	Occurs when a transaction is aborted.
CommitTransaction	Occurs when a transaction is committed.
Error	Occurs when an exception is unhandled.

Working with the `System.Web.UI.UserControl` Class

The `System.Web.UI.UserControl` class is based on the `System.Web.UI.TemplateControl` class and supports Web user controls in code. The hierarchy of this class is as follows:

```
System.Object
    System.Web.UI.Control
        System.Web.UI.TemplateControl
            System.Web.UI.UserControl
```

You can find the significant public properties of `System.Windows.Forms.UserControl` objects in Table 20.8 and their significant public method in Table 20.9 (this class has no noninherited events). Note that as with other Web controls, these tables do not list the significant properties, methods, and events `UserControl` inherits from the `System.Web.UI.Control` class, such as the `Click` event; you can see them in Tables 12.1, 12.2, and 12.3.

20

TABLE 20.8   Significant Public Properties of `System.Windows.Forms.UserControl` Objects

Property	Means
Application	Returns the HTTP `Application` object for the Web user control.
Attributes	Returns all attribute name and value pairs for the Web user control.

TABLE 20.8   continued

Property	Means
IsPostBack	Returns True if the user control is used after a postback or if it is being accessed for the first time.
Request	Returns the HTTP Request object.
Response	Returns the HTTP Response object.
Server	Returns the Server object.
Session	Returns the user session information.

TABLE 20.9   Significant Public Method of System.Windows.Forms.UserControl Objects

Method	Means
InitializeAsUserControl	Initializes the Web user control.

We've completed our look at Web user controls. As you can see, they're much like Windows user controls except that you embed them in Web applications. Next, we're going to turn to today's final topic: multithreading.

Supporting Multithreading

Sometimes it seems that your programs are required to perform two tasks at once; for example, they must perform some time-consuming task (such as downloading from the Internet or managing a large database) while also handling input from the user to keep the user interface going. And, in fact, it *is* possible to let your code do two—and more—things at the same time, with multithreading.

NEW TERM   A *thread* is the name for a stream of execution, and when you have multiple threads going at once, you have multiple streams of execution going in your code, executing different parts of your code at the same time. What actually happens is the computer divides processing time into *slices*, and when you start a new thread, that thread gets some time slices, which means that thread's code can execute (the program itself is also running a thread, called the *main thread*, to execute its own code).

For example, if you don't want to let your user interface freeze up when it's time to perform some huge behind-the-scenes task, you would launch another thread to take care of that task while the main thread in your application maintains the user interface. (In Visual Basic .NET, you should not use threads you launch to handle user-interface elements.) Let's look at an example, making all this information concrete.

Creating Threads

Our threading example is named MultiThreading in the code for this book, and you can see it at work in Figure 20.12. This example does just what we've been discussing— launches a thread to take care of a time-consuming task, while making sure that the user interface still reacts to the user. The time-consuming task here is simply to loop from 1 to the value you set in the top text box in the MultiThreading example, which is set to 100,000,000 by default:

```
For intLoopIndex As Integer = 1 To Maximum
    intTotal += 1
Next intLoopIndex
```

FIGURE 20.12

The MultiThreading example.

This task will be performed in a new thread when the user clicks the Start button you see in Figure 20.12. When the thread completes its task, it will signal the main thread using a custom event, and the total the thread has counted to will appear in the text box at the bottom of the window, as you see in the figure.

To follow along in this example, create a new Windows application named MultiThreading now. To handle the time-consuming task with a new thread, we'll create an entirely new, self-contained object, so create a new class named counter now by selecting the Project, Add Class menu item. Here's what this class looks like when you create it:

```
Public Class counter

End Class
```

20

This class will count from 1 to the value in its public data member named Maximum in a method named Count:

```
Public Class counter
    Public Maximum As Integer

    Sub Count()
        Dim intTotal As Integer = 0

        For intLoopIndex As Integer = 1 To Maximum
            intTotal += 1
        Next intLoopIndex
            .
            .
            .
    End Sub
End Class
```

When the loop is finished, the value we've counted to will be stored in the intTotal variable, and we can communicate with the main thread, letting it know what that value is, with an event which we'll name DoneCounting. We simply declare this event and use the RaiseEvent method to make it happen:

```
Public Class counter
    Public Maximum As Integer
    Public Event DoneCounting(ByVal Number As Integer)

    Sub Count()
        Dim intTotal As Integer = 0

        For intLoopIndex As Integer = 1 To Maximum
            intTotal += 1
        Next intLoopIndex

        RaiseEvent DoneCounting(intTotal)
    End Sub
End Class
```

Now all we'll have to do in the main thread is launch a new thread, start the counter object's Count method, and handle the DoneCounting event when it occurs. Until that event occurs, we're free to handle user interface events, so the program will not appear to freeze from the user's point of view.

NEW TERM How do we set up a new thread to run the Count method of a counter object when the user clicks the Start button? In code, we create an object of the counter class named counterObject, and when the user clicks the Start button, we pass the *address* of that object's Count method to the Thread class's constructor to create a new thread object, Thread1 (the procedures you pass to the Thread constructor this way may not take any arguments):

```
Dim counterObject As New counter

Private Sub Button1_Click(ByVal sender As System.Object, _
    ByVal e As System.EventArgs) Handles Button1.Click
    Thread1 = New System.Threading.Thread(AddressOf counterObject.Count)
    .
    .
    .
End Sub
```

Next, we clear the text in the program's bottom text box (which will display the value counted to) and set the Maximum data member of the counterObject to the value the user wants us to count to (as set in the top text box you see in Figure 20.12). To handle the event that occurs when the Count method is finished counting, the DoneCounting event, we also connect an event handler named DoneCountingEventHandler to that event by using the AddHandler statement:

```
Dim counterObject As New counter

Private Sub Button1_Click(ByVal sender As System.Object, _
    ByVal e As System.EventArgs) Handles Button1.Click
    Thread1 = New System.Threading.Thread(AddressOf counterObject.Count)
    TextBox2.Text = ""
    counterObject.Maximum = Val(TextBox1.Text)
    AddHandler counterObject.DoneCounting, AddressOf DoneCountingEventHandler
    .
    .
    .
End Sub
```

In the DoneCountingEventHandler event handler, we simply display the count the Count method counted to in the bottom text box:

```
Dim counterObject As New counter

Private Sub Button1_Click(ByVal sender As System.Object, _
    ByVal e As System.EventArgs) Handles Button1.Click
    Thread1 = New System.Threading.Thread(AddressOf counterObject.Count)
    TextBox2.Text = ""
    counterObject.Maximum = Val(TextBox1.Text)
    AddHandler counterObject.DoneCounting, AddressOf DoneCountingEventHandler
    .
    .
    .
End Sub

Sub DoneCountingEventHandler(ByVal Number As Integer)
    TextBox2.Text = Number
End Sub
```

20

All that remains is to start the new thread, and we can do that by using the Thread class's Start method like this:

```
Dim counterObject As New counter

Private Sub Button1_Click(ByVal sender As System.Object, _
    ByVal e As System.EventArgs) Handles Button1.Click
    Thread1 = New System.Threading.Thread(AddressOf counterObject.Count)
    TextBox2.Text = ""
    counterObject.Maximum = Val(TextBox1.Text)
    AddHandler counterObject.DoneCounting, AddressOf DoneCountingEventHandler
    Thread1.Start()
End Sub

Sub DoneCountingEventHandler(ByVal Number As Integer)
    TextBox2.Text = Number
End Sub
```

And that's it! Now when the user clicks the Start button, the value in the top text box is placed into the Maximum data member of the counterObject, the Count method is launched in a new thread (leaving the main part of the program free to respond to user events), and when Maximum is reached, the DoneCounting event occurs, displaying the final count in the bottom text box. You can see the results in Figure 20.12. All in all, not very difficult to implement.

Suspending Threads

While a thread is running, you can also suspend it, which makes it stop running until it is resumed. While the thread is counting to 100,000,000, you can suspend it by using the Thread class's Suspend method. That happens when the user clicks the Suspend button you see in Figure 20.12.

```
Private Sub Button2_Click(ByVal sender As System.Object, _
    ByVal e As System.EventArgs) Handles Button2.Click
    Thread1.Suspend()
End Sub
```

Now the user can click the Start button to start the new thread and click the Suspend button before the thread finishes its task. Doing so makes the thread stop counting and wait until it is resumed again, which we'll do next.

Resuming Threads

After counting has been suspended, the user can resume the new thread operation by clicking the Resume button you see in Figure 20.12, which uses this code:

```
Private Sub Button3_Click(ByVal sender As System.Object, _
    ByVal e As System.EventArgs) Handles Button3.Click
    Thread1.Resume()
End Sub
```

The user can click the Start button to start the new thread and suspend it with the Suspend button. While the thread is suspended, nothing happens, but when the user clicks the Resume button, the thread starts again, completes the count, and displays the final value in the bottom text box.

Stopping Threads

You can also stop a thread altogether by using its `Abort` method. Here's how that works when you click the Cancel button in the MultiThreading example:

```
Private Sub Button4_Click(ByVal sender As System.Object, _
    ByVal e As System.EventArgs) Handles Button4.Click
    Thread1.Abort()
End Sub
```

When the thread is counting and the user clicks this button, the new thread stops working and is deallocated. You can't start the thread so that it takes up where it left off in this case.

Making Threads Sleep

In addition, you can make threads "go to sleep," suspending execution for a specified amount of time. You do so by passing the number of milliseconds (1/1000ths of a second) you want the thread to sleep to the thread's `Sleep` method. Here's how that works in the MultiThreading example when the user clicks the Sleep button, making the thread sleep for 10 seconds:

```
Private Sub Button5_Click(ByVal sender As System.Object, _
    ByVal e As System.EventArgs) Handles Button5.Click
    Thread1.Sleep(10 * 1000)
End Sub
```

> **Note**
>
> In practice, the precision with which Windows programs can measure time intervals is greater than a millisecond. In fact, `Sleep(1)` will give you the same interval as `Sleep(10)`.

20

Prioritizing Threads

 You have more control over threads than we've seen so far. You can also set how much time they get with respect to other threads by setting their *priority*. You can read or set the priority of a thread by using its `Priority` property, setting it to one of the values in the `ThreadPriority` enumeration:

- `ThreadPriority.AboveNormal`—Assigns higher priority to a thread.
- `ThreadPriority.BelowNormal`—Assigns lower priority to a thread.
- `ThreadPriority.Highest`—Assigns highest priority to a thread.
- `ThreadPriority.Lowest`—Assigns lowest priority to a thread.
- `ThreadPriority.Normal`—Assigns average priority to a thread.

Here's what that code looks like in the MultiThreading example, where we set the thread's priority to `BelowNormal` when the user clicks the Low Priority button:

```
Private Sub Button6_Click(ByVal sender As System.Object, _
    ByVal e As System.EventArgs) Handles Button6.Click
    Thread1.Priority = System.Threading.ThreadPriority.BelowNormal
End Sub
```

In practice, however, setting a thread's priority often makes less difference than you might think. If the computer isn't doing much else, for example, lower priority threads end up executing about as fast as higher priority ones. The speed depends on how Windows schedules individual tasks.

Finding a Thread's State

As we've seen, threads can be suspended, they can be running, they can be stopped, and so on. You can determine the state of a thread by using the `ThreadState` property, which can hold a combination of the values in the `System.Threading.Threadstate` enumeration:

- `System.Threading.Threadstate.Initialized`—The thread was initialized, but it hasn't started.
- `System.Threading.Threadstate.Ready`—The thread is ready.
- `System.Threading.Threadstate.Running`—The thread is running.
- `System.Threading.Threadstate.Standby`—The thread is in standby.
- `System.Threading.Threadstate.Terminated`—The thread has terminated.
- `System.Threading.Threadstate.Transition`—The thread is in transition between two states.
- `System.Threading.Threadstate.Unknown`—The thread state is unknown.
- `System.Threading.Threadstate.Wait`—The thread is waiting.

Let's round off our preliminary look at threads by looking at the properties, methods, and events of the `Thread` class itself.

Using the Thread Class

The Thread class supports threads in Visual Basic .NET. The hierarchy for this class is as follows:

```
System.Object
    System.Threading.Thread
```

You can find the significant public properties of Thread objects in Table 20.10 and their significant public methods in Table 20.11 (this class has no noninherited events).

TABLE 20.10   Significant Public Properties of Thread Objects

Property	Means
IsAlive	Indicates whether the thread has been started and is alive.
IsBackground	Returns or sets whether this is a background thread.
Name	Returns or sets the thread's name.
Priority	Returns or sets the thread's priority.
ThreadState	Returns the thread's state.

TABLE 20.11   Significant Public Methods of Thread Objects

Method	Means
Abort	Aborts the thread.
Interrupt	Interrupts threads in the WaitSleepJoin state.
Join	Waits for a thread to complete or be terminated.
Resume	Resumes thread execution for threads that have been suspended.
Start	Begins execution of the thread.
Suspend	Suspends thread execution.

NEW TERM   As we've seen, threads operate largely by themselves. Sometimes, that's not good enough. For example, two threads may be working with the same data, and you might not want the second thread to work with that data until the first thread is finished with it. In such cases, you have to *synchronize* your threads.

20

Synchronizing Threads

Sometimes, it's important to coordinate the actions of threads in your applications. For example, if you have a thread working in a database and create some intermediate result in each record, you won't want a second thread to start working with those results until they're ready. A good way to let threads communicate with each other is to use events, and we've seen how to do that already.

There are two more ways to synchronize threads in Visual Basic .NET: using the SyncLock statement and the Join method. We'll see both of them at work in the Synchronizer example in the code for this book. This example uses two threads to increment a single value, and because both threads operate on a single data item, we'll get a chance to synchronize those threads here. This example uses a class named counter as the MultiThreading example did, but this counter class is much simpler, just containing a single data member named intTotal:

```
Public Class counter
    Public intTotal As Integer
End Class
```

Now, in the application's main form, we can create an object of this class, counterObject, and two threads, Thread1 and Thread2:

```
Public Class Form1
    Inherits System.Windows.Forms.Form
    Dim counterObject As New counter
    Dim Thread1 As New System.Threading.Thread(AddressOf CounterProcedure1)
    Dim Thread2 As New System.Threading.Thread(AddressOf CounterProcedure2)
        .
        .
        .
```

Note that we've given Thread1 the address of a Sub procedure named CounterProcedure1, and Thread2 the address of a Sub procedure named CounterProcedure2. We can write both of these Sub procedures to read the intTotal data member of the counterObject object, increment that data, wait a short time, and write the new value back to intTotal data member when the user clicks a button marked Start:

```
Public Class Form1
    Inherits System.Windows.Forms.Form
    Dim counterObject As New counter
    Dim Thread1 As New System.Threading.Thread(AddressOf CounterProcedure1)
    Dim Thread2 As New System.Threading.Thread(AddressOf CounterProcedure2)
#Region " Windows Form Designer generated code "

    Private Sub Button1_Click(ByVal sender As System.Object, _
        ByVal e As System.EventArgs) Handles Button1.Click
        Thread1.Start()
        Thread2.Start()
        TextBox1.Text = counterObject.intTotal
    End Sub

    Private Sub CounterProcedure1()
        For intLoopIndex As Integer = 1 To 50
```

```
            Dim tempValue = counterObject.intTotal
            Thread1.Sleep(1)
            counterObject.intTotal = tempValue + 1
        Next intLoopIndex
    End Sub

    Private Sub CounterProcedure2()
        For intLoopIndex As Integer = 1 To 50
            Dim tempValue = counterObject.intTotal
            Thread2.Sleep(1)
            counterObject.intTotal = tempValue + 1
        Next intLoopIndex
    End Sub

End Class
```

Each Sub procedure increments `intTotal` 50 times, and because we have two threads, we should end up with a value of 100. However, we do have a problem, as you can see in Figure 20.13; we end up with a number around 50 (the actual value will vary).

FIGURE 20.13

The Synchronizer example, first attempt.

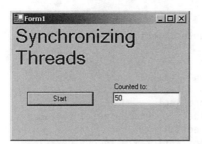

What's going on? When `Thread1` has copied the value in `counterObject.intTotal` to a variable named `tempValue` and is sleeping, the other thread, `Thread2`, increments the actual value in `counterObject.intTotal`. Then, when `Thread1` wakes up, it will increment the value it stored a millisecond ago, `tempValue` (instead of using the new value in `counterObject.intTotal`, which was just incremented by the other thread, which is now sleeping), and overwrite `counterObject.intTotal` with its own, out-of-date value. In this way, it overwrites the new value stored in `counterObject.intTotal` by the other thread, which means the two threads are interfering with each other.

We can fix this problem by synchronizing the threads. You could do that with events, setting a Boolean variable when it's safe for the other thread to proceed. Or you could give each thread a name by assigning text to the threads' `Name` properties and add code to block one thread while the other is incrementing `counterObject.intTotal`. But there's an easier way: You can simply restrict access to `counterObject.intTotal` by using the `SyncLock` statement. To use this statement, you pass it an expression that you want to lock, such as an object (the type of expression you lock must be a reference type, such as a class, a

20

module, an array, or an interface). When you do, access to that object will be denied to all other threads until you use the End SyncLock statement. Here's how you use SyncLock:

```
SyncLock Expression
    [sensitive code]
End SyncLock
```

This means that we can fix the problem in the Synchronizer example by locking access to counterObject when a thread is working with it like this:

```
Public Class Form1
    Inherits System.Windows.Forms.Form
    Dim counterObject As New counter
    Dim Thread1 As New System.Threading.Thread(AddressOf CounterProcedure1)
    Dim Thread2 As New System.Threading.Thread(AddressOf CounterProcedure2)
#Region " Windows Form Designer generated code "

    Private Sub Button1_Click(ByVal sender As System.Object, _
        ByVal e As System.EventArgs) Handles Button1.Click
        Thread1.Start()
        Thread2.Start()
        Thread1.Join()
        Thread2.Join()
        TextBox1.Text = counterObject.intTotal
    End Sub

    Private Sub CounterProcedure1()
        For intLoopIndex As Integer = 1 To 50
            SyncLock counterObject
                Dim tempValue = counterObject.intTotal
                Thread1.Sleep(1)
                counterObject.intTotal = tempValue + 1
            End SyncLock
        Next intLoopIndex
    End Sub

    Private Sub CounterProcedure2()
        For intLoopIndex As Integer = 1 To 50
            SyncLock counterObject
                Dim tempValue = counterObject.intTotal
                Thread2.Sleep(1)
                counterObject.intTotal = tempValue + 1
            End SyncLock
        Next intLoopIndex
    End Sub

End Class
```

Now only one thread at a time has access to counterObject and, therefore, to counterObject.intTotal. When one thread is using counterObject, the other thread will wait.

But we're not finished yet. We still have to make sure both threads have finished before displaying the total count in the application's text box. In the MultiThreading example, we created a custom event that occurred when the new thread was finished. But there is another way to determine when a thread has finished its work: You can use a `Thread` object's `Join` method. When you call a thread's `Join` method, it returns only when that thread has finished (allowing that thread's flow of execution to join the current thread) or has been terminated. Here are the various forms of this method:

- `Join()`—Waits for a thread to finish or be terminated.
- `Join(TimeOut As Integer)`—Waits for the thread to finish/terminate or for a specific timeout, specified as a number of milliseconds, to elapse. Returns `True` if the thread died; `False` if the call timed out.
- `Join(TimeOut As TimeSpan)`—Waits for the thread to finish/terminate or for a specific timeout, given as a `TimeSpan` object, to elapse. Returns `True` if the thread died; `False` if the call timed out.

Here's how we use the `Join` method in the Synchronizer example to make sure both threads are done before displaying the total count:

```
Private Sub Button1_Click(ByVal sender As System.Object, _
    ByVal e As System.EventArgs) Handles Button1.Click
    Thread1.Start()
    Thread2.Start()
    Thread1.Join()
    Thread2.Join()
    TextBox1.Text = counterObject.intTotal
End Sub
```

Now when you run the Synchronizer example and click the Start button, both threads will increment `intTotal` by 50, and they won't interfere with each other, giving you a total of 100, as you see in Figure 20.14.

FIGURE 20.14

The Synchronizer example, second attempt.

20

We've now completed our look at threading.

Summary

Today, we looked at three important topics: user controls for use in Windows applications, Web user controls for use in Web applications, and multithreading.

User controls act like mini Windows forms, allowing you to place other controls in them or not as you prefer. You can handle the events of the user control itself, like the Click event, to create your own control, or add Windows controls to a user control to create a composite control.

User controls also support properties, methods, and events like any control, and we've seen how to add them to user controls today. We've also seen how to add user controls to forms in other applications to put those user controls to work.

Web user controls are much like standard user controls, except they're designed to be used in Web applications. We saw that the process of creating Web user controls in code is very much like the way you create user controls, and we created virtually the same controls for Web use as for Windows use, including the same properties, methods, and events.

We saw, however, that how you put Web user controls to work in a Web form is different from the corresponding user controls. You add a user control to the toolbox and drag it onto a Windows form, but you drag a Web user control directly from the Solution Explorer to a Web form.

We also looked at multithreading today, seeing how to create threads, start them, and give them work to do behind the scenes. Besides starting a thread, you can suspend it, resume it, stop it, and make it sleep a specified number of milliseconds.

In the MultiThreading example, we saw how to use custom events to communicate between threads, and that's a technique often used when you want to make sure the user interface isn't interrupted by the background task.

We also looked at synchronizing threads through the use of the SyncLock statement and Join method. You can use SyncLock to restrict thread access to items such as objects, as we've seen today, allowing you to synchronize thread operations. You can use the Join method to determine when a thread has finished or has terminated, and that's useful when you need to wait for a thread to finish.

And that's it for today's work. Tomorrow, we're going to start working with Windows servers and Web services and seeing how to deploy your applications.

Q&A

Q Can I derive new controls from user controls as I can from standard controls?

A Yes, you can inherit from a user control, creating a new control to which you can add new properties, methods, and events. In the Solution Explorer, select the user control. From the Project menu, select Add Inherited Control, opening the Add New Item dialog. In the Name box, enter the name of the derived control you want to create and click Open, opening the Inheritance Picker window. Under Component Name, double-click the name of the control you want to inherit from and click OK. You'll see that the new, derived user control appears in the Solution Explorer.

Q Even though I am not supposed to, can I use threads to work with user interface controls?

A You actually can, but it's risky. Microsoft recommends you execute methods of a form or control only in the thread in which the form or control was created. If you do work with user elements in a thread, don't use the SyncLock statement. Often, however, you'll find that your program hangs if you use threads that are not the main thread to handle user interface controls.

Workshop

This workshop tests whether you understand the concepts you saw today. It's a good idea to make sure you can answer these questions before pressing on to tomorrow's work.

Quiz

1. How do you create a new user control?

2. You want to add a user control to a Windows form but can't seem to find it in the Add References dialog. What could be wrong?

3. When you want to add a Web user control to a Web form, where do you drag that control from?

4. What is the purpose of the Thread class's Join method?

5. What priority do you give a thread when you want to give it the least time compared to other threads?

20

Quiz Answers

1. You can select the File, New Project menu item to open the New Project dialog and then select the Windows Control Library item. You can also add a new user control to an application by selecting the Project, Add User Control menu item.

2. You may not have compiled the user control to make it available to other projects. You can compile it by selecting the Build, Build Solution menu item.

3. From the Solution Explorer.

4. The Join method allows you to determine when a thread has finished or been terminated. You use it when you want to wait for a thread to finish executing before continuing for your code.

5. You can assign the value ThreadPriority.Lowest to the thread's Priority property.

Exercises

1. Create a user control that displays an alarm clock, modeled on the Timers application in Day 6, "Windows Forms: Working with List Boxes, Combo Boxes, Picture Boxes, Scrollbars, Splitters, Tool Tips, and Timers." Let the user set the time when he or she wants the alarm to start beeping and include Alarm On and Alarm Off buttons. (**Extra credit:** Modify your alarm clock into an appointment calendar that allows the user to keep track of important dates.)

2. Create a new Windows application that uses a thread to increment a counter and a custom event to display the current count in a text box. Let the user start and end the thread with Start and Stop buttons, and also implement Suspend and Resume buttons. (**Extra credit:** Implement two synchronized threads to increment the same counter value.)

DAY 21

Creating Windows Services, Web Services, and Deploying Applications

Today, we're going to complete our grand tour of Visual Basic .NET by looking at ways to create Windows services and Web services and deploy Visual Basic applications. All these techniques are powerful, and they'll add a lot to our Visual Basic arsenal. Here's an overview of today's topics:

- Creating a Windows service
- Writing to event logs from Windows services
- Creating a Windows service installer
- Communicating with a Windows service from other applications
- Creating a Web service
- Using a Web service

- Accessing Web methods
- Deploying your applications

NEW TERM *Windows services* are applications that usually run in the background while you're doing other things. They don't have a user interface that's always open like standard Windows applications, although they frequently have a user interface you can open by right-clicking or double-clicking an icon in the taskbar. These applications provide you with some service, often connected to device drivers such as printer device drivers, audio devices, data providers, CD burners, and so on. You can also interact with Windows services from your own applications, as we'll see today.

NEW TERM *Web services* are similar services for the Web. A Web service is a Web component that can be called by Web applications and return data, such as data from a database. These services do their work on the Web, which means you can create business objects to implement custom logic, such as running credit checks on the user before considering a loan. You can use Web services as a middle-tier business object that works with and passes on data in a three-tier data Web application, for example.

After you've created your applications, the next step is to deploy them. Visual Basic .NET applications are designed to be installed with the Windows installer program, which use Microsoft Installer (.msi) files. We'll see how to create .msi files for applications today. To install an application, you just copy the .msi file and double-click it, and the Microsoft Windows installer will do the rest.

We'll start our tour by looking at ways to create Windows services.

Creating Windows Services

Windows services usually provide support services rather than act as a front-line application. These services run in the background and usually don't have a user interface except for, perhaps, a control panel that you can open by double-clicking a notify icon in the taskbar. (See Day 6, "Windows Forms: Working with List Boxes, Combo Boxes, Picture Boxes, Scrollbars, Splitters, Tool Tips, and Timers," for more details on notify icons and how to create them.) Their life cycle is different from standard Windows applications; they typically start automatically when you start your computer and quit only when you shut down.

As far as we're concerned in Visual Basic .NET, Windows services are based on the `ServiceBase` class, and that class provides most of the support we'll need. To create a working Windows service, you should override the `OnStart` and `OnStop` methods (their names make them look like event handlers, but they're methods), which are called when the service starts and stops, respectively. For example, you might start a `Timer` object in the `OnStart` method to make control return to your service regularly so that it can check whether it's supposed to be doing something.

You can configure a service to start automatically when the computer boots, or start manually using a tool built into Windows, the Service Control Manager (SCM). And you might also want to override the `OnPause` and `OnContinue` event handlers as well to handle occasions when the service is paused and resumed.

NEW TERM   A single Windows service executable can contain multiple services, but you need an *installer* for each of them; we'll see how to create Windows service installers today. Most frequently, Windows services run under the System account in Windows. On the other hand, when you install a Windows service, you can use a `ServiceProcessInstaller` object to set up the service to run under a specific user's account. Let's see how this works in practice; the code for this book contains an example, WindowsService1, and we'll look at how that application works here.

To create a new Windows service project, select the File, New, Project menu item; then select the Windows Service icon in the Templates box of the New Project dialog and give this new service the name `WindowsService1`. By doing so, you create a new Windows service project, as you see in Figure 21.1. The name for this new service, using the default Visual Basic .NET has given it, is `Service1`, as you can see in the Properties window in the figure.

FIGURE 21.1

A new Windows service.

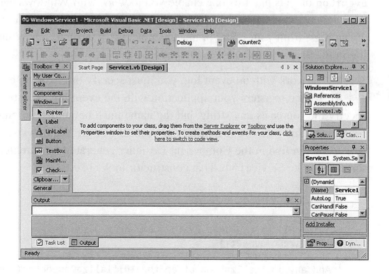

As with any other Visual Basic .NET project, you can design the Windows service visually—at least, up to a point. Our Windows service isn't going to do much; it's just going to write entries to an event log. To make this happen, click the Components tab in the toolbox now and drag an `EventLog` object to the Windows service designer, as you see in Figure 21.2. Set the event log's `Log` property to the name of the log; in this case, we'll use `NewLog1`. Also make sure the Windows service's `AutoLog` property is set to `True` (that's the default).

FIGURE 21.2

Adding an event log to a Windows service.

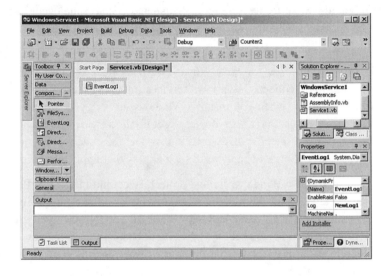

`EventLog` objects like this one enable you to work with Windows event logs, which can record data about software or hardware events. You can read from logs, write to logs, and delete logs, from your code. In this example, we'll write to our Windows service's event log in the `OnStart` and `OnStop` methods.

NEW TERM To work with an event log, you must specify or create an event *source*. The event source registers your application with the event log as a source of data; you can specify the source as any string, but the name must be unique among other registered sources. In this case, we'll register our event log in the Windows service's constructor, which we can find in the Component Designer generated code region of the Windows service's code, Service1.vb. That constructor looks like this:

```
Public Sub New()
    MyBase.New()

    ' This call is required by the Component Designer.
    InitializeComponent()

    ' Add any initialization after the InitializeComponent() call

End Sub
```

In this example, we'll create a source named VBSource1. After the new source is created, we can assign its name to our EventLog object's Source property like this:

```
Public Sub New()
    MyBase.New()

    ' This call is required by the Component Designer.
    InitializeComponent()

    ' Add any initialization after the InitializeComponent() call

    If Not EventLog1.SourceExists("VBSource1") Then
        EventLog1.CreateEventSource("VBSource1", "NewLog1")
    End If

    EventLog1.Source = "VBSource1"

End Sub
```

Next, we set the Source property of the event log to VBSource1 in the Properties window to connect the source to the event log. At this point, we're ready to write to our event log when the service starts and stops. You can do that in the OnStart and OnStop methods, which look like this in Service1.vb:

```
Protected Overrides Sub OnStart(ByVal args() As String)
    ' Add code here to start your service. This method should set things
    ' in motion so your service can do its work.
End Sub

Protected Overrides Sub OnStop()
    ' Add code here to perform any tear-down necessary to stop your service.
End Sub
```

How do you actually write text to a log? You can use the log's WriteEntry method, as we'll do here. In our example, we'll insert a message into the log corresponding to the event that has occurred, like this:

```
Protected Overrides Sub OnStart(ByVal args() As String)
    EventLog1.WriteEntry("Starting WindowsService1.")
End Sub

Protected Overrides Sub OnStop()
    EventLog1.WriteEntry("Stopping WindowsService1.")
End Sub
```

When our Windows service starts, our code will write "Starting WindowsService1." to event log NewLog1, and when the service stops, our code will write "Stopping WindowsService1." to the log.

21

We've created our Windows service, but to install that service, we need an installer. To create one, click the Add Installer link in the description section of the Properties window (this link is visible at bottom right in Figure 21.2). This creates ProjectInstaller.vb with two objects in it, ServiceProcessInstaller1 and ServiceInstaller1, as you see in Figure 21.3.

FIGURE 21.3

Creating an installer for a Windows service.

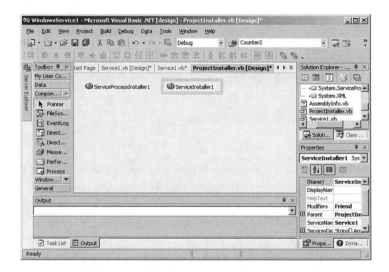

ServiceInstaller objects let Windows know about the service by writing Windows Registry values for the service to a Registry subkey in the HKEY_LOCAL_MACHINE\ System\CurrentControlSet\Services Registry key; the service is identified with its ServiceName value in this subkey. ServiceProcessInstaller objects handle the individual processes started by your service.

To install a Windows service, you have to specify the account the service is to run under; in our example, just click the ServiceProcessInstaller1 object and set its Account property to LocalSystem. You can also set this property to LocalService, NetworkService, or User. Note that to set up the service to run under a specific account, you set Account to User (also, be sure to set the Username and Password properties of the ServiceProcessInstaller1 object in that case).

Next, click the ServiceInstaller1 object and make sure its ServiceName property is set to the name of this service, Service1 (it should already be set to that name). You can use the ServiceInstaller1 object's StartType property to specify how to start the service; here are the possibilities, from the ServiceStartMode enumeration:

- ServiceStartMode.Automatic—The service should be started automatically at system startup.

- `ServiceStartMode.Disabled`—The service is disabled, so it cannot be started.

- `ServiceStartMode.Manual`—The service can only be started manually, by using either the Service Control Manager or an application.

The safest of these possibilities while testing a new Windows service is `Manual`, so set the `StartType` property of the `ServiceInstaller1` object to `Manual` now.

Finally, we'll build and install our new Windows service, `Service1`. To build the service, select the Build, Build WindowsService1 menu item, which creates WindowsService1.exe. To install this service, you can use the InstallUtil.exe tool that comes with Visual Basic .NET. (You can also deploy Windows services with setup packages in Visual Basic .NET. See today's discussion on deploying applications for more information on deployment, and see the "Q&A" section at the end of today's discussion for using deployment projects to install Windows services.) For example, you can find InstallUtil.exe in Windows 2000 in the C:\WINNT\Microsoft.NET\Framework\v*xxxxxxx* directory, where *xxxxxxx* is the .NET version number.

Using InstallUtil.exe, here's how you install WindowsService1.exe at the DOS command prompt (the command line here is split onto two lines only because it's too long for the page width; make it one line when you type it), and what you see when you do:

```
C:\WINNT\Microsoft.NET\Framework\xxxxxxxxxx>installutil
c:\vbnet2003\day21\WindowsService1\bin\WindowsService1.exe

Microsoft (R) .NET Framework Installation utility Version xxxxxxxxxx
Copyright (c)Microsoft Corporation 1998-2002. All rights reserved.

Running a transacted installation.

Beginning the Install phase of the installation.
See the contents of the log file for the
c:\vbnet2003\day21\windowsservice1\bin\windowsservice1.exe assembly's progress.
The file is located at c:\vbnet2003\day21\windowsservice1\bin\windowsservice1.
InstallLog.
Installing assembly
'c:\vbnet2003\day21\windowsservice1\bin\windowsservice1.exe'.
Affected parameters are:
   assemblypath = c:\vbnet2003\day21\windowsservice1\bin\windowsservice1.exe
   logfile = c:\vbnet2003\day21\windowsservice1\bin\windowsservice1.InstallLog
Installing service Service1...
Service Service1 has been successfully installed.
Creating EventLog source Service1 in log Application...

The Install phase completed successfully, and the Commit phase is beginning.
See the contents of the log file for the
c:\vbnet2003\day21\windowsservice1\bin\windowsservice1.exe assembly's progress.
The file is located at c:\vbnet2003\day21\windowsservice1\bin\windowsservice1.
InstallLog.
```

21

```
Committing assembly
'c:\vbnet2003\day21\windowsservice1\bin\windowsservice1.exe'.
Affected parameters are:
   assemblypath = c:\vbnet2003\day21\windowsservice1\bin\windowsservice1.exe
   logfile = c:\vbnet2003\day21\windowsservice1\bin\windowsservice1.InstallLog

The Commit phase completed successfully.

The transacted install has completed.

C:\WINNT\Microsoft.NET\Framework\xxxxxxxxxx>
```

And that's it! This code installs the new Windows service. If InstallUtil hadn't been able to install the new service without problems, it would have removed the nonworking service. Now that our service is installed, the next step is to use the Service Control Manager to start the service. Here's how you start the Service Control Manager in an operating system like Windows 2000:

- In Windows 2000 Professional, right-click My Computer on the desktop and select the Manage item. In the dialog that opens, open the Services and Applications node and click the Services entry.

- In Windows 2000 Server, click Start, select Programs, click Administrative Tools, and then click Services.

For example, you can see the Service Control Manager for Windows 2000 Professional in Figure 21.4. You can see the newly installed service, Service1, listed in the Service Control Manager in the figure.

FIGURE 21.4

The Service Control Manager.

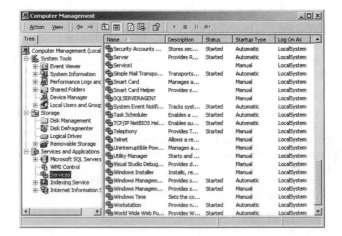

The next step is to actually start the new service, so right-click Service1 in the Service Control Manager now and select the Start item in the menu that opens. This starts the service, as you see in Figure 21.5, where Service1 is listed as Started.

FIGURE 21.5

Starting a Windows service.

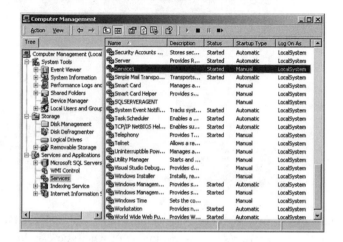

> **Tip**
>
> A Windows service with errors in it can make Windows unstable, so be careful when testing Windows services. Until you're sure a Windows service is working properly, you should keep its start mode as Manual so that it doesn't start again automatically if you reboot. If you do get into a cycle where a problematic Windows service is starting automatically when you boot and causing Windows to hang, try holding down the F8 key to boot Windows in safe mode.

To stop the service, right-click Service1 in the Service Control Manager and select the Stop item.

At this point, we've started and stopped our new service, so it should have written to our event log, NewLog1. You can check whether it has from inside Visual Basic .NET. To check, just open the Server Explorer's Event Logs node, as you see in Figure 21.6, and look at the entry for VBSource1 in NewLog1. In the Server Explorer in Figure 21.6, you can see the two entries our service has written to the event log: Starting WindowsService1. and Stopping WindowsService1.. Our Windows service is a success.

21

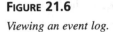

FIGURE 21.6

Viewing an event log.

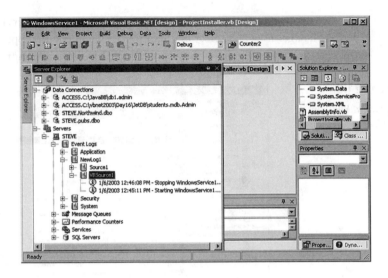

And that's it! Our new Windows service did what it was supposed to: It wrote to the event log. Of course, that's just the beginning of what you can do with Windows services.

Interacting with Windows Services from Other Applications

How do you interact with a Windows service from another application? All you need to do is drag a `ServiceController` object from the Components tab of the toolbox to a form in a Windows application. Then you set these properties:

- `MachineName` — The name of the computer on which the service is running or just "." for the local computer.
- `ServiceName` — The name of the service with which you want to work.

By default, `MachineName` is set to the name of the local machine, so if your service is on the local machine, you don't need to set this property. Next, you add a reference to `System` and `System.ServiceProcess` DLLs by right-clicking the current project in the Solution Explorer, selecting the Add Reference item, clicking the .NET tab in the Add Reference dialog, and selecting System.dll. Next, click Select, select System.ServiceProcess.dll and click Select, then click OK to close the Add Reference dialog. Also, you must include an `Imports` or `Using` statement in your application's code for both the `System` and `System.ServiceProcess` namespaces. Now you can access the properties and methods that are built in to, or those you've added to, your service by using the `ServiceController` object like this:

```
Imports System
Imports System.ServiceProcess

Public Class Form1
        .
        .
        .
    Dim Controller1 As New System.ServiceProcess.ServiceController("Service1")

    If Controller1.CanStop Then
        MsgBox(Controller1.ServiceName & " may be stopped.")
    End If
```

That's all it takes to access a Windows service from code. You can also implement events in a Windows service and, using ServiceController objects, handle those events in other applications.

It's also important to know that you can uninstall a Windows service with InstallUtil.exe just as you can install it. Just use the /u option to uninstall. Here's what you see when you uninstall our Windows service:

```
C:\WINNT\Microsoft.NET\Framework\v1.1.4322>installutil
c:\vbnet2003\day21\WindowsService1\bin\WindowsService1.exe /u

Microsoft (R) .NET Framework Installation utility Version 1.1.4322.12
Copyright (c)Microsoft Corporation 1998-2002. All rights reserved.

The uninstall is beginning.
See the contents of the log file for the
c:\vbnet2003\day21\windowsservice1\bin\windowsservice1.exe assembly's progress.
The file is located at c:\vbnet2003\day21\windowsservice1\bin\windowsservice1.
InstallLog.
Uninstalling assembly
'c:\vbnet2003\day21\windowsservice1\bin\windowsservice1.exe'.
Affected parameters are:
    assemblypath = c:\vbnet2003\day21\windowsservice1\bin\windowsservice1.exe
    logfile = c:\vbnet2003\day21\windowsservice1\bin\windowsservice1.InstallLog
Removing EventLog source Service1.
Service Service1 is being removed from the system...
Service Service1 was successfully removed from the system.

The uninstall has completed.

C:\WINNT\Microsoft.NET\Framework\v1.1.4322>
```

That provides the framework you need to create Windows services; now you're able to write behind-the-scenes code and access that code when it's needed. Now that we have our Windows service working, let's look at the properties, methods, and events that make Windows services work.

21

Working with the ServiceBase Class

The ServiceBase class is the base class for Windows services. The hierarchy of this class is as follows:

```
System.Object
    System.MarshalByRefObject
        System.ComponentModel.Component
            System.ServiceProcess.ServiceBase
```

You can find the significant public properties of ServiceBase objects in Table 21.1 and their significant protected methods in Table 21.2 (this class has no noninherited events; note that although the items in Table 21.2 look like events, they're actually methods you can override and customize).

TABLE 21.1   Significant Public Properties of ServiceBase Objects

Property	Means
AutoLog	Specifies whether to record Start, Stop, Pause, and Continue commands in the event log automatically.
CanPauseAndContinue	Returns or sets whether you can pause and continue the service.
CanShutdown	Returns or sets whether the service should be notified at system shutdown.
CanStop	Returns or sets whether the service can be stopped.
EventLog	Returns an event log you can write to.
ServiceName	Returns or sets the name used to identify the service.

TABLE 21.2   Significant Protected Methods of ServiceBase Objects

Method	Means
OnContinue	Called when a service continues after being paused.
OnPause	Called when a service pauses.
OnPowerEvent	Called when the computer's power status changes, as when notebooks go into suspended mode.
OnShutdown	Called when the system is shutting down.
OnStart	Called when the service starts.
OnStop	Called when a service stops running.

Working with the EventLog Class

The EventLog class supports access to Windows event logs used by Windows services. The hierarchy of this class is as follows:

```
System.Object
    System.MarshalByRefObject
        System.ComponentModel.Component
            System.Diagnostics.EventLog
```

You can find the significant public class (that is, shared) methods of EventLog in Table 21.3, the significant public properties of EventLog objects in Table 21.4, their significant methods in Table 21.5, and their significant event in Table 21.6.

TABLE 21.3   Significant Public Class (Shared) Methods of the EventLog Class

Method	Means
CreateEventSource	Creates an event source that enables an application to write to a log.
Delete	Deletes a log.
DeleteEventSource	Removes an application's event source registration.
Exists	Returns True if a log exists.
GetEventLogs	Returns an array of event logs.
LogNameFromSourceName	Returns the name of the log with which a source is registered.
SourceExists	Checks for a specific event source.
WriteEntry	Writes an entry in the log.

TABLE 21.4   Significant Public Properties of EventLog Objects

Property	Means
Entries	Returns the contents of the log.
Log	Returns or sets the name of the log.
LogDisplayName	Returns the log's display name.
MachineName	Returns or sets the name of the log's computer.
Source	Returns or sets the source name to use when writing to the log.

21

TABLE 21.5   Significant Public Methods of `EventLog` Objects

Method	Means
BeginInit	Starts initialization of an event log.
Clear	Clears all entries from the log.
Close	Closes the log.
EndInit	Ends initialization of an event log.
WriteEntry	Writes an entry in the event log.

TABLE 21.6   Significant Public Event of `EventLog` Objects

Event	Means
EntryWritten	Occurs when data is written to an event log.

Working with the `ServiceProcessInstaller` Class

`ServiceProcessInstaller` objects are responsible for installing the specific processes in a Windows service. The hierarchy of this class is as follows:

```
System.Object
    System.MarshalByRefObject
        System.ComponentModel.Component
            System.Configuration.Install.Installer
                System.Configuration.Install.ComponentInstaller
                    System.ServiceProcess.ServiceProcessInstaller
```

You can find the significant public properties of objects of the `ServiceProcessInstaller` class in Table 21.7, their significant methods in Table 21.8, and their significant events in Table 21.9. Note that these tables include the properties, methods, and events inherited from the `Installer` and `ComponentInstaller` classes.

TABLE 21.7   Significant Public Properties of `ServiceProcessInstaller` Objects

Property	Means
Account	Returns or sets the account type for this service.
HelpText	Returns help text for service options.
Installers	Returns the installers used.
Parent	Returns or sets the parent installer.
Password	Returns or sets the password for a user account.
Username	Returns or sets a user account.

TABLE 21.8 Significant Public Methods of `ServiceProcessInstaller` Objects

Method	Means
Install	Writes service information to the Registry.
Rollback	Rolls back service information written to the Registry.
Uninstall	Removes an installation.

TABLE 21.9 Significant Public Events of `ServiceProcessInstaller` Objects

Event	Means
AfterInstall	Occurs after the installation.
AfterRollback	Occurs after the installations are rolled back.
AfterUninstall	Occurs after uninstallation operations.
BeforeInstall	Occurs before the `Install` method has run.
BeforeRollback	Occurs before the installers are rolled back.
BeforeUninstall	Occurs before uninstall operations.
Committed	Occurs after all the installers have committed their installations.
Committing	Occurs before the installers commit their installations.

Working with the `ServiceInstaller` Class

`ServiceInstaller` objects install Windows services. The hierarchy of this class is as follows:

```
System.Object
  System.MarshalByRefObject
    System.ComponentModel.Component
      System.Configuration.Install.Installer
        System.Configuration.Install.ComponentInstaller
          System.ServiceProcess.ServiceInstaller
```

You can find the significant public properties of objects of the `ServiceInstaller` class in Table 21.10, their significant methods in Table 21.11, and their significant events in Table 21.12. Note that these tables include the properties, methods, and events inherited from the `Installer` and `ComponentInstaller` classes.

21

TABLE 21.10   Significant Public Properties of ServiceInstaller Objects

Property	Means
DisplayName	Holds the display name for this service.
HelpText	Returns help text for the installers.
Installers	Returns the installers themselves.
Parent	Returns or sets the parent installer.
ServiceName	Holds the name of this service.
ServicesDependedOn	Specifies any services that must be running to support this service.
StartType	Specifies when this service should be started.

TABLE 21.11   Significant Public Methods of ServiceInstaller Objects

Method	Means
Commit	Commits the installation when overridden.
Install	Installs the service by writing data to the Registry.
Rollback	Rolls back a service's data written to the Registry.
Uninstall	Uninstalls the service.

TABLE 21.12   Significant Public Events of ServiceInstaller Objects

Event	Means
AfterInstall	Occurs after the installers have installed.
AfterRollback	Occurs after the installations are rolled back.
AfterUninstall	Occurs after all the installers finish their uninstallations.
BeforeInstall	Occurs just before the each installer's Install method runs.
BeforeRollback	Occurs before the installers are rolled back.
BeforeUninstall	Occurs before the installers uninstall.
Committed	Occurs after all the installers commit their installations.
Committing	Occurs before the installers commit their installations.

We've completed our look at Windows services; next up are Web services.

Creating Web Services

As you can gather from their name, Web services are all about providing callable services on the Web. These services can be used by other applications; for example, if you want to retrieve data from a data source on the Web in a managed way, using a Web service is a good way to do so. Even a Windows application can call the methods you put into a Web service, allowing you to integrate Web access into your Windows applications easily. Web services are often used to implement multitiered, distributed data applications like that, and we'll create a Web service much like that today.

This example is called WebServices1 in the code for this book, and the idea here is to let it work with the authors table in the SQL pubs sample database. In particular, we'll implement two methods in this Web service: GetAuthors, to return a dataset holding the authors table, and SetAuthors, to update that table in the pubs database when needed.

We can use a Windows application to call these methods, making our Web service the middle tier of a distributed data application. Although this Web service will simply pass on data as needed, you could make it apply various rules to the data; for example, you could check whether the items in a database table are in stock in a warehouse and mark items that are not available as out of stock.

To follow along, create a new Web service project now by selecting the File, New, Project menu item. Then select the ASP.NET Web Service icon and give this project the name WebServices1 to create the new Web service project that you see in Figure 21.7.

FIGURE 21.7

A new Web service project.

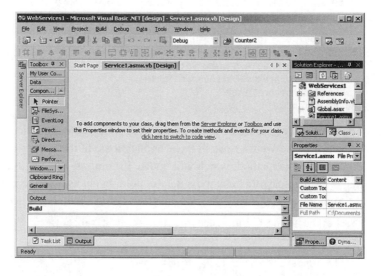

The Visual Basic .NET code file for the new Web service is Service1.asmx.vb, and the name of the new Web service is Service1. (Don't confuse the Web service name with the name of the project, WebServices1; the name Service1 is the way you refer to the

21

service in code.) When you open Service1.asmx.vb in Visual Basic .NET, you'll see that this new service is derived from the WebService class:

```
Imports System.Web.Services

<System.Web.Services.WebService(Namespace :=
    "http://tempuri.org/WebServices1/Service1")> _
Public Class Service1
    Inherits System.Web.Services.WebService
        .
        .
        .
```

Now that we've created our Web service, we can set up our connection to the authors table. As usual, you just need to drag a data adapter—you can use an SqlDataAdapter object here—to the Web service designer and use the Data Adapter Configuration Wizard to connect the data adapter to the authors table. Next, you select the Data, Generate Dataset menu item, which will create a new dataset class, DataSet1. This is the dataset class we'll use to access the authors table in the Web service.

To expose methods from a Web service and make them accessible outside the service, you use the <WebMethod()> attribute when declaring those methods. For example, in the GetAuthors method, we want to return a dataset filled with the authors table, so we add this code in Service1.asmx.vb now:

```
<WebMethod(Description:="Returns the authors table")> _
Public Function GetAuthors() As DataSet1
    Dim AuthorsTable As New DataSet1
    SqlDataAdapter1.Fill(AuthorsTable)
    Return AuthorsTable
End Function
```

The GetAuthors method will be available to code in other applications after we've add a reference to the Web service in those applications. In the same way, we can implement the SetAuthors method, which will update the authors table with changes the user has made. We can pass this method a dataset holding changes to the authors table and update the authors table by using the data adapter's Update method as needed like this:

```
<WebMethod(Description:="Updates the authors table")> _
Public Function UpdateAuthors(ByVal _
    UpdatedRecords As DataSet1) As DataSet1
    If (UpdatedRecords Is Nothing) Then
        Return Nothing
    Else
        SqlDataAdapter1.Update(UpdatedRecords)
        Return UpdatedRecords
    End If
End Function
```

This code implements the GetAuthors and SetAuthors methods. To make this Web service available to applications, build the service now by selecting the Build, Build WebServices1 menu item.

The next step is to put this new Web service to work. To do that, add a new Windows application to this solution that will connect to the Web service by selecting the File, Add Project, New Project menu item. In the Add New Project dialog, select the Windows Application icon, name this new Windows application WebServicesWindowsApplication, and click OK. That opens the Windows application you see in Figure 21.8. In addition, make this Windows application the startup project by selecting the Project, Set as StartUp Project menu item.

FIGURE 21.8

A new Windows application.

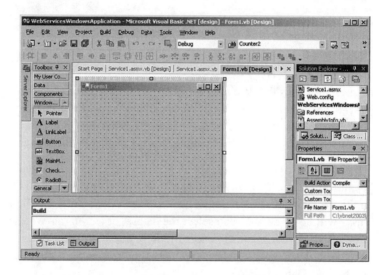

To get access to the GetAuthors and SetAuthors methods, we need to add a reference to our Web service. To do that, right-click the WebServicesWindowsApplication entry in the Solution Explorer and select the Add Web Reference menu item, which opens the Add Web Reference dialog listing the available Web service locations. To add a reference to a Web service, you can enter the URL for the service's .vsdisco (discovery) file in the Address box in the Add Web Reference dialog. Or you can browse to the service you want by clicking the link in the Add Web Reference dialog for the server you want to use and then clicking the name of the service you want to use, which is Service1 for us. Either technique opens our Web service's entry in the Add Web Reference dialog, as you see in Figure 21.9. To add a reference to this Web service to our Windows application, click the Add Reference button.

FIGURE 21.9

*The Add Web
Reference dialog.*

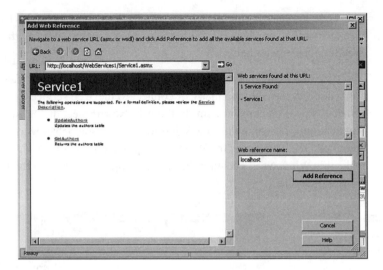

This action adds the Web reference that will give us access to the GetAuthors and
SetAuthors methods. We'll put these methods to work now. To hold the data returned
from the Web service, add a data grid to the Windows application and put two buttons
below the data grid with the captions "Get Data" and "Set Data".

Next, drag a DataSet object (*not* a data adapter) from the Data tab of the toolbox to the
main form in the Windows application. Doing so opens the Add Dataset dialog you see
in Figure 21.10. In this dialog, make sure the Typed Dataset radio button is selected
(as it will be by default) and select the dataset object in our Web service, DataSet1,
from the drop-down list. Note that the fully qualified name of DataSet1 is
WebServicesWindowsApplication.localhost.DataSet1, and that's the way it appears
in the Add Dataset dialog.

To create the new dataset, DataSet11, click the OK button in the Add Dataset dialog. You
need to bind DataSet11 to the data grid in the Windows application, so set the data grid's
DataSource property to DataSet11 and its DataMember property to authors.

When the user clicks the Get Data button, we can fill DataSet11 with data sent to us
from the Web service. Here's how it works. When the user clicks the Get Data button, we
can create an object, service, of our Web service class:

```
Private Sub Button1_Click(ByVal sender As System.Object, _
    ByVal e As System.EventArgs) Handles Button1.Click
    Dim service As New WebServicesWindowsApplication.localhost.Service1
         .
         .
         .
End Sub
```

FIGURE 21.10

The Add Dataset dialog.

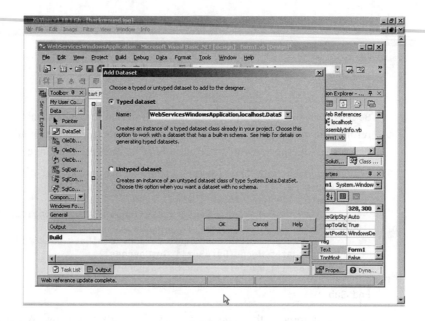

The `service` object here allows us to use the methods we've built into our Web service. The process is as simple as that. For example, we can fill the Windows application's `DataSet11` object with the dataset returned from the Web service's `GetAuthors` method by using the `Merge` method like this:

```
Private Sub Button1_Click(ByVal sender As System.Object, _
    ByVal e As System.EventArgs) Handles Button1.Click
    Dim service As New WebServicesWindowsApplication.localhost.Service1
    DataSet11.Merge(service.GetAuthors())
End Sub
```

And that's how it works: You create an object corresponding to the Web service, as you would with any reference added to your application, and then you're free to use that object's methods, accessing the Web service in your code.

We can also update the authors table as needed with the changes the user makes in the data grid. Recall that when the user makes such changes, they are reflected immediately in the dataset the data grid is bound to. To get only the changed records, we can use the dataset's `GetChanges` method this way:

```
Private Sub Button2_Click(ByVal sender As System.Object, _
    ByVal e As System.EventArgs) Handles Button2.Click
    If DataSet11.HasChanges() Then
        Dim dsUpdates As New _
            WebServicesWindowsApplication.localhost.DataSet1
        dsUpdates.Merge(DataSet11.GetChanges())
```

21

```
        .
        .
        .
        End If
End Sub
```

Now that we have a dataset object with the changes, we can use the Web service's `SetAuthors` method to update the authors table in the pubs database. That method returns the changed records, and we can merge them into the Windows application's dataset so that those records will no longer be marked as changed:

```
Private Sub Button2_Click(ByVal sender As System.Object, _
    ByVal e As System.EventArgs) Handles Button2.Click
    If DataSet11.HasChanges() Then
        Dim service As New WebServicesWindowsApplication.localhost.Service1
        Dim dsUpdates As New _
            WebServicesWindowsApplication.localhost.DataSet1
        dsUpdates.Merge(DataSet11.GetChanges())
        DataSet11.Merge(service.SetAuthors(dsUpdates))
    End If
End Sub
```

And that completes the code we need; we're ready to go now. When you run this example and click the Get Data button, the data from the authors table appears in the data grid, as you see in Figure 21.11. And if you make changes to the data in the data grid and click the Set Data button, those changes will be sent to the authors table in the pubs database.

FIGURE 21.11

Using a Web service.

And that's it! As you can see, it takes some work to create and connect to a Web service, but it's worthwhile. As far as the user is concerned, the connection to the Web is maintained entirely behind the scenes; all the user has to do is click buttons. All in all, this is a very impressive showing for Visual Basic .NET. We'll look at the `WebService` class used with Web services next.

Working with the WebService Class

The System.Web.Services.WebService class is the base class for Web services. The hierarchy of this class is as follows:

```
System.Object
   System.ComponentModel.MarshalByValueComponent
      System.Web.Services.WebService
```

You can find the significant public properties of objects of the WebService class in Table 21.13 (this class has no noninherited methods or events).

TABLE 21.13 Significant Public Properties of WebService Objects

Property	Means
Application	Returns the HTTP application object for the HTTP request.
Context	Returns the HttpContext object for the HTTP request.
Server	Returns the HttpServerUtility object for the HTTP request.
Session	Returns the HttpSessionState object for the HTTP request.
User	Returns an ASP.NET server User object.

Finally, it's time to look at how to deploy Visual Basic .NET applications.

Deploying Your Applications

When you're done creating and testing your application, it's time to deploy it in the field. You can deploy your applications in many ways, and Visual Basic .NET gives you plenty of options. For example, you can create a Windows installer file, with the extension .msi. Just copy the .msi file to the target computer and double-click it (assuming the target computer contains both the Windows installer application and has the .NET Framework installed) to install your application.

We'll look at how this process works as our final Visual Basic .NET topic. In this case, we'll create an .msi file for an application named BigApp2005. This exciting application displays a message box with the message "Welcome to Big App 2005!" when the user clicks a Click Me! button (and that's all BigApp2005 does):

```
Private Sub Button1_Click(ByVal sender As System.Object, _
    ByVal e As System.EventArgs) Handles Button1.Click
    MsgBox("Welcome to Big App 2005!")
End Sub
```

You can see BigApp2005 at design time, including the Click Me! button, in Figure 21.12.

21

FIGURE 21.12

Big App 2005.

What you actually distribute is the .exe file, BigApp2005.exe, so select the Build, Build BigApp2005 menu item now, building BigApp2005.exe. That's the executable file we'll actually deploy.

Our task now is to create an installer file for BigApp2005, and we'll name that installer file BigApp.msi. To do that, select the File, Add Project, New Project menu item, opening the Add New Project dialog you see in Figure 21.13.

FIGURE 21.13

The Add New Project dialog.

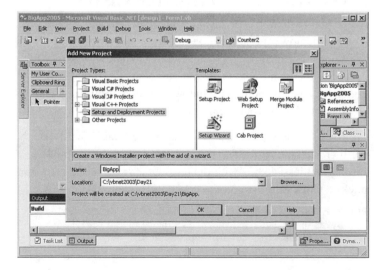

Select the Setup and Deployment Projects icon in the Project Types box and the Setup Wizard icon in the Templates box, as you see in Figure 21.13. The Setup Wizard enables you to create deployment projects in the easiest possible way (although you can also create deployment projects without the Setup Wizard, using the deployment project templates you see in Figure 21.13).

Give the new deployment project the name BigApp, as you see in Figure 21.13, and click OK to open the Setup Wizard, as you see in Figure 21.14.

FIGURE 21.14

The Setup Wizard, first pane.

Now click Next to move to the second pane in the wizard, as you see in Figure 21.15. The Setup Wizard supports different types of deployment projects, including those for Windows and Web applications.

For our example, select the Create a Setup for a Windows Application radio button and click Next to open the third pane in the Setup Wizard, which you see in Figure 21.16. In the third pane, you specify exactly what files you want to deploy. For example, you can deploy just the application itself, or the program and its source code, and so on. In this case, we'll deploy the works—everything in the BigApp2005 application—so select all items, as you see in Figure 21.16.

21

FIGURE 21.15

The Setup Wizard, second pane.

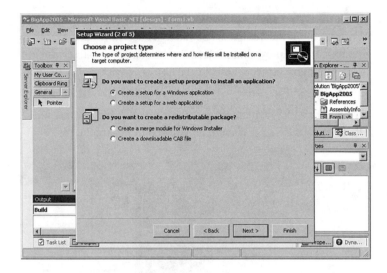

FIGURE 21.16

The Setup Wizard, third pane.

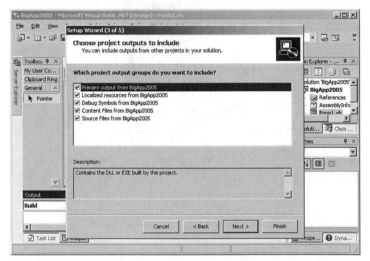

Now click Next to move to the fourth pane of the Setup Wizard, as you see in Figure 21.17. In this pane, you can specify other files you also want to be deployed, such as help and documentation files, licensing agreements, and so forth.

In this case, we're not going to include any additional files with the deployment package, so click Next to bring up the fifth pane of the Setup Wizard, which you see in Figure 21.18. This is the last pane of the Setup Wizard, and to create the installer file, you just need to click Finish.

FIGURE 21.17

*The Setup Wizard,
fourth pane.*

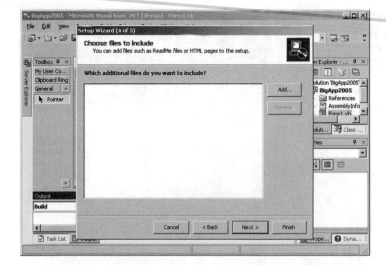

FIGURE 21.18

*The Setup Wizard, fifth
pane.*

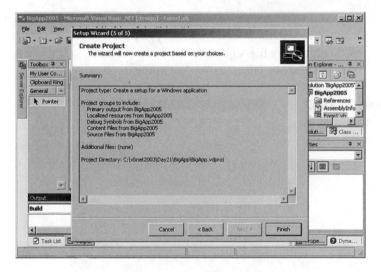

When the Setup Wizard closes, you'll see the file structure of the setup project displayed
in the IDE, as you see in Figure 21.19. You can move files around just by dragging them
to specify where they should be installed on the user's machine. You can set the name of
the application that the Windows installer will display when it installs by setting the
setup project's `ProductName` property. You can also set the `Manufacturer` property to the
name of your company.

21

FIGURE 21.19

*The setup project in
the IDE.*

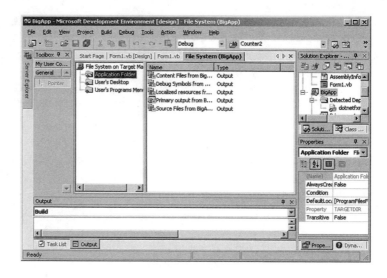

After you've created the setup project, select the Build, Build Solution menu item; this
creates BigApp.msi, which is the file you use to deploy BigApp2005. To deploy the
application, copy BigApp.msi to the target machine. When you double-click that file, the
Windows installer opens, as you see in Figure 21.20.

FIGURE 21.20

*The Windows installer,
first pane.*

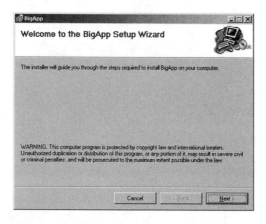

Continue by clicking Next in the Windows installer to move on to its second pane. Here,
you can specify the place to install the application, as you see in Figure 21.21.

After you specify the place to install the application, clicking Next two more times
installs the application, as you see in Figure 21.22.

FIGURE 21.21

The Windows installer, second pane.

FIGURE 21.22

Installing BigApp.

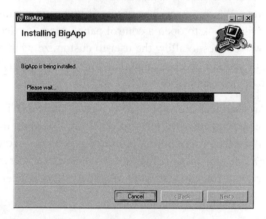

You've installed BigApp2005. Now you can double-click the newly installed BigApp2005.exe and it'll run, as you see in Figure 21.23.

FIGURE 21.23

Running BigApp2005.

21

We've now created an installation package for our application and installed that application. The process is similar for creating installation files for Web applications. For Web applications, you select the Create a Setup for a Web Application option in the second pane of the Setup Wizard instead of Create a Setup for a Windows Application.

Summary

Today, we looked at three important topics in Visual Basic .NET: using Windows services, using Web services, and deploying your applications.

Windows services enable you to create applications that run in the background and give you the option of having them started automatically when the computer starts. Windows services can have a user interface, but that interface is not usually showing when the program is running. Often, Windows services use notify icons in the taskbar so that the user can double-click or right-click to open a control panel. Many device drivers use control panels with Windows services to allow the user to customize what happens with that device driver, such as starting or stopping a data provider like SQL Server, setting volume level for audio devices, and so on.

We saw that Windows services are supported in Visual Basic .NET much like the other types of projects we've worked with. These projects are based on the `ServiceBase` class, and that class gives you the programming foundation you need. You can override various methods of the `ServiceBase` class, including both `OnStart` and `OnStop` to handle various Windows service actions. You can start your Windows service when `OnStart` is called and stop it when `OnStop` is called.

You need an installer for every Windows service you want to implement. As we saw, that usually involves an object of both the `ServiceProcessInstaller` and `ServiceInstaller` classes in Visual Basic .NET.

As we've seen, your Windows service can write to an event log, which is maintained by Windows. In Visual Basic .NET, event logs are supported by the `EventLog` class. To use an object of this class, you use its `CreateEventSource` method to create an event source and then assign that source to the event log's `Source` property. You can write to the event log by using the event log's `WriteEntry` method.

To indicate when a Windows service should be started, you can use the service's `StartType` property. `ServiceStartMode.Automatic` means that the service is to be started automatically when the computer is booted, `ServiceStartMode.Disabled` means that it cannot be started, and `ServiceStartMode.Manual` means that the service can only be started manually, by either a user using the Service Control Manager or by an application. When you're testing a Windows service under development, the best choice is manual so that a problematic service doesn't automatically start when the computer (re)boots.

We used InstallUtil.exe to install our Windows service today and the Service Control Manager to start and stop it. After you've debugged an installed service, you can set it to start automatically when the computer starts. You can also use InstallUtil.exe to uninstall a Windows service, by using the /u option on the command line, as we also saw today.

Next, we looked at working with Web services in Visual Basic .NET. Both these and Windows services operate in the background, but Web services are designed to be called by other processes through IIS.

Web services typically expose methods that may be called by other applications. The example we saw today allowed you to call two methods, GetAuthors and SetAuthors, to get and set the data in the authors table of the pubs SQL Server sample database.

Visual Basic .NET enables you to create Web service projects using its Web service template, which is based on the WebService class. To expose methods from a Web service and make them accessible outside the service, you use the <WebMethod()> attribute. For example, here's how we set up the GetAuthors method, which returns the authors table in a dataset:

```
<WebMethod(Description:="Returns the authors table")> _
    Public Function GetAuthors() As DataSet1
        .
        .
        .
End Function
```

To access a Web method in a Web service, you first have to add a Web reference to that service. You can do that by right-clicking a project in the Solution Explorer, selecting the Add Web Reference menu item, and browsing to the Web service you want in the Add Web Reference dialog. After you've added the Web reference, you're free to create a new object of that service's class, as we did today, and call the Web methods of that object. In our code, we saw how to call the GetAuthors and SetAuthors methods this way.

Finally, we looked at ways to deploy Visual Basic .NET applications. In particular, we looked at creating Windows installer files (.msi files). To create a setup application, you can add a setup and deployment project to the current project. You can select from various options when you're creating a setup project; the easiest of these is to use the Setup Wizard, as we did today.

The Setup Wizard will guide you through the steps needed to create the new setup project for your applications. After the setup project has been created, select the Build, Build Solution menu item to create the .msi file that the Windows installer will use to install your application. You just need to copy the .msi file to the target computer and double-click it to open it in the Windows installer (as long as the target computer has the Windows installer and .NET Framework installed). You can also create a small application specifically to launch your .msi file if you prefer.

21

And that's it! With the deployment of our applications, we've finished our grand tour of Visual Basic .NET. We've come far in the past 21 days, from the beginning essentials all the way up through some pretty advanced topics. We began in Day 1, "Getting Started with Visual Basic .NET!" with on overview of the primary Visual Basic .NET tool, the IDE itself. From there, we worked through the Visual Basic .NET language's syntax, Windows applications, object-oriented programming, file handling, graphics, and Web applications. We added special emphasis on handling databases with Visual Basic .NET, spending four days on the topic, because database work is such a large part of Visual Basic .NET, and one of the primary reasons that people use it in the first place. We also looked at a number of advanced topics: user controls, Web user controls, distributed data applications, Windows services, and more.

Over the past three weeks, we've added hundreds of techniques and skills to our programming arsenal. We've seen what Visual Basic .NET has to offer; all that remains now is to put this remarkable tool to work. Happy programming.

Q&A

Q How can I set up a Windows service to be paused and restarted?

A You must specify whether a service may be paused and resumed by using the `CanPauseAndContinue` property of the `ServiceBase` class. By default, this property is set to `False`, so if you want to pause and resume your service, set this property to `True`.

Q How can I customize a setup and deployment project I've added to a Windows service project so the Windows service will be installed on the target machine?

A You can do this by adding a *custom action* to the setup project. Here's how that process works: In the Solution Explorer, right-click the setup project, select View, and then select Custom Actions, making the Custom Actions dialog appear. In the Custom Actions dialog, right-click the Custom Actions item and choose Add Custom Action, making the Select Item in Project dialog appear. Double-click the Application Folder in the list box, opening that folder; then select Primary Output from *ServiceName* (Active), where *ServiceName* is the name of your service; and click OK. The primary output (that is, the Windows service itself) is added to all four custom action folders: Install, Commit, Rollback, and Uninstall. To build the setup project, right-click that project in the Solution Explorer and select Build.

Workshop

This workshop tests whether you understand the concepts you saw today. It's a good idea to make sure you can answer these questions before pressing on to tomorrow's work.

Quiz

1. What methods are called in a Windows service when the service starts and stops?

2. What classes do you use to handle the installation of Windows services?

3. What component can you drag from the toolbox to interact with a Windows service?

4. What attribute do you use when you declare a Web method in a Web service to make that method accessible outside the service?

5. What do you need to do in a Windows application before working with the methods of a Web service?

Quiz Answers

1. The `OnStart` and `OnStop` methods, which you can override to add your own code.

2. The `ServiceInstaller` and `ServiceProcessInstaller` classes.

3. A `ServiceController` object.

4. To expose methods from a Web service and make them accessible outside the service, you use the `<WebMethod()>` attribute.

5. You need to add a Web reference to the Web service to the Windows application and create an object corresponding to that service. Then you can call the Web service's members using that object.

Exercises

1. Create a Windows service named Daytimer and add a notify icon to it. When the user double-clicks the notify icon in the taskbar, display a message box with the current time (use the `NotifyIcon1_DoubleClick` event).

2. Create a new Web service to match the Windows service you created in Exercise 1. In this case, have the Web service implement a Web method named `GetTime` and have that method return the current time on the Web server as a `String`.

21

PART VI

In Review

Advanced Topics

In Part VI, we took a look at some advanced topics—user controls, Web user controls, multithreading, Windows services, Web services, and how to deploy your applications. There was a lot going on here, so let's take a look at these topics in review.

As discussed in Day 20, user controls are much like miniature Windows forms. You can add Windows controls to a user control at design time to put together your own composite control. Or, if you prefer, you can draw the appearance of a user control yourself and use the events of that control, such as the Click event, to create a totally new control.

Visual Basic .NET 2003 gives you a great deal of support for creating user controls; to create a user control, you use the File, New Project menu item and select the Windows Control Library item in the New Project dialog. When you click the OK button in the New Project dialog, the new user control is created.

At design time, a new user control looks like a Windows form—you can add your own controls to the user control or give it a custom appearance in code. As with any other Windows control, user controls can support properties, methods, and events. After you've created and customized your user control, you build it and add it to your applications.

Web user controls are very much like Windows user controls, except that you use them in Web applications. Programming them is very similar in many ways to standard user controls. To show how that programming works, we created a new Web application and added a Web user control to the application using the Project, Add Web User Control menu item.

At design time, a new Web user control looks like a standard Web form. As with standard user controls, you can add other controls such as text boxes and buttons to your Web use control, as we did in Day 20 before adding our new Web user control to a Web page. Once created, these controls can let you reuse your code in multiple Web forms.

Threads are simply streams of execution. As we've discussed, your computer's processing time is divided into slices. When you start a new thread, that thread gets some time slices so that the thread's code can execute. Time slices can be allocated between your threads, giving each some processor time.

Threads are great if you don't want your user interface to come to a halt when it's time to perform some background work. To perform that work, you only need to launch a new thread and specify the code you want that thread to execute. To start a new thread, you create an object of the Thread class and pass the address of the procedure you want the thread to execute to the thread's constructor. That looked like this in Day 20:

```
Dim Thread1 As New System.Threading.Thread(AddressOf CounterProcedure1)
```

When the thread completes its task, you saw that there are various ways of signaling the main thread, such as using a custom event. In addition, we worked through threads in some detail, seeing how to suspend, resume, prioritize, sleep, and synchronize them in code. As you've seen, threads represent a very powerful aspect of Visual Basic .NET programming.

Windows services, which you saw in Day 21, are applications that you let run in the background. Unlike most of the other applications in this book, they're not user interface-oriented (although commercial Windows services often do have a user interface you can open by right-clicking or double-clicking an icon in the taskbar). These services are often used with device drivers such as printer device drivers, or audio device drivers, and let you customize their operation.

You saw how to build install, and run a Windows service. You can override various methods in a Windows service, including both OnStart and OnStop to handle various Windows service actions. You can start your Windows service when OnStart is called and stop it when OnStop is called. You also need an installer for every Windows service, which you can create with objects of the ServiceProcessInstaller and ServiceInstaller classes.

Our Windows service only wrote to a log file, but you also saw how you can interact with a Windows service from your own code running in the foreground.

Web services are similar services for the Web. Technically speaking, a Web service is a Web component that can be called by Web applications and that can return data. It works on the Web, so it is accessible over the Internet, letting you interact easily with Web-based applications from Windows applications. Web services are often used, for example, as middle-tier business objects that check data before sending it on in a three-tier data Web application, for example.

As for Windows services, there is a great deal of support for creating Web services in Visual Basic .NET 2003. You can create a new Web service with the File, New, Project menu item, selecting the ASP.NET Web Service icon. To expose methods from a Web service and make them accessible outside the service, you use the `<WebMethod()>` attribute when declaring those methods.

To get access to those Web methods, you add a reference to your Web service. To do that, you right-click an application in the Solution Explorer and select the Add Web Reference menu item; Visual Basic .NET 2003 will let you browse to the Web service. After you've added a reference to a Web service, you can call that service's methods in your code.

The final topic we looked at was how to deploy your applications. We took a look at various options and built a Windows installer to get an idea how they work. To deploy your application, you add a setup and deployment project to your application in the design phase. You can control how your application is deployed manually, or you can use the Setup Wizard, as we did in Day 21.

When the setup project has been created, you select the Build, Build Solution menu item to create a .msi file. To use the .msi file to install your application, you just double-click it in Windows, launching the Windows Installer and installing your application.

And that's it—that takes us up through all 21 days. We've packed a great deal into our grand tour of Visual Basic .NET 2003—all that's left is to make use of the new skills in your arsenal. Happy programming!

INDEX

Visual J#, 12
Visual Studio .NET 2003, 12
VScrollBar class, 284-285

W

Web Application icon
(ASP.NET), 507
Web applications, 19-20, 497
    browser programming in
        JavaScript, 528-530
    creating, 507
        ASP.NET, 498
        HTML, 503-507
        mobile applications,
            527-528
        multiform applications,
            524-527
        Solution Explorer files,
            508-509
        Web forms, 498-502,
            509-517
    customizing Web pages in
        HTML, 518-522
    databases
        complex data binding,
            817-835
        Internet Explorer,
            837-839
        master-detail data forms,
            835-837
        navigating data, 813-817
        simple data binding,
            811-812
    detecting browser capabili-
        ties, 531
    embedding Visual Basic code
        in Web pages, 531-534
    preserving data between
        servers, 522
    preserving data in clients,
        523
    preserving data in servers,
        523-524
    running, 517-518
Web configuration file, 31
Web controls, creating Web
    applications
    HTML client controls, 502
    HTML server controls, 501
    server controls, 499-500
    validation controls, 502
Web forms. *See also* Web

Server controls
    ad rotators, 664-668
    background property, 510
    bgColor property, 509
    bottomMargin property, 510
    calendar controls, 659-663
    check boxes, 578-580
        creating, 580-581
        lists, 582-589
    creating Web applications,
        498-499
        adding controls, 511-513
        events, 513-517
        flow layout mode, 509
        grid layout mode, 509
        properties, 510-511
        Web controls, 499-502
    designers, 40
    drop-down lists, 625-629
    extension, 30
    hyperlinks, 630-634
    image buttons, 615-618
    image controls, 612-615
    leftMargin property, 510
    link buttons, 634-637
    list boxes, 618-620
        adding items at runtime,
            623-625
        multiple-selection,
            622-623
        single-selection, 620-621
    PageLayout property, 509
    panels, 604-608
    radio buttons, 589-591
        creating, 591-592
        lists, 593-596
    rightMargin property, 510
    tables, 596-604
    text property, 509
    title property, 510
    topMargin property, 510
    validation controls, 642-645
        comparison, 647-650
        custom, 655-657
        range, 650-651
        regular expression,
            651-654
        required field, 645-647
        summaries, 657-659
Web Hosting subtab, 55
Web Server controls, 537, 541.
    See also Web forms
    access keys, 545
    ad rotators, 664-668

adding at runtime, 548-552
border style, 547-548
buttons, 552-553
    command, 554-555
    creating, 554
calendar, 659-663
check box lists, 582-583
    CheckBoxList class,
        584-589
    ListControl class,
        583-584
    ListItem class, 584
check boxes, 578-581
Control class, 538
disabling, 541-542
drop-down lists, 625-629
enabling, 541-542
fonts, 546-547
hyperlinks, 630-634
image, 612-615
image buttons, 615-618
labels, 561-564
link buttons, 634-637
list boxes, 618-625
literals, 564-566
moving at runtime, 543-545
panels, 604-608
placeholders, 566-568
radio buttons, 589-596
tables, 596-604
text boxes, 556-561
tool tips, 545
validation, 642-645
    comparison, 647-650
    custom, 655-657
    range, 650-651
    regular expression,
        651-654
    required field, 645-647
    summaries, 657-659
visibility, 542
XML control, 569-573
Web services, 24, 882
    creating, 896-902
    WebService class, 903
Web user controls, 860-864
    System.Web.UI.UserControl
        class, 865-866
    TemplateControl class,
        864-865
WebCentral .NET ISP, 55